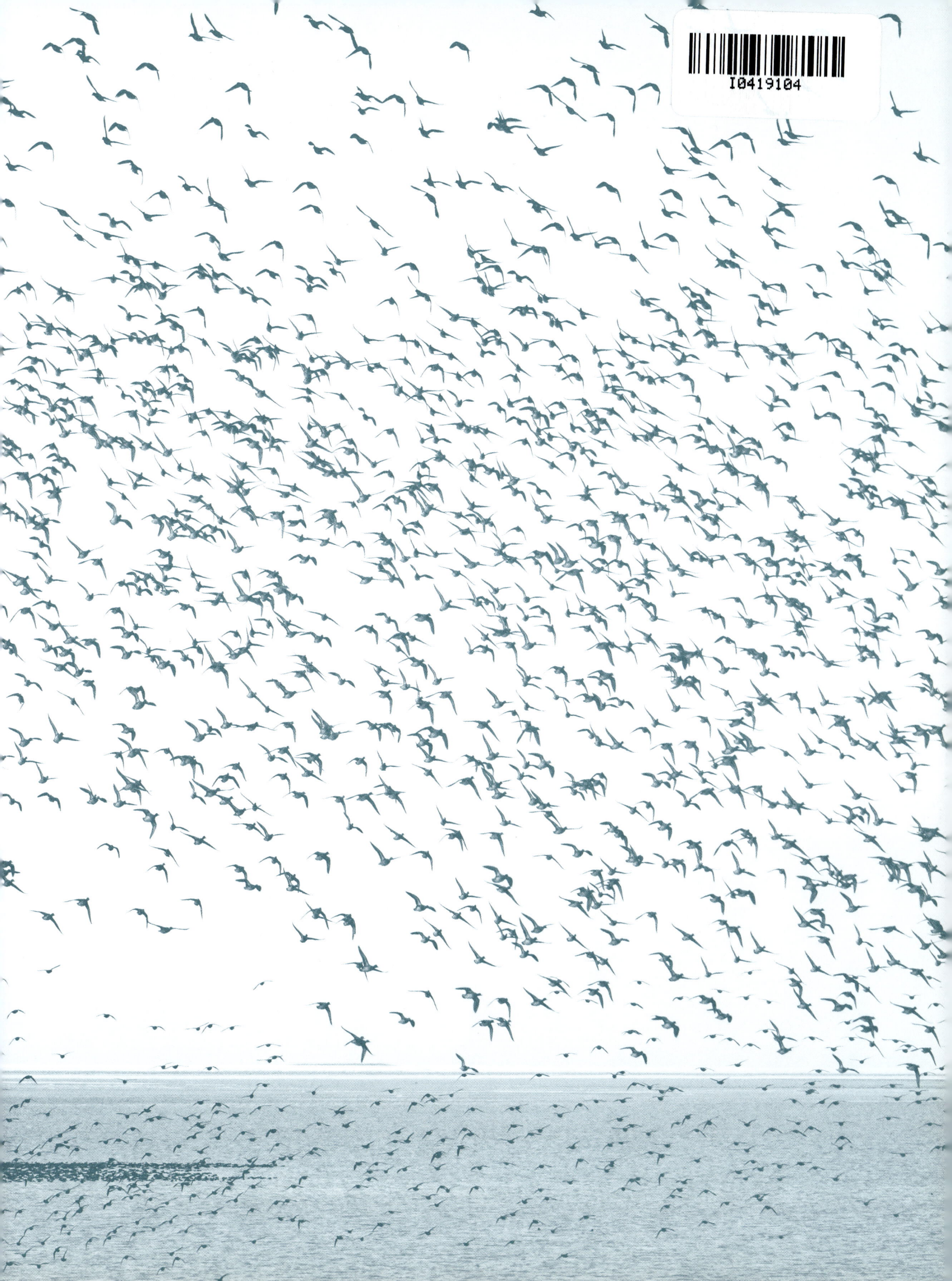

PRESERVING GREATNESS

GREAT SALT LAKE IN PHOTOGRAPHS

PRESERVING GREATNESS

GREAT SALT LAKE
IN PHOTOGRAPHS

CHRIS CARLSON

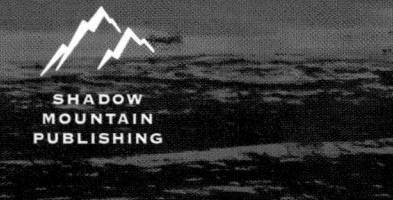

SHADOW
MOUNTAIN
PUBLISHING

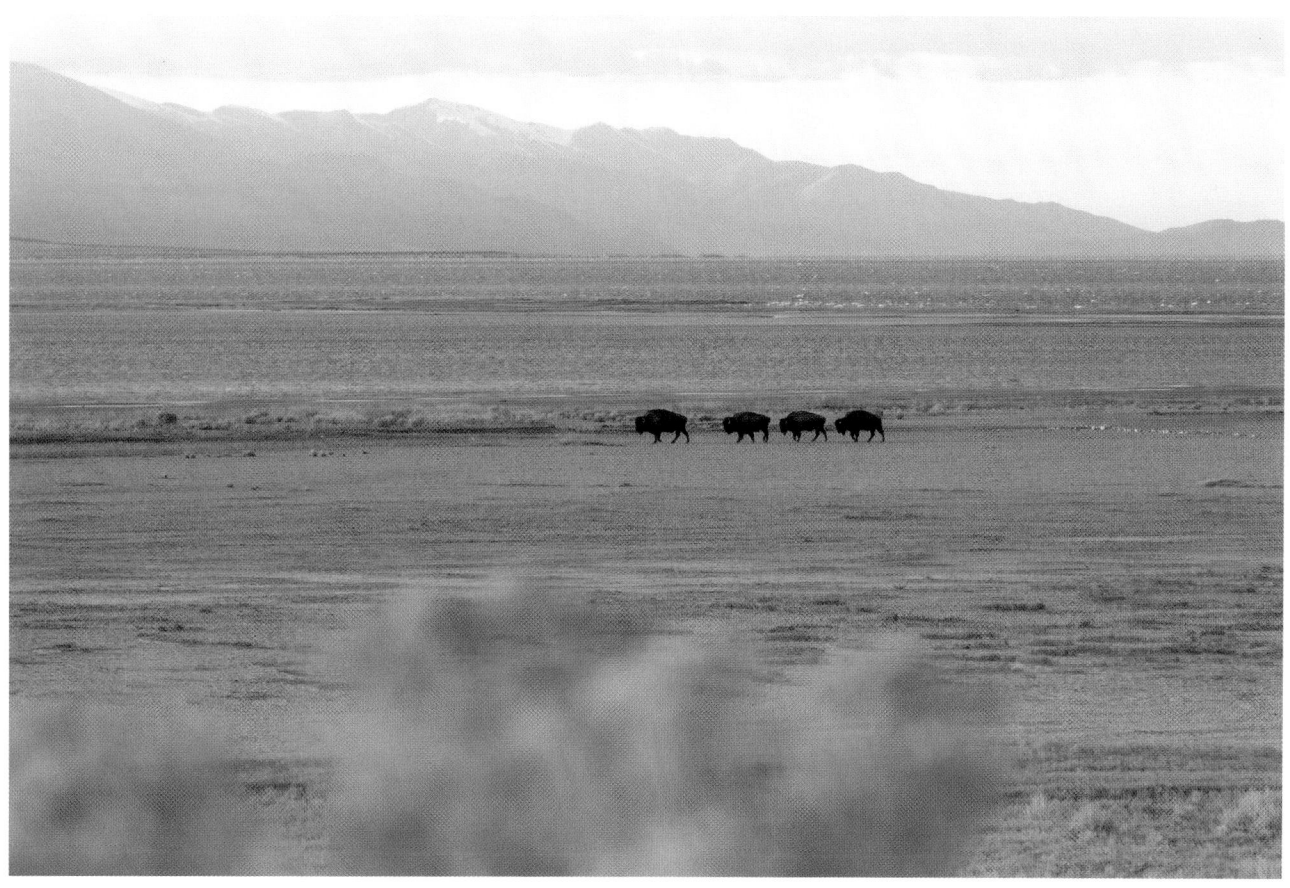

To my wife, Audrey, and my two sons, Jonah and Samuel.
I could not ask to be a part of a better herd.
The greatest things in my life have come because of you.

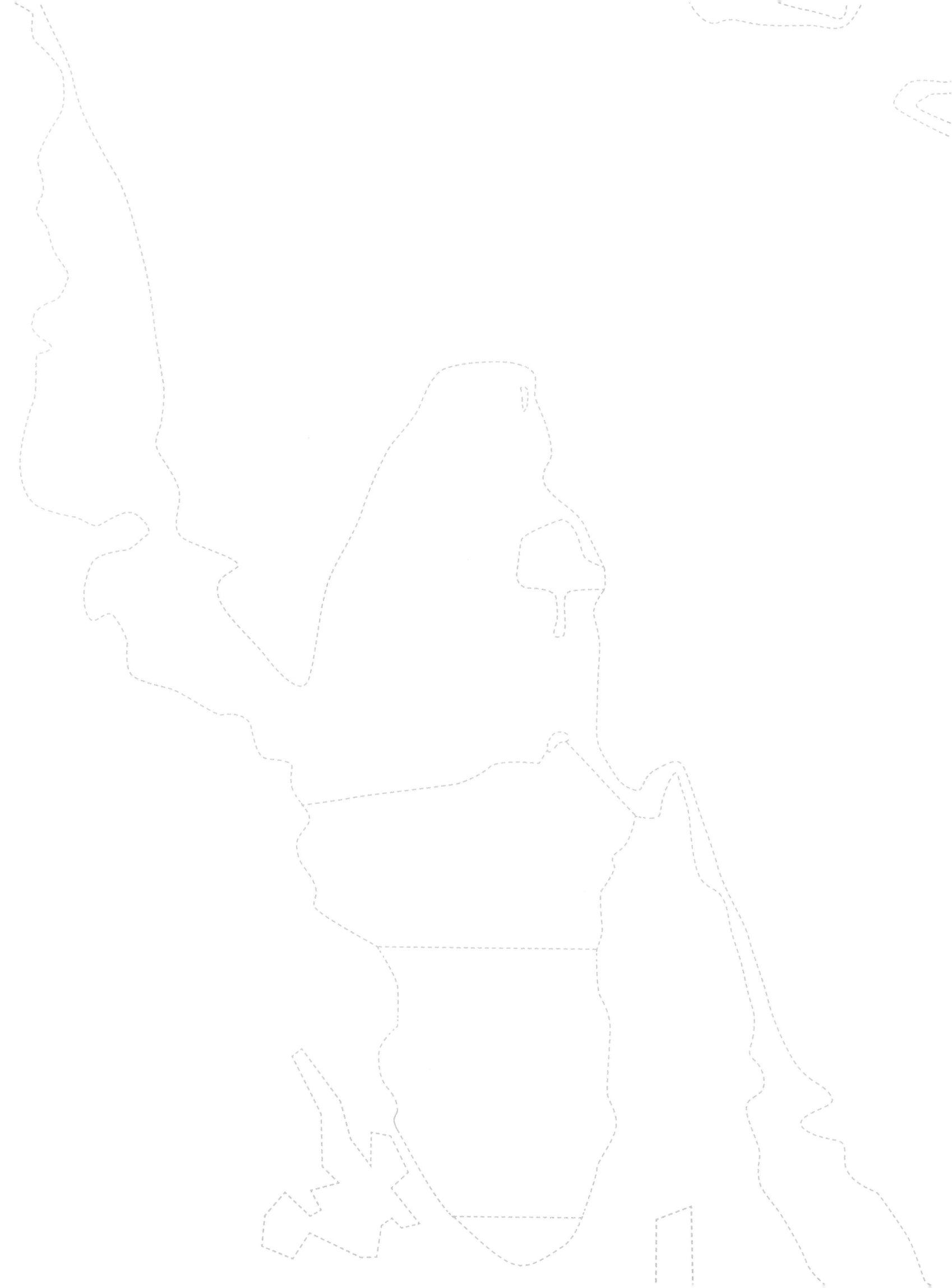

CONTENTS

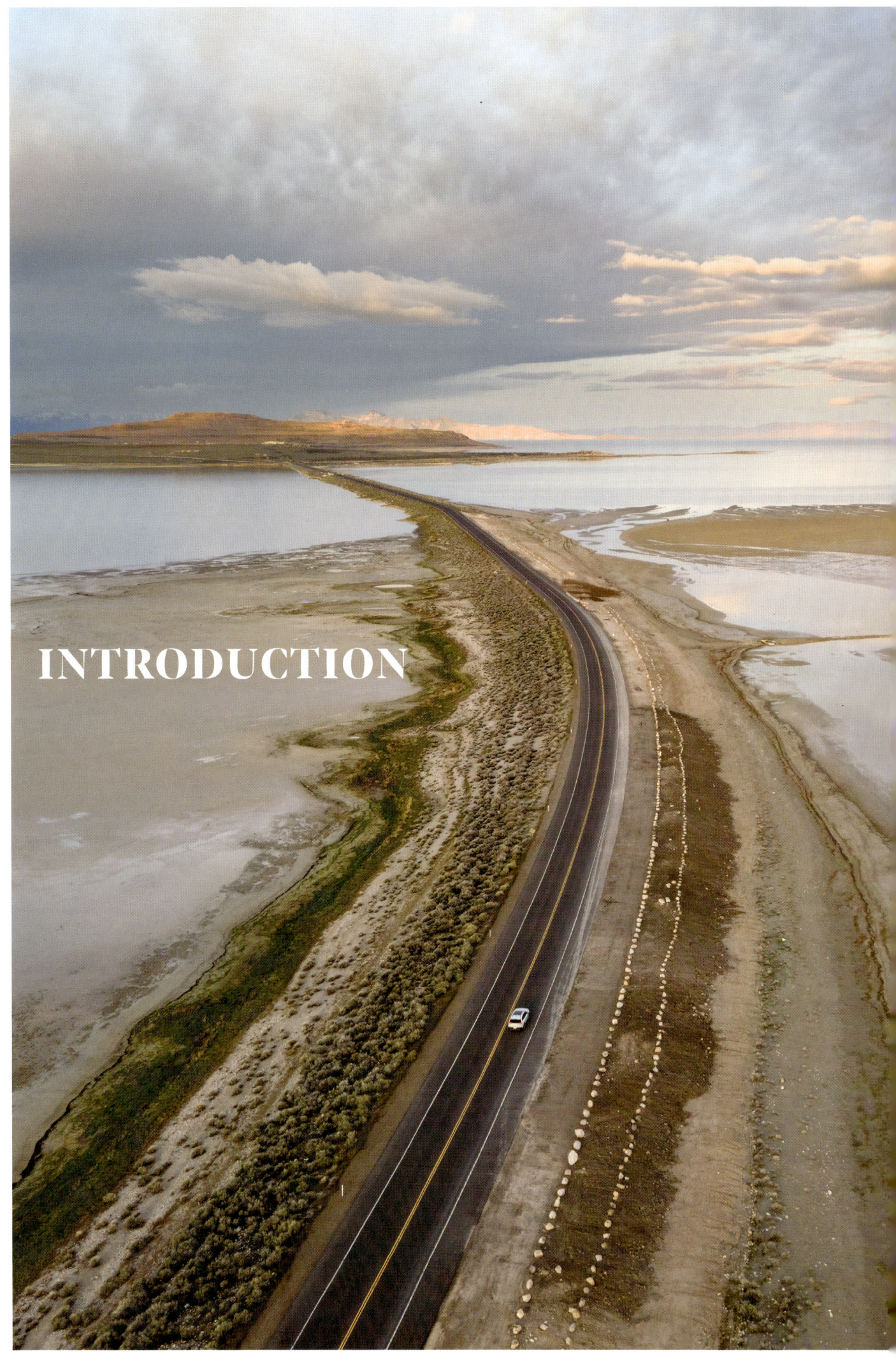

INTRODUCTION

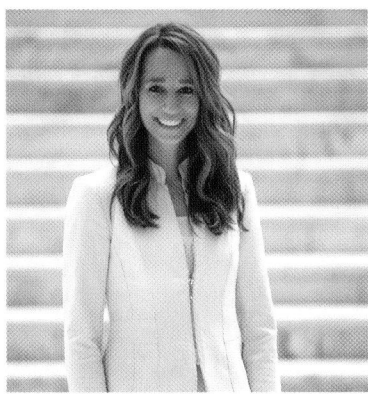

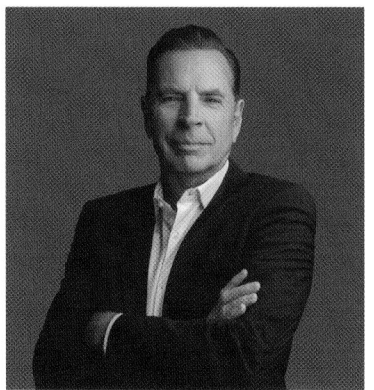

I'm a Utah girl at heart.

In my role as the First Lady of Utah, I launched a service-based initiative called "Show Up." Why? Because when needs arise, that's exactly what the people of the great state of Utah do! And that is exactly what is needed—right now—to preserve the greatness of the Great Salt Lake. Far more than a stunning natural canvas, the Great Salt Lake fuels our quality of life—from the multibillion-dollar impact on our economy to the quality of our world-famous snow.

As you turn the pages of this book and soak in the beauty of Chris Carlson's uniquely stunning photographs of the Great Salt Lake, my hope is that it moves both your heart to treasure it and your hands to act to preserve it. I'm calling on all Utahns to show up as advocates for its protection and community builders to preserve our state's beauty, opportunity, and prosperity for future generations.

ABBY COX

First Lady of Utah and Advocate for Legacy

I know a thing or two about preserving greatness.

From the moment the flame went out at the closing ceremony of the 2002 Olympic Winter Games, Utah went to work; preserving and maintaining the world-class venues to train the next generation of Olympians and transform our amazing state into the home of winter sport. These tireless efforts paid off as we secured the bid to bring the Games back to Utah in 2034.

However, the home of "The Greatest Snow on Earth" owes its world-famous title to the Great Salt Lake. The magic of our powder days is born from the lake's unique salinity and those perfect northwesterly winds that sculpt snowflakes into memories that last a lifetime.

Simply put, we can't preserve our state as the home of winter sport if we don't preserve the greatness of the Great Salt Lake. The two are forever tied together—what a responsibility and what an opportunity! With vivid detail, Chris Carlson's photographs inspire me to join others in preserving and championing the Great Salt Lake—to 2034 and beyond.

FRASER BULLOCK

President and CEO, Salt Lake City—Utah Committee for the Games

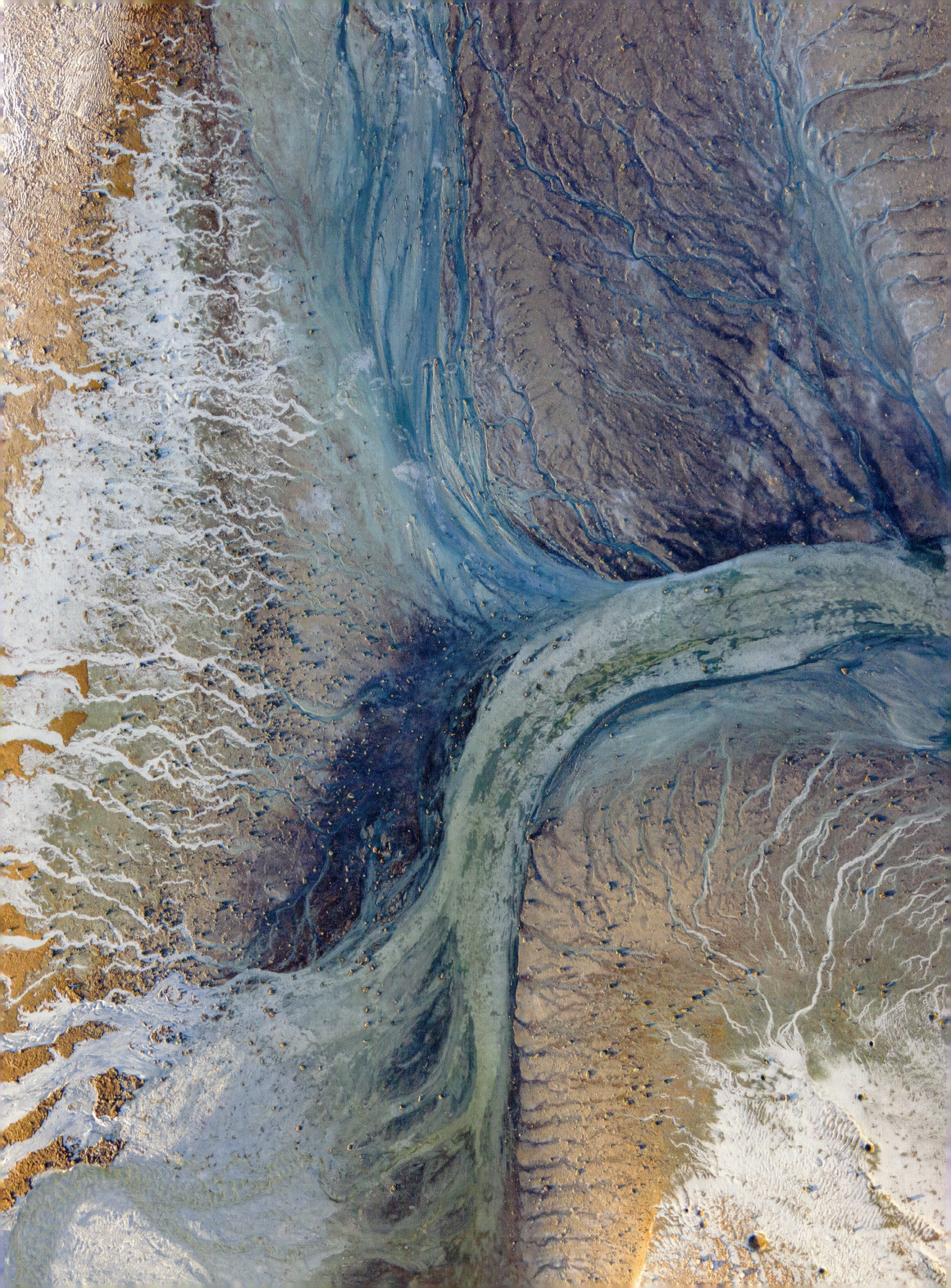

A Journey Through Loss and Memory

THIS PROJECT BEGAN during an incredibly challenging period of my life. My father was in the grip of Alzheimer's disease, a cruel illness that slowly stripped away his memories, piece by piece. I watched, heartbroken, as this brilliant, vibrant man—who had once been my guide, my teacher, my hero—began to fade into a fog of forgotten moments. The disease took more than just his memories; it took the very essence of who he was, until even his body forgot how to eat. In the final days, there was a profound helplessness in knowing I could not hold onto what was slipping away. When he passed, I felt a deep and consuming grief—a grief not just for his loss, but for the loss of all the stories, experiences, and memories he carried within him.

In the depths of that sorrow, I found myself drawn to Great Salt Lake. Its vast, ever-changing landscape became a sanctuary, a place where I could be alone with my thoughts and emotions. The lake offered a kind of solace, an open space to feel the full weight of my grief. Photographing its shores became more than just a creative pursuit; it transformed into a means of healing. Every visit to the lake, every shutter click, felt like a meditation—a way to make sense of the loss, a way to channel my pain into something tangible and lasting. I spent countless hours shooting, reshooting, editing, and refining, searching for the right way to capture what I was feeling.

As time passed, the lake began to reveal itself to me in new ways. I began to see its greatness not merely in its expanse but in its quiet resilience, its capacity to endure and change. The lake was not just a body of water but a living, breathing entity with its own stories, its own struggles, its own significance. Its beauty was undeniable, but so too was its fragility. With every photograph, my sense of advocacy deepened. Friends and family began to ask why I was so captivated by this place. What was it about the lake that held me so firmly in its grasp?

I realized I was compelled to capture the essence of Great Salt Lake—not just to showcase its beauty, but to raise awareness of its precarious state. I felt an urgency to create a visual record that might stir others to care, to act, to remember. I wanted these images to speak to the heart, to remind people of what might be lost if we do not pay attention.

This journey didn't begin with the intention of creating a book. I was driven by a simple, profound need to express, to document, and to hold onto something in the face of loss. But as the collection of photographs grew, capturing so many facets of the lake's character and soul, a book began to feel like a natural evolution. It became a way to share my personal journey with others, inviting them to see Great Salt Lake with fresh eyes—as a place worth remembering, preserving, and fighting for.

To those who have taken the time to purchase or even simply leaf through this book, I offer my deepest thanks. Your interest in these images means more to me than words can express. You have become a part of this journey—a journey of memory, of loss, and of finding unexpected beauty in the face of change. Thank you for letting these photographs tell their story to you. I hope they inspire you to view Great Salt Lake with the same sense of wonder and urgency that has driven me throughout this project.

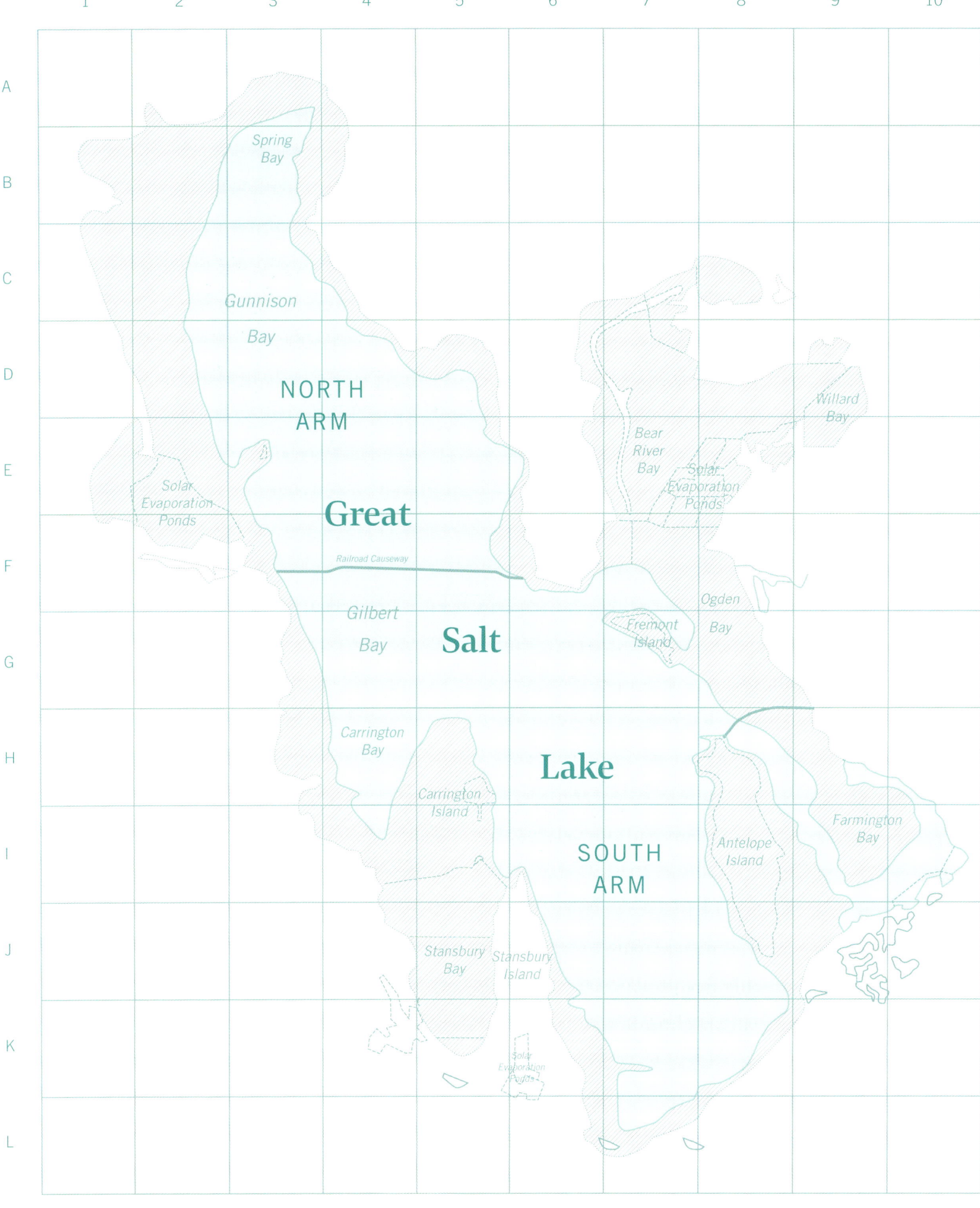

GREAT SALT LAKE

GREAT SALT LAKE is one of the largest saltwater lake in the Western Hemisphere, typically covering an area between 1,700 and 3,300 square miles (4,403 and 8,547 square kilometers)— roughly the size of Connecticut. At its fullest, the lake stretches approximately 75 miles (121 km) long and 35 miles (56 km) wide with an average depth of about 13 feet (4 meters) and a maximum depth of 33 feet (10 m). It features an irregular shape with numerous bays and inlets, divided into the North Arm and South Arm by a railroad causeway. Situated north-west of Salt Lake City, Utah, the lake is bordered by the Wasatch Mountains to the east, the Promontory Mountains to the north, and the Hogup Mountains to the west. Antelope Island is the largest of the lake's eleven islands, which also include notable others like Fremont Island, Stansbury Island, and Gunnison Island, each contributing to the lake's unique geographical and ecological story.

The map on this page is laid out on a grid. As you view photographs in this book, each photograph will be labeled with the date it was taken and the grid coordinates on this map so that you can understand when and where each was taken.

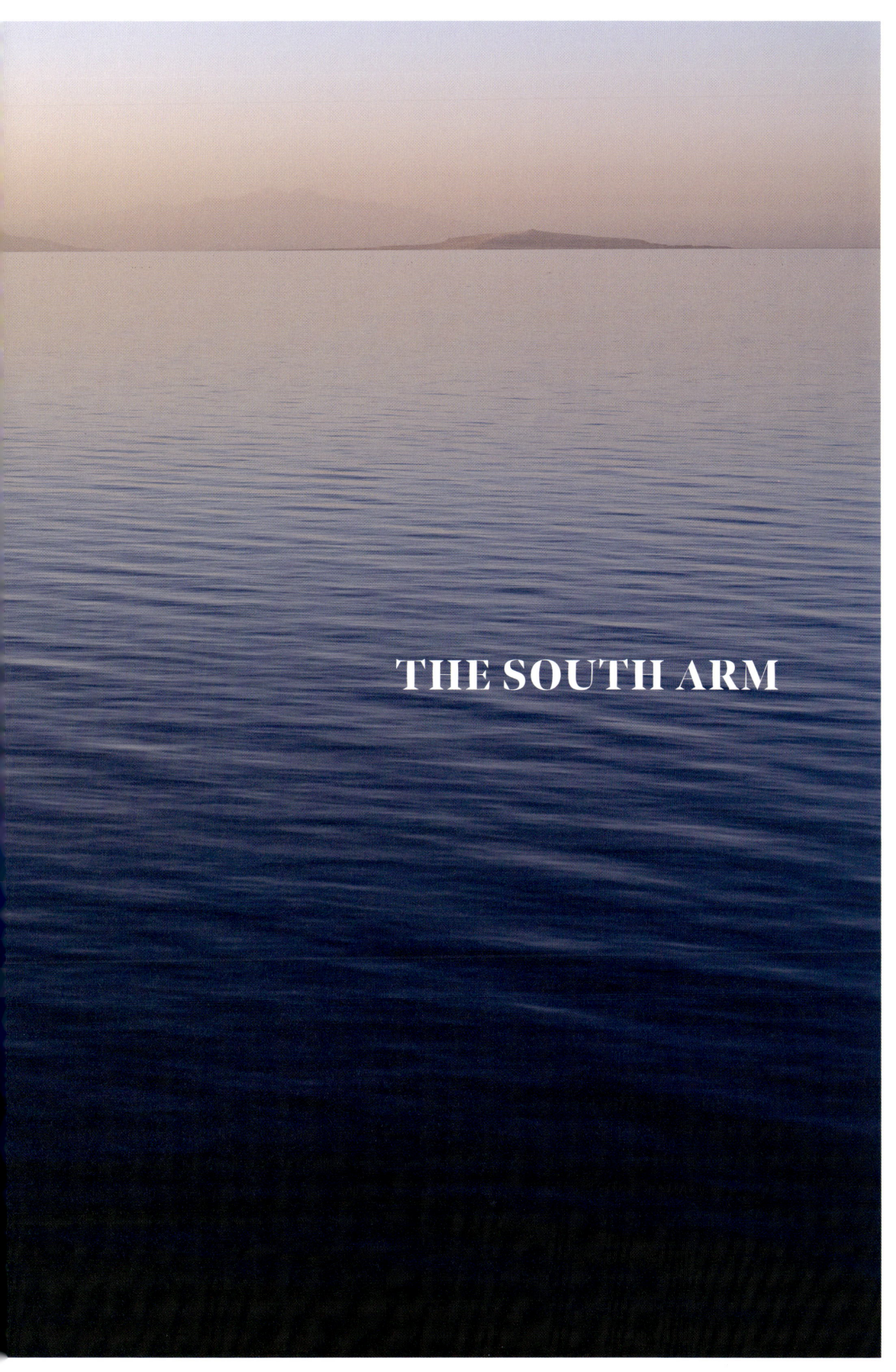

THE SOUTH ARM

01.

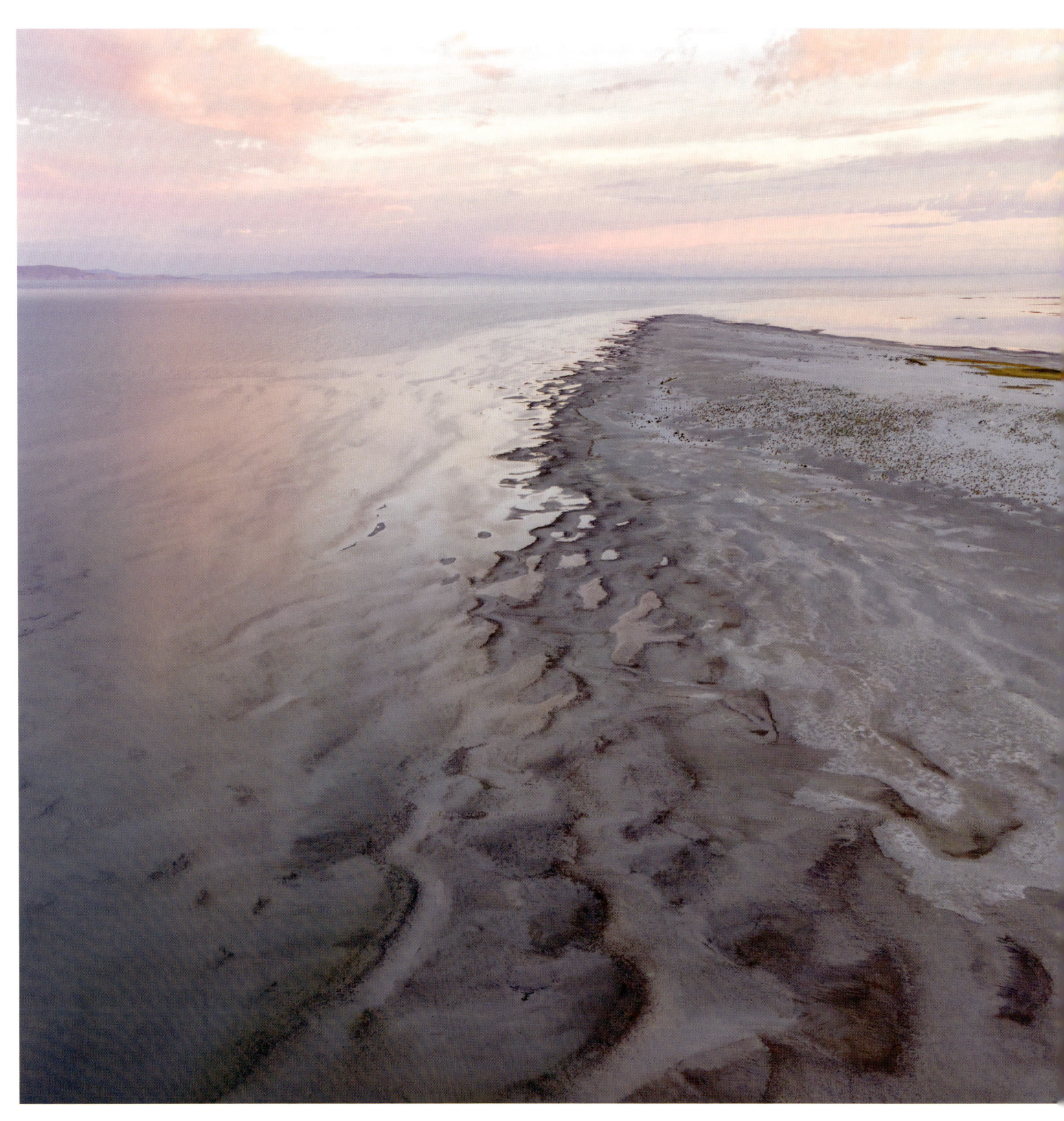

Gilbert Bay of Great Salt Lake | J8 | 09.10.2023

PREVIOUS PAGE: The South Arm of Great Salt Lake from Promontory Point | F6 | 10.05.2024

Nature's Resilient Sanctuary

THE SOUTH ARM OF GREAT SALT LAKE is a testament to nature's enduring spirit. This vast expanse, spanning 1,700 square miles (4403 sq km) with depths reaching 33 feet (10 m), is an ecological marvel—a sanctuary where life thrives despite and because of the briny waters. Indigenous nations like the Shoshone, Goshute, and Ute discovered sustenance and spiritual connection here. Early settlers marveled at this saline sea, finite yet infinite, weaving stories and traditions that echo across time.

The Jordan River, Bear River, Weber River, and smaller water sources like Lee Creek breathe vitality into this place, their merging flows nurturing a rich food web. Microbialites, ancient and vital components of the lake's ecosystem, are abundant in the South Arm. These "living rocks," formed by microbial communities that trap and bind sediments, provide essential nutrients and a primary food source for brine shrimp and brine flies. This, in turn, supports millions of migratory birds. The microbialites are not only critical for the lake's food web but also serve as indicators of the health of the entire ecosystem. They bring the sun's energy into the lake through photosynthesis, fueling the entire lake system. Millions of birds, such as avocets and eared grebes, arrive annually, drawn by this abundant feast.

Antelope Island, the crown jewel of Great Salt Lake's many islands, embodies the greatness of the South Arm. Its rugged beauty and diverse wildlife—bison, pronghorn antelope, myriad birds—reflect the lake's grandeur. From 6,596 feet (2,010 m) atop Antelope Island's Frary Peak, one can experience panoramic views that showcase the South Arm's vast expanse and seemingly endless horizon, while lower, locals gather at Ladyfinger Point and Buffalo Point to marvel at sunsets painting the sky in oranges and pinks.

To the north, Fremont Island whispers of history and mystery, a quiet refuge preserving the past because of its isolation and lack of human visitors. To the west, Stansbury Island beckons with its geological wonders and colorful evaporation ponds ripe for exploration. Each island enriches the South Arm's story with layers of allure and discovery.

The lush wetlands of Farmington Bay, a vibrant green contrasting the salty waters, filter life into the lake while providing crucial habitat for migratory waterfowl and shorebirds. On the southern shores, Black Rock's dark basalt form juts outward, a dramatic silhouette against the mirrored surface at sunset.

Great Salt Lake State Park stands as the gateway of the South Arm, inviting visitors to begin their journeys into this unique ecosystem. The park's programs deepen understanding of the lake's significance, while relics like Saltair's resort whisper nostalgically of joyful eras past.

Our relationship with the South Arm is a delicate balance between use and preservation. Industries draw from its resources, while conservationists strive to maintain ecological harmony. Challenges like water diversion, climate change, and pollution loom large, threatening this fragile ecosystem. This place is a reminder of nature's resilience and the interconnectedness of life.

ANTELOPE ISLAND

Antelope Island is a sanctuary of ecological diversity and recreational splendor. Home to free-roaming bison, pronghorn antelope, mule deer, and numerous bird species, the island's varied ecosystems—from grassy plains to salt marshes—support a rich array of wildlife. It offers scenic trails for hiking, biking, and horseback riding, while its white sandy beaches invite visitors to float in the buoyant, saline waters of Great Salt Lake. The historic Fielding Garr Ranch adds a layer of cultural significance, providing insights into the region's pioneer history. One of Antelope Island's most intriguing features is its fluctuating connection to the mainland. During periods of low water levels, land bridges emerge, transforming the island into an accessible extension of the shore.

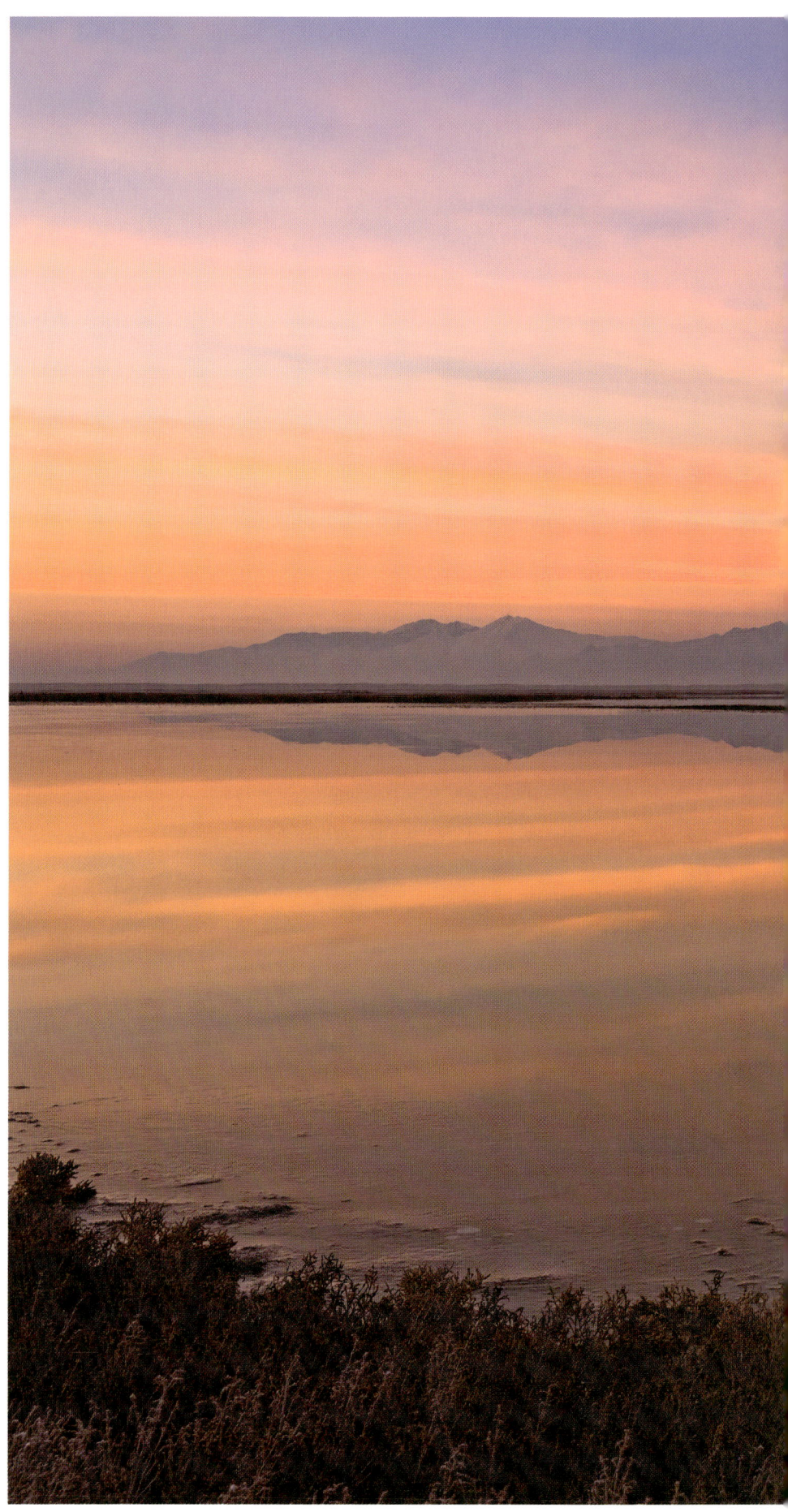

Sunrise, Antelope Island | H8 | 01.28.2024

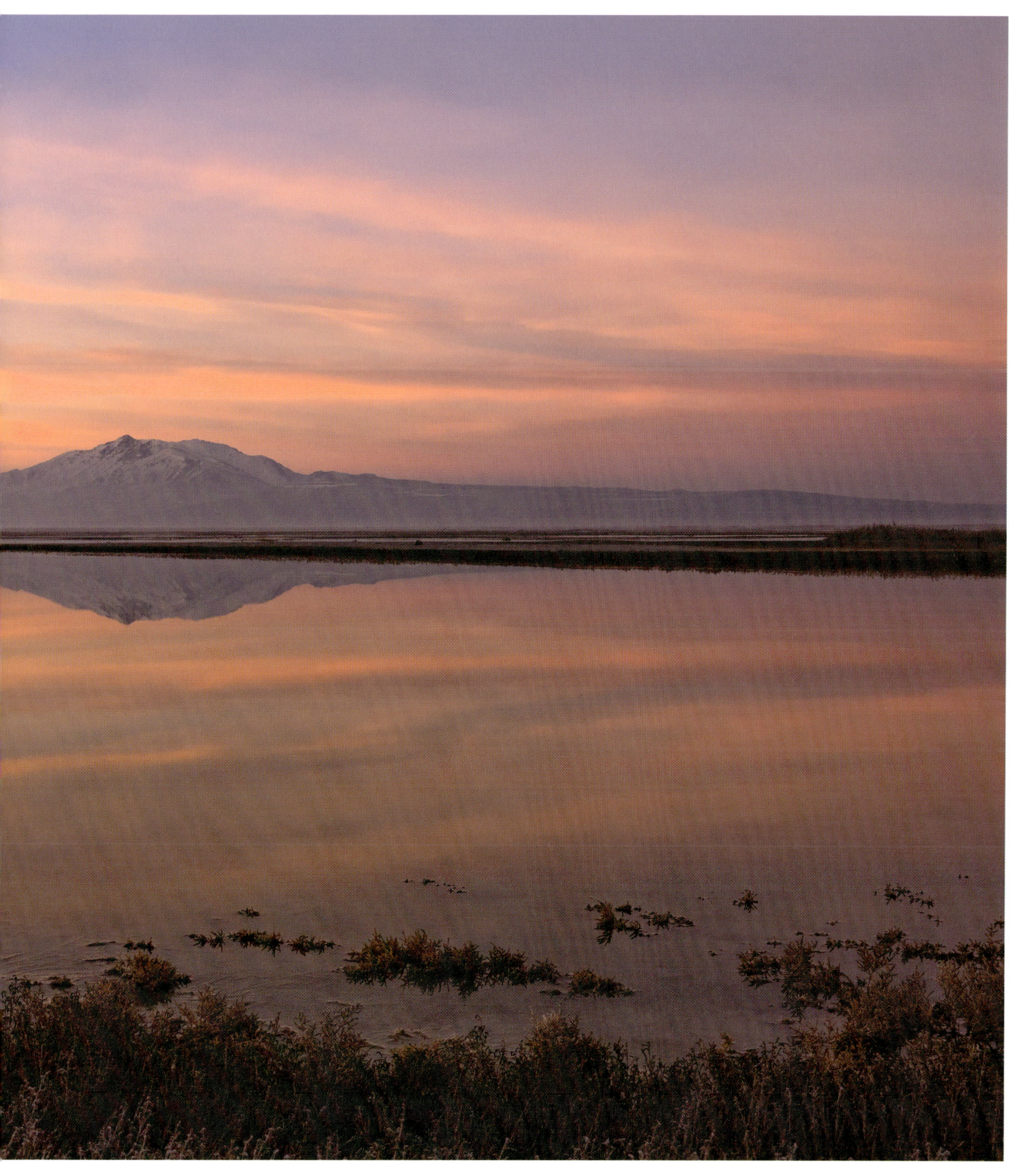

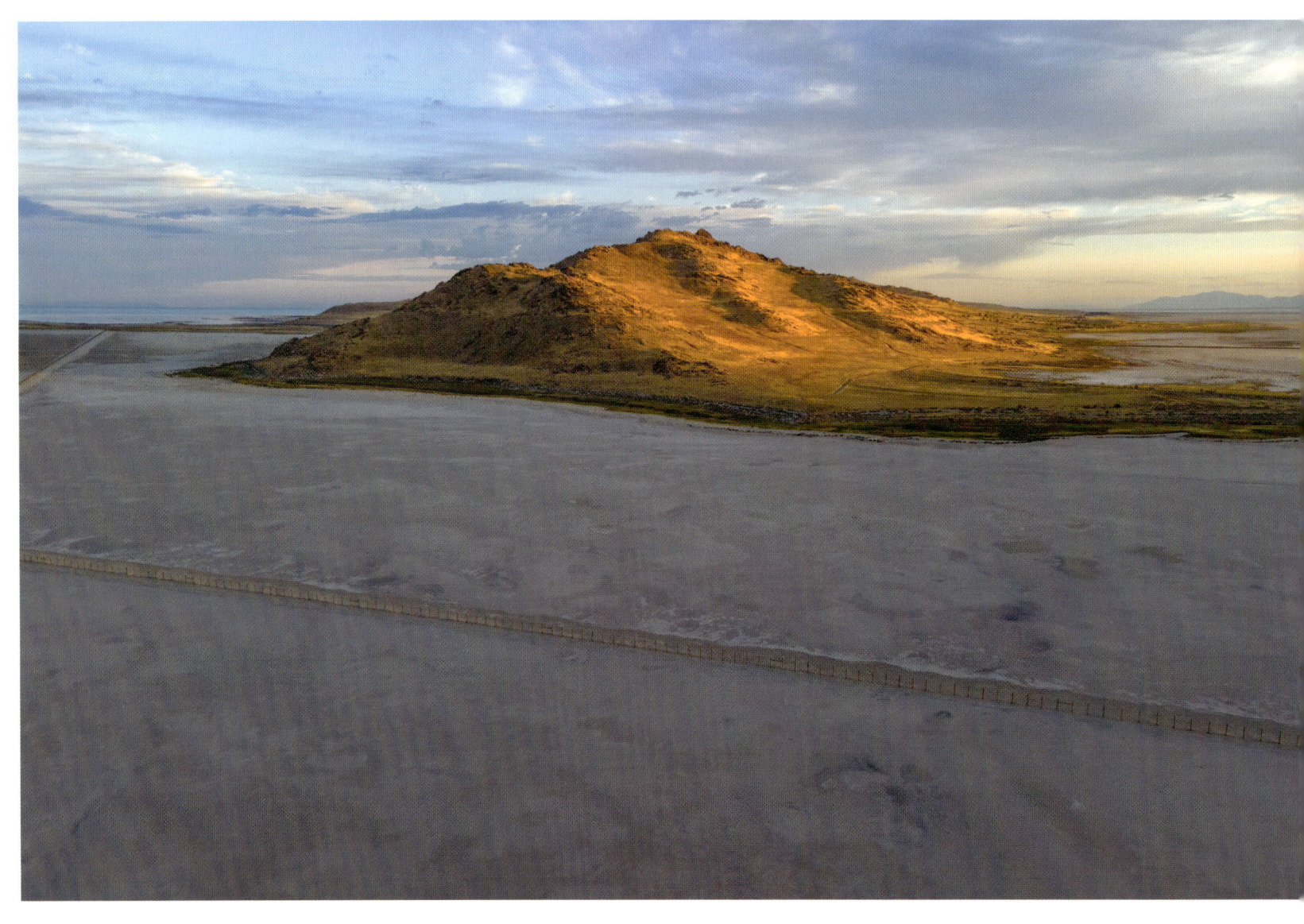

Sunrise, southern tip of Antelope Island | J8 | 09.10.2023

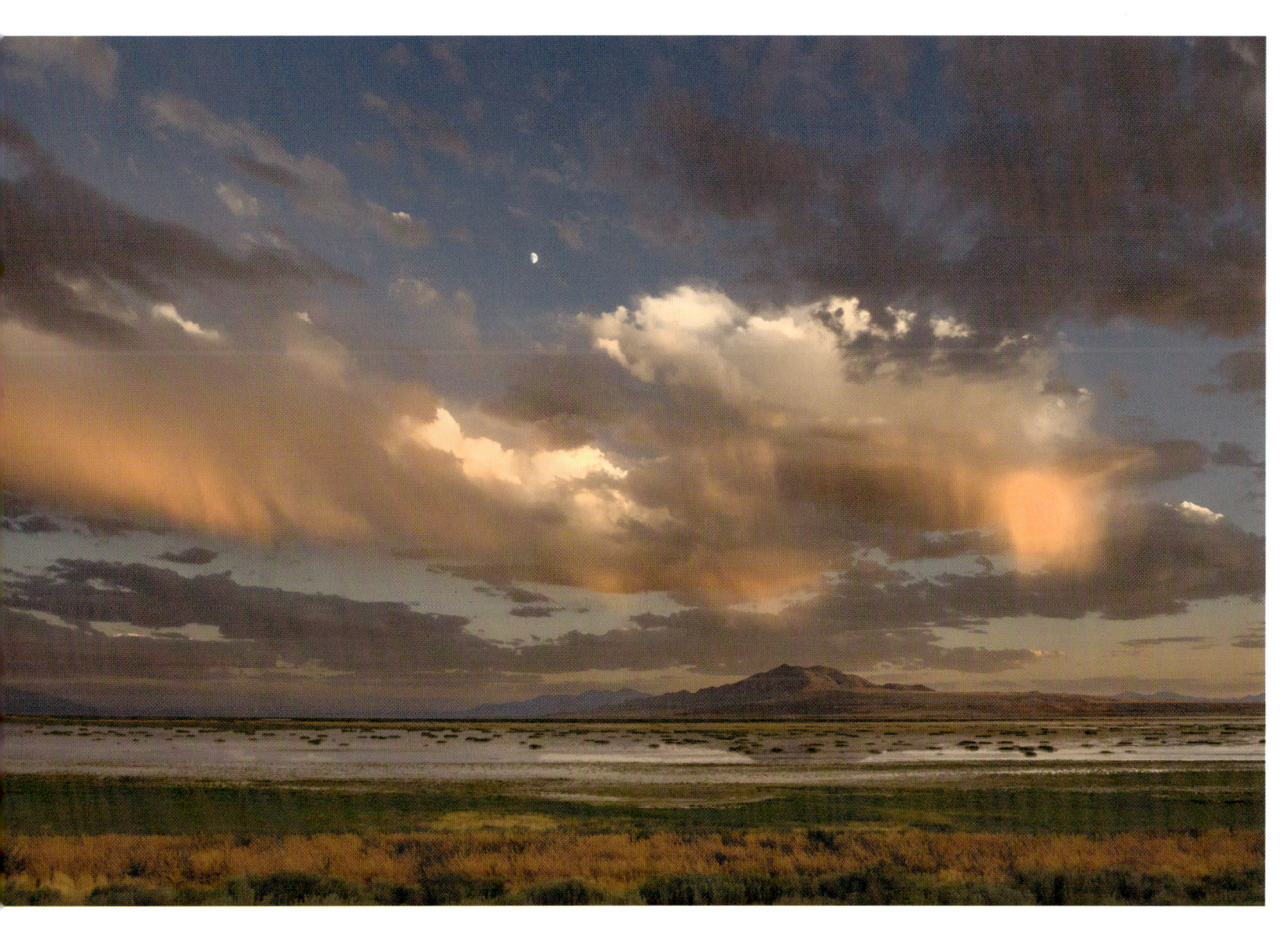

Sunset and breaking storm, Farmington Bay | H8 | 07.20.2023

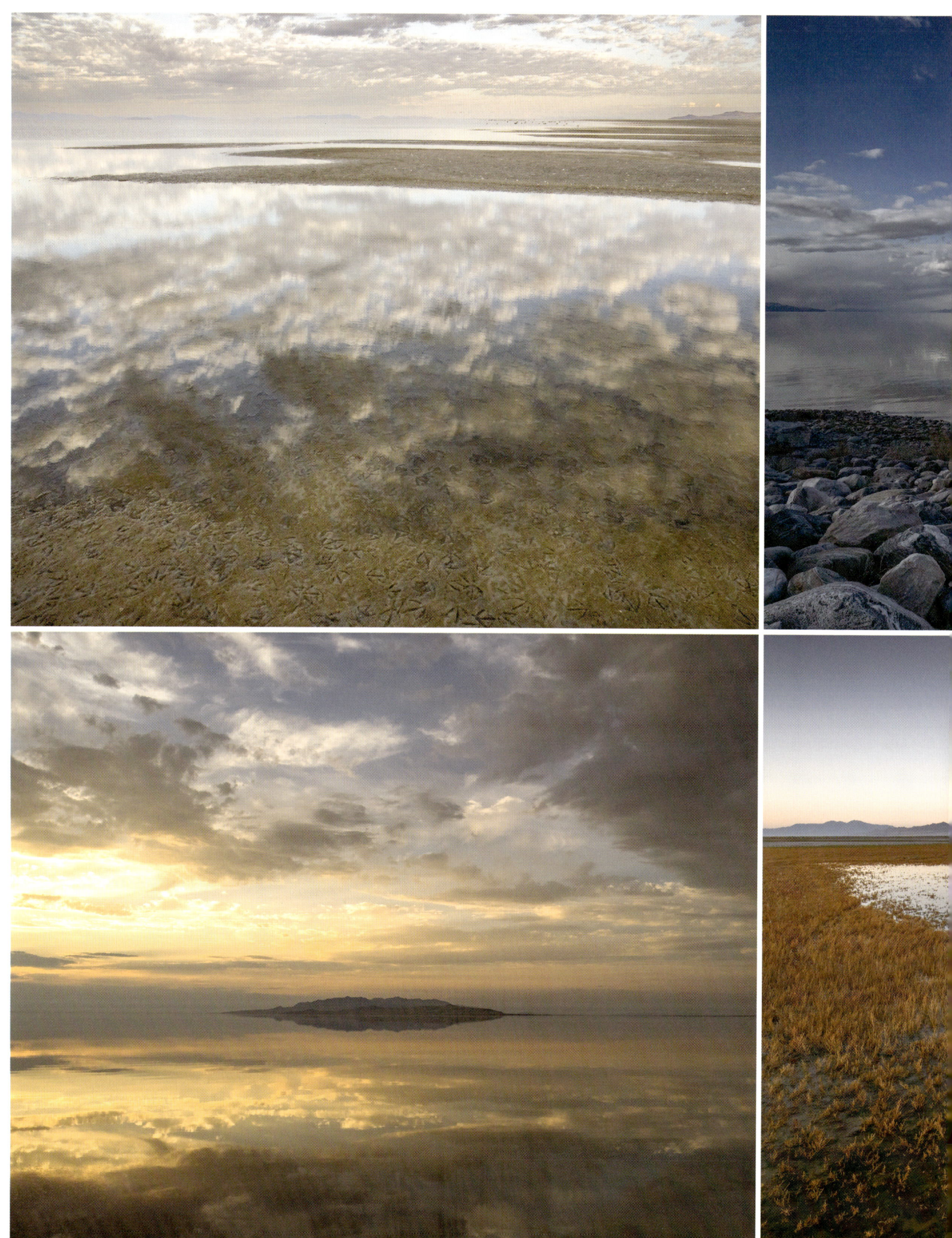

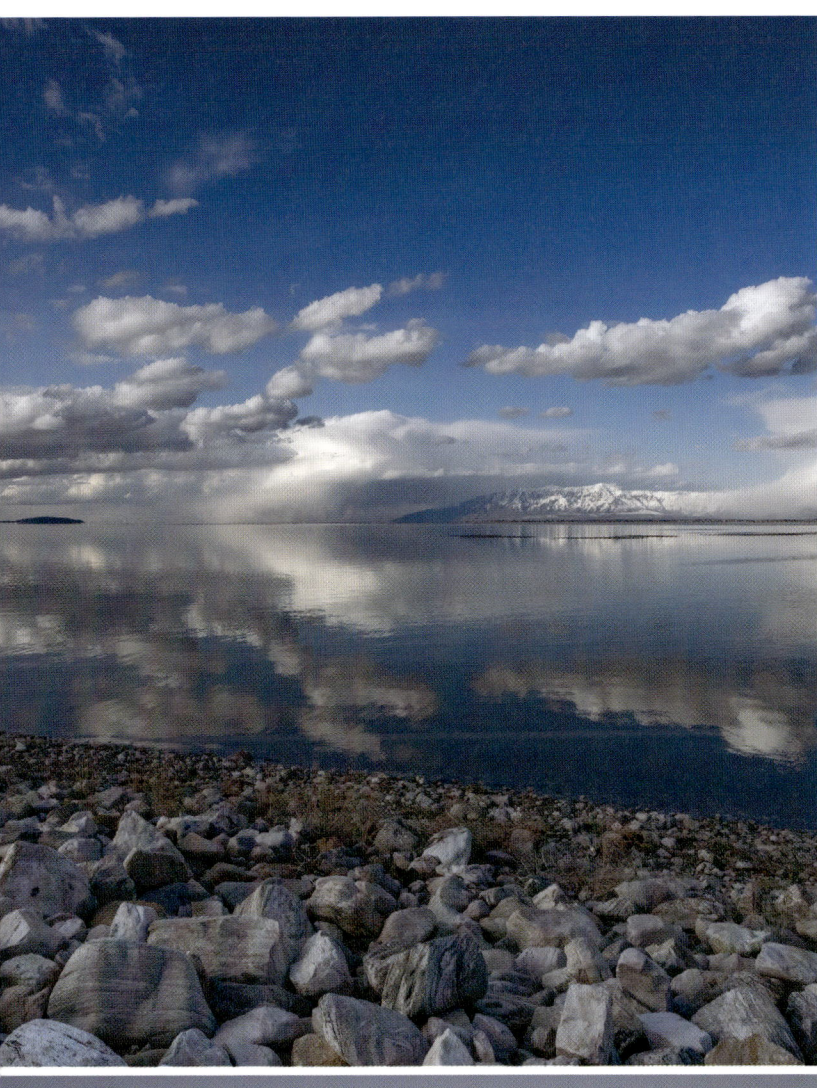

THE LAKE AS A MIRROR

When the weather is perfectly calm, Great Salt Lake transforms into a stunning natural mirror, reflecting the sky and surroundings with remarkable clarity. The surface of the water becomes glass-like, creating an illusion where the horizon seems to vanish, blending seamlessly with the expanse above. This mirror effect captures the colors of the sky, from the soft pastels of dawn to the fiery hues of sunset, producing a breathtakingly serene and ethereal landscape. The stillness amplifies the reflections of distant mountains, clouds, and even the slightest ripples, making the lake appear as a boundless, tranquil surface that mesmerizes and captivates anyone fortunate enough to witness this extraordinary phenomenon.

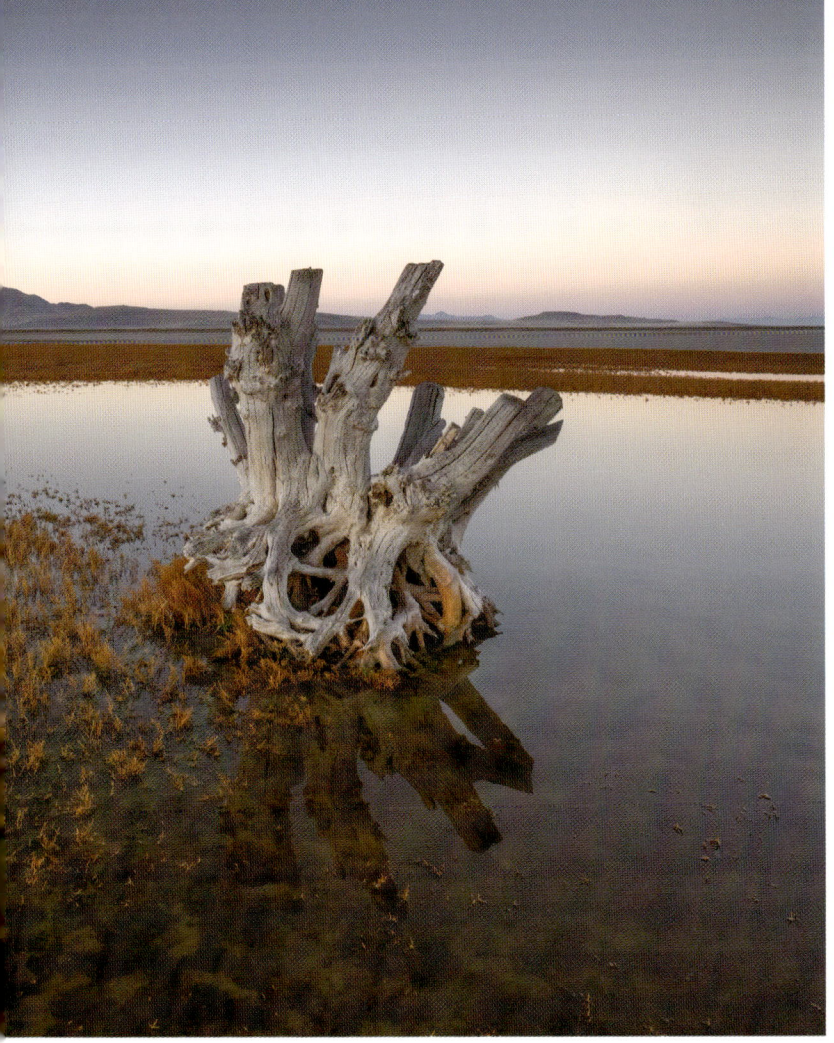

Bird footprints and cloud mirror, Antelope Island
H8 | 08.26.2023

Cloud mirror from Antelope Island
H8 | 04.14.2023

Fremont Island and Promontory Point
H8 | 07.18.2021

Tree of the past, near the causeway to Antelope Island
H8 | 09.02.2023

FOLLOWING PAGE: Tumbleweed and gradients, Farmington Bay | H8 | 09.23.2023

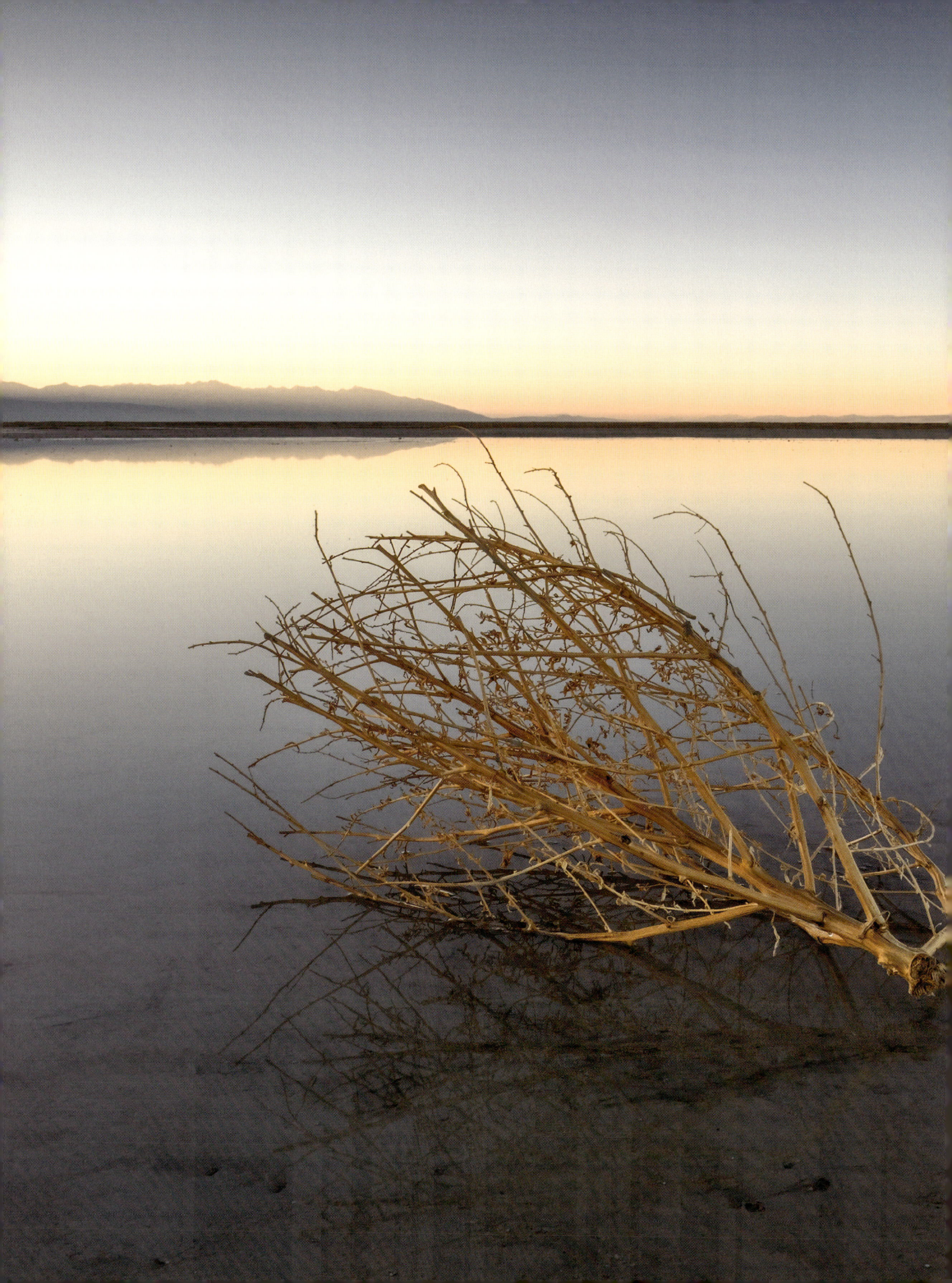

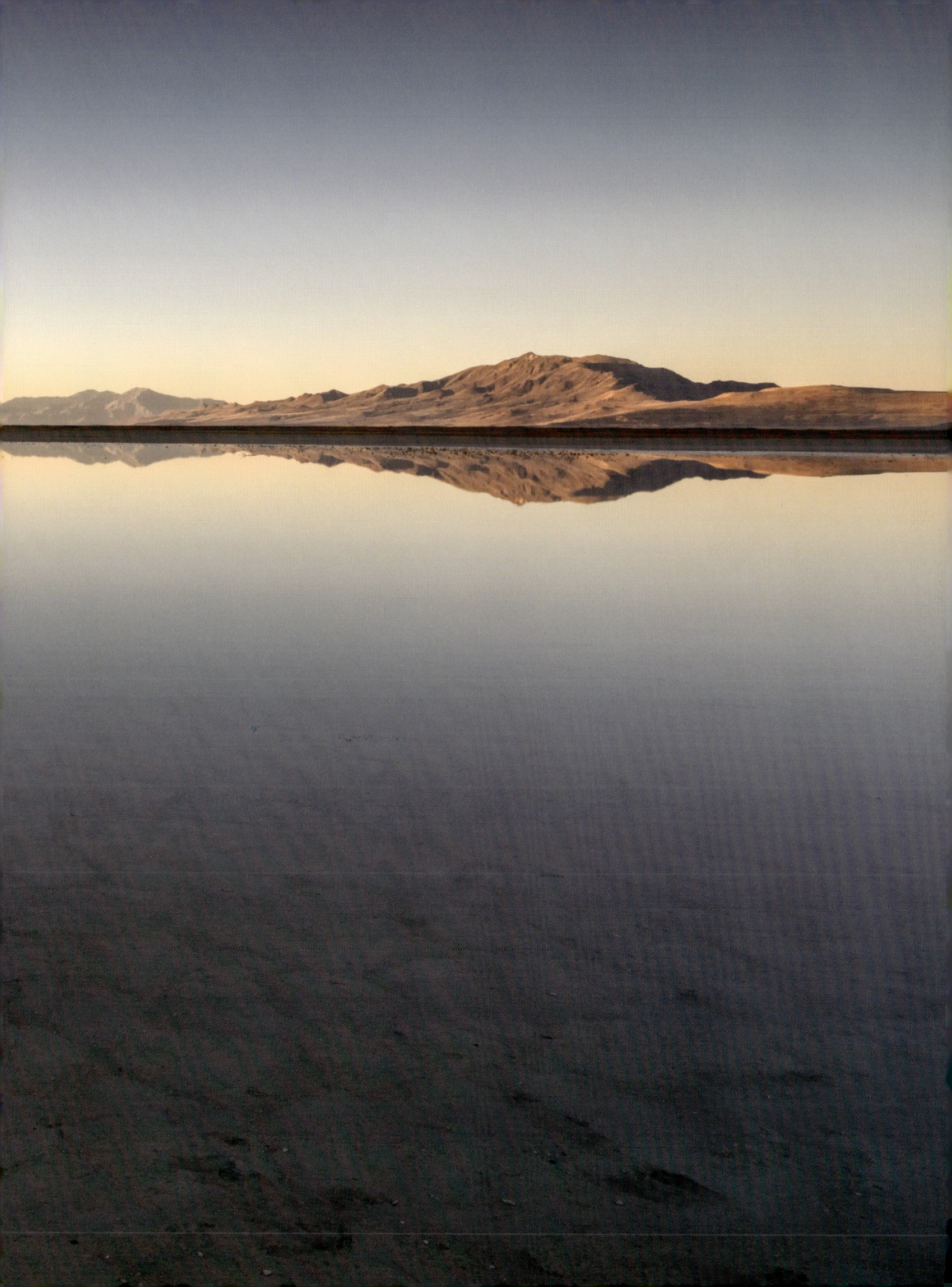

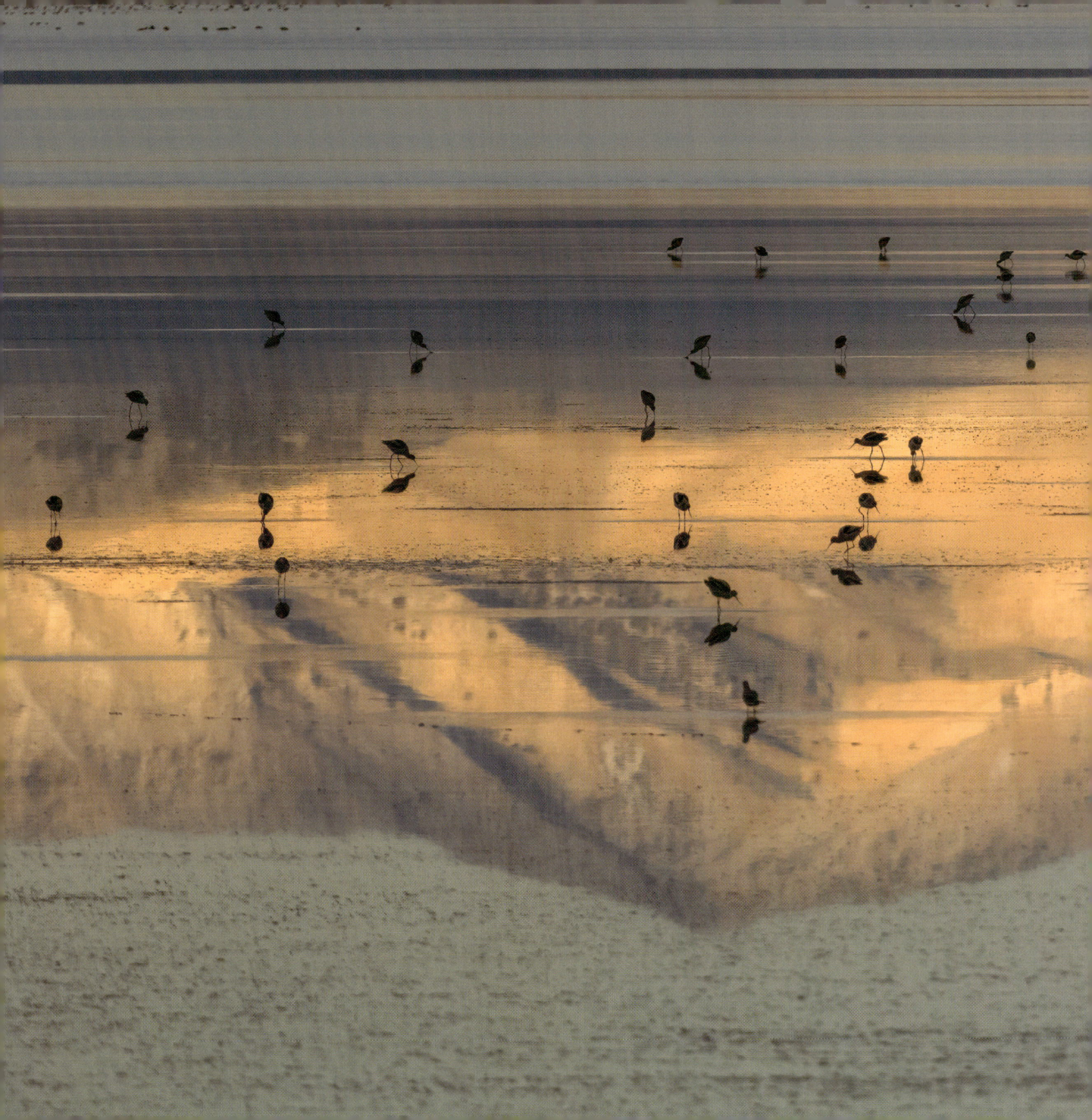

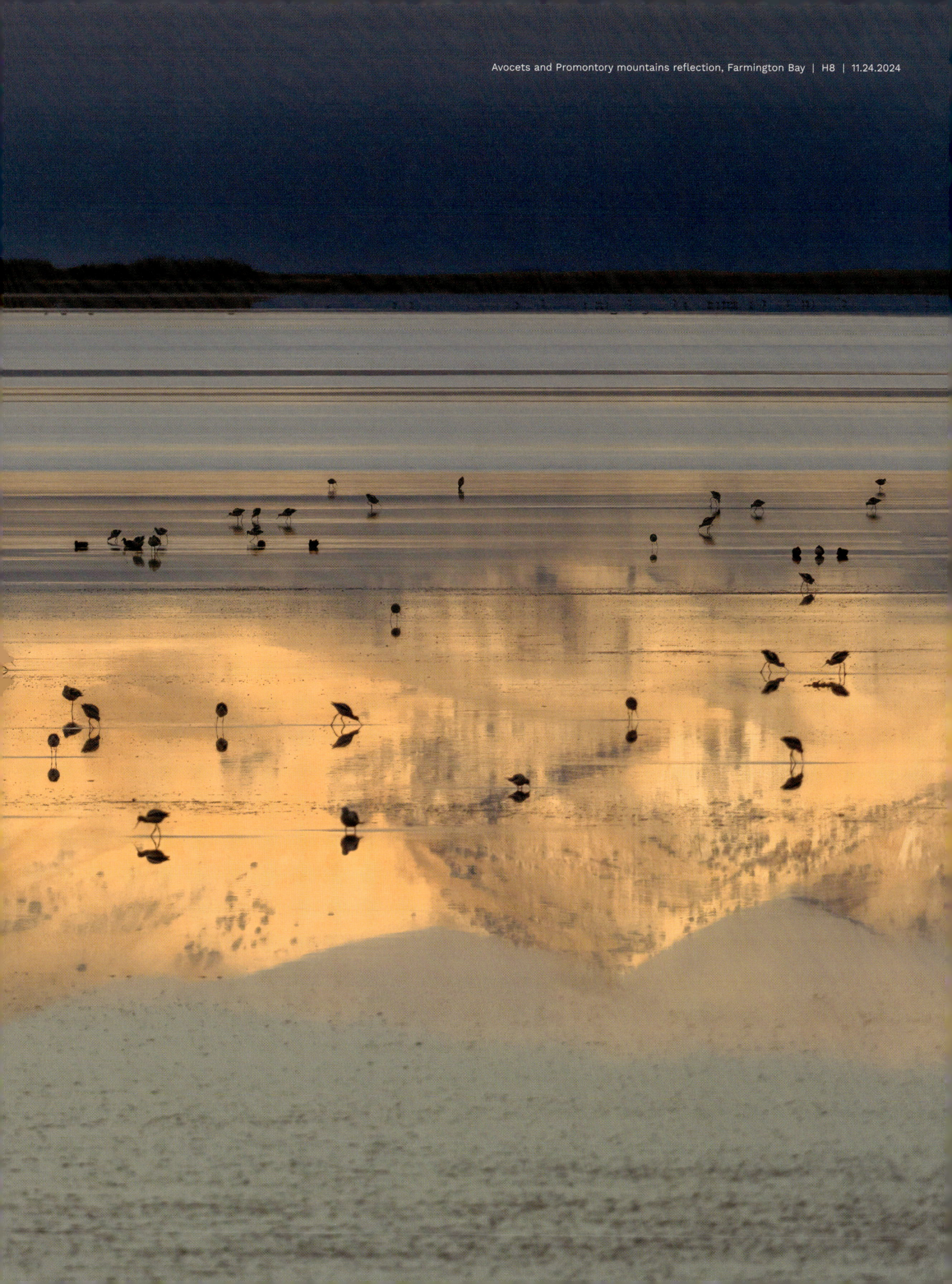

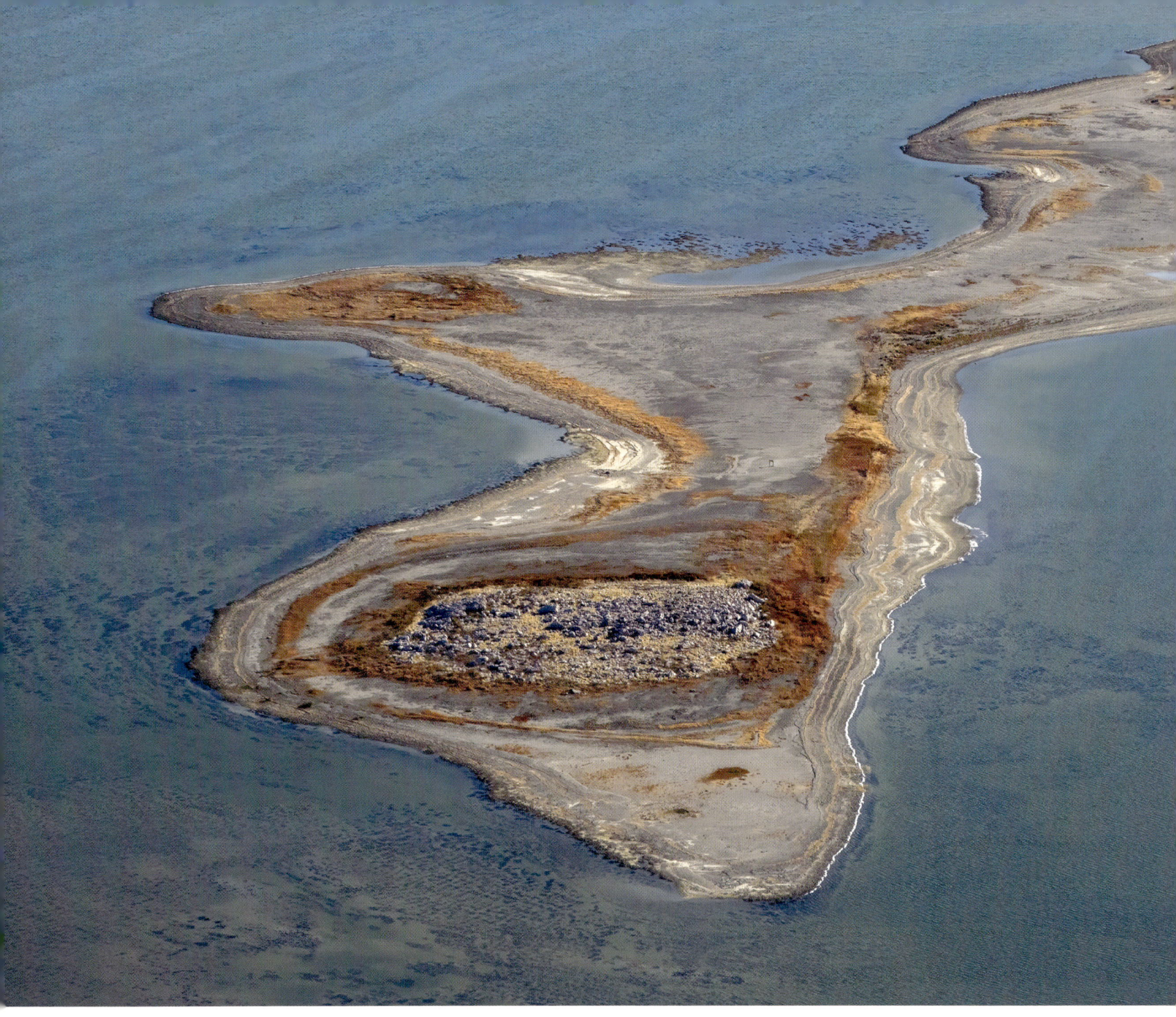

EGG ISLAND

Historically, Egg Island is a nesting site off Antelope Island for 5,000–8,000 gulls from April through June. During these months, gulls lay their eggs and hatch their young. Once the chicks mature, the gulls leave the island. Recently, due to insufficient water levels, Egg Island has not been fully separated from Antelope Island. This lack of separation has led gulls to nest elsewhere to avoid predators like coyotes.

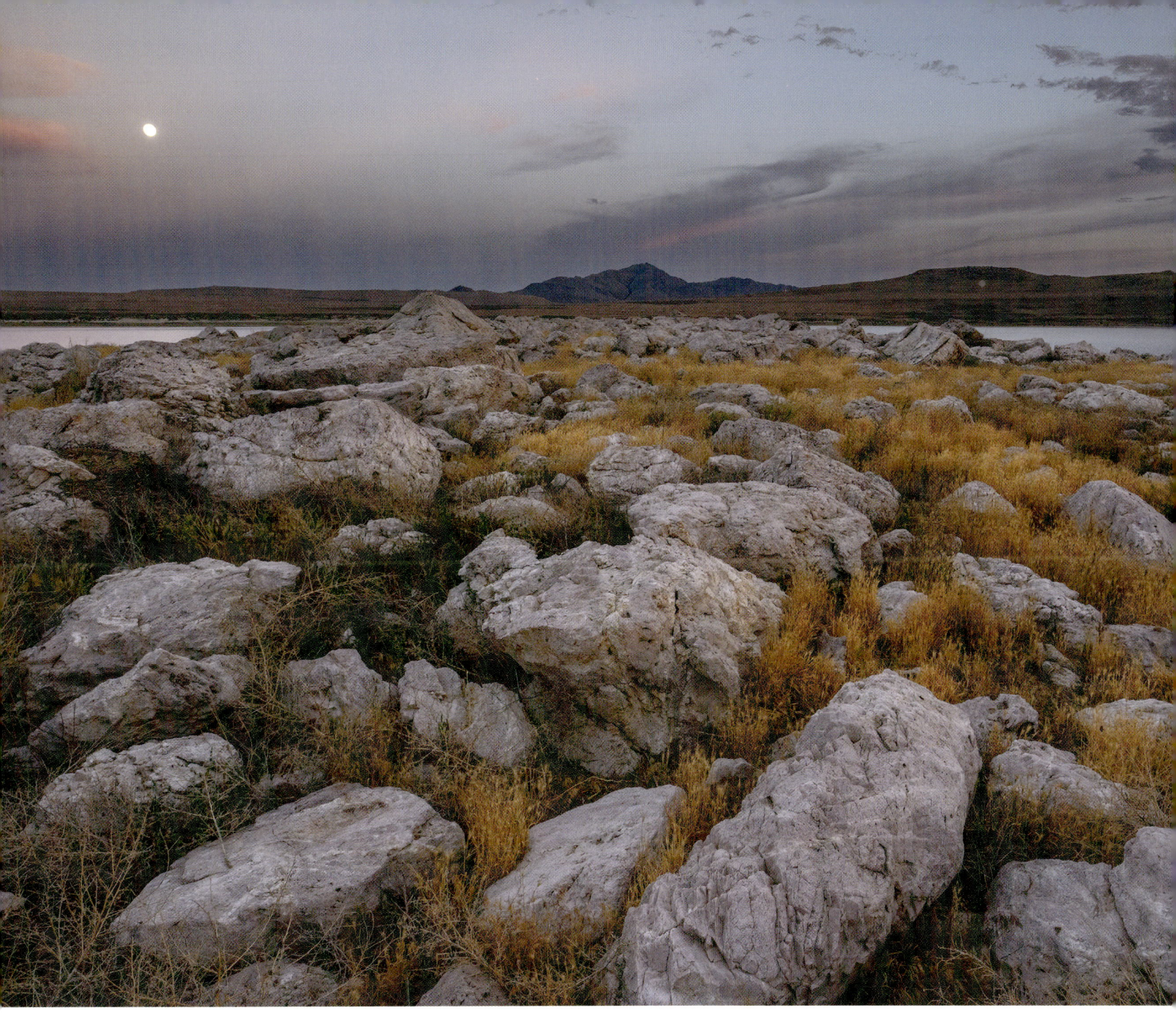

Egg Island from 5,000 feet (1,524 m) | H8 | 10.13.2023

Egg Island at night | H8 | 06.02.2023

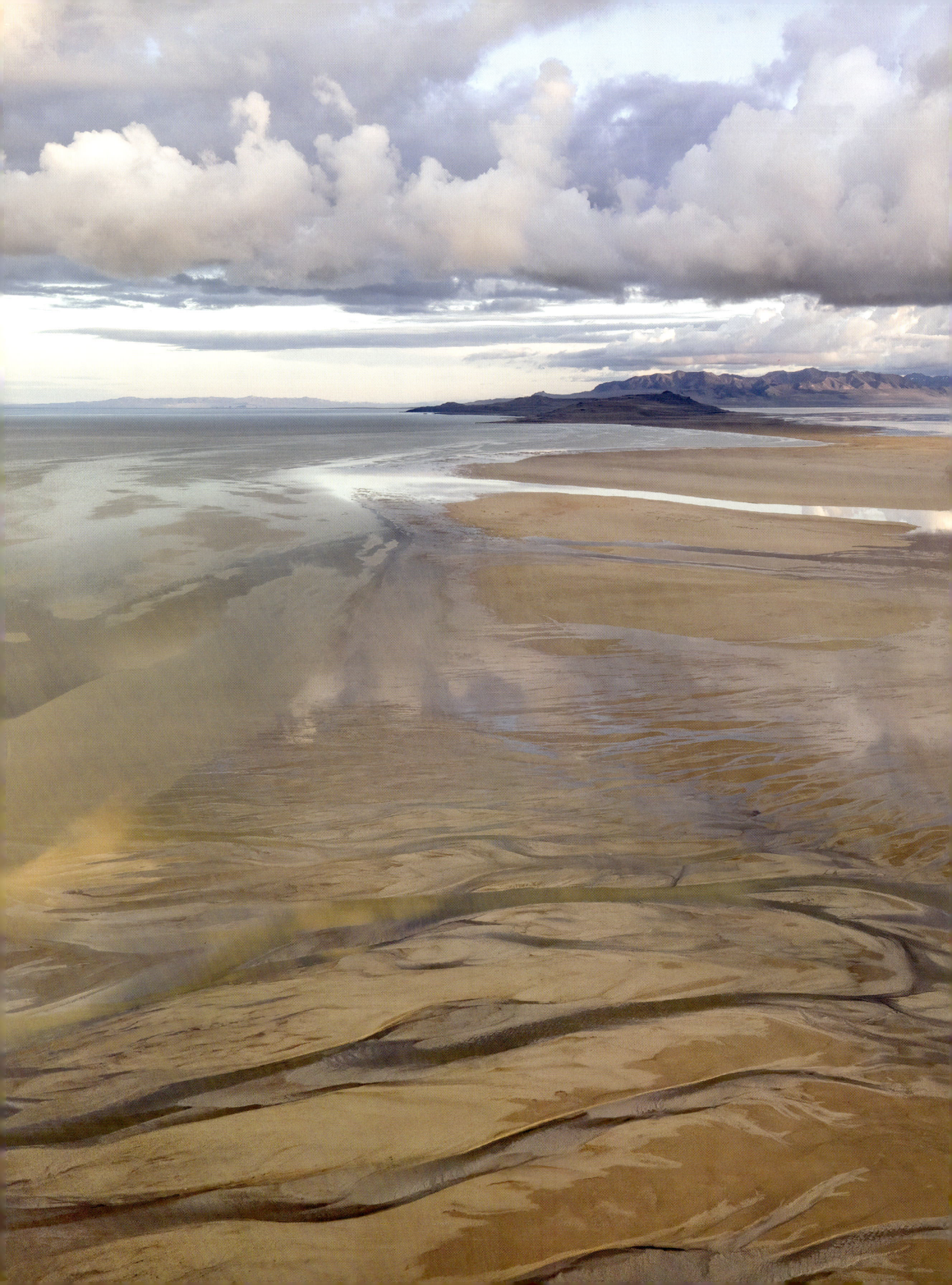

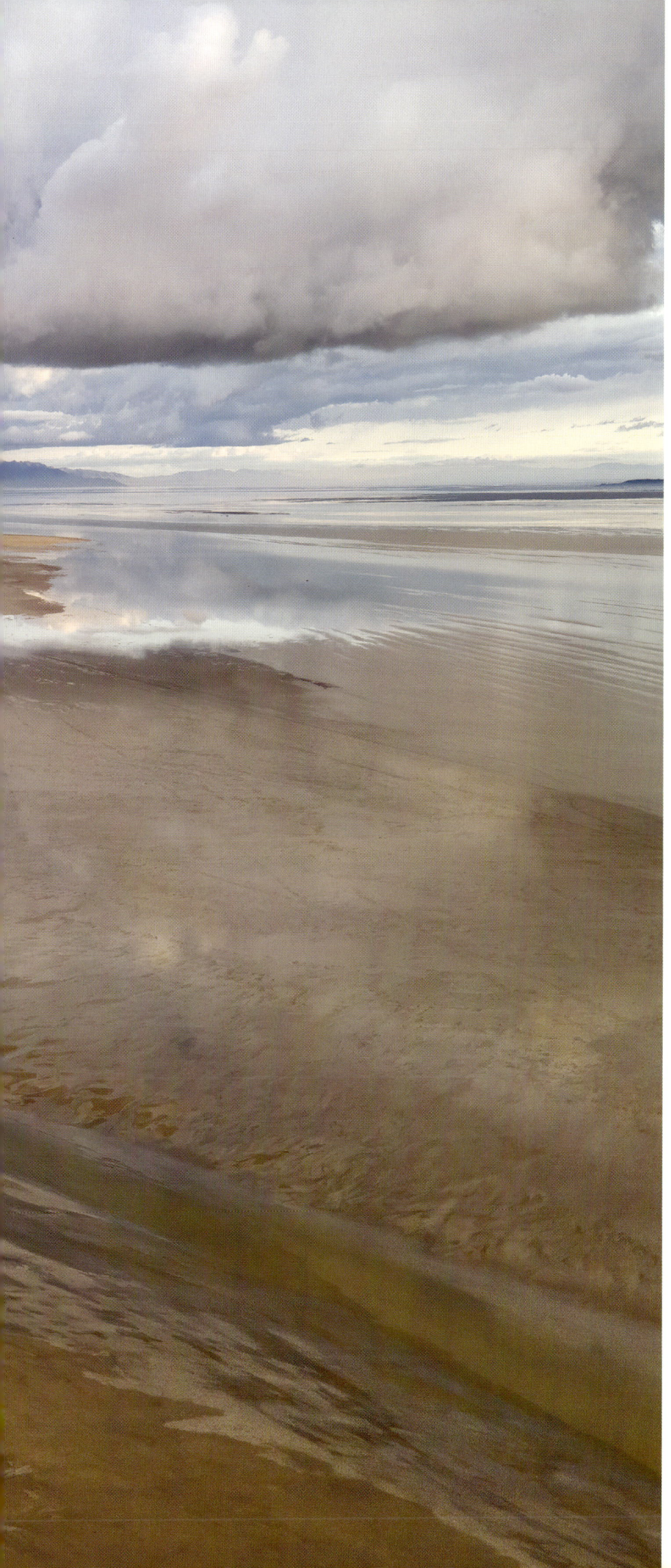

SPRING RUNOFF

Delicate, branching patterns are formed by seasonal runoff, where melting snow and rainwater carve channels through the mudflats, carrying sediments that are deposited along the way. These veins guide the water flow toward Great Salt Lake, gradually building up and altering the terrain. Calm weather enhances the visibility of these patterns, as the still water highlights the contrast between wet and dry areas, creating a surreal, reflective surface that mirrors the sky and clouds.

Spring runoff moving across the mudflats between Antelope and Fremont islands | H8 | 05.07.2023

FOLLOWING PAGE: Healthy water, South arm
F6 | 10.13.2023

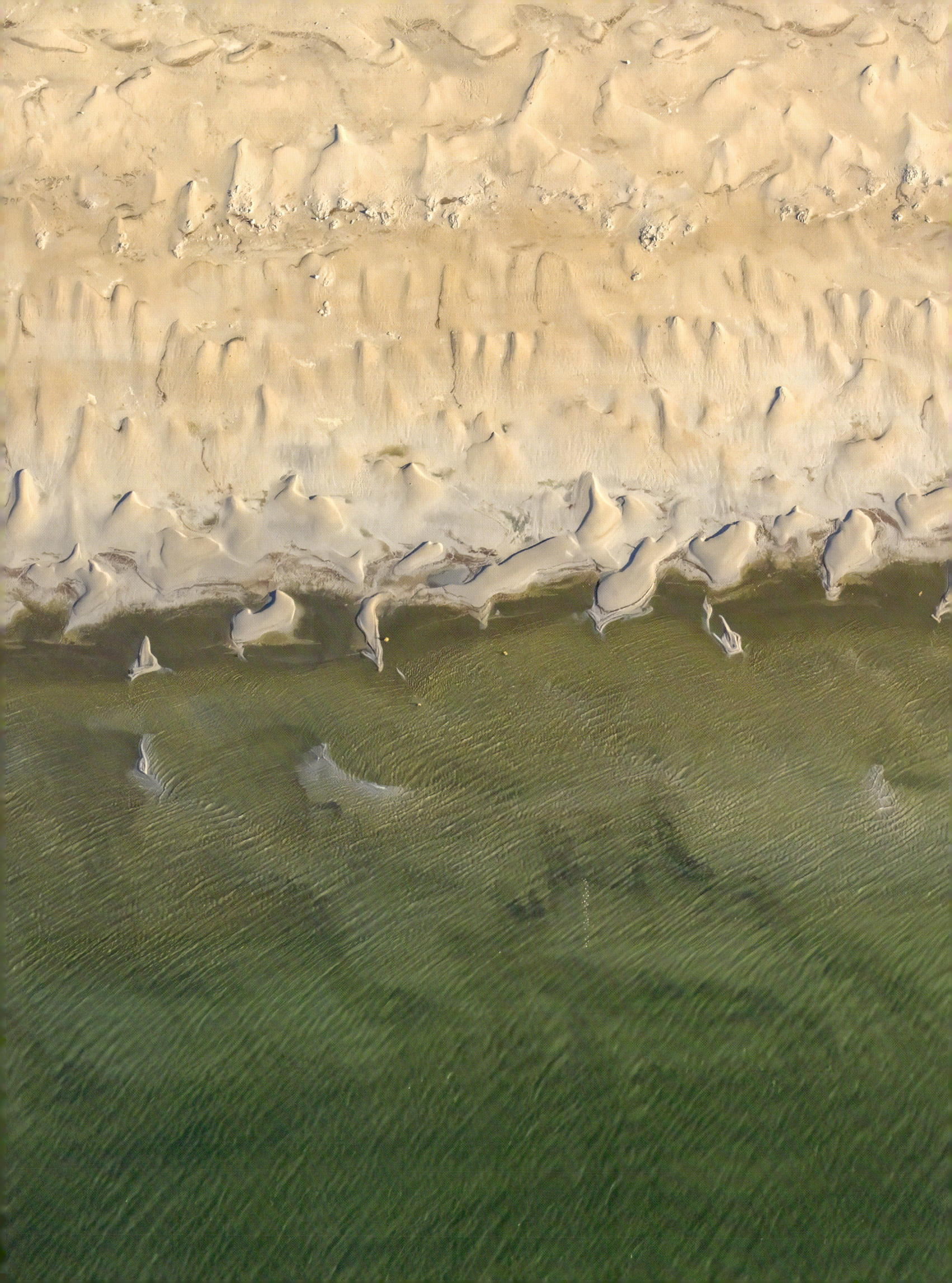

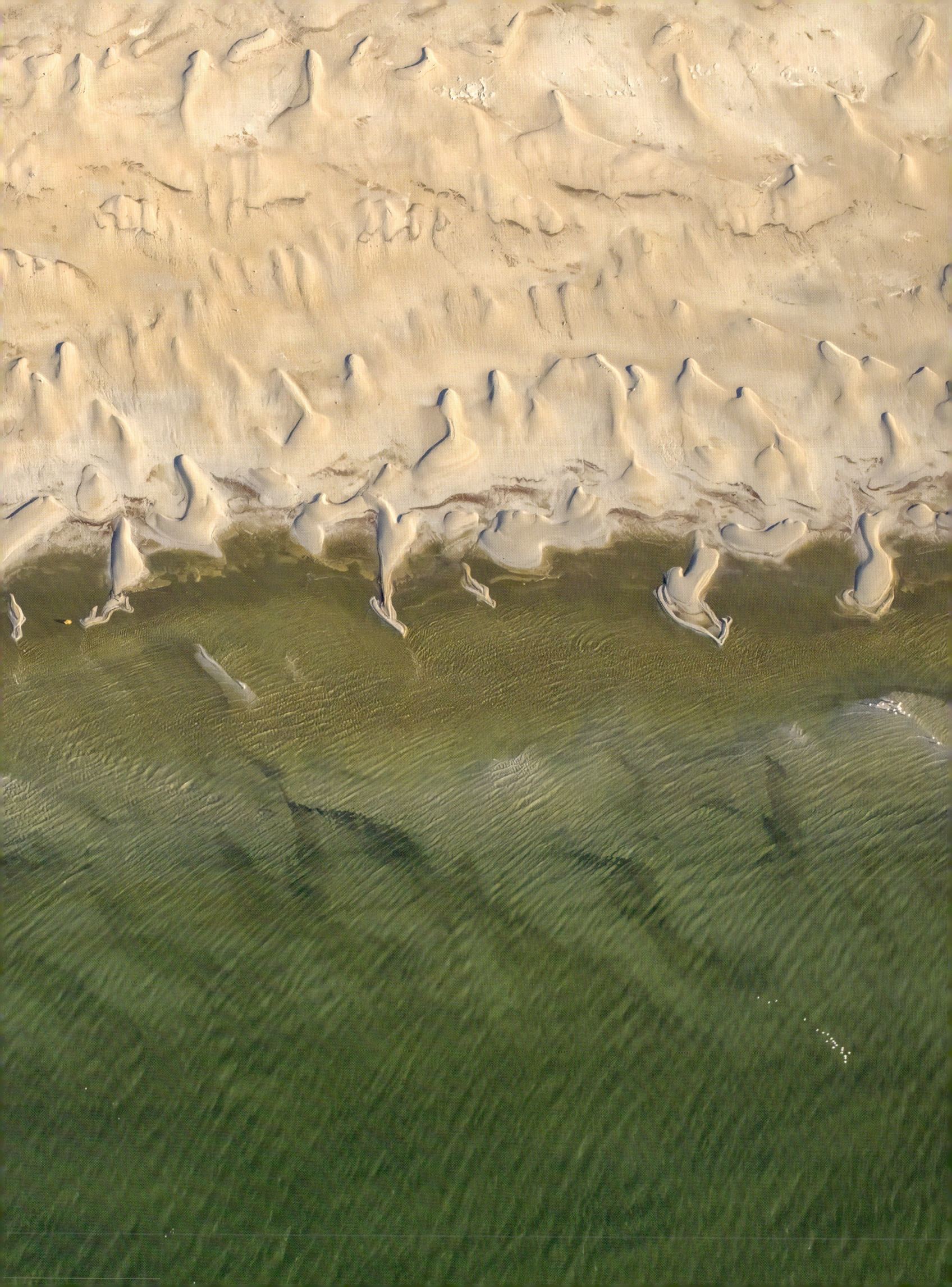

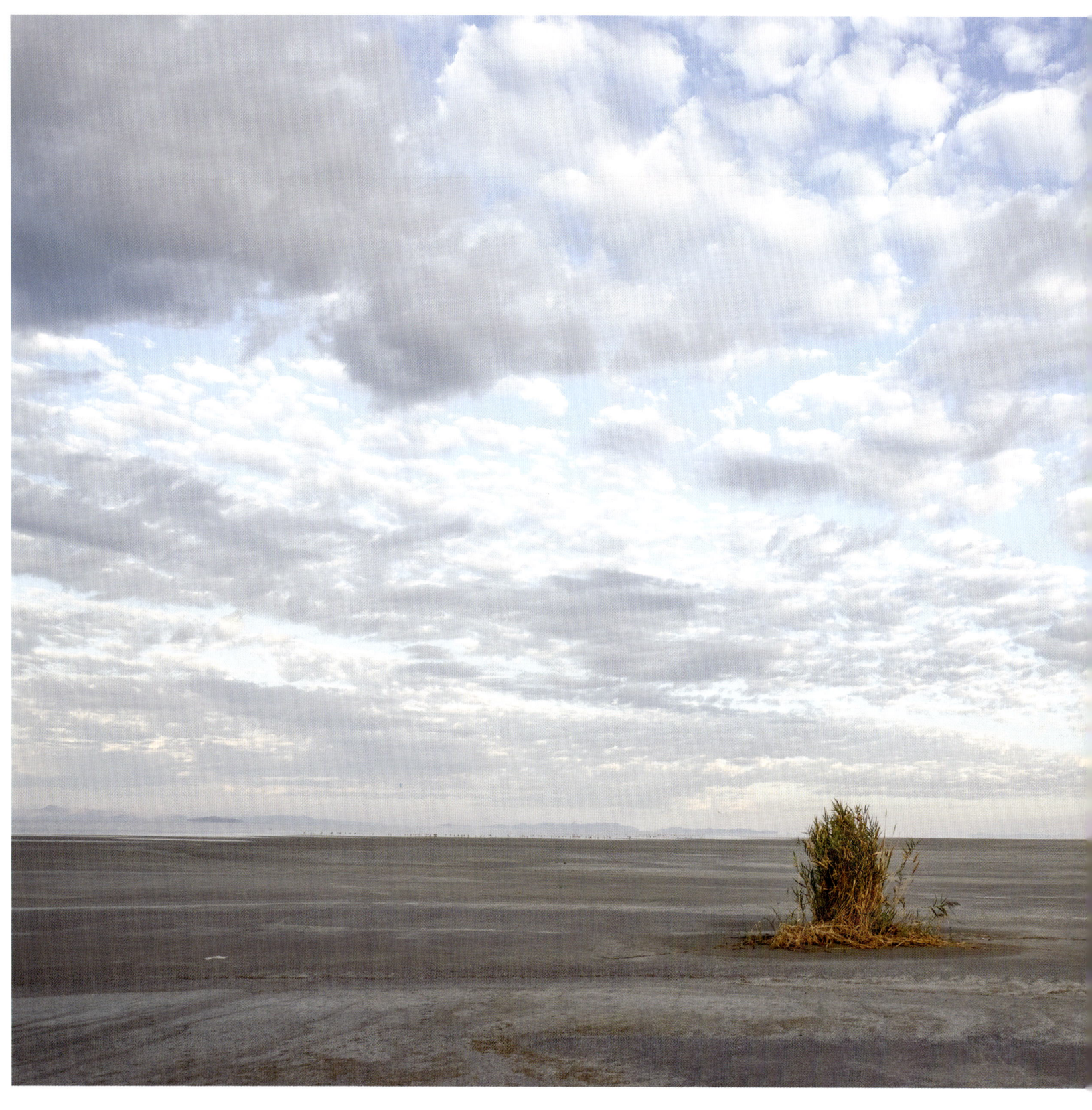

Phragmites, an invasive plant, growing in the middle of a mudflat | G8 | 08.26.2023

PLANT GROWTH

Great Salt Lake hosts a variety of unique plants, especially in its wetland areas. One can find cattails with their tall, reedy stalks and distinctive brown spikes, and bulrushes, which have slender stems topped with clustered flowers. Saltgrass forms dense mats along the shores, while pickleweed, a succulent plant, thrives in the salty mudflats. Phragmites, a variety of invasive perennial reed grass, are also common, towering over other vegetation. All these plants are crucial for the local ecosystem, providing habitat and food for wildlife and helping stabilize the soil and cycle nutrients.

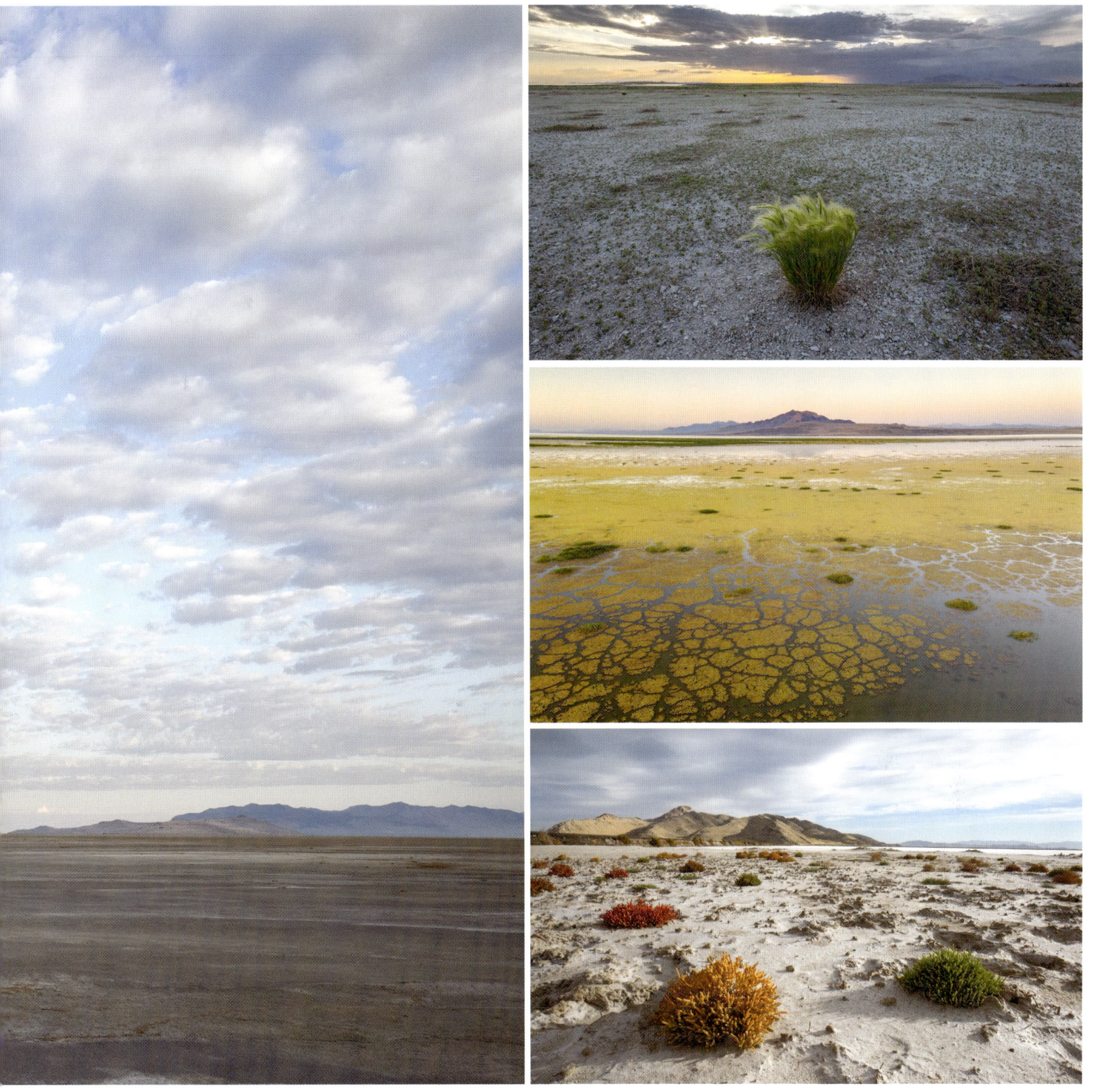

Salt grass between Antelope Island and Egg Island | H8 | 06.02.2023

Early summer plant growth in Farmington Bay | H8 | 06.01.2023

Pickleweed in fall, Stansbury Island | K6 | 09.30.2023

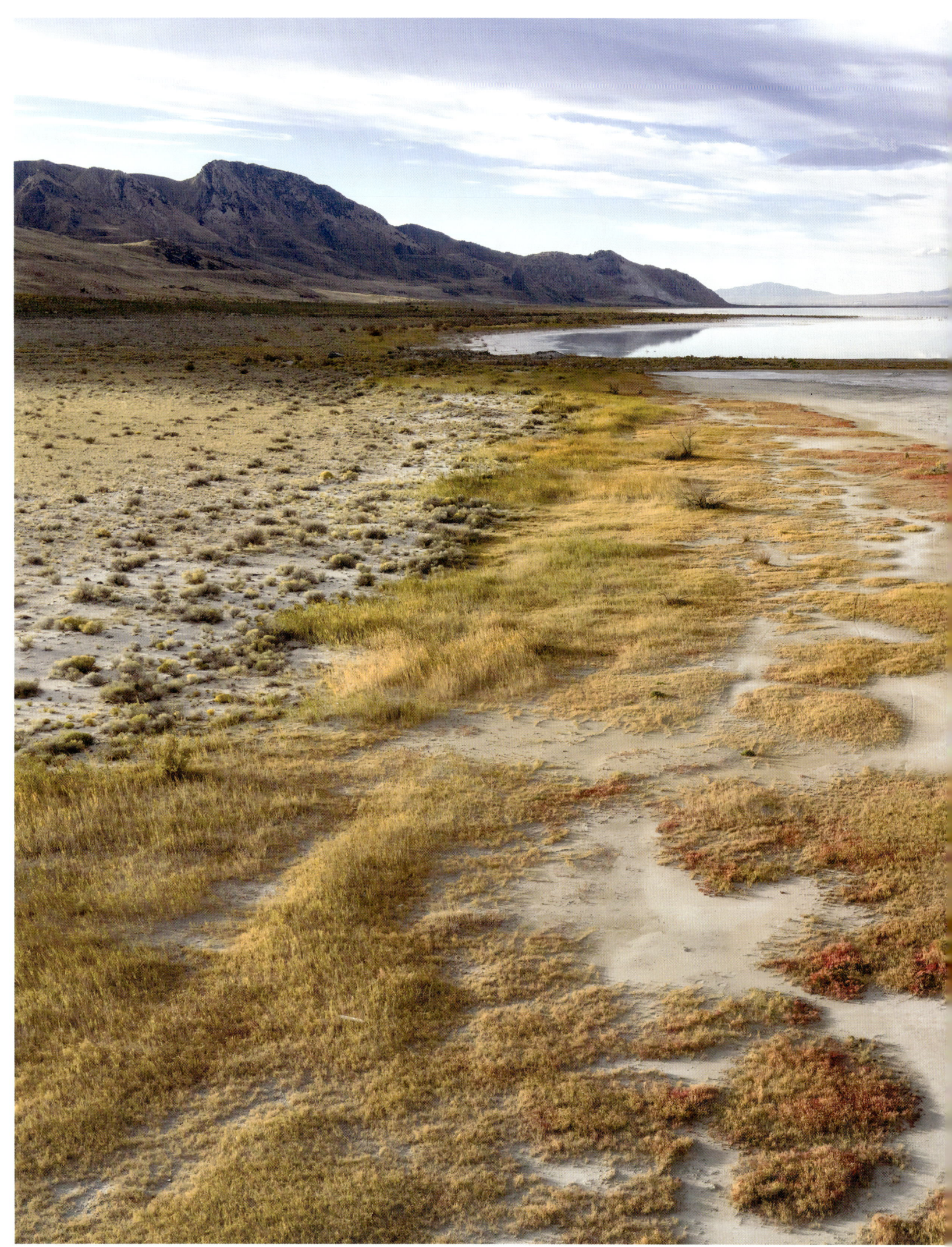

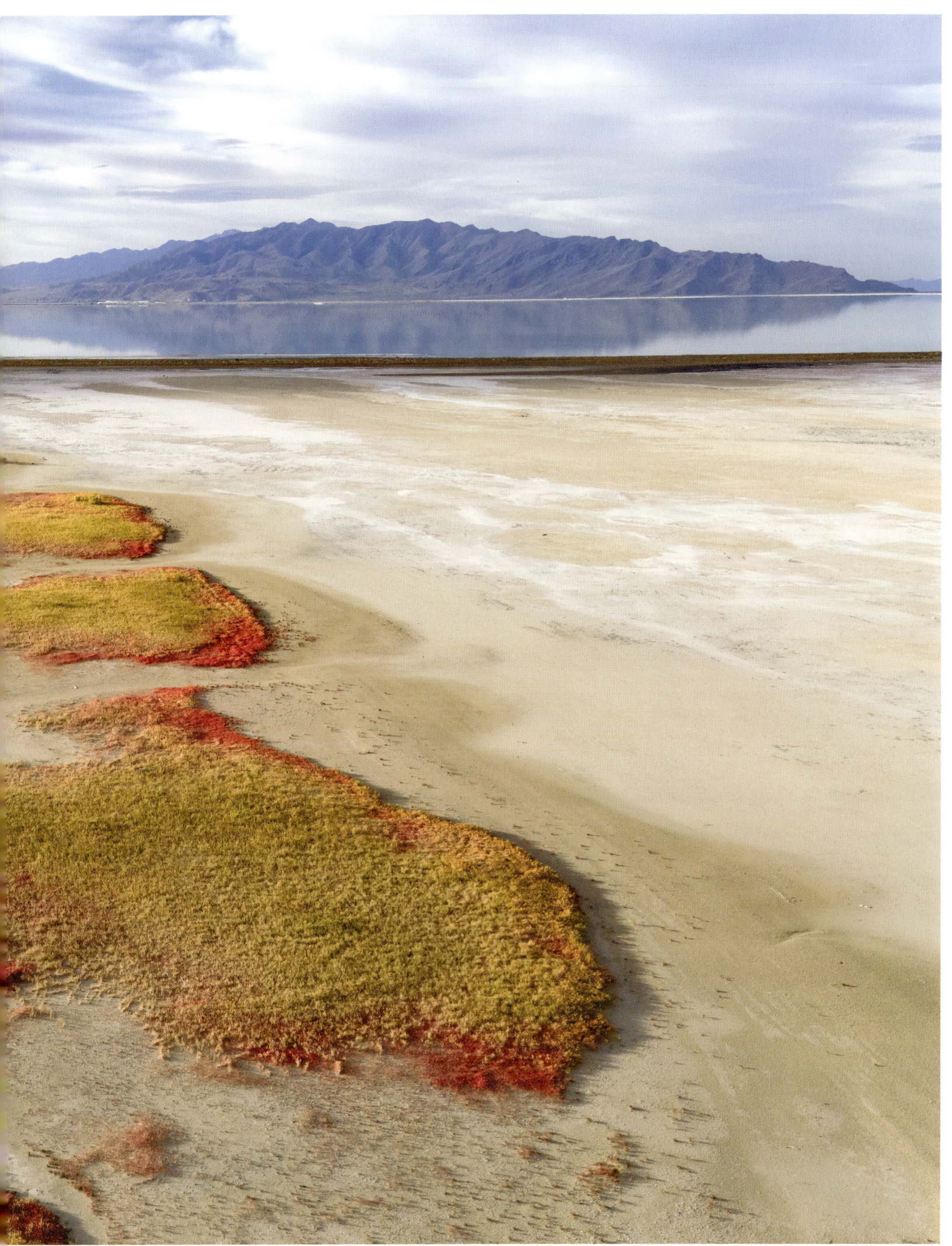

Fall colors, Stansbury Bay | J5 | 09.30.2023

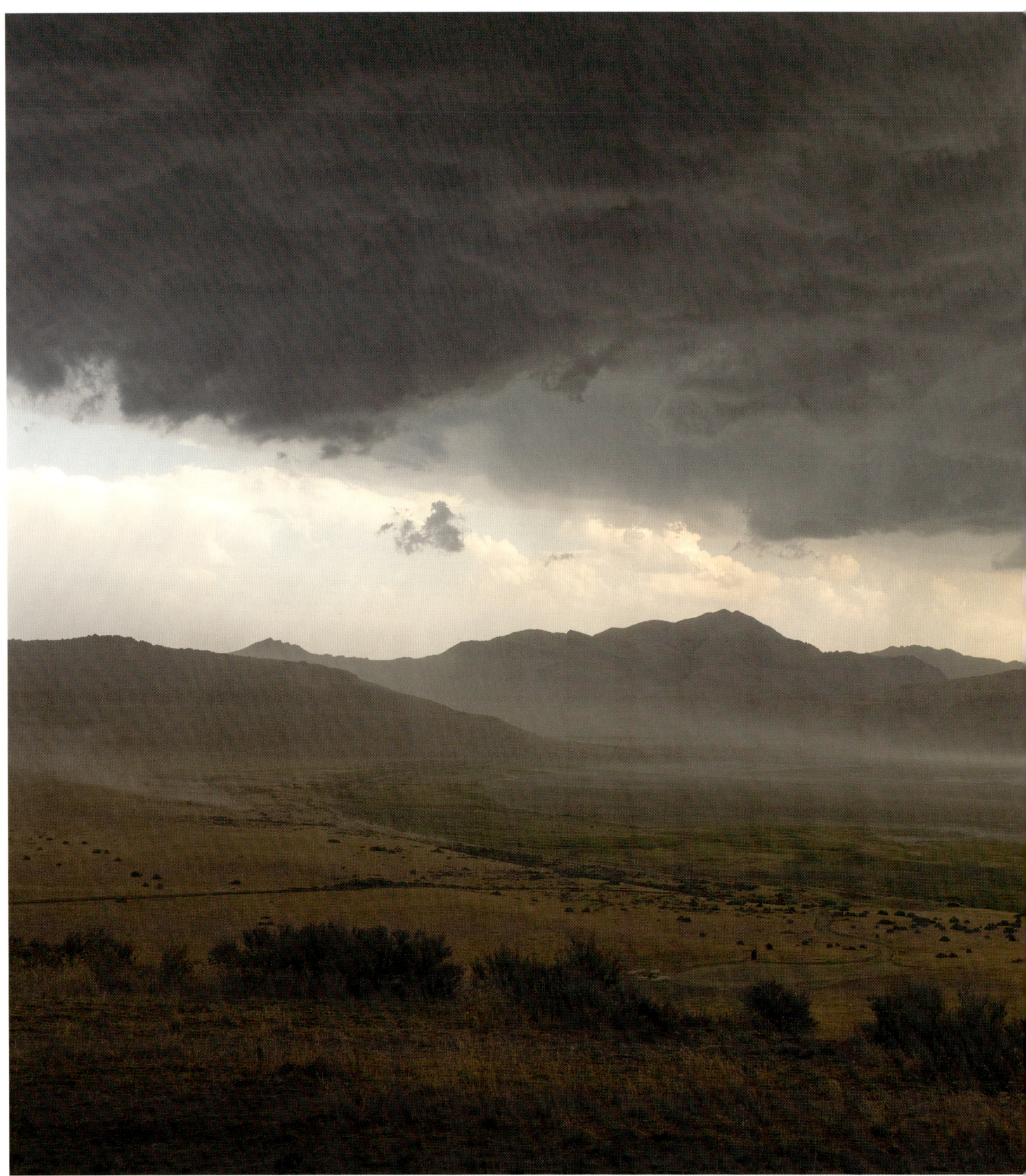

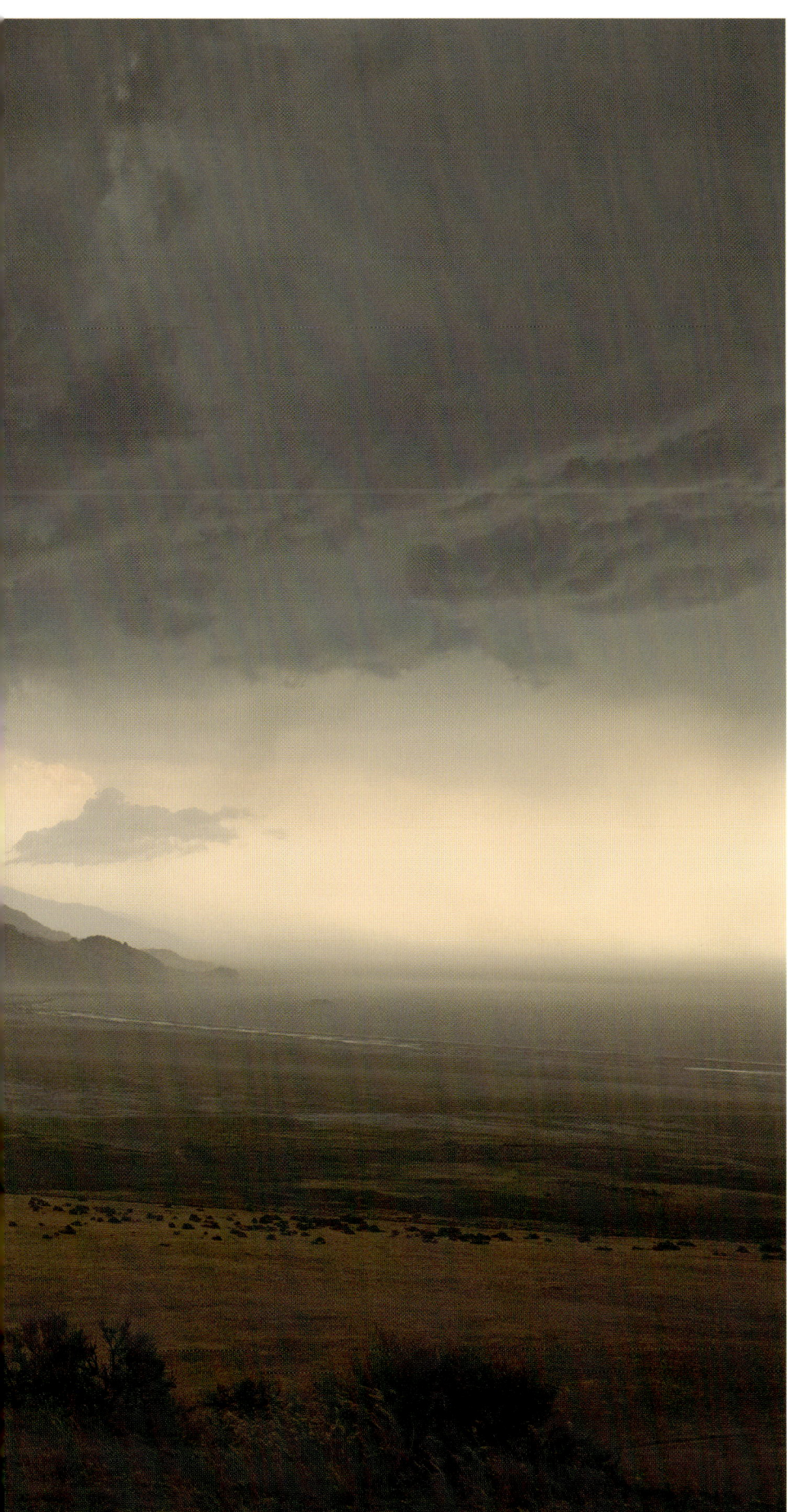

BREAKING STORMS

When storms break over Great Salt Lake, the landscape transforms dramatically as dark clouds gather and winds whip across the water, creating a sense of intense power. Lightning often illuminates the sky, and rain falls in heavy sheets, penetrating the lake's surface. The air is filled with the scent of wet earth and salt. As storms recede, vibrant rainbows often appear against the retreating clouds, and the setting sun casts a golden glow over the tranquil waters. The mood shifts from tumultuous to serene, highlighting the lake's dynamic nature and breathtaking beauty.

Storm over Frary Peak, Antelope Island
H8 | 07.27.2024

FOLLOWING PAGE:
Storm clouds and rainbow over Farmington Bay
H8 | 11.15.2024

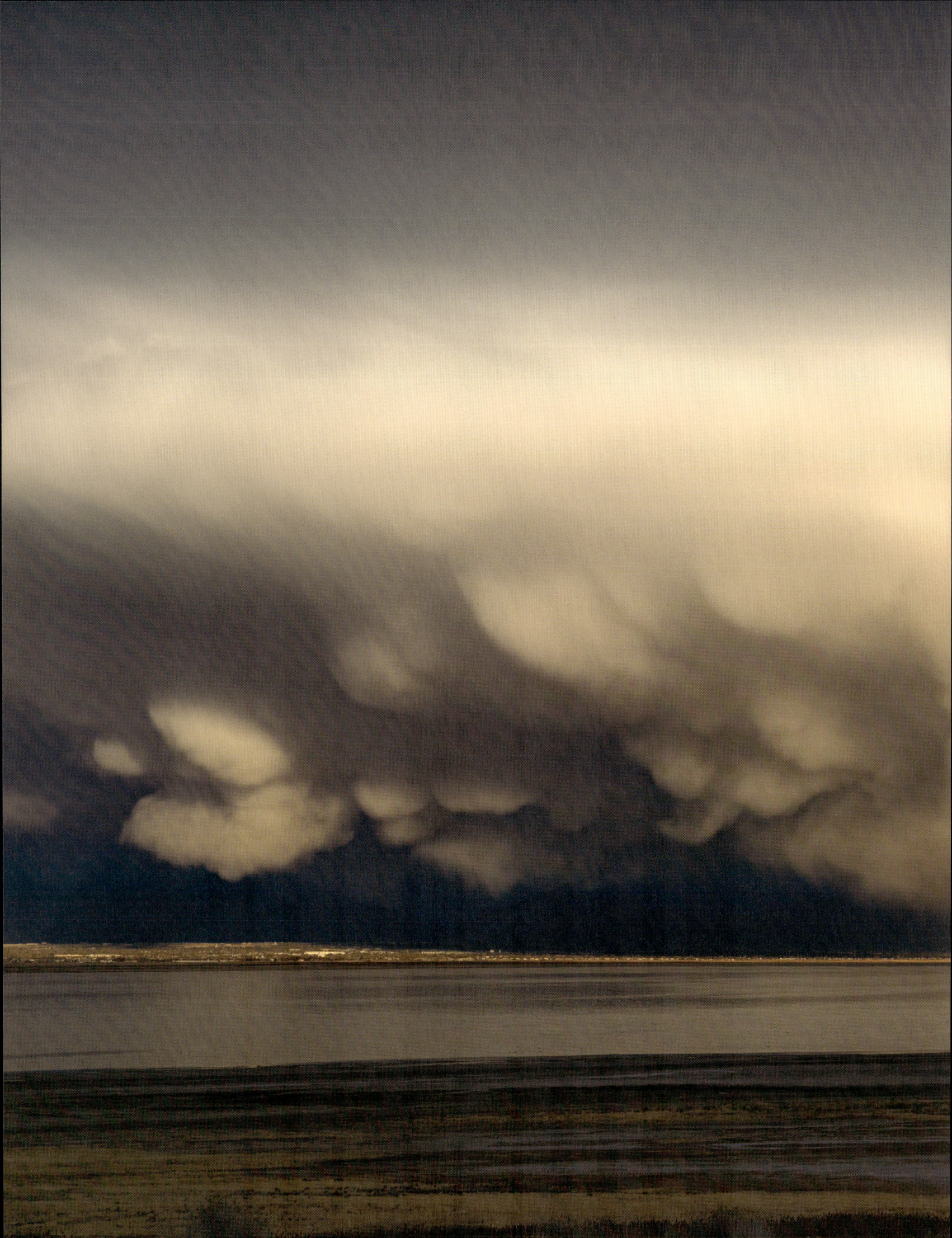

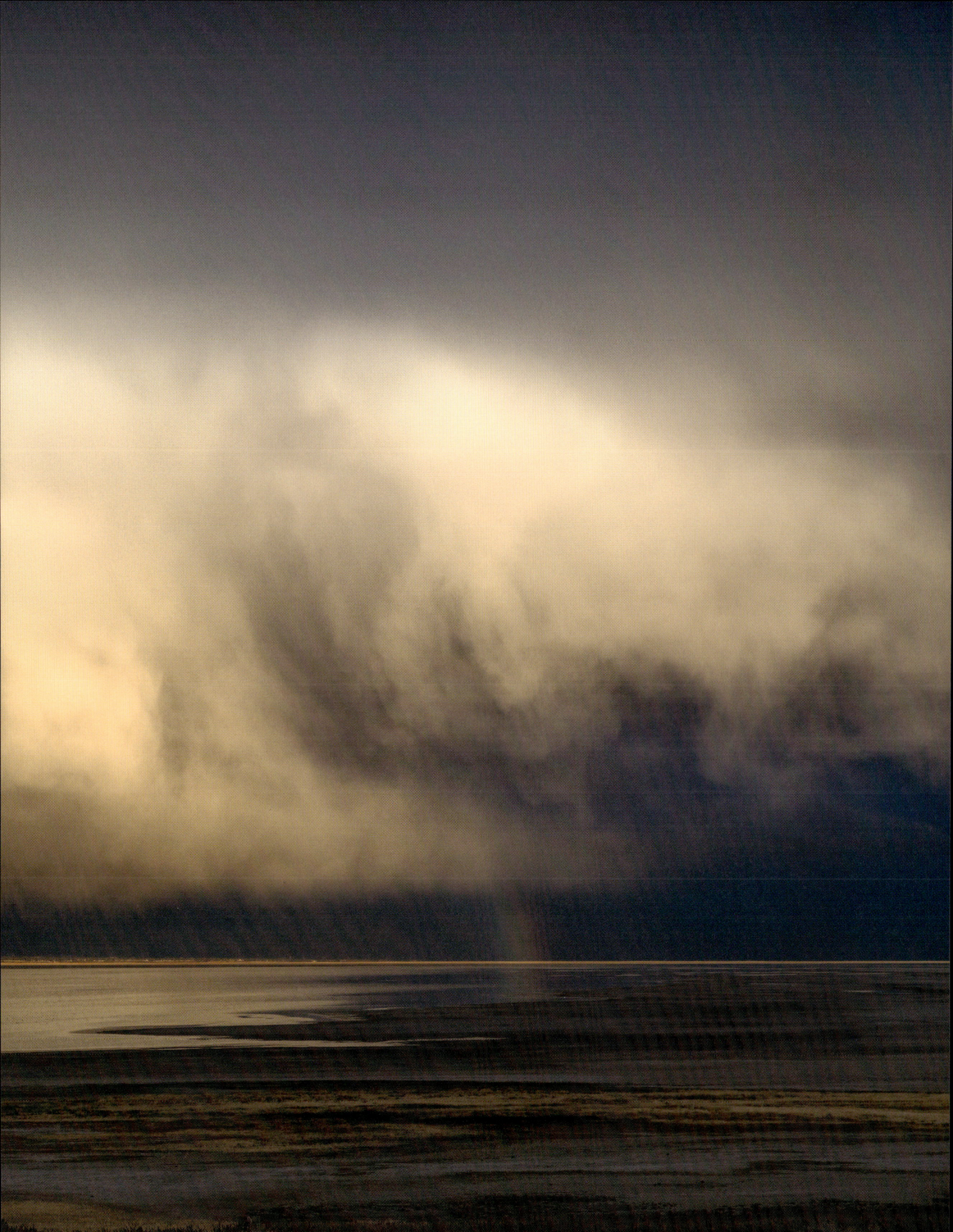

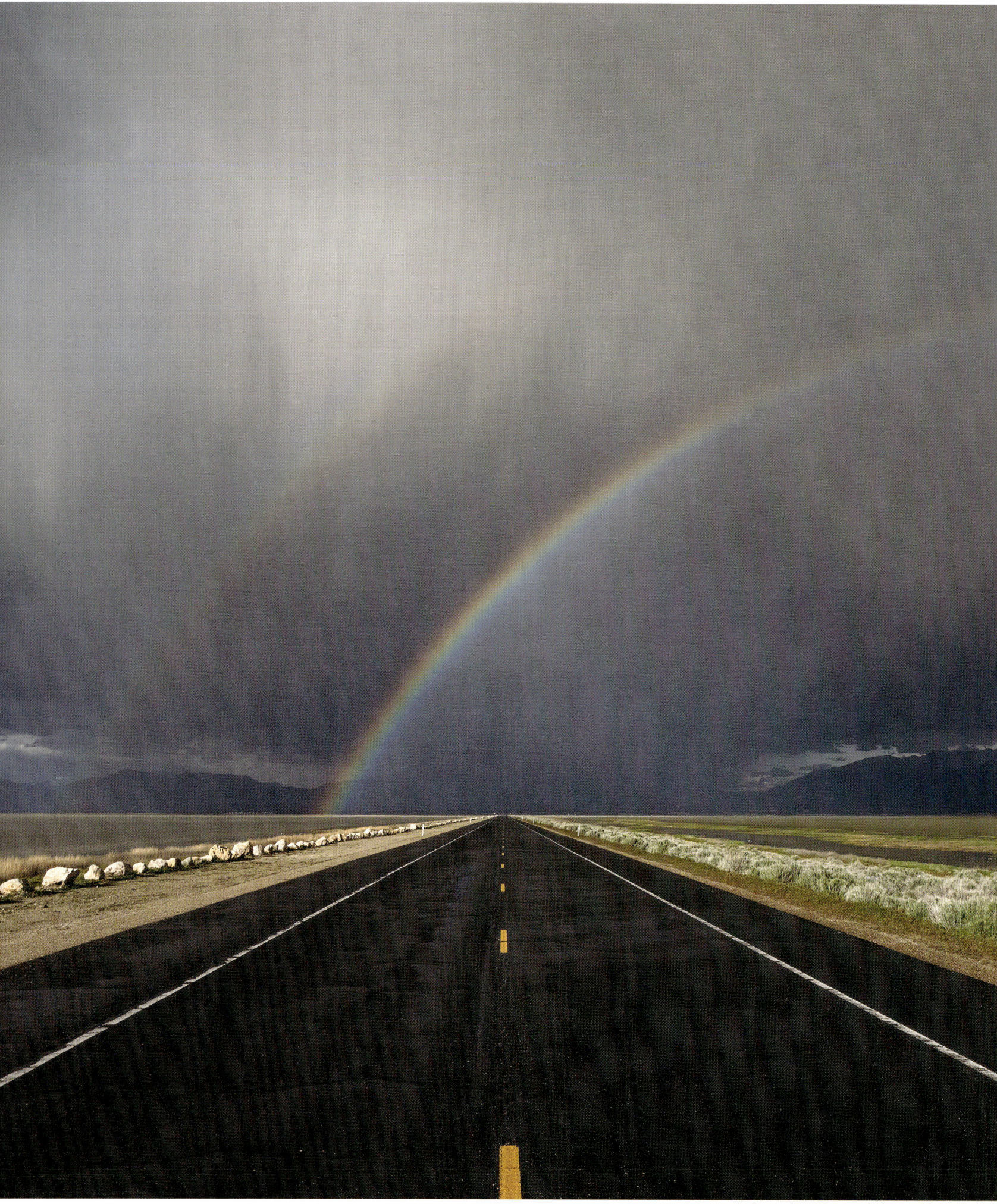

Double rainbow, Antelope Island causeway | H8 | 04.29.2024

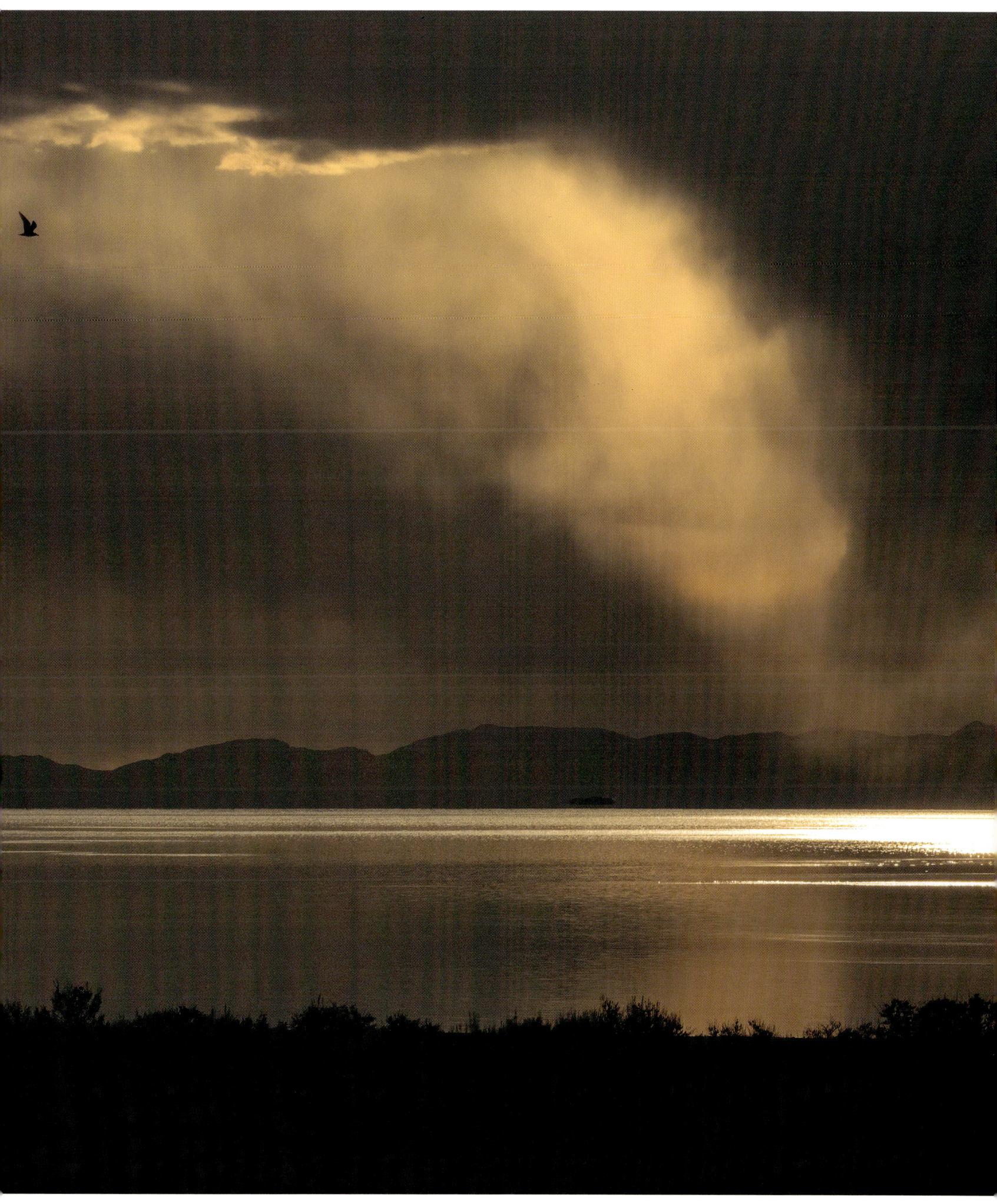

Bird and breaking storm | H8 | 04.14.2023

FOLLOWING PAGE: White Rock Bay right after a thunderstorm | H8 | 03.20.2023

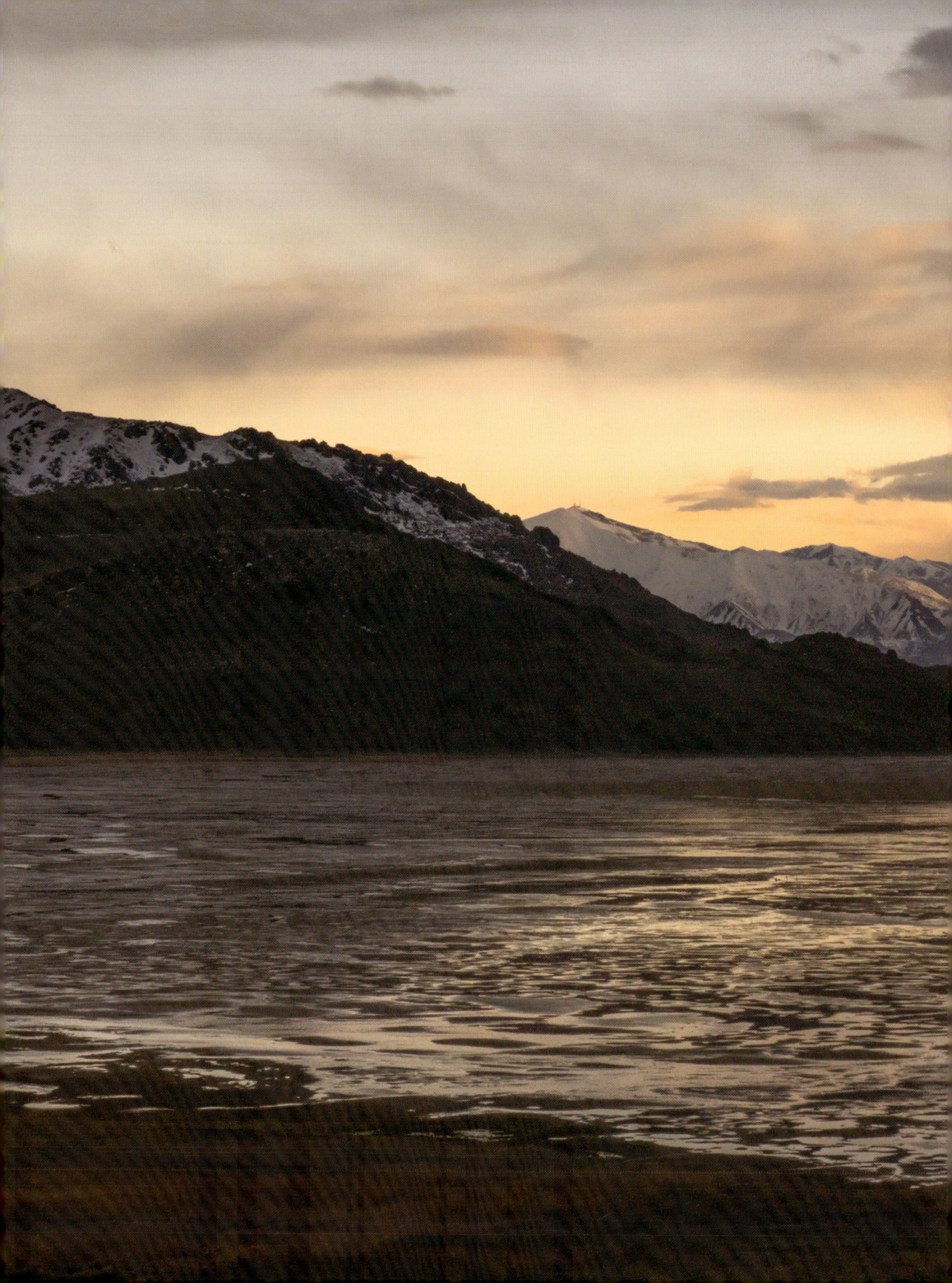

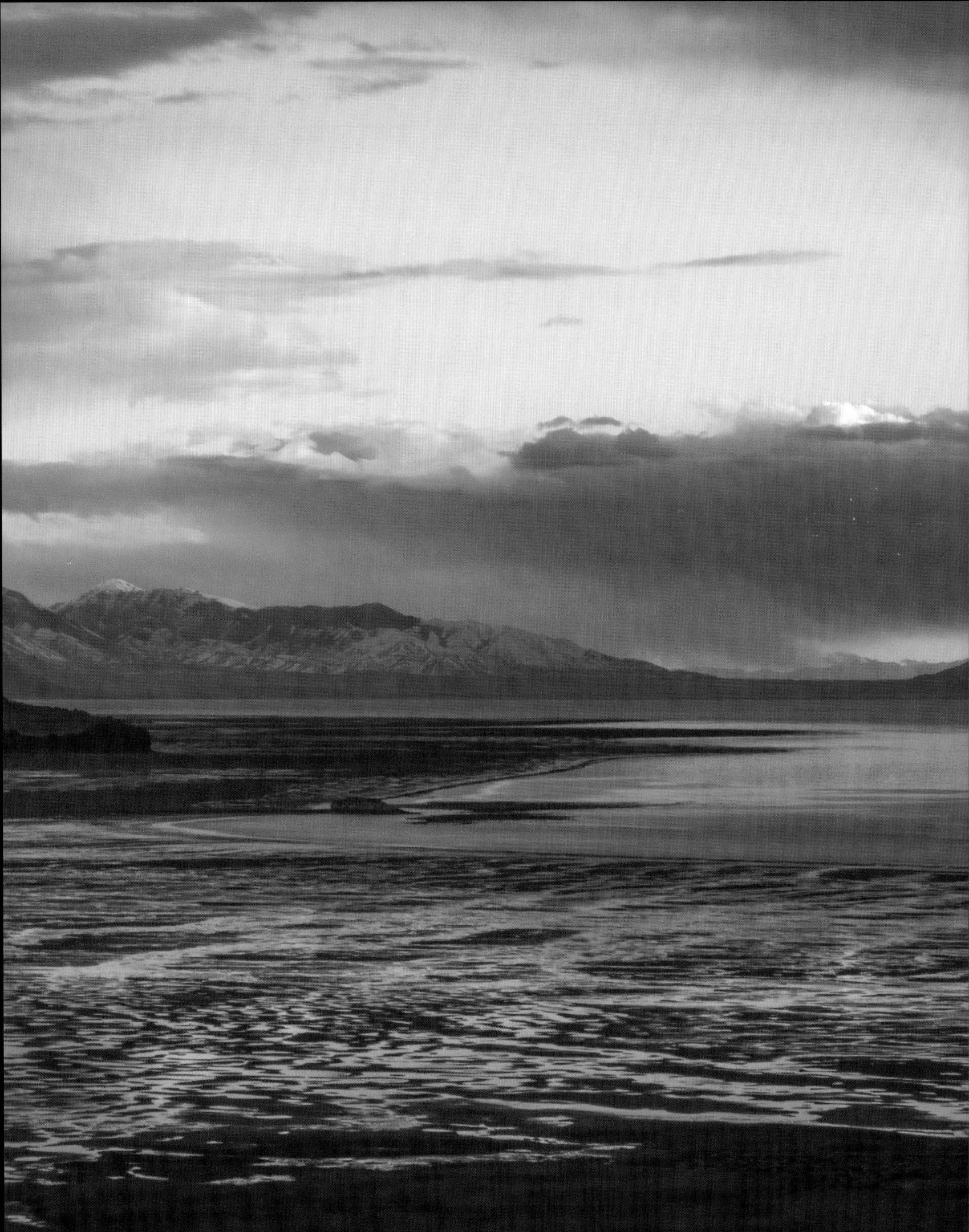

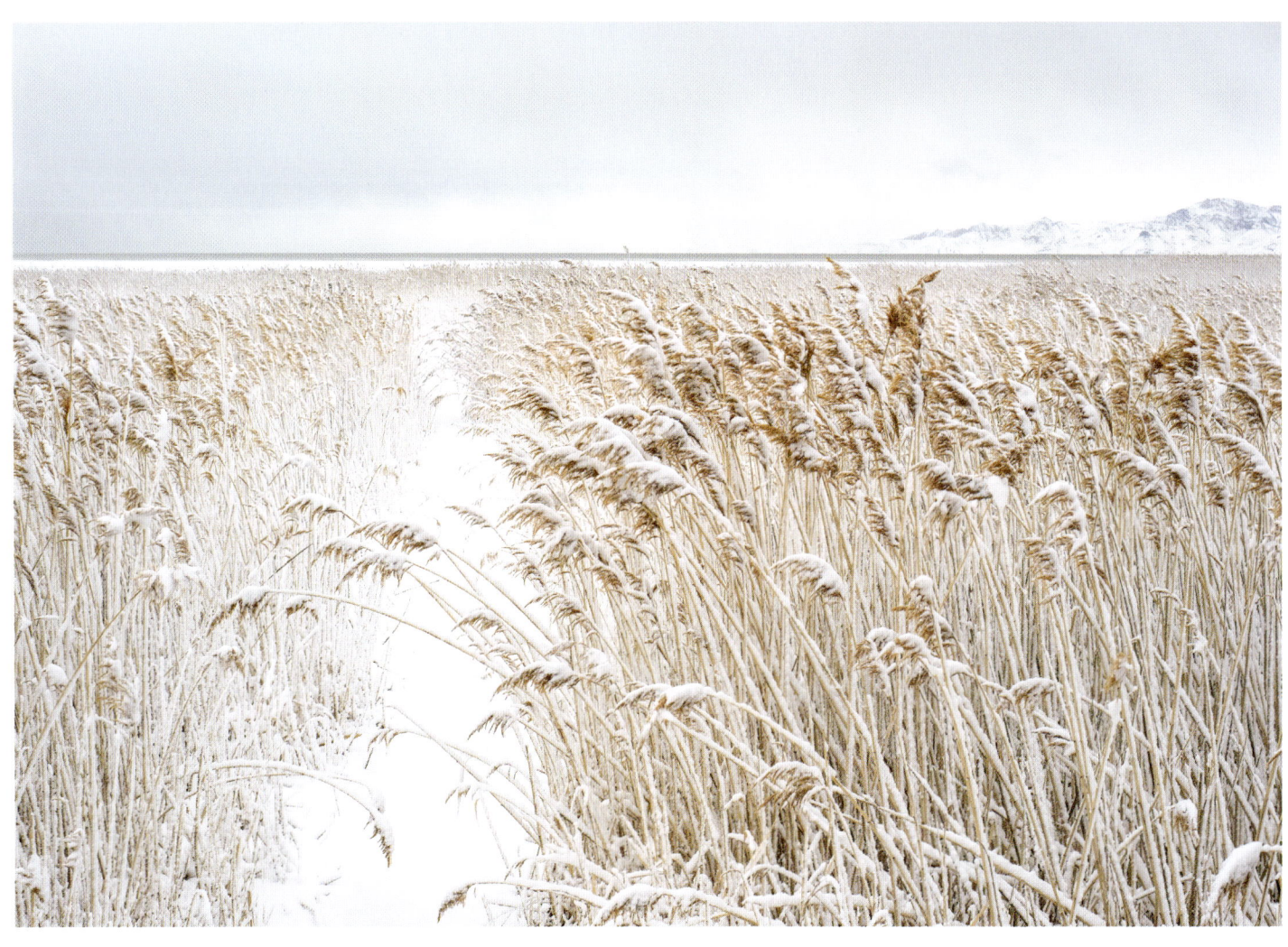

WINTER

Winter on the shores of Great Salt Lake is serene and starkly beautiful. The landscape can be partially frozen, with snow often covering the mudflats and salt crusts, creating a pristine, almost otherworldly appearance. Winter storms bring strong winds that whip across the water and snow that blankets the frozen parts of the lake. The surrounding mountains provide a dramatic backdrop to the reflective lake surface, especially at sunrise and sunset.

Moments after a snowstorm, White Rock Bay. | H8 | 03.02.2024

Hoarfrost and boardwalk, Great Salt Lake Shorelands Preserve | H10 | 12.18.2024

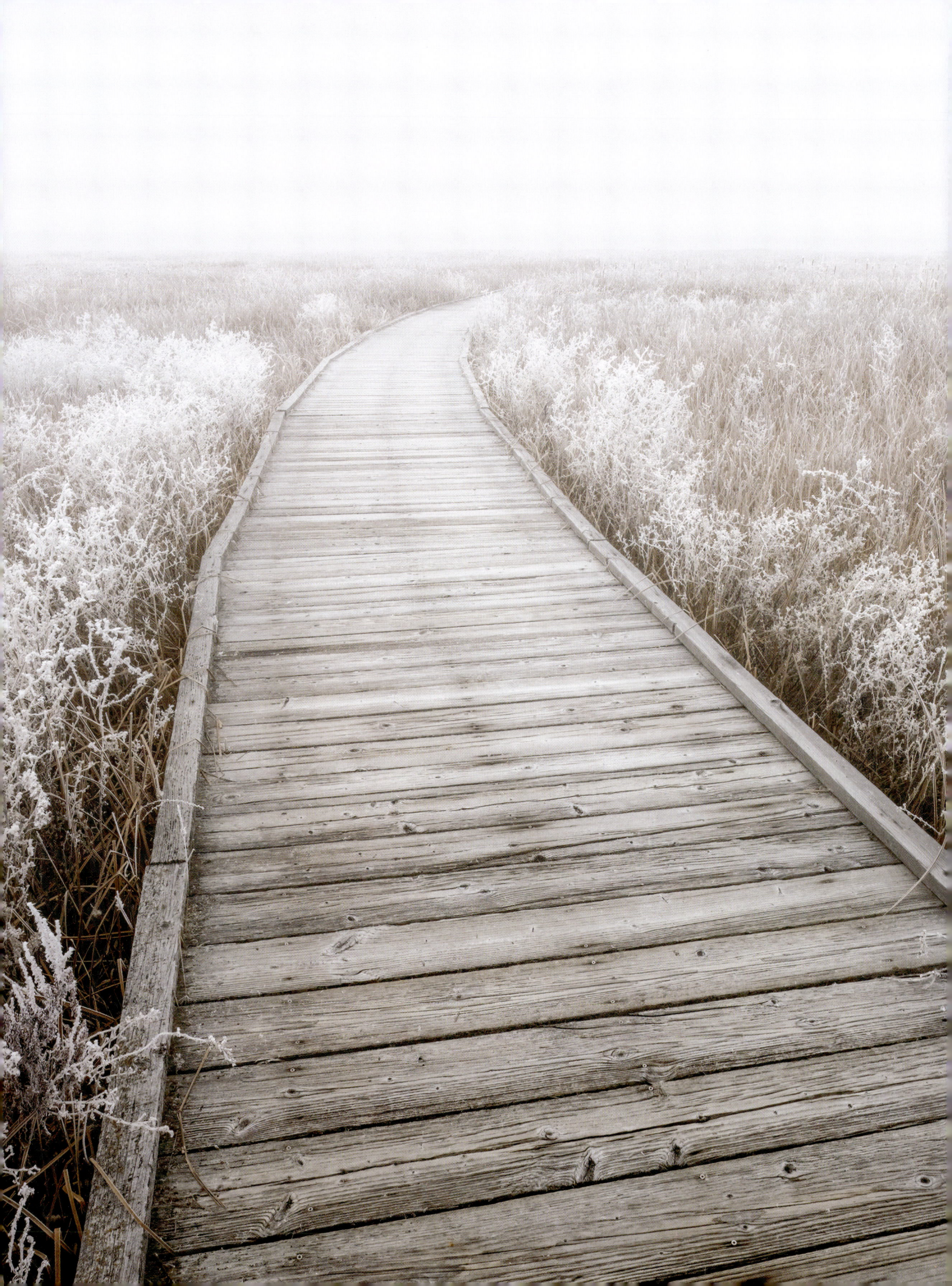

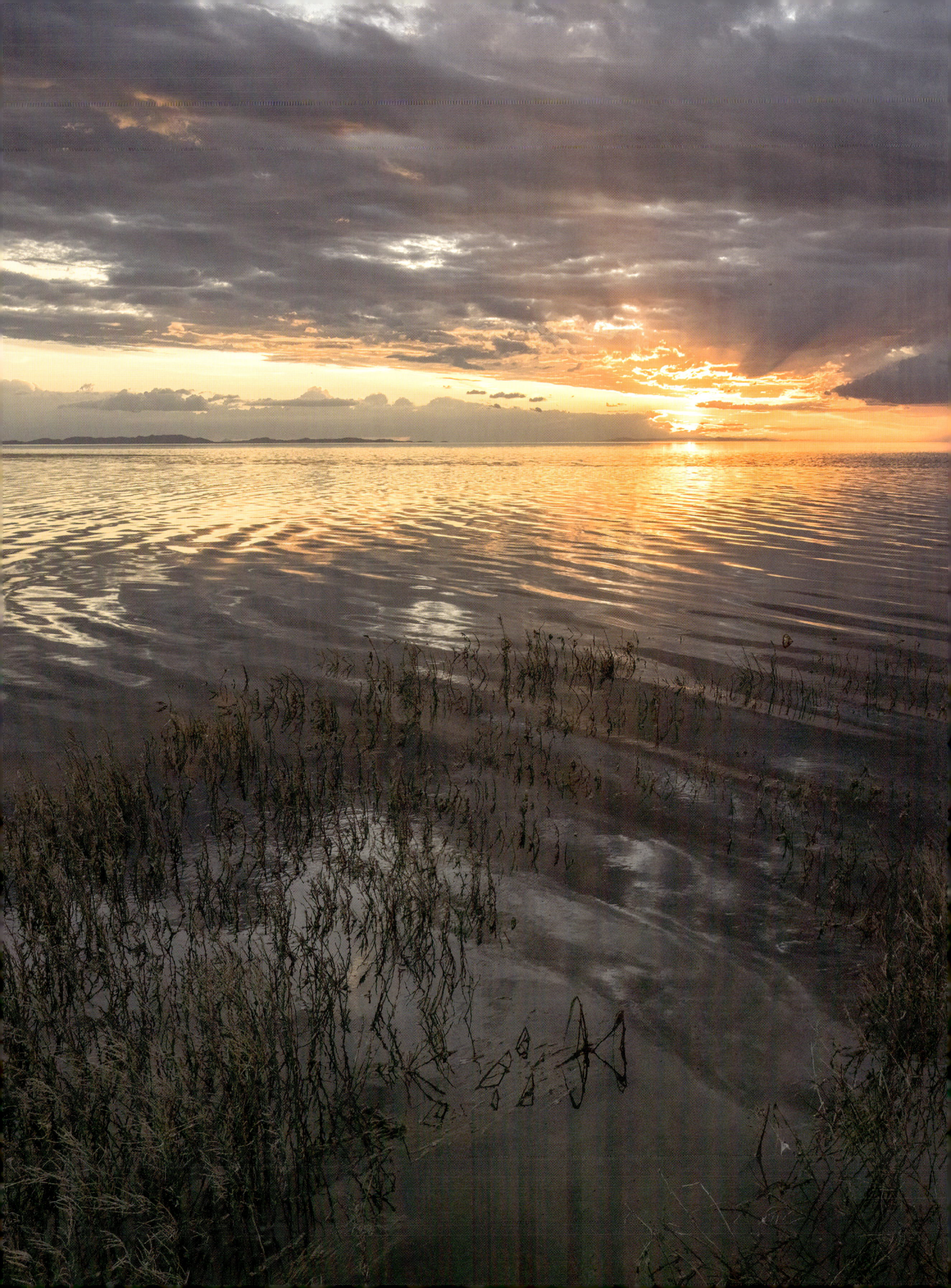

THE BEST SUNSETS

Sunsets at Great Salt Lake are among the most mesmerizing in the world, with a blend of vibrant colors and serene reflections creating breathtaking spectacles that are divine in nature. The best places to experience sunset around the lake include the summit of Frary Peak, Buffalo Point, and Ladyfinger Point, all on Antelope Island. Each of these locations offers expansive views of the horizon and the reflective waters of Gilbert Bay and most of the South Arm. The Great Salt Lake Marina also provides a stunning vantage point, with the added bonus of viewing Antelope Island in the distance.

Gilbert Bay sunset from Egg Island | H8 | 06.02.2023

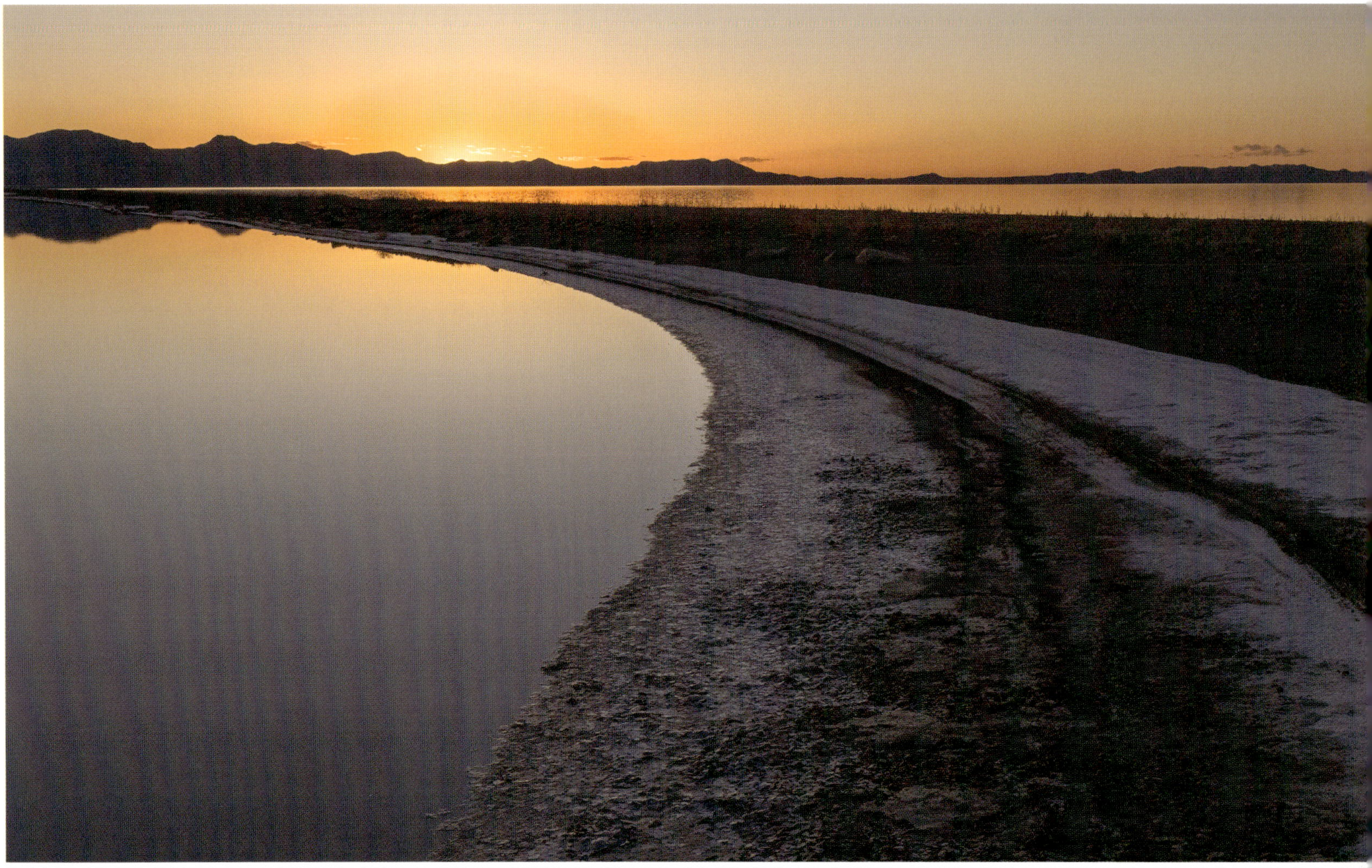

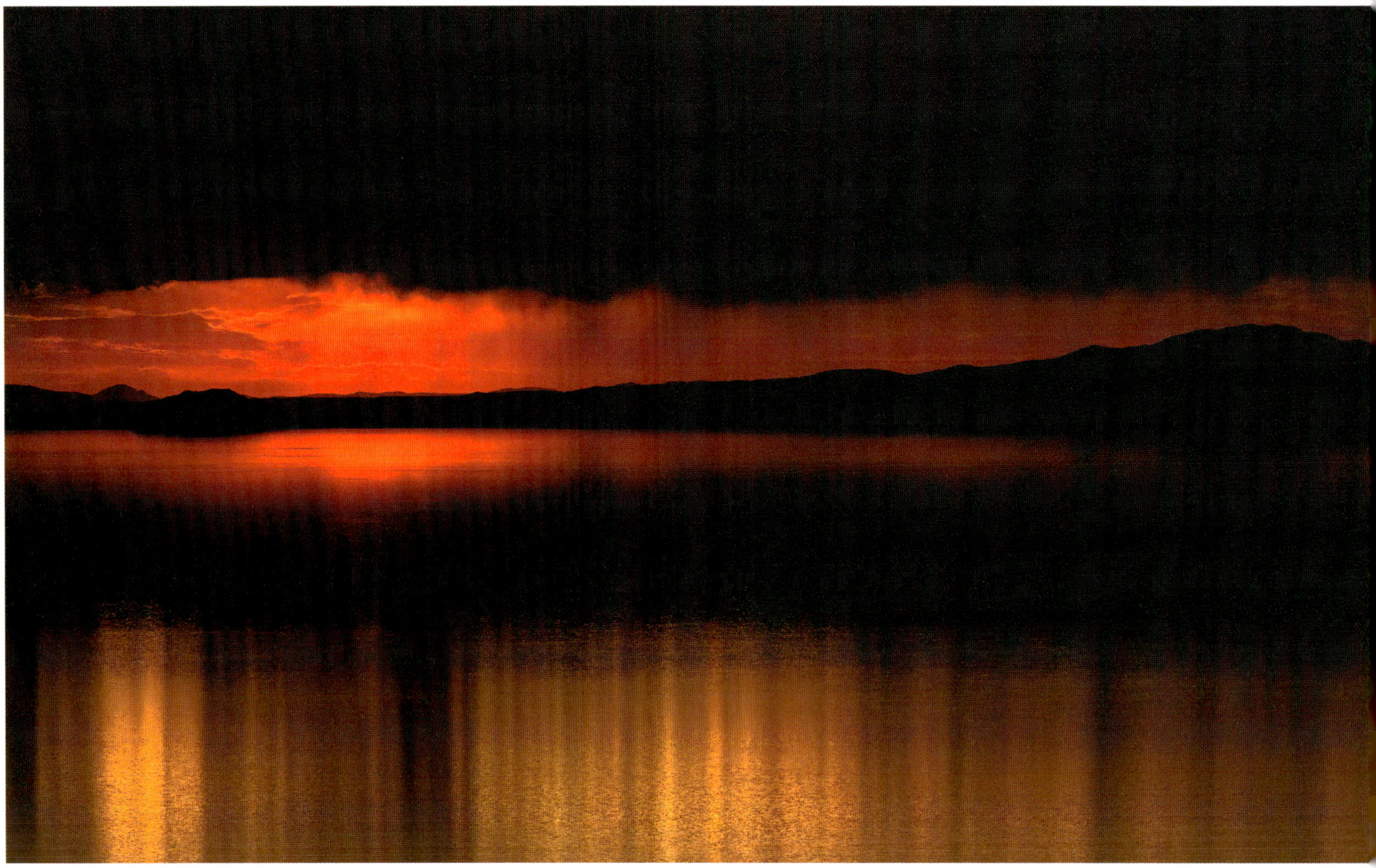

Salty shoreline, Stansbury Bay | J5 | 04.20.2024

Storm and sunset, Gilbert Bay | H8 | 07.15.2022

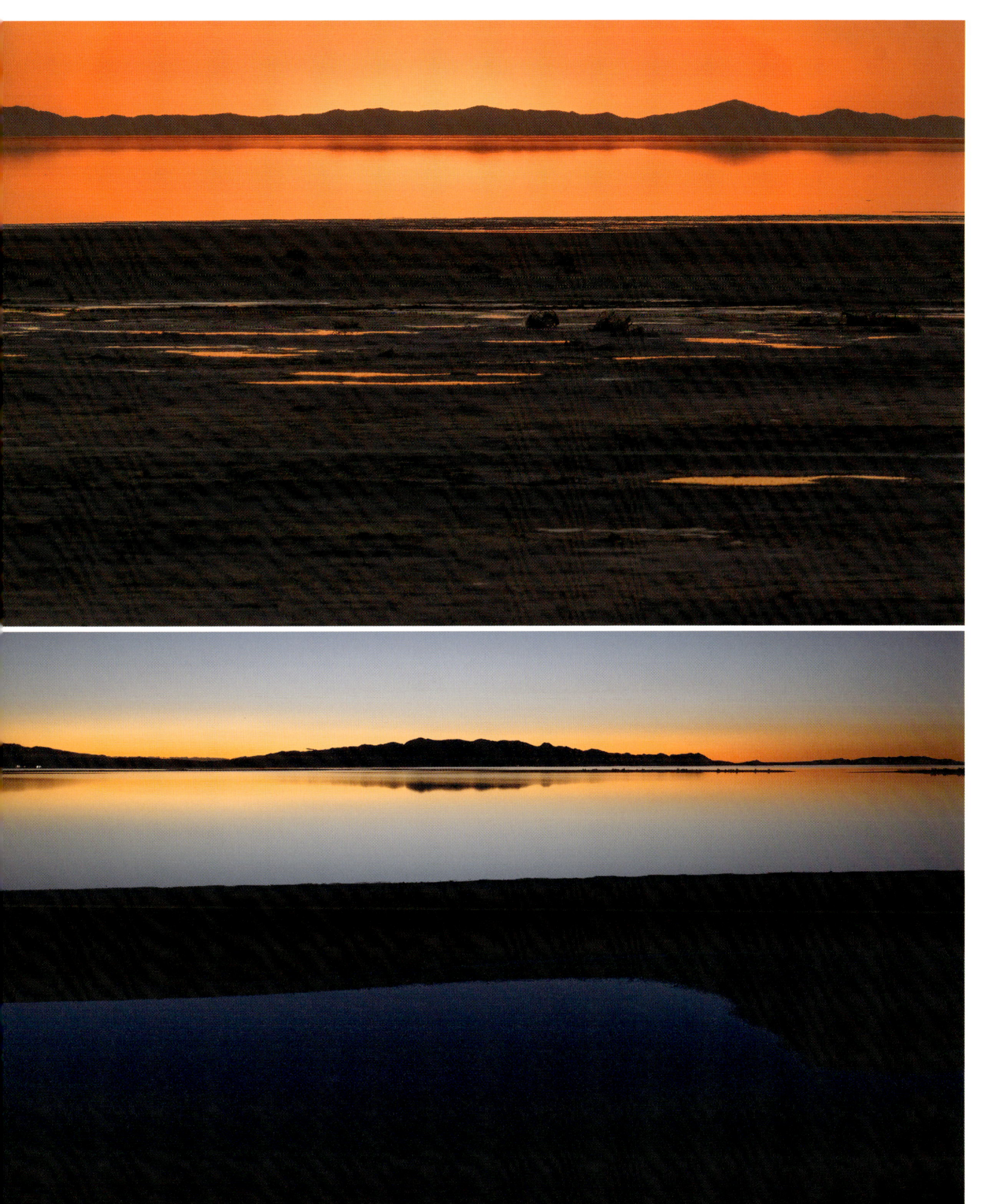

Sun puddles, dusk at White Rock Bay | H8 | 07.02.2023
Blue hour, Stansbury Bay | J5 | 04.20.2024

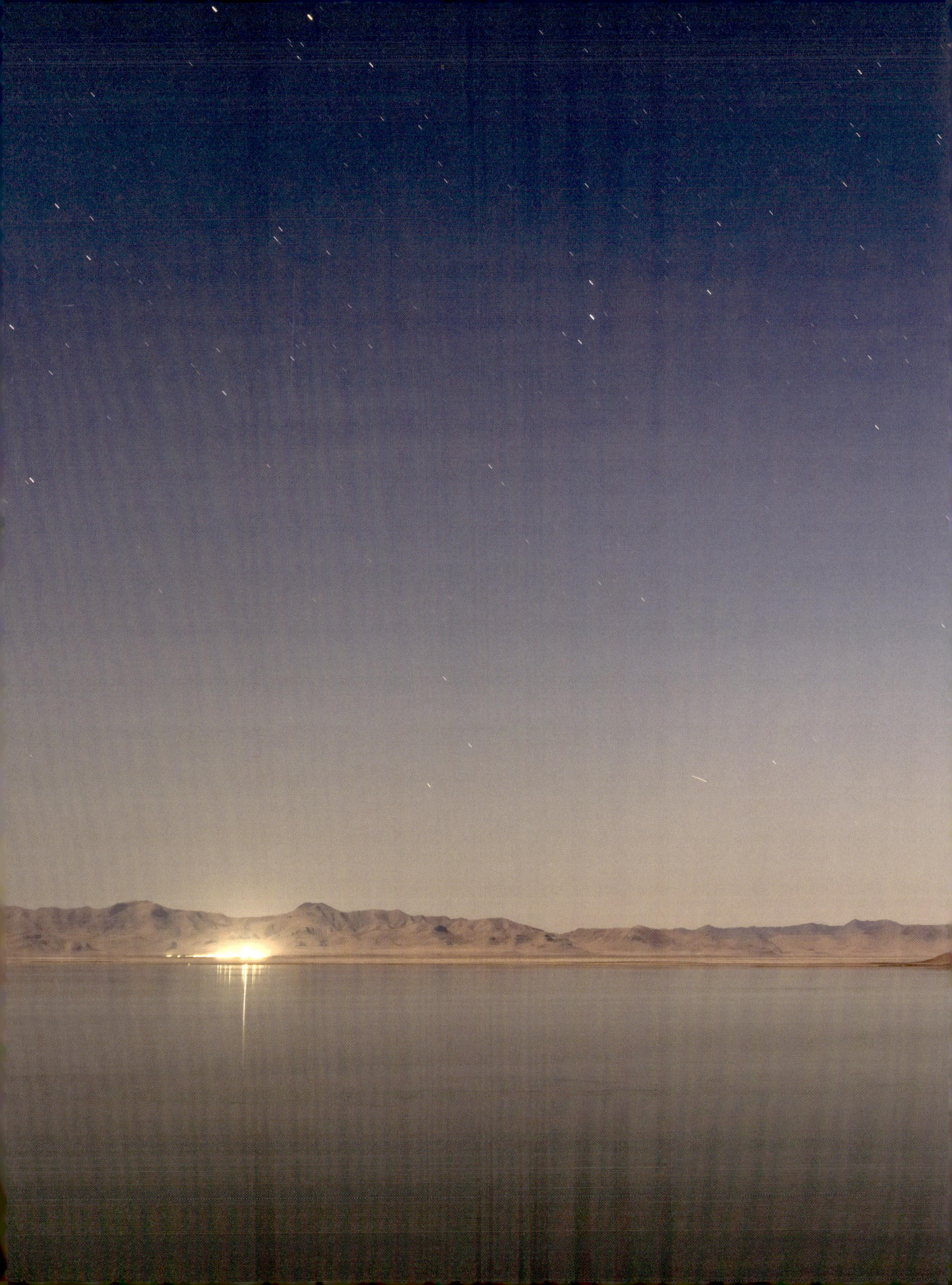

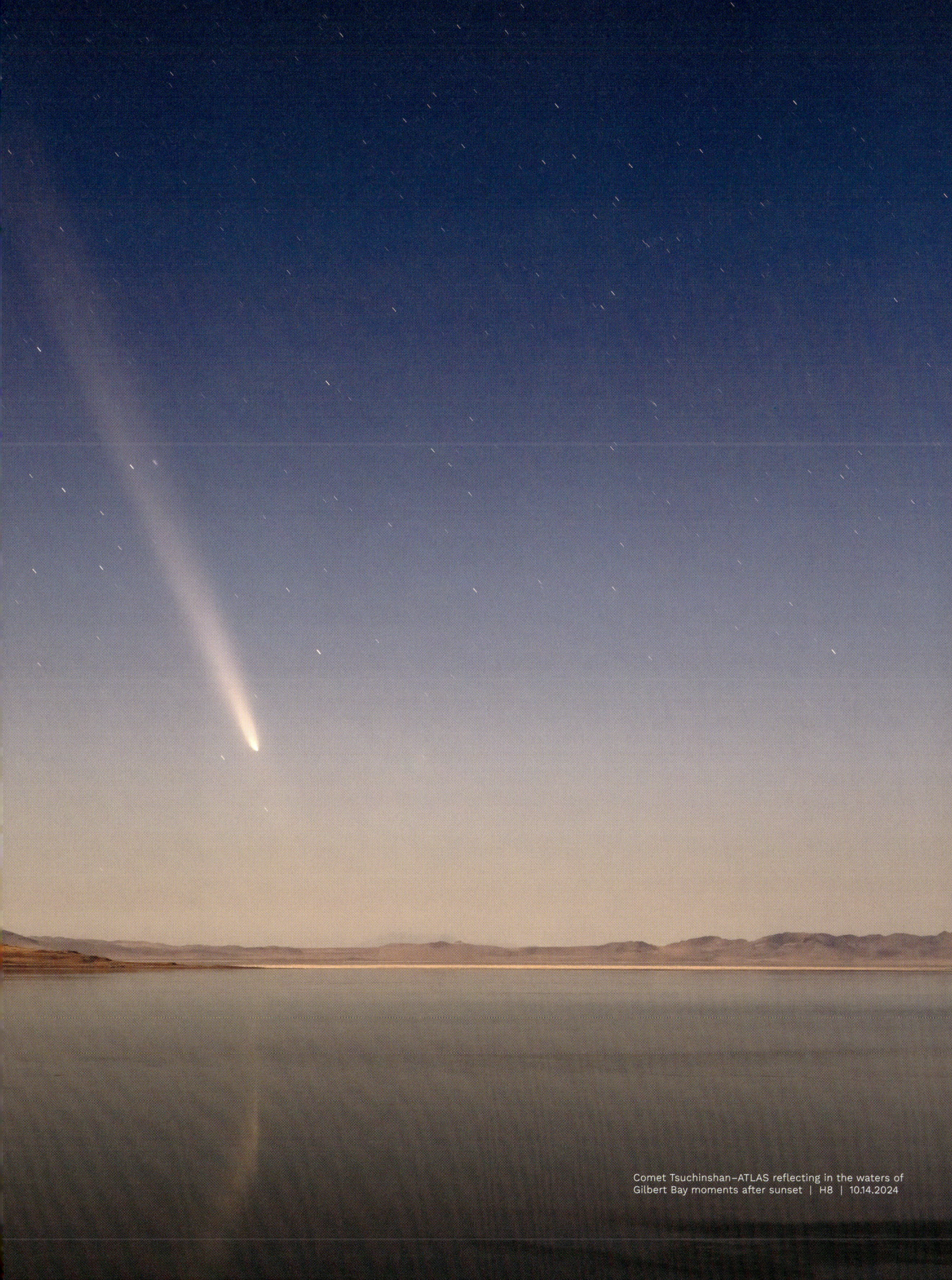

Comet Tsuchinshan–ATLAS reflecting in the waters of
Gilbert Bay moments after sunset | H8 | 10.14.2024

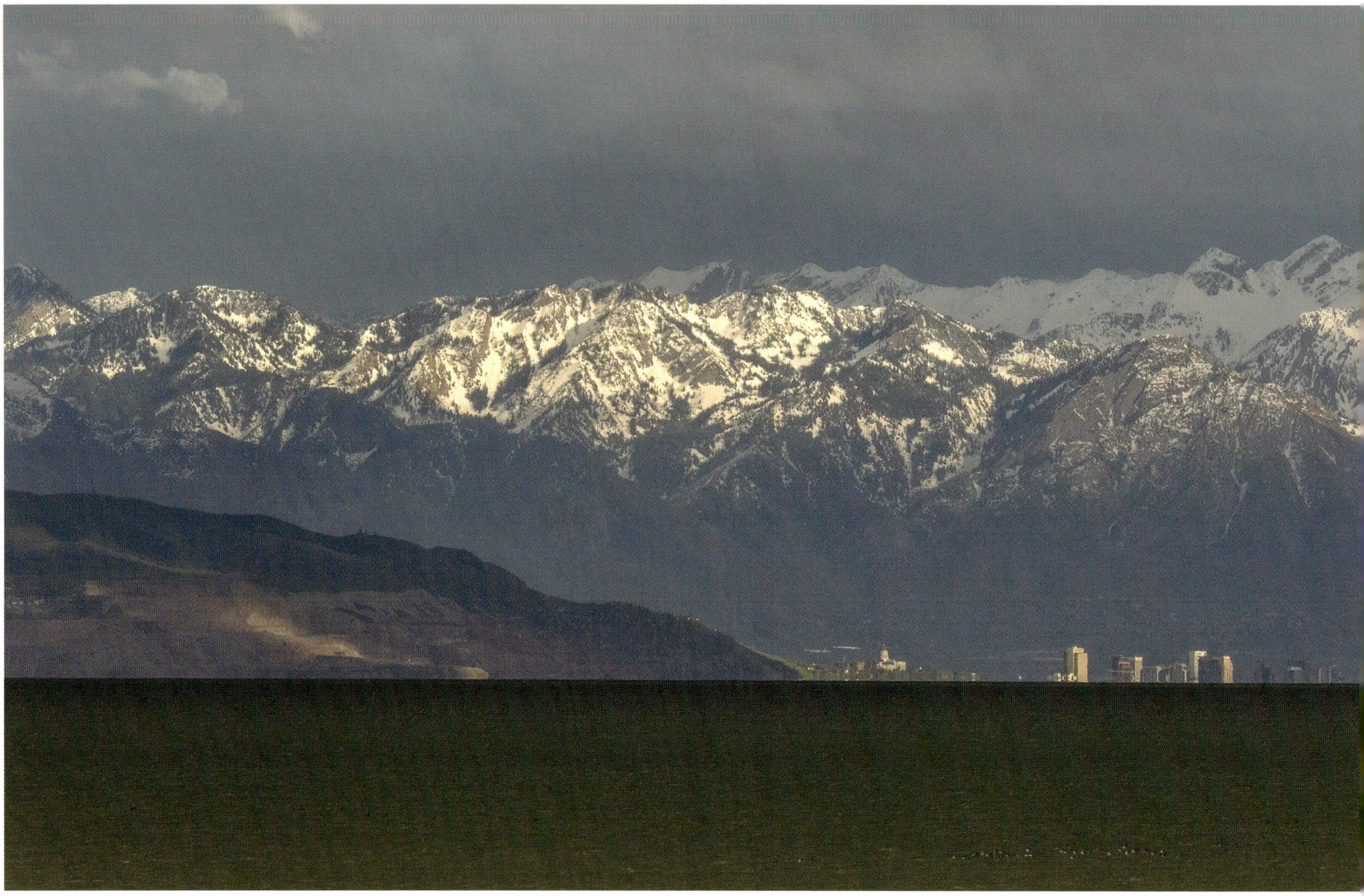

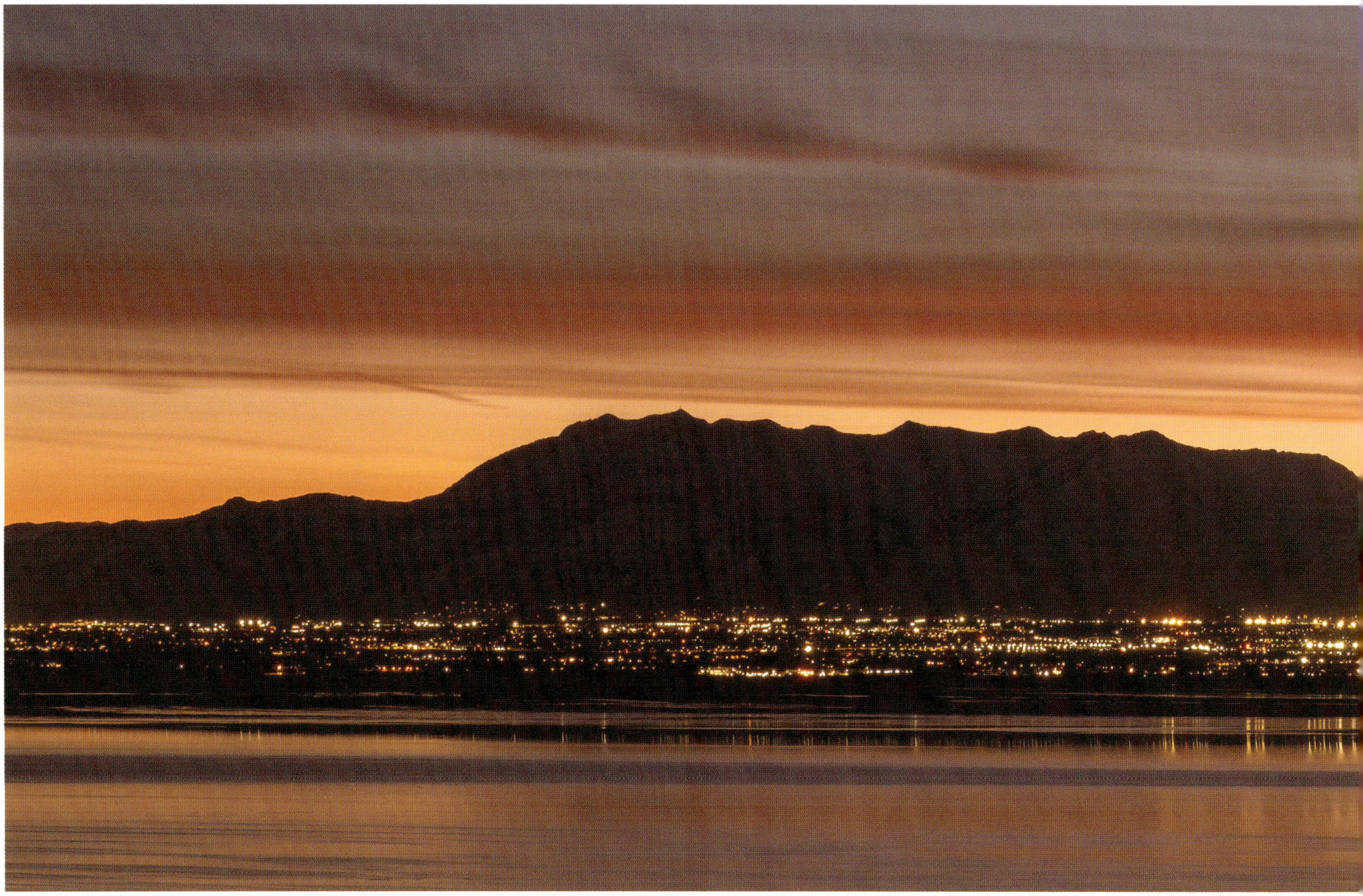

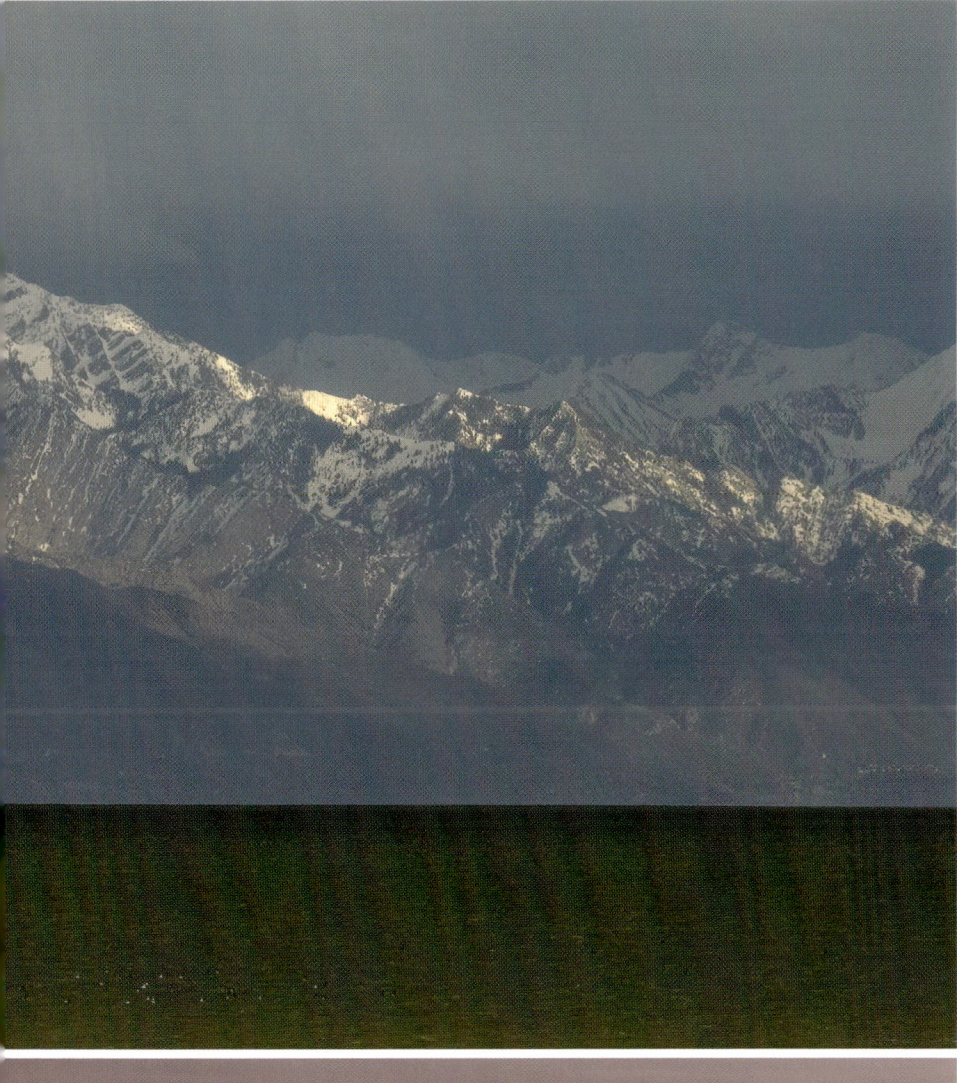

Farmington Bay and Salt Lake City | H8 | 04.29.2024

Farmington Bay with Syracuse and Ogden in the background | H8 | 03.19.2023

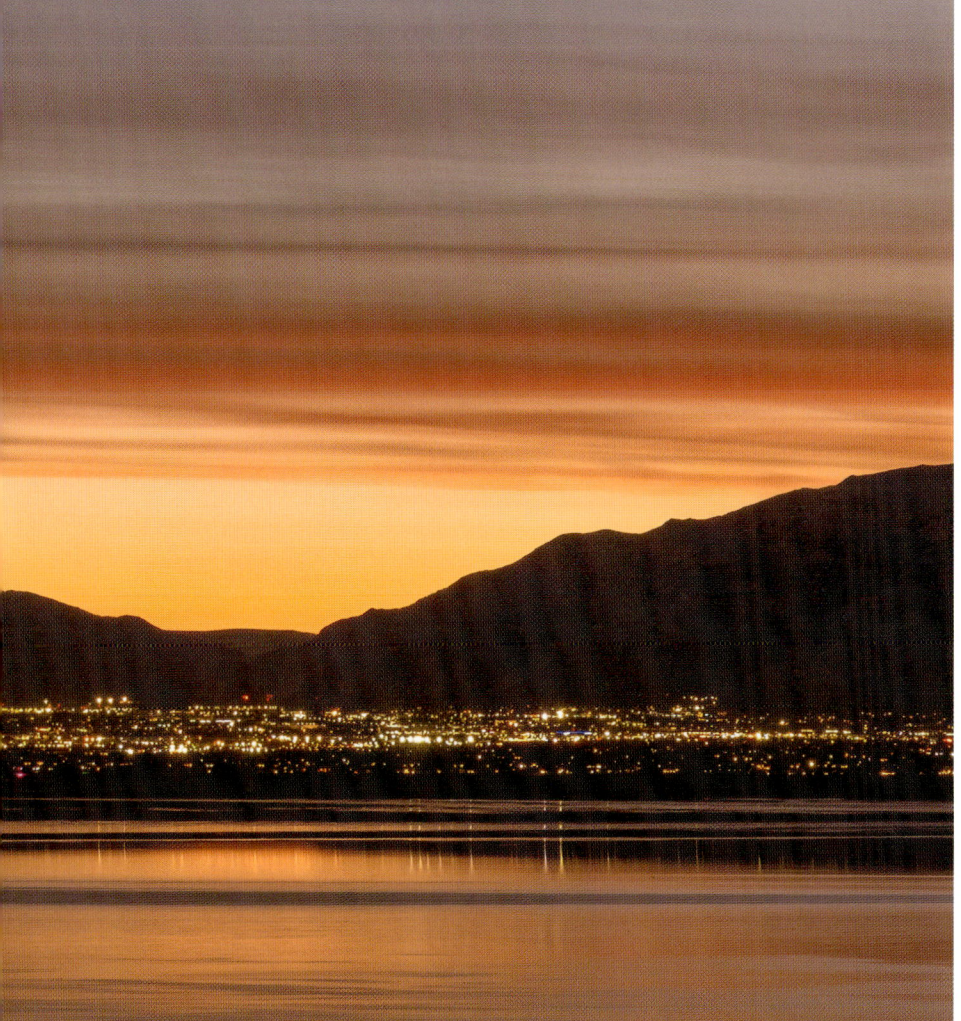

LIVING NEAR THE LAKE

Living near Great Salt Lake offers Utah's residents a unique and enriching experience. The lake's vast, reflective waters and diverse ecosystems provide endless opportunities for outdoor recreation, such as hiking, cycling, bird-watching, and kayaking. The lake's stunning landscapes, especially during sunrise and sunset, offer breathtaking views that have become part of daily life. Those who live near the lake appreciate the smell that often comes in with gentle breezes and fierce winds.

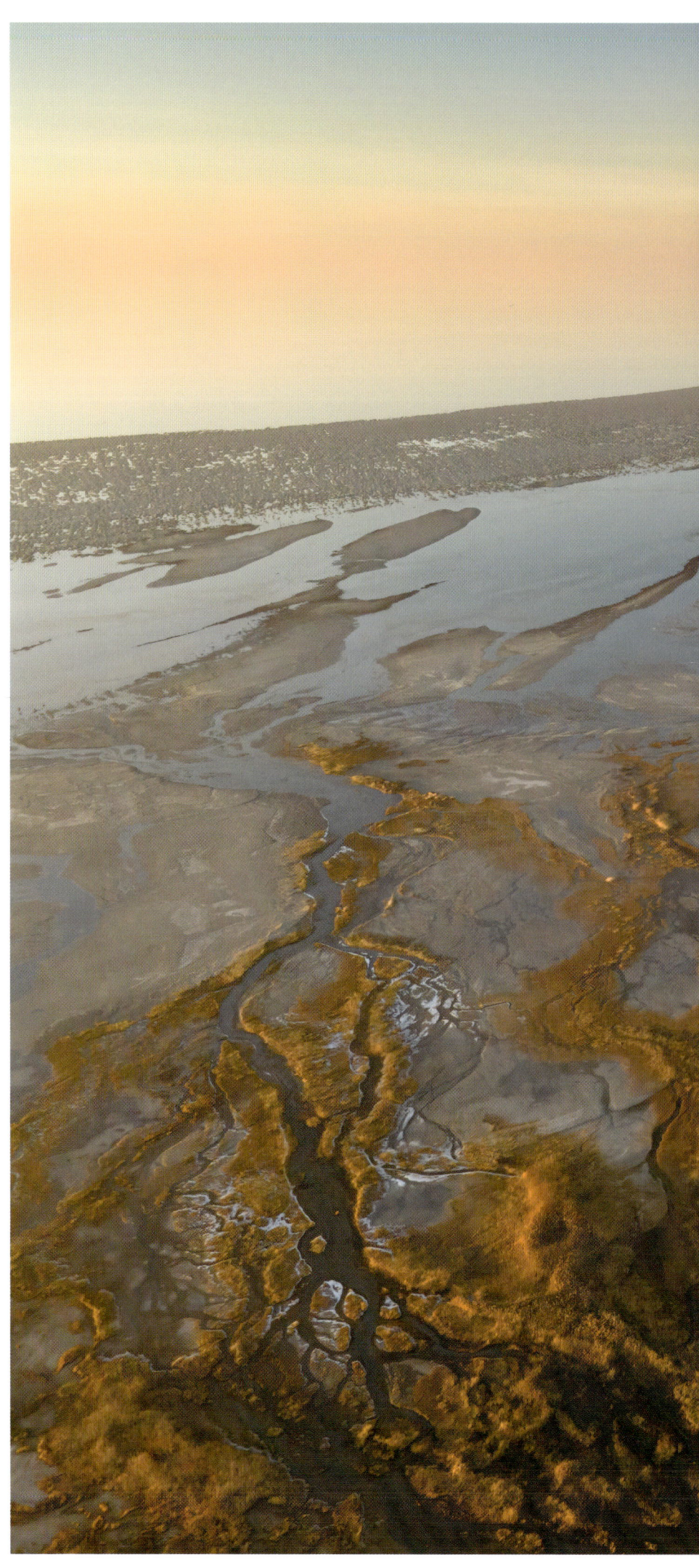

LEE CREEK

This delta forms where Lee Creek deposits
sediments into the lake, creating channels
and plumes. Lighter areas show recent
deposits, while darker ones have older,
organic-rich sediments. Bright patches are
salt minerals from high evaporation. The
meandering channels and water pools reflect
changing flow patterns influenced by seasons
and climate. Vegetation and wetlands thrive,
supporting wildlife. Antelope Island emerges
on the horizon.

Lee Creek | K8 | 11.20.2022

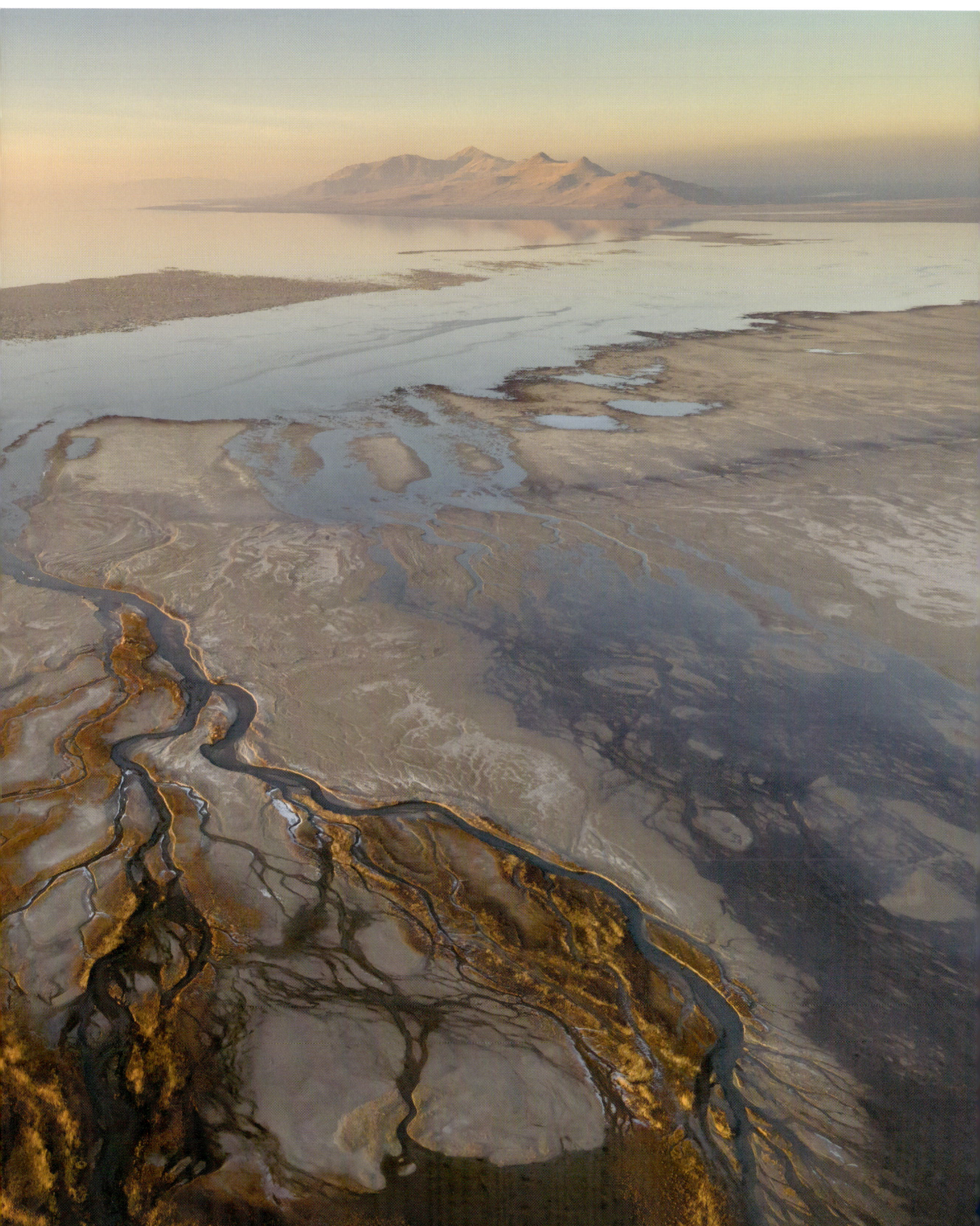

EXPOSED MICROBIALITES

Microbialites are essential to Great Salt Lake's ecosystem, providing habitats for tiny creatures like brine shrimp and brine flies, which are crucial food for birds, akin to coral reefs in the ocean. They recycle nutrients, enhancing the lake's productivity, and their cyanobacteria use sunlight to produce energy and oxygen, supporting the food chain. These structures also indicate environmental changes and help sequester carbon dioxide. When exposed, microbialites dry out, reducing their ability to produce oxygen and shelter organisms, affecting the entire food chain and altering their role in trapping sediments and minerals.

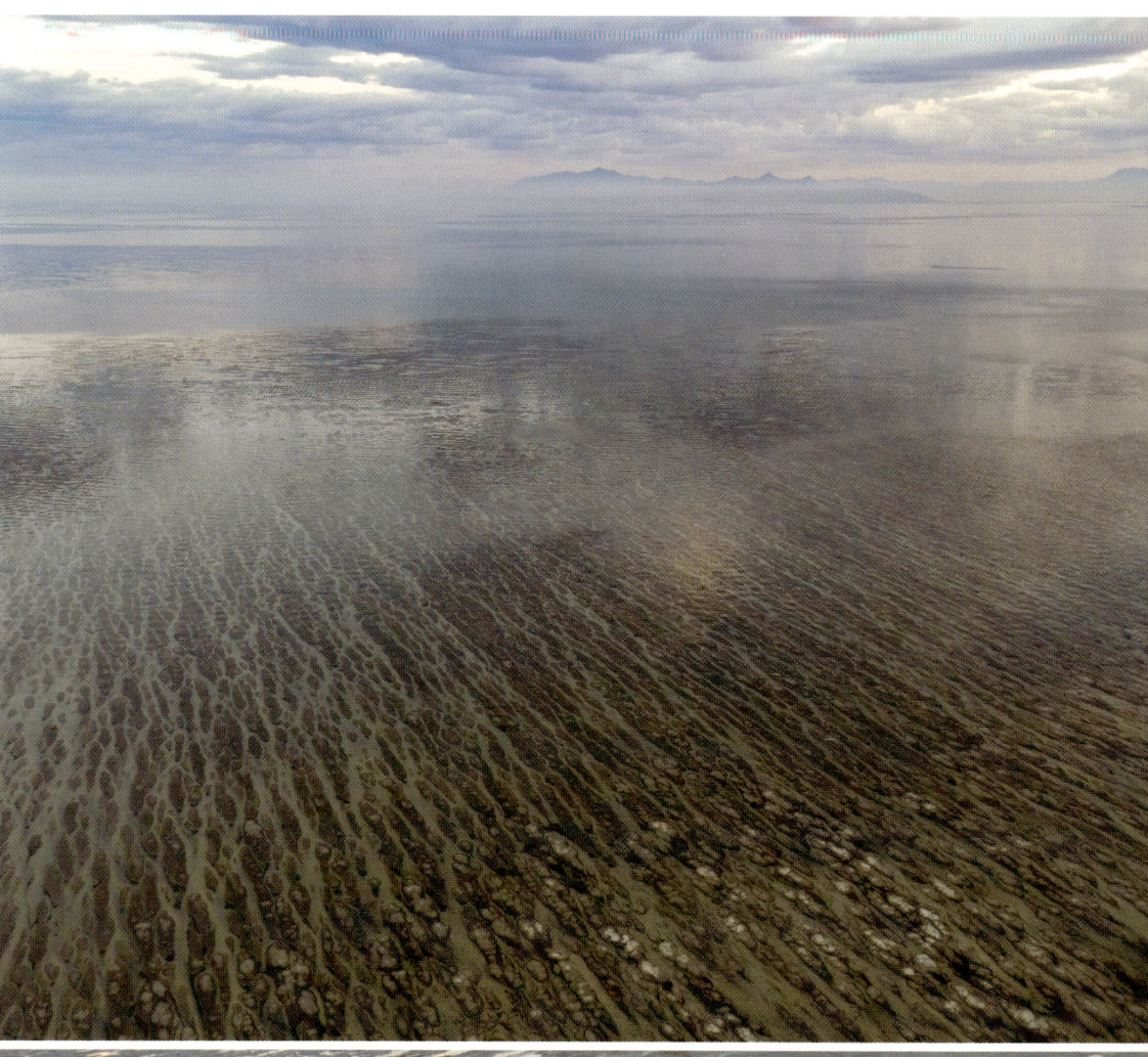

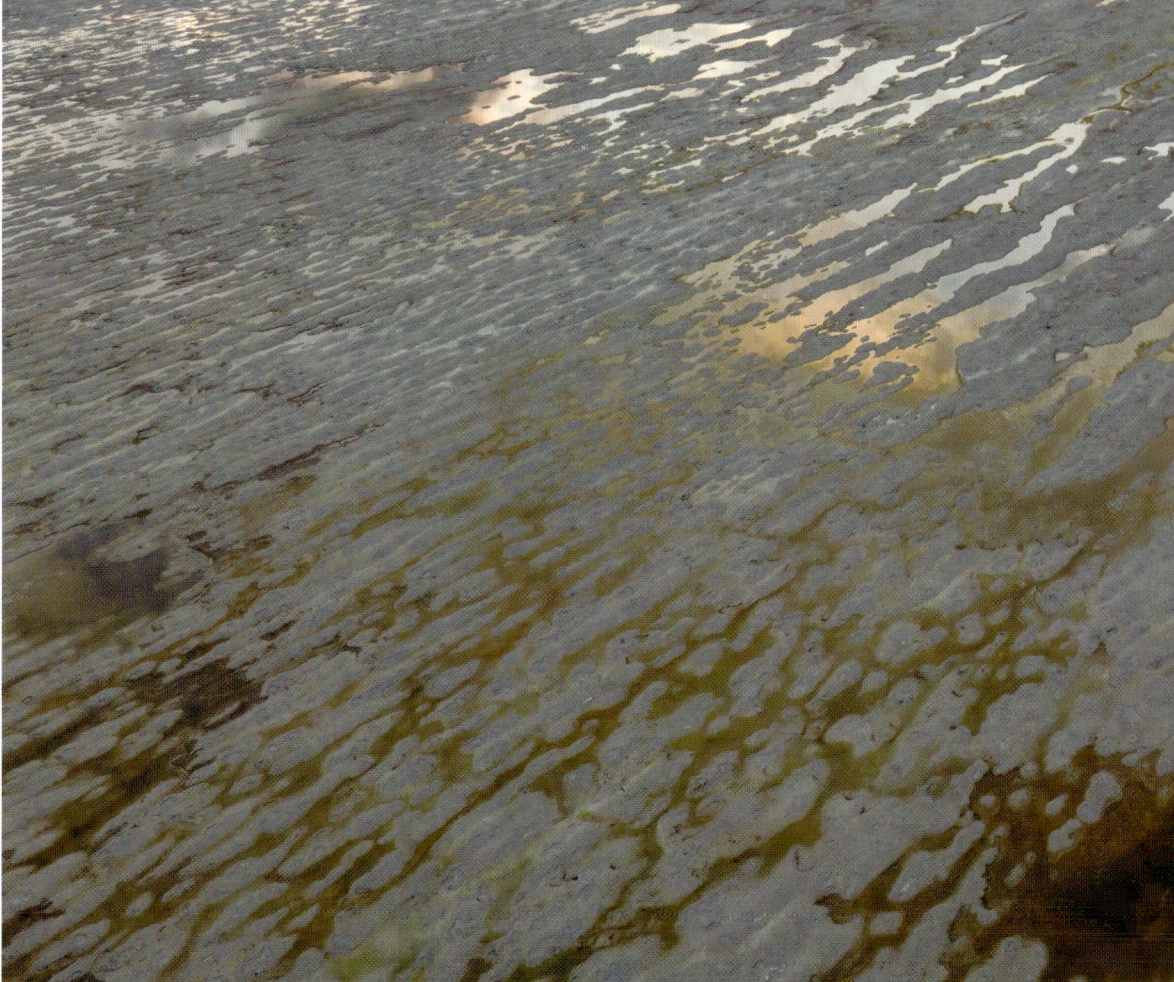

Microbialites under water
K7 | 10.21.2023

Exposed microbialites from the air
K8 | 11.18.2023

OPPOSITE: Exposed mircrobialites
K8 | 11.18.2023

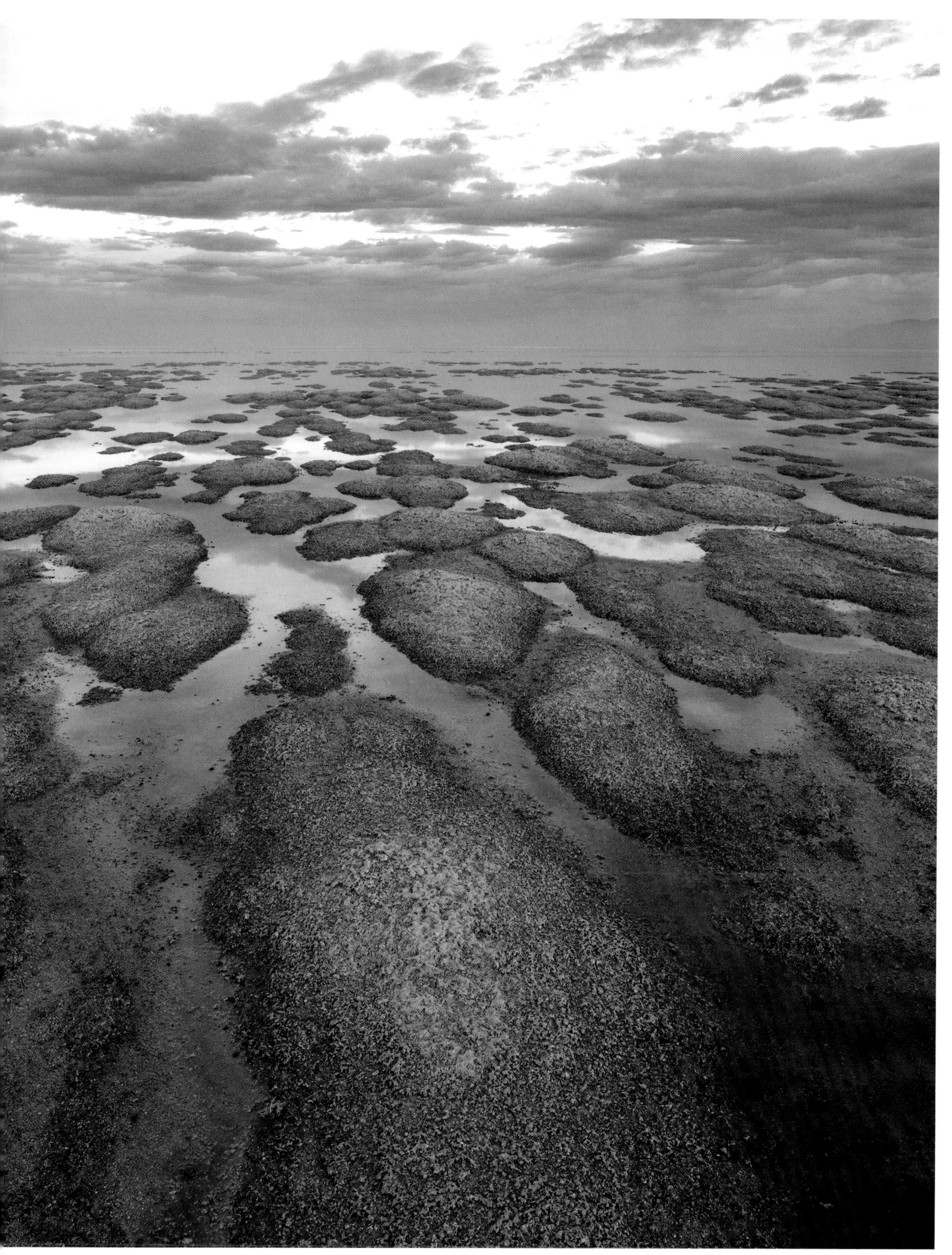

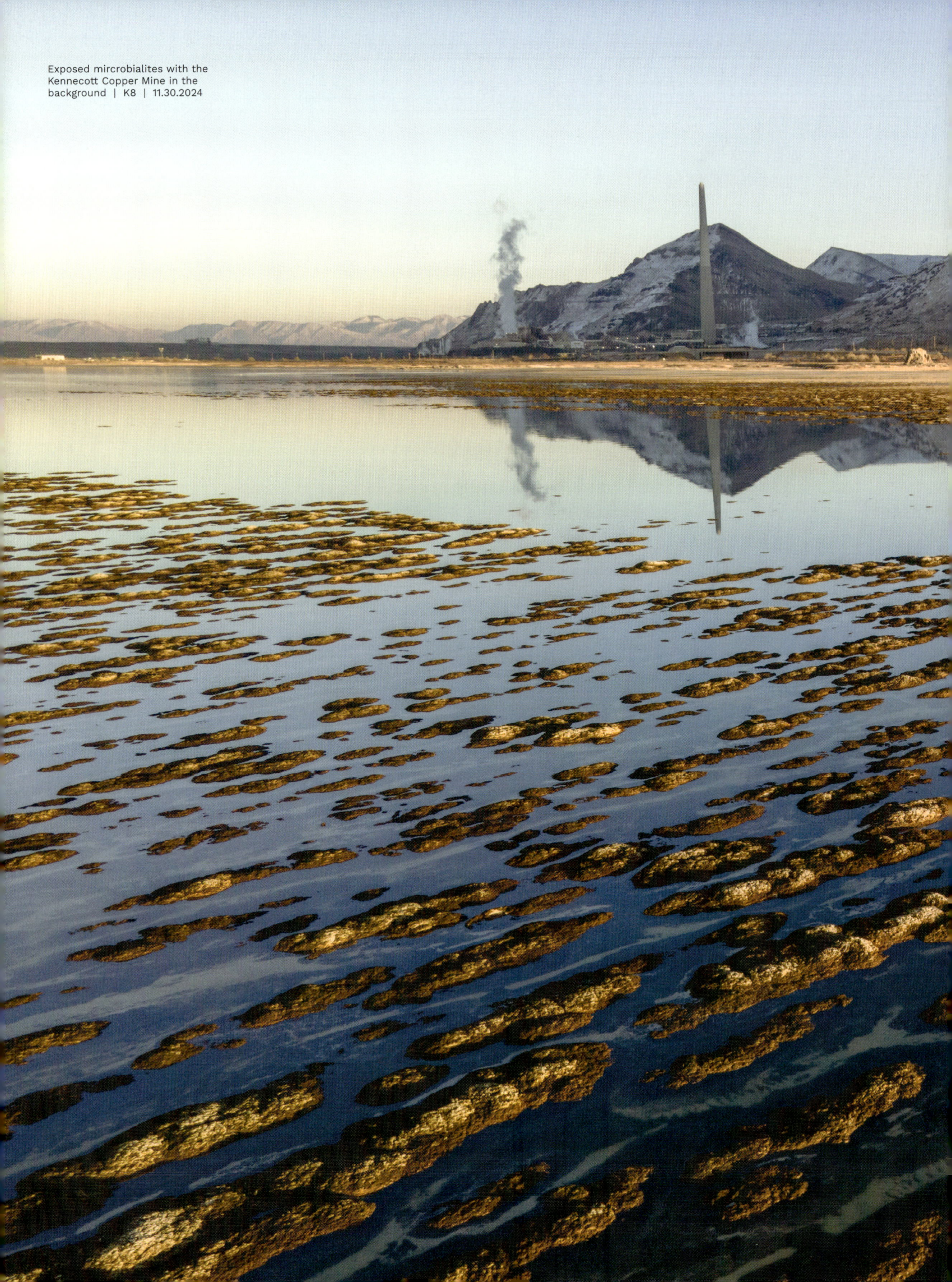

Exposed mircrobialites with the
Kennecott Copper Mine in the
background | K8 | 11.30.2024

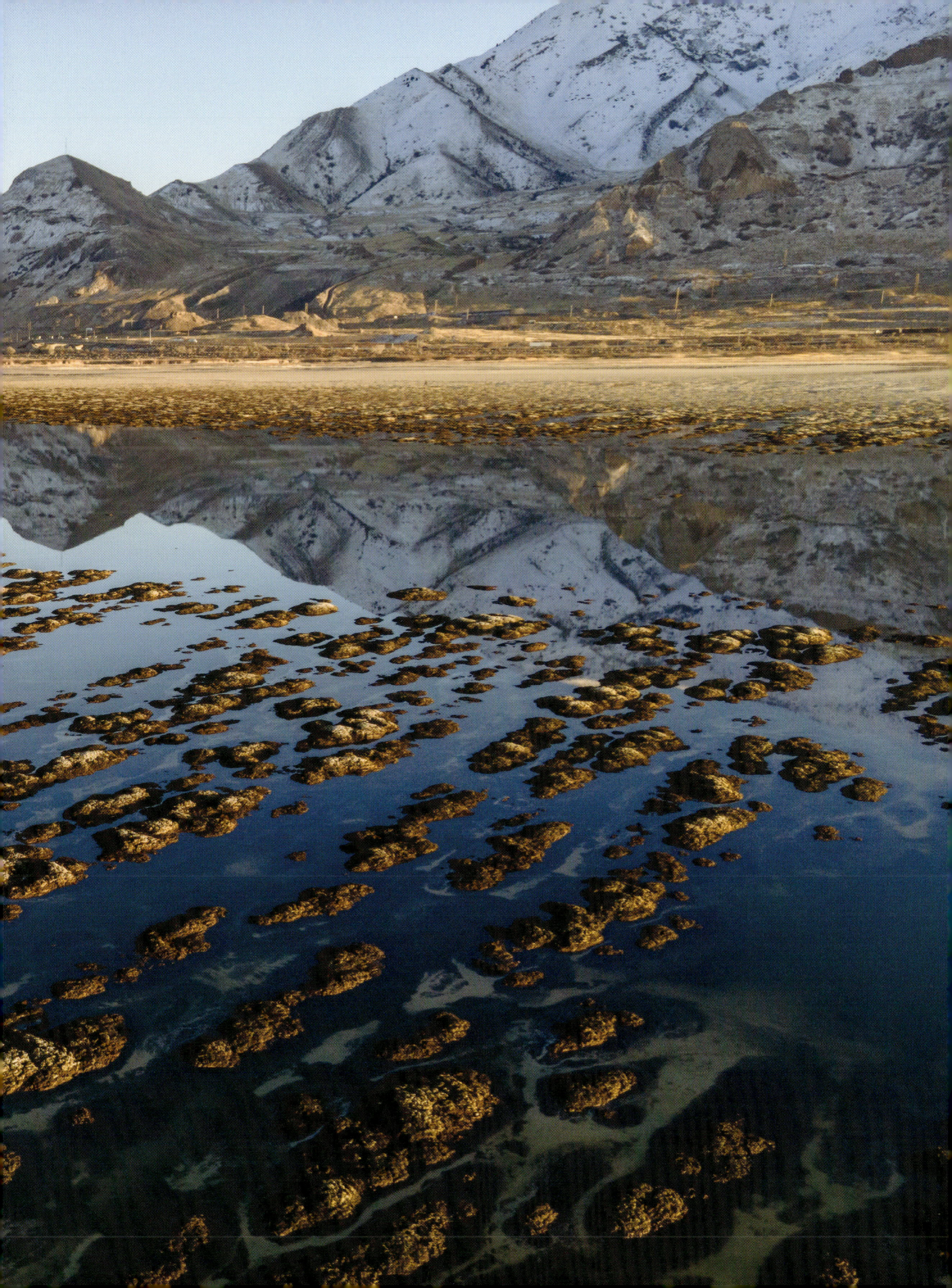

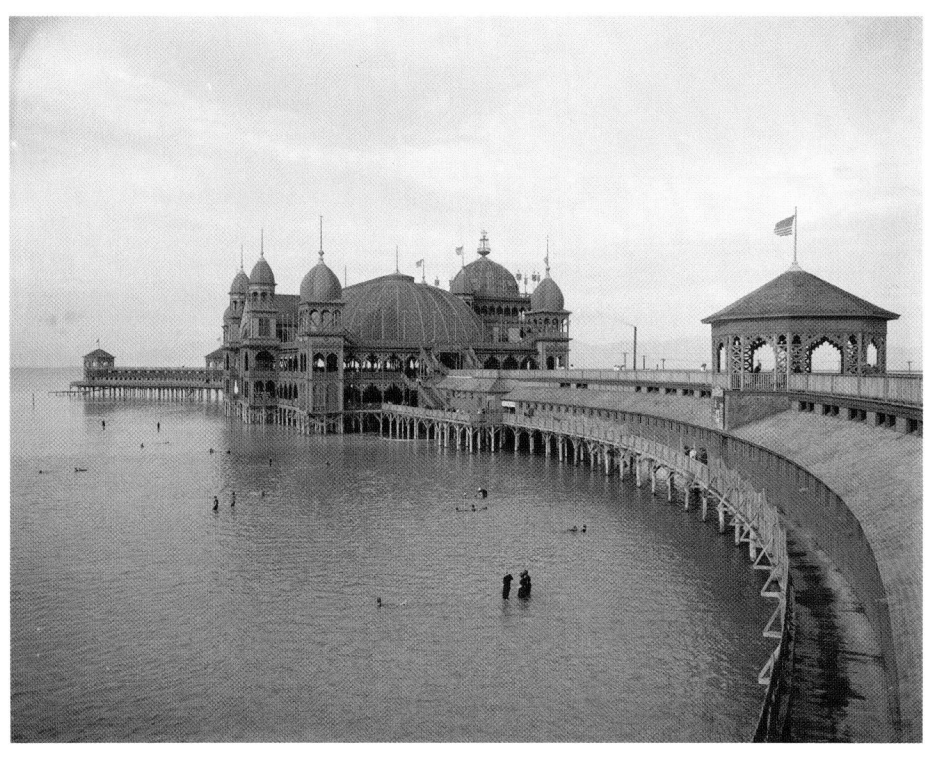

SALTAIR

The old Saltair, built in 1893 on Great Salt Lake's shores, was a grand Moorish Revival–style resort offering dance pavilions, swimming, and amusement rides. Despite its popularity, it faced challenges such as fires, fluctuating lake levels, and economic difficulties, leading to its decline and eventual abandonment, with only the original foundations remaining. The new Saltair, constructed in 1981 a few miles east of the original location, pays homage to the original with some similar architectural elements and serves as a modern venue for concerts and events.

Remnants of old Saltair | K8 | 11.20.2022

New Saltair | K8 | 11.18.2023

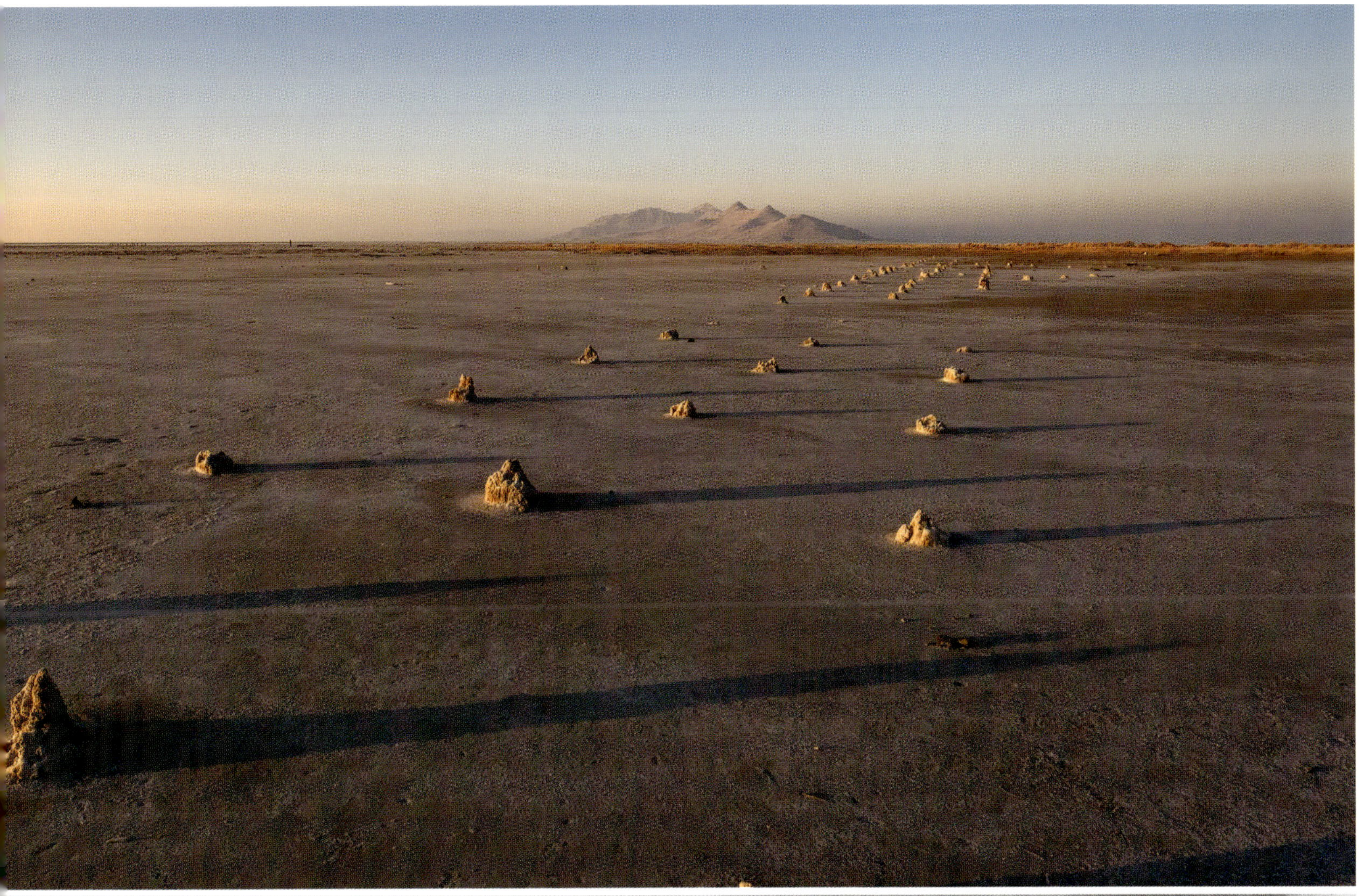

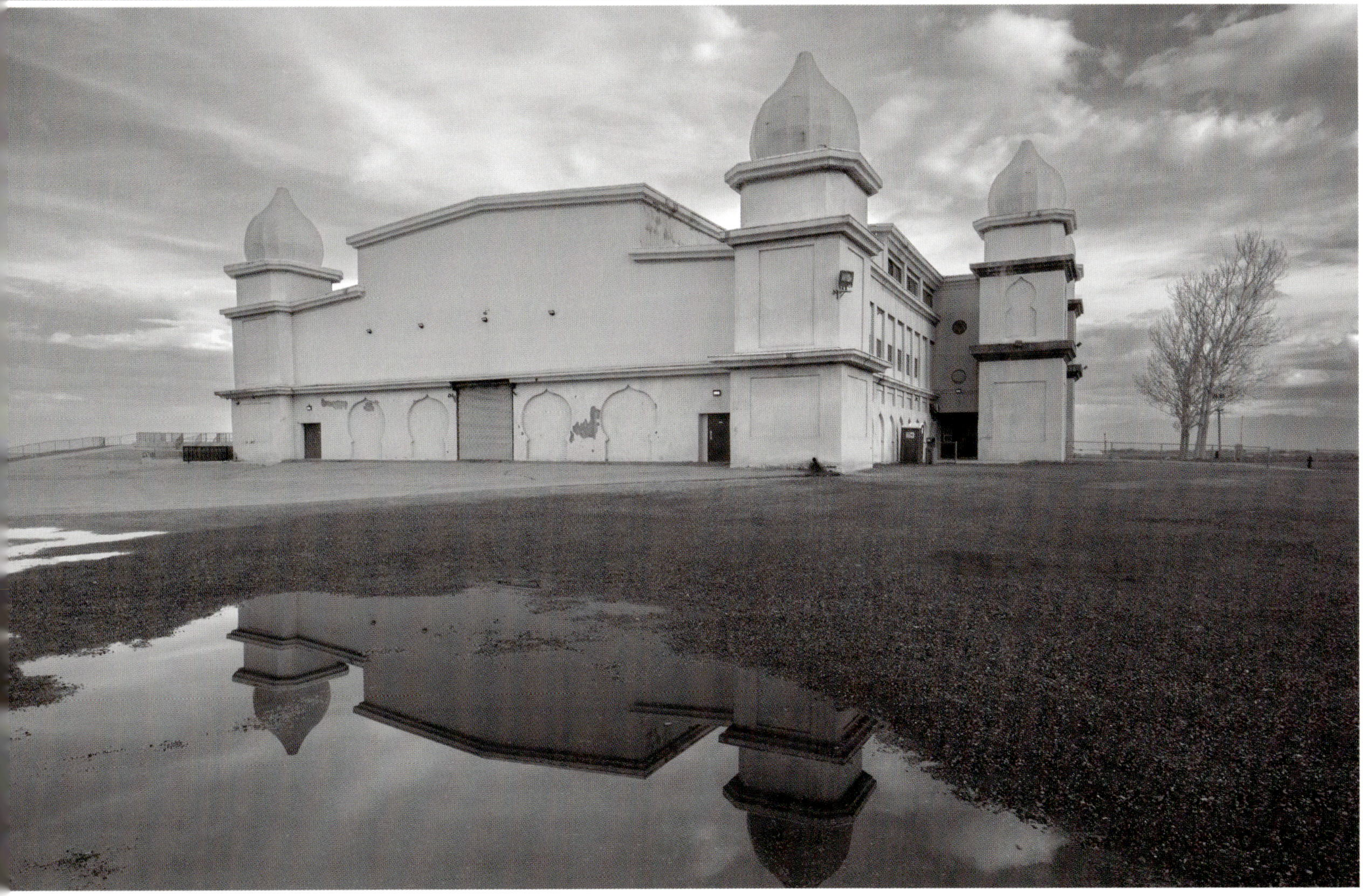

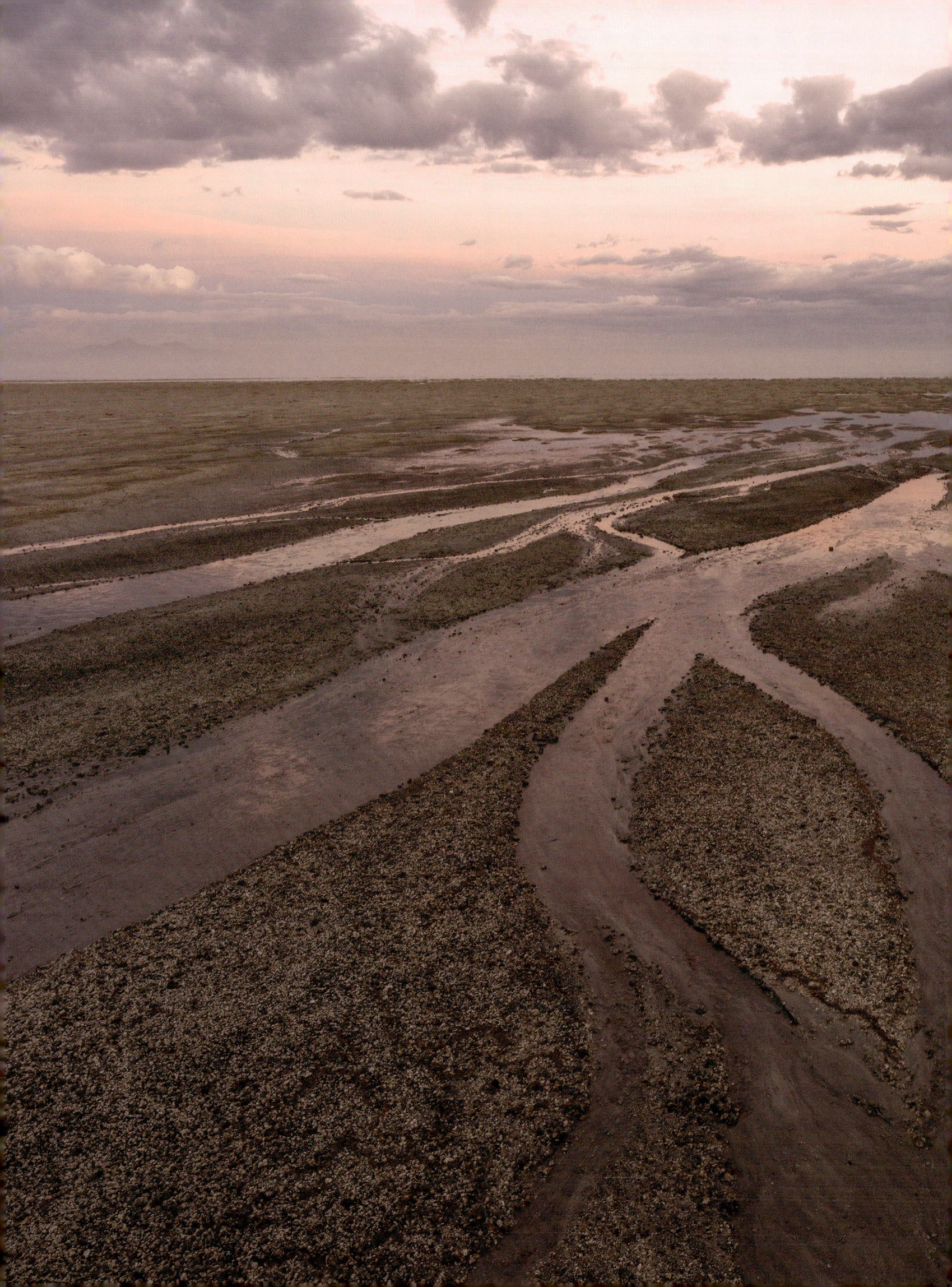

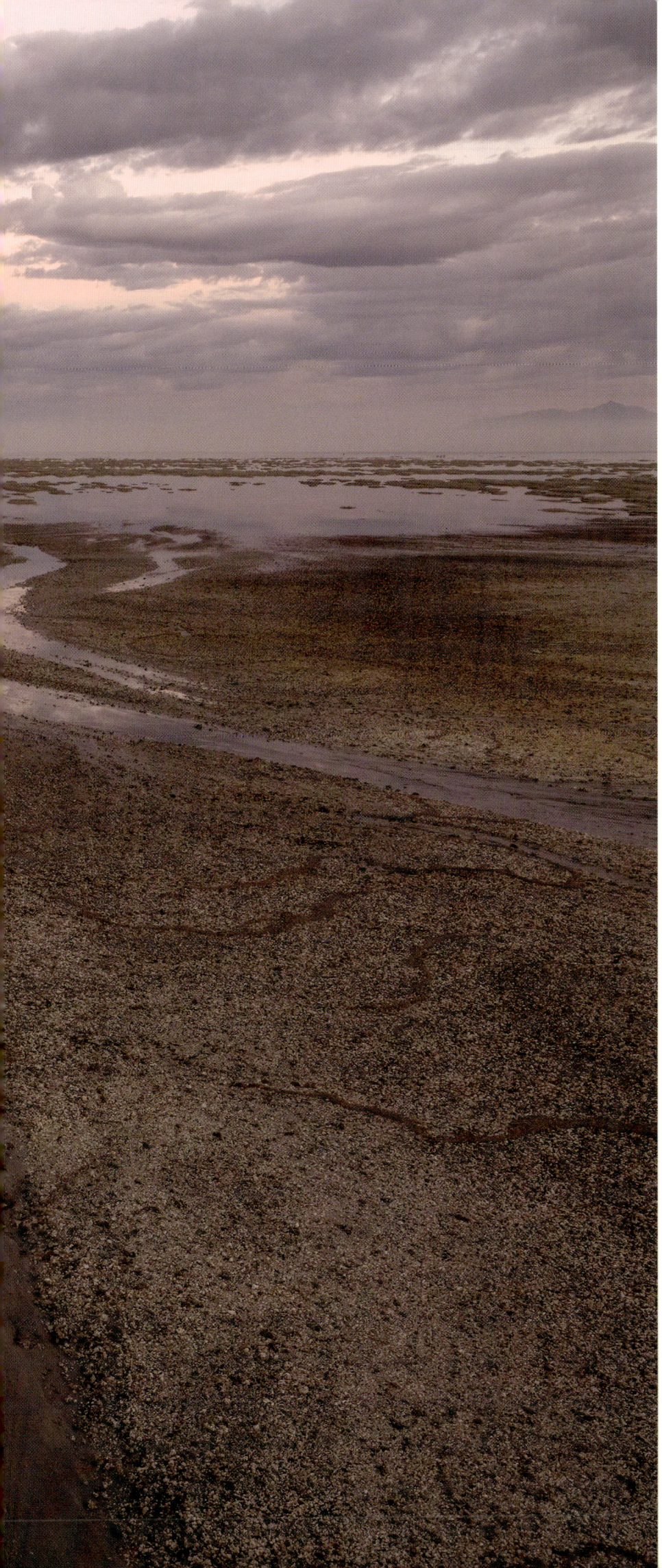

SEDIMENT TRANSPORT

The landscape of Great Salt Lake on the south shore is dynamic and ever-changing, shaped by water and sediment movement. Intricate patterns and textures are created with layers of fine silt and sand deposited by the lake's gentle currents and winds. These features reveal how the lake's fluctuating water levels continually reshape its shores, offering a glimpse into the natural processes at work.

Water veins | K8 | 11.18.2023

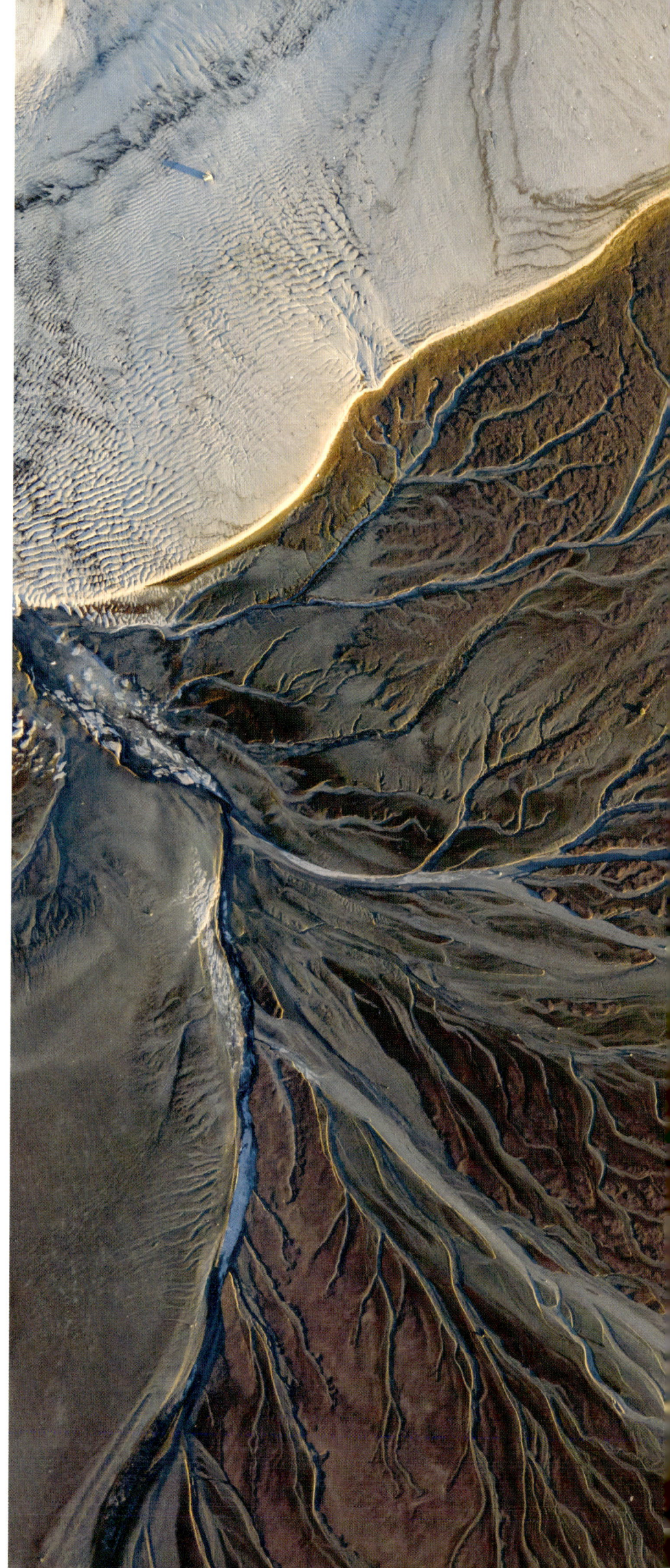

Sediment delta on the south shore
K8 | 11.28.2024

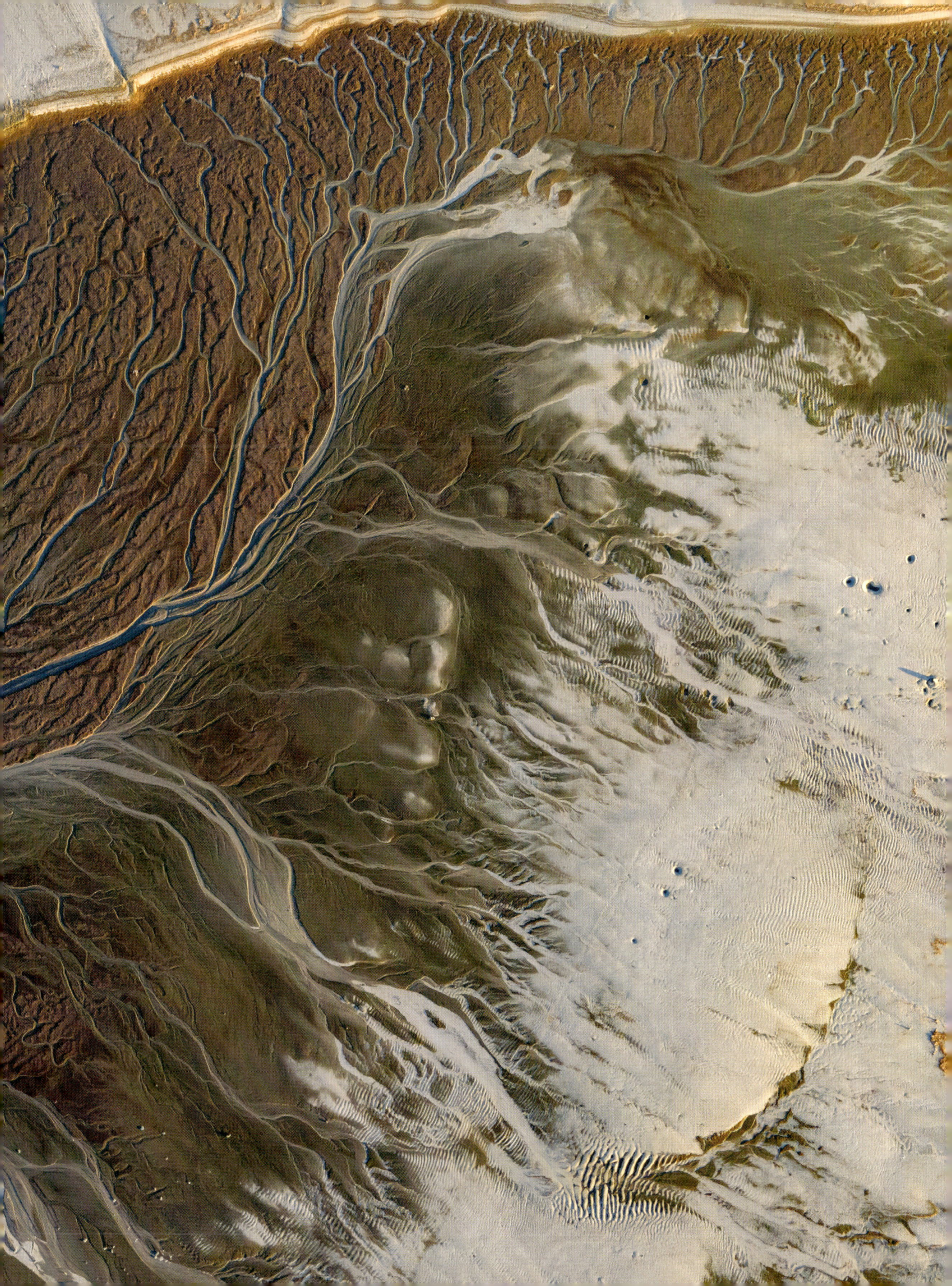

MORNINGS ON GREAT SALT LAKE
Great Salt Lake in the morning can transform
into a serene and almost otherworldly
landscape. The horizon blends seamlessly
with the water, creating a sense of infinite
space and peaceful solitude, the moon adding
a touch of celestial elegance.

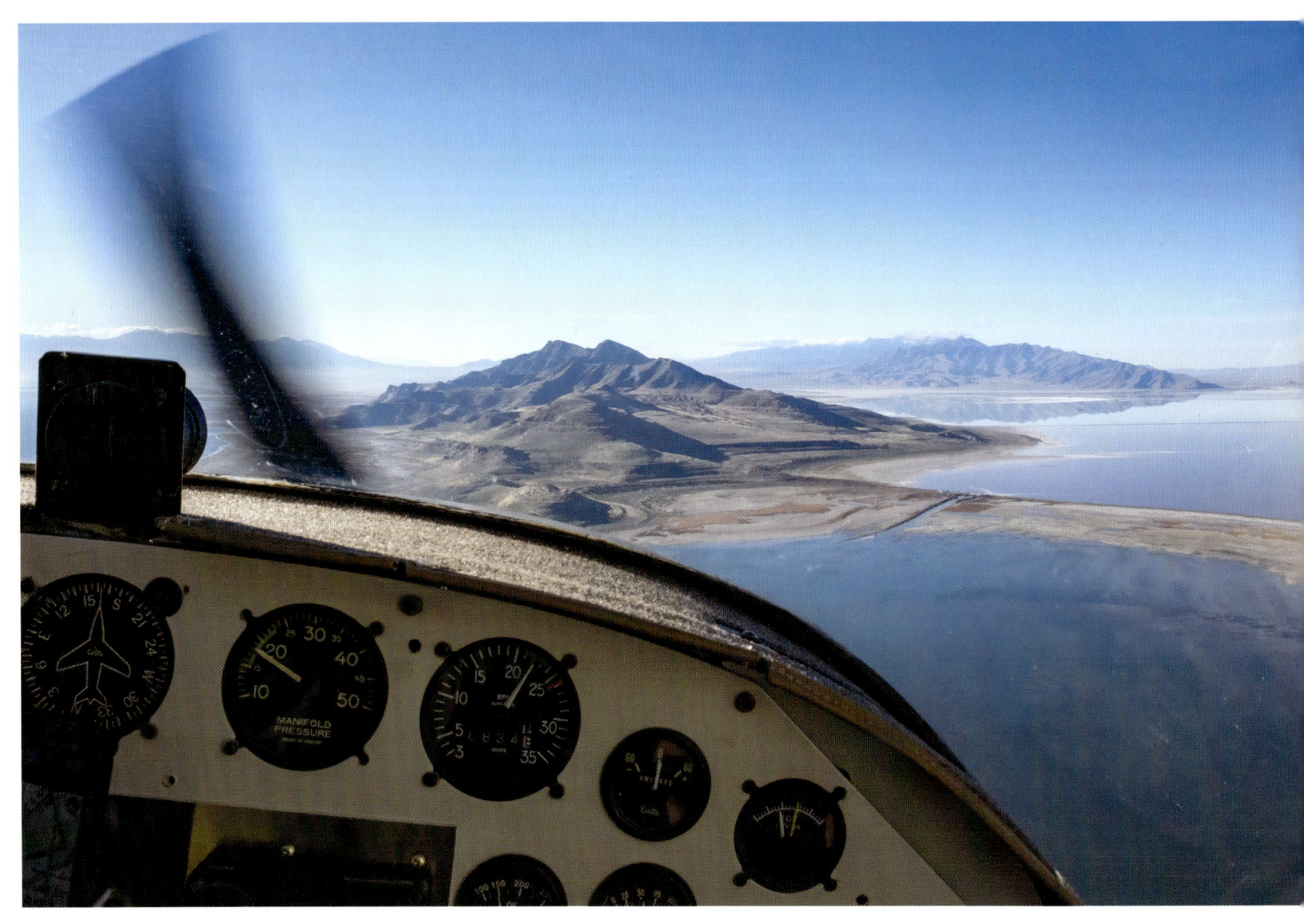

North end of Stansbury Island from the air | H6 | 10.13.2013

PREVIOUS PAGE: Predawn gradient and moon | K8 | 12.22.2023

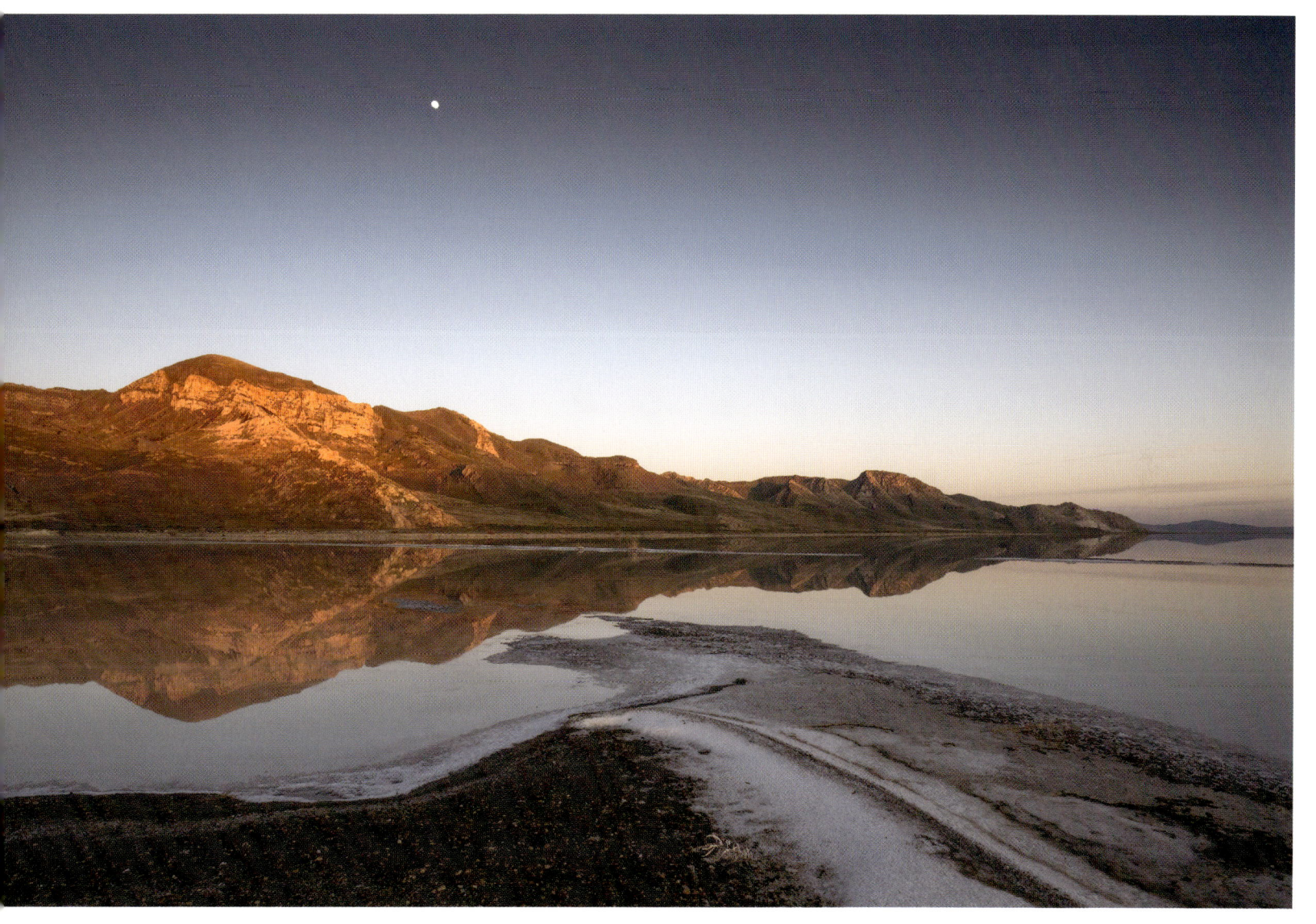

Stansbury Island and moon | J5 | 04.20.2024

STANSBURY ISLAND

Stansbury Island, named after Howard Stansbury, the first Euro-American to extensively explore and survey Great Salt Lake, is called Ya'han-go-a by native Western Shoshone people. The island is rich in history, with petroglyphs scattered across its landscape and two significant caves likely used seasonally by the Goshute people. Stansbury is still classified as an island even though it is now connected to the mainland due to the receding lake and the construction of a causeway. Spanning about 11.5 miles (18.5 km) in length and less than 5 miles (8 km) in width, it features several freshwater seeps along its eastern mountainous area. Castle Rock, the island's peak, rises 6,647 feet (2,026 m) above sea level, towering over 2,400 feet (732 m) above the lake's surface.

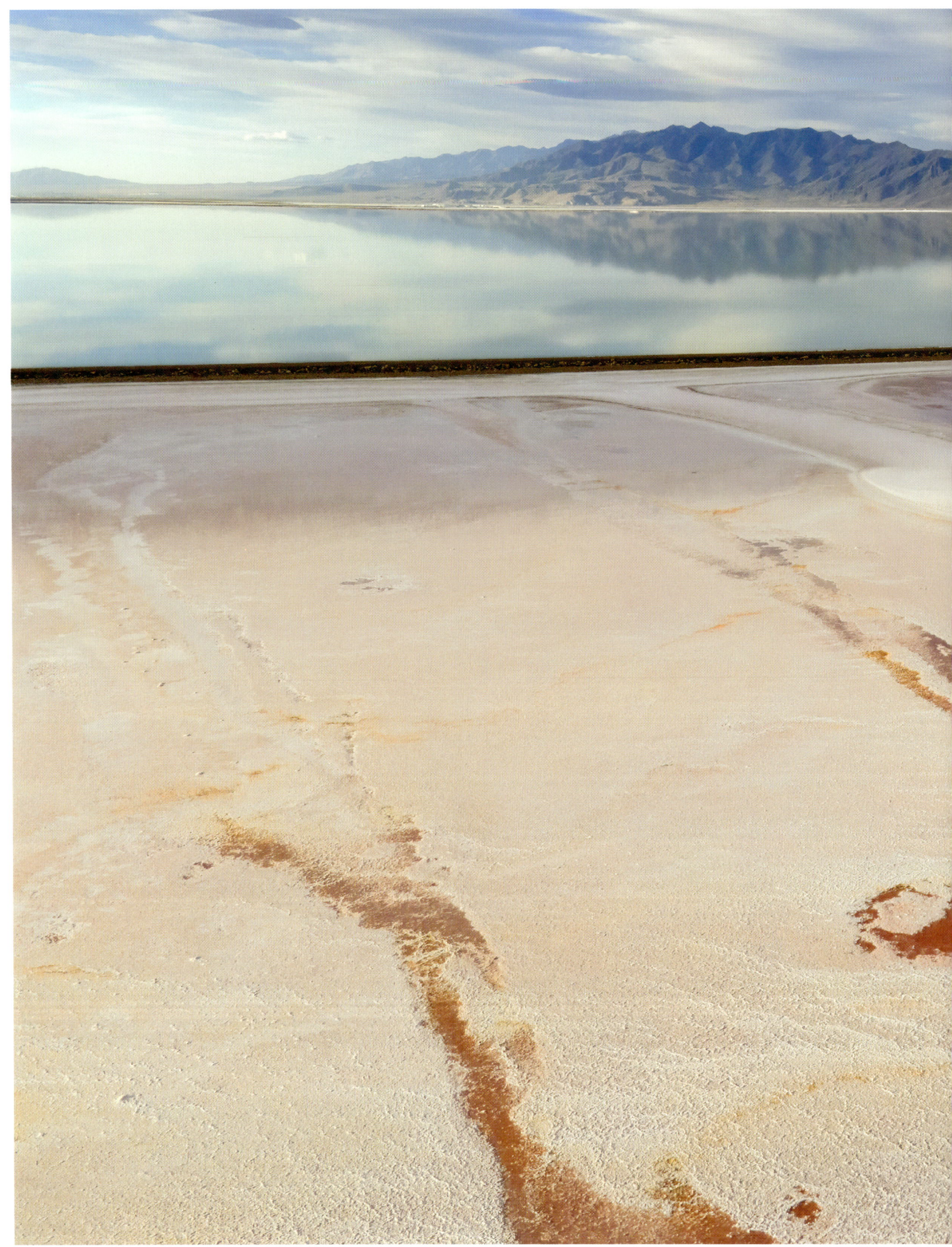

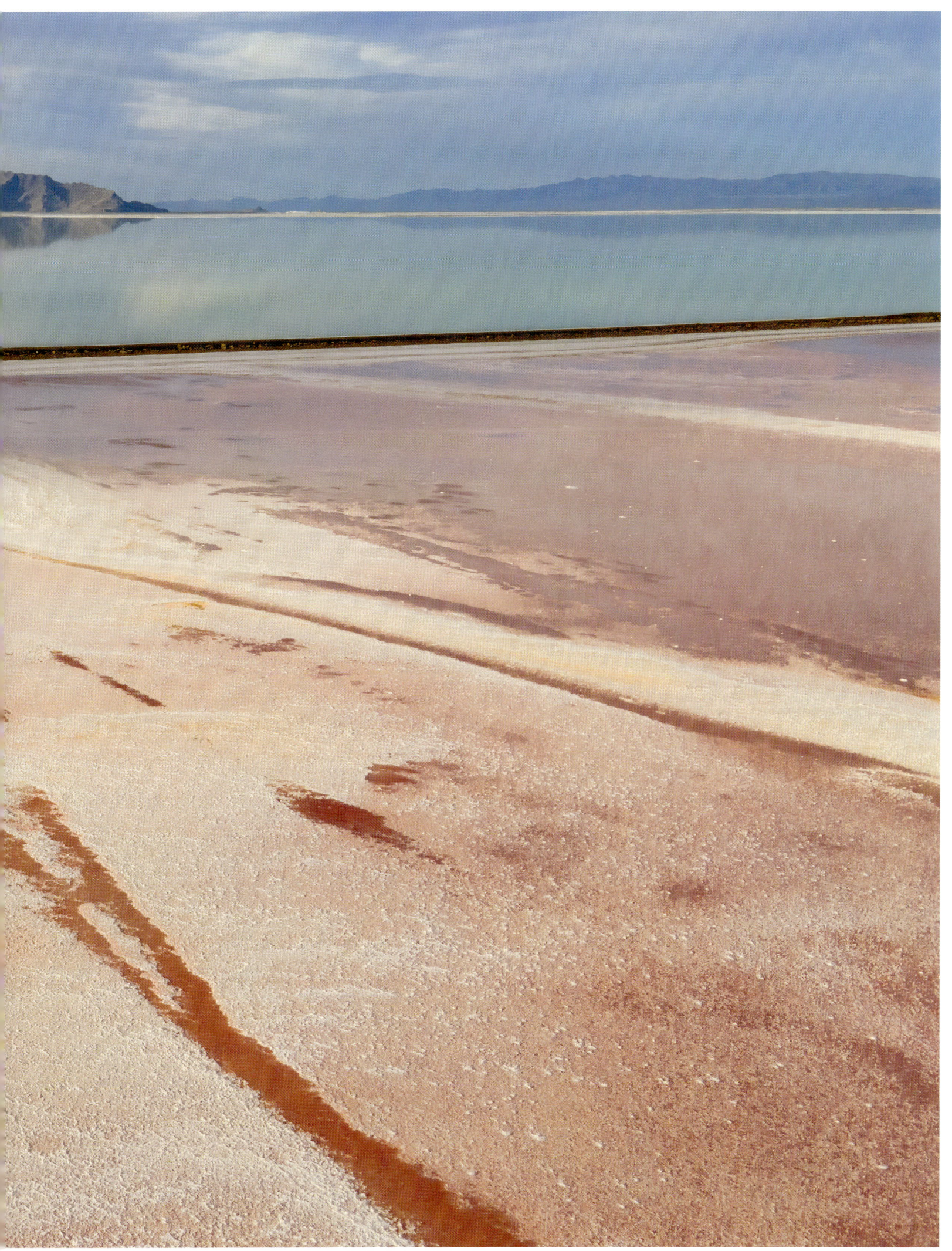

The divided Stansbury Bay, Oquirrh Mountains in the background | J5 | 09.30.2023

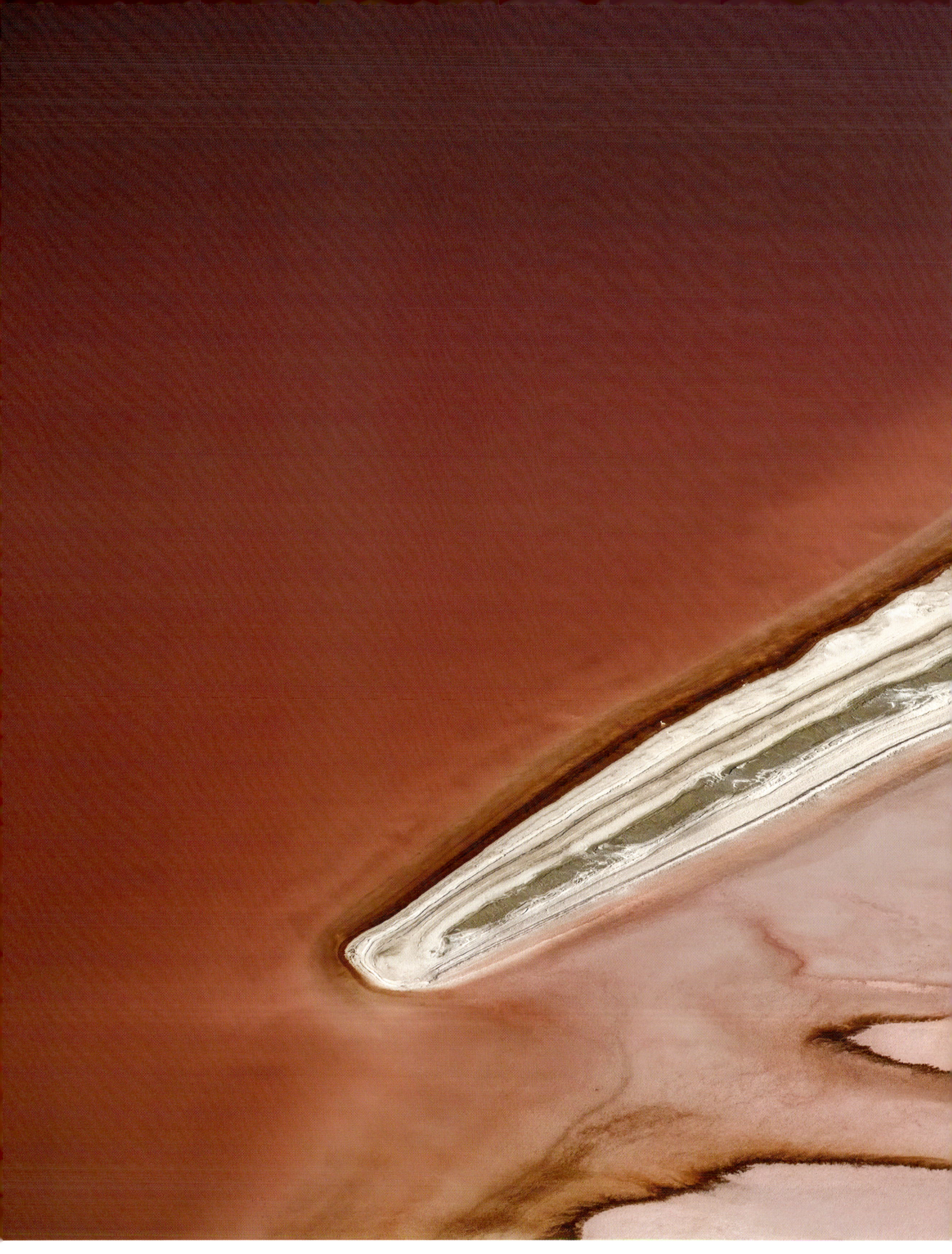

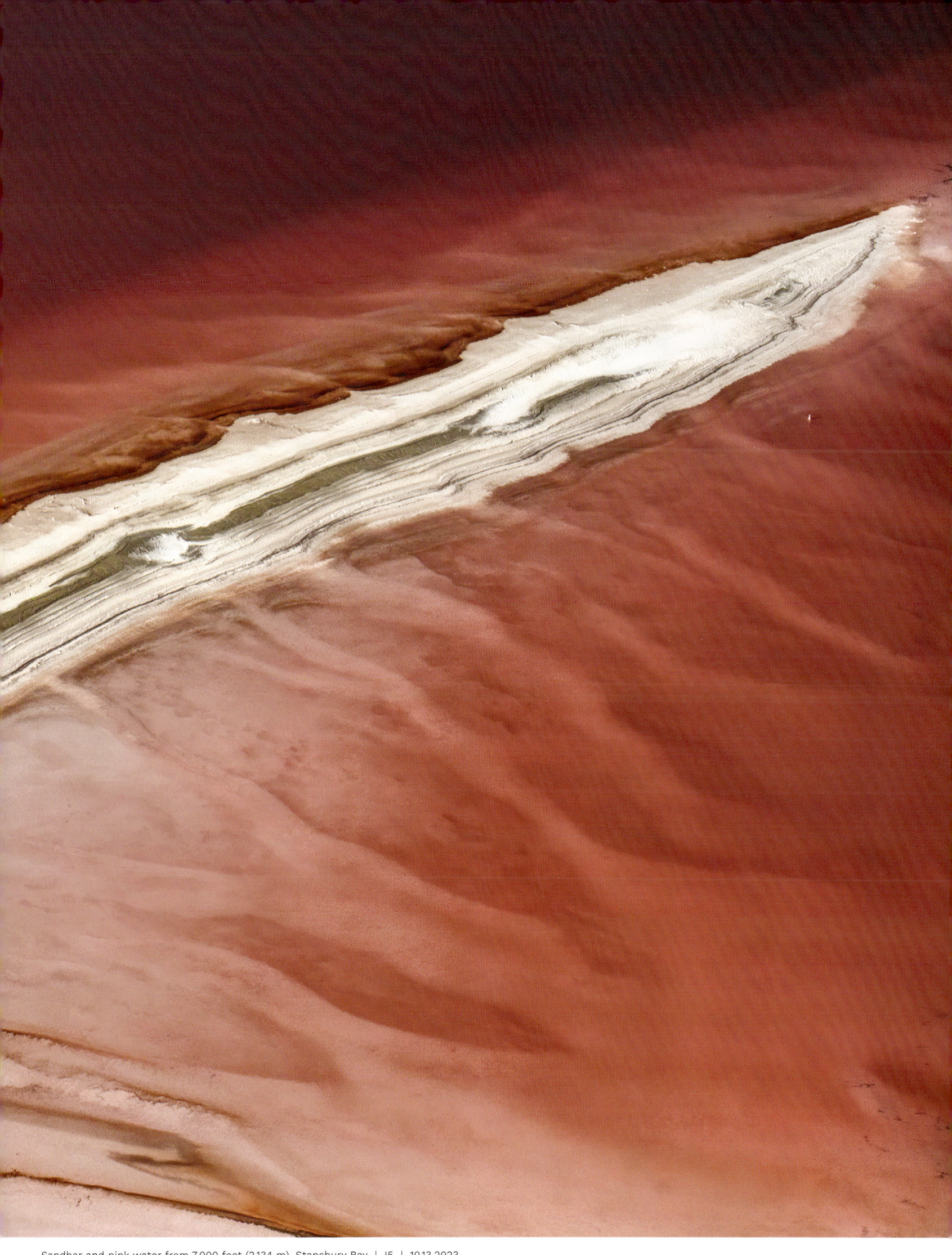

Sandbar and pink water from 7,000 feet (2,134 m), Stansbury Bay | I5 | 10.13.2023

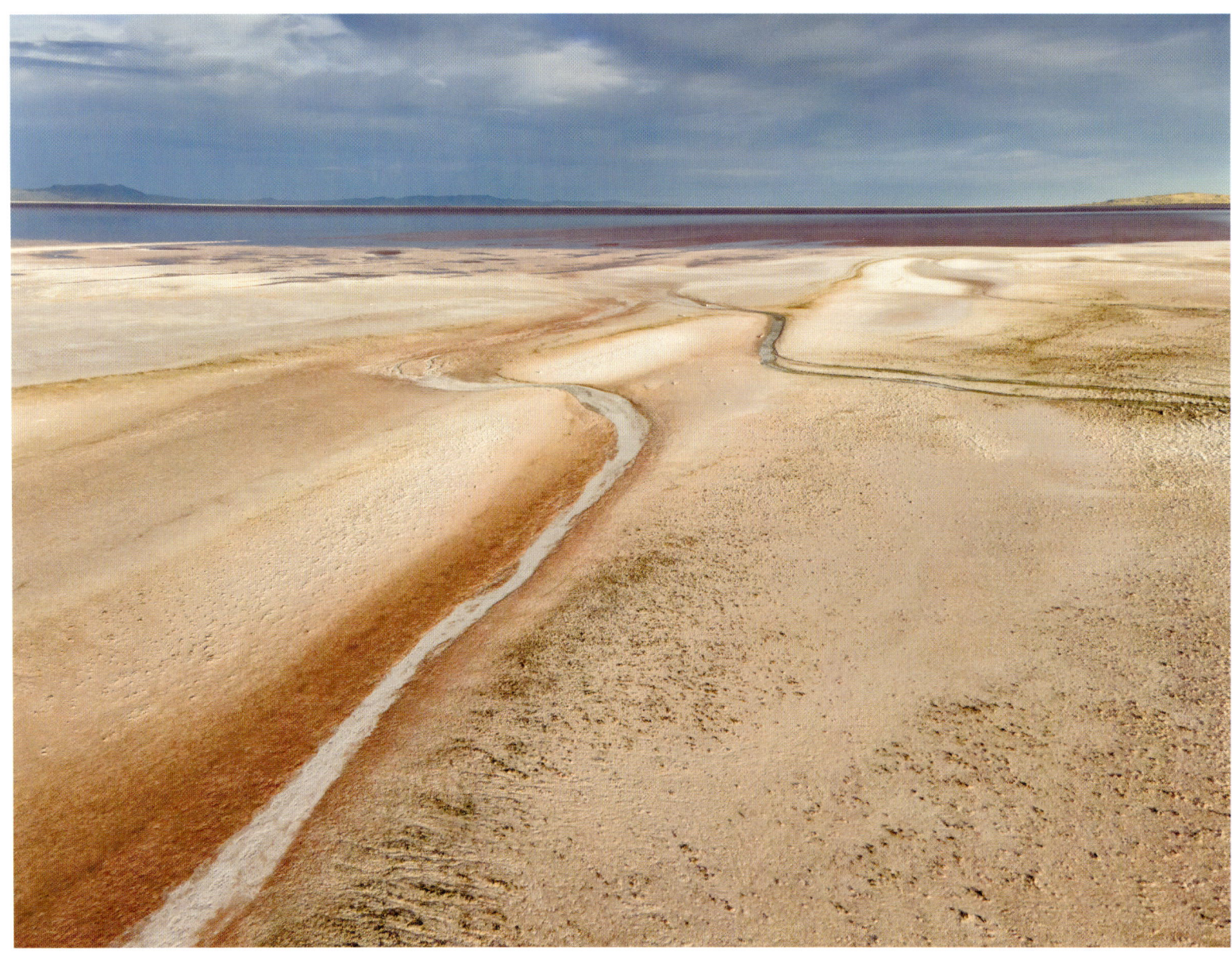

SALT, SALT, SALT

Stansbury Bay features highly variable salinity levels influenced by seasonal changes, precipitation, and water inflows. The salinity can range from 5 to 27 percent (hypersalinity), depending on environmental conditions and freshwater input. This high salinity supports specialized microorganisms and brine shrimp, vital to the lake's ecosystem. The bay is also central to Utah's mineral industry, with companies like Morton Salt and Cargill extracting industrial-grade salt through large evaporation ponds. The pink color of the water, sand, and shoreline in Stansbury Bay is due to tiny salt-loving microorganisms, like certain bacteria and algae, which produce pink pigments. This natural phenomenon creates the distinctive pink hues you see along the shoreline.

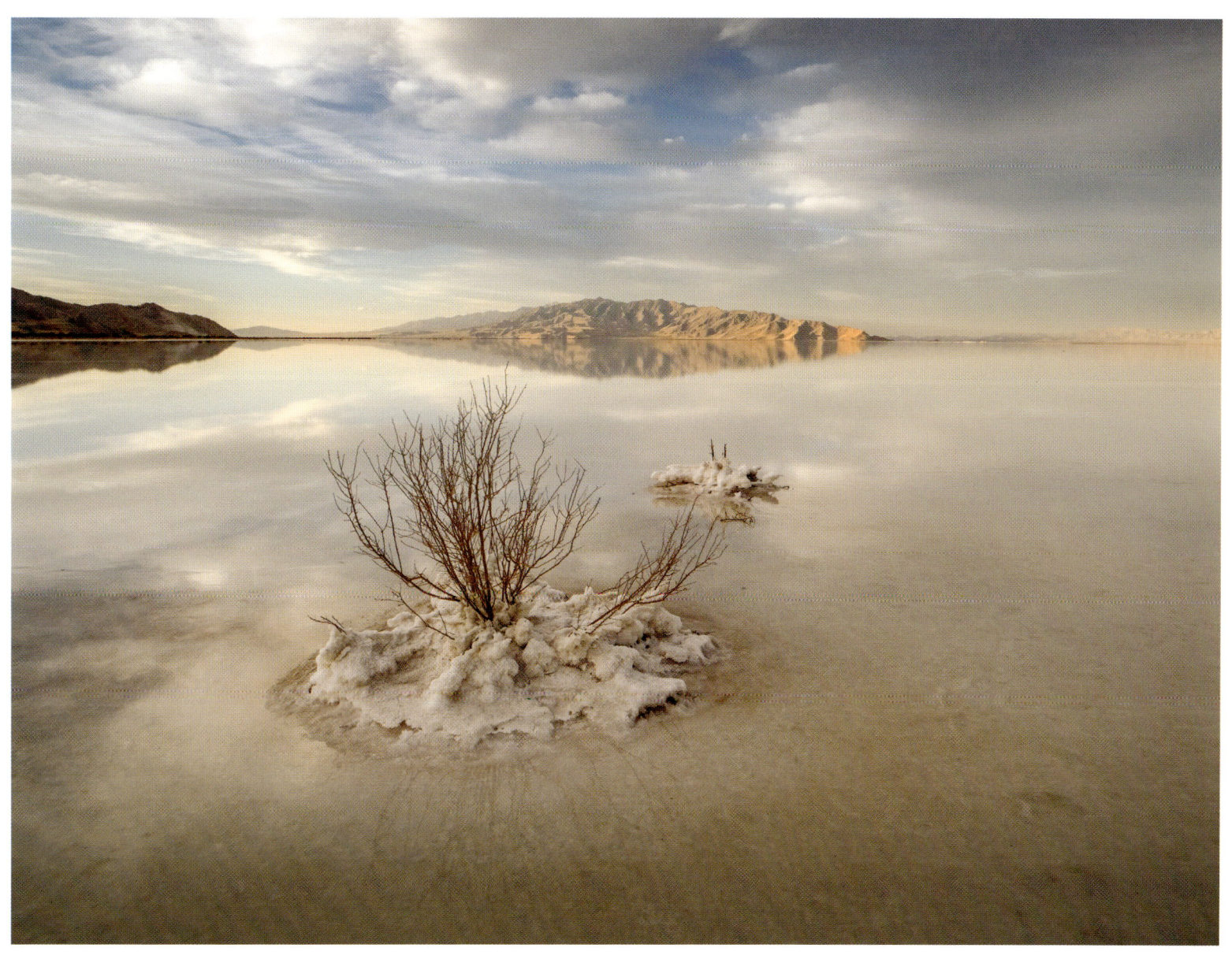

Pink water and soil, Stansbury Bay | J5 | 09.30.2023
Salt-encrusted shrubs, Stansbury Bay | J5 | 09.30.2023

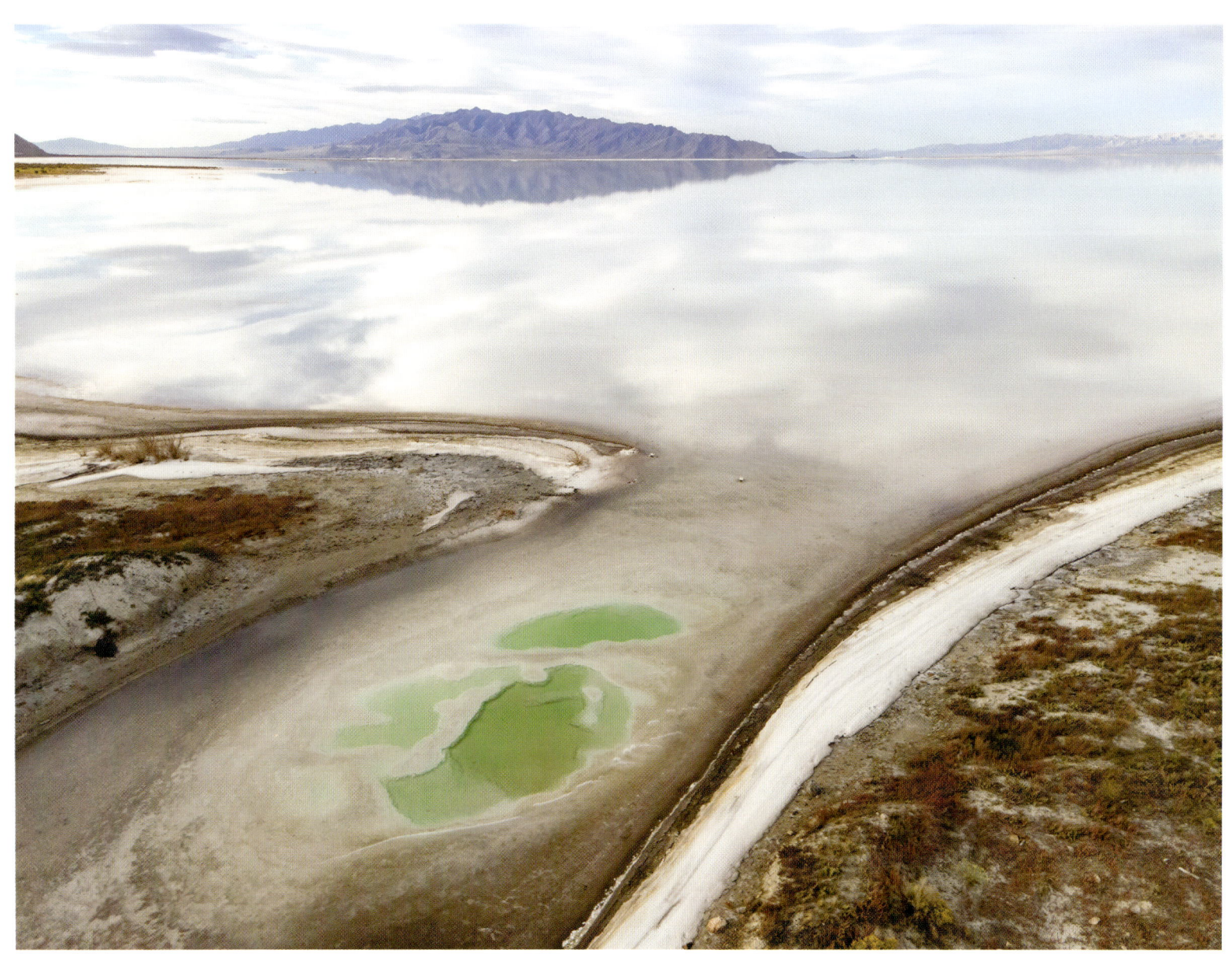

Hypersaline pools underwater, Stansbury Bay | J5 | 09.30.2023

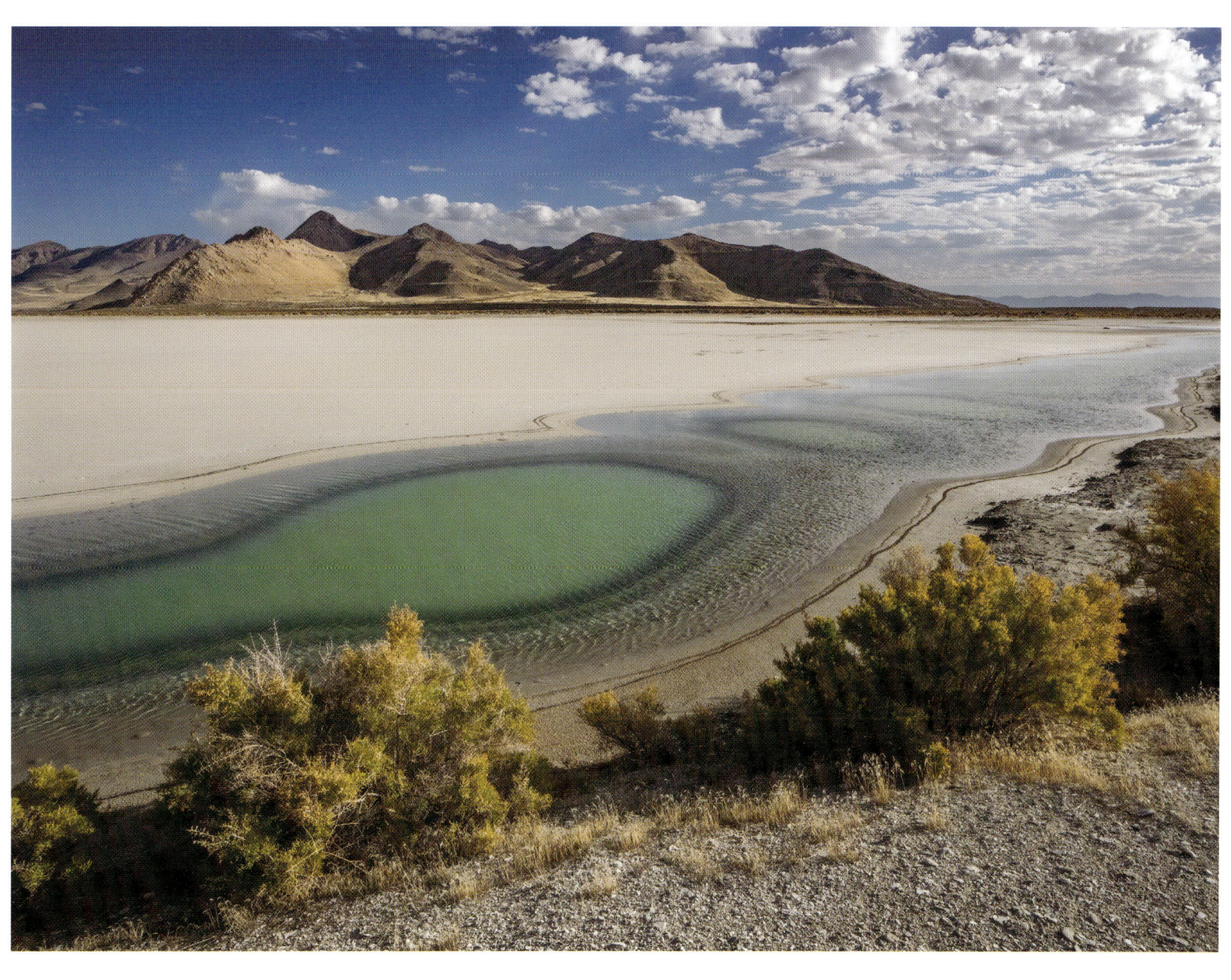

Hypersaline pools, Stansbury Bay | J5 | 10.21.2023

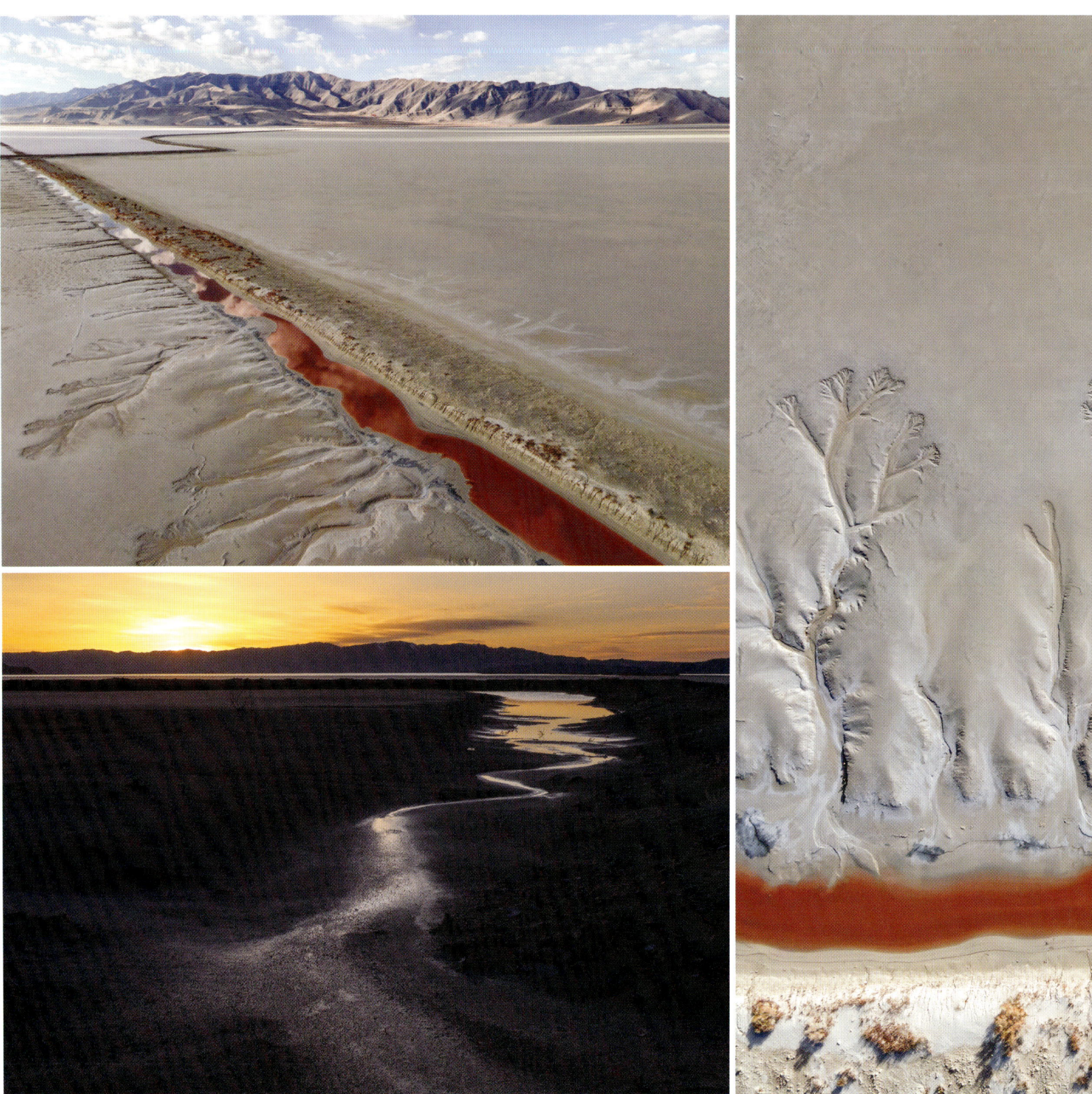

BRINE TRANSFER

In Stansbury Bay, brine is transferred to evaporation ponds using a system of channels and pumps. These brine channels are typically shallow, man-made ditches or canals lined with materials to prevent seepage. They direct the highly saline water from the lake into large, shallow evaporation ponds. The water in these ponds evaporates under the sun, leaving behind concentrated salts and minerals, which are then harvested. The channels are designed to manage the flow of brine efficiently, ensuring maximum evaporation and salt recovery.

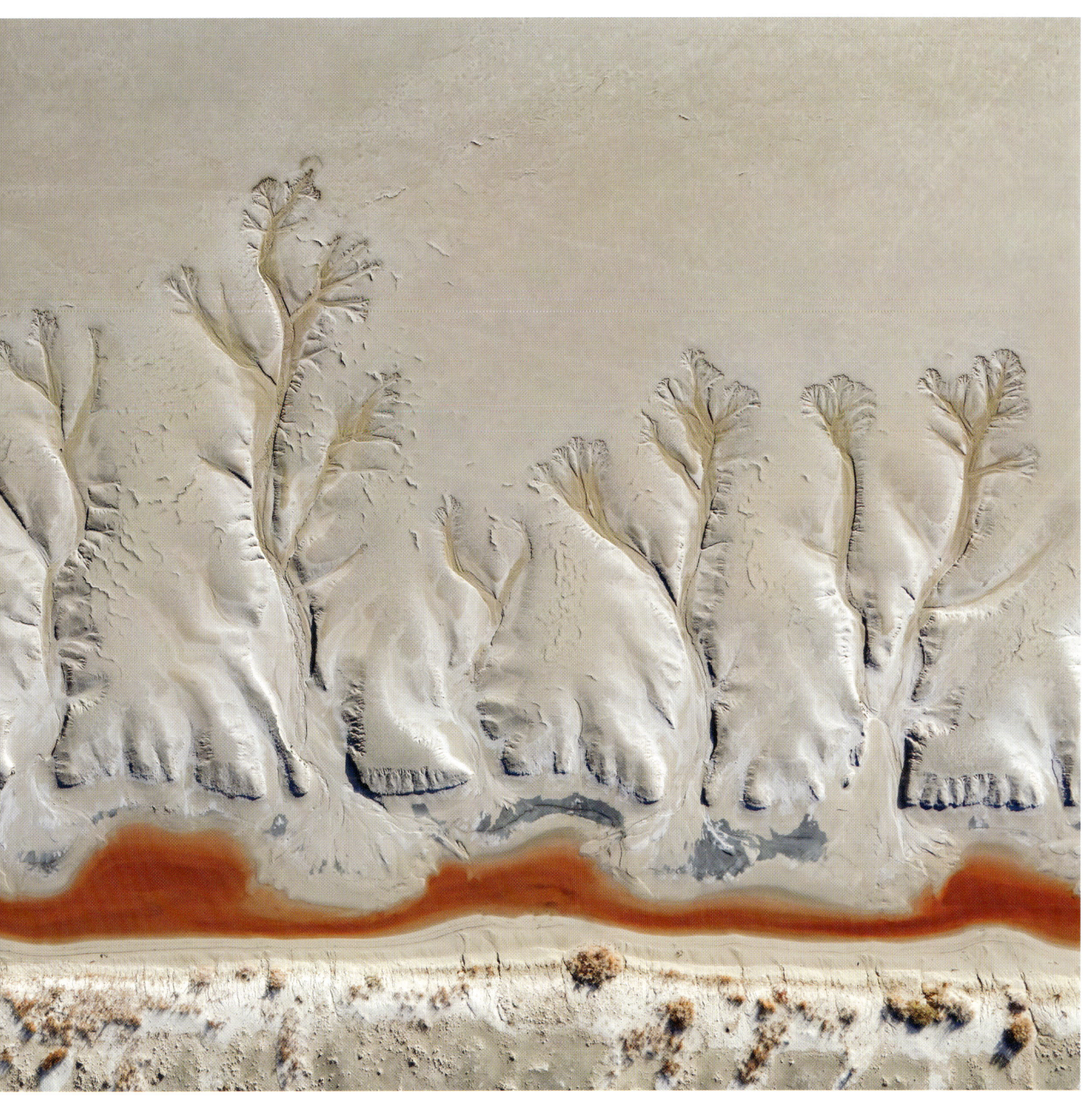

Red brine channel and Oquirrh Mountains | K5 | 10.23.2023
Evaporating brine channel | K5 | 02.25.2023
Fractal erosion patterns and brine channel | K5 | 10.23.2023

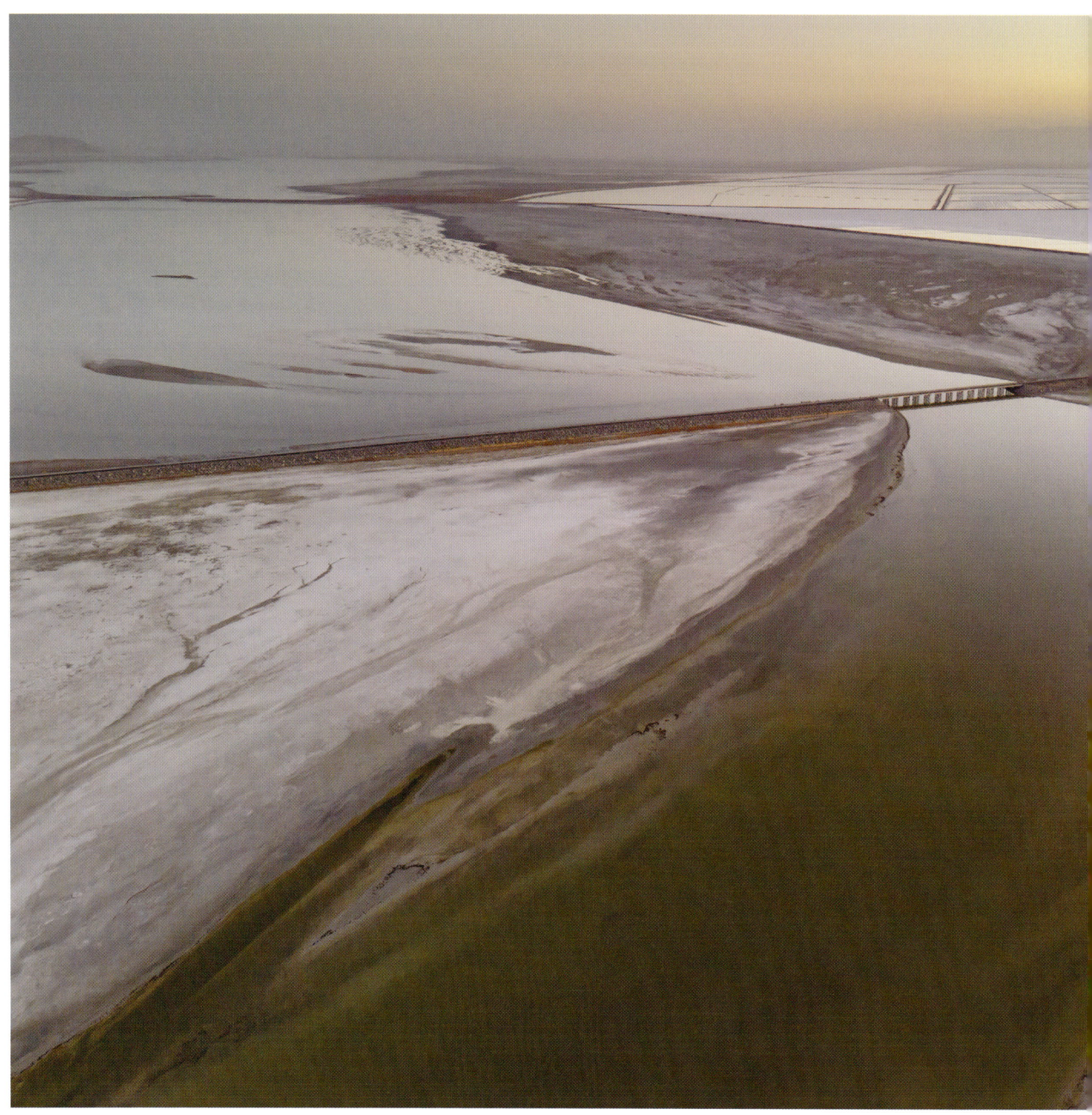

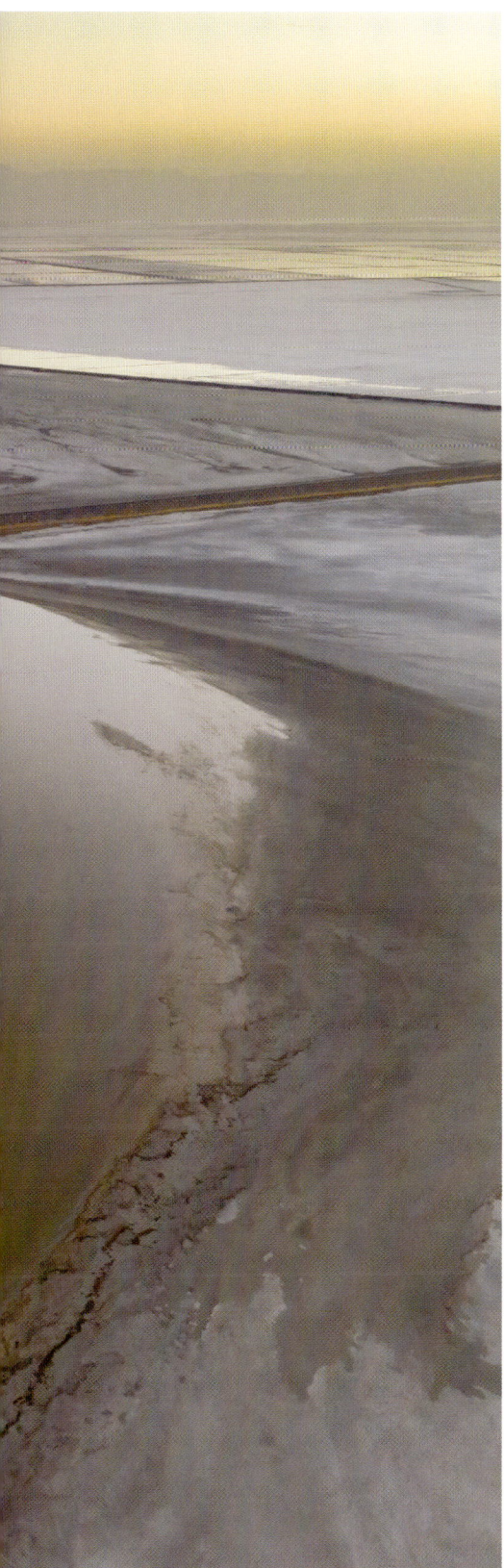

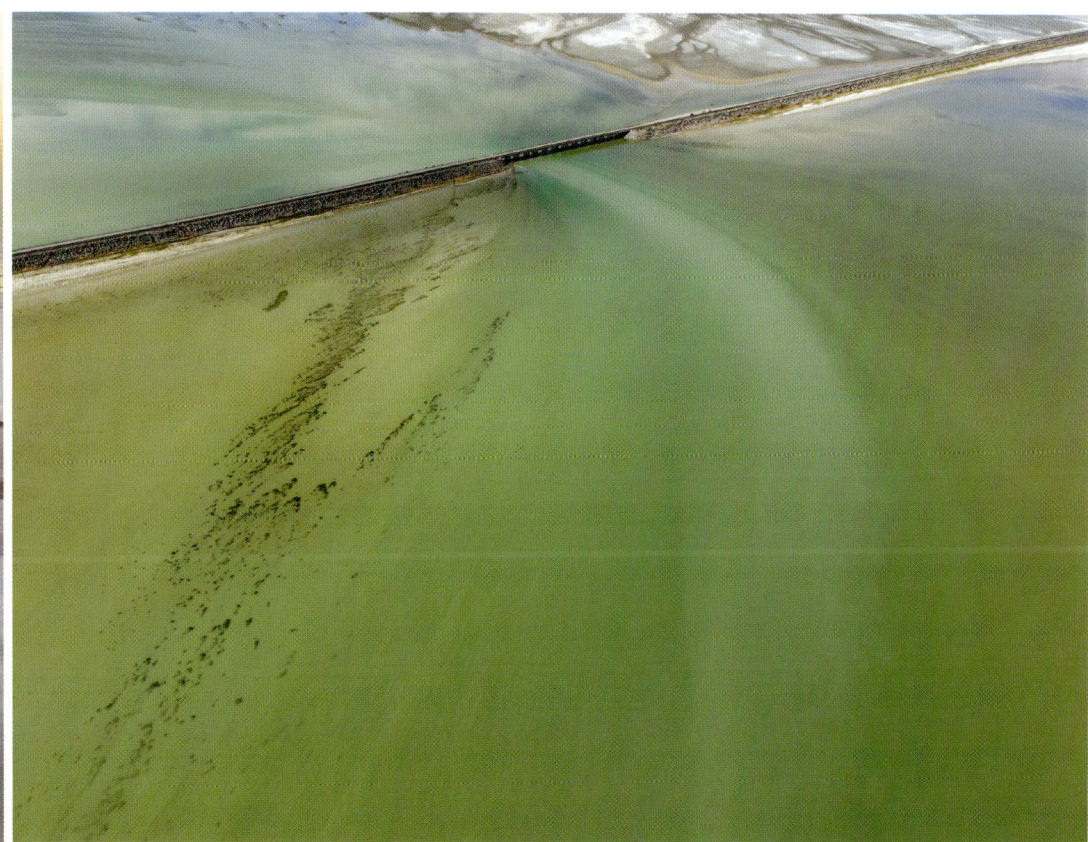

THE BEAR RIVER

The Bear River is crucial to Great Salt Lake, supplying about 60 percent of its freshwater inflow and serving as its largest tributary. This freshwater input is vital for maintaining the lake's water levels and reducing its salinity to support a diverse ecosystem. Millions of migratory birds rely on the lake's wetlands for feeding and breeding. The Bear River's 350-mile (563-km) journey from the Uinta Mountains through Wyoming and Idaho to Great Salt Lake creates a critical freshwater oasis in the desert, supporting over 200 bird species and contributing significantly to the Bear River Migratory Bird Refuge. The river enters the northeastern arm of Great Salt Lake through this refuge near Brigham City. Efforts to divert the Bear River for municipal and agricultural use pose significant risks to the lake, potentially lowering its levels and affecting the entire ecosystem.

Bear River inlet in fall | F7 | 10.05.2024

Bear River inlet in spring | F7 | 06.03.2024

WILLARD BAY

Willard Bay is a vital part of the Great Salt Lake ecosystem, providing an essential habitat for various wildlife, including numerous bird species that use the bay for feeding and nesting. It supports recreational activities like boating, fishing, and camping, which boost the local economy. Additionally, Willard Bay supplies crucial irrigation water to surrounding agricultural areas, sustaining local farming operations in northern Utah's arid climate. The bay acts as a freshwater buffer against Great Salt Lake's high salinity levels, helping to balance the ecosystem. Maintaining and protecting Willard Bay is crucial for supporting both ecological and human needs in the region.

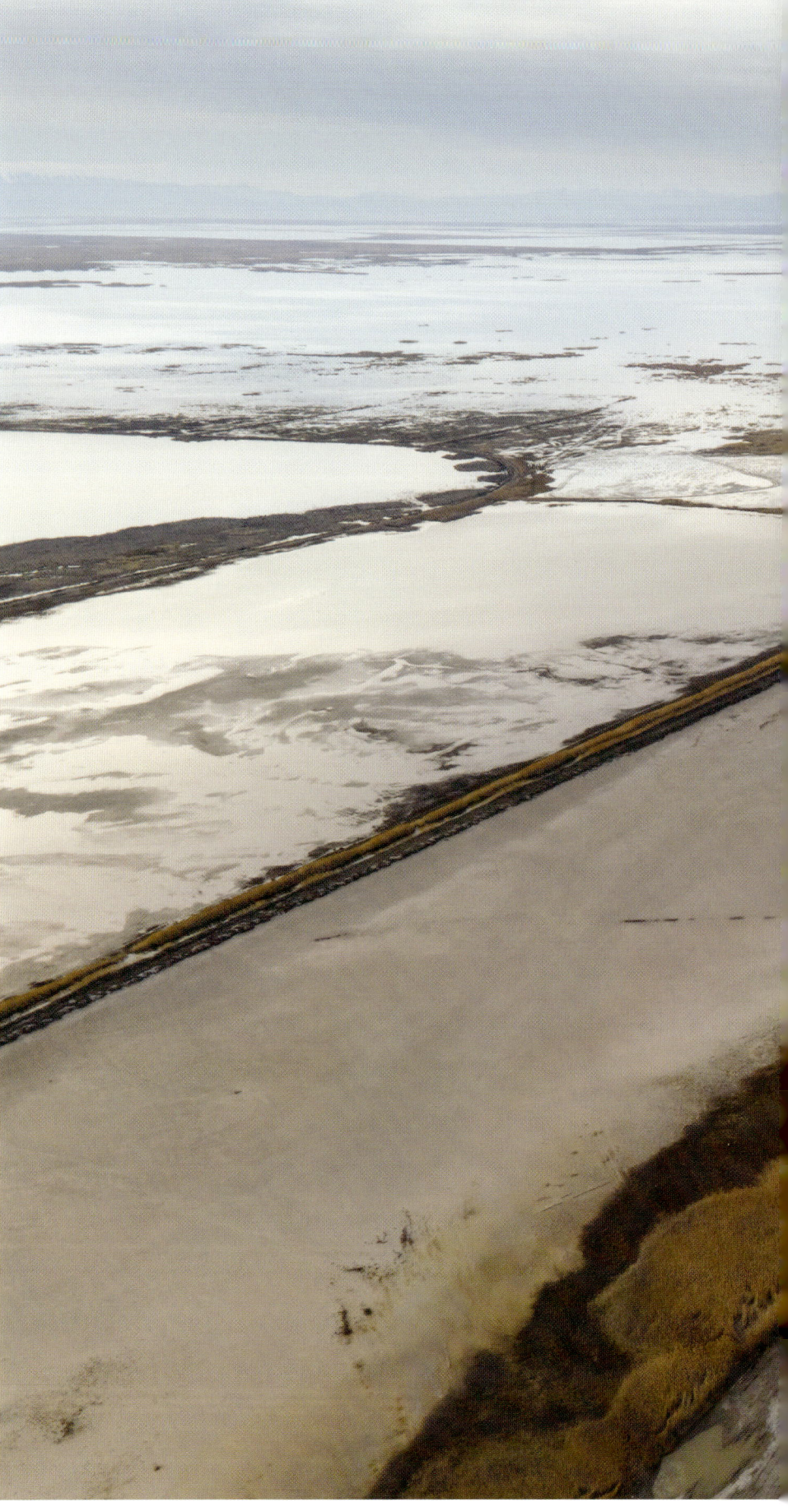

The fresh water of Willard Bay | E9 | 03.09.2024

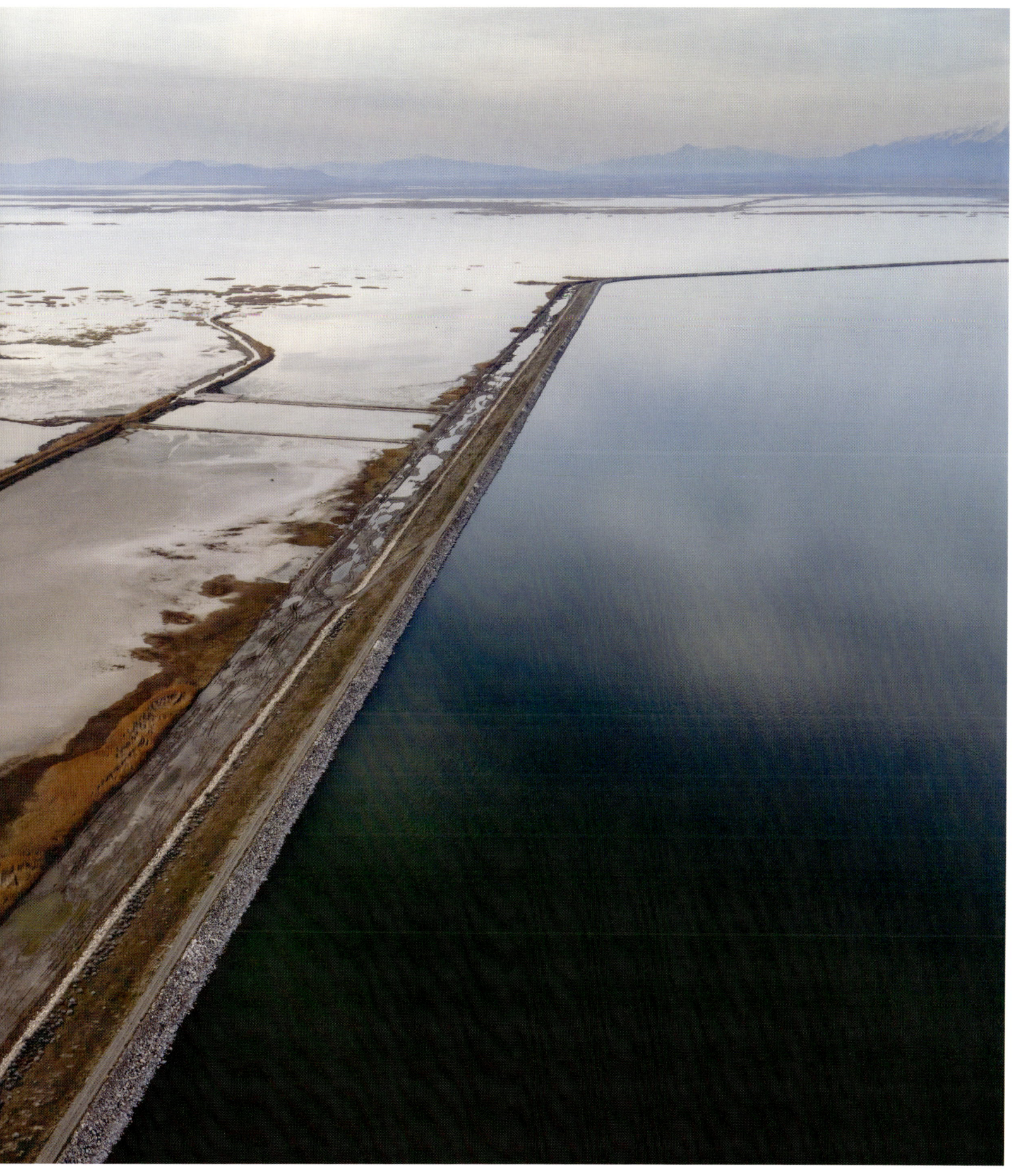

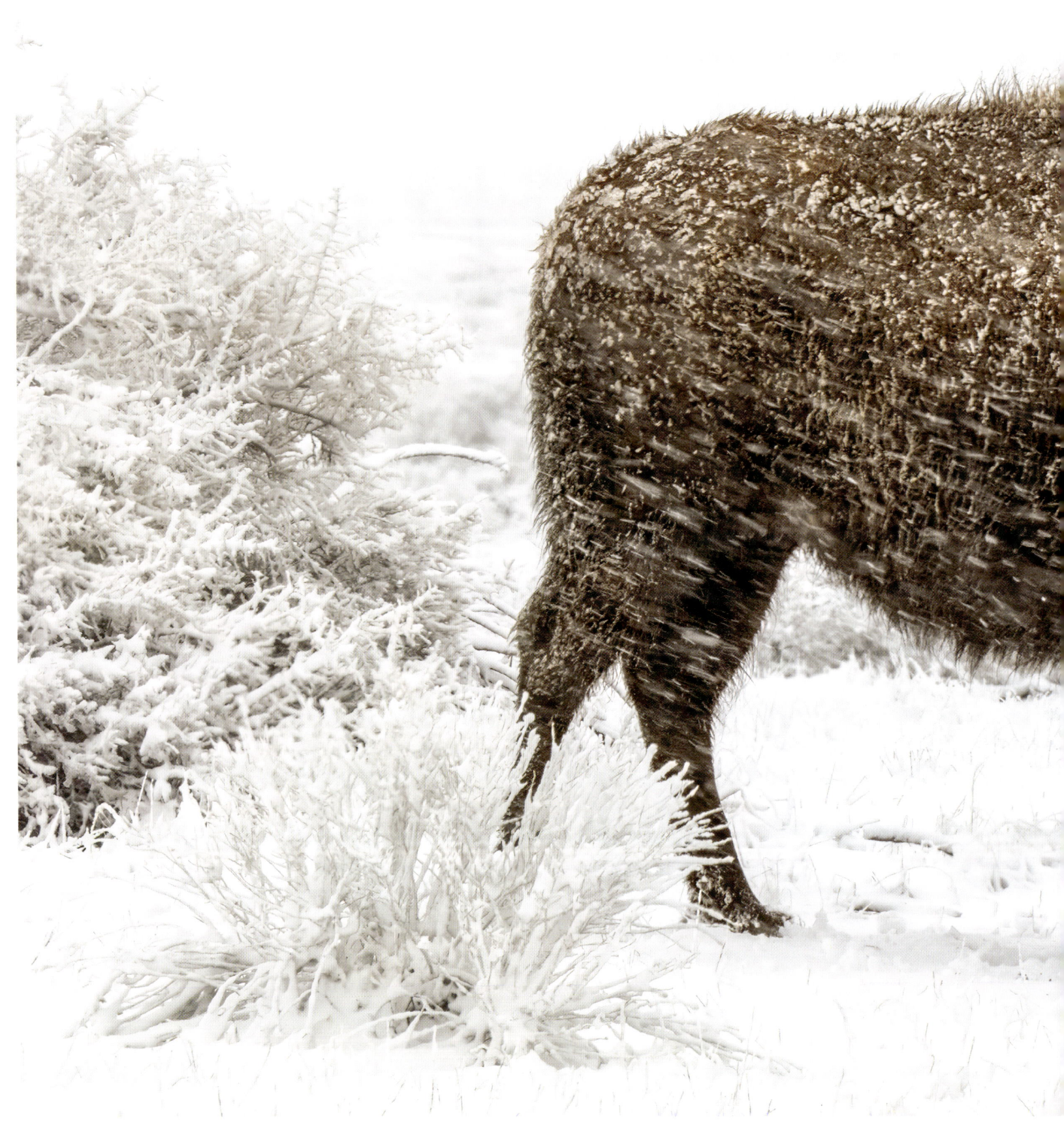

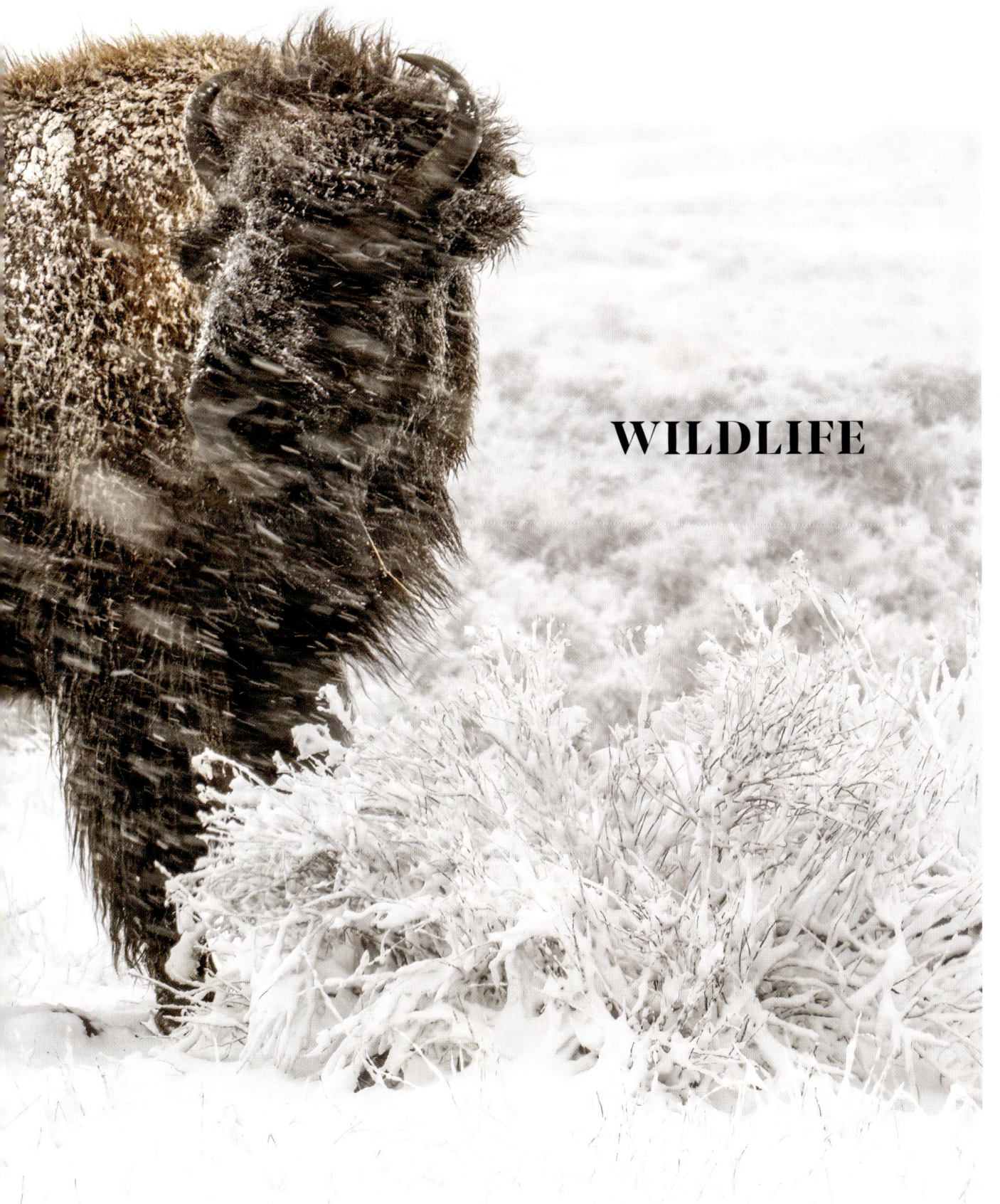

WILDLIFE

02.

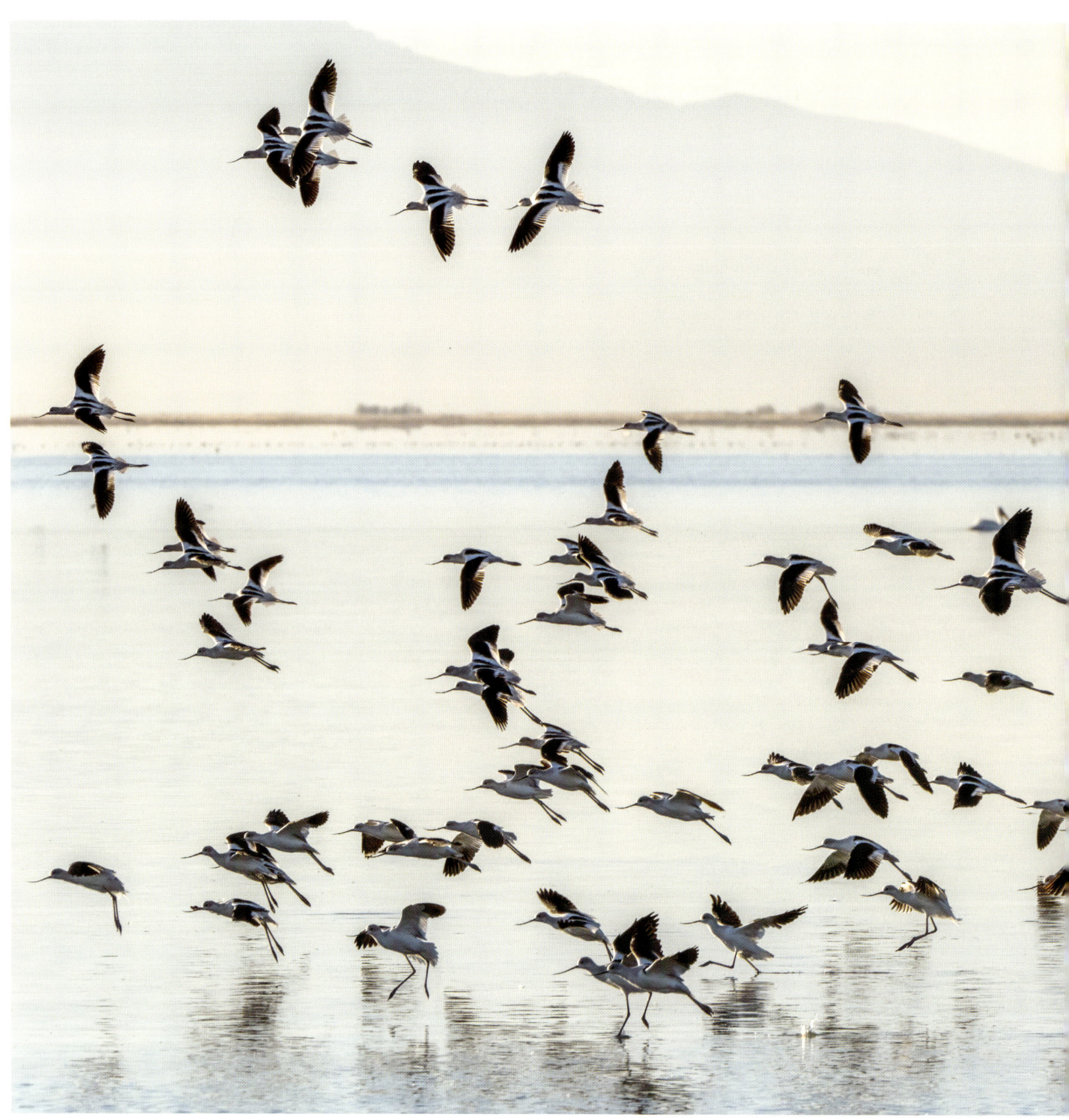

A Haven for Diversity

WHAT MAKES GREAT SALT LAKE so great for wildlife? Its sheer size and diverse habitats create a haven for a multitude of species. The lake's fluctuating salinity levels and varying water depths support a wide range of life forms, from tiny brine shrimp and majestic American White Pelicans to massive American Bison.

The lake is a vital habitat for a wide variety of mammals and bird species, making it an ecological treasure. For mammals, the diverse habitats around the lake—including marshes, grasslands, and islands—support species like bison, pronghorn, and mule deer. These mammals find shelter and forage in the varied terrain, making the Great Salt Lake region a crucial sanctuary for terrestrial wildlife. For birds, the lake's vast, shallow waters and surrounding wetlands provide essential breeding grounds, resting spots, and feeding areas during migration. Species such as the American Avocet, Wilson's Phalarope, and Eared Grebe thrive here, relying on the abundant brine shrimp and insects.

Great Salt Lake is a critical habitat supporting over 250 bird species, making it one of North America's most vital avian habitats. The lake plays a crucial role in the Pacific Flyway, a major north-south migratory route. Each year, up to 10 million migratory birds visit the lake to rest, refuel, and breed.

The lake's hypersaline environment supports unique microbial communities that are essential to a thriving food web, benefiting numerous bird species. Critical invertebrates like brine shrimp and brine flies form the foundation of this food web, sustaining millions of migratory birds. Additionally, the brine shrimp industry is economically significant, with Great Salt Lake producing about 40 percent of the world's brine shrimp eggs, which are crucial for global aquaculture.

Great Salt Lake's ecological importance and its role in supporting such a diverse array of wildlife underscore the need for ongoing conservation efforts. Preserving this unique habitat ensures that it will continue to be a haven for wildlife and a crucial stopover for migratory birds on the Pacific Flyway.

The greatness of Great Salt Lake lies in its ability to sustain such a rich and varied ecosystem. Each species, from the soaring American White Pelican to the tiny brine shrimp, plays a vital role in maintaining the health and balance of this unique environment. Through understanding and appreciation, we can ensure the preservation of this extraordinary natural treasure for generations to come.

American Avocets in flight | H8 | 09.23.2023

PREVIOUS PAGE: Bison in blizzard, Antelope Island | H3 | 03.02.2024

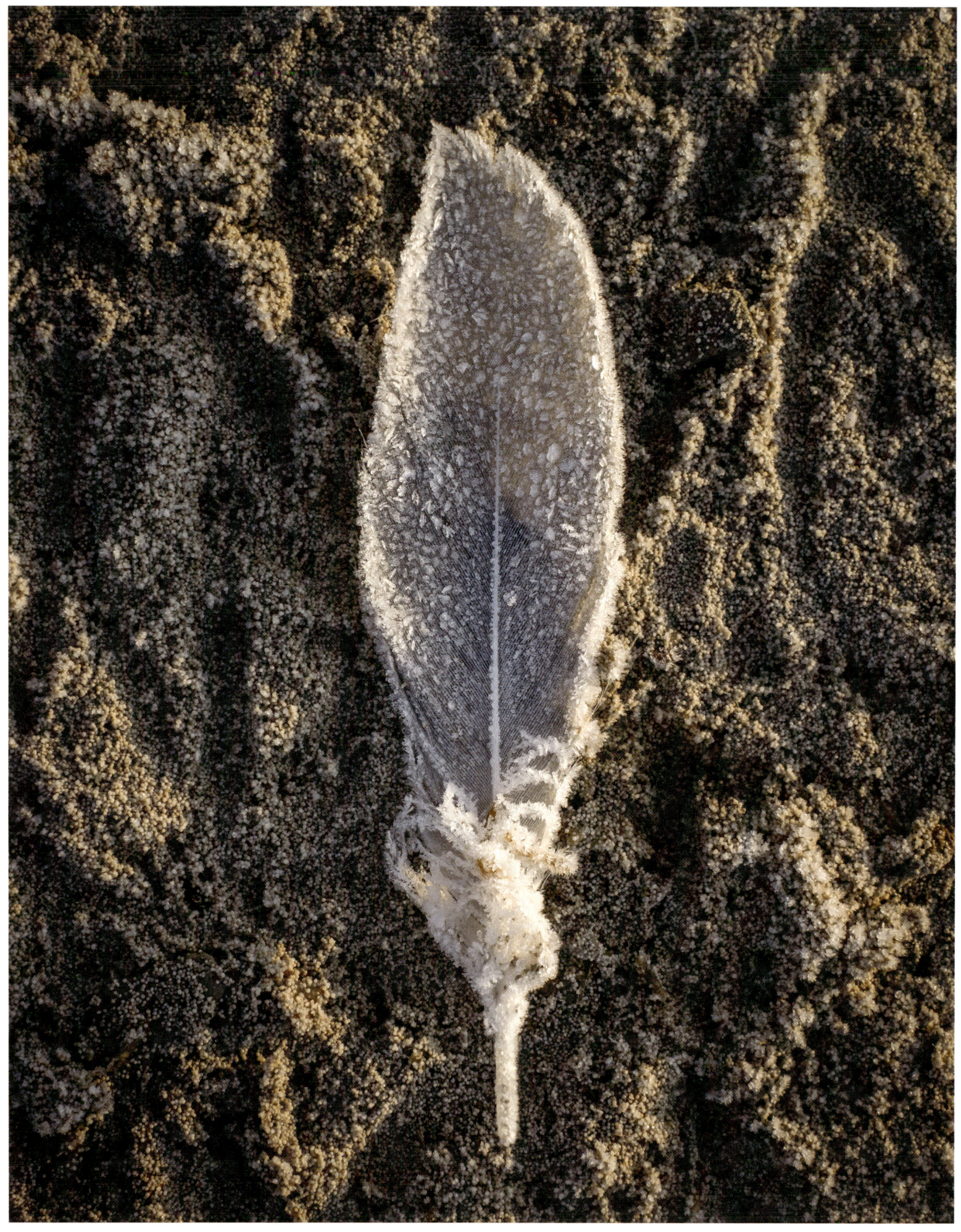

Frozen feather, south shore of Great Salt Lake | K8 | 12.31.2023

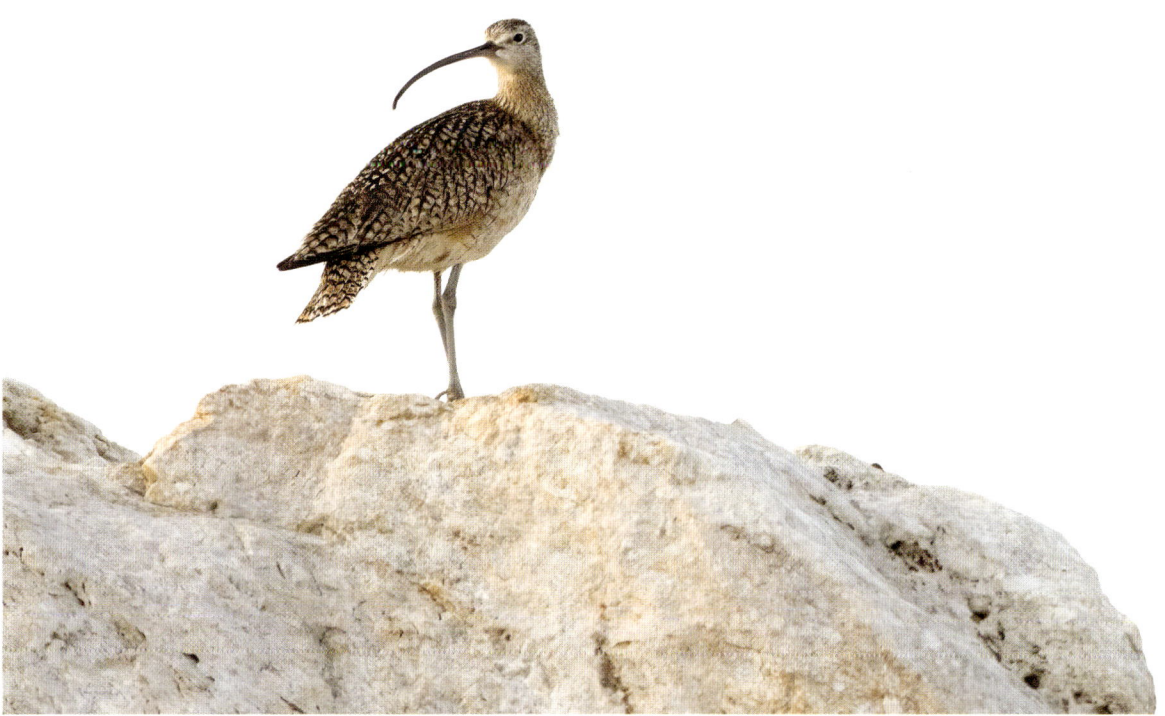

LONG-BILLED CURLEW
The Long-billed Curlew (*Numenius ameri-canus*), North America's largest shorebird, is distinguished by its extraordinarily long, thin, curved bill. This speckled bird adeptly probes mud and sand for aquatic inver-tebrates on wintering grounds and hunts grasshoppers in breeding grasslands around Great Salt Lake. The genus name, *Numenius*, meaning "of the new moon," reflects the bill's crescent shape, which enables it to access food other birds cannot reach.

Long-billed Curlew at Ladyfinger Point, Antelope Island | H8 | 05.21.2023

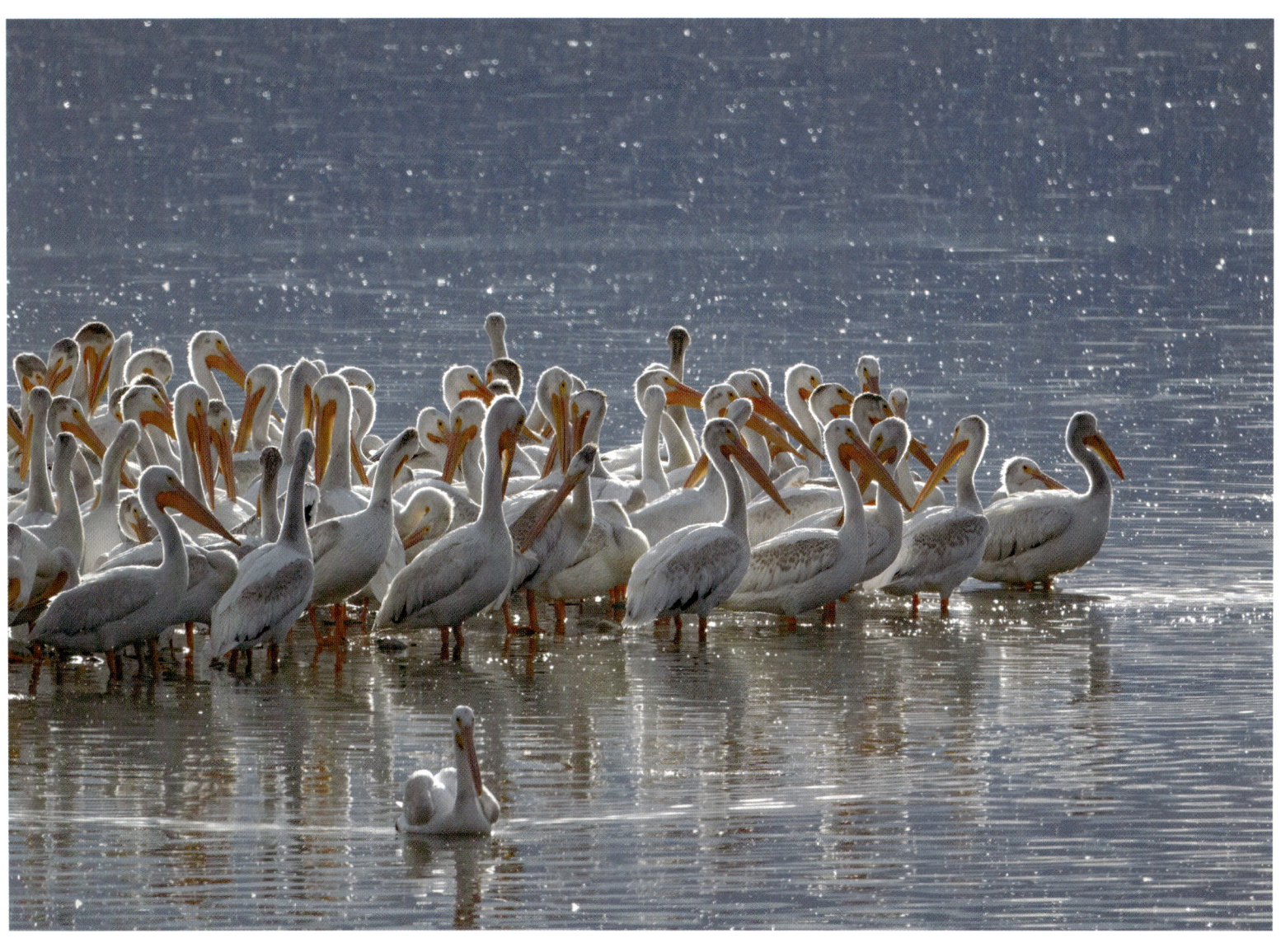

AMERICAN WHITE PELICAN

The American White Pelican (*Pelecanus erythrorhynchos*), one of North America's largest birds, is a majestic sight at Great Salt Lake. Primarily nesting on Gunnison Island and recently on Hat Island, these pelicans need about 150 pounds (68 kg) of food to raise each chick. They forage mainly by day in winter, switching to night foraging during the breeding season, often catching larger fish. Recent observations indicate a significant decline in pelican numbers on Gunnison Island, likely due to low water levels which provide predators access to the island.

American White Pelicans in Gilbert Bay | H8 | 09.04.2023

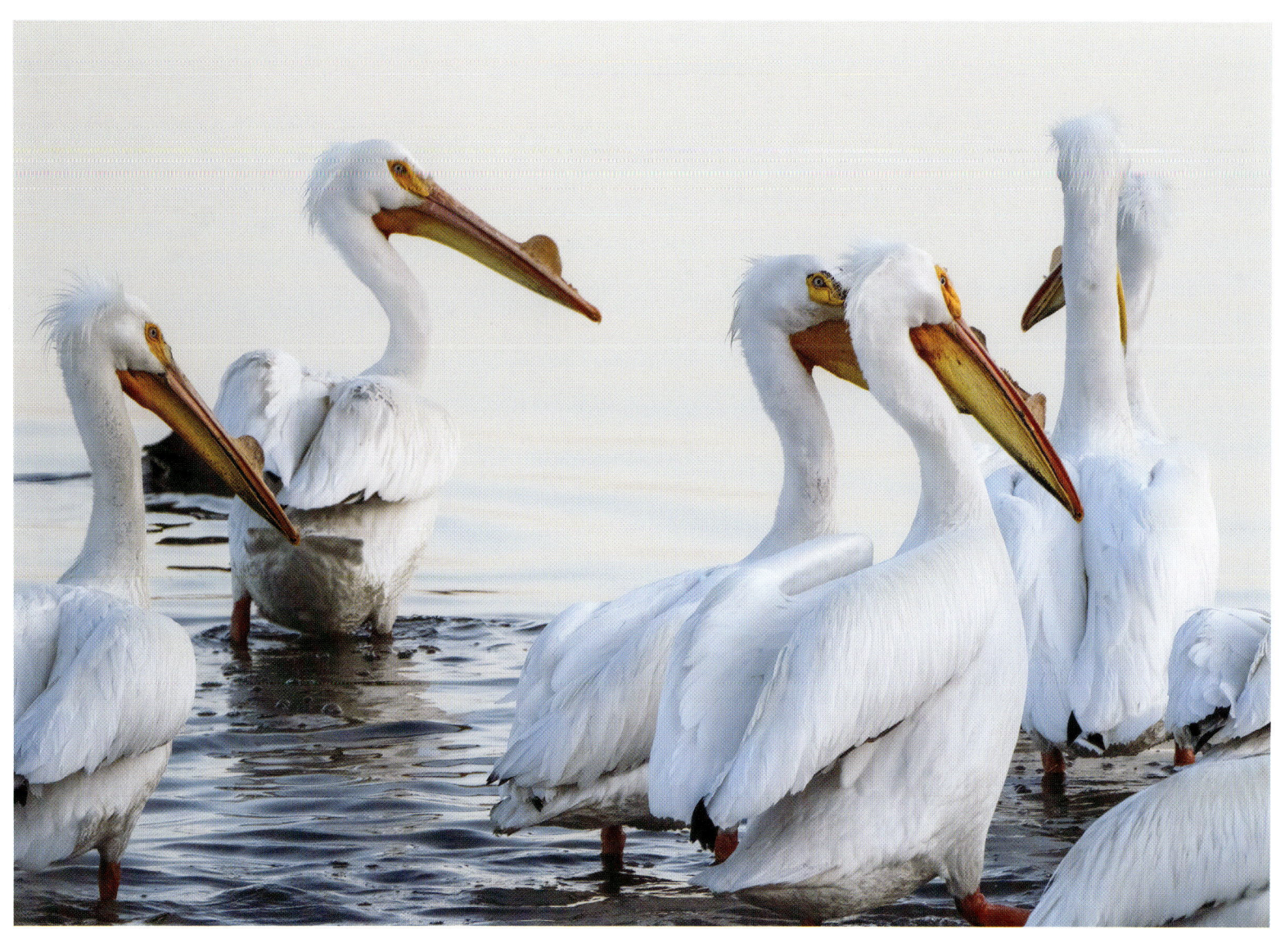

American White Pelicans in Farmington Bay | 18 | 04.15.2023

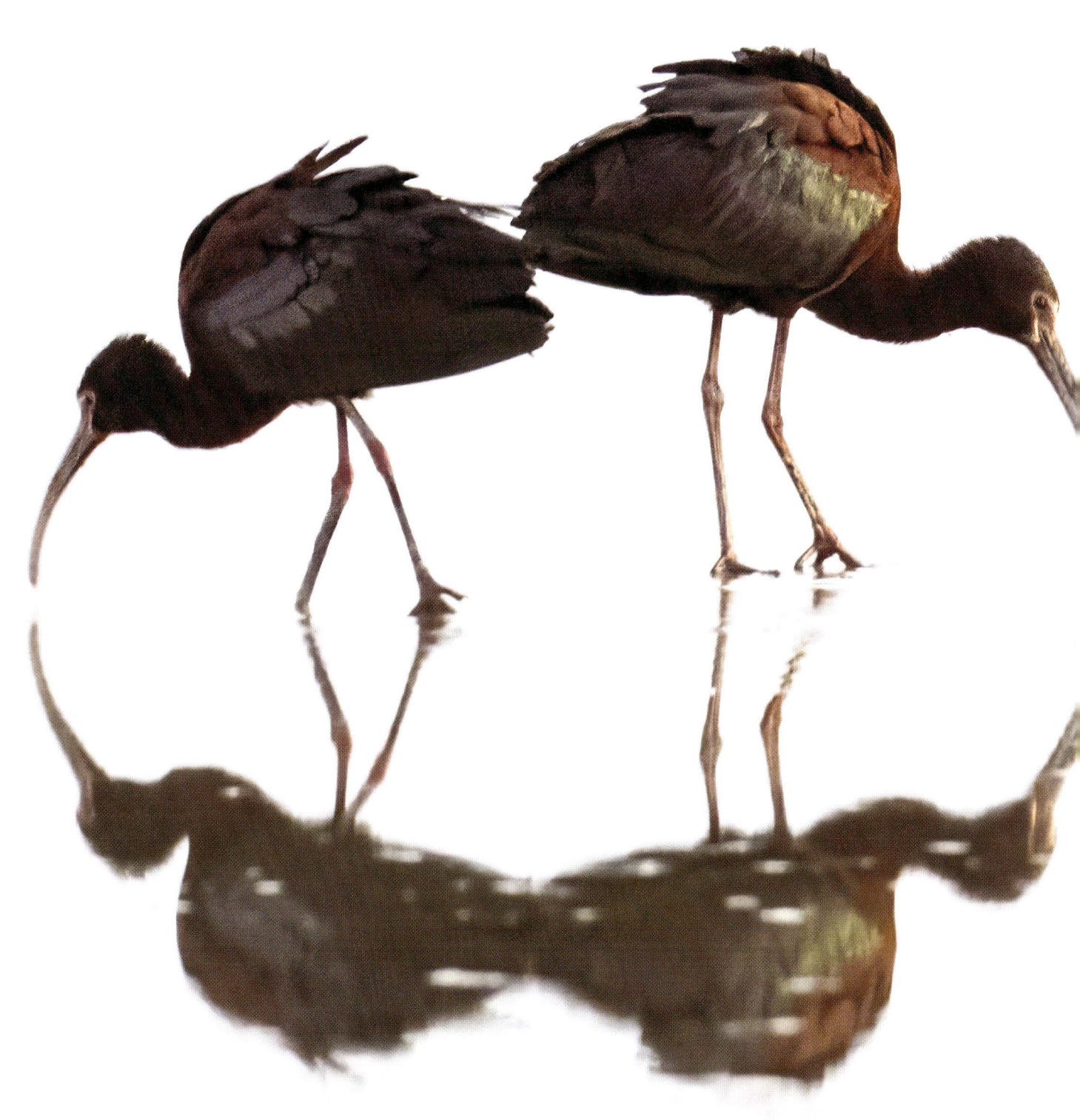

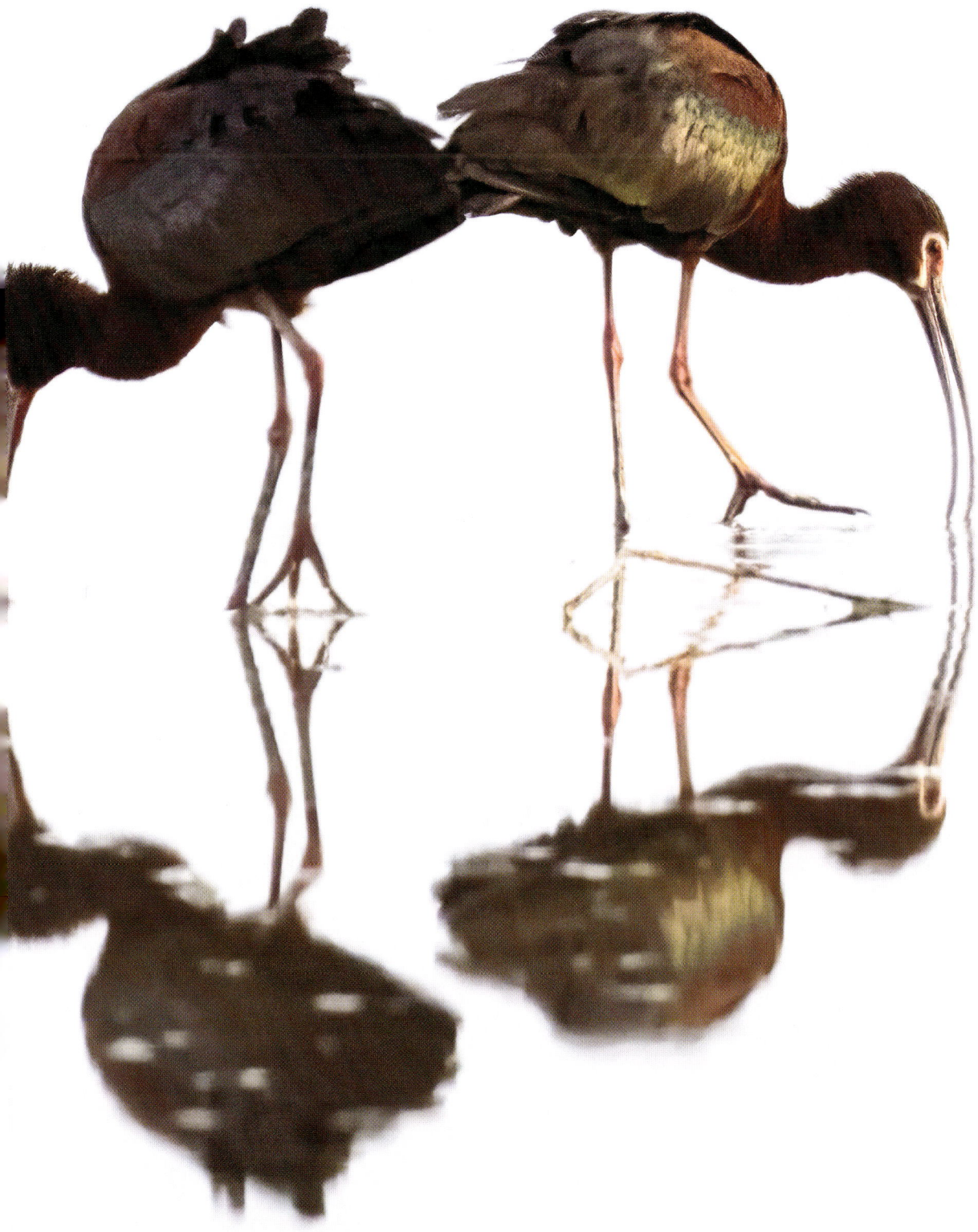

White-faced Ibis from the Antelope Island causeway | H8 | 05.07.2023

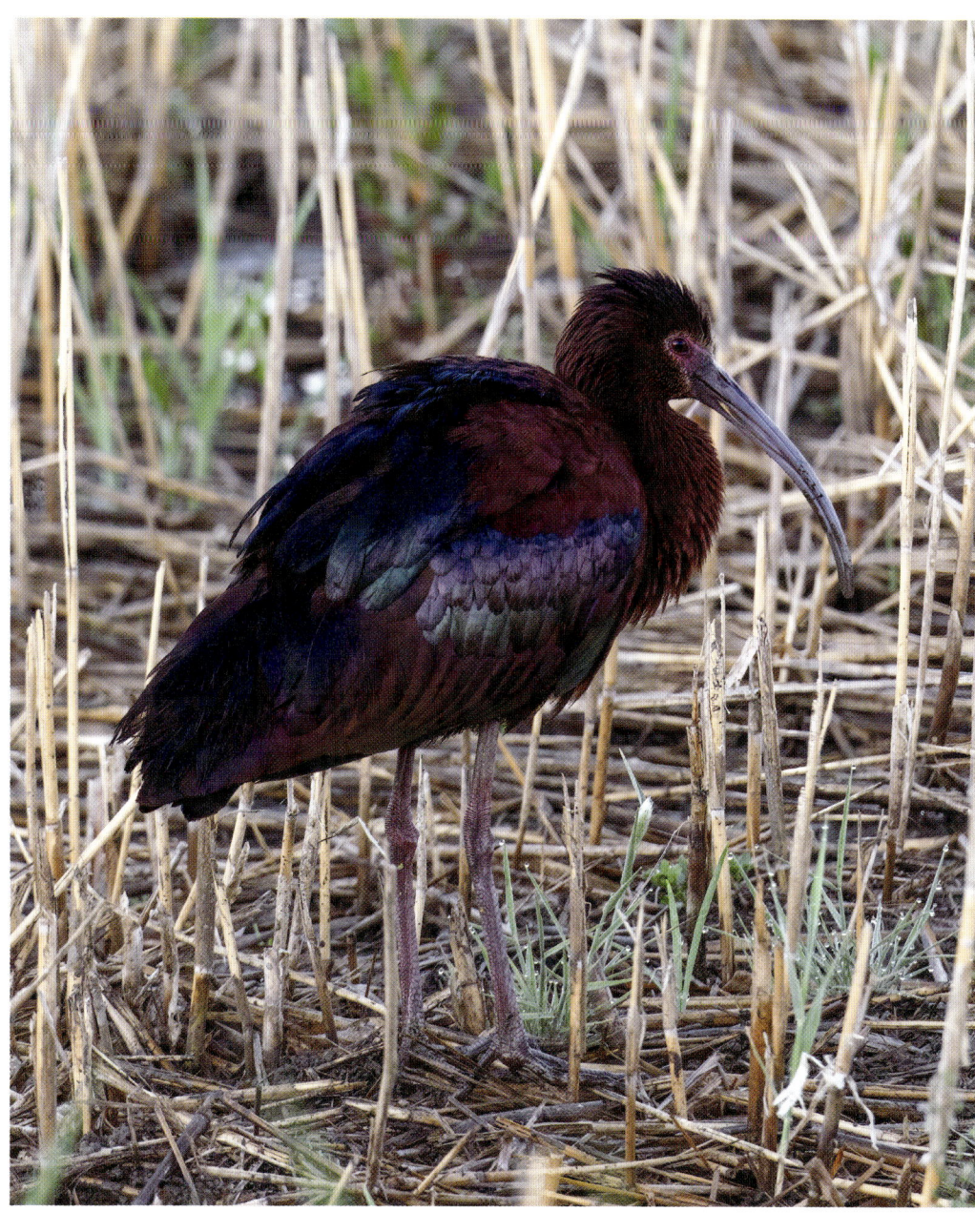

WHITE FACED IBIS

The White-faced Ibis (*Plegadis chihi*), with its shimmering purple, green, and bronze plumage, is a striking presence in the wetlands of Great Salt Lake. During breeding season, its ruby-red eyes and white facial mask add to its allure. Approximately 27,000 breeding adults form one of the world's largest populations in the lake's emergent marshes. These birds often incorporate human-made objects into their nests, showcasing their resourcefulness. Their long, curving bills are perfect for foraging at the edges of marshes and wet farm fields around Great Salt Lake.

WILSON'S PHALAROPE

The Wilson's Phalarope (*Phalaropus tricolor*) is a fascinating bird known for its unique behavior and role reversal in breeding, where the more brightly colored females court males, and the males incubate eggs and care for the chicks. Phalaropes are exceptional swimmers, often spinning in circles on the water's surface to create whirlpools that draw aquatic invertebrates up for easy feeding. Great Salt Lake serves as a critical stopover for hundreds of thousands of Wilson's Phalaropes during their migration to South America, providing rich food resources like brine shrimp and brine flies that are essential for their journey. The lake supports a significant portion of the North American population, making it a vital habitat for the species.

Magnificent color of the White-faced Ibis,
Farmington Bay | J9 | 06.29.2024

Wilson's Phalarope in shallow water
H8 | 08.02.2023

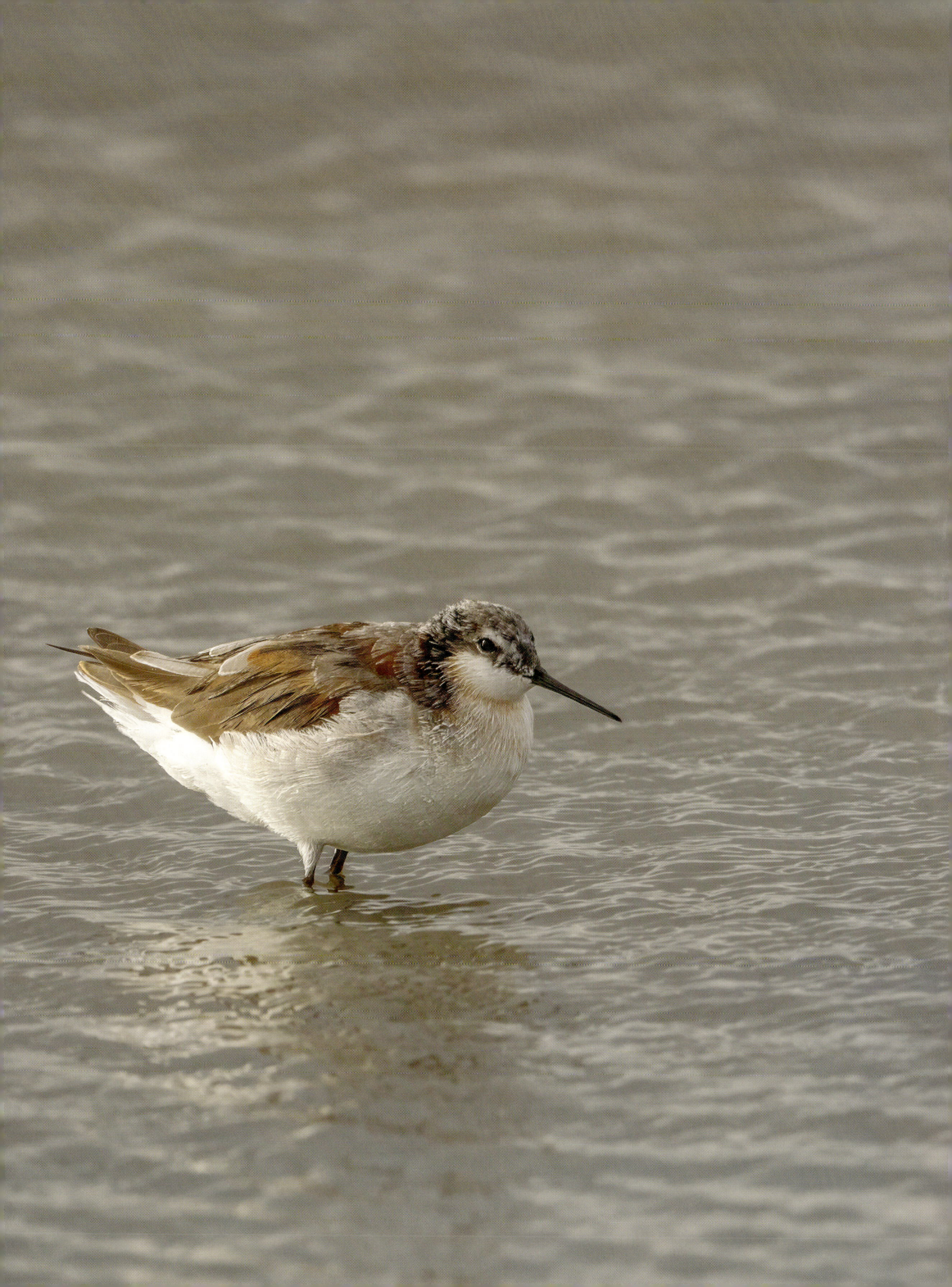

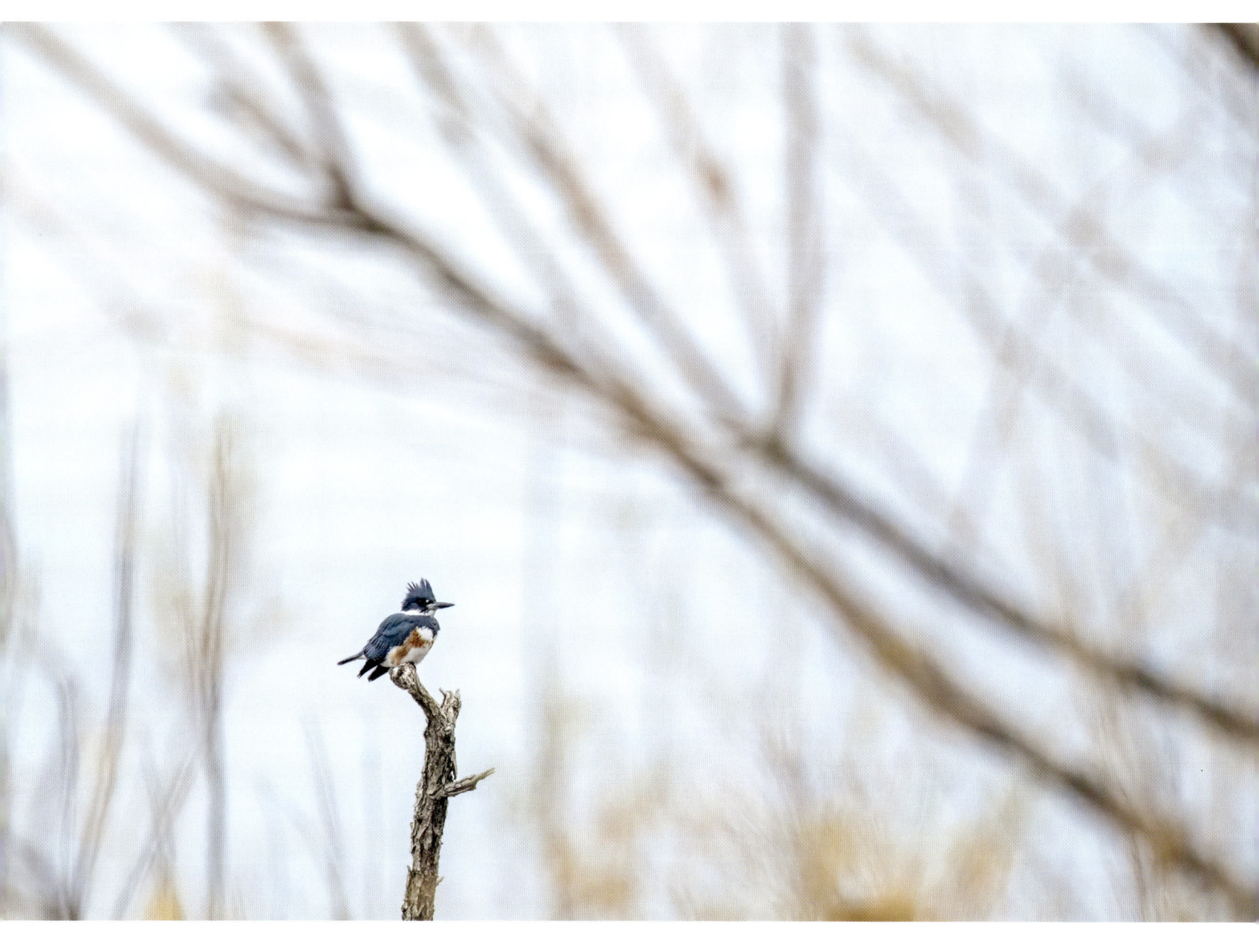

BELTED KINGFISHER

The Belted Kingfisher (*Megaceryle alcyon*), often seen around Great Salt Lake, is notable for its unique reversal of typical avian coloration—females are more vibrantly colored than males, sporting an additional chestnut band across their lower bellies. These birds are adept fishers, frequently observed hovering over the lake's waters before diving headfirst to catch fish. They nest in burrows dug into sandy banks near the water, and their loud, rattling call is a familiar sound along the lake's shores.

Female Belted Kingfisher, Farmington Bay | J9 | 12.03.2023

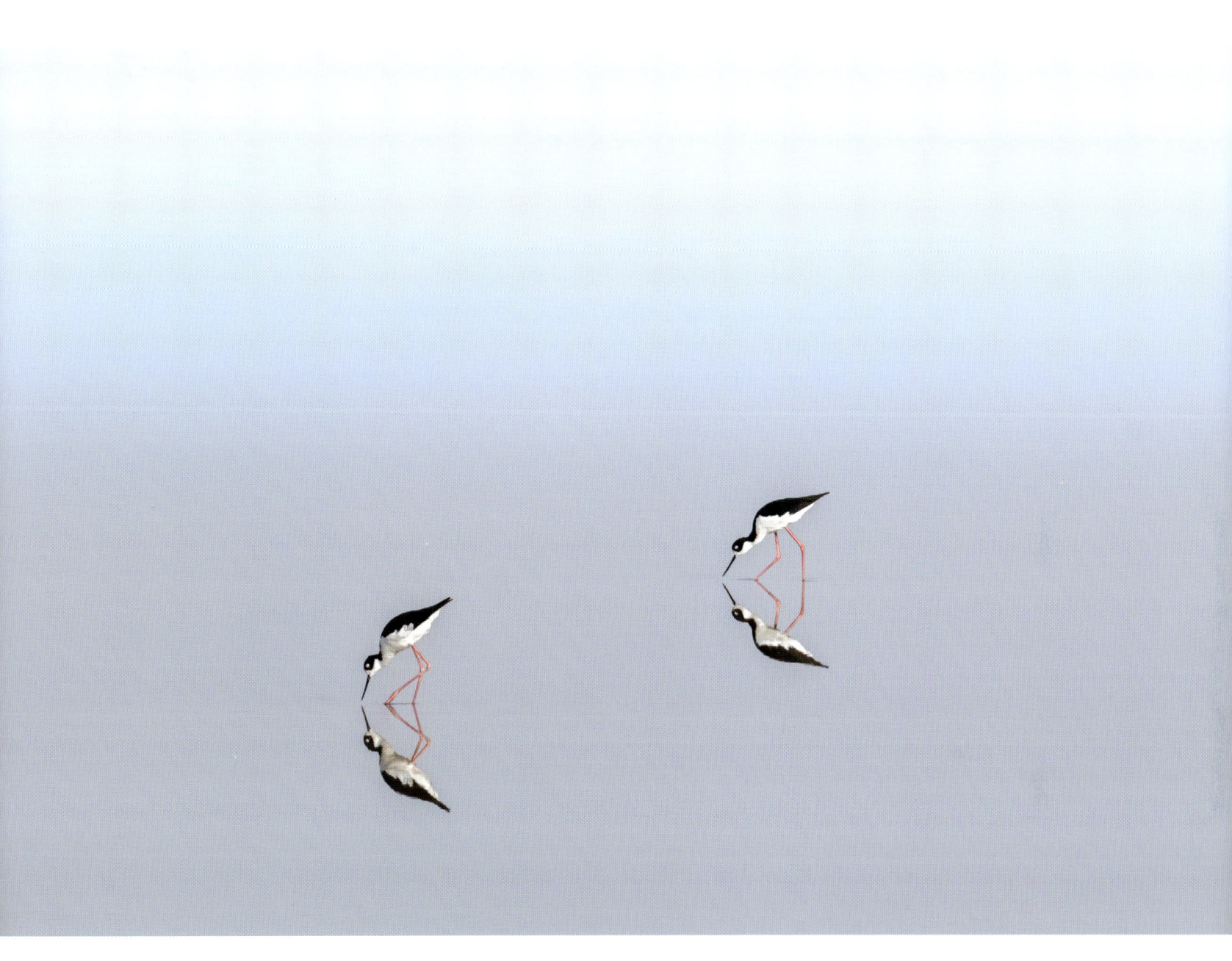

BLACK-NECKED STILT

Black-necked Stilts (*Himantopus mexicanus*) are visually striking with their contrasting black-and-white plumage, long pink legs, and thin black bills. The lake's protected wetlands, managed by organizations like the Utah Department of Natural Resources; US Fish and Wildlife Service; and The Nature Conservancy, provide essential breeding and nesting sites. Great Salt Lake hosts large populations of Black-necked Stilts, with peak counts showing up to 65,000 birds.

Black-necked Stilts, Farmington Bay | J9 | 09.10.2023

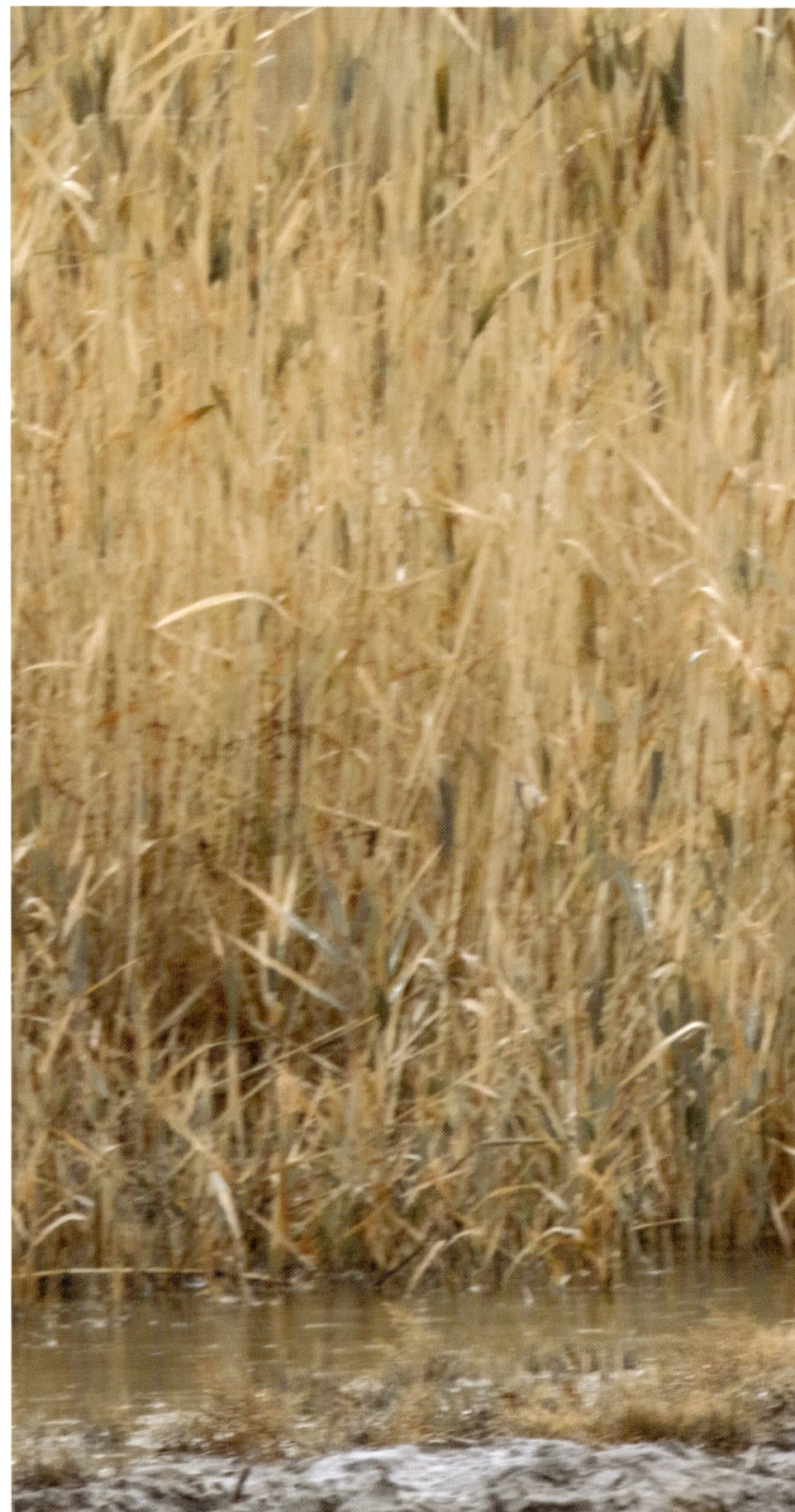

GREAT BLUE HERON

Great Salt Lake is a vital habitat for the Great Blue Heron (*Ardea herodias*), particularly those residing in the rookery at Farmington Bay. This expansive body of water provides abundant food sources, including fish, amphibians, and invertebrates that are essential for the herons' diet. The Farmington Bay area hosts one of the largest rookeries in the region. Here, the blue herons build their nests, creating a safe haven for raising their young. The proximity to the lake ensures that herons have easy access to feeding grounds, supporting their reproductive success and overall population health.

Great Blue Heron landing, Farmington Bay | J9 | 12.02.2023

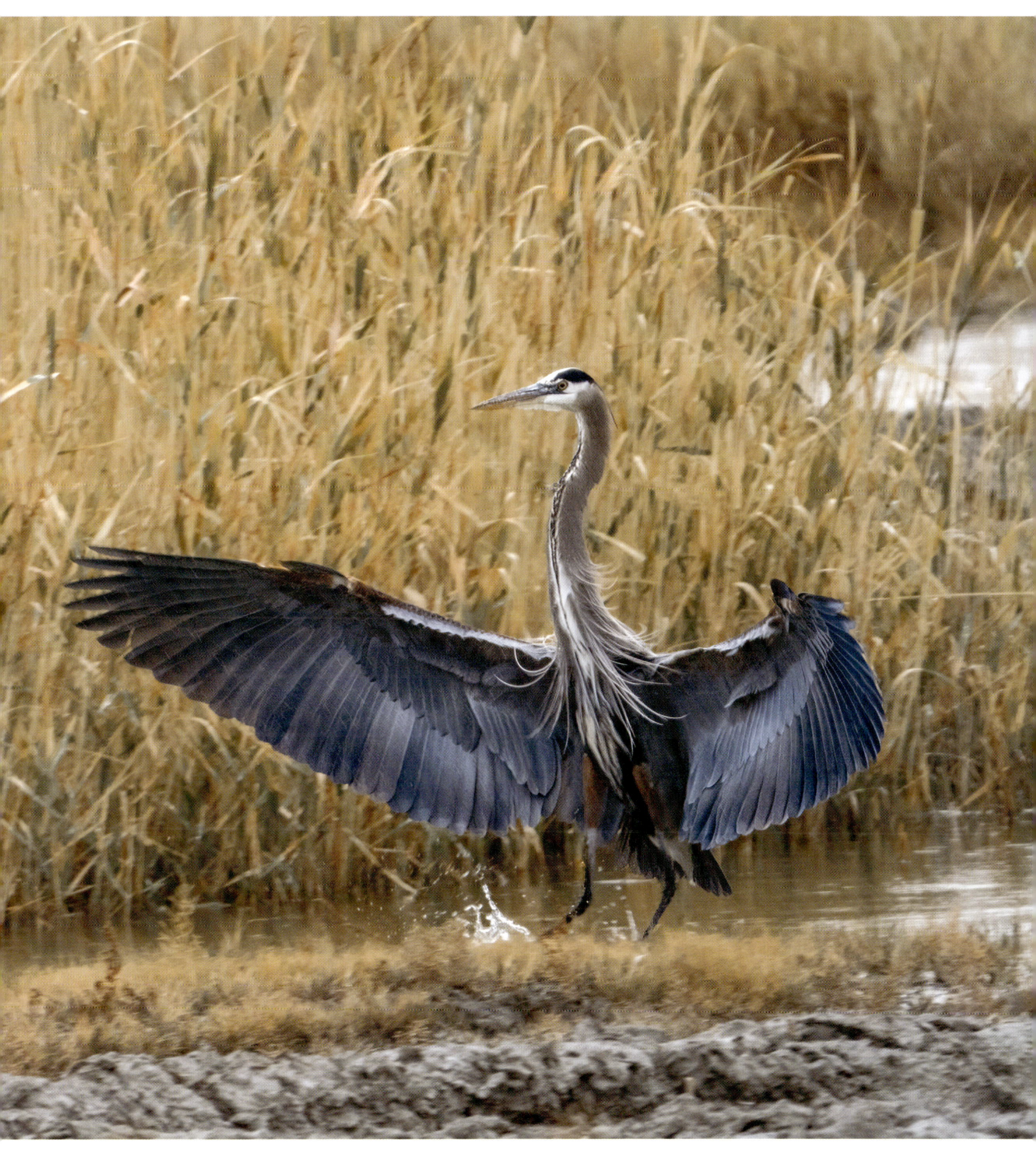

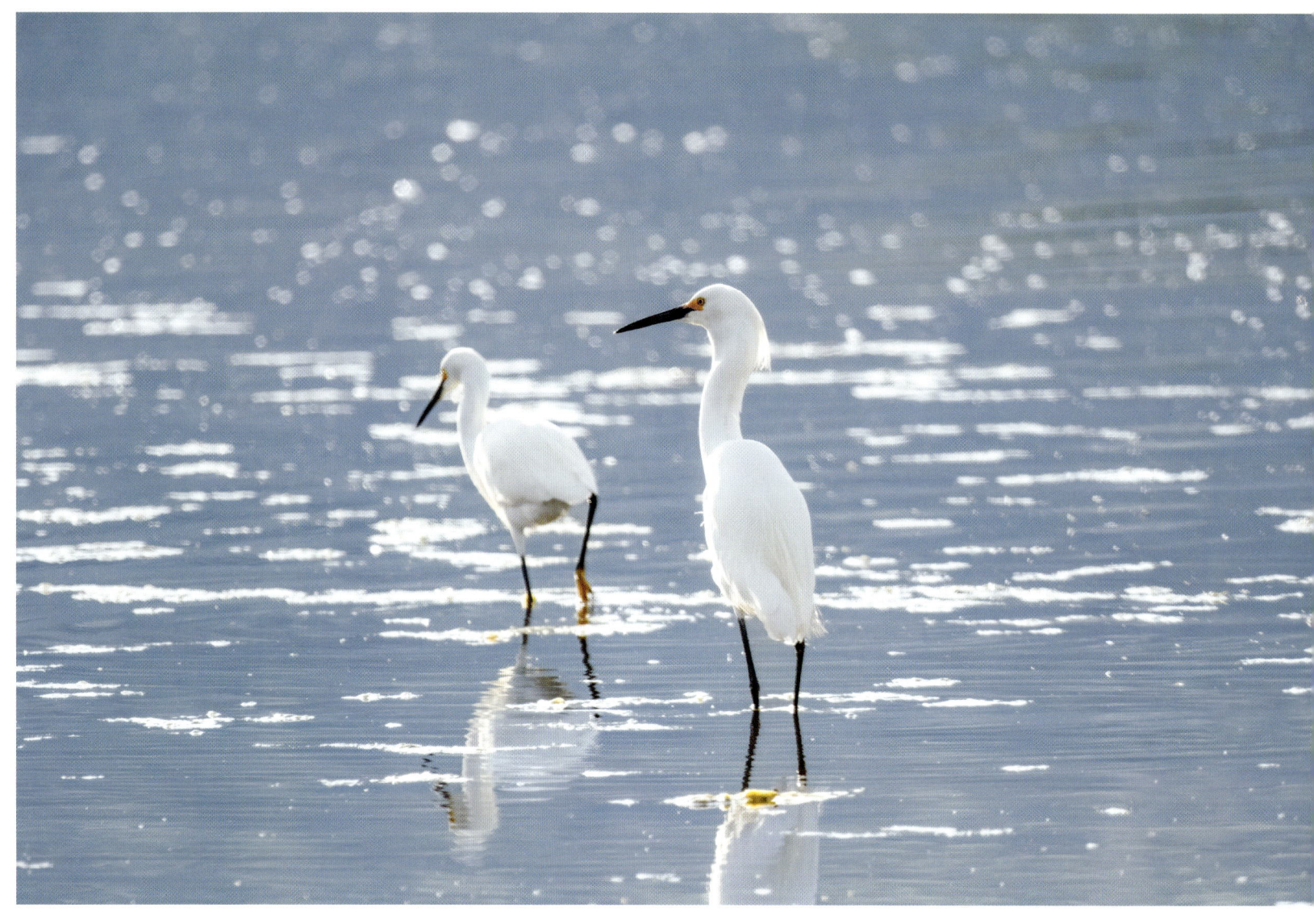

SNOWY EGRET

Snowy Egrets (*Egretta thula*) captivate observers with their elegant white plumage, slender black legs, and bright yellow feet, often called "golden slippers." These medium-size herons are known for their dynamic foraging techniques, using their feet to stir up prey in shallow waters and employing various hunting methods to catch fish, insects, and crustaceans.

Snowy Egret, Farmington Bay | J9 | 05.29.2023

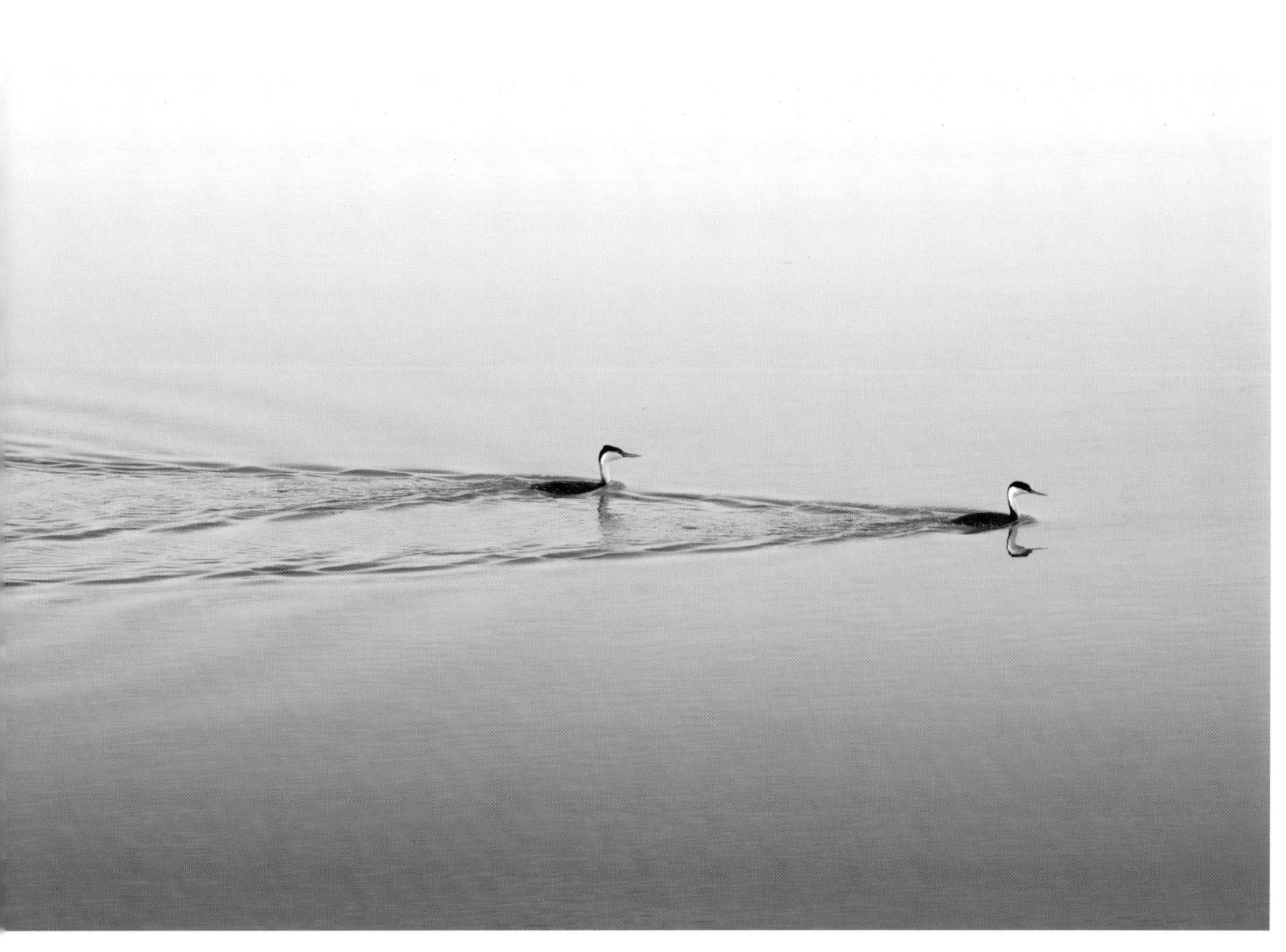

Clark's Grebes, Bear River Migratory Bird Refuge | C8 | 04.16.2023

CLARK'S GREBE

Clark's Grebes (*Aechmophorus clarkii*) find Great Salt Lake an ideal habitat for building floating nests anchored to emergent vegetation. They are particularly fascinating due to their intricate courtship displays, often described as ballet-like, involving synchronized "rushing" across the water. Additionally, they show remarkable adaptability, foraging farther from shore and in deeper waters compared to their close relatives, the Western Grebes.

EARED GREBE

Around 90 percent of North America's
Eared Grebe (*Podiceps nigricollis*) population
depends on Great Salt Lake, especially in the
fall when they gather to feed on its abundant
brine shrimp. Each grebe consumes up to
30,000 brine shrimp daily, enabling them
to double their weight and prepare for the
long journey south. More Eared Grebes
tend to die when the lake's water levels are
low, such as in 2022, because reduced water
levels limit the availability of brine shrimp,
forcing the birds to compete more fiercely
for food. Lower water levels also expose the
birds to higher concentrations of pollutants
and make them more vulnerable to disease
outbreaks, such as West Nile virus, which
has previously caused significant die-offs
among Eared Grebes at the lake.

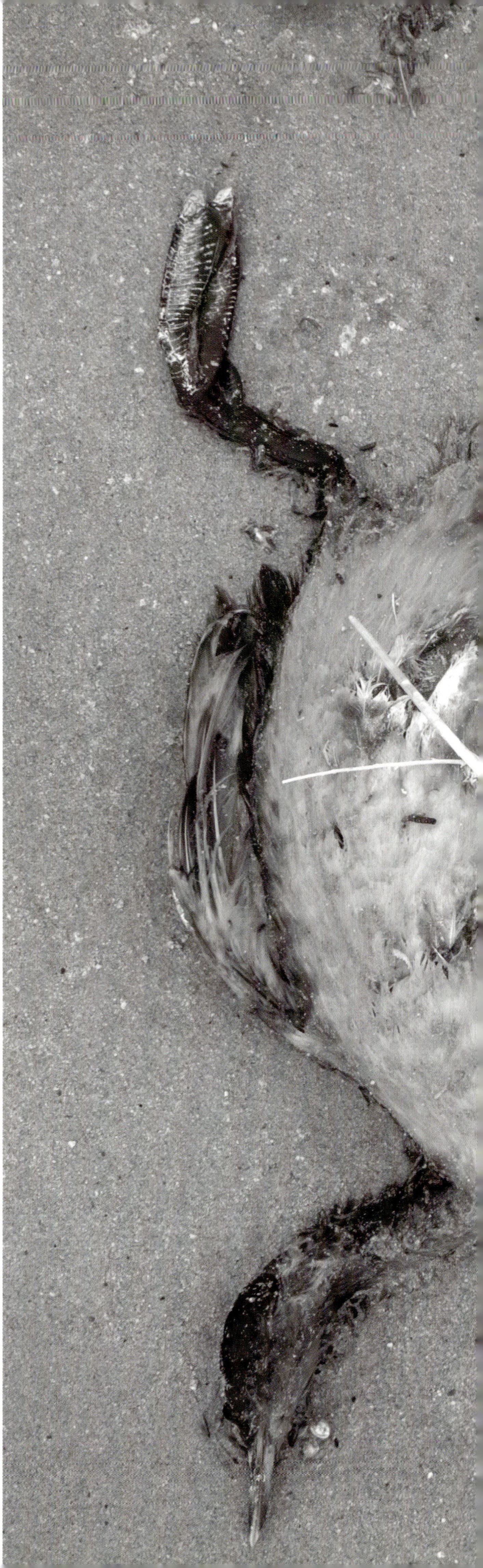

Dead Eared Grebes, south shore of Great Salt Lake
K8 | 04.04.2023

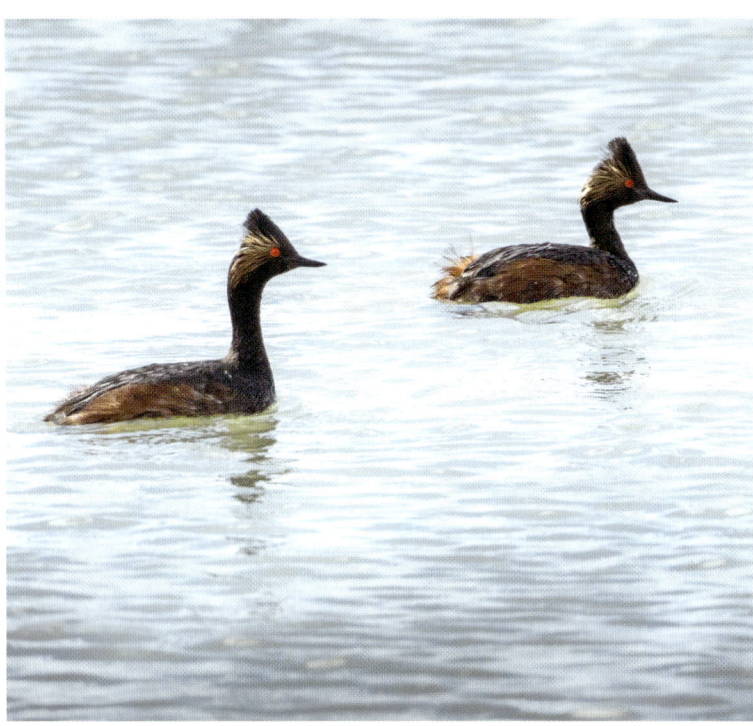

Eared Grebes, Farmington Bay | H8 | 05.10.2024

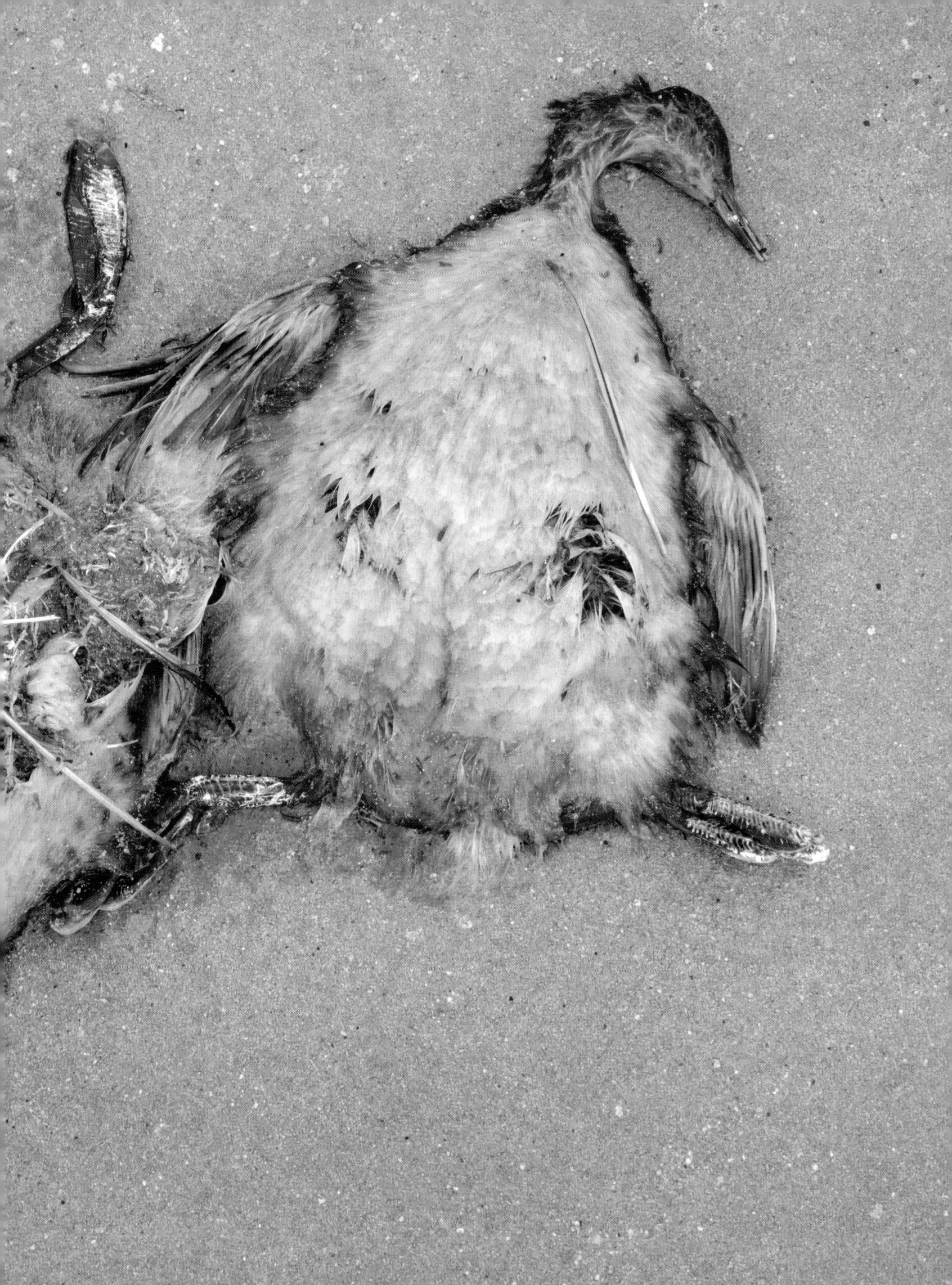

GREEN-WINGED TEAL

Green-winged Teals (*Anas crecca*) are fascinating birds, with their striking cinnamon-colored heads and bright green wing patches. They are the smallest dabbling ducks in North America. They're known for their agile flight and diverse diet, which includes seeds, aquatic insects, and crustaceans. Great Salt Lake's shallow waters and extensive wetlands provide abundant food and safe nesting sites, making the lake a critical stopover during migration and an essential wintering ground for these small ducks.

Green-winged Teals, Farmington Bay | H8 | 01.07.2024

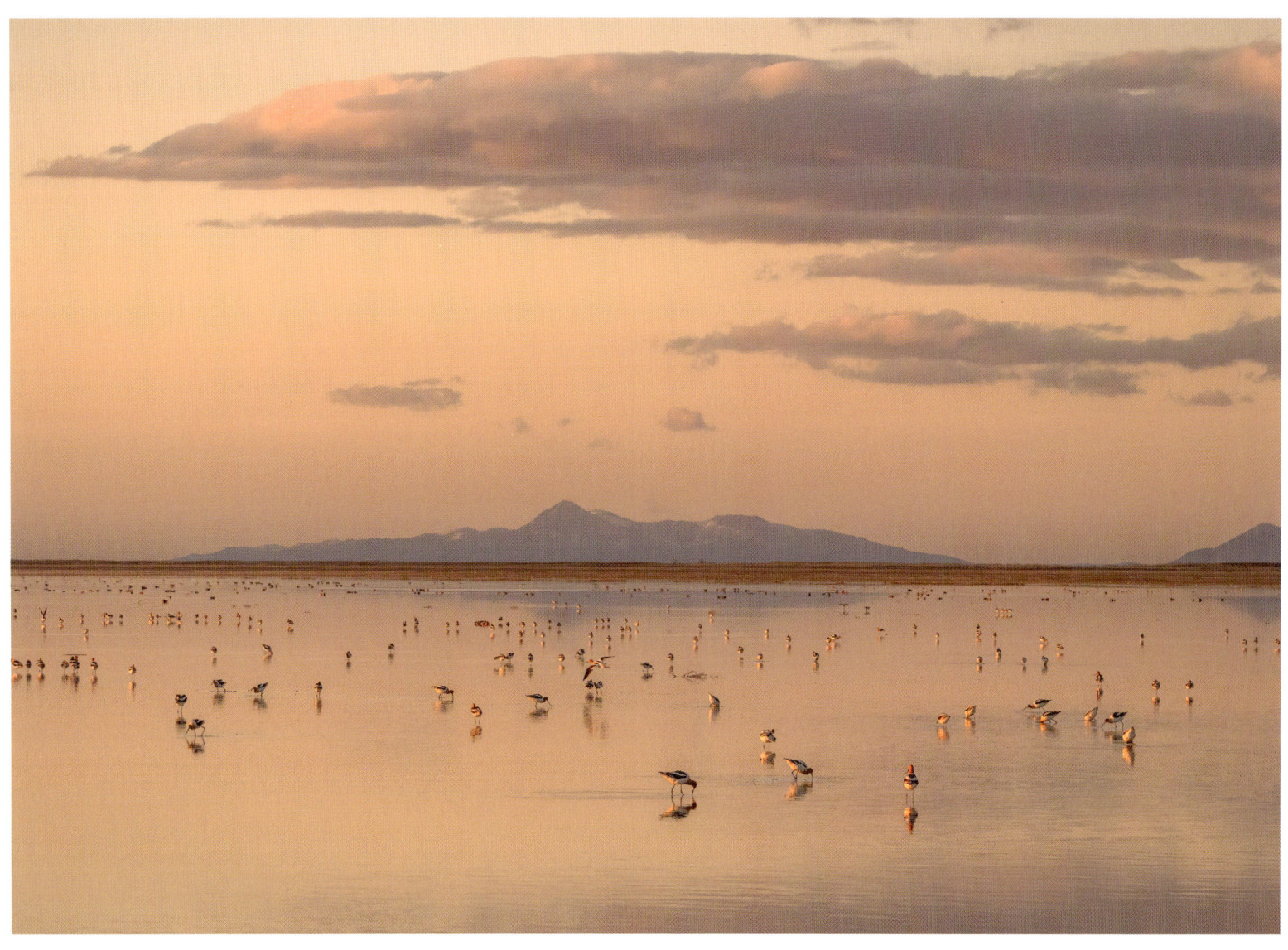

AMERICAN AVOCET

The American Avocet (*Recurvirostra americana*) epitomizes elegance, gliding through shallow waters with its long legs and swishing its slender, upturned bill to catch aquatic invertebrates. In summer, it sports a striking black-and-white body with a rusty head and neck, which turns grayish white in winter. Known for its unique predator response, the avocet emits call notes that rise in pitch, simulating the Doppler effect and making its approach seem faster. Remarkably, avocet chicks leave the nest within 24 hours of hatching, able to walk, swim, and dive to evade predators. Great Salt Lake serves as a crucial breeding ground for these birds, supporting about 50 percent of the North American population during their migration. Fourteen percent of the continental breeding population relies on its wetlands, making it an indispensable habitat for their survival and reproduction.

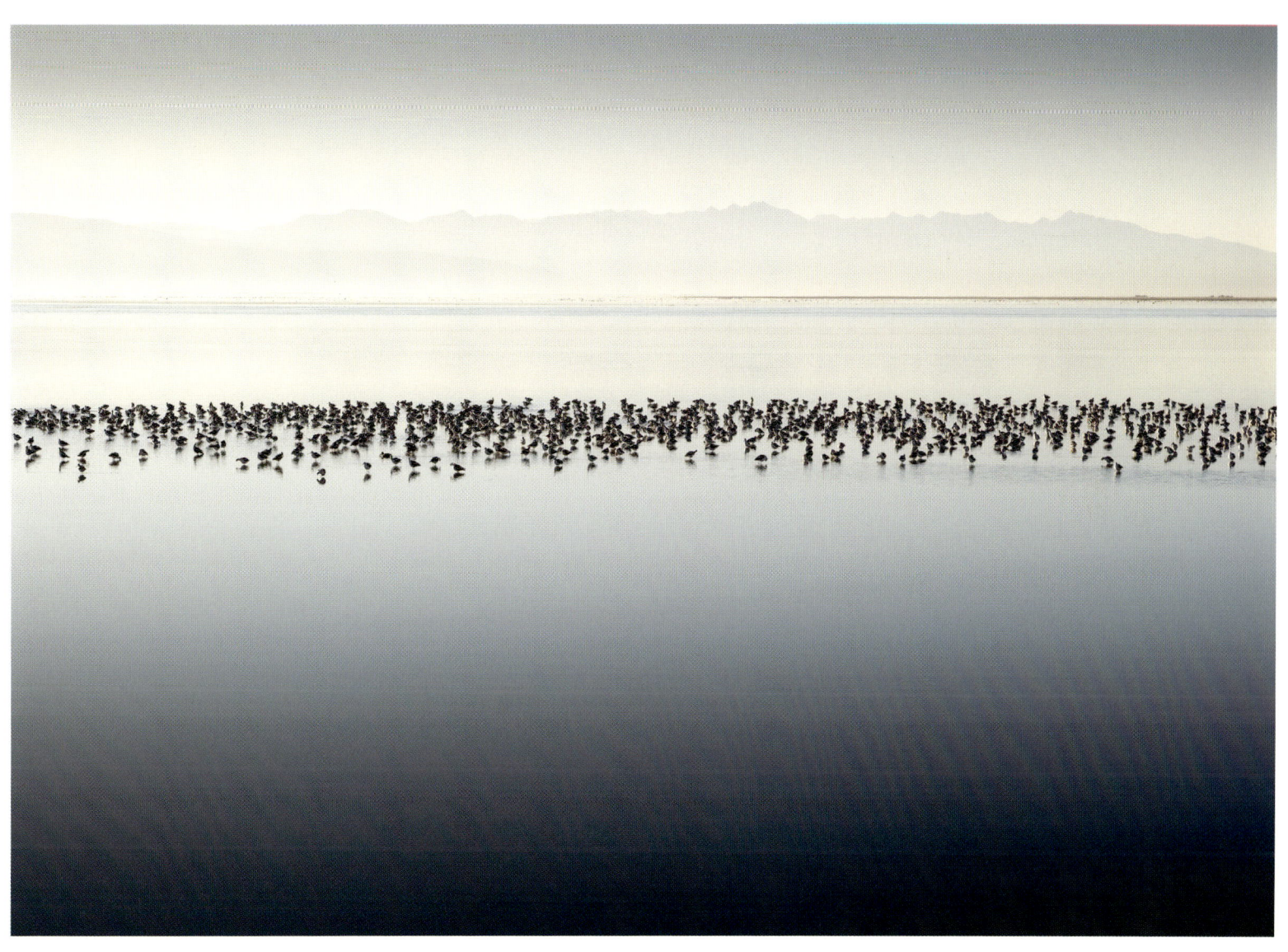

Feeding American Avocets, Farmington Bay | H8 | 04.01.2024

Birds of a feather flock together (American Avocets) | H8 | 09.23.2023

FOLLOWING PAGE: Hundreds of non-breeding American Avocets, Farmington Bay | H8 | 09.04.2023

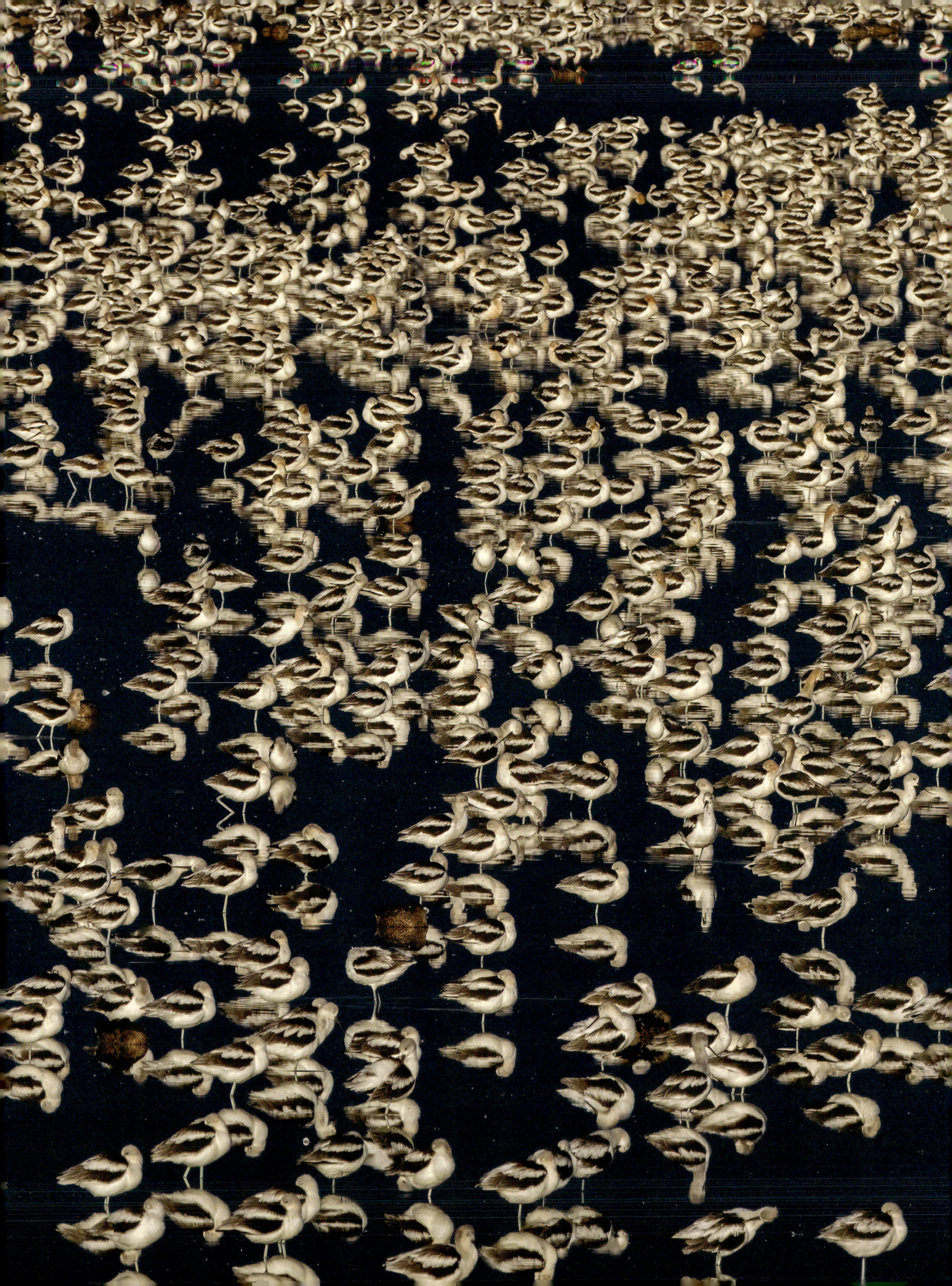

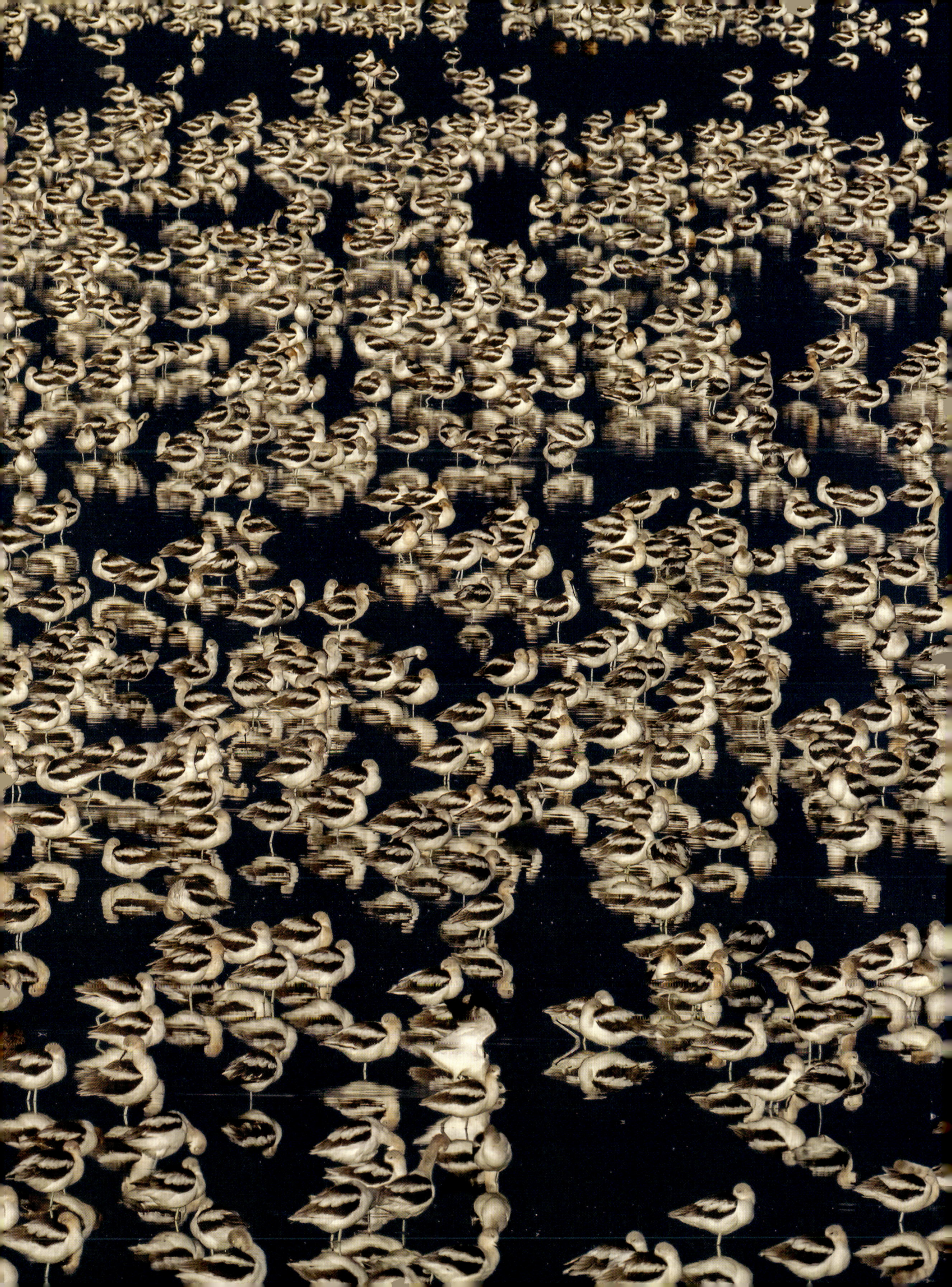

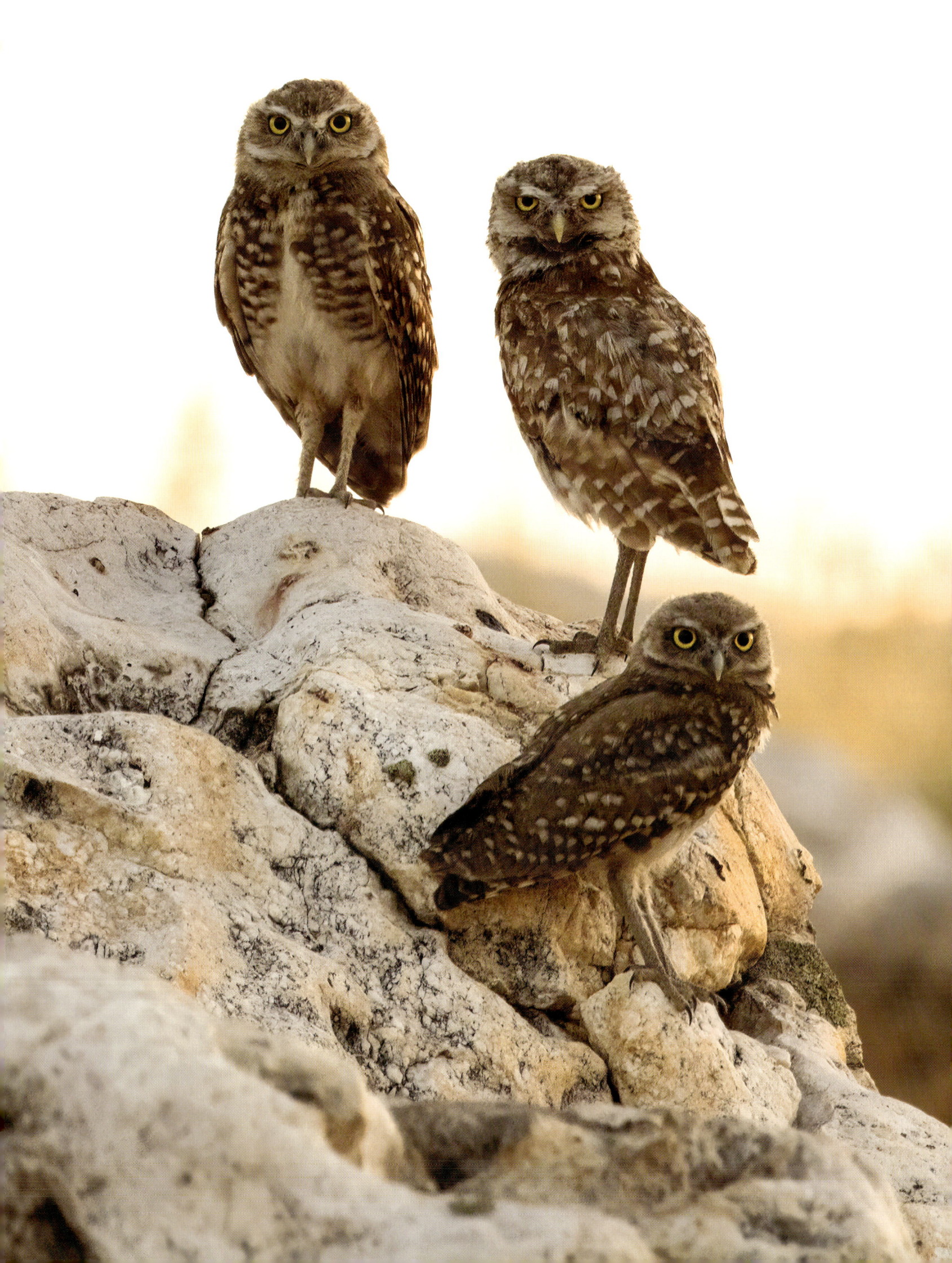

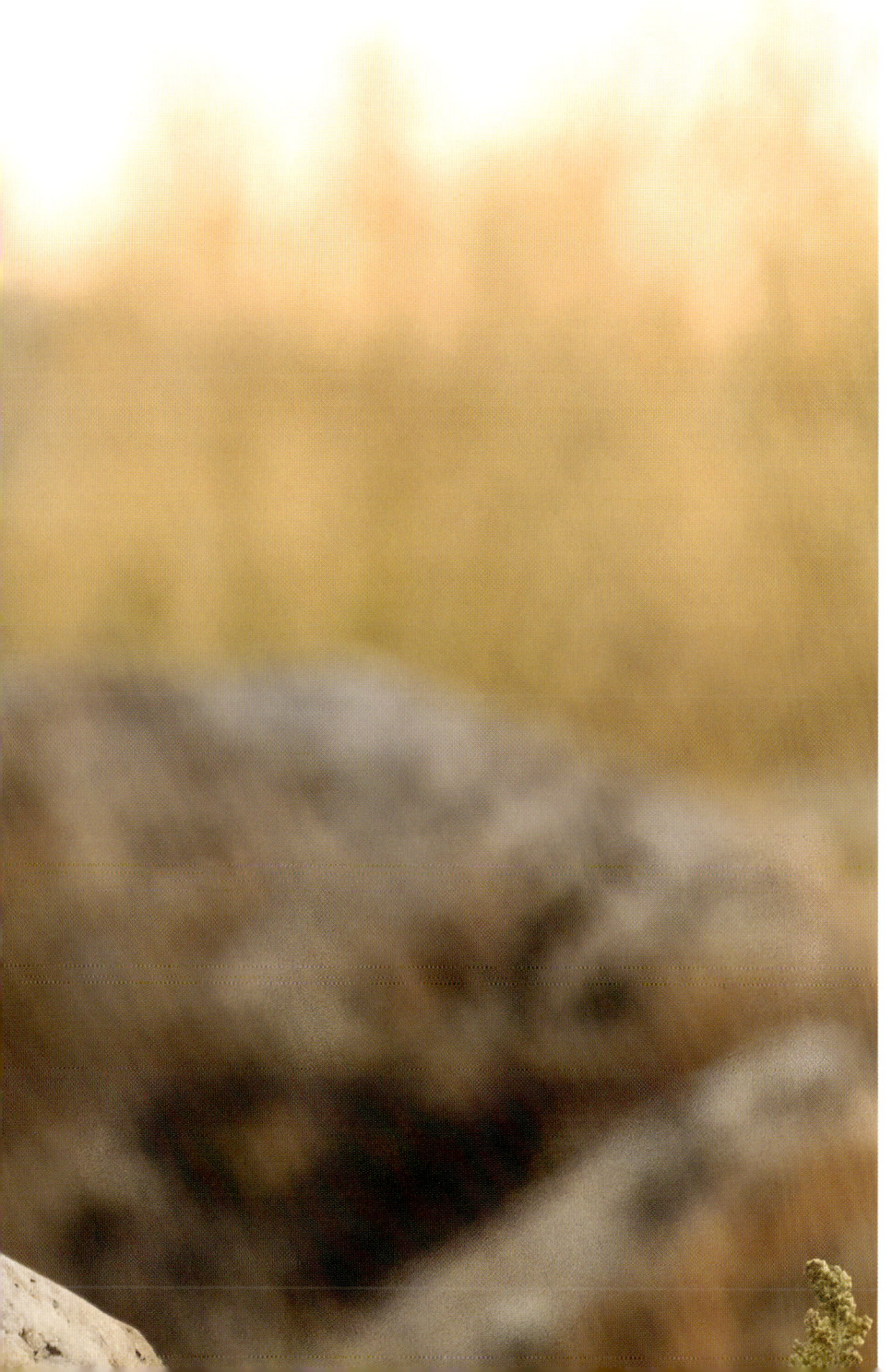

BURROWING OWL

Burrowing Owls (*Athene cunicularia*) are fascinating for their unique daytime activity and preference for underground nesting in abandoned animal dens. Their expressive behaviors and distinct yellow eyes make them a favorite among bird watchers. Antelope Island is an ideal habitat for these owls because of its open grasslands and available nesting sites. Park staff have installed artificial burrows to support their breeding, ensuring a safe environment for raising young. The island provides ample food and minimal disturbance, and efforts by organizations like HawkWatch International to monitor these nests further enhance the owls' successful breeding on the island.

Burrowing Owls, Antelope Island | H8 | 08.30.2023

AMERICAN KESTREL

American Kestrels (*Falco sparverius*), North America's smallest and most colorful falcons, captivate bird-watchers with their unique slate-blue heads, rusty red backs, and exceptional hunting skills. Despite their small size, they exhibit fierce predatory behavior, utilizing their ability to see ultraviolet light to track small mammals. Conservation efforts, including the installation of nest boxes by organizations like The Nature Conservancy and HawkWatch International, ensure that kestrels thrive in this unique ecosystem.

American Kestrel, Hooper, Utah
G9 | 11.11.2023

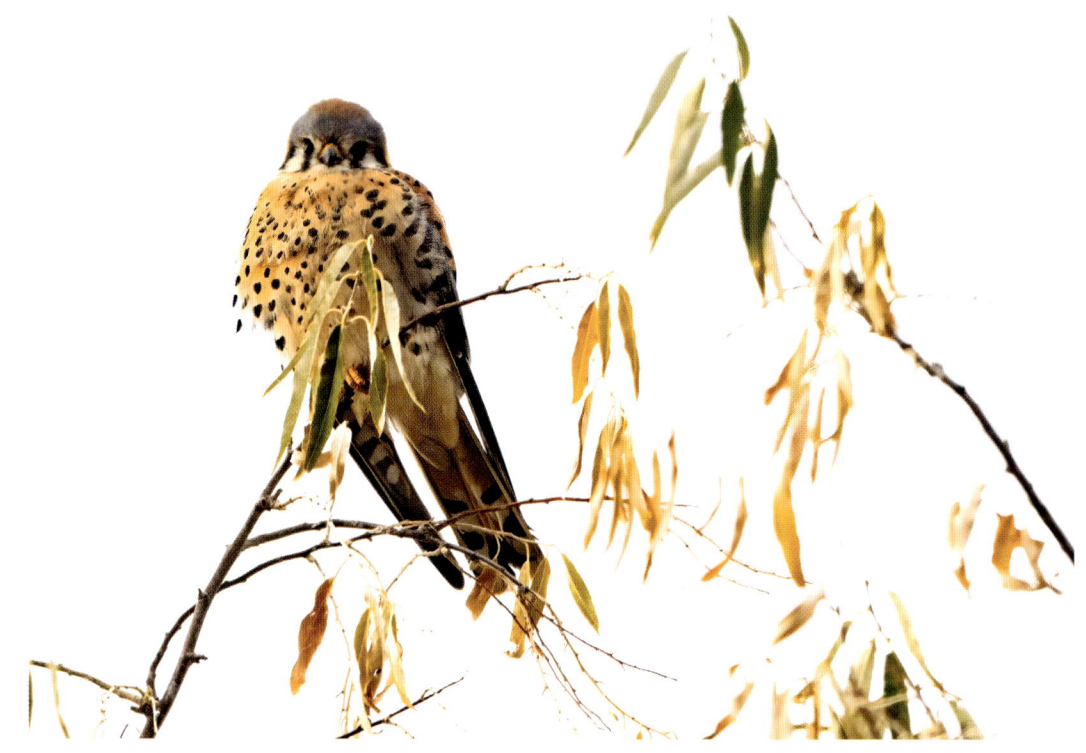

NORTHERN HARRIER

Northern Harriers (*Circus hudsonius*) thrive in the Great Salt Lake biome, which supplies a rich prey base of small mammals, birds, and insects that they hunt using their low, slow flight and keen hearing, aided by their owlish facial disk. Their unique behaviors, such as males mating with several females and providing most of the food for their mates and offspring, set them apart from other raptors.

Female Northern Harrier, south end of Antelope Island | J9 | 12.03.2024

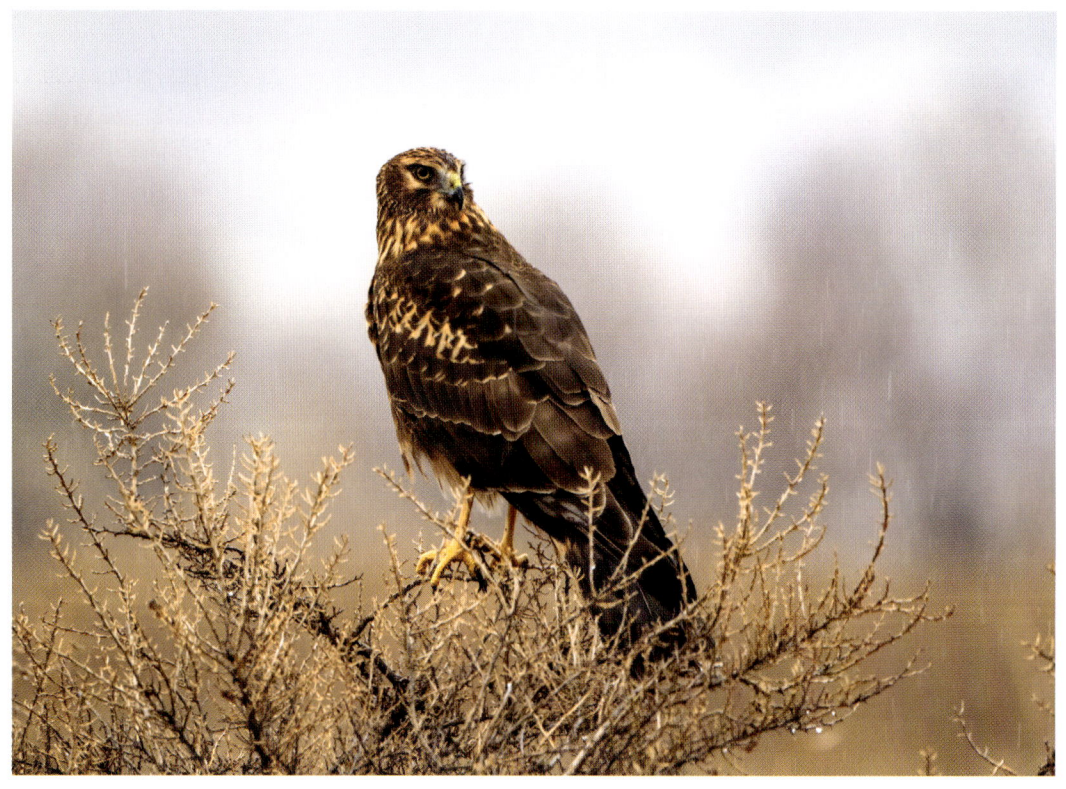

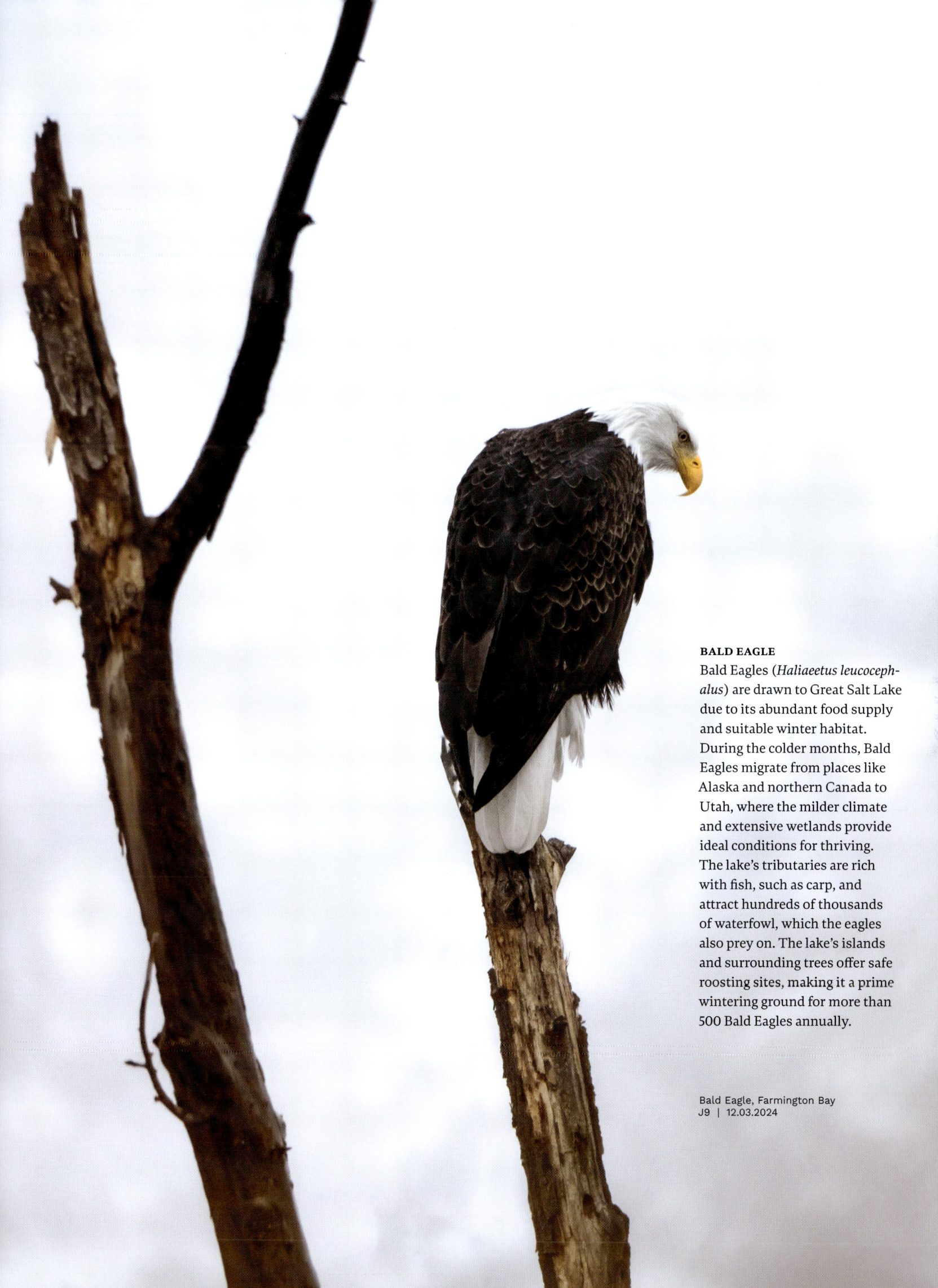

BALD EAGLE

Bald Eagles (*Haliaeetus leucocephalus*) are drawn to Great Salt Lake due to its abundant food supply and suitable winter habitat. During the colder months, Bald Eagles migrate from places like Alaska and northern Canada to Utah, where the milder climate and extensive wetlands provide ideal conditions for thriving. The lake's tributaries are rich with fish, such as carp, and attract hundreds of thousands of waterfowl, which the eagles also prey on. The lake's islands and surrounding trees offer safe roosting sites, making it a prime wintering ground for more than 500 Bald Eagles annually.

Bald Eagle, Farmington Bay
J9 | 12.03.2024

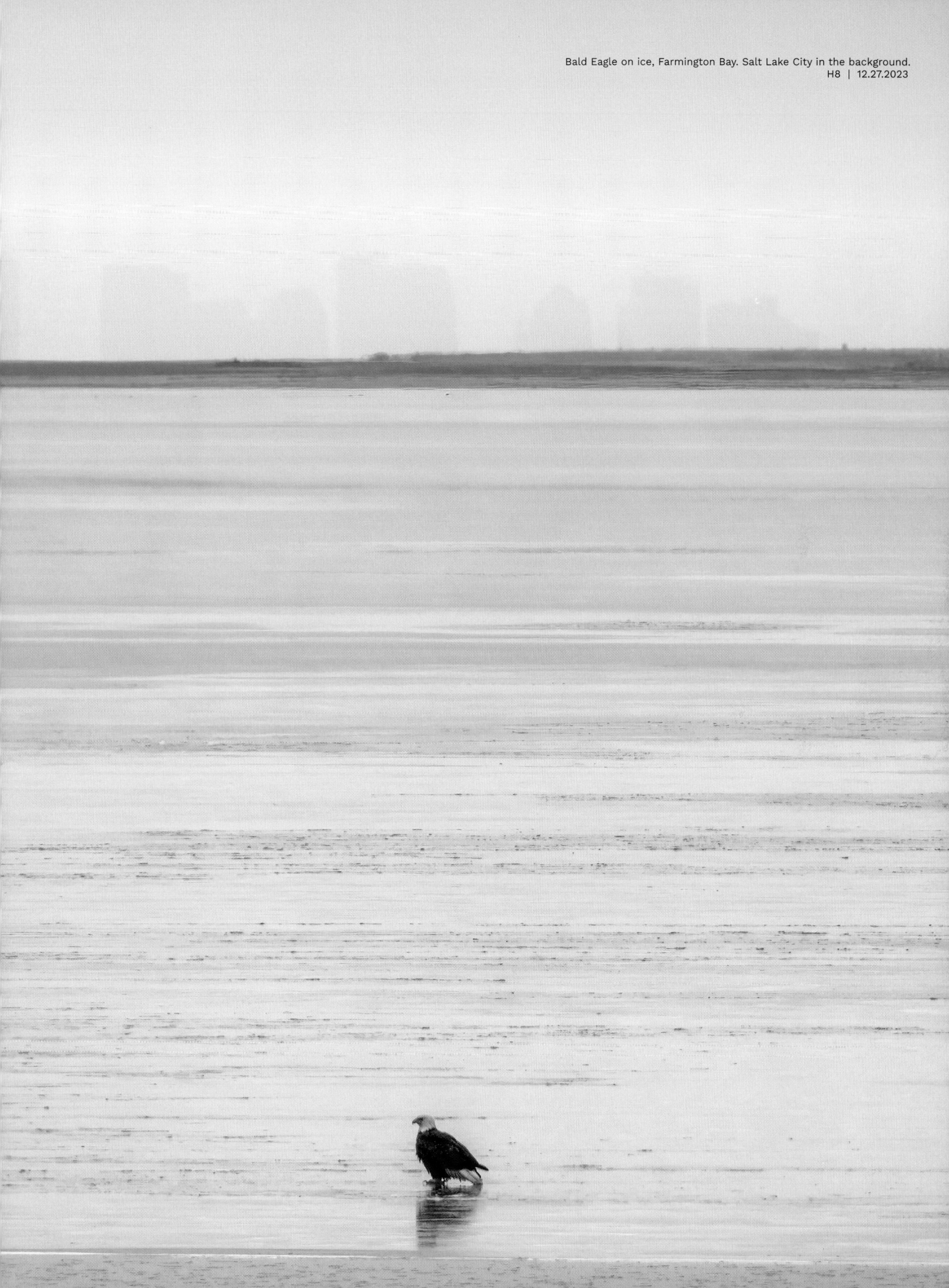

Bald Eagle on ice, Farmington Bay. Salt Lake City in the background.
H8 | 12.27.2023

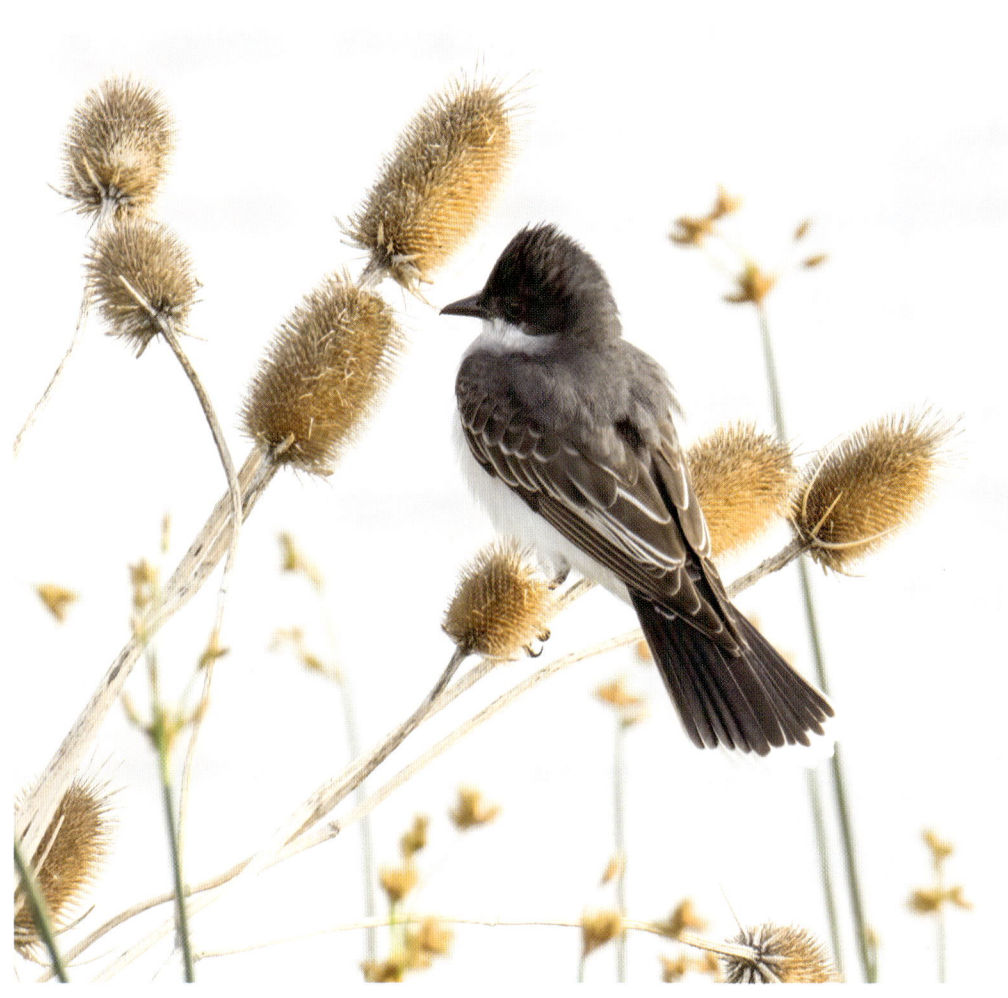
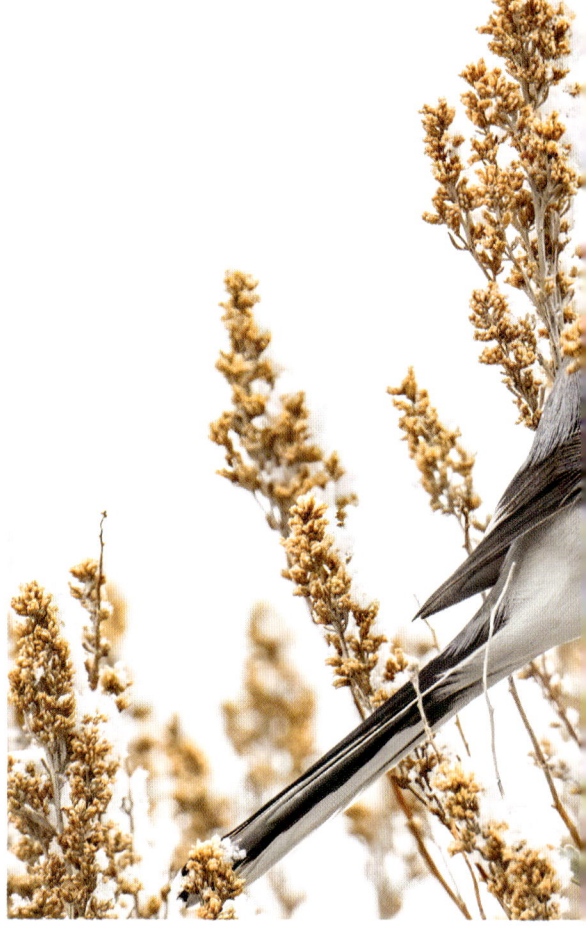

KINGBIRD

Both Western Kingbirds (*Tyrannus verticalis*) and Eastern Kingbirds (*Tyrannus tyrannus*) thrive around Great Salt Lake, but they exhibit separate characteristics. Western Kingbirds, with their gray heads and bright yellow bellies, are aggressive defenders of their territory, often seen perching on utility lines and fences to catch flying insects midair. In contrast, Eastern Kingbirds have dark gray upperparts and a white-tipped tail. They display a fearless attitude by harassing larger birds to protect their nests.

Eastern Kingbird, Farmington Bay | J9 | 05.29.2023

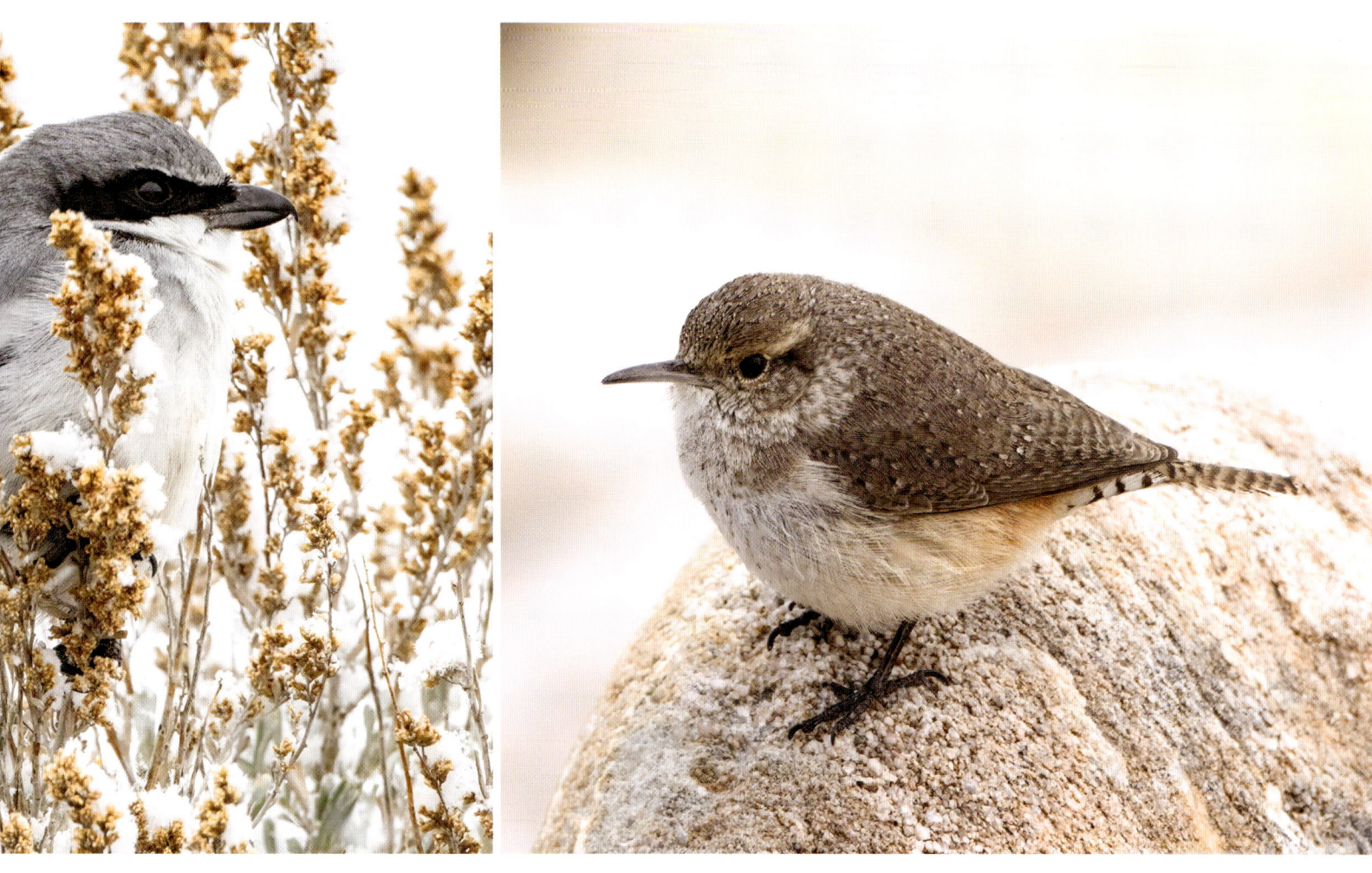

LOGGERHEAD SHRIKE

Loggerhead Shrikes (*Lanius ludovicianus*), known as "butcher birds," are fascinating due to their unique predatory behavior of impaling prey on thorns or barbed wire, compensating for their lack of raptor talons. These small songbirds have impressive black, white, and gray plumage and exhibit raptor-like hunting methods, preying on insects, birds, lizards, and small mammals, which are found in abundance on Antelope Island.

ROCK WREN

Rock Wrens (*Salpinctes obsoletus*) are particularly interesting due to their distinctive behavior and adaptability to rocky environments. These small, energetic birds are known for their constant bobbing motion and loud, melodious calls, often heard in rocky outcrops. They build their nests in crevices among rocks, using pebbles to line their nests and create pathways, unique among songbirds. Antelope Island provides an ideal habitat for Rock Wrens with its rocky terrain and abundant insect population, offering ample nesting sites and food sources.

Loggerhead Shrike, Antelope Island | H8 | 12.02.2023

Rock Wren, Antelope Island | H8 | 12.10.2023

CALIFORNIA GULL

The California Gull (*Larus californicus*) holds a special place in Utah's history and culture and has become more than just a common sight but also a state symbol. This bird is celebrated in local folklore through the "Miracle of the Gulls" in 1848, when flocks of California Gulls saved early settlers' crops from a devastating cricket infestation, an event commemorated by the Seagull Monument in downtown Salt Lake City.

California Gull, Great Salt Lake State Park K8 | 07.27.2023

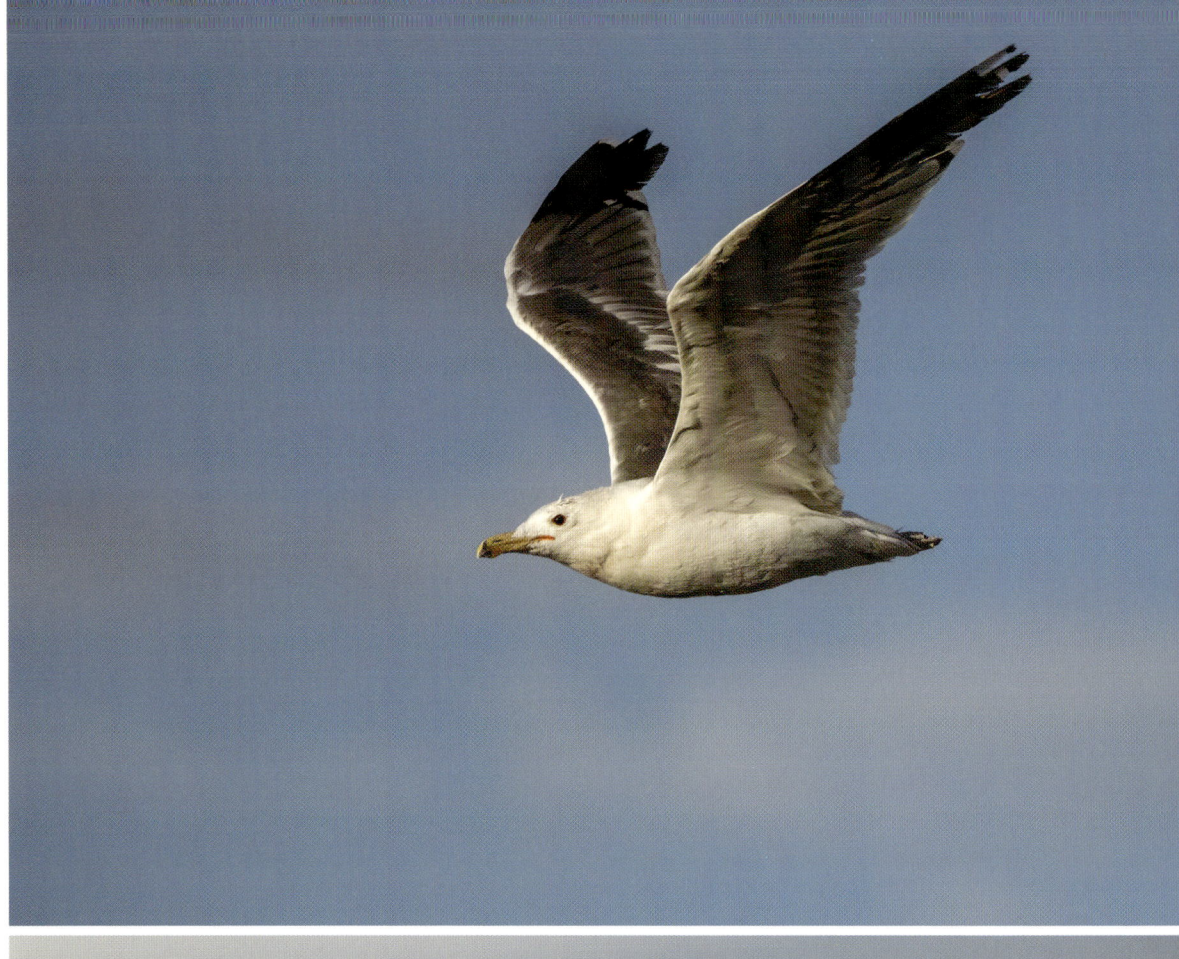

WESTERN MEADOWLARK

Western Meadowlarks (*Sturnella neglecta*) are well-known for their beautiful songs, a signature sound of the open grasslands around Great Salt Lake and on its islands. Their songs consist of a series of clear, flute-like whistles, often described as a cheerful and bright melody. Males sing from prominent perches, such as fence posts or shrubs, to establish territory and attract mates. These vocal displays are crucial not only for mating but also for communicating with other meadowlarks in the area.

Singing Western Meadowlark, Antelope Island | H8 | 03.22.2024

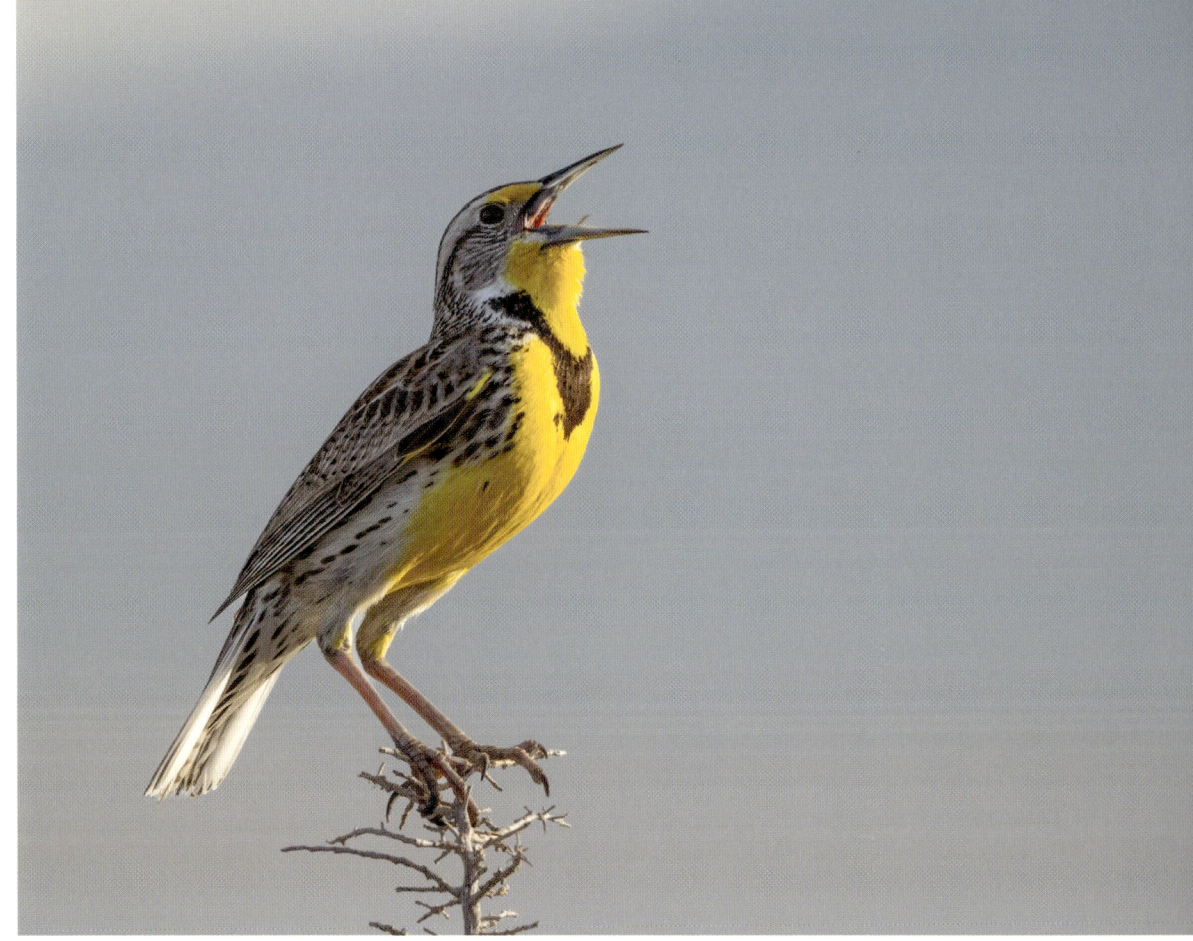

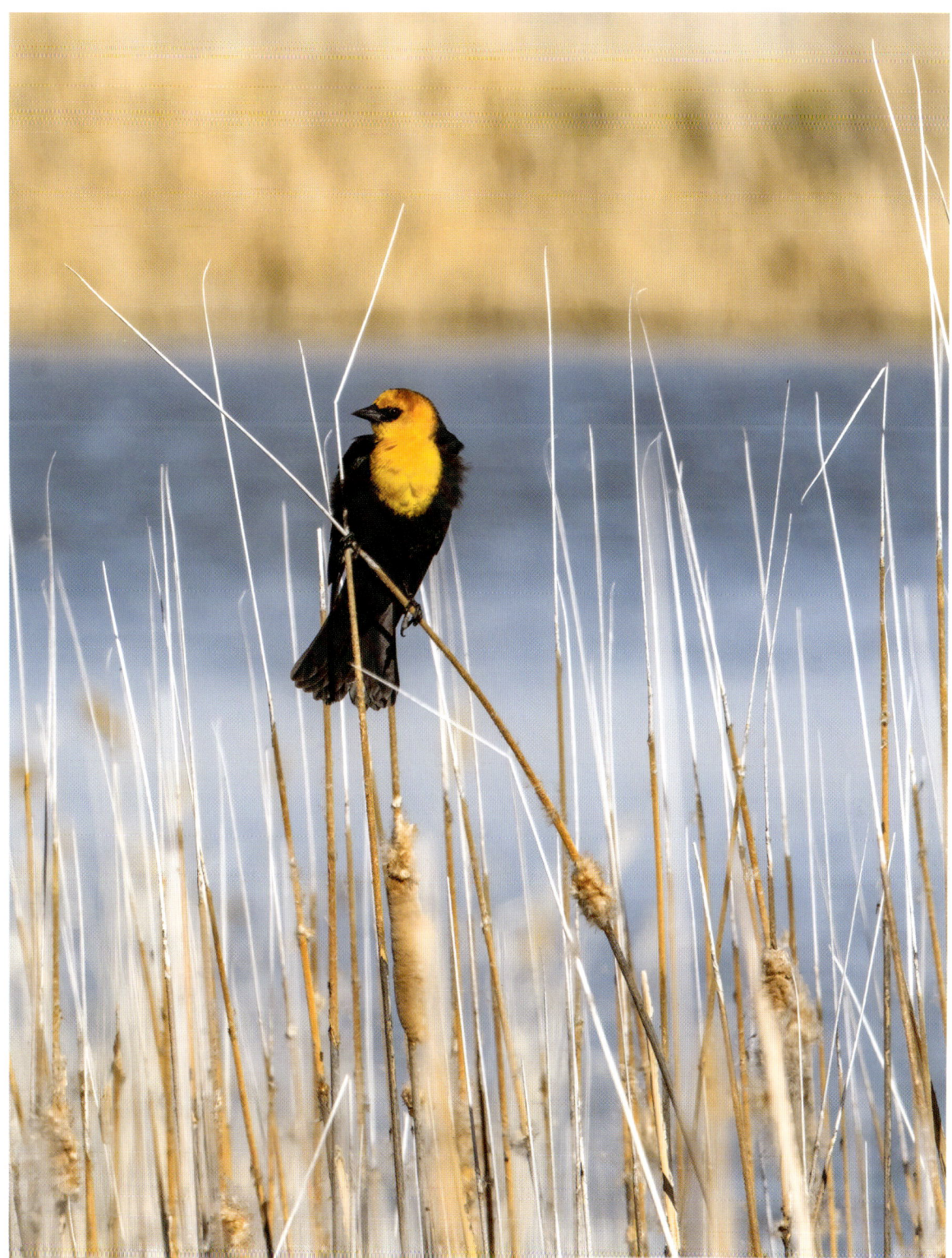

YELLOW-HEADED BLACKBIRD

Yellow-headed Blackbirds (*Xanthocephalus xanthocephalus*) are captivating due to their vivid coloring and unique behavior. Males display bright yellow heads and chests contrasted with jet-black bodies, making them easily recognizable. Their raspy, mechanical songs add a distinctive sound to the shores of Great Salt Lake.

Male Yellow-headed Blackbird, Bear River Migratory Bird Refuge | C8 | 04.16.2023

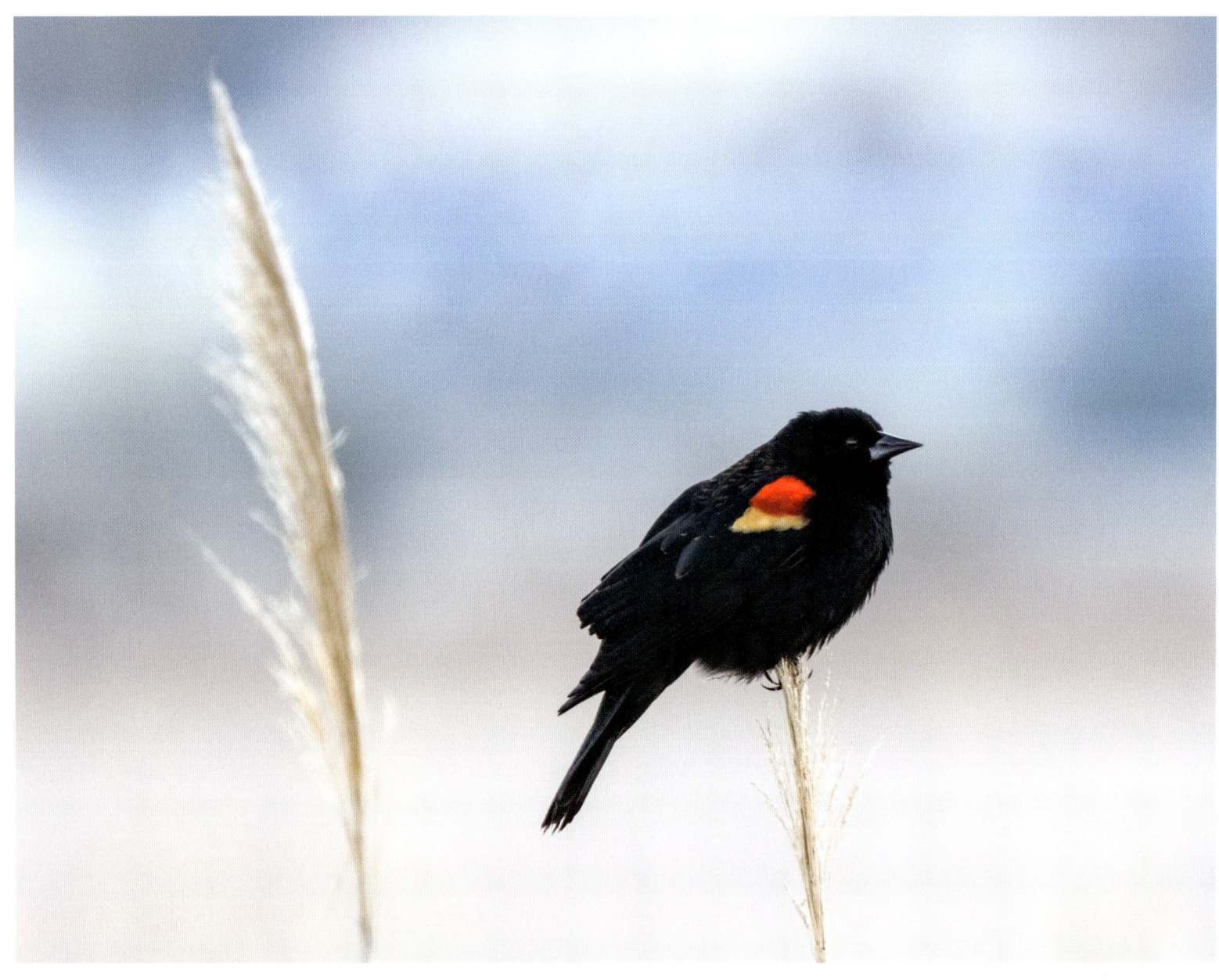

Male Red-winged Blackbird, Farmington Bay | J9 | 11.17.2024

RED-WINGED BLACKBIRDS
Red-winged Blackbirds (*Agelaius phoeniceus*) are striking songbirds recognized for the males' glossy black feathers and vibrant red and yellow shoulder patches. These birds thrive in wetland habitats, where they feed on insects, seeds, and grains, which is why they thrive around Great Salt Lake.

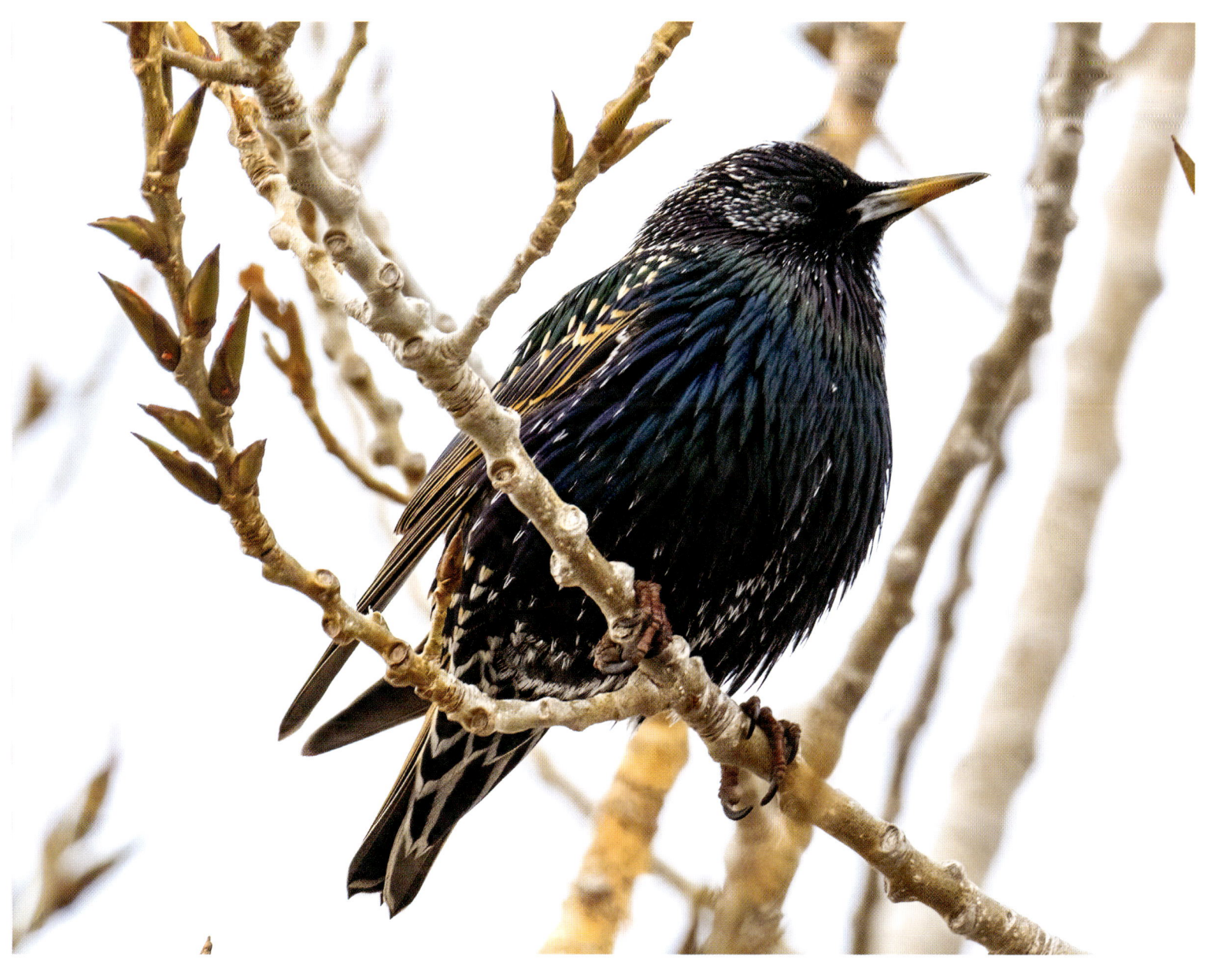

EUROPEAN STARLINGS

European Starlings (*Sturnus vulgaris*) are common around Great Salt Lake, thriving in wetlands, agricultural fields, and urban areas. One of the most fascinating behaviors they display in this region is their mesmerizing murmurations—synchronized, twisting flocks that are especially visible during fall and winter evenings. These aerial displays serve to confuse predators, maintain group warmth, and scout for safe roosting spots.

European Starling, Antelope Island | H8 | 12.22.2024

AMERICAN BISON

The American Bison (*Bison bison*) herd on Antelope Island is one of the largest and oldest publicly owned bison herds in the United States, with the population fluctuating between 550 and 700 animals. The island provides an ideal habitat for bison due to its expansive dry grass prairie, which offers abundant forage and no significant predators. This environment allows the bison to thrive and reproduce, with around 150 to 200 calves born each year. The island's isolation on Great Salt Lake also helps protect the herd from disease and genetic mixing with other bison populations, preserving unique genetic markers.

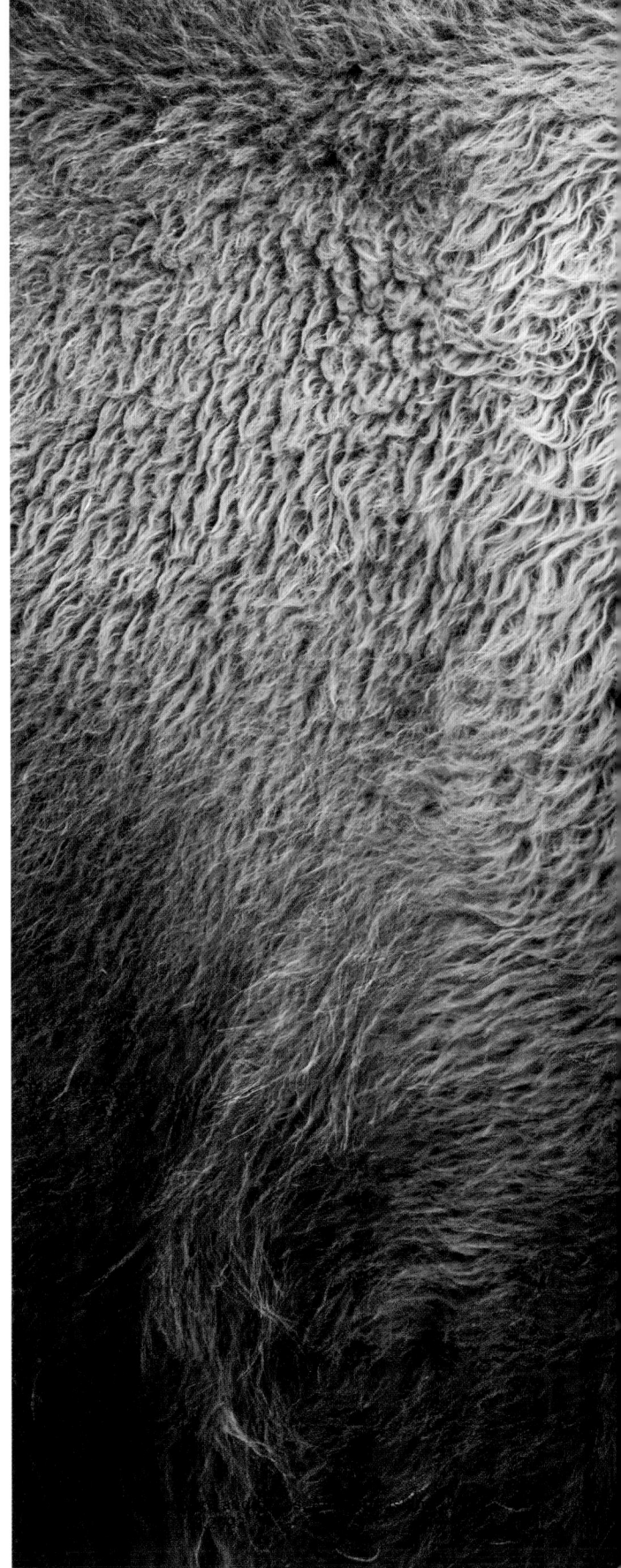

Fur texture and horns, Antelope Island | H3 | 03.19.2023

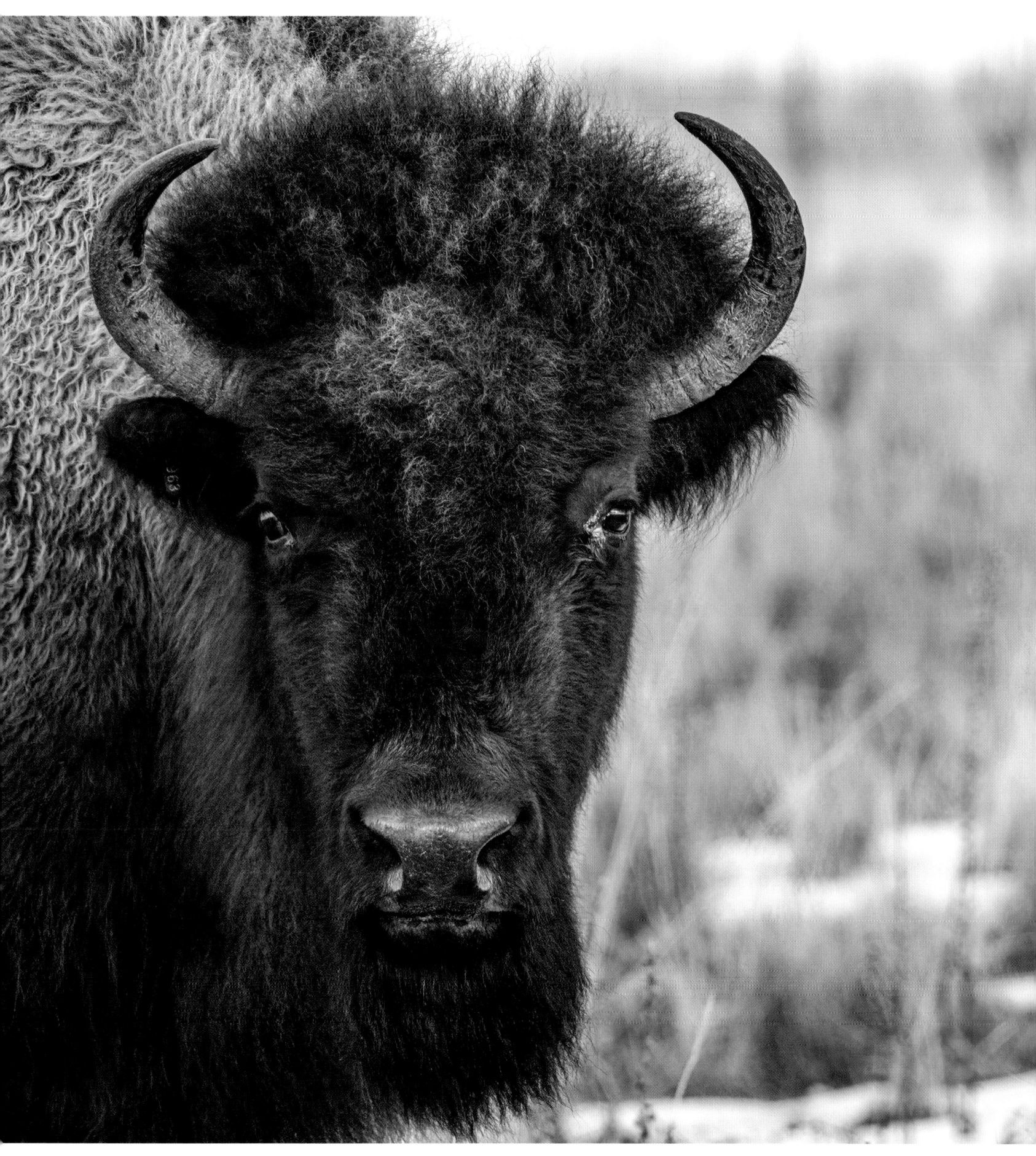

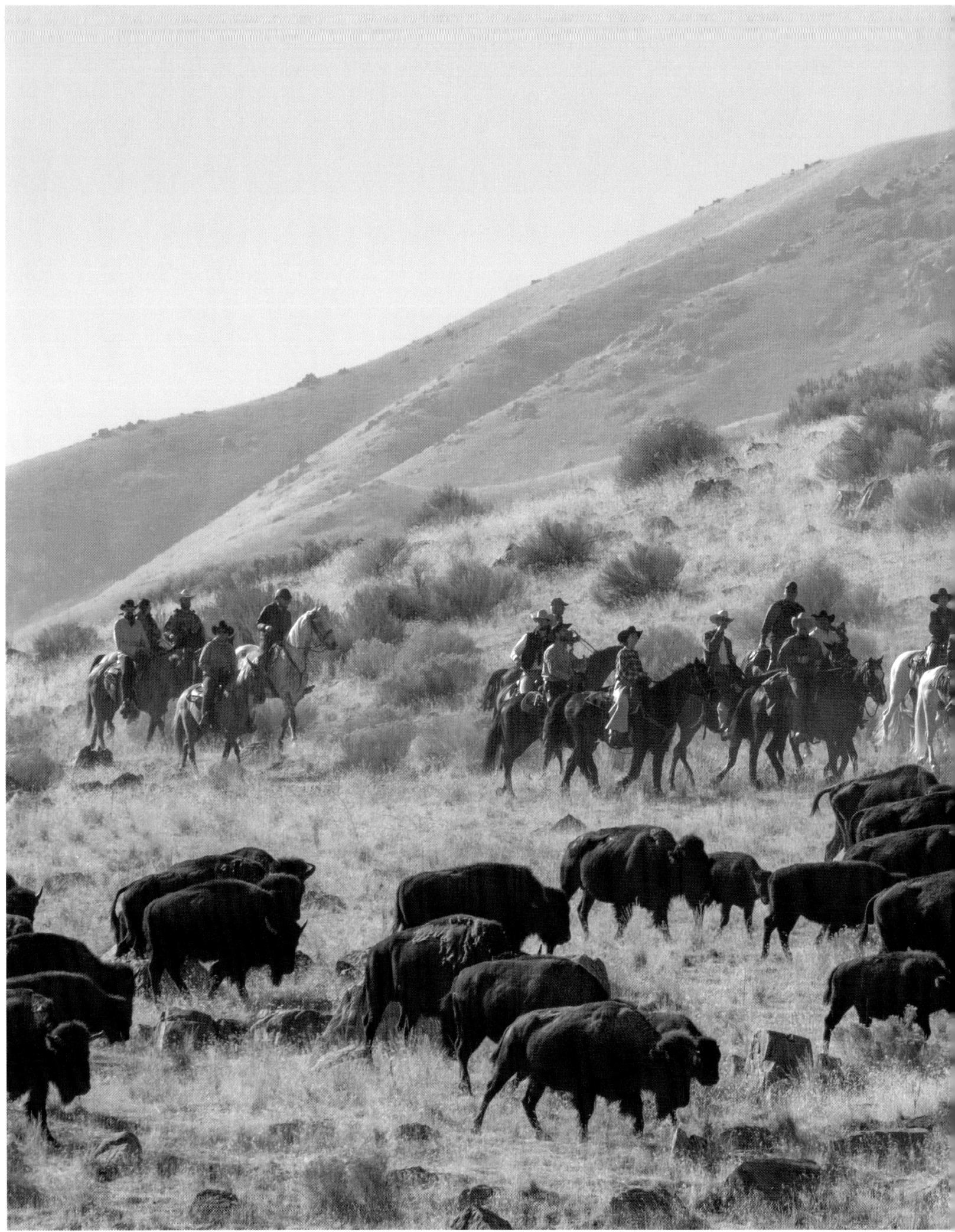

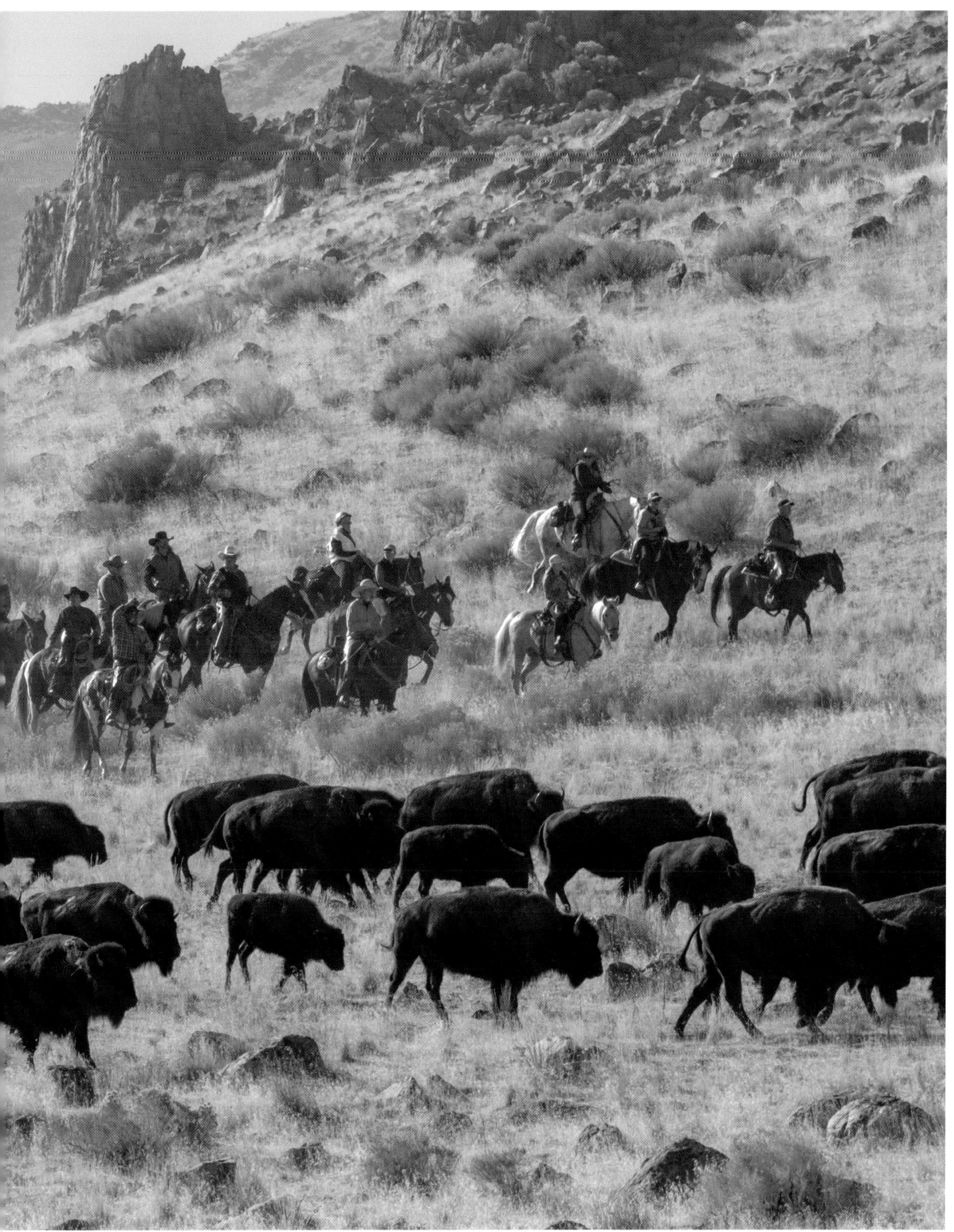

The annual bison roundup | H8 | 10.24.2024

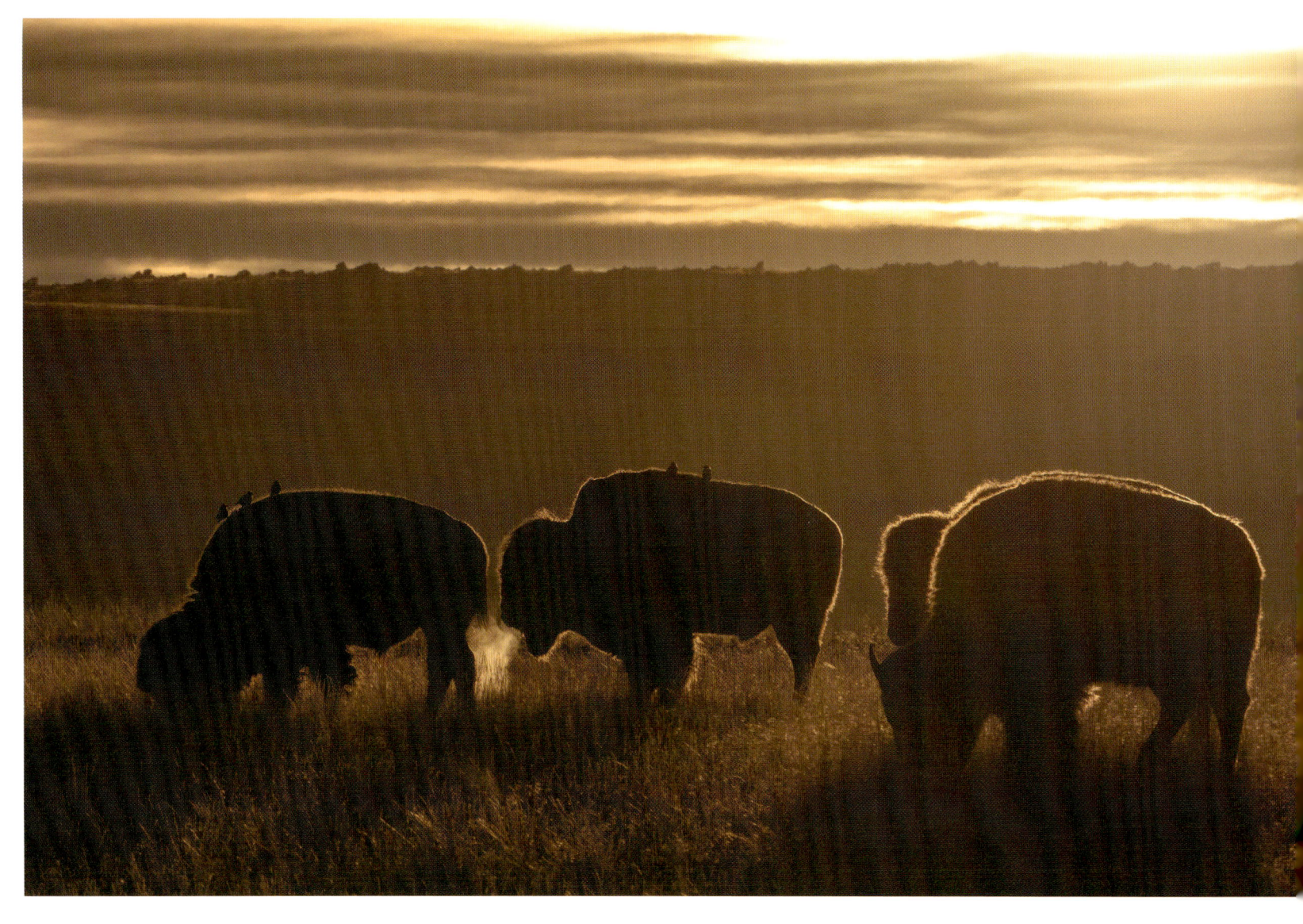

Bison breath, Antelope Island | H3 | 01.27.2024

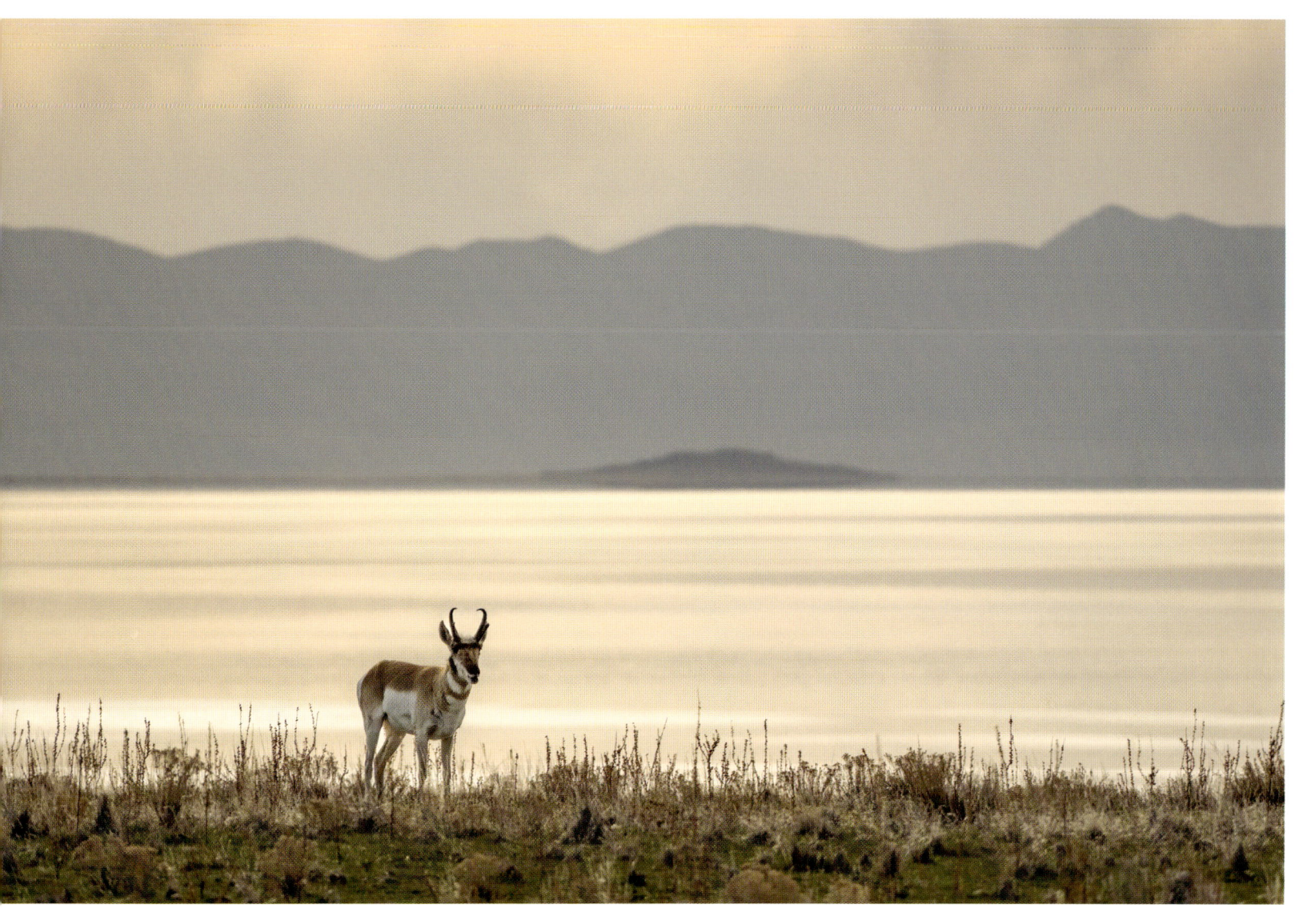

PRONGHORN ANTELOPE

The Pronghorn Antelope (*Antilocapra americana*) on
Antelope Island thrive due to the island's expansive
grasslands and minimal human disturbance. Reintroduced
in the 1990s, the Pronghorn population has flourished due
to the isolated nature of the island, with current numbers
sitting at around 200 antelope.

Horns on the horizon, Antelope Island | H3 | 05.10.2024

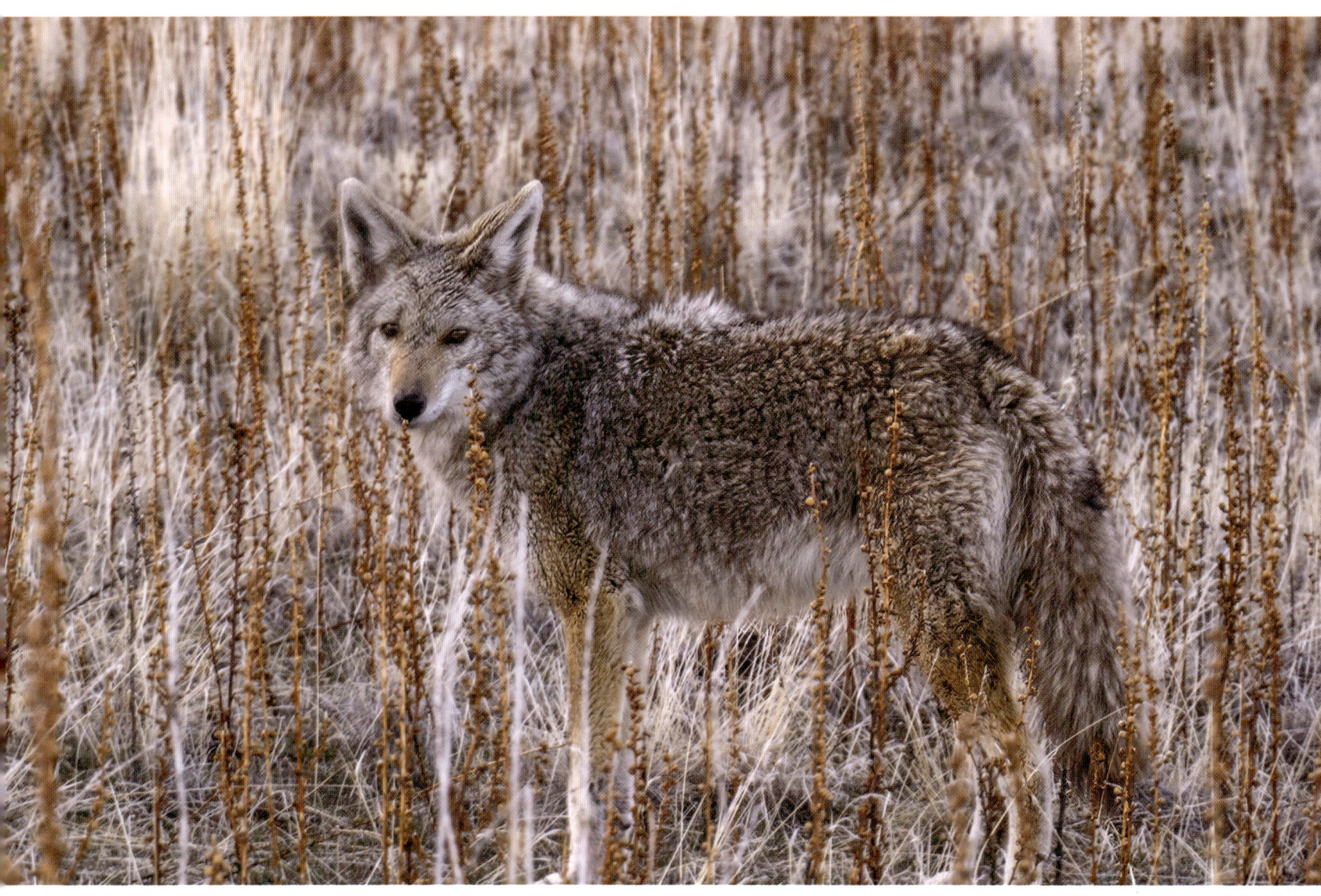

COYOTES

Coyotes (*Canis latrans*) thrive around Great Salt Lake, particularly on Antelope Island, due to its diverse habitats and abundant food sources. The mix of wetlands, grasslands, and minimal human disturbance creates an ideal environment for these opportunistic predators. Coyotes are most active during sunrise and sunset, taking advantage of lower light conditions to hunt small mammals, birds, and insects. Their remarkable adaptability and intelligence allow them to utilize both hunting and scavenging techniques, often patrolling the shores for sick or injured waterfowl, especially during winter when diseases like botulism can affect duck populations. Their complex social structures, varied vocalizations, and ability to thrive in a wide range of environments make them a fascinating subject for observation.

Camouflage, Antelope Island
H3 | 03.20.2023

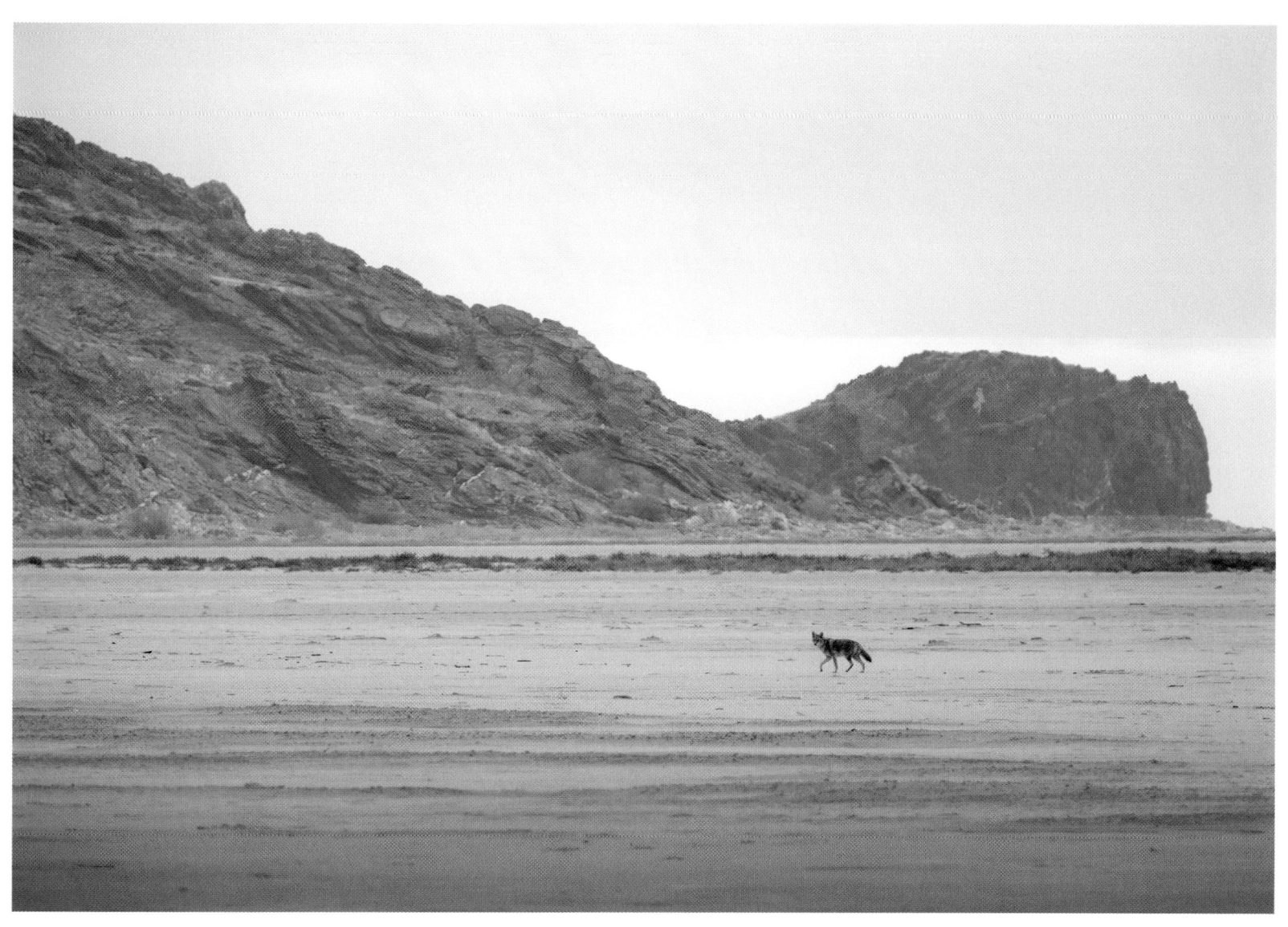

Scavenging on the beach, White Rock Bay
H3 | 12.27.2024

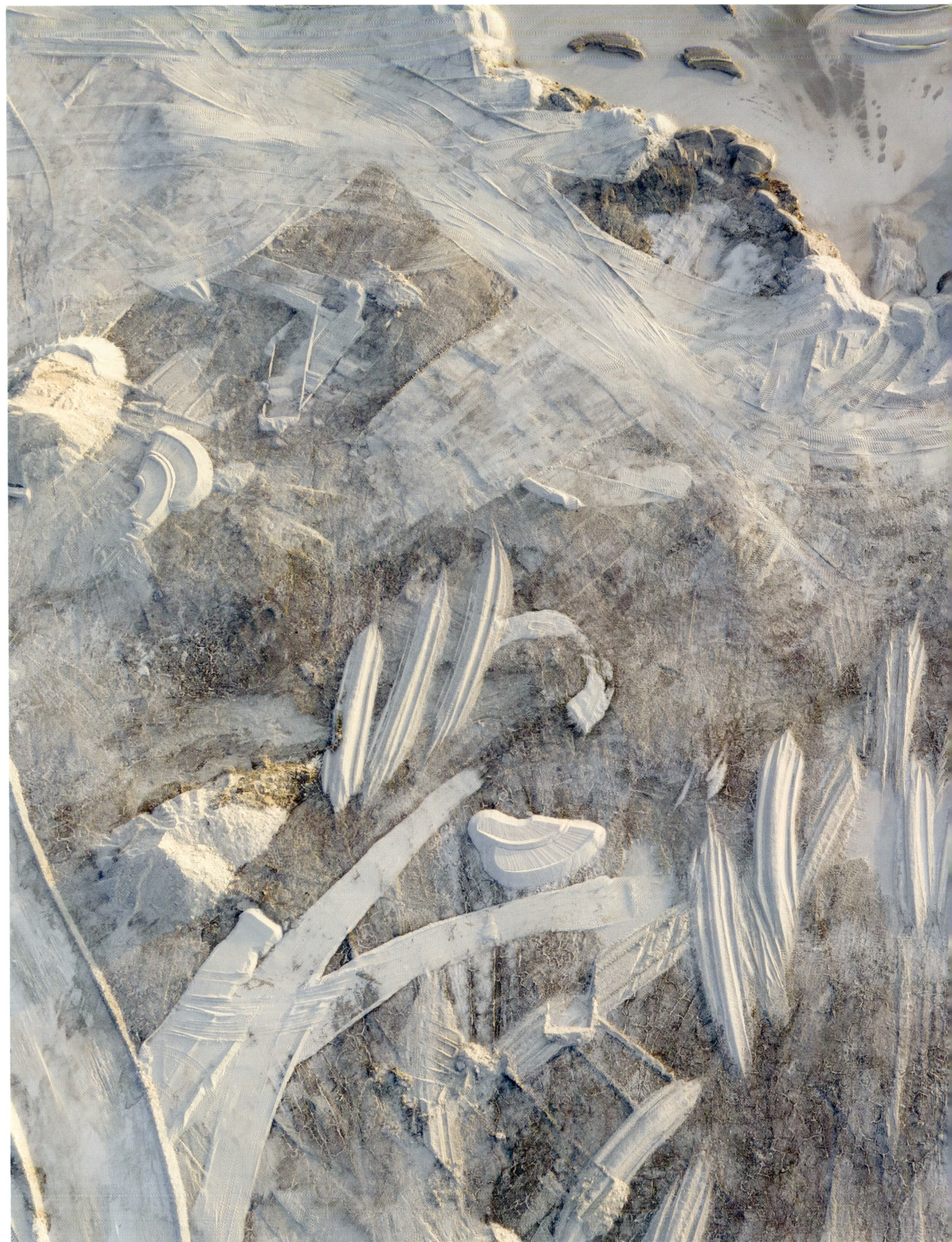

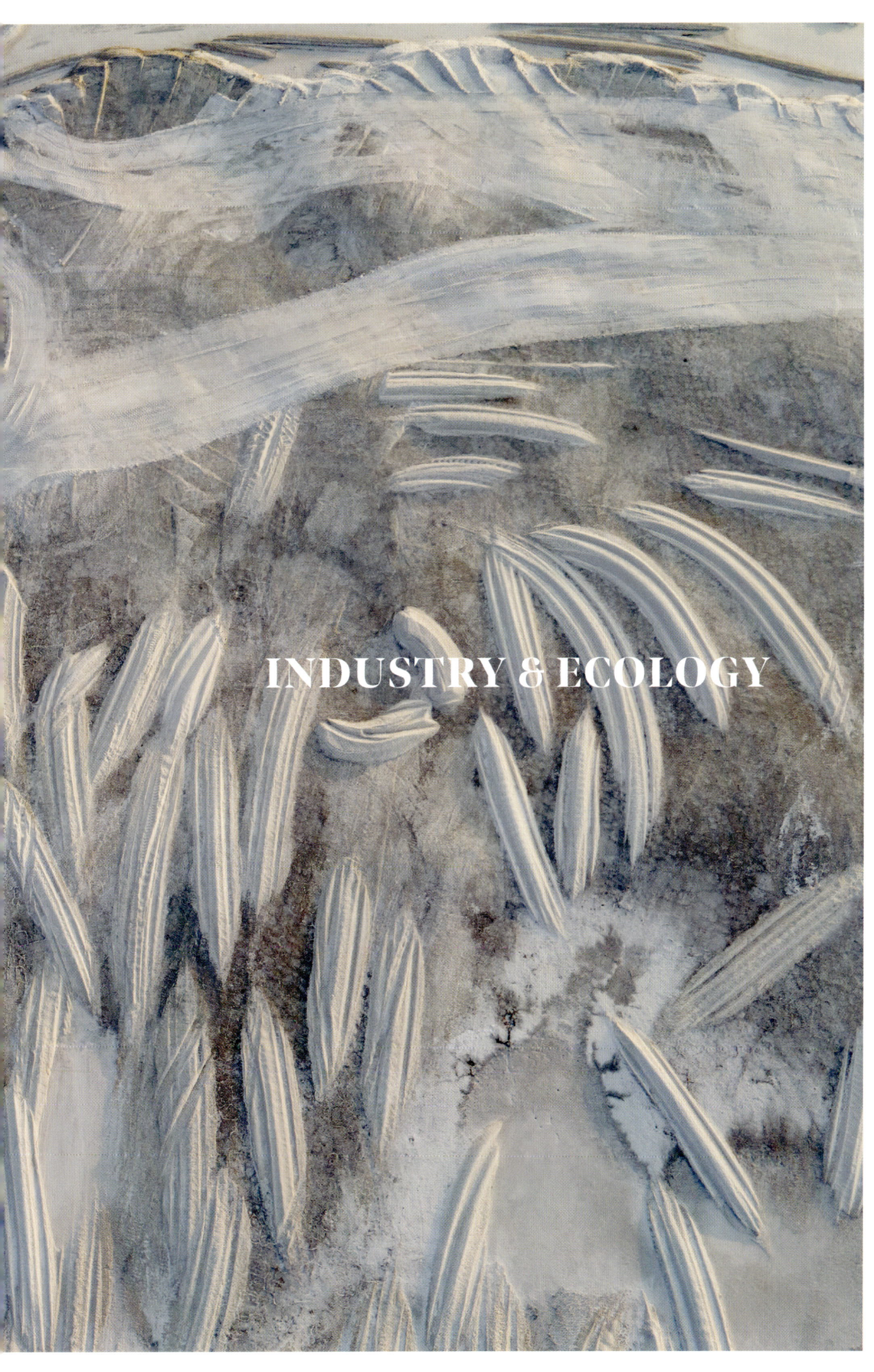

INDUSTRY & ECOLOGY

03.

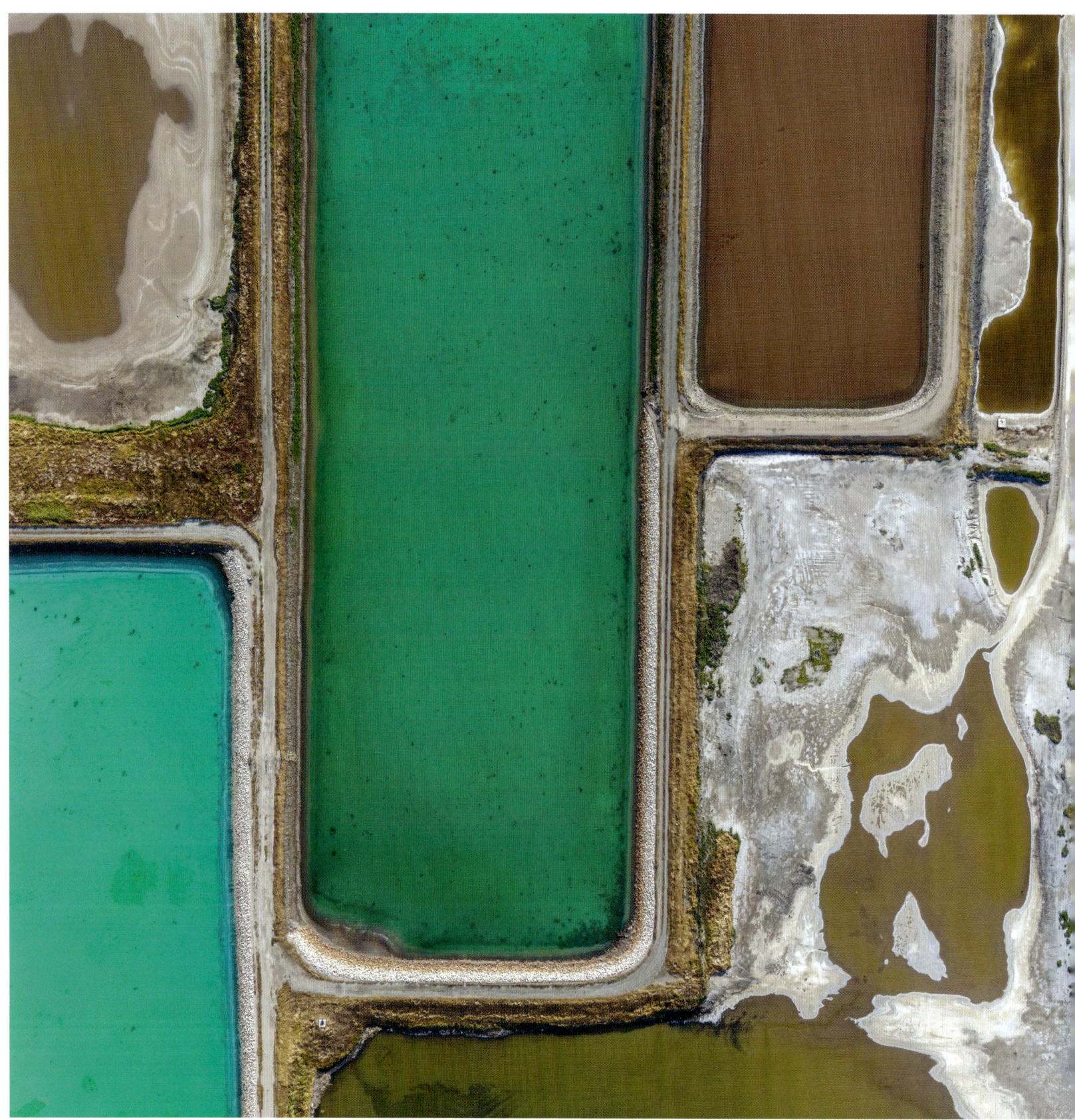

Great Salt Lake's Dilemma

GREAT SALT LAKE, with its perfect conditions for industrial use, is both a blessing and a burden. Its unique environment provides abundant resources that industries can draw from, yet this very exploitation poses significant threats to its ecological balance. Keeping the lake great means living up to our responsibilities as its caretakers, ensuring that industrial activities are regulated and sustainable.

Imagine the vast expanse of the lake, stretching out under a broad sky, divided by the structures of salt production. Morton Salt and Cargill have mastered the art of harvesting this essential mineral. Morton Salt's facility in Grantsville, Utah, has been in operation since 1918. The process begins by drawing saltwater into large, shallow ponds where the sun and wind evaporate the water, leaving behind pure salt crystals. These crystals are then harvested, washed, crushed, and screened into various forms, from the salt that graces our tables to industrial-grade salt that keeps our roads safe in winter.

Cargill's operations paint a similar picture of industry harmonizing with the environment. Spanning 10,000 acres, its ponds have scaled to meet demand. From the air, these vast evaporation ponds look like a colorful quilt, each section a different shade of white, pink, red or green depending on the minerals being concentrated.

Magnesium extraction is another significant industry, with US Magnesium producing 70,000 tons (63,500 tonnes) annually. Operating on the southwestern shore, US Magnesium is the only primary producer of magnesium metal in North America. However, this site has faced environmental challenges, becoming an Environmental Protection Agency Superfund site (a polluted area the US government cleans up because it's dangerous to people or the environment). The EPA has mandated measures to mitigate these impacts, including barrier walls and soil vapor assessments.

The extraction of other minerals, such as sulfate of potash (SOP), is also critical. Compass Minerals utilizes the lake's resources to produce this high-value fertilizer, essential for agriculture worldwide. Additionally, the lake is a significant source of brine shrimp, with operations like Great Salt Lake Artemia providing up to 40 percent of the global supply. These shrimp are crucial for aquaculture, feeding fish and other marine species in farms around the globe, thus supporting global food production.

The economic impact of these industries is profound. Collectively, they contribute approximately $1.9 billion annually to Utah's economy and support over 7,700 jobs. The lake's influence extends to enhancing the state's ski industry by contributing to lake effect snow, adding another $1.2 billion and 20,000 jobs to the state's economy.

The greatness of Great Salt Lake lies in its ability to integrate ecological diversity with economic vitality. Each industry, from salt production to brine shrimp harvesting, exemplifies the lake's value. As these industries continue to evolve, the challenge remains to balance economic activities with ecological preservation, ensuring that the lake remains a vital and sustainable resource in the future. This means meaningful regulation and a commitment to sustainable practices to truly honor our role as caretakers of the lake.

Brine storage ponds, Compass Minerals | E8 | 06.03.2024
PREVIOUS PAGE: Piles of salt, Morton Salt | K6 | 05.21.2023

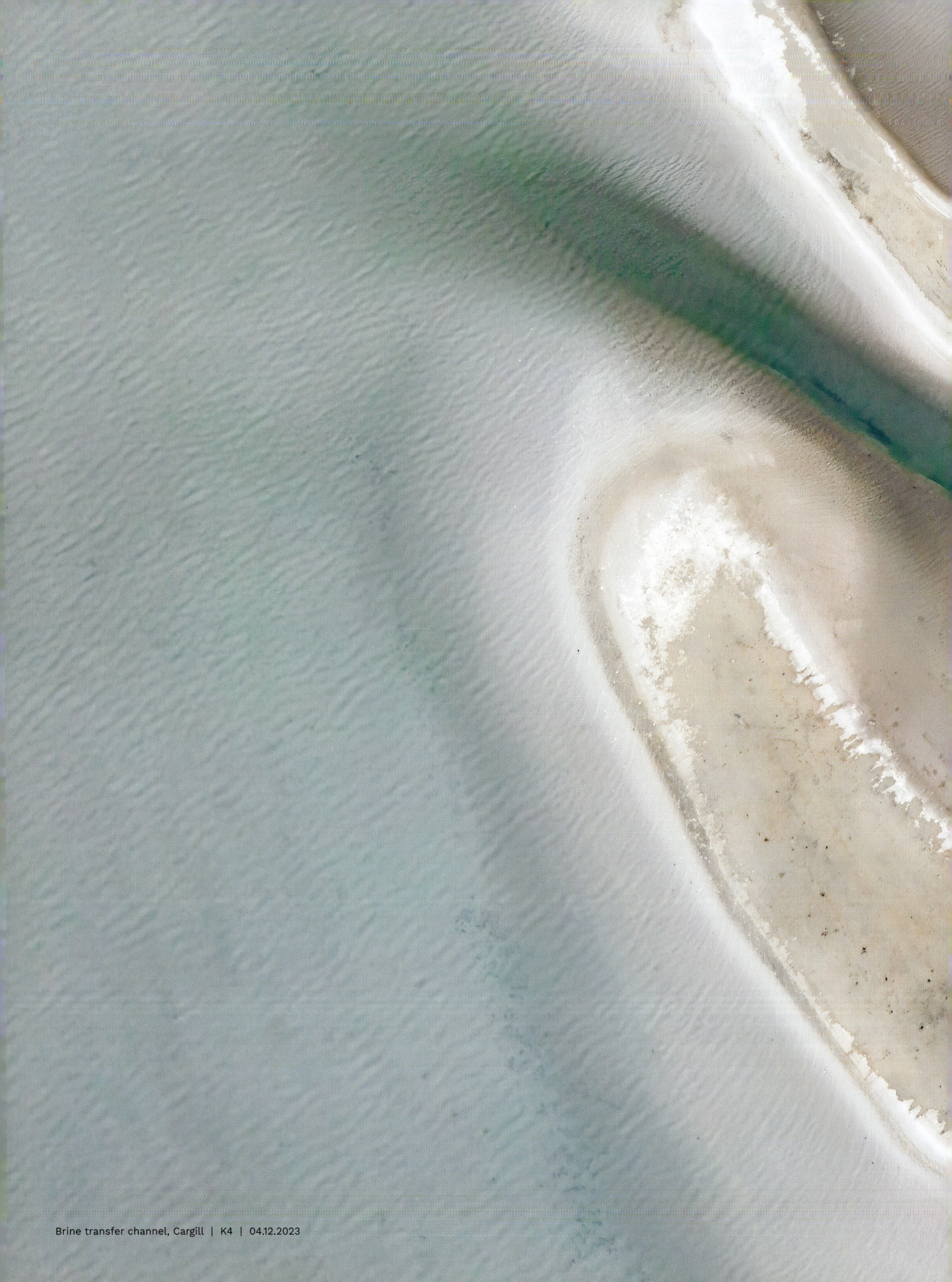

Brine transfer channel, Cargill | K4 | 04.12.2023

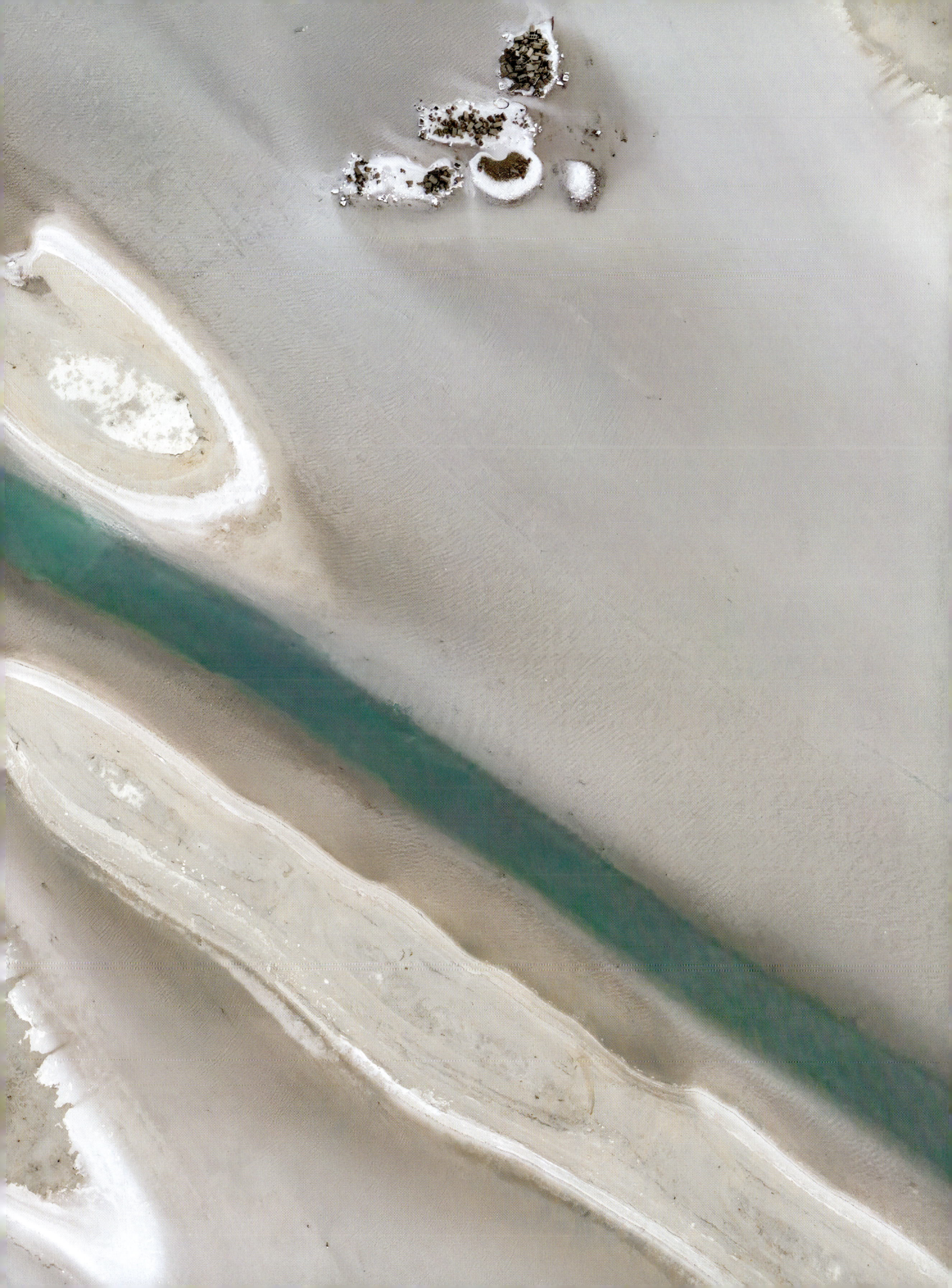

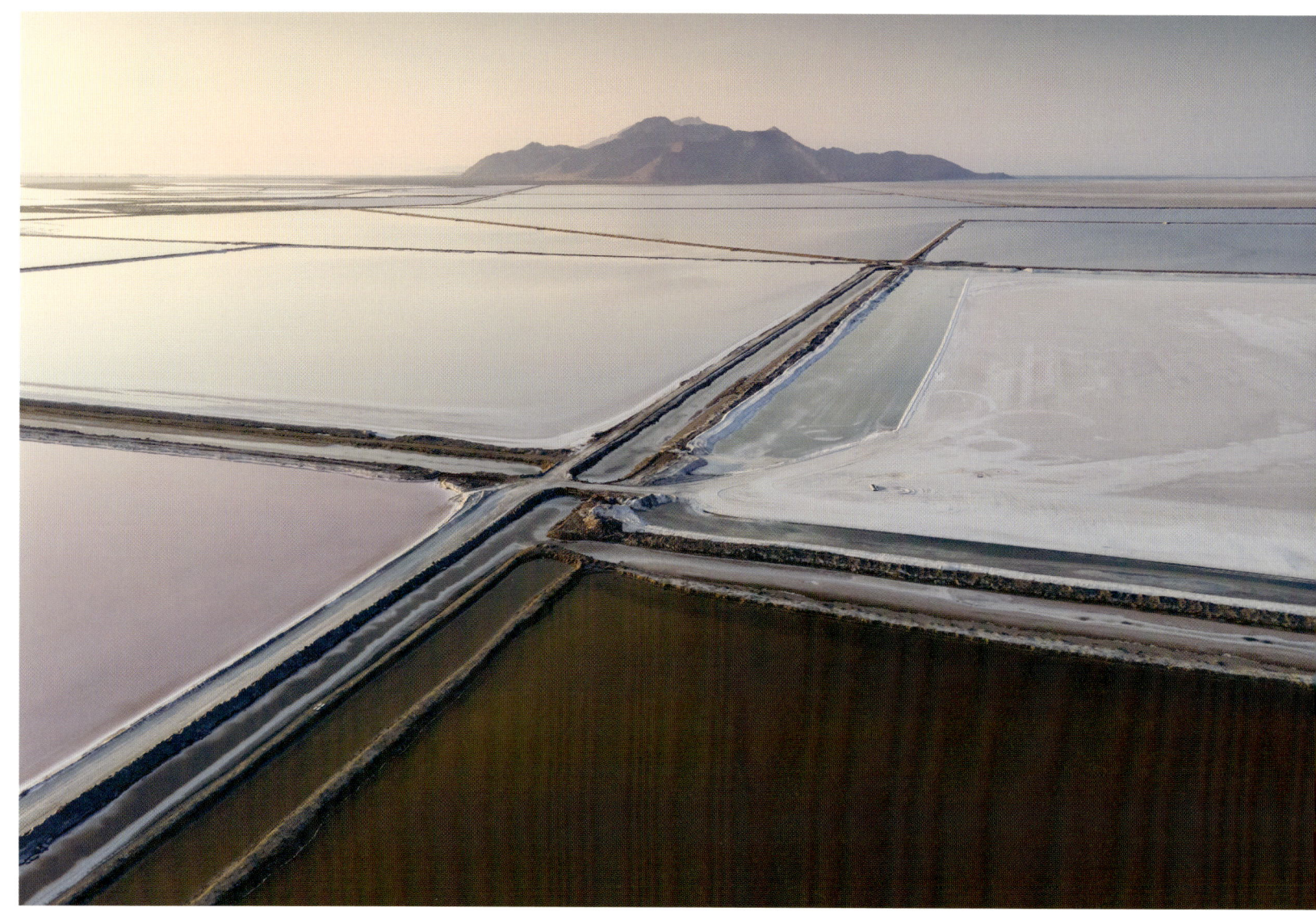

HOW SALT IS HARVESTED FROM GREAT SALT LAKE

Mining salt from Great Salt Lake is an intricate process that leverages the unique properties of the lake's saline-rich environment. Great Salt Lake is one of the largest sources of mineral salts in the world, and the extraction process begins with the creation of vast evaporation ponds. These ponds, which can span thousands of acres, are essentially shallow pools where lake water is channeled and allowed to evaporate under the hot Utah sun. As the water evaporates, it leaves behind concentrated brine, which is progressively moved through a series of ponds to further increase its salinity.

Once the brine reaches a critical concentration, the salt begins to crystallize. Workers then use specialized machinery to harvest the salt crystals from the pond beds. This raw salt is initially coarse and impure, so it undergoes several stages of washing and purification to remove impurities and achieve the desired quality. The purified salt is then dried and processed into various forms, such as table salt, road salt, or industrial salt, depending on its intended use.

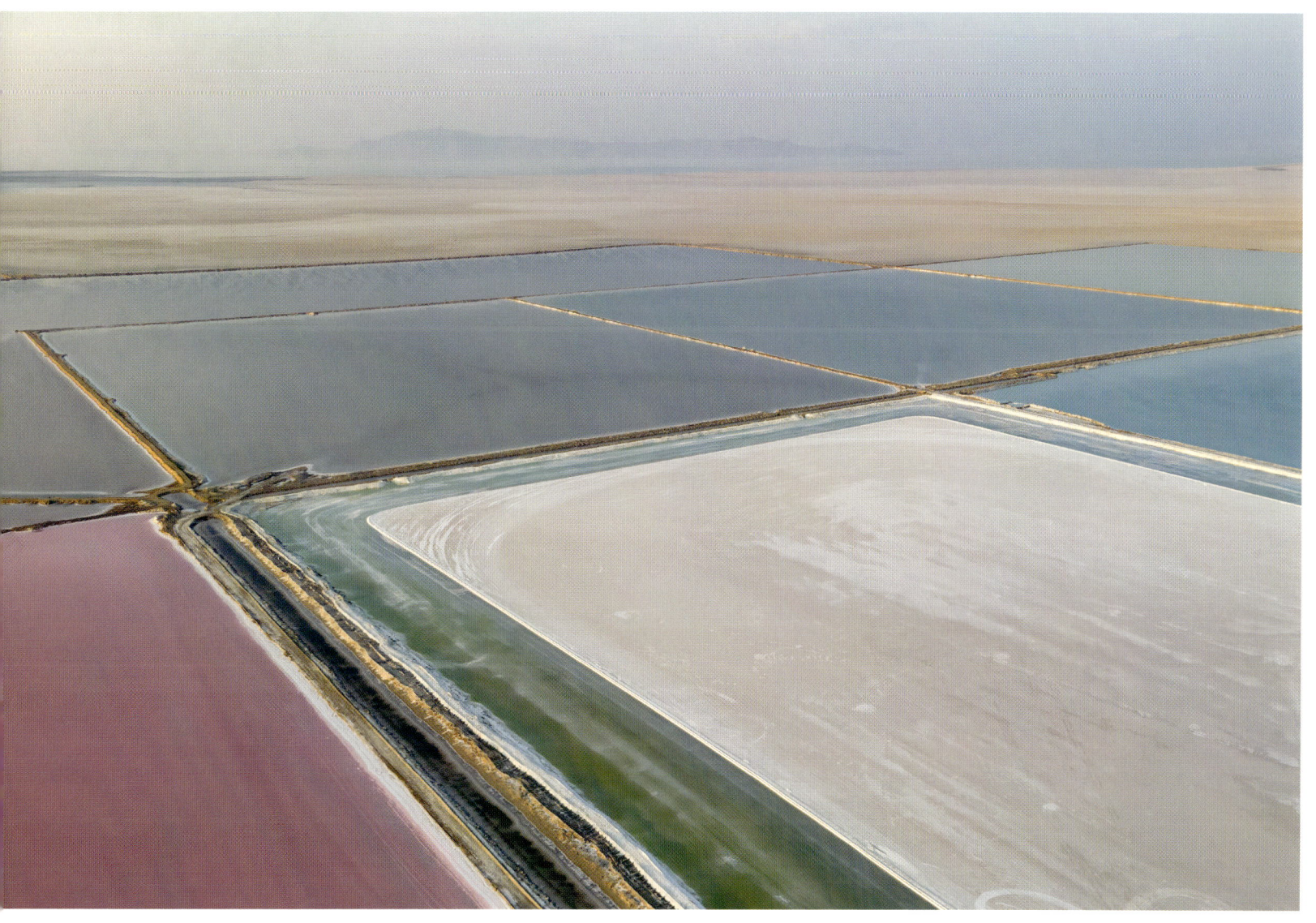

Morton Salt evaporation ponds
K6 | 05.21.2023

Morton Salt evaporation ponds
K6 | 05.21.2023

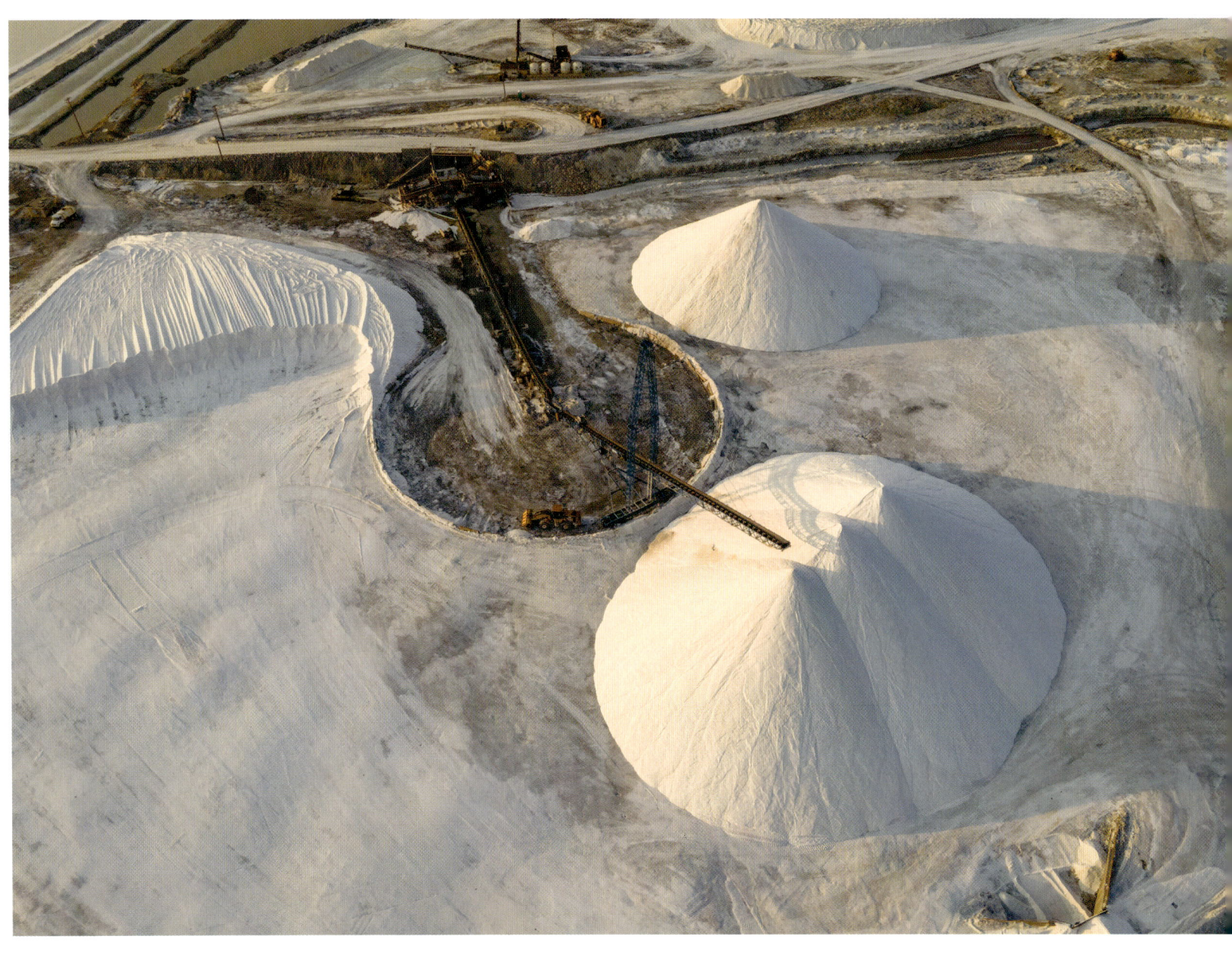

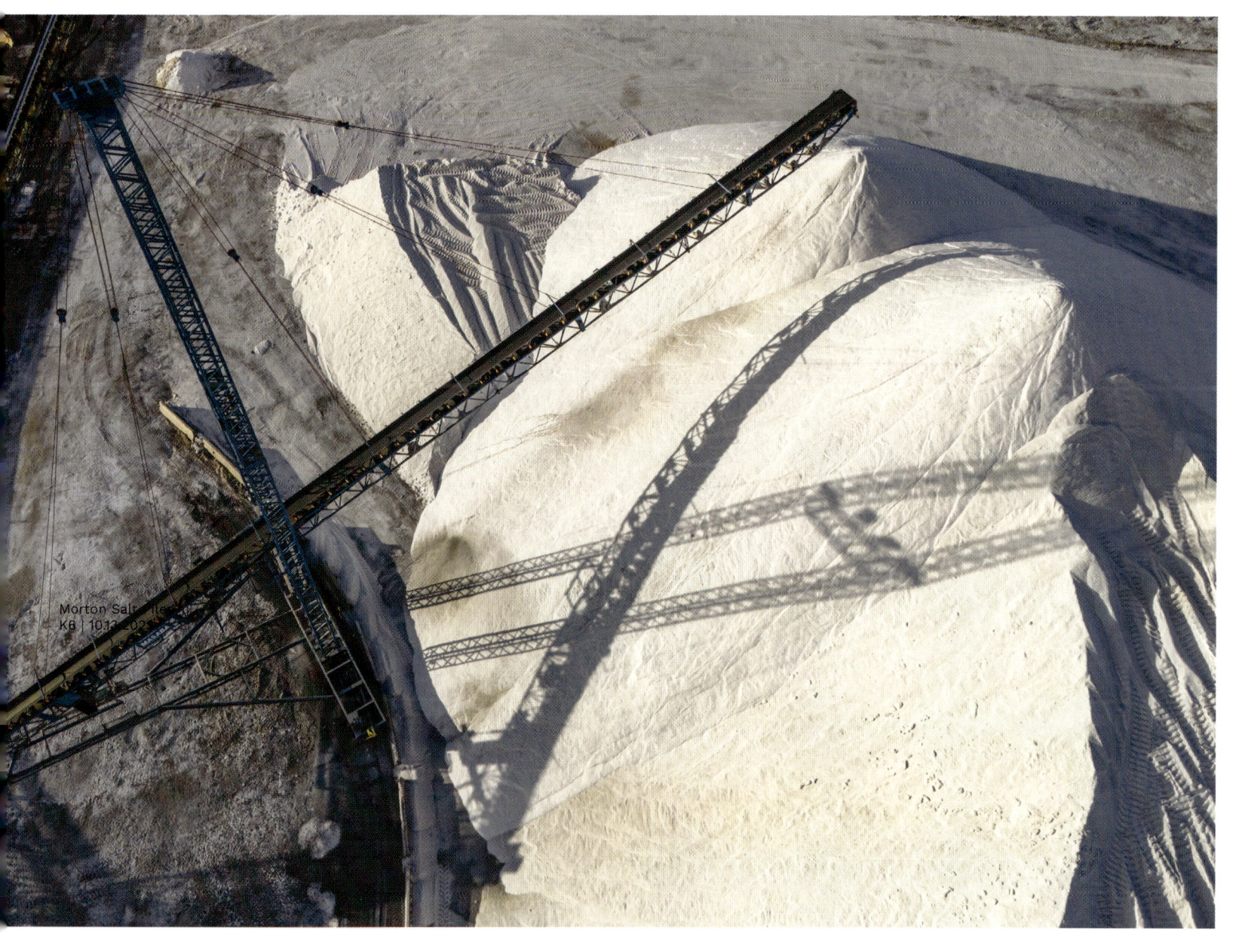

Morton Salt piles
K6 | 10.13.2023

Morton salt piles | K6 | 10.13.2023
Morton Salt conveyer belt | K6 | 04.20.2024

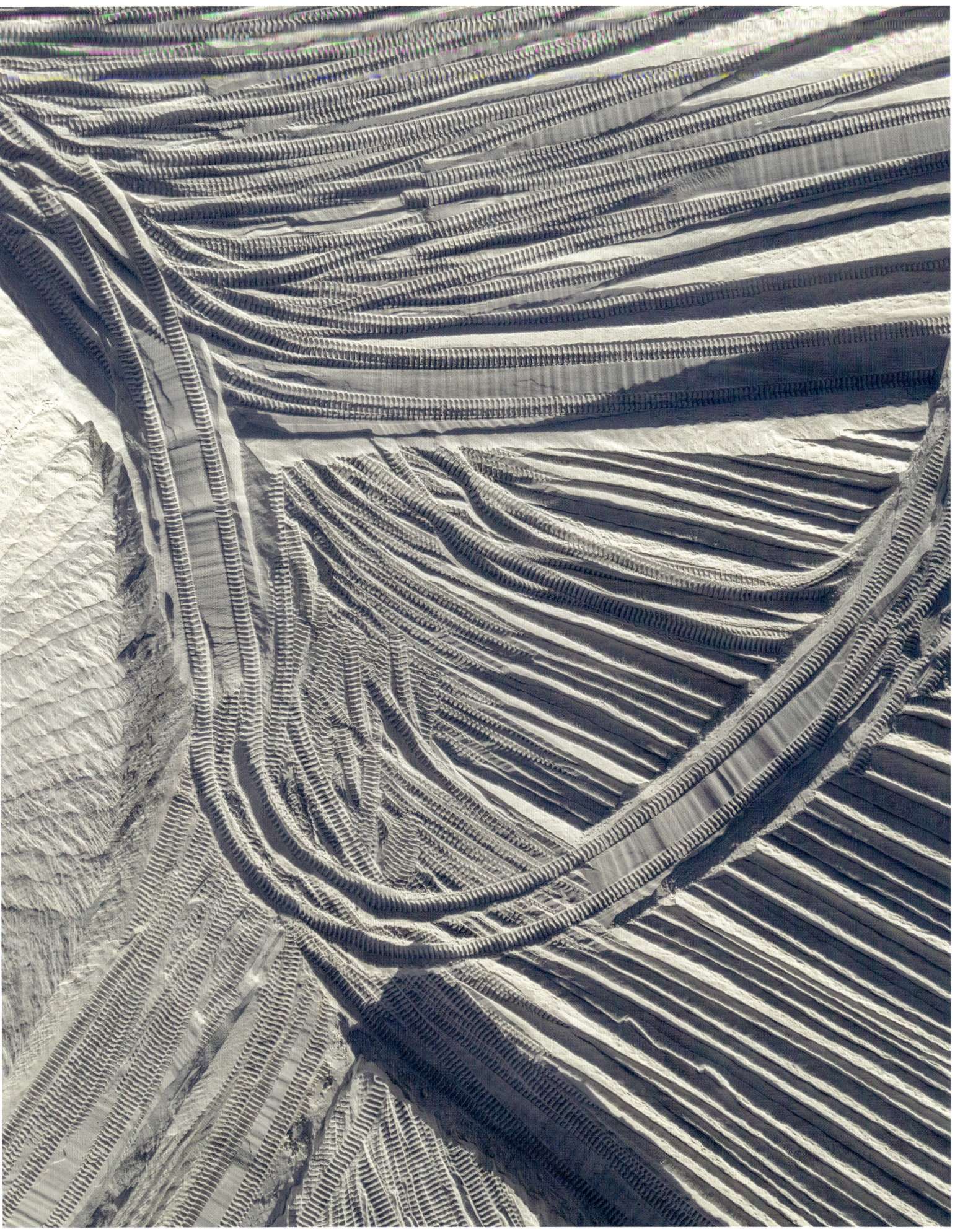

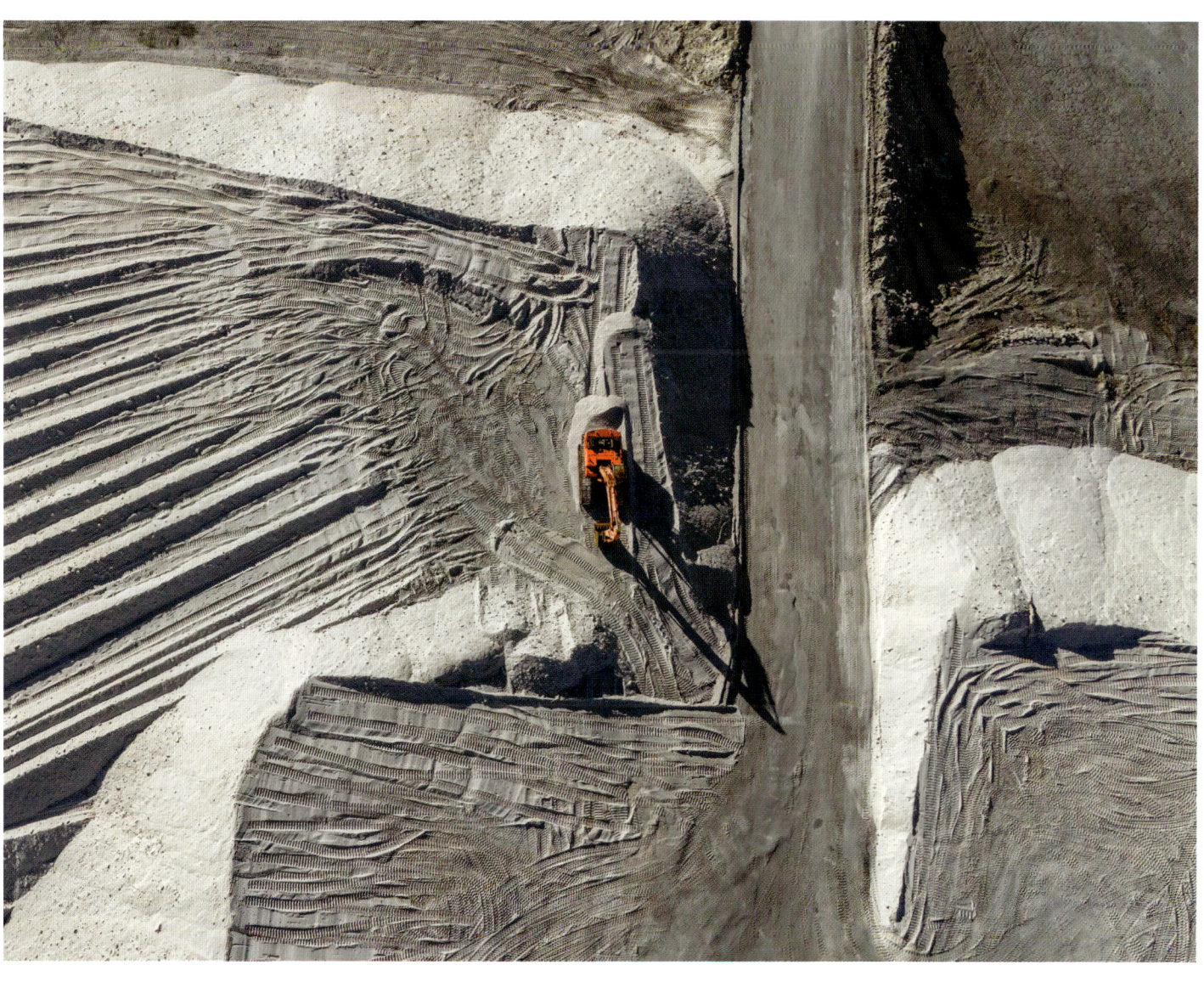

Dozer tracks on a salt pile, Morton Salt | K6 | 04.20.2024
Harvesting machinery, Cargill | K5 | 02.25.2024

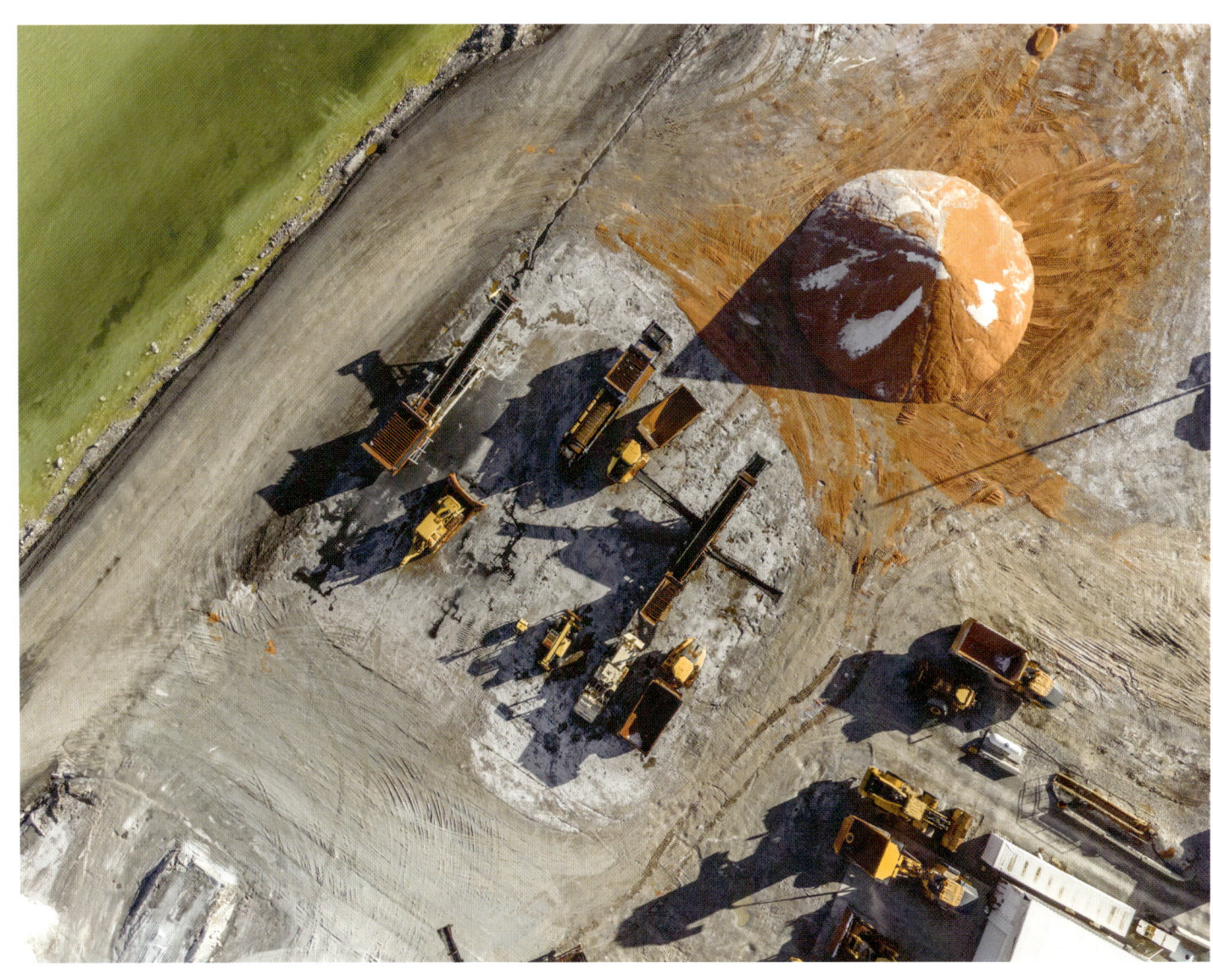

Harvesting machinery, Cargill | K5 | 02.25.2024
Salt scraping, Cargill | K5 | 02.25.2024

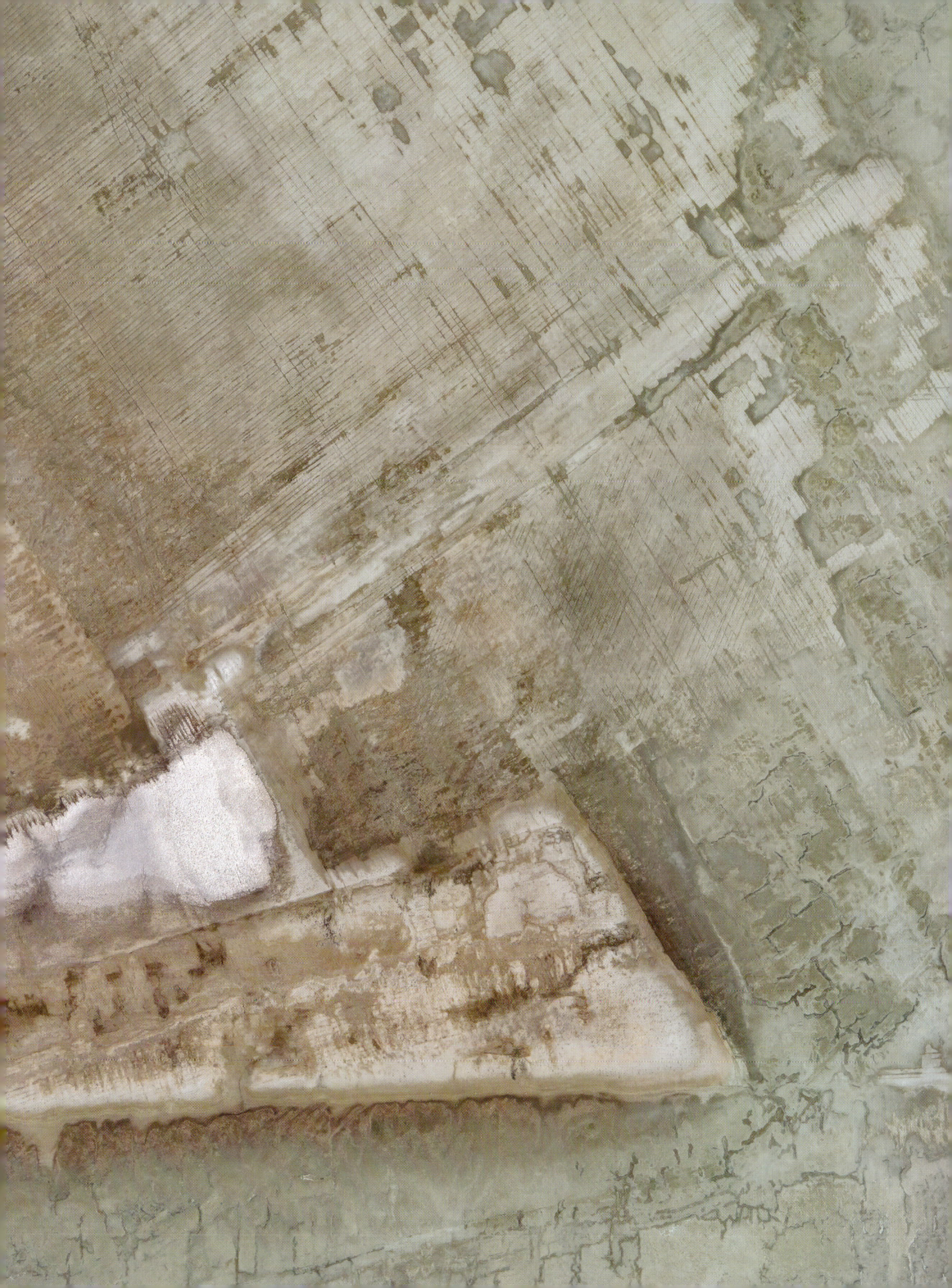

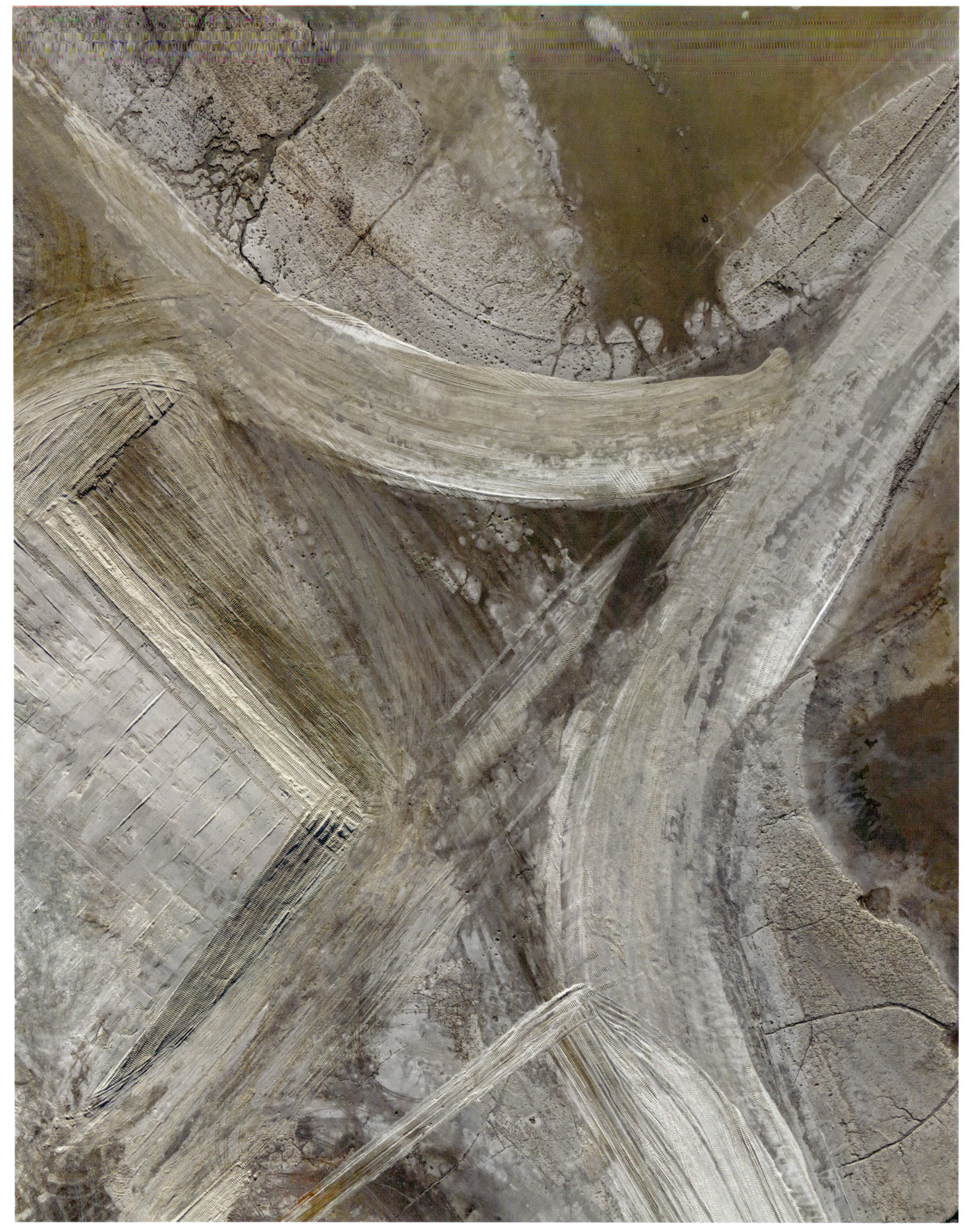

Salt scraping, Cargill | K5 | 02.25.2024

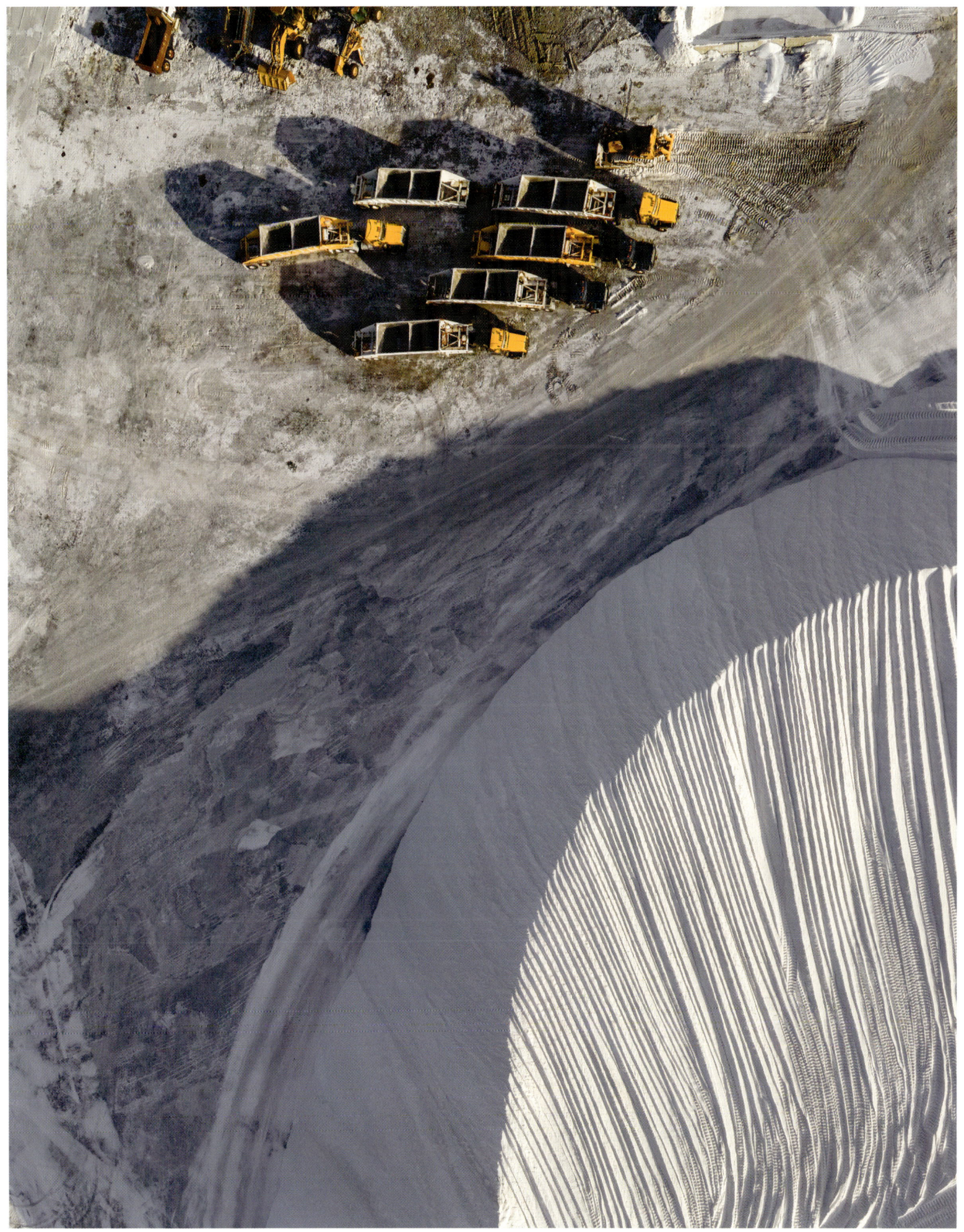

Harvesting machinery, Morton Salt | K6 | 04.20.2024

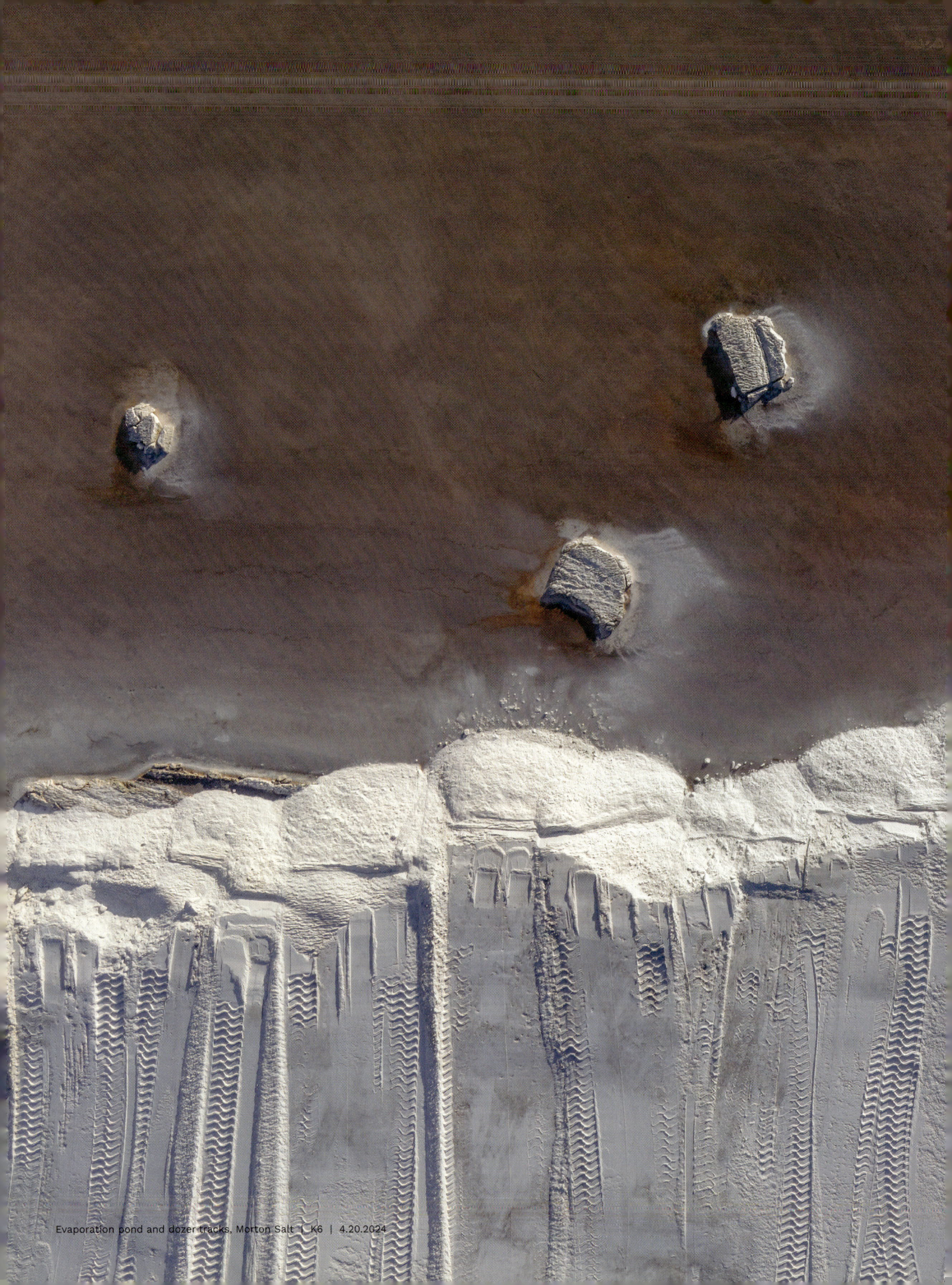

Evaporation pond and dozer tracks, Morton Salt | K6 | 4.20.2024

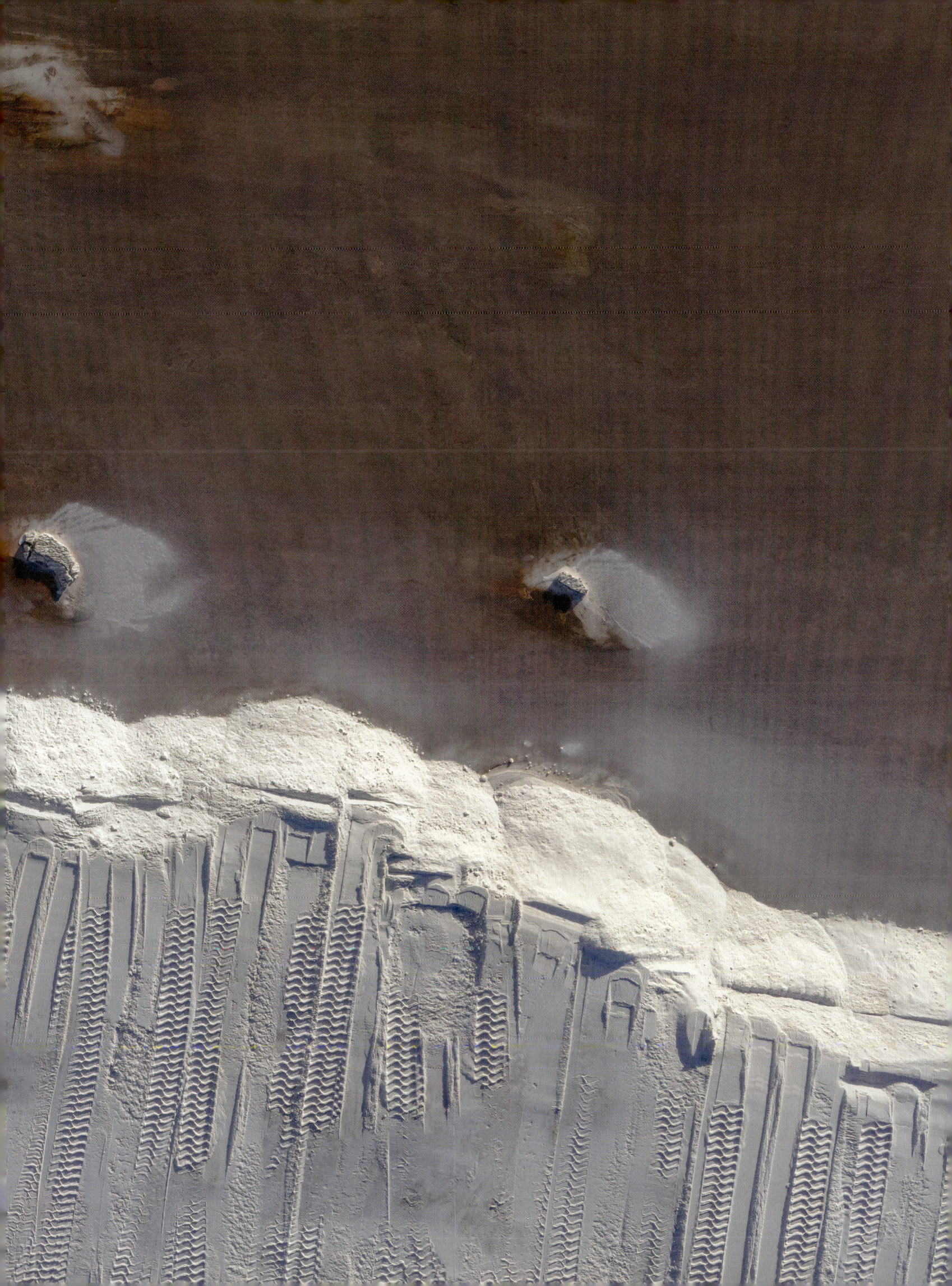

HOW MAGNESIUM IS HARVESTED AT GREAT SALT LAKE

At US Magnesium in Utah, the production of magnesium from Great Salt Lake is a complex and highly specialized process that capitalizes on the lake's rich mineral content. The process begins with the extraction of magnesium chloride–rich brine from the lake. This brine is concentrated through a series of solar evaporation ponds, much like the salt extraction process. The sun and wind help evaporate the water, leaving behind increasingly concentrated magnesium chloride. These evaporation ponds cover a vast area, spanning thousands of acres, to ensure sufficient production capacity.

Crucial components of this process are the deep brine storage tanks, which play several key roles in ensuring efficient and stable magnesium production. These tanks serve as reservoirs for the concentrated brine, providing a buffer to manage fluctuations in brine concentration and production rates. They ensure a continuous and consistent feed of high-concentration magnesium chloride to the electrolytic cells where the actual magnesium extraction occurs.

Once the brine reaches the desired concentration and quality, it undergoes electrolysis at the US Magnesium plant. During this process, an electric current is passed through the magnesium chloride, causing it to decompose into magnesium metal and chlorine gas. Magnesium metal collects at the cathode, while chlorine gas is released at the anode. This raw magnesium is then collected and cast into ingots or further processed into various forms.

Unfortunately, US Magnesium has faced significant environmental compliance issues. The company has been involved in several legal and regulatory battles due to improper waste disposal practices. The EPA and the Department of Justice (DOJ) have reached settlements with US Magnesium to address violations of hazardous waste regulations. These settlements require the company to implement extensive process modifications to reduce environmental impacts, including constructing barrier walls and filtration plants to treat wastewater and providing financial assurance for future cleanup and closure costs. These measures aim to mitigate the environmental damage caused by the facility's operations and protect the health of workers and the surrounding ecosystem.

As of December of 2024, US Magnesium's leadership is now overseen by a court-appointed receiver following legal and environmental compliance issues, as ordered by a Utah judge. This action aligns with broader efforts by the Utah Legislature to enforce stricter environmental regulations, particularly around Great Salt Lake.

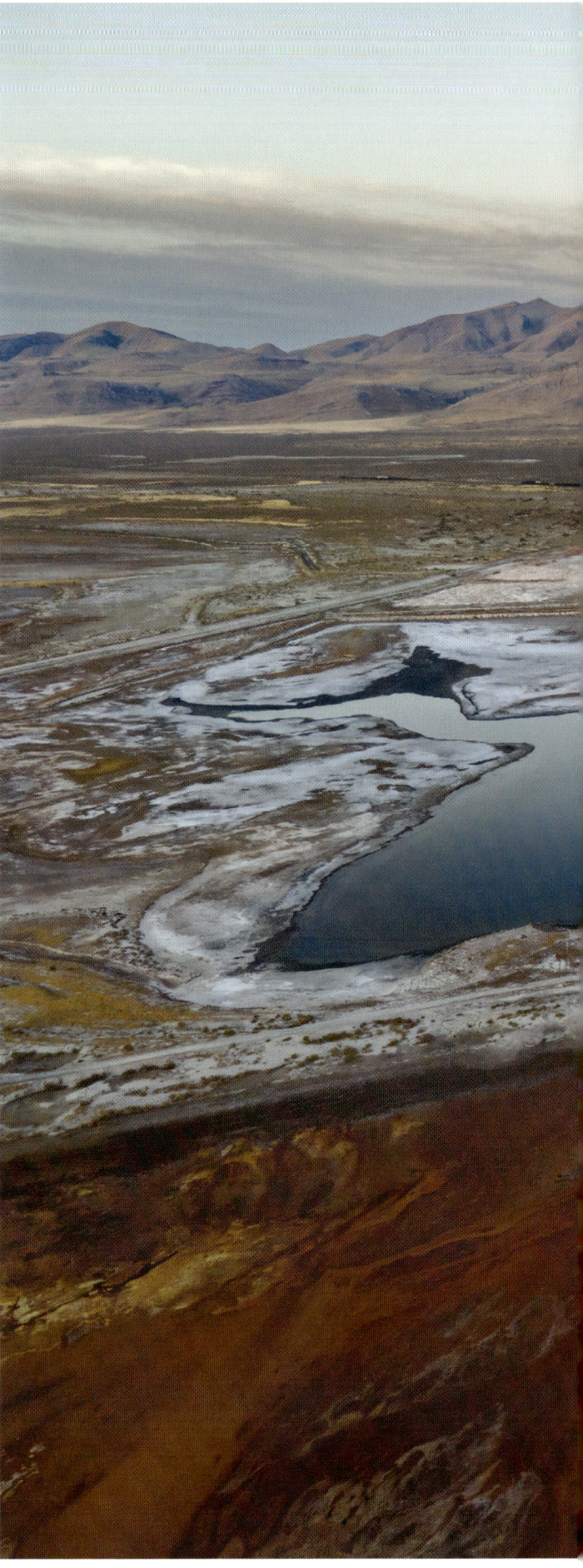

US Magnesium facility | 14 | 03.24.2024

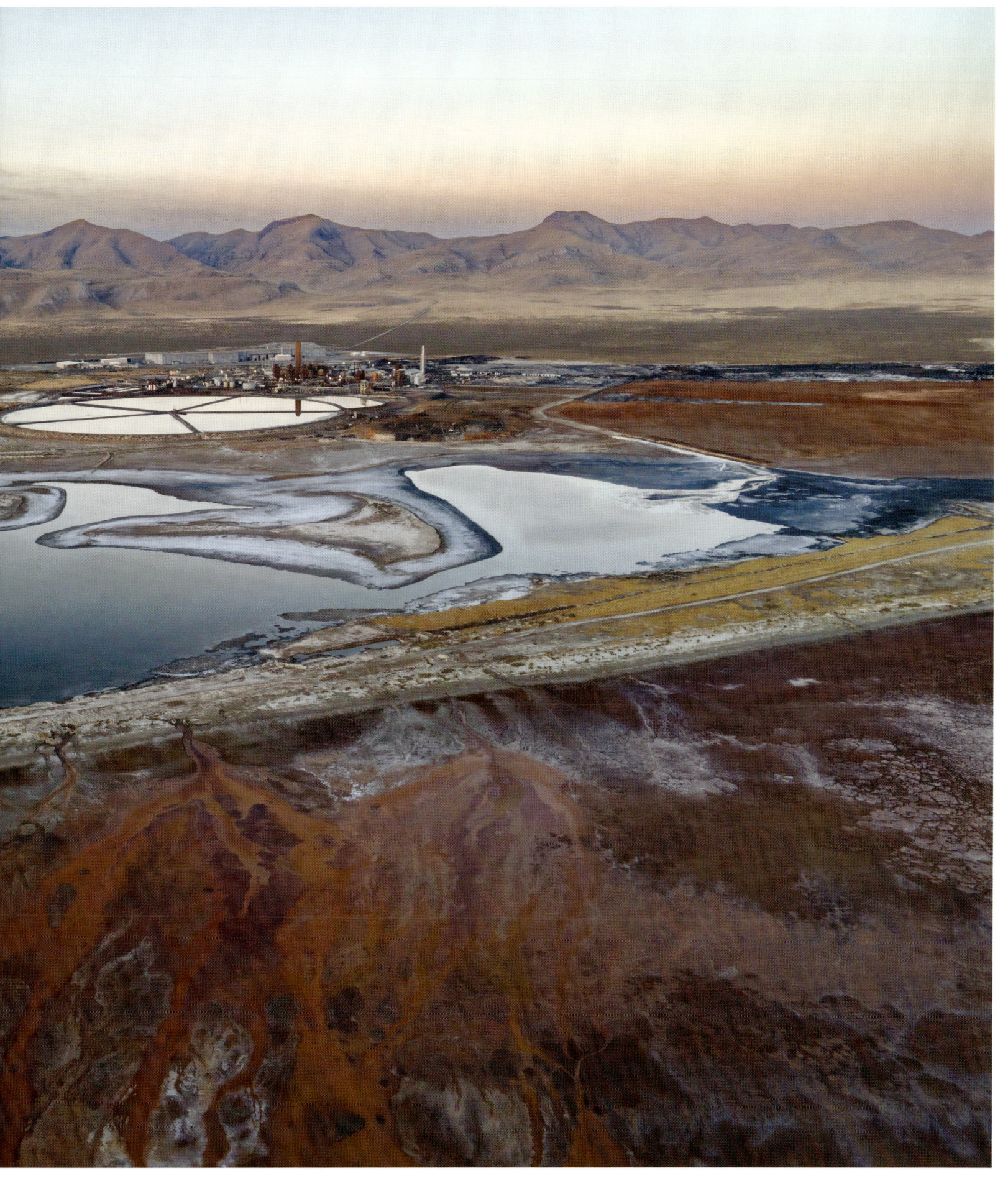

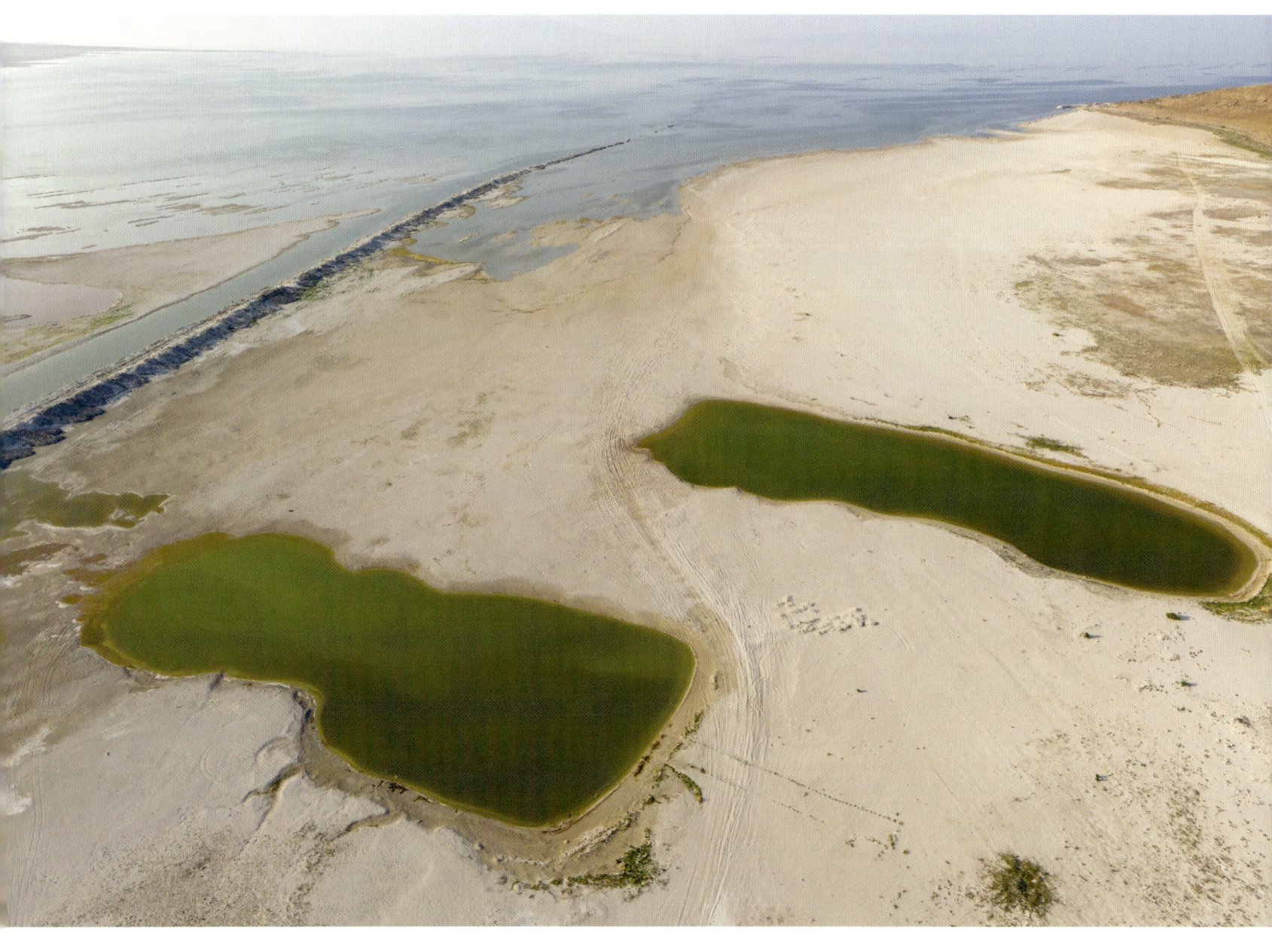

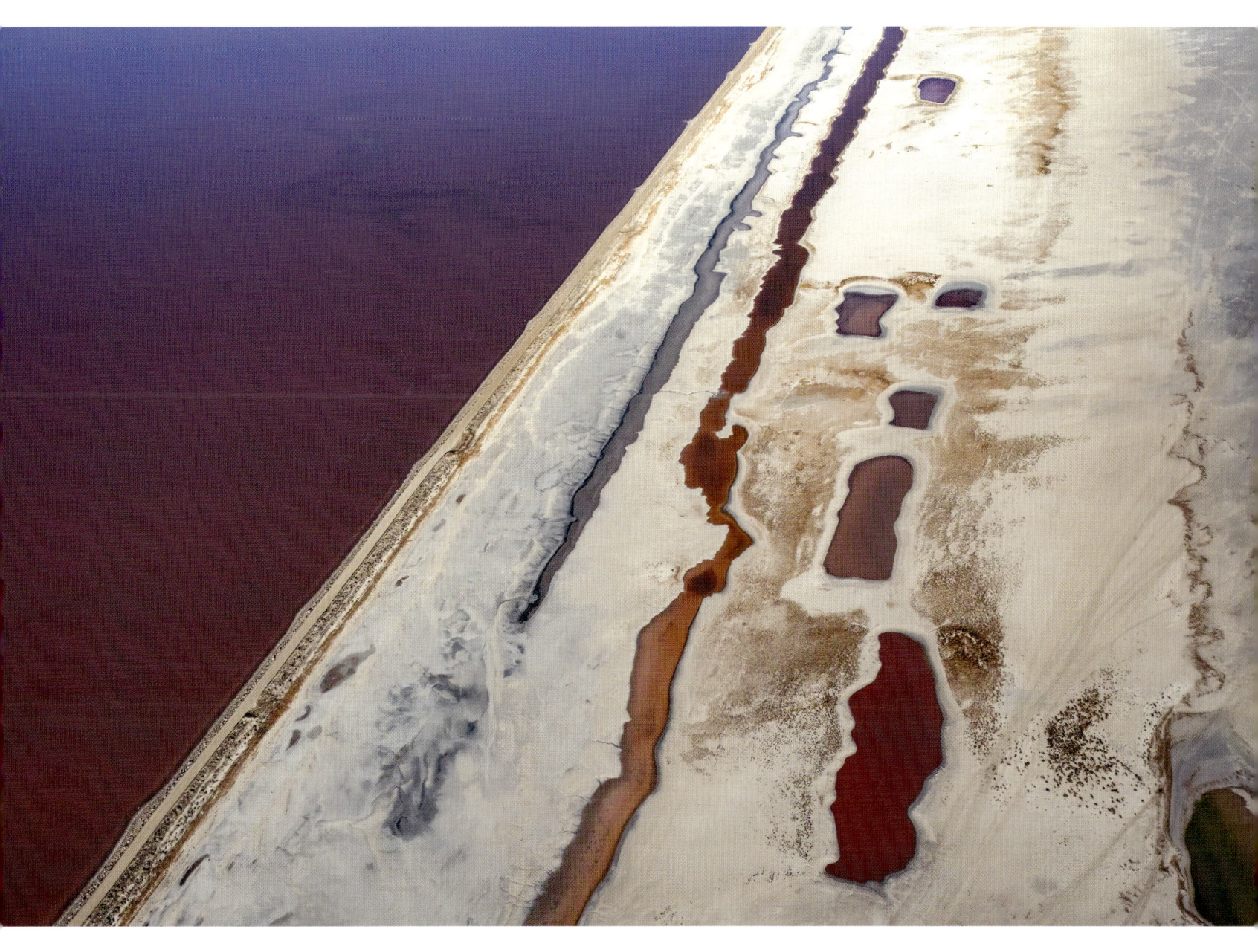

Brine pools from 656 feet (200 m), US Magnesium | I5 | 05.21.2023

Brine pools next to Stansbury Bay from 7,000 feet (2,134 m), US Magnesium | I5 | 10.13.2023

FOLLOWING PAGE: Deep brine storage from 100 feet (30 m), US Magnesium | I4 | 10.12.2024

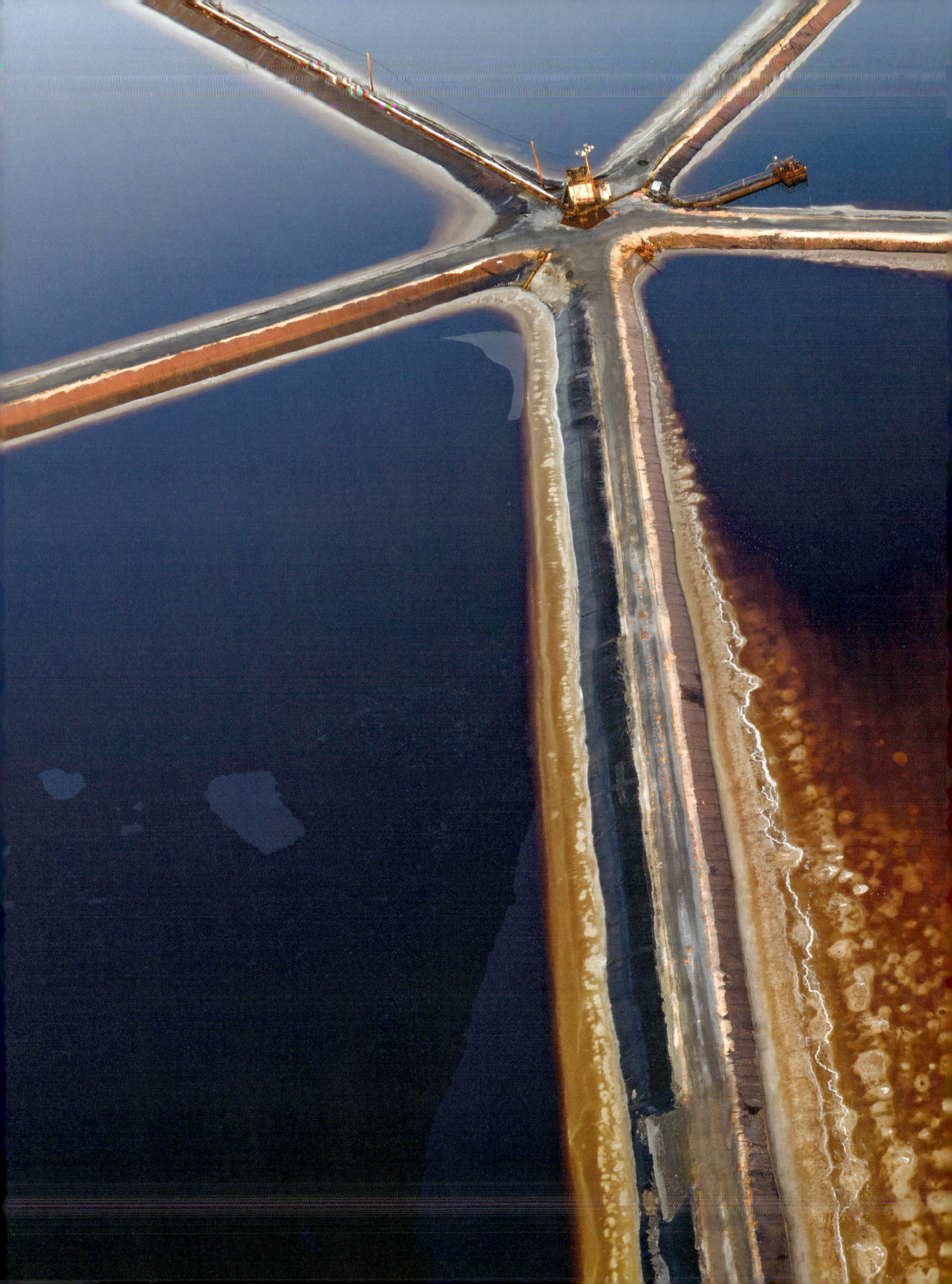

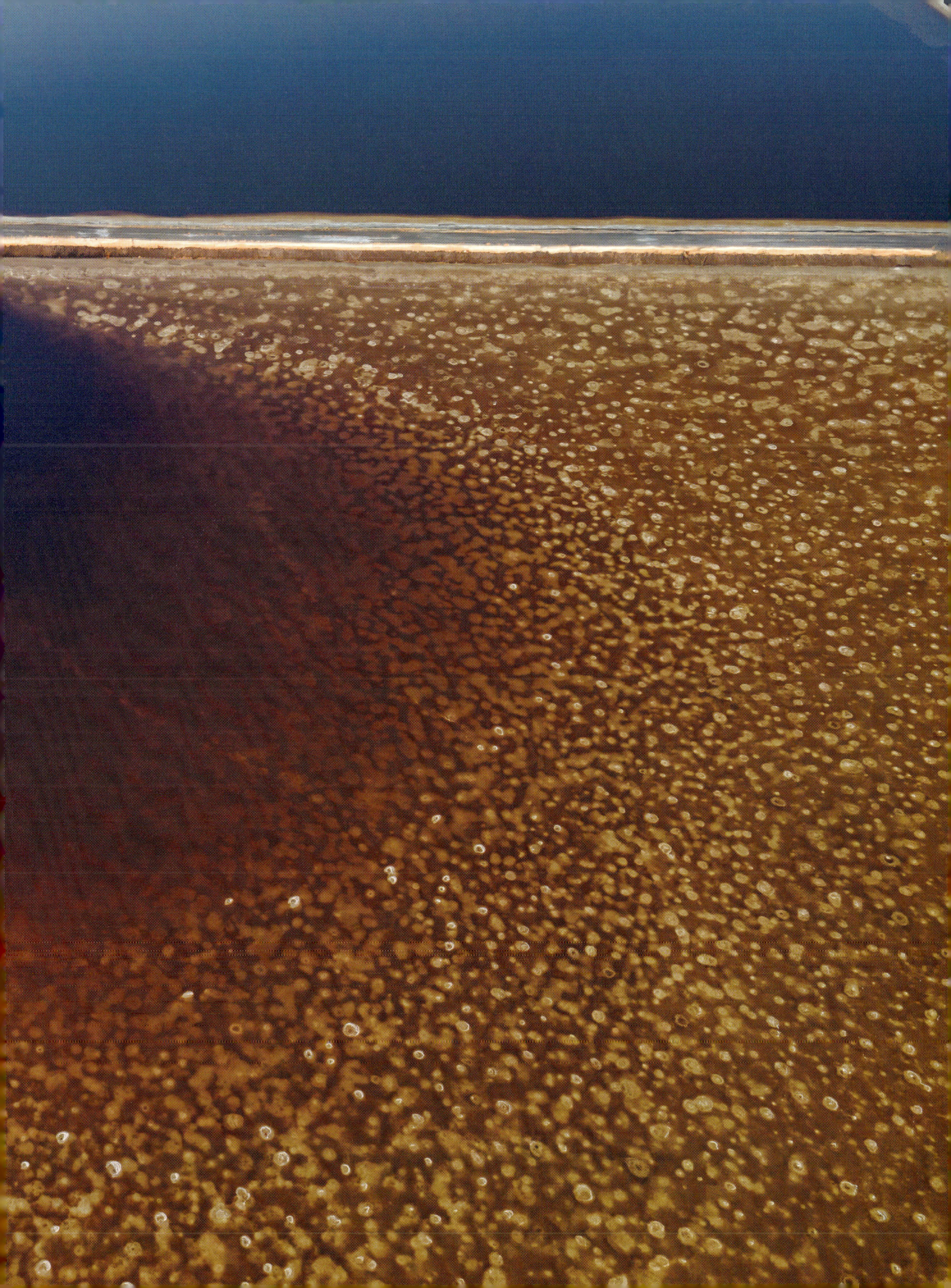

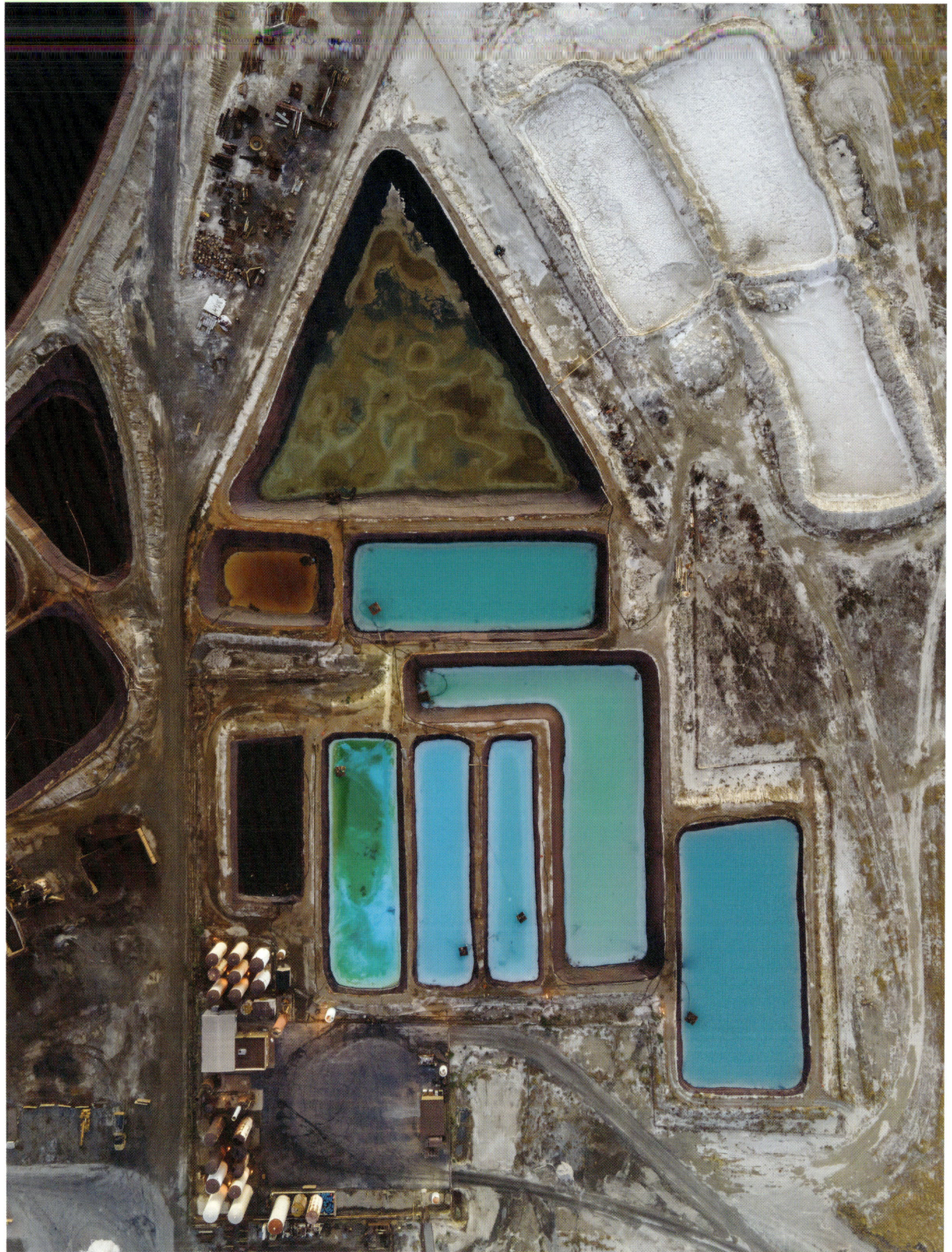

US Magnesium, brine storage ponds from 656 feet (200 m) | I4 | 10.12.2024

US Magnesium, iron oxide cat | I4 | 03.12.2024

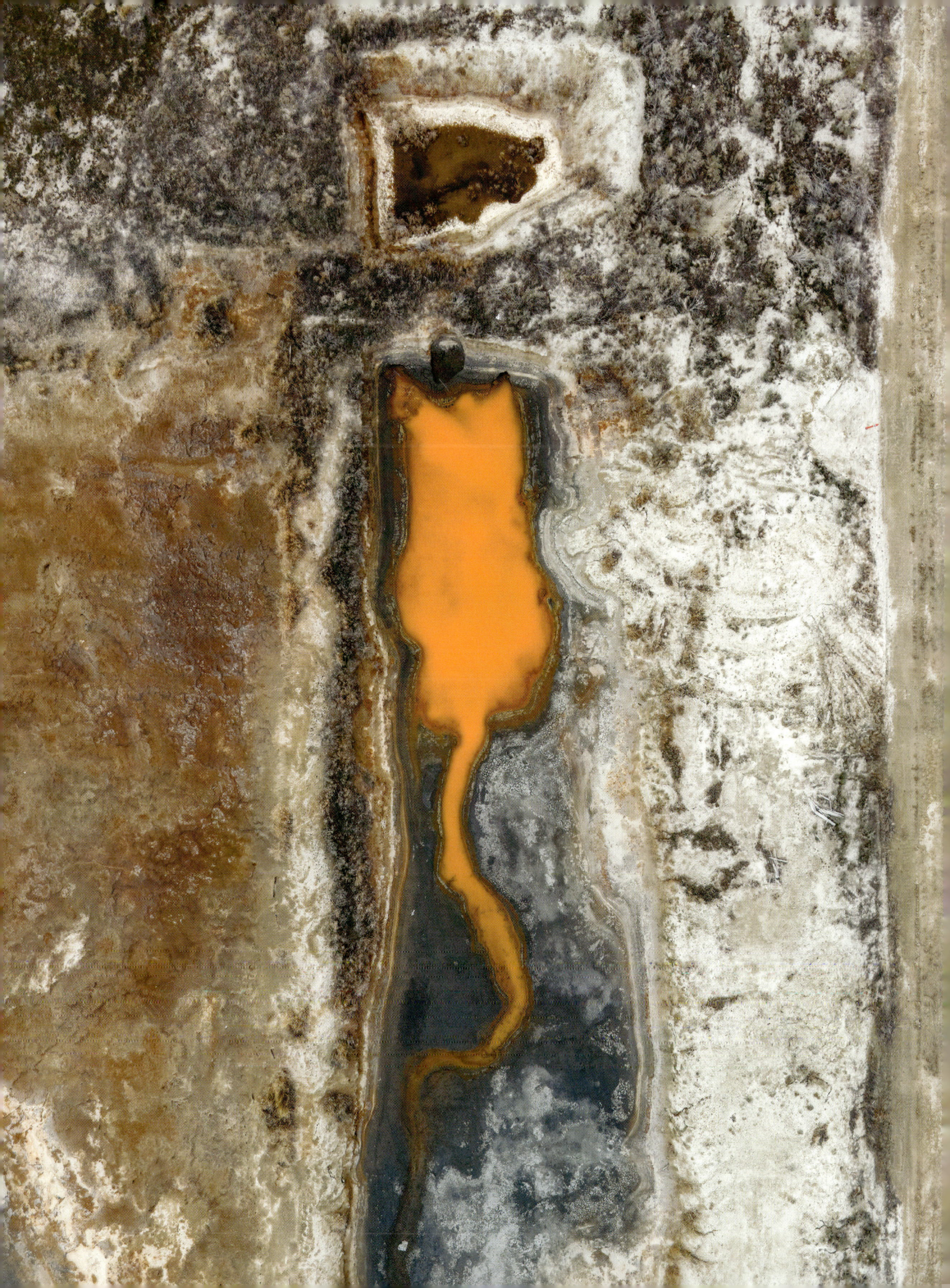

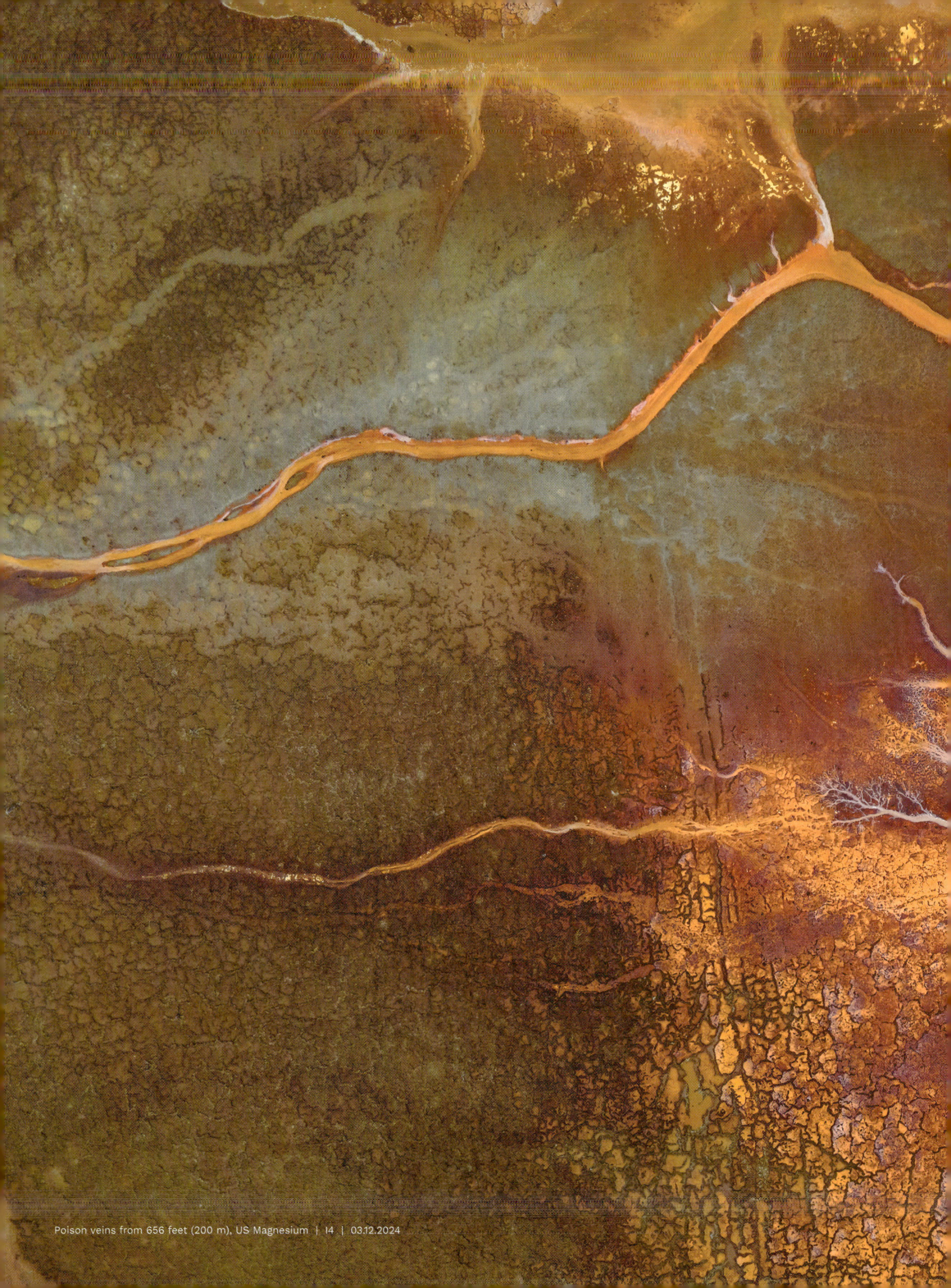

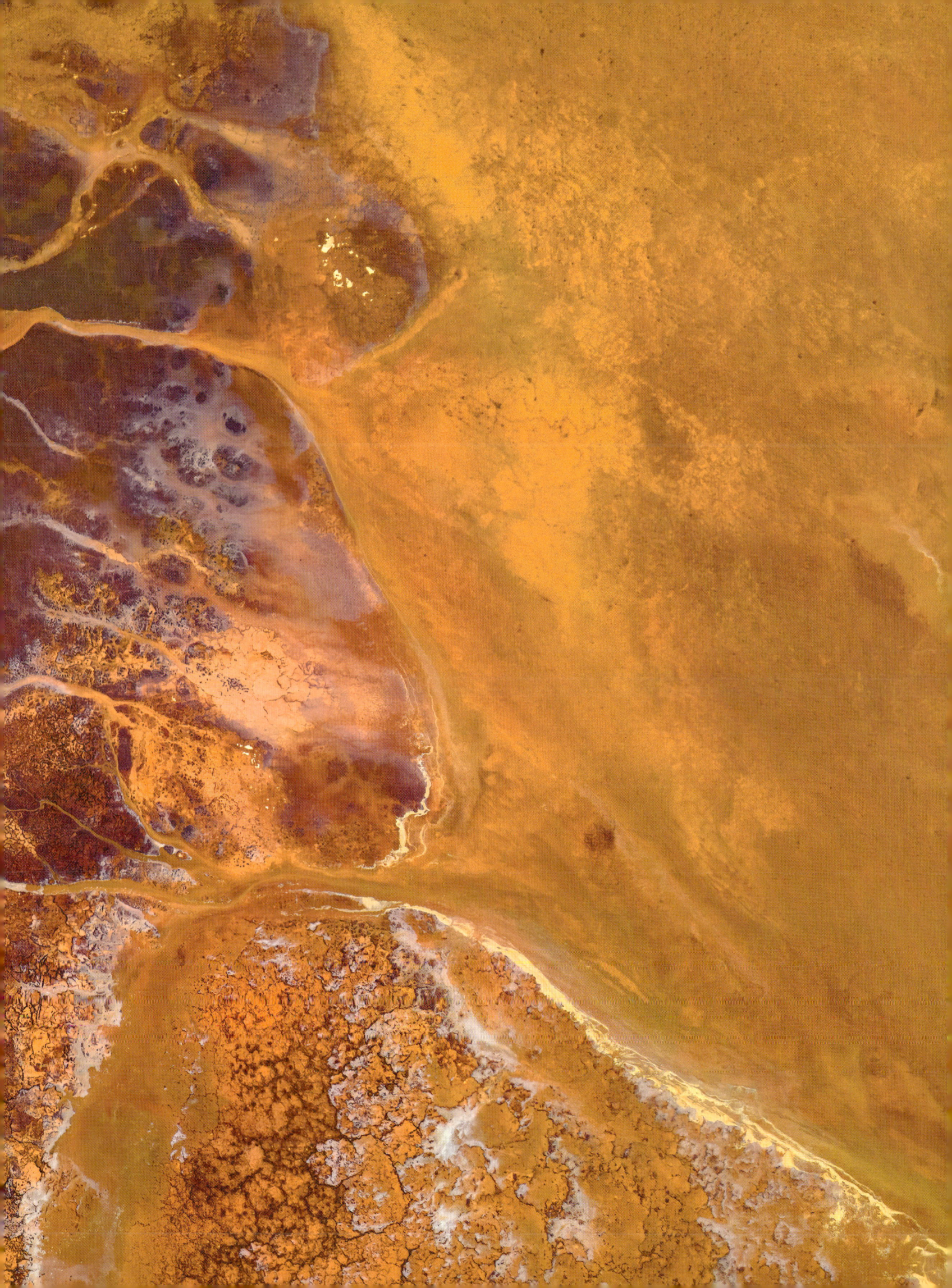

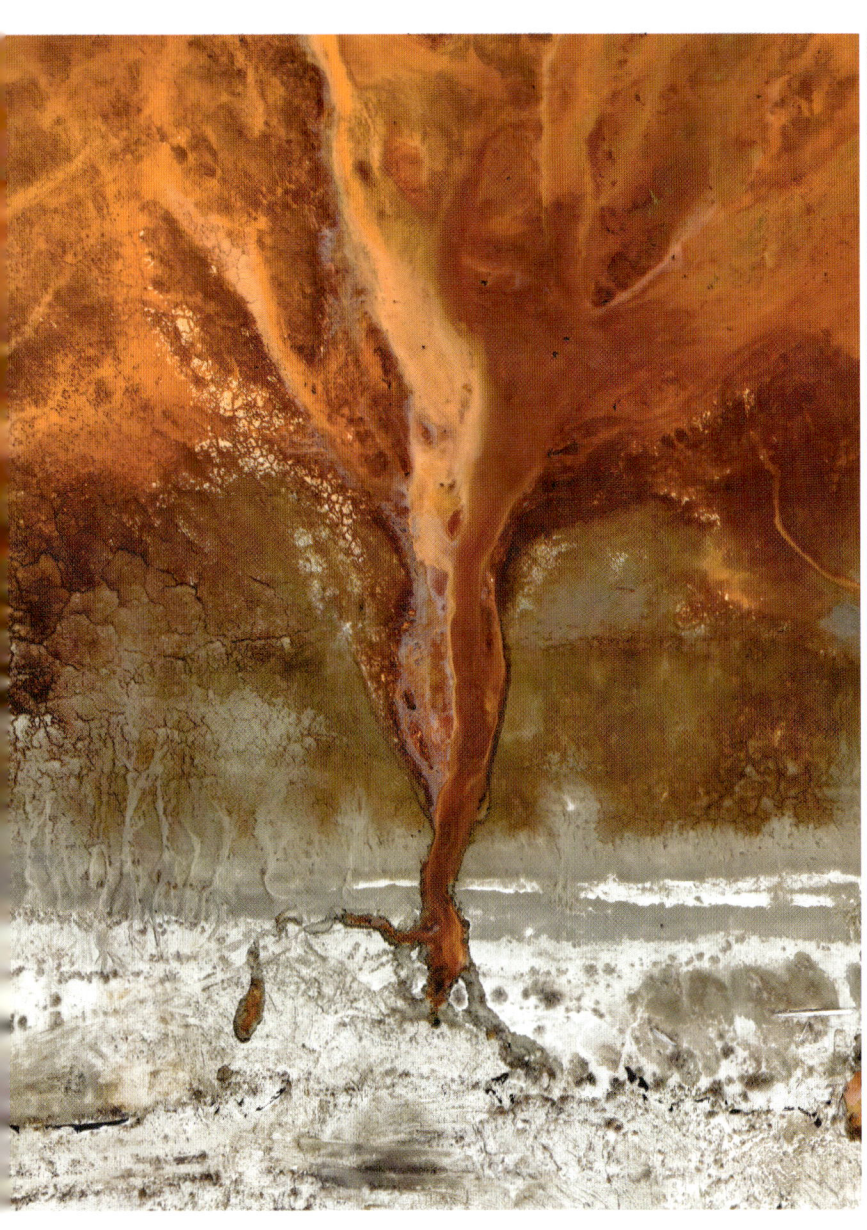
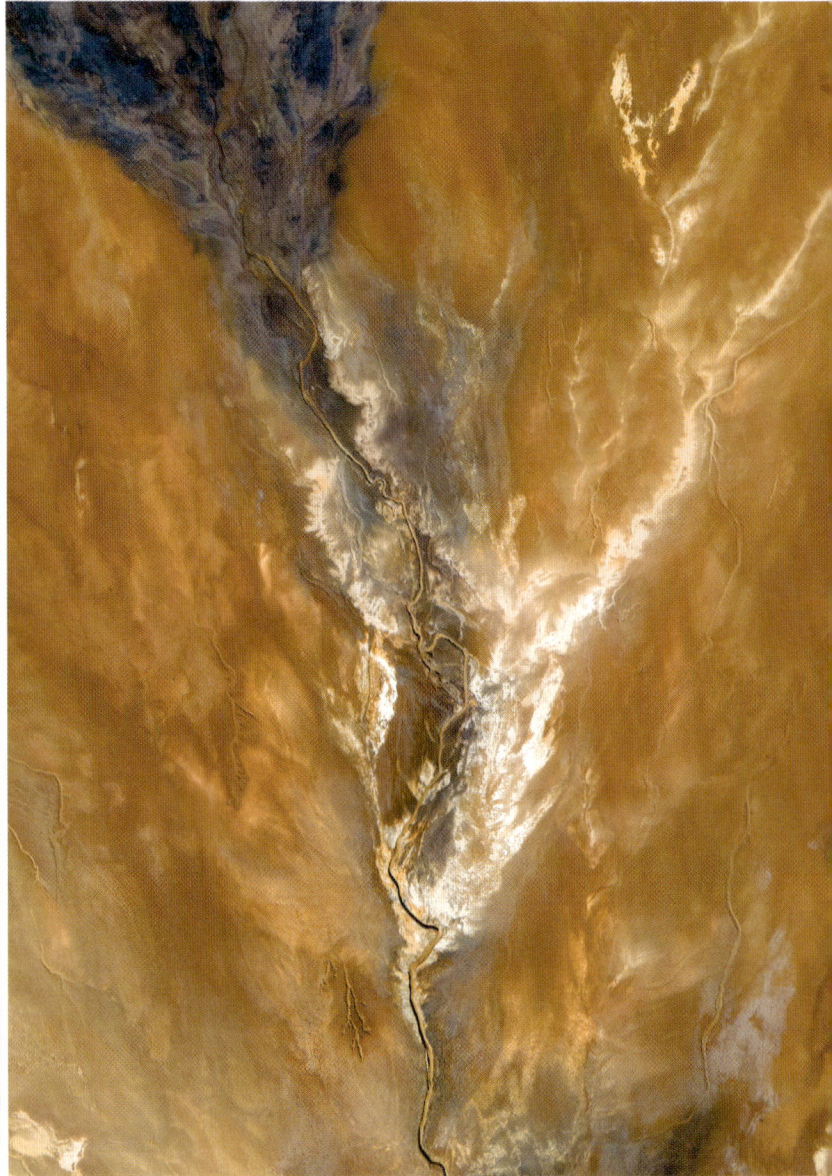

US Magnesium, iron oxides and other metal contaminants from 246 feet (75 m) | I4 | 03.29.2024

US Magnesium, industrial discharge and contaminants from 548 feet (167 m) | I4 | 04.03.2024

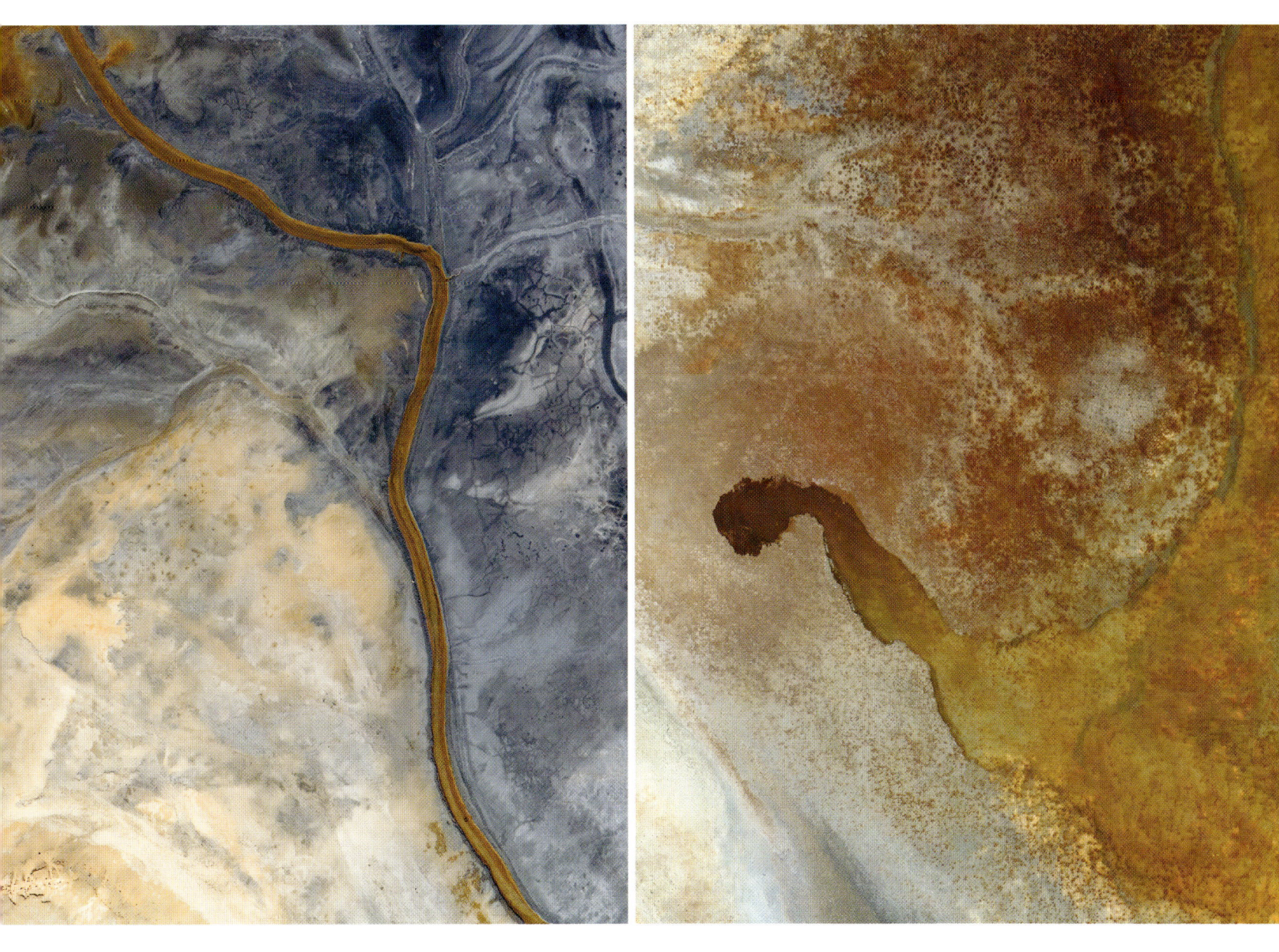

US Magnesium, oxidating river of waste from 656 feet (200 m) | I4 | 04.03.2024
US Magnesium, the waste of industrial might, 656 feet (200 m) | I4 | 04.03.2024

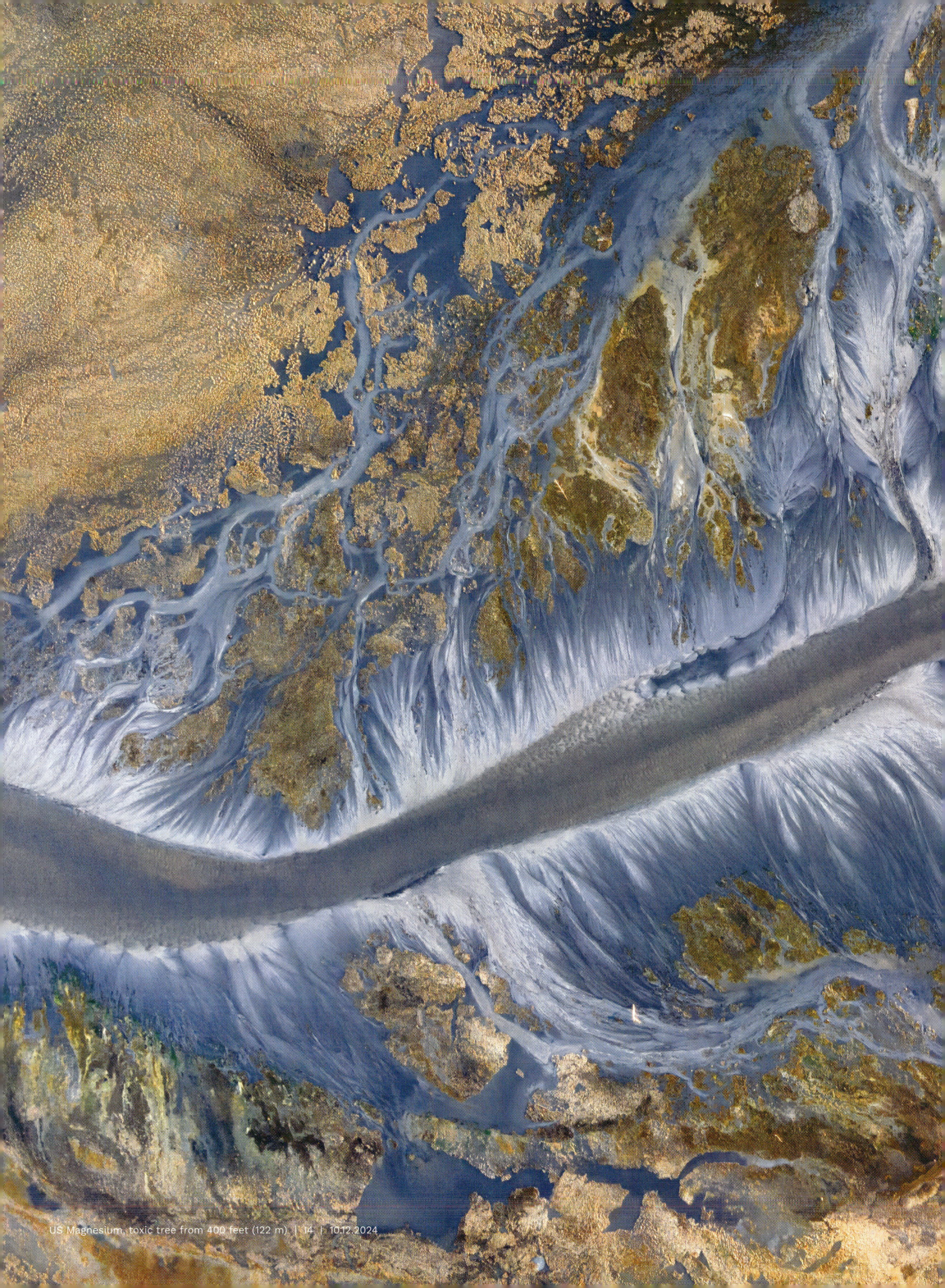

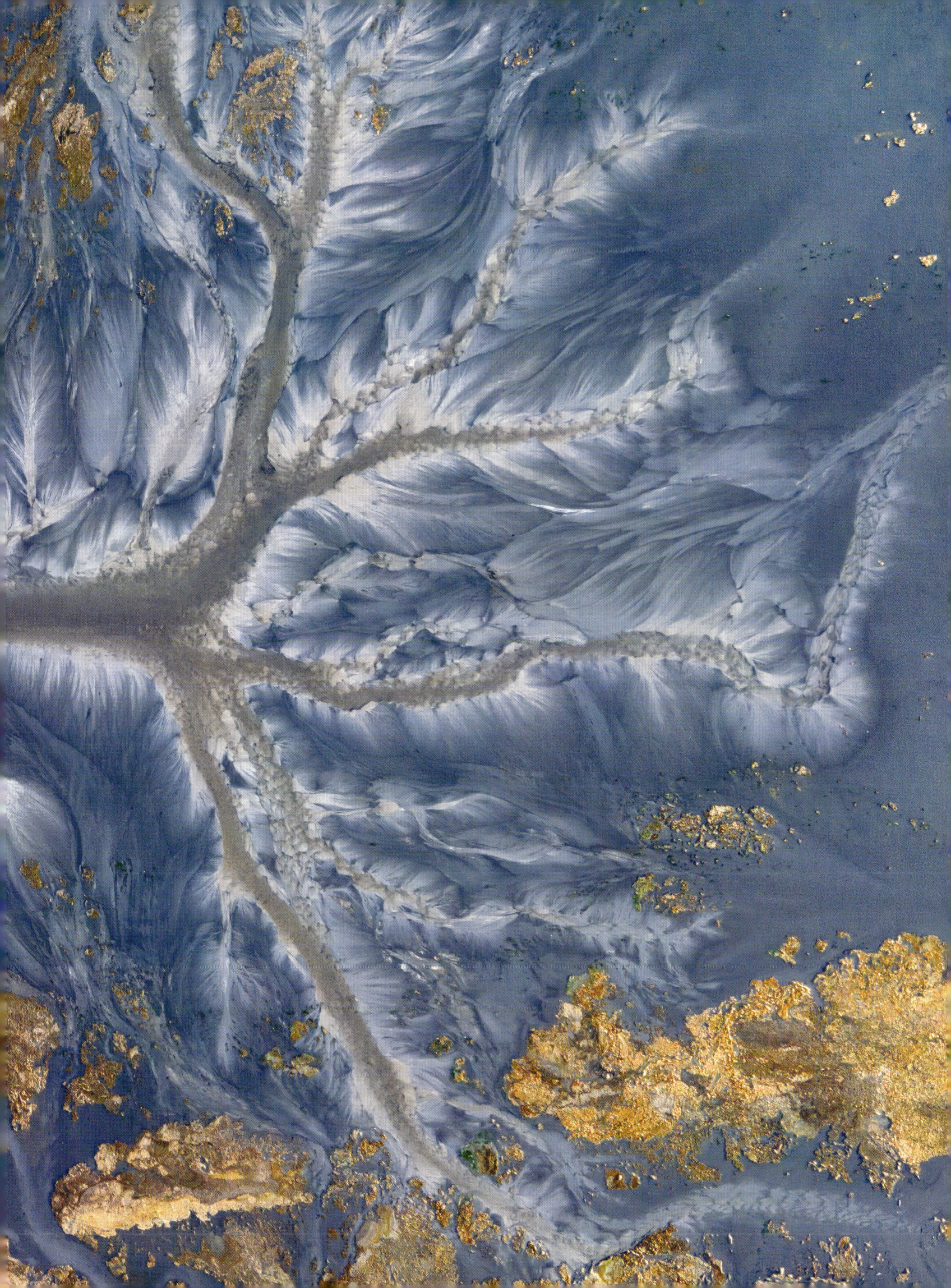

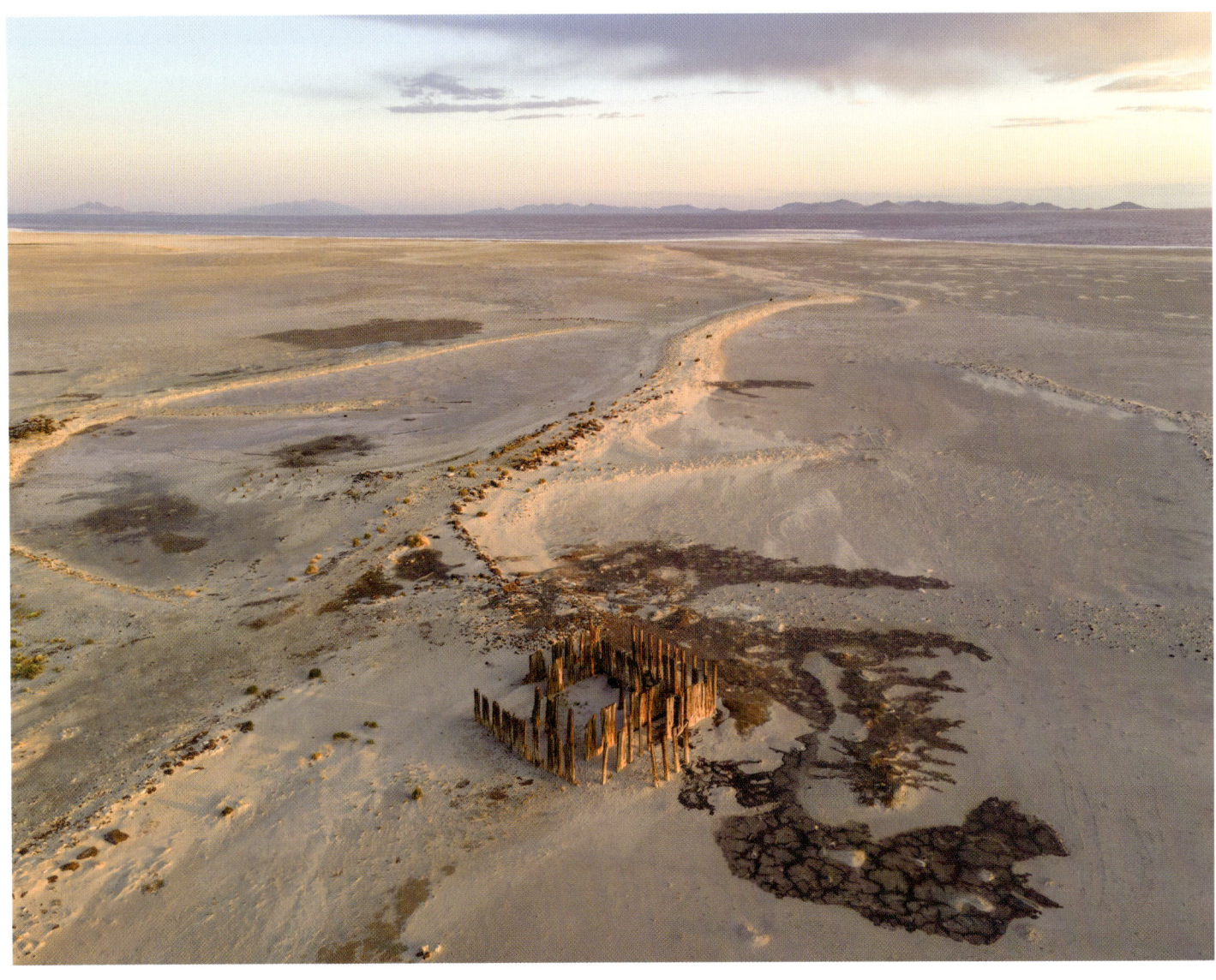

ROZEL POINT OIL FIELD

This area, with its naturally occurring crude oil seeps, has been intriguing geologists and oil prospectors for decades. Picture a landscape where oil bubbles up naturally from the earth, a testament to the ancient organic-rich sediments lying beneath. These seeps, active for millions of years, are a reminder of a time when the region was a lush, thriving ecosystem during the Miocene to Pliocene Epochs. The real boom at Rozel Point came between 1978 and 1980 when Amoco drilled 13 wells, striking oil at the West Rozel oil field. This discovery was exciting but challenging. The oil here is found in fractured basalt at considerable depths, and the operation faced hurdles like high water content and hefty costs. Despite these obstacles, the field stands as a remarkable chapter in Utah's oil exploration saga, illustrating the relentless human pursuit to tap into the earth's hidden resources.

Today, Rozel Point is more than just an industrial relic; it's an environmental case study. The natural tar seeps mix with the hypersaline waters of Great Salt Lake, creating a unique and colorful landscape. This interaction offers scientists valuable insights into how petroleum-rich environments affect local ecosystems. The site's dramatic contrasts—black tar against the sparkling blue of the lake—tell a story of both natural beauty and the enduring impacts of human industry. This blend of geology, history, and environmental science makes Rozel Point a captivating and complex part of Great Salt Lake's vast and varied narrative

Rozel Point oil field | D4 | 06.23.2023

Tar and pelican skeleton, Rozel Point oil field | D4 | 04.07.2024

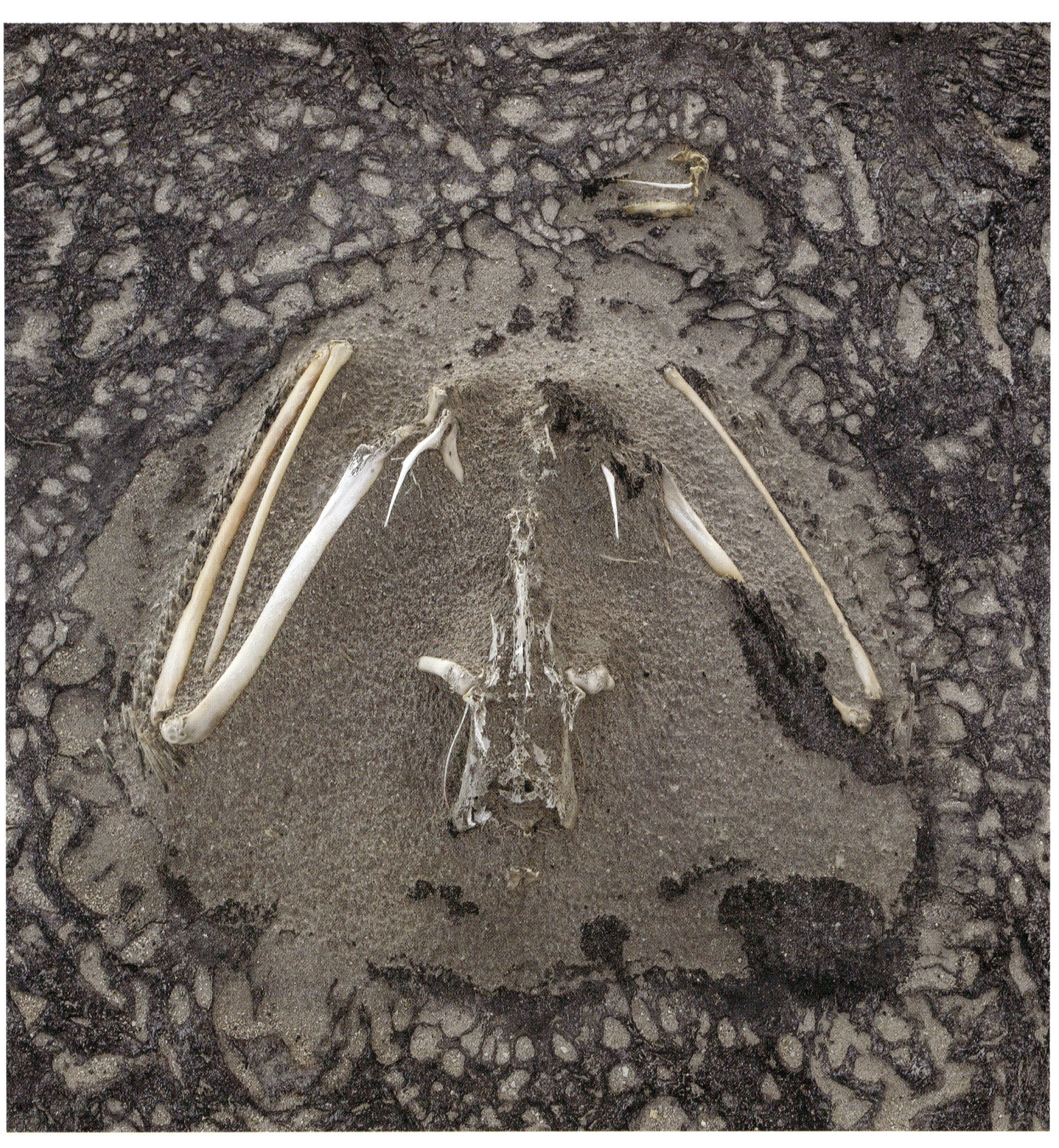

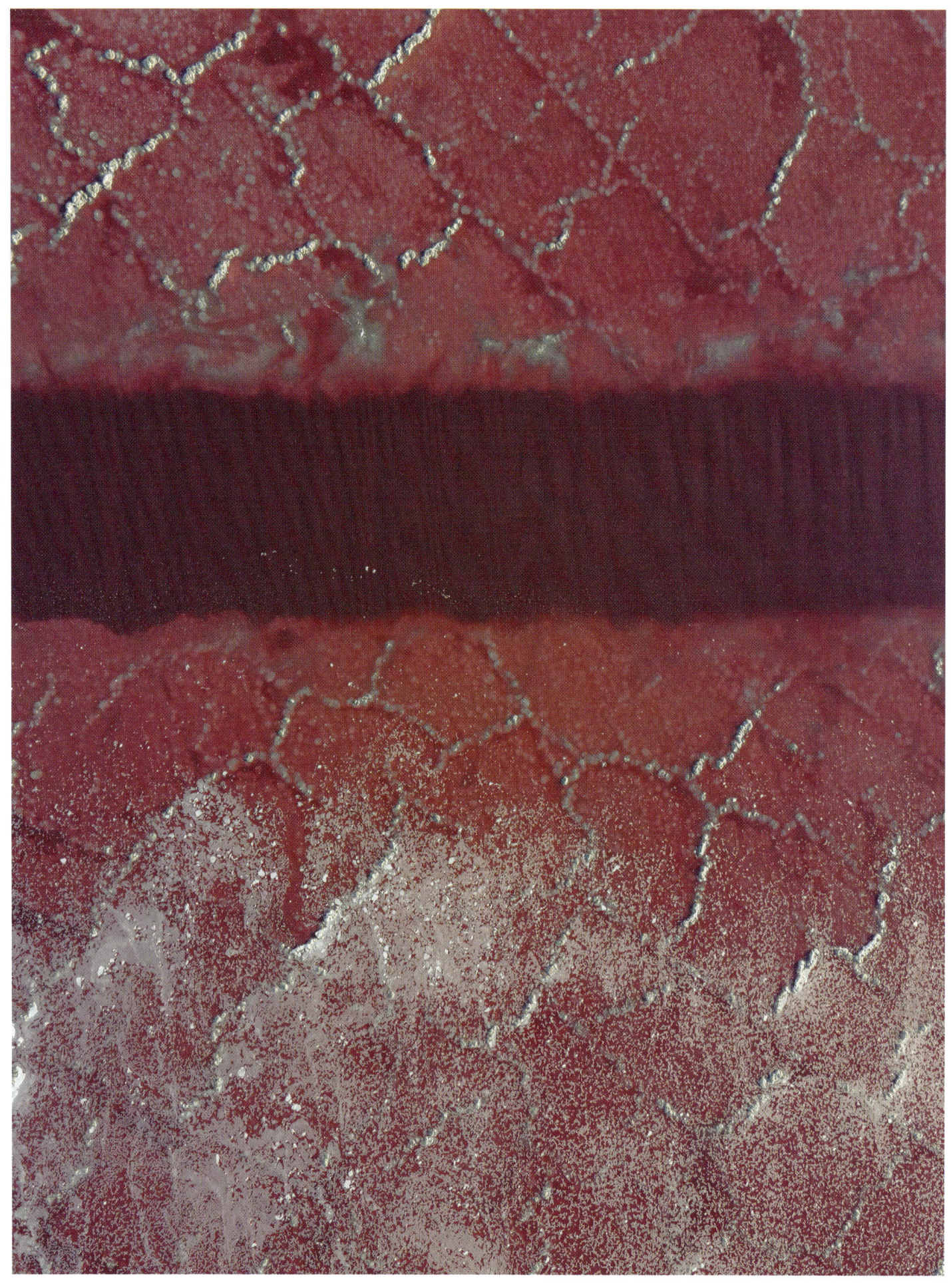

The Behrens Trench from above | F6 | 10.13.2023

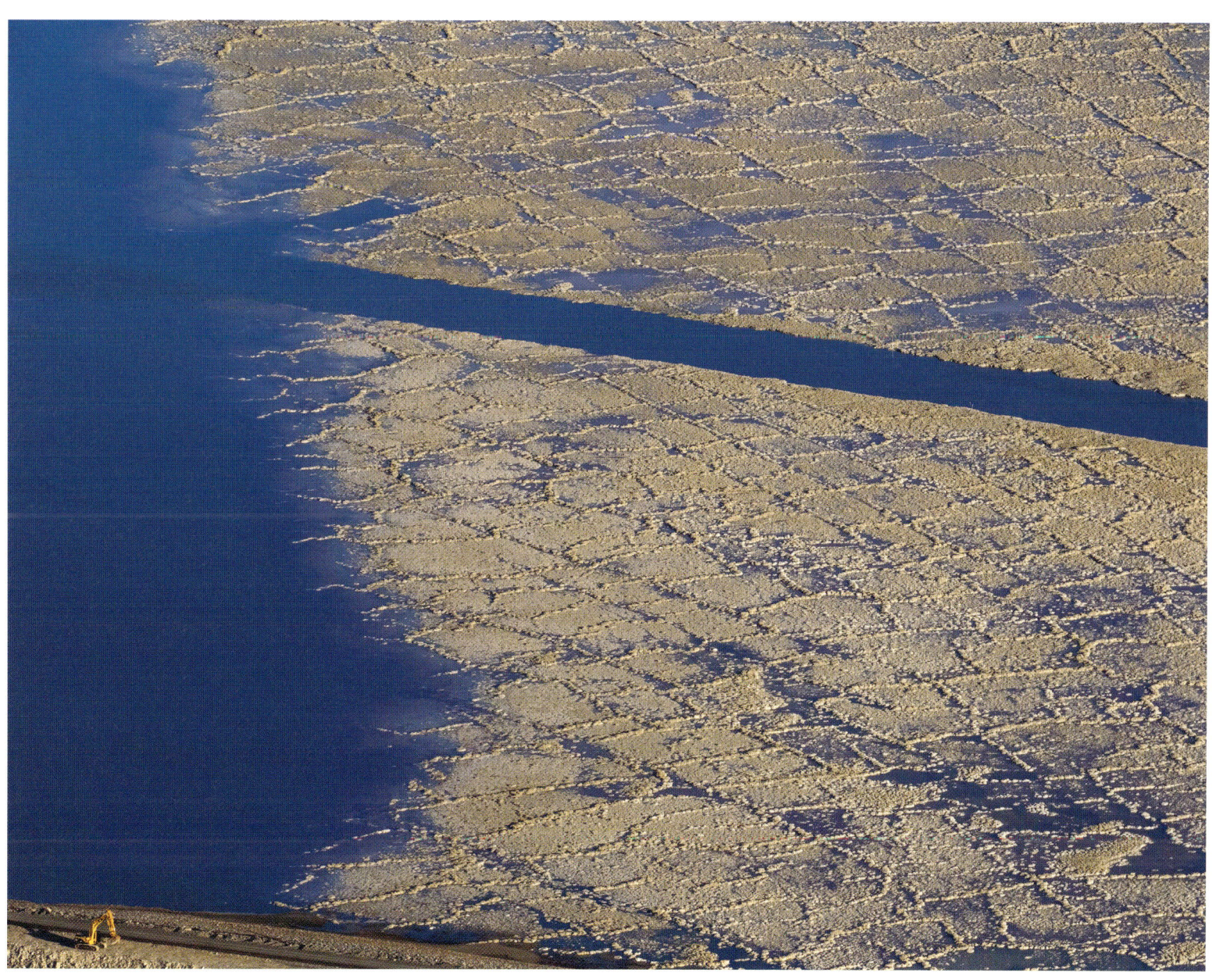

THE BEHRENS TRENCH

The Behrens Trench, constructed in 1991 by the Great Salt Lake Minerals and Chemicals Company, is a unique canal designed to transport liquid brine across Great Salt Lake. Unlike typical canals, it moves denser, salt-laden brine within the lake's water, creating a "water within water" flow. The trench, which runs underwater, is cut into the lake bottom and continuously slopes downward as it heads eastward. The brine, released from solar evaporation ponds, remains contained within the canal due to its higher density. It takes about a week for brine to travel the 21 miles (34 km) to the east end, where it is pumped over the railroad tracks of the causeway into a conventional canal. This canal continues east along the shore of Promontory Point toward additional ponds and a processing plant northwest of Ogden.

Backhoe near the east end of the Behrens Trench | F6 | 10.13.2023

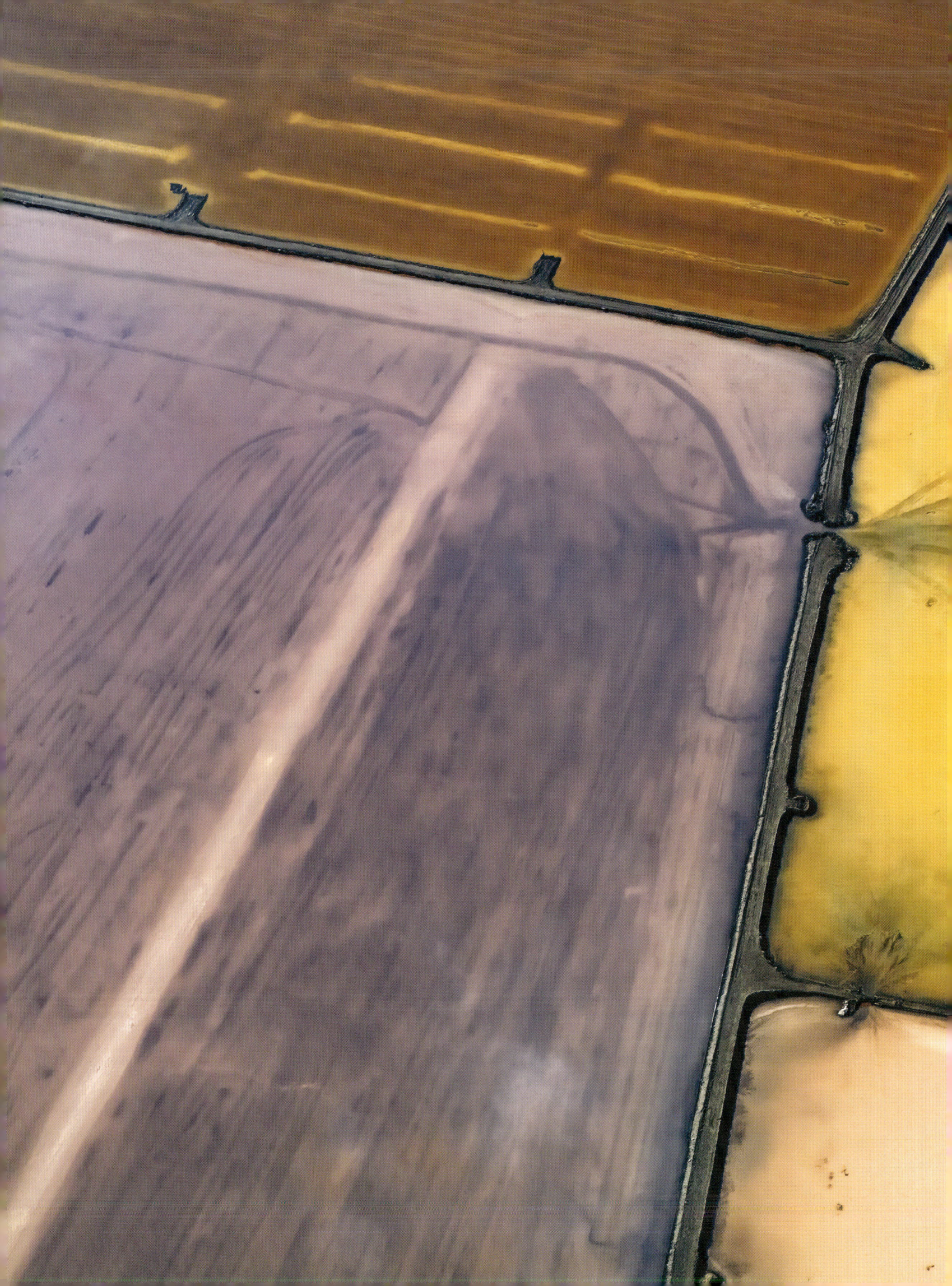

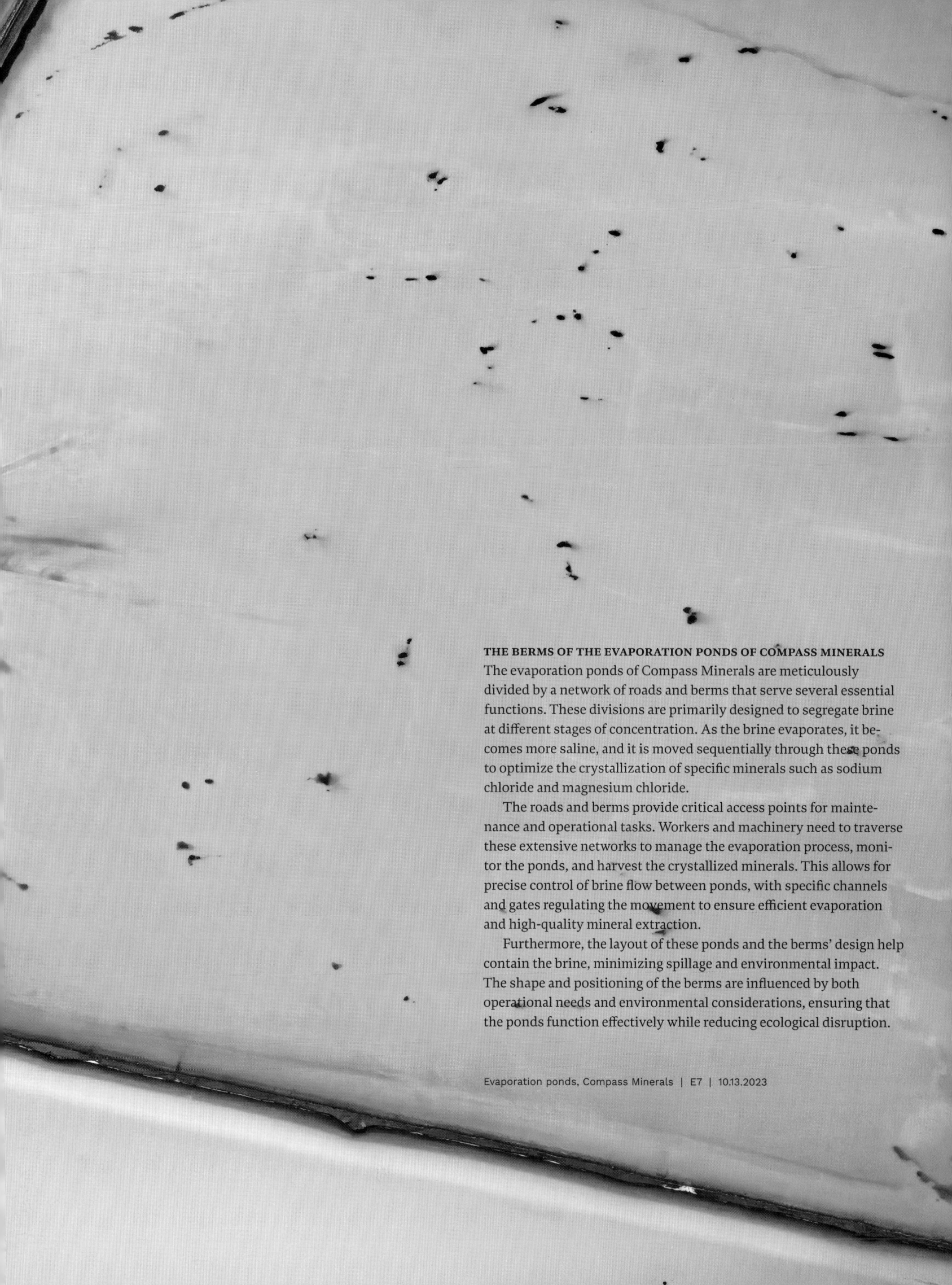

THE BERMS OF THE EVAPORATION PONDS OF COMPASS MINERALS
The evaporation ponds of Compass Minerals are meticulously divided by a network of roads and berms that serve several essential functions. These divisions are primarily designed to segregate brine at different stages of concentration. As the brine evaporates, it becomes more saline, and it is moved sequentially through these ponds to optimize the crystallization of specific minerals such as sodium chloride and magnesium chloride.

The roads and berms provide critical access points for maintenance and operational tasks. Workers and machinery need to traverse these extensive networks to manage the evaporation process, monitor the ponds, and harvest the crystallized minerals. This allows for precise control of brine flow between ponds, with specific channels and gates regulating the movement to ensure efficient evaporation and high-quality mineral extraction.

Furthermore, the layout of these ponds and the berms' design help contain the brine, minimizing spillage and environmental impact. The shape and positioning of the berms are influenced by both operational needs and environmental considerations, ensuring that the ponds function effectively while reducing ecological disruption.

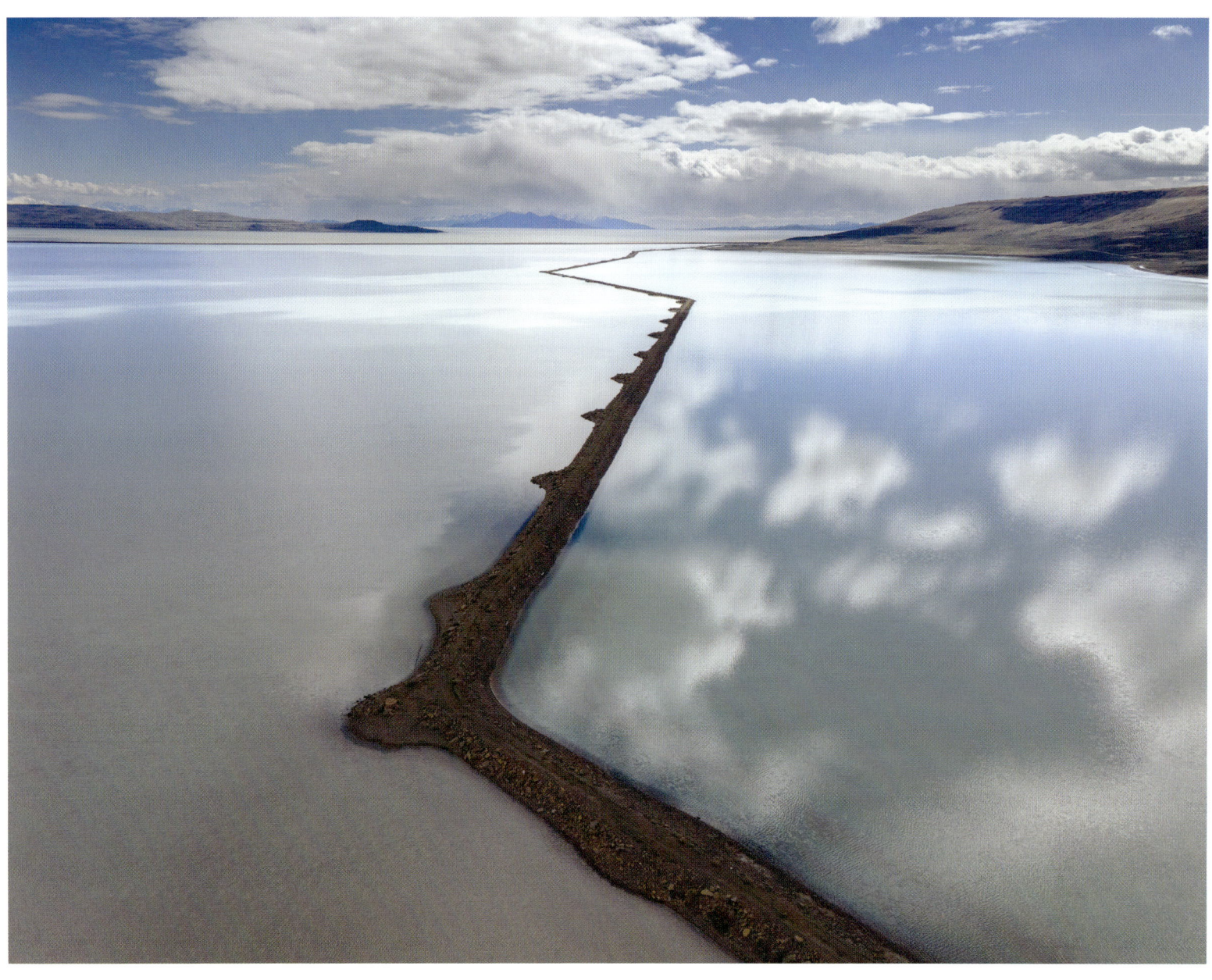

THE SAME EVAPORATION PONDS AT DIFFERENT TIMES OF YEAR

The bright and varied colors of the evaporation ponds at Compass Minerals come from a mix of mineral concentrations, microbial activity, and chemical reactions. As water evaporates, the minerals in the brine become more concentrated, changing the water's color. Certain salt-loving microorganisms, like algae and bacteria, produce pigments that can turn the water red, pink, green, or yellow. Additionally, metals in the water can oxidize, adding to the color variations. Factors like sunlight and temperature also influence these colors, creating a vibrant and ever-changing landscape. Throughout the year, these ponds change color due to seasonal variations in temperature and sunlight, which affect the growth of microorganisms and the rate of evaporation. In warmer months, increased evaporation and microbial activity can intensify colors, while cooler months may see more subdued hues. This dynamic interplay results in a constantly shifting and visually striking palette.

Evaporation pond berm, Compass Minerals | E7 | 04.07.2024
Evaporation pond berm, Compass Minerals | E7 | 10.23.2023

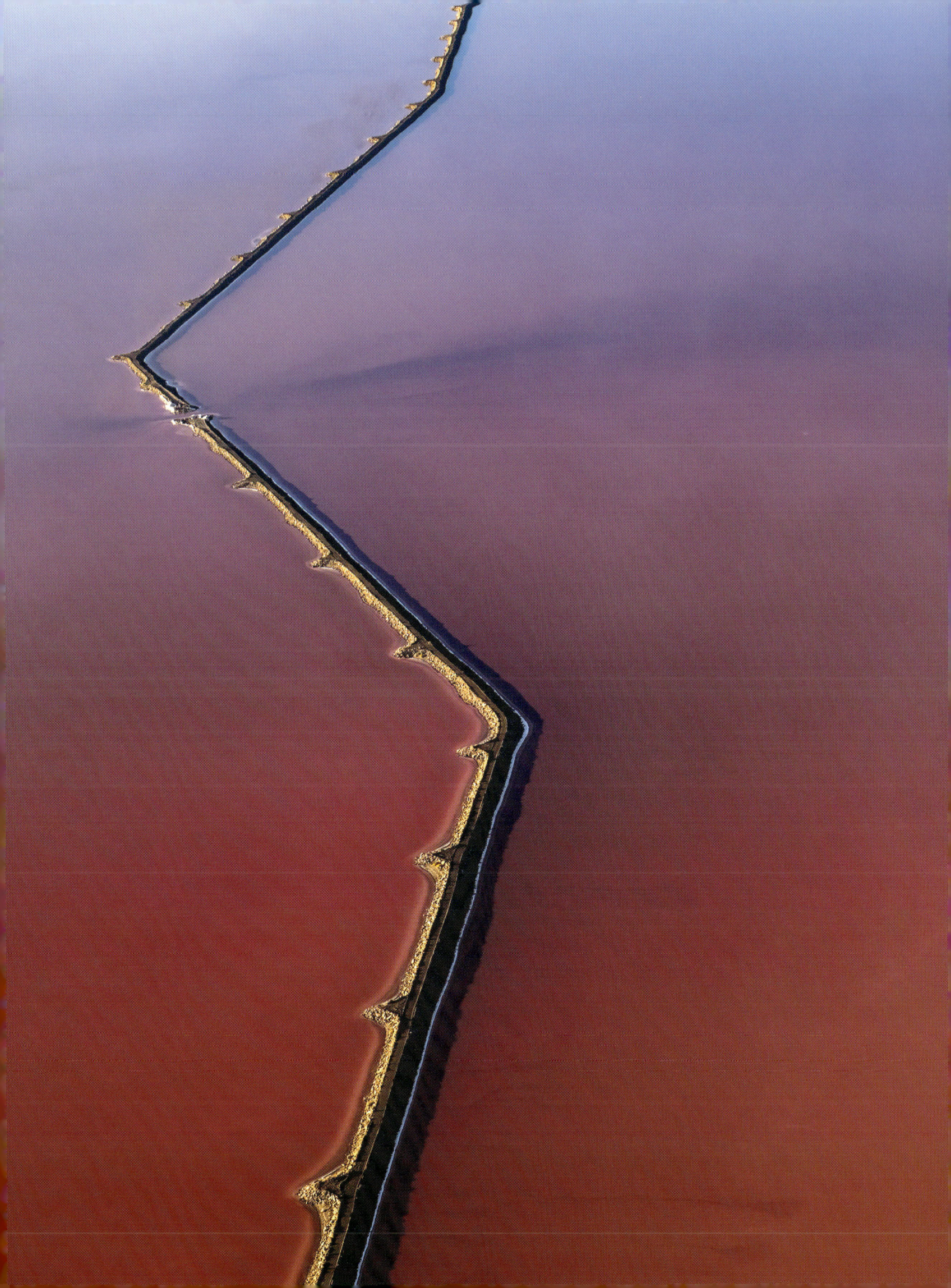

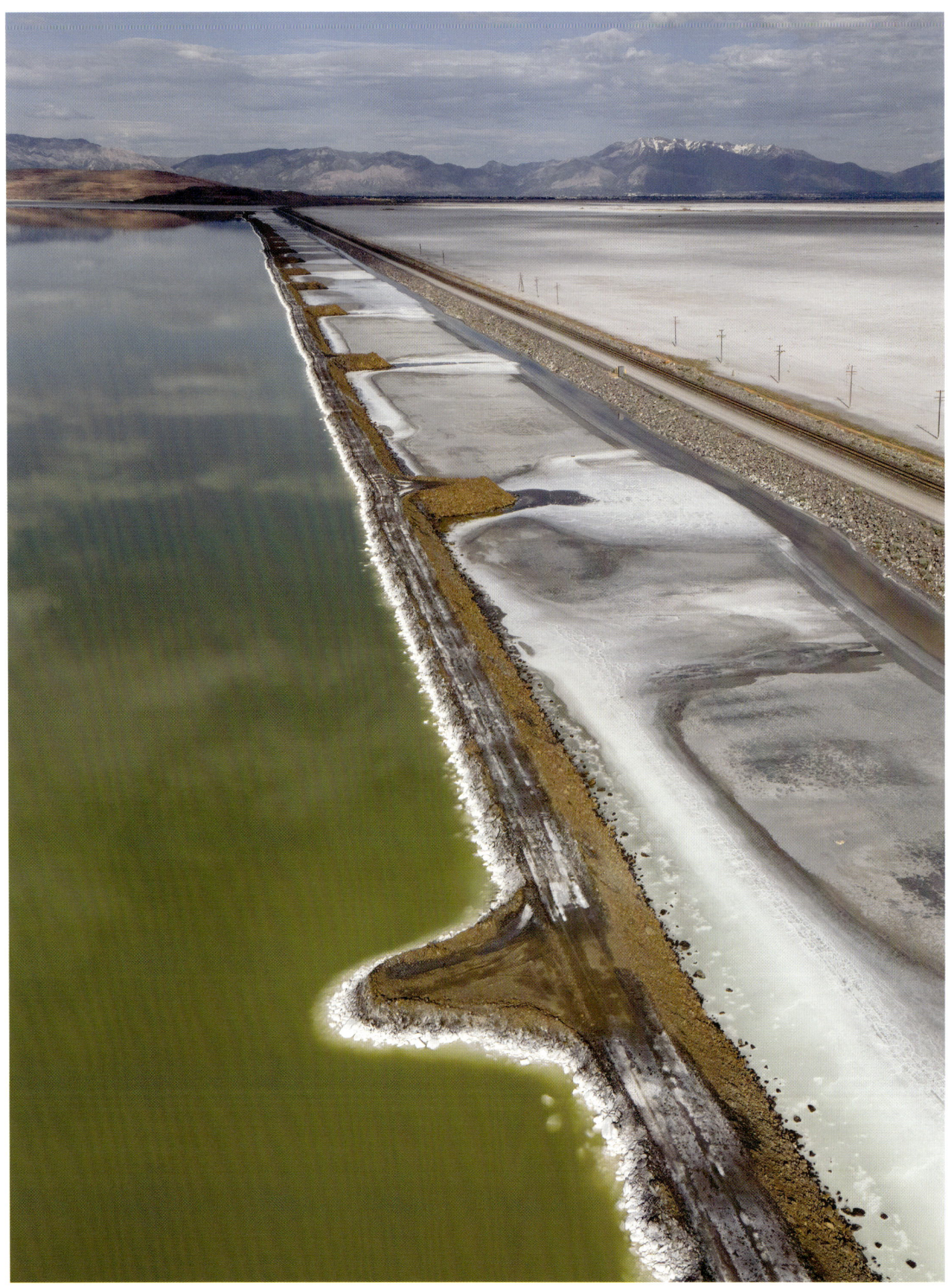

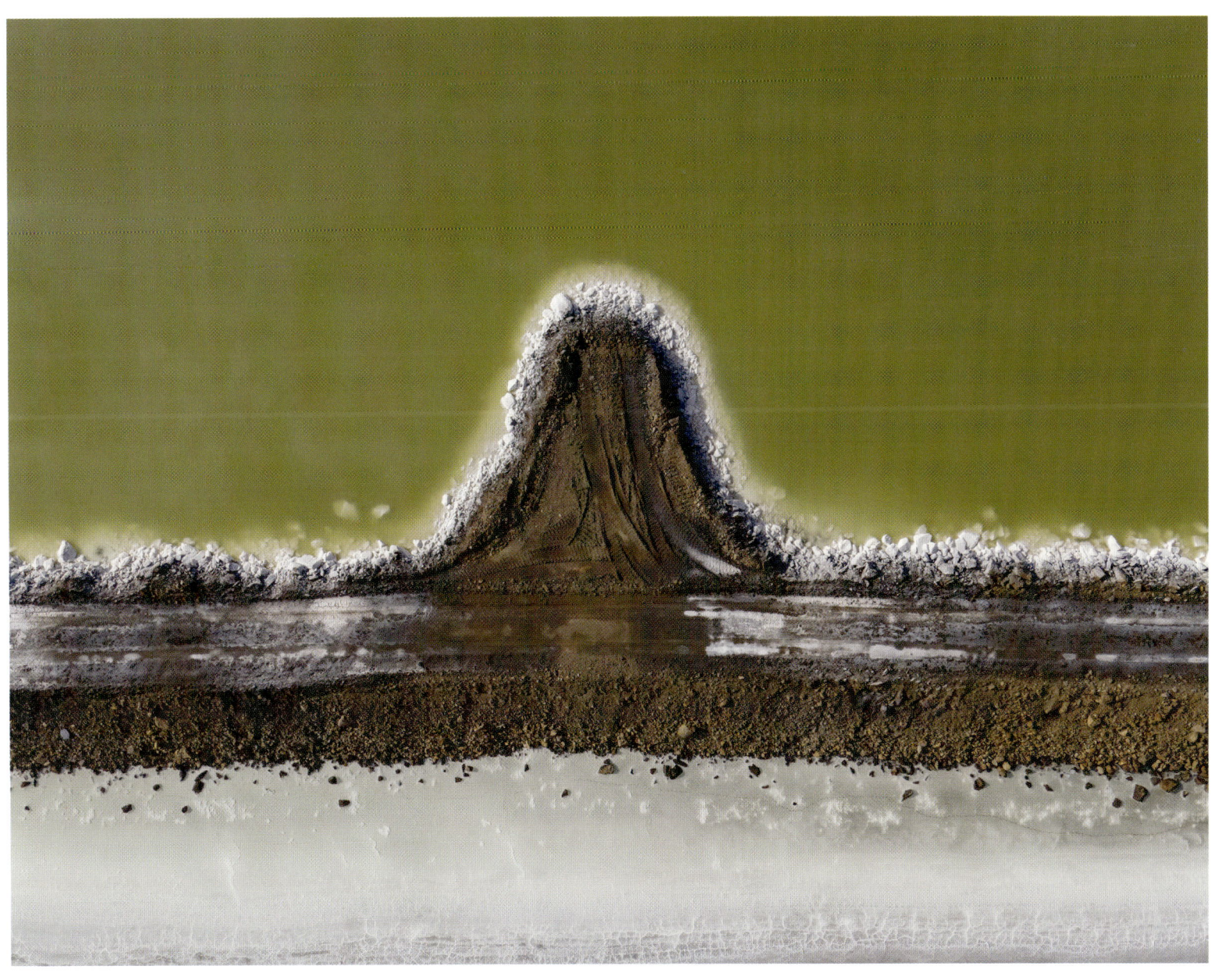

SEPARATING GREAT SALT LAKE FROM INDUSTRIAL OPERATIONS
The evaporation ponds of Compass Minerals, particularly near
the Bear River inlet, are separated from Great Salt Lake through a
network of berms and canals designed to contain the dense, salt-
laden brine. These structures ensure that the brine remains isolated,
preventing it from mixing with the lake's water. The berms and roads
facilitate maintenance and operational tasks while also minimizing
brine leakage by sealing the ponds with inert materials.

The divide between Compass Minerals and Great Salt Lake | F7 | 06.03.2024
Compass Minerals berm detail | F7 | 06.03.2024

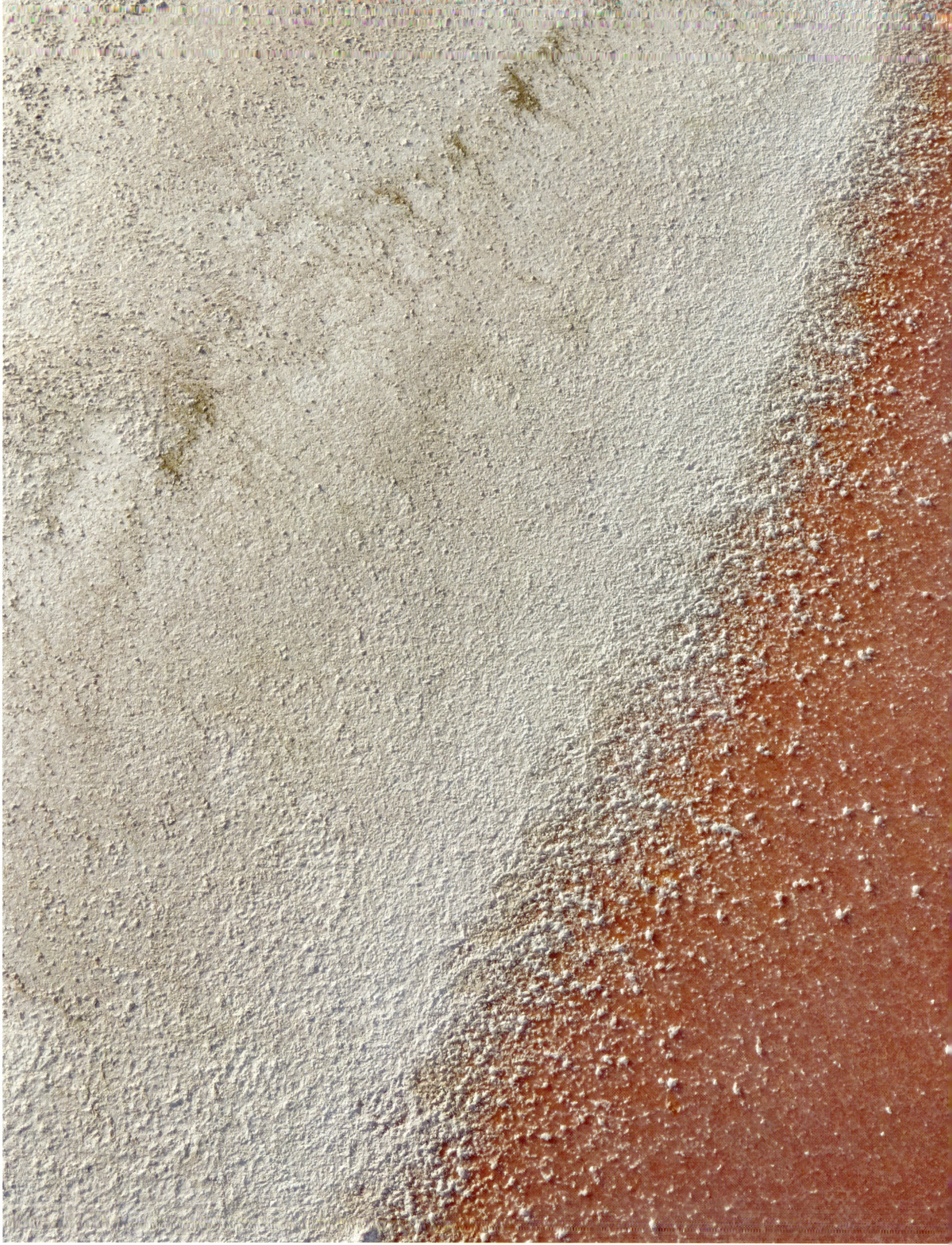

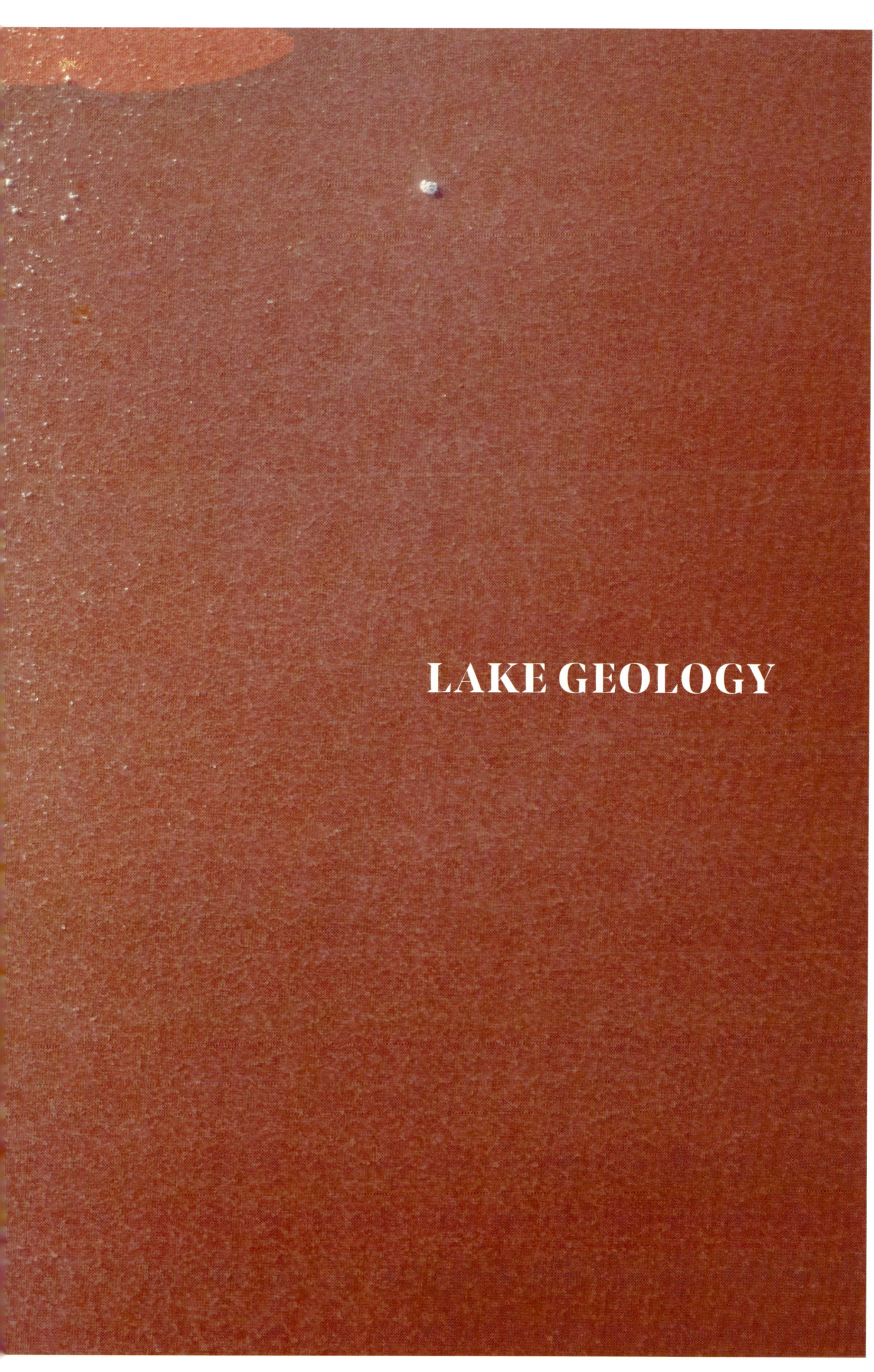

LAKE GEOLOGY

04.

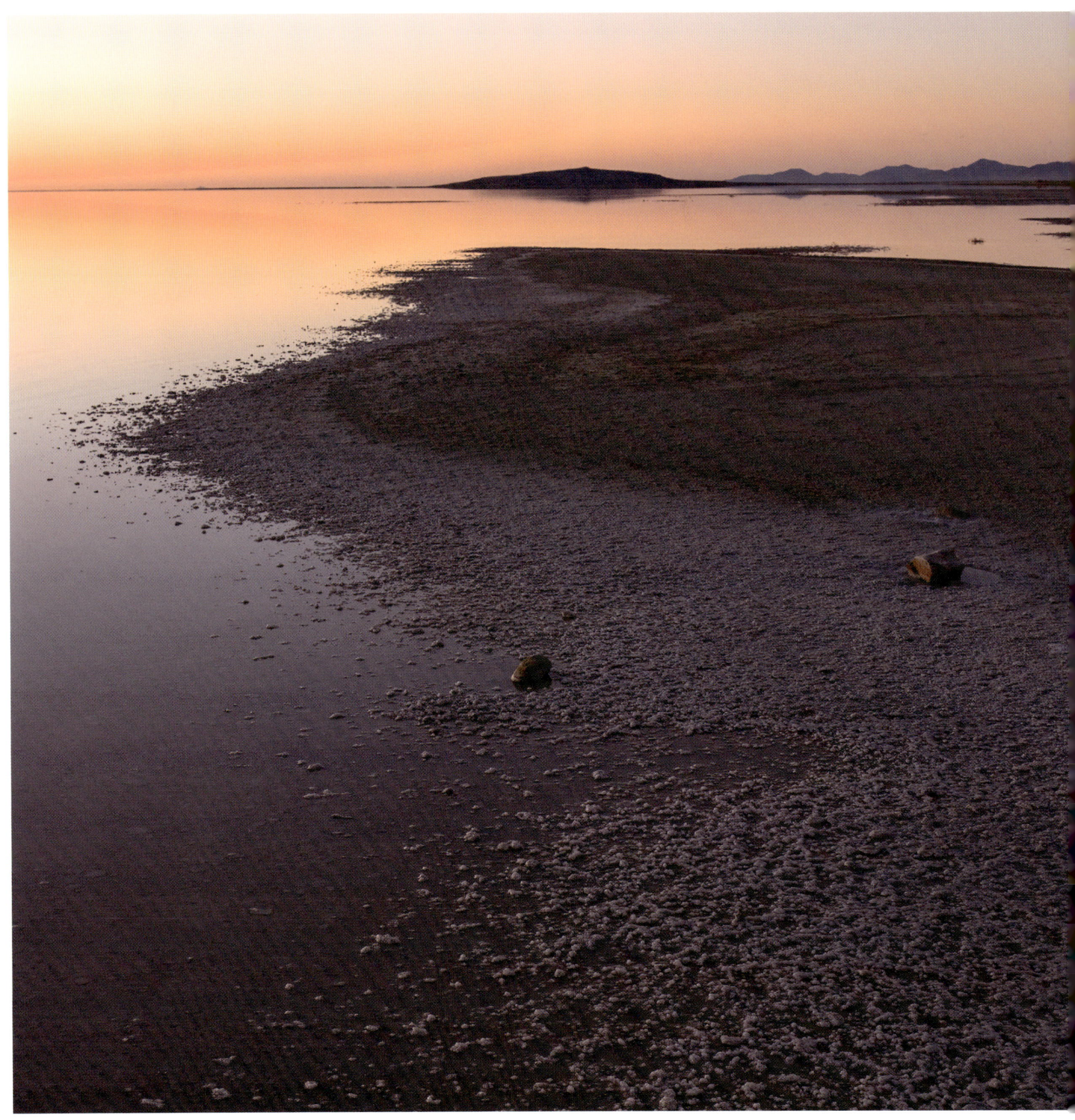

A Tapestry of Textures

GREAT SALT LAKE IS A MARVEL OF NATURE, offering a diverse palette of textures that capture the imagination and tell the story of its dynamic environment. From the grainy sands of its beaches to crystalline structures of salt, the lake is a sensory experience that is both visually and tactilely rich, each texture adding to the greatness of this unique ecosystem.

The shores of Great Salt Lake are lined with coarse, gritty sand and mud, a mix of eroded rock particles and mineral deposits. Walking along the beaches, one can feel the uneven soil shift underfoot, a reminder of the lake's ancient geological processes. The soil varies in color from pale white to darker, more mineral-rich hues, reflecting the diverse sources of sediment that feed into the lake.

Salt is perhaps the most defining texture of Great Salt Lake. The water's high salinity leads to salt flats, where the ground is covered in a thick crust of white salt crystals. These flats can appear smooth and unbroken from a distance but reveal a rough, jagged surface up close. The salt crystals are sharp and angular, starkly contrasting the lake's smooth waters.

The lake is surrounded by various rock formations, from the rugged outcrops of Antelope Island to the smooth, water-worn stones found along the shoreline. These rocks range in texture from rough, volcanic basalt of Black Rock to smoother, sedimentary stones that have been polished by wind and water over millennia. Each rock tells a story of the lake's volcanic and sedimentary history, adding richness and complexity to the story of Great Salt Lake.

The water of the lake is unique in its salinity. It feels denser than freshwater, with a slight oiliness that comes from its high mineral content. The surface can be calm and glassy, reflecting the sky and creating a mirror-like effect, or it can be rippled and rough, depending on the wind and weather conditions. The water's texture changes with the seasons and weather, offering a constantly shifting landscape that is both mesmerizing and vital for the ecosystem's health.

The deltas where rivers like the Jordan, Bear, and Weber enter the lake are rich with textures. Here, the veins of the river deltas spread out in intricate networks, carrying sediment and nutrients into the lake. These deltas are dynamic, with constantly shifting sands and silt creating new patterns and textures as the water flows. This vital interaction between water and land is crucial for supporting the diverse life forms that depend on the lake.

The edges of the lake are dotted with pools and springs that add to the textural diversity. These small bodies of water can be smooth and clear or muddy and murky, depending on their mineral content and the surrounding landscape. Some are bright pink, yellow, or orange. The springs often create mounds of deposits where minerals precipitate out of the water, adding another layer of texture to the environment.

Great Salt Lake's textures tell a story of natural forces at work. Each element—from the gritty sands and sharp salt crystals to the smooth rocks and dense water—contributes to a detailed picture that reflects the lake's geological and ecological complexity. Exploring these textures offers a tactile connection to the lake's ancient past and its ever-changing present, underscoring the greatness of this unique and vital natural wonder.

The textured shores of Stansbury Bay | J5 | 04.20.2024
PREVIOUS PAGE: Salt and pink brine, Stansbury Bay | J5 | 09.30.2023

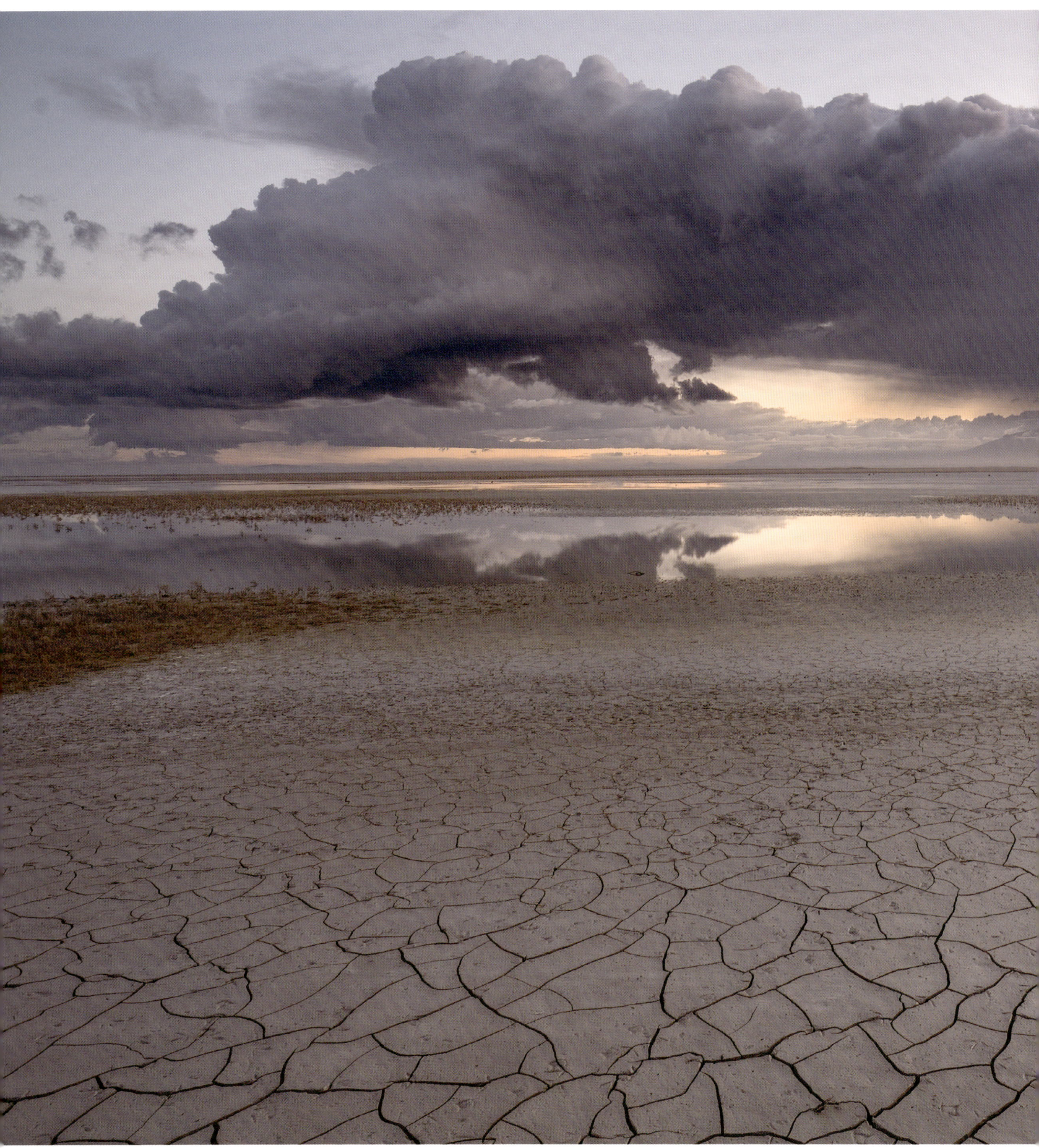

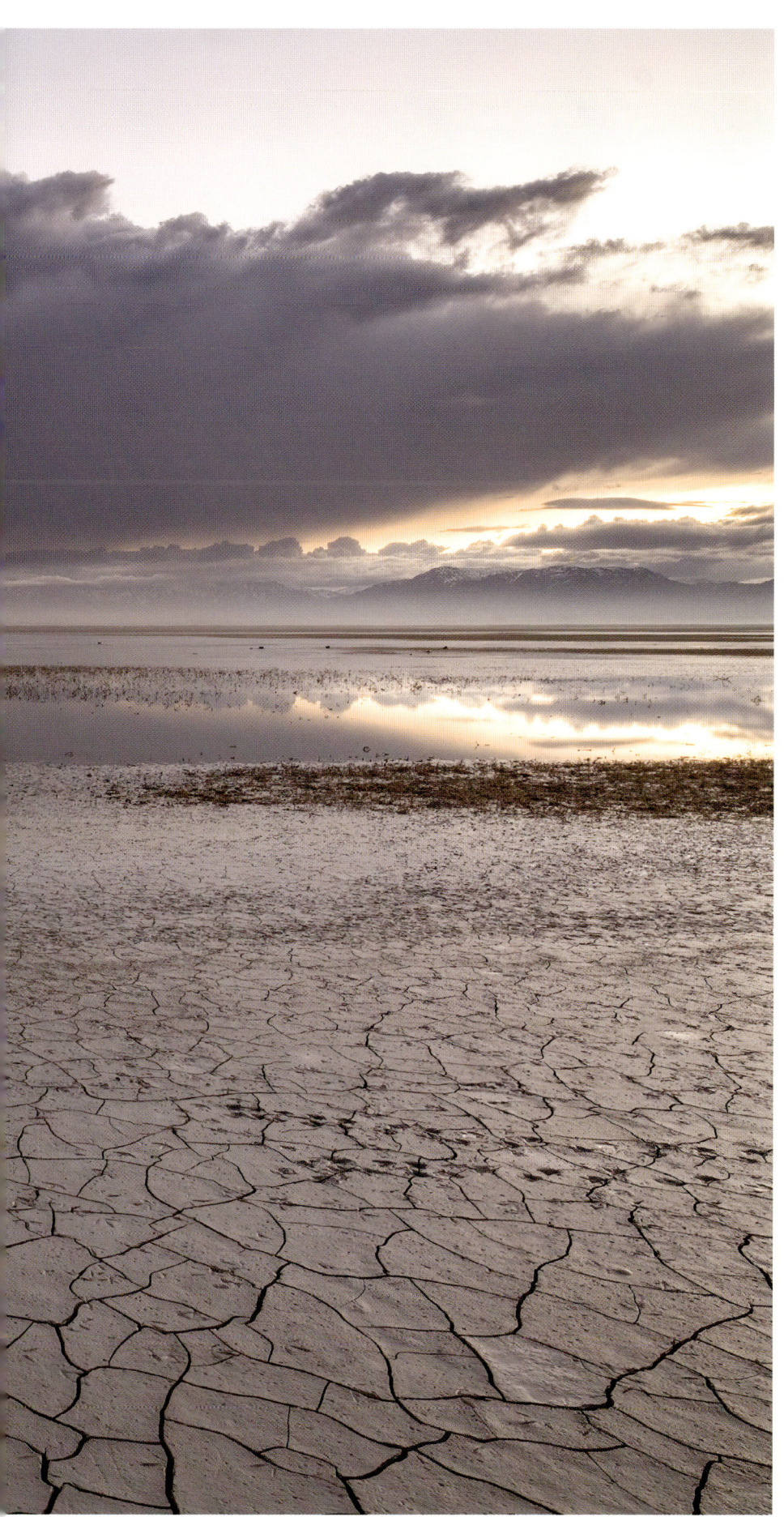

CRACKED SOIL

The phenomenon of cracked soil around Great Salt Lake is indicative of significant environmental stress. The primary causes include prolonged drought and extensive water diversion for agriculture and urban use, leading to reduced lake levels and dry lakebeds. High rates of evaporation, especially in summer, exacerbate this drying, leaving behind salt which further hardens and cracks the soil. The lake's high salinity affects the soil's physical properties, intensifying the cracking as it dries. Additionally, human activities such as industrial mineral extraction and land use changes around the lake disrupt the natural water balance, furthering the drying and cracking of the soil.

Storm clouds and mud cracks | H8 | 05.07.2023

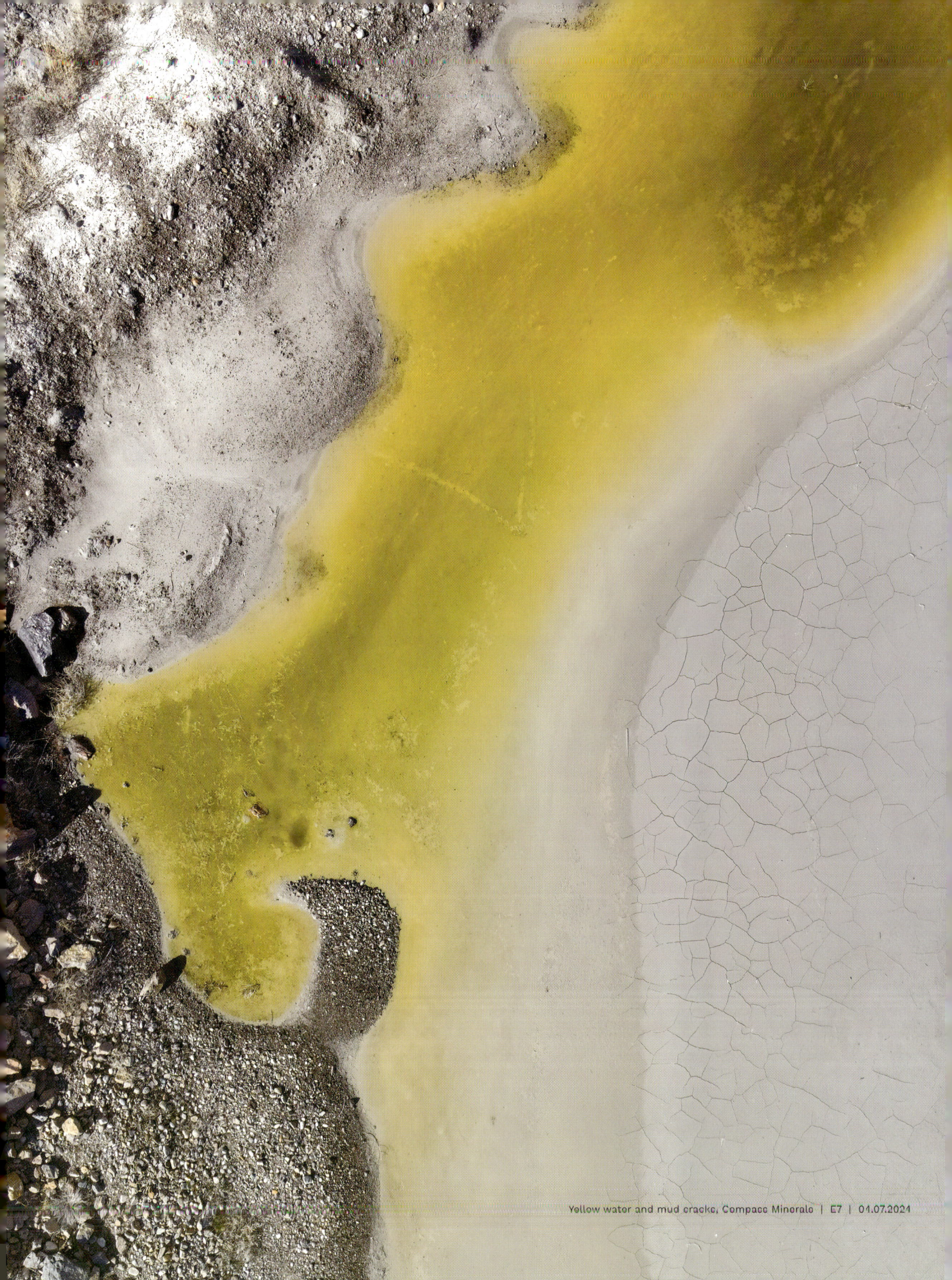

Yellow water and mud cracks, Compass Minerals | E7 | 01.07.2024

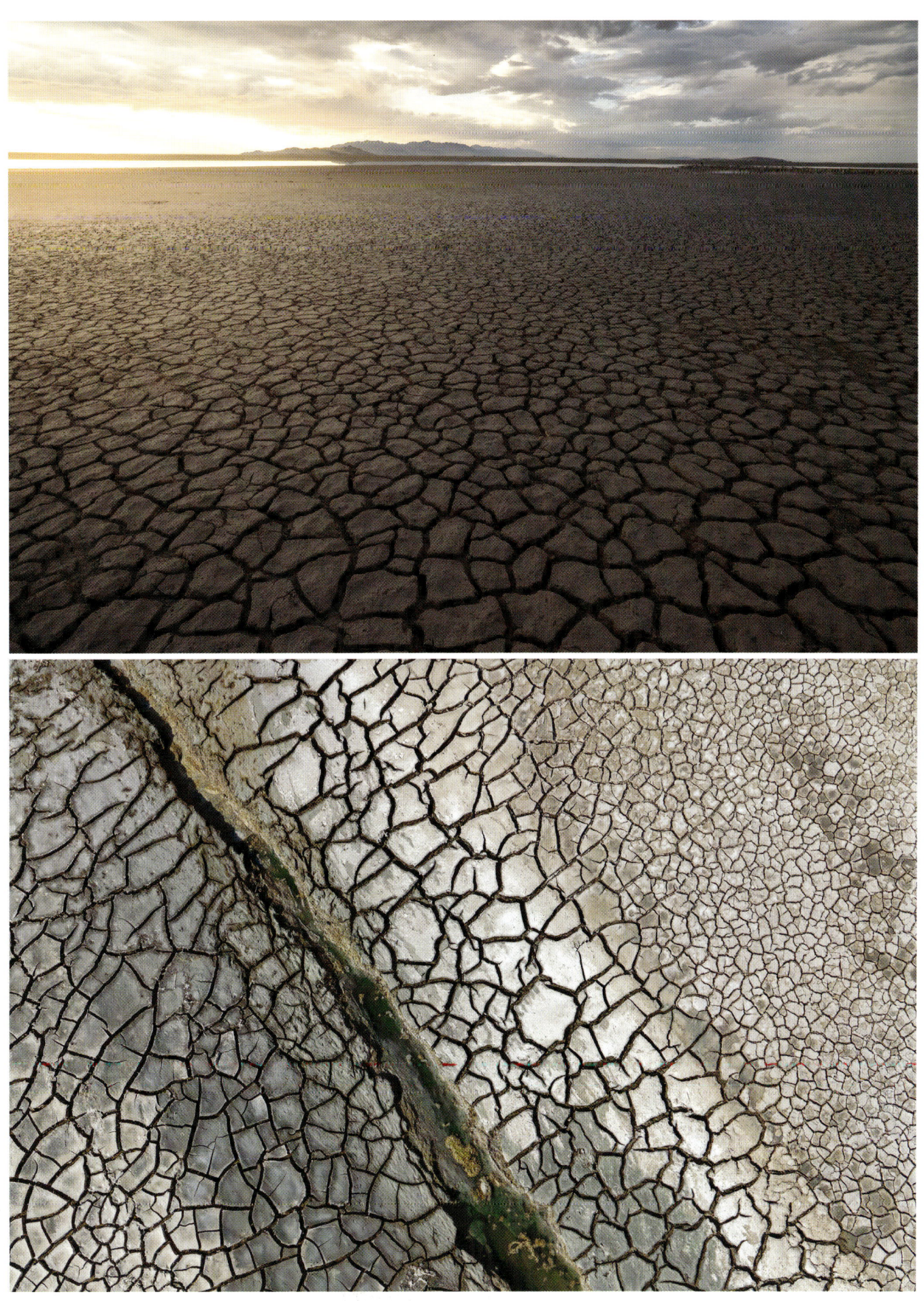

Mudflats between Antelope Island and Fremont Island | H8 | 09.04.2023

Mud cracks and stream near Compass Minerals | F7 | 06.03.2024

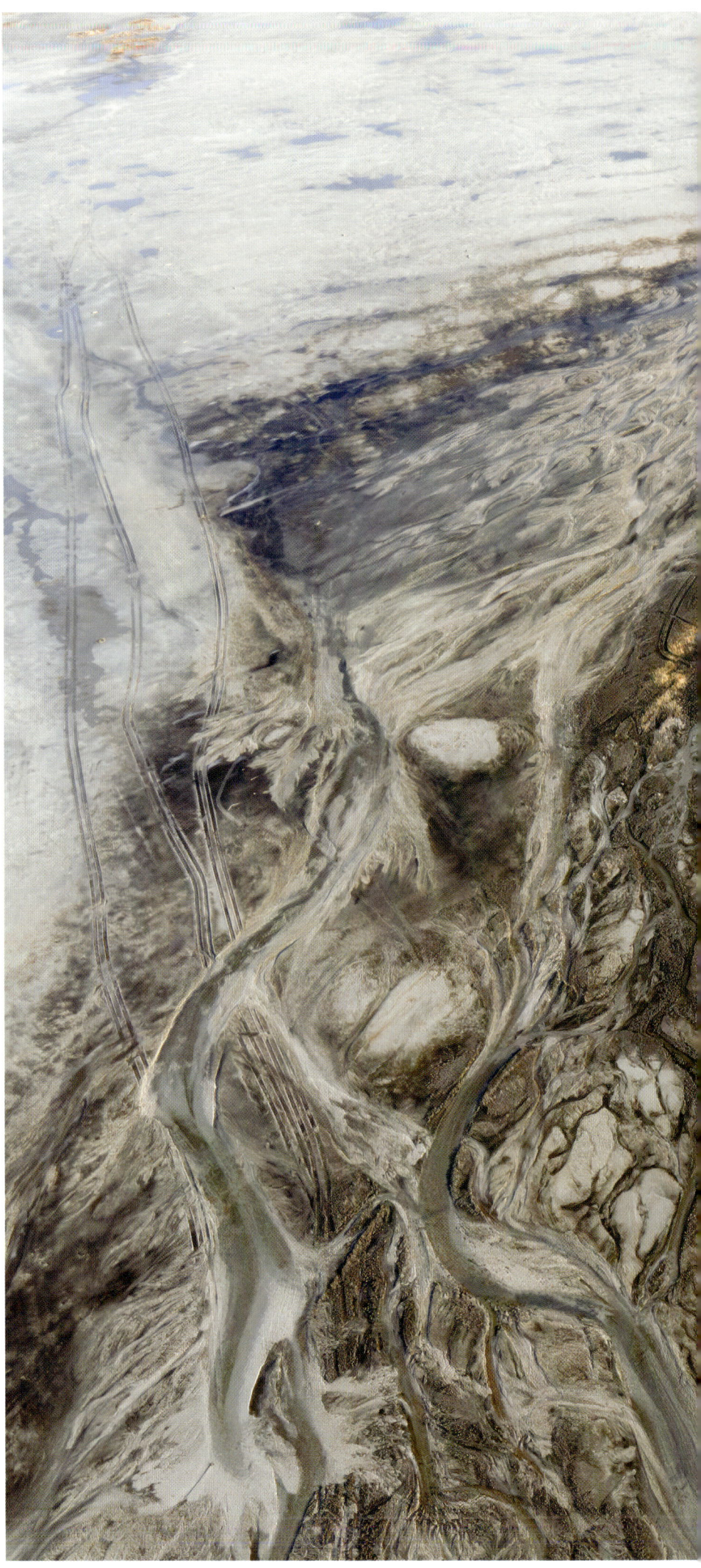

MUDFLATS AND DELTAS

The mesmerizing, tree-like patterns of mudflats and deltas around Great Salt Lake are created by a mix of natural forces. As rivers and streams flow into the lake, they slow down and deposit sediments, forming these unique landscapes. High evaporation rates leave salts and minerals behind, adding to their distinctive look. Wind and water erosion further shapes these formations, while climate change and human activities, like water diversion and industrial work, affect the water flow and sediment buildup.

Lee Creek delta | K8 | 03.08.2024

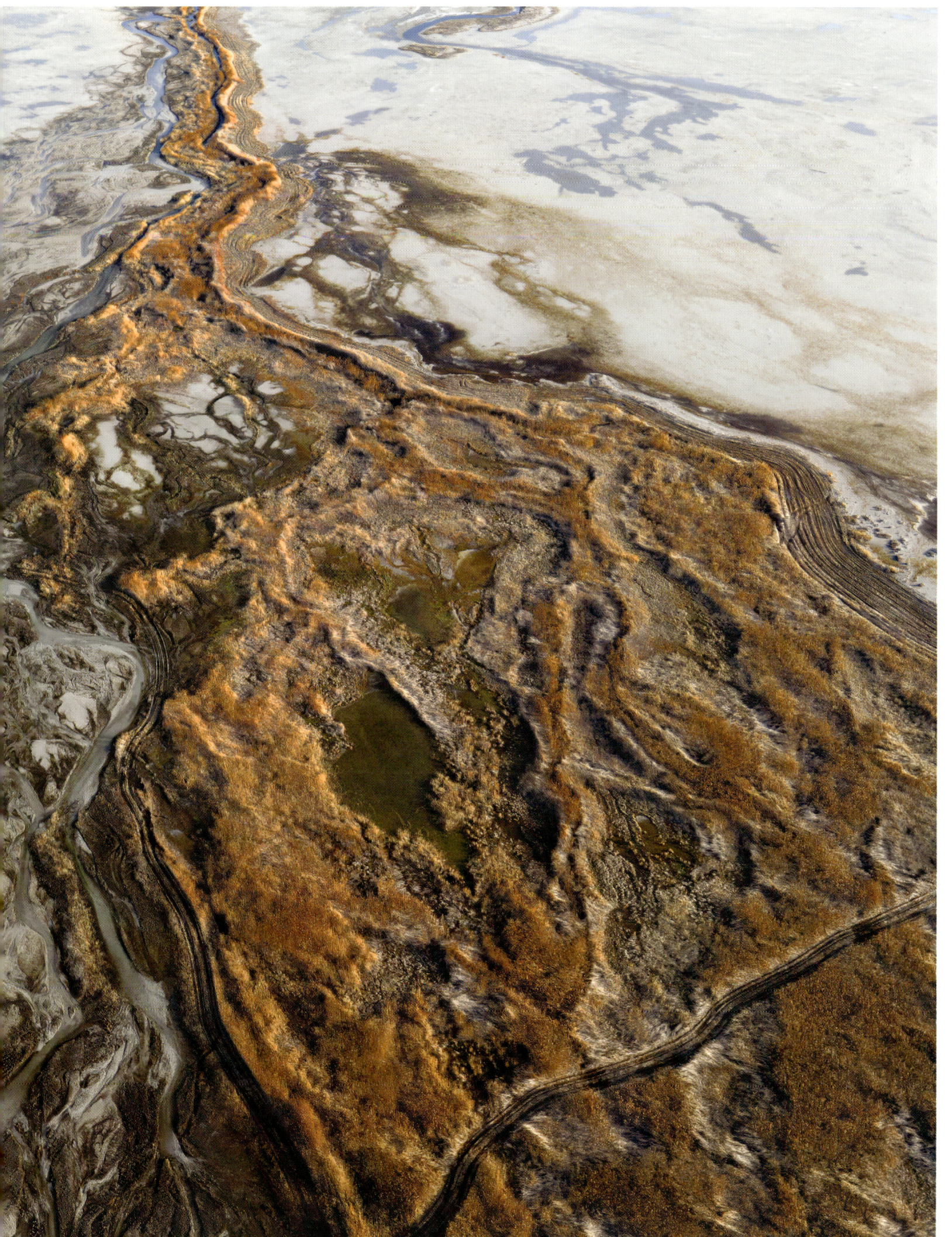

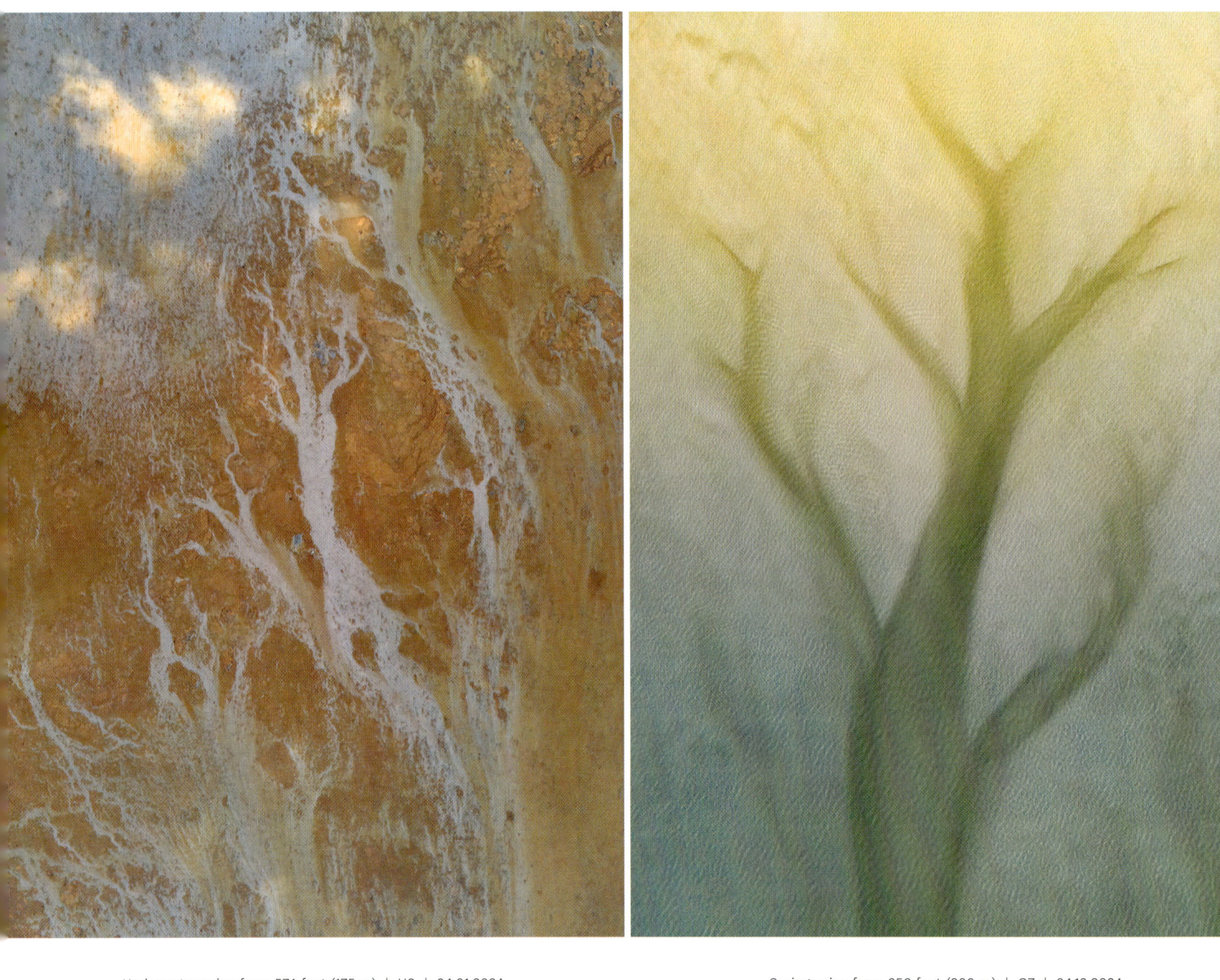

Underwater veins from 574 feet (175 m) | H8 | 04.01.2024

Spring veins from 656 feet (200 m) | G7 | 04.13.2024

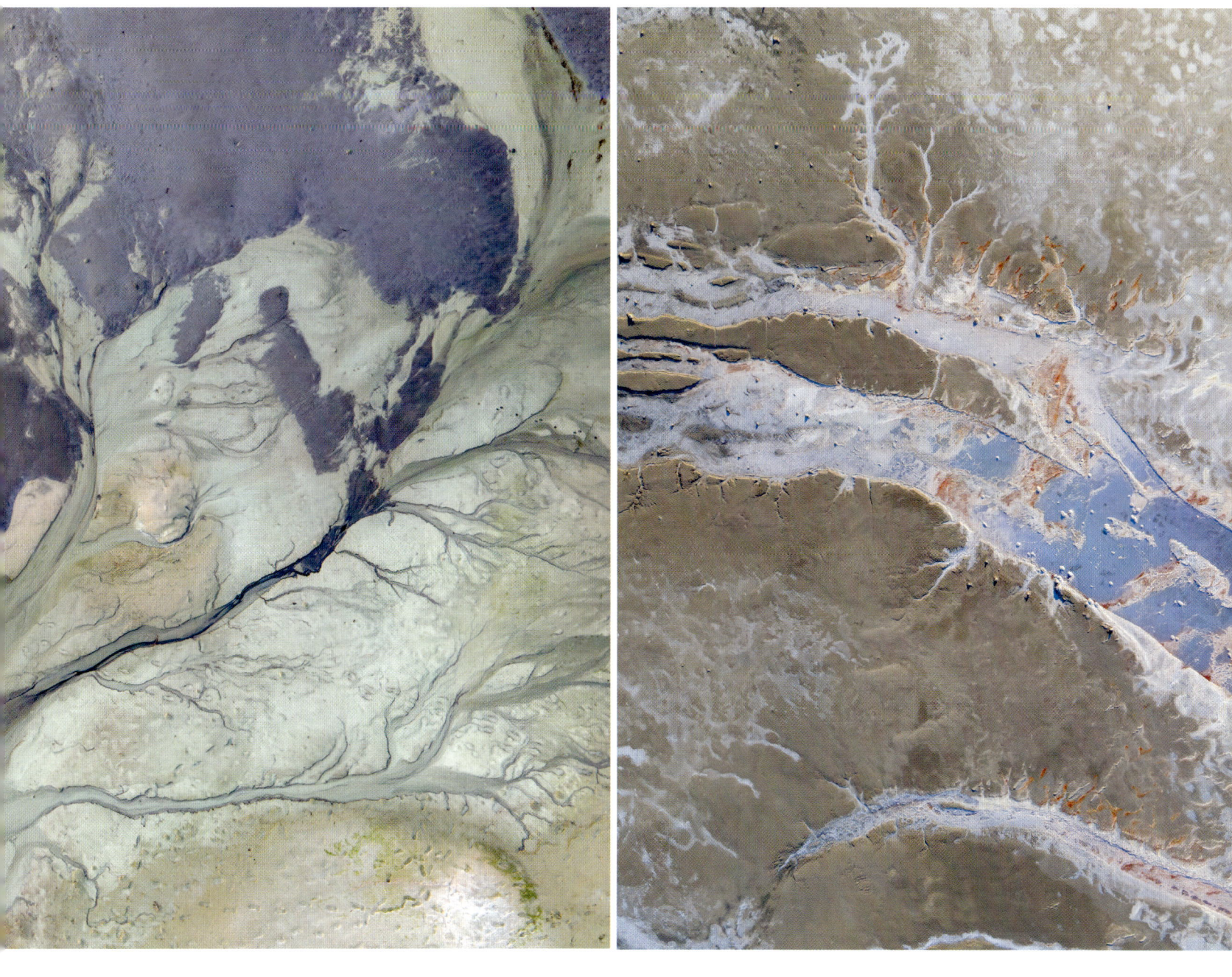

Blue water veins and footprints | K8 | 12.31.2023

Dried delta in Spring Bay | B3 | 07.16.2023

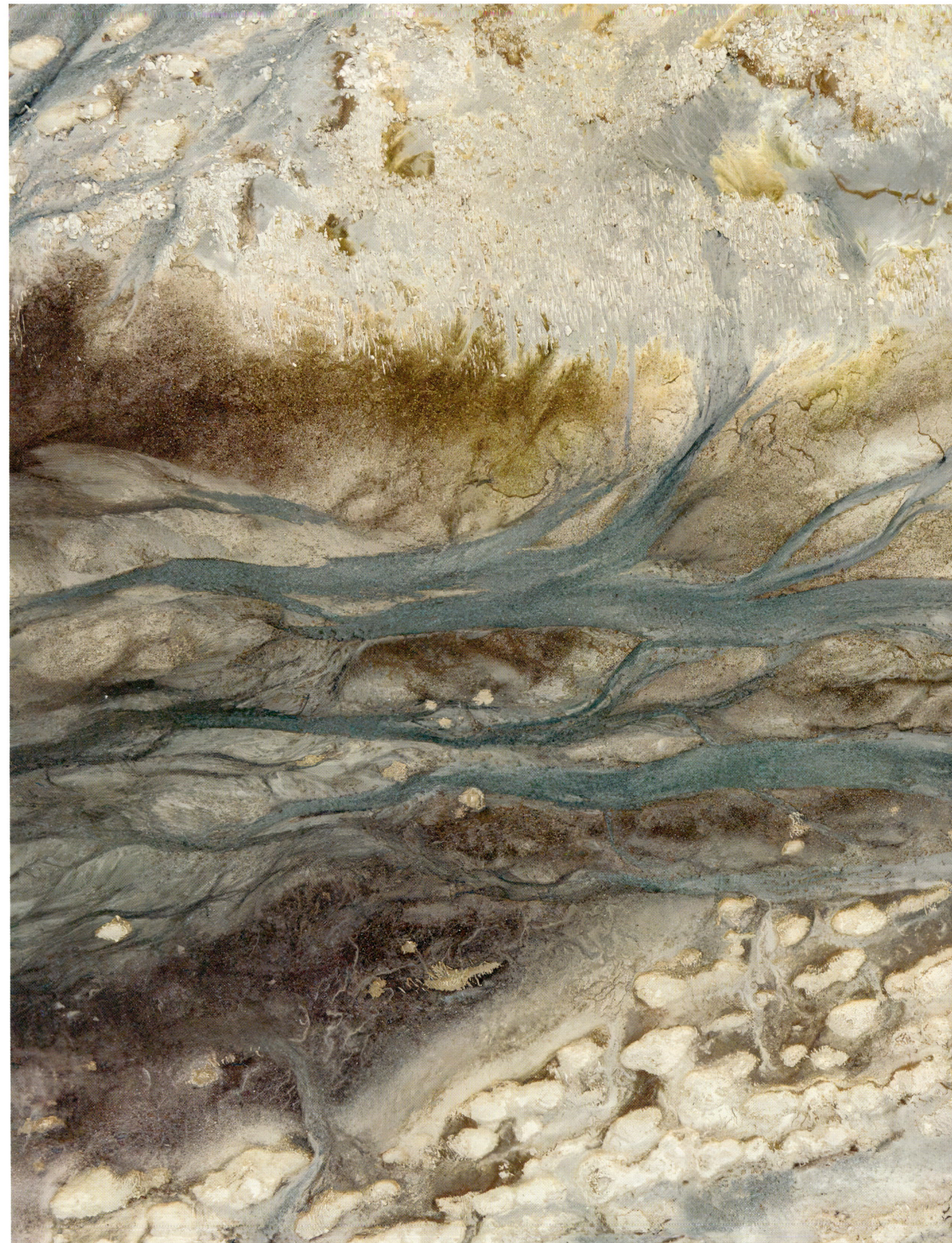

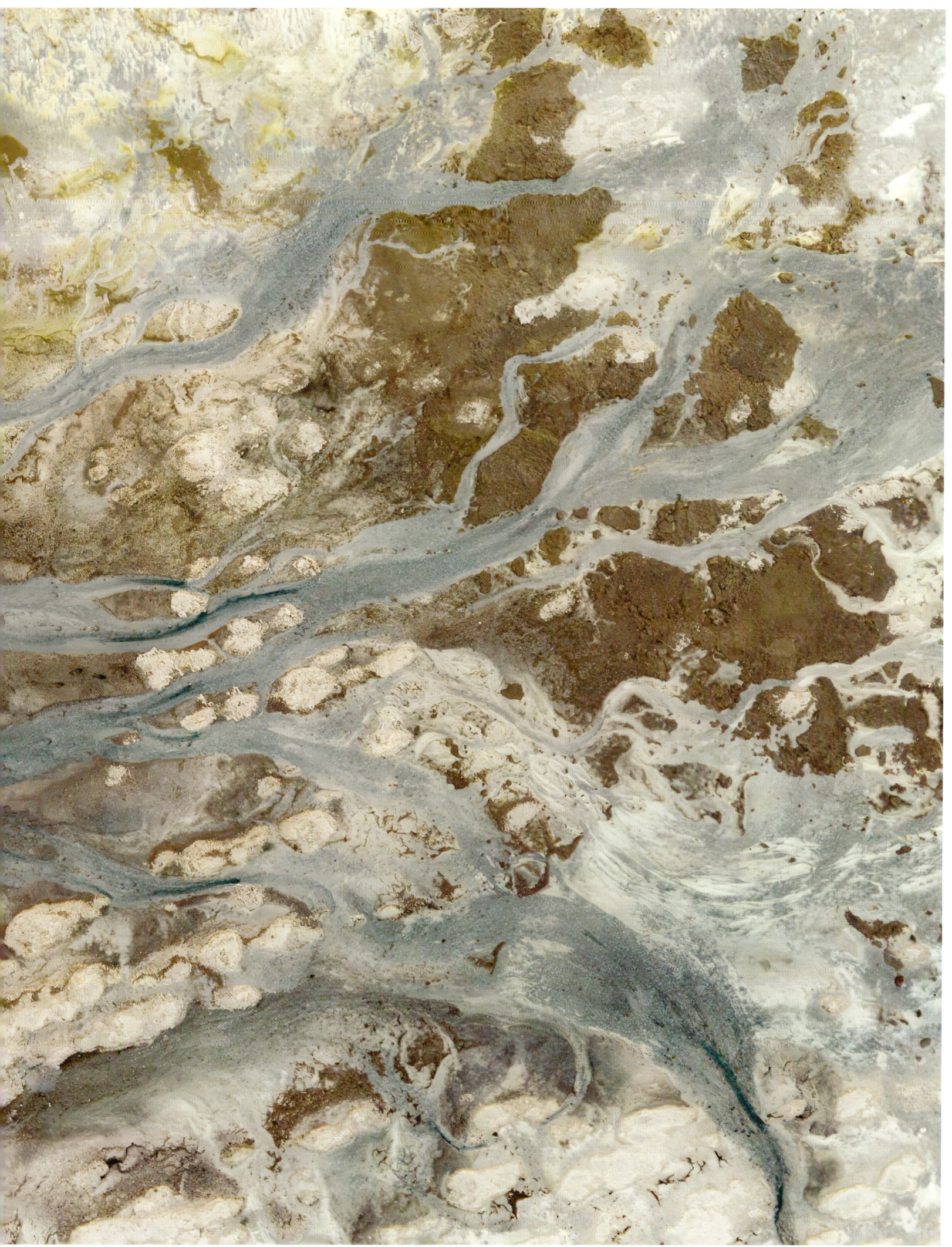

South shore water veins from 164 feet (50 m) | K8 | 11.18.2023

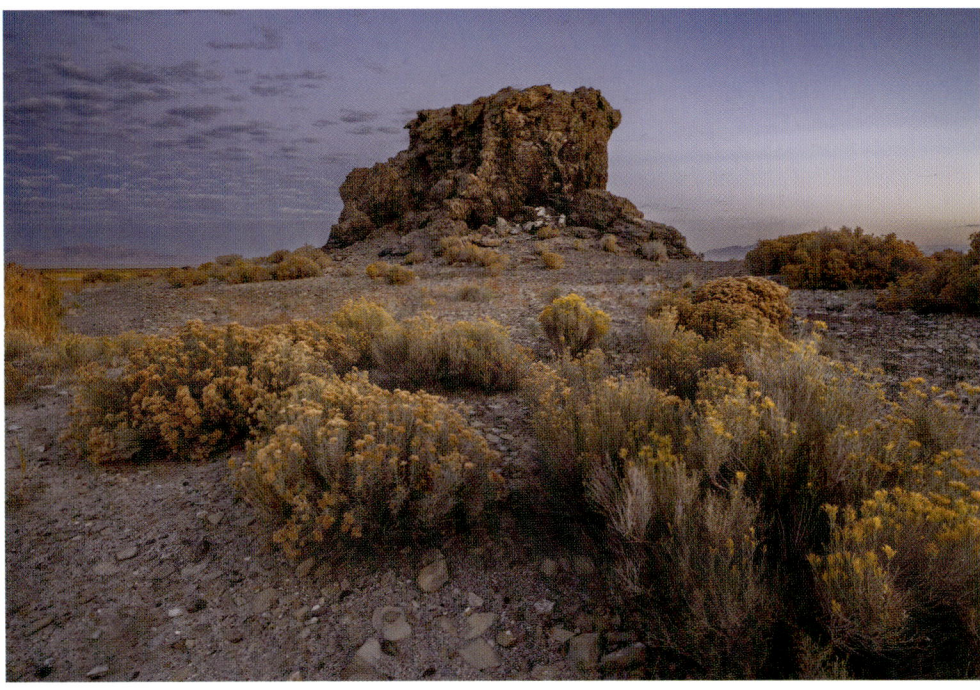

BLACK ROCK

Black Rock emerged over 13,000 years ago when it rolled off the Oquirrh Mountains during the Lake Bonneville time period. As the ancient lake drained, this limestone formation became visible, alternating between a peninsula and an island depending on lake levels. Since 1847, Black Rock has been a significant site for outdoor recreation and inspiration for artists. Notable Utah artists such as Alfred Lambourne and James Taylor Harwood captured its unique and striking appearance in their works, establishing it as a beloved subject in Utah's artistic heritage. Recently, efforts to restore and preserve Black Rock have led to its inclusion in the National Register of Historic Places in 2021, recognizing its historical and natural significance.

Black Rock | K8 | 10.21.2023

Black Rock | K8 | 04.02.2023

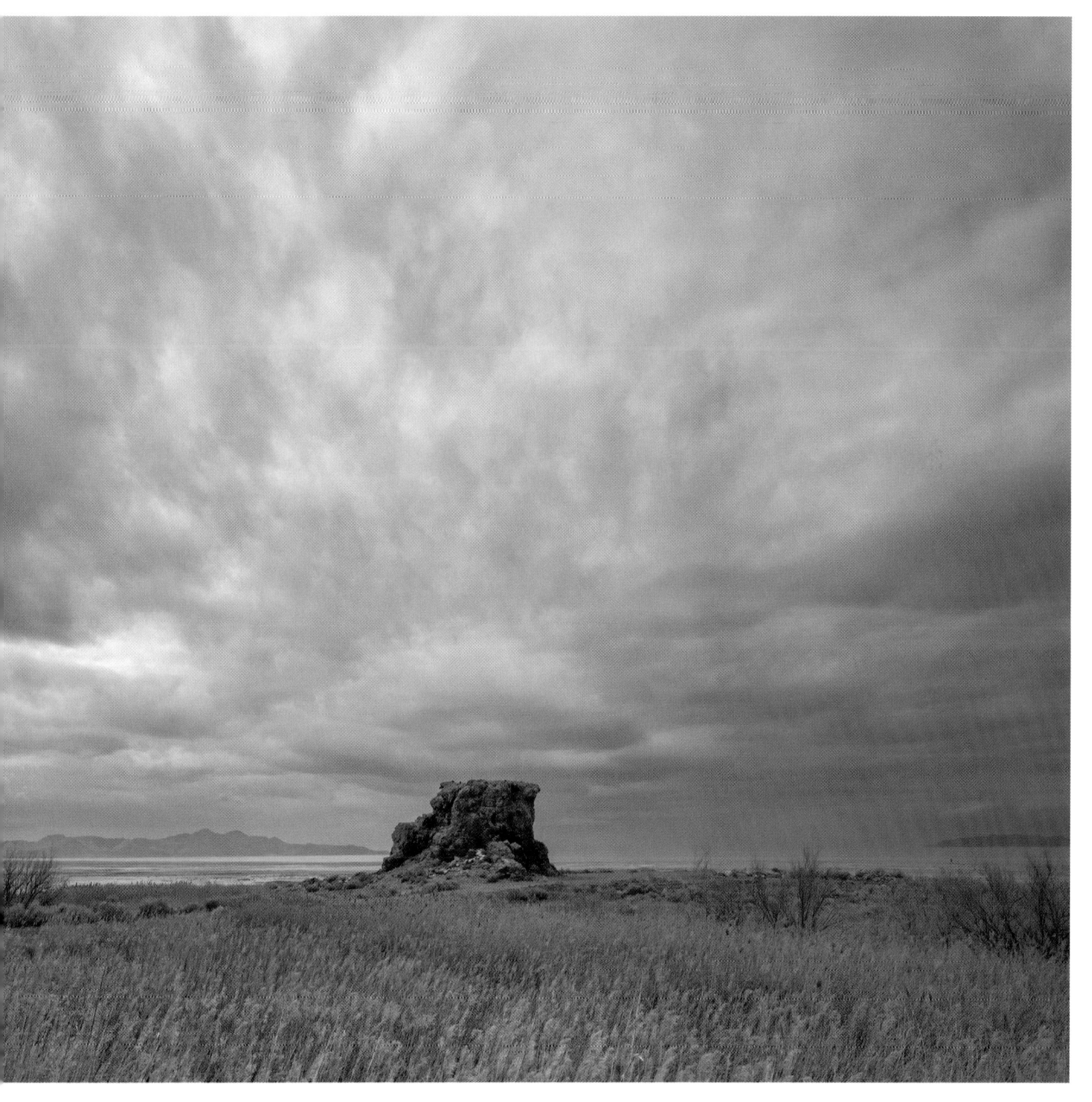

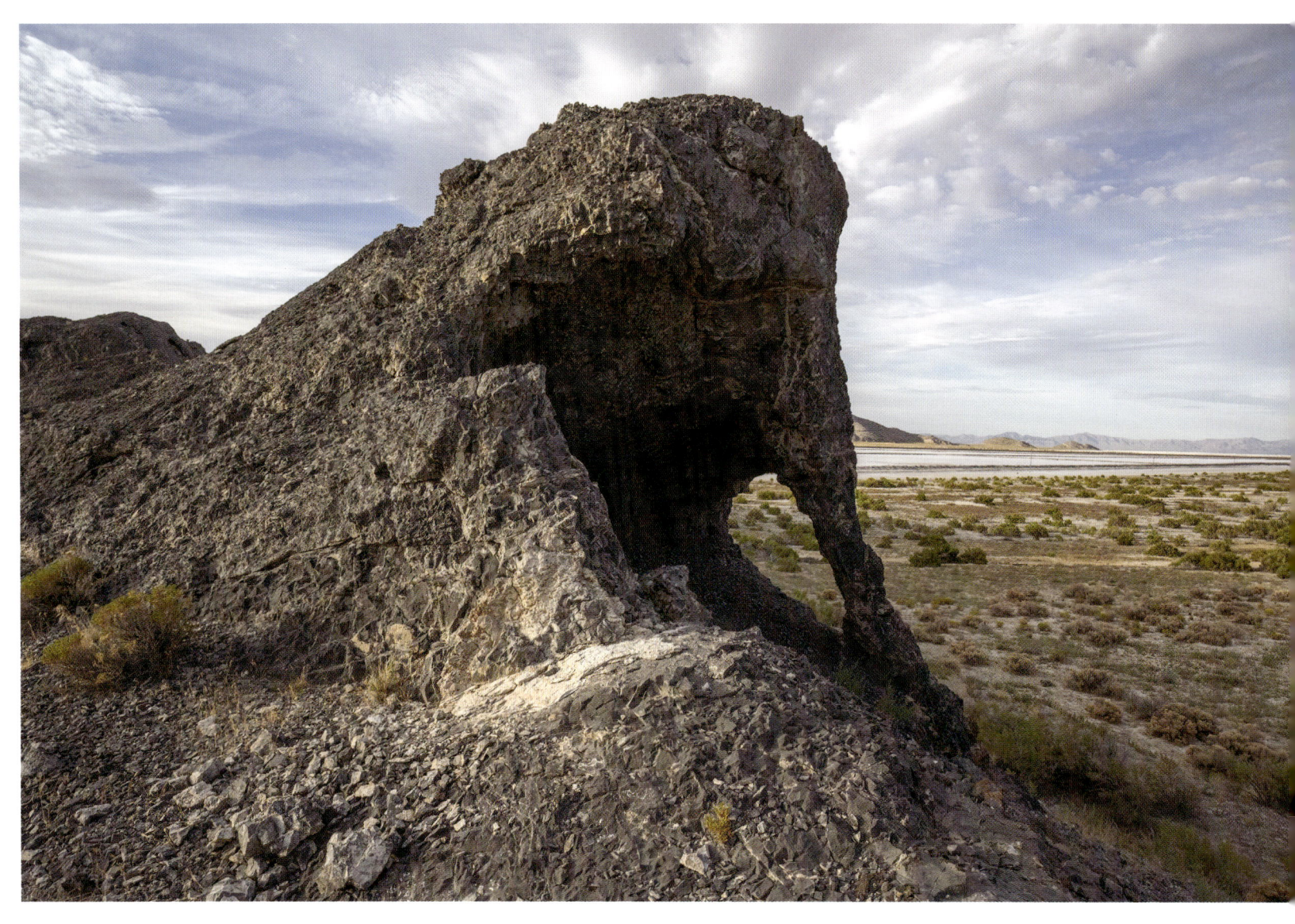

Elephant Rock | F3 | 08.19.2023

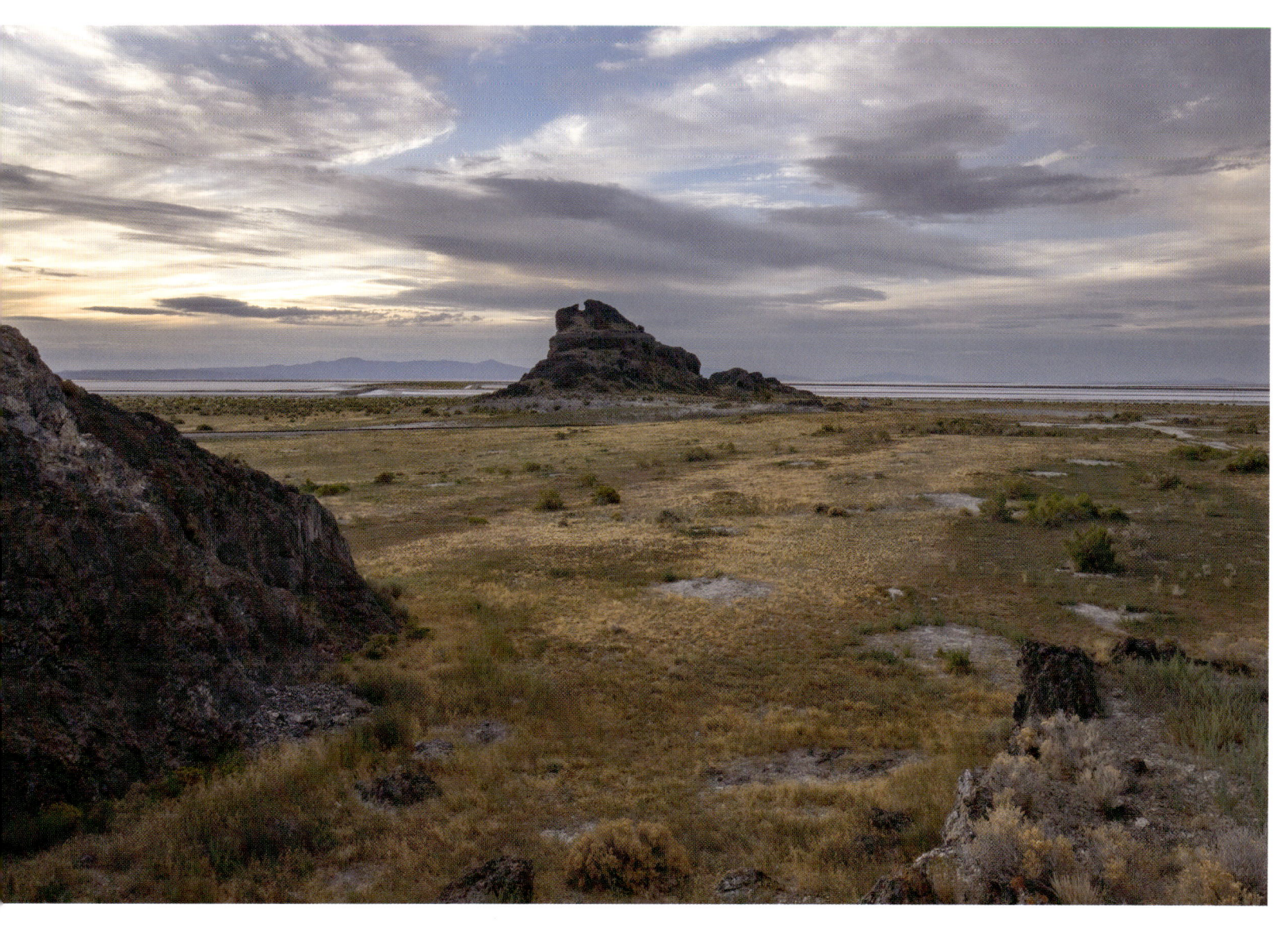

Gunsight Point | F3 | 08.19.2023

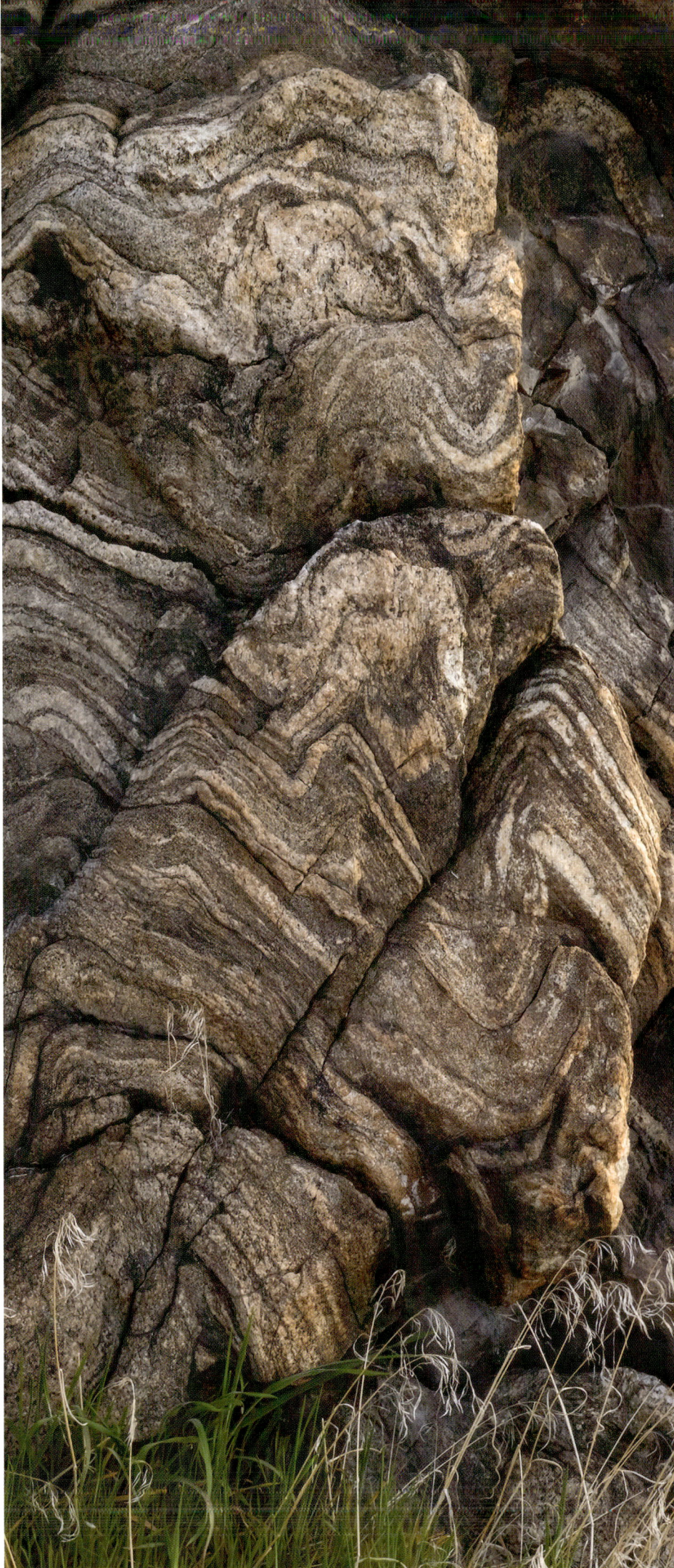

THE FARMINGTON CANYON COMPLEX

The Farmington Canyon Complex on Antelope Island is a geological marvel, showcasing some of the oldest rocks in Utah, dating back 1.7 to 2.5 billion years. These Precambrian metamorphic rocks, including schist, gneiss, and quartzite, were formed deep within the Earth's crust and later exposed through tectonic activity and erosion. This complex offers valuable insights into early crustal development and tectonic processes, making it a key site for geological study.

Farmington Canyon Complex gneiss | 18 | 03.22.2024

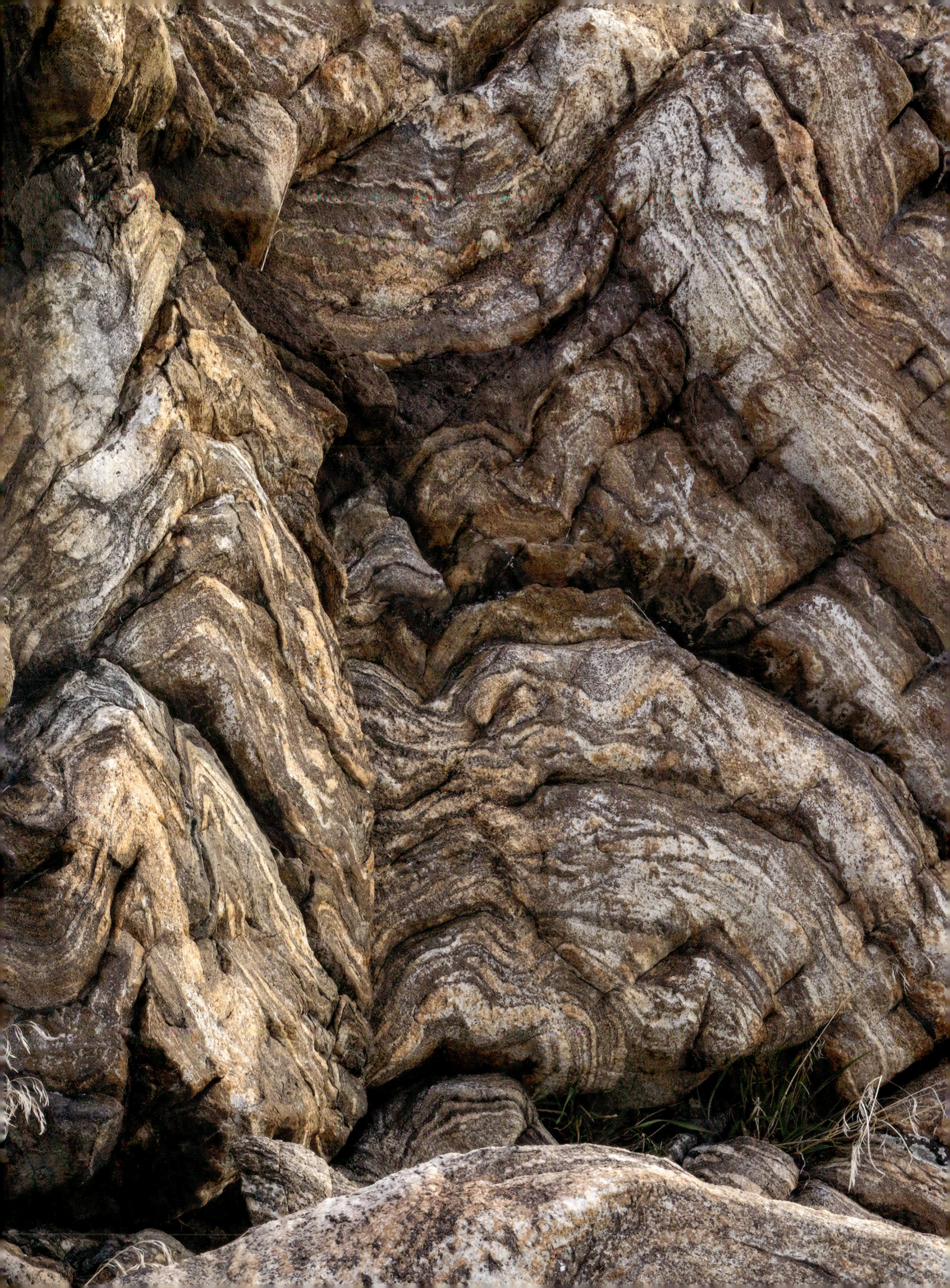

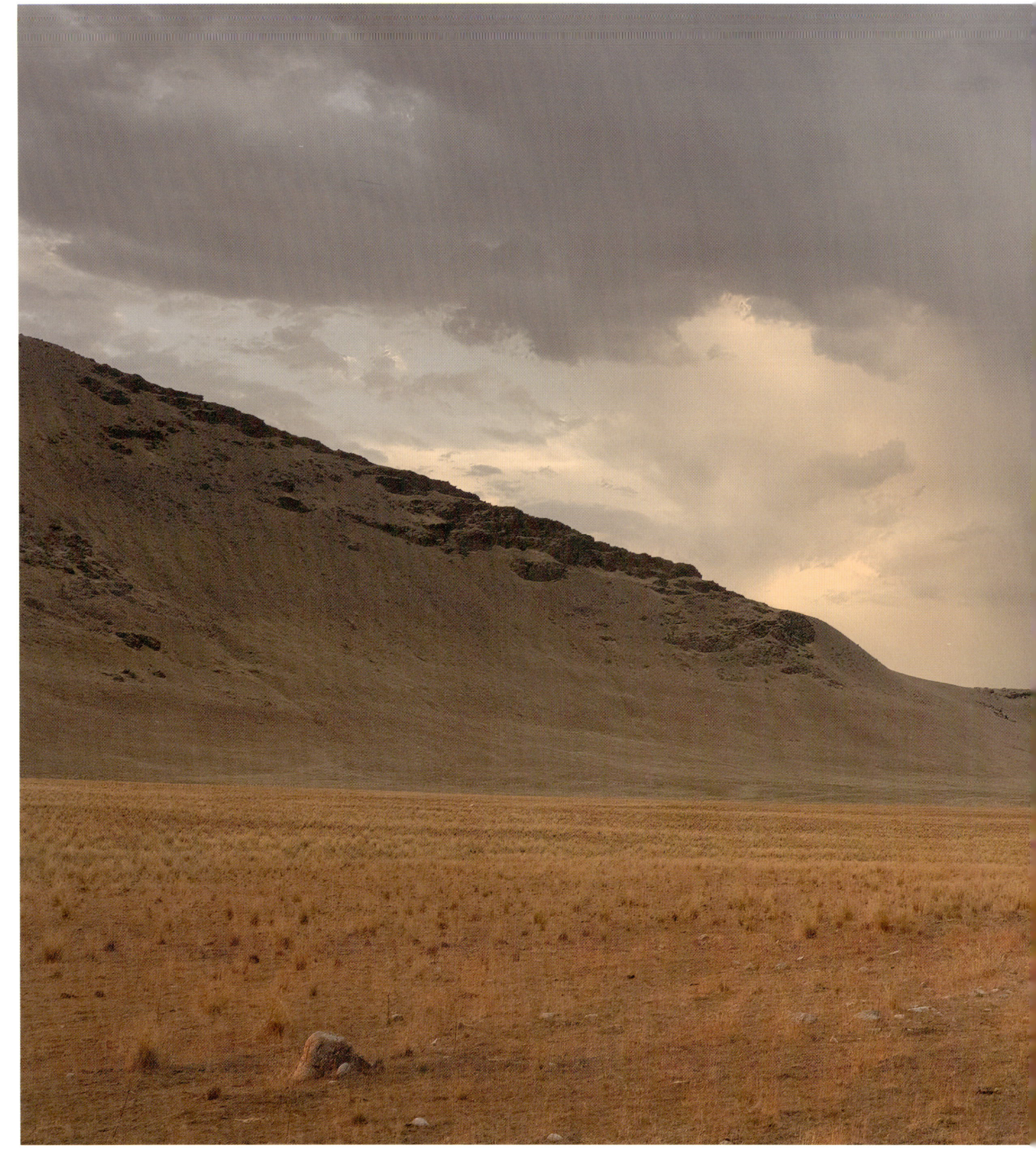

Split Rock, Antelope Island | I8 | 07.27.2024

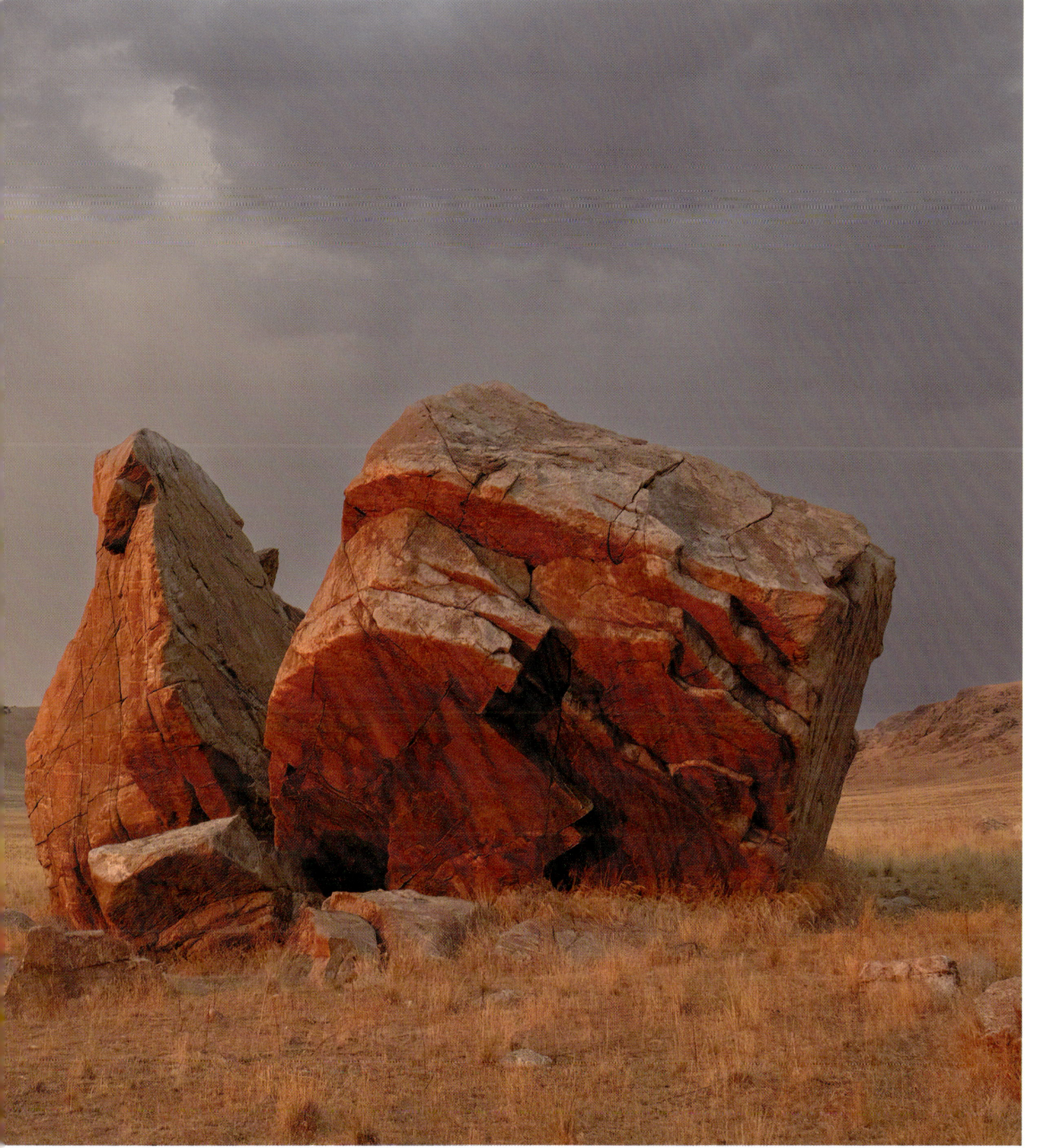

SPLIT ROCK, ANTELOPE ISLAND
This prominent rock formation appears to be split in half, and its unique structure is thought to have resulted from natural weathering processes over thousands of years. The forces of wind, water, and temperature changes likely contributed to the rock's division, creating the striking visual that stands out on the landscape of Antelope Island.

SALT CRYSTALLIZATION

Salt crystallization around Great Salt Lake occurs through several intriguing processes, each contributing to the lake's unique and dynamic landscape. The most common type of crystallization is the formation of halite (sodium chloride) crystals, which happens when the lake's hypersaline water becomes supersaturated with salt, leading to precipitation. These halite crystals often form cubic or hopper-shaped structures, growing on the lakebed, in splash zones, and around objects protruding from the water.

Another significant process involves the formation of bladed selenite crystals, a variety of gypsum (calcium sulfate dihydrate). These crystals emerge from the lake sediments and can sometimes be seen with inclusions of lake muds. Additionally, the unique environment of Great Salt Lake leads to the creation of "dirty diamonds," which are selenite crystals found within the lake's gray, claylike soil. These crystals, known for their hexagonal lenticular shape, add to the fascinating mineral diversity of the lake.

Salt crust from 164 feet (50 m), Compass Minerals
F7 | 06.03.2024

Salt mounds and pink playa from 7,000 feet (2,134 m)
E2 | 10.13.2023

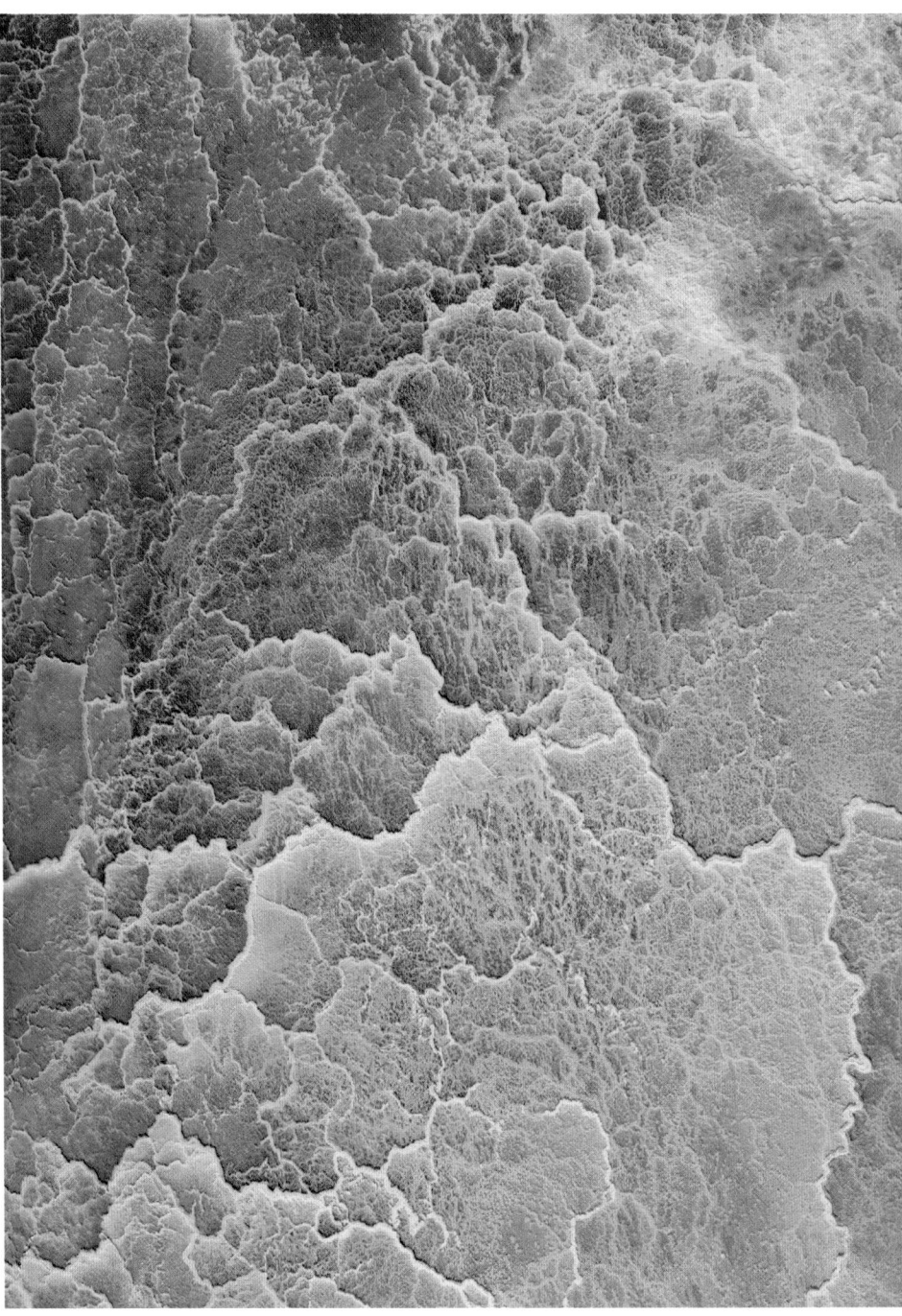

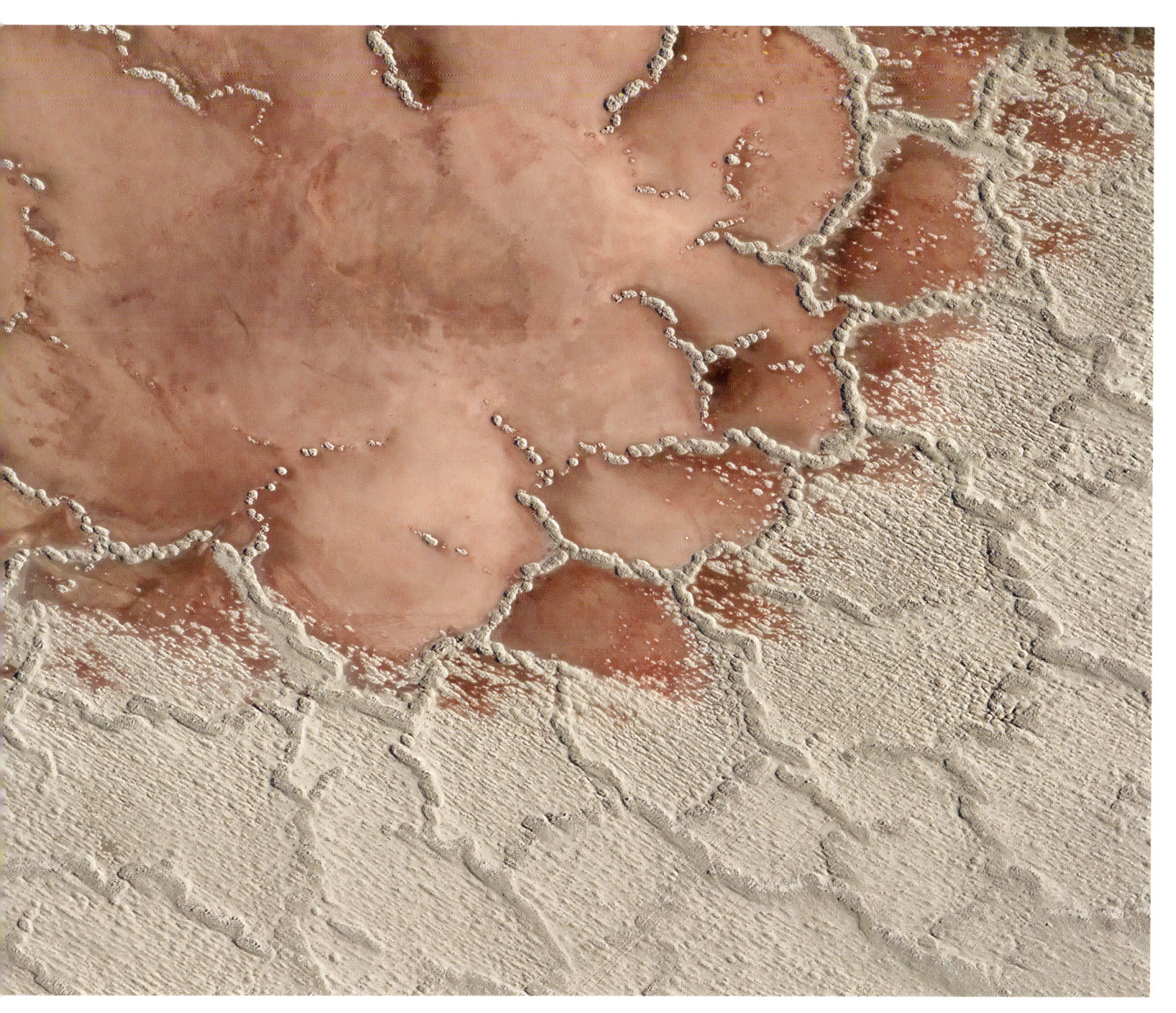

FOLLOWING PAGE: Salt crust from 164 feet (50 m), Compass Minerals | F7 | 06.03.2024

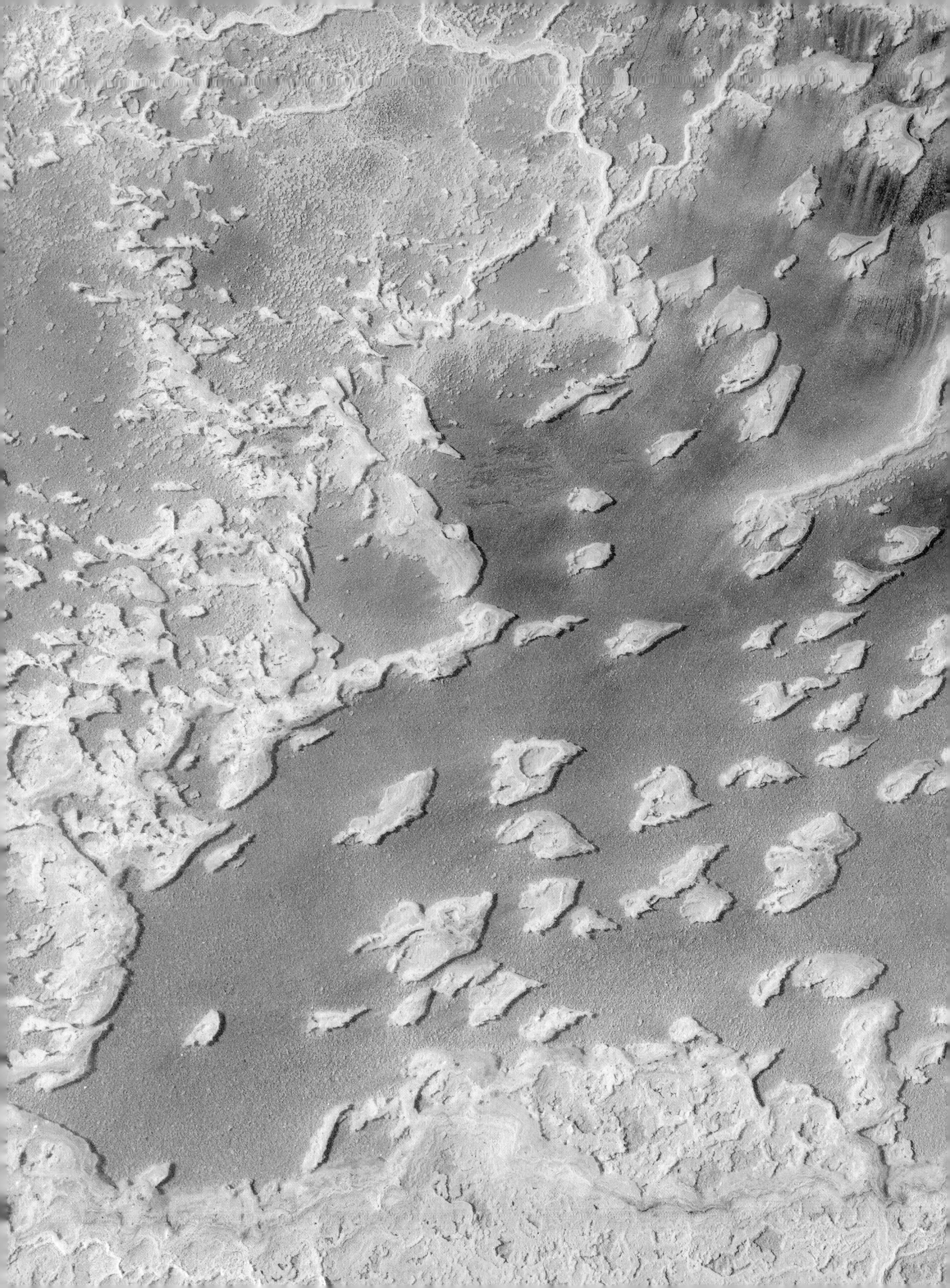

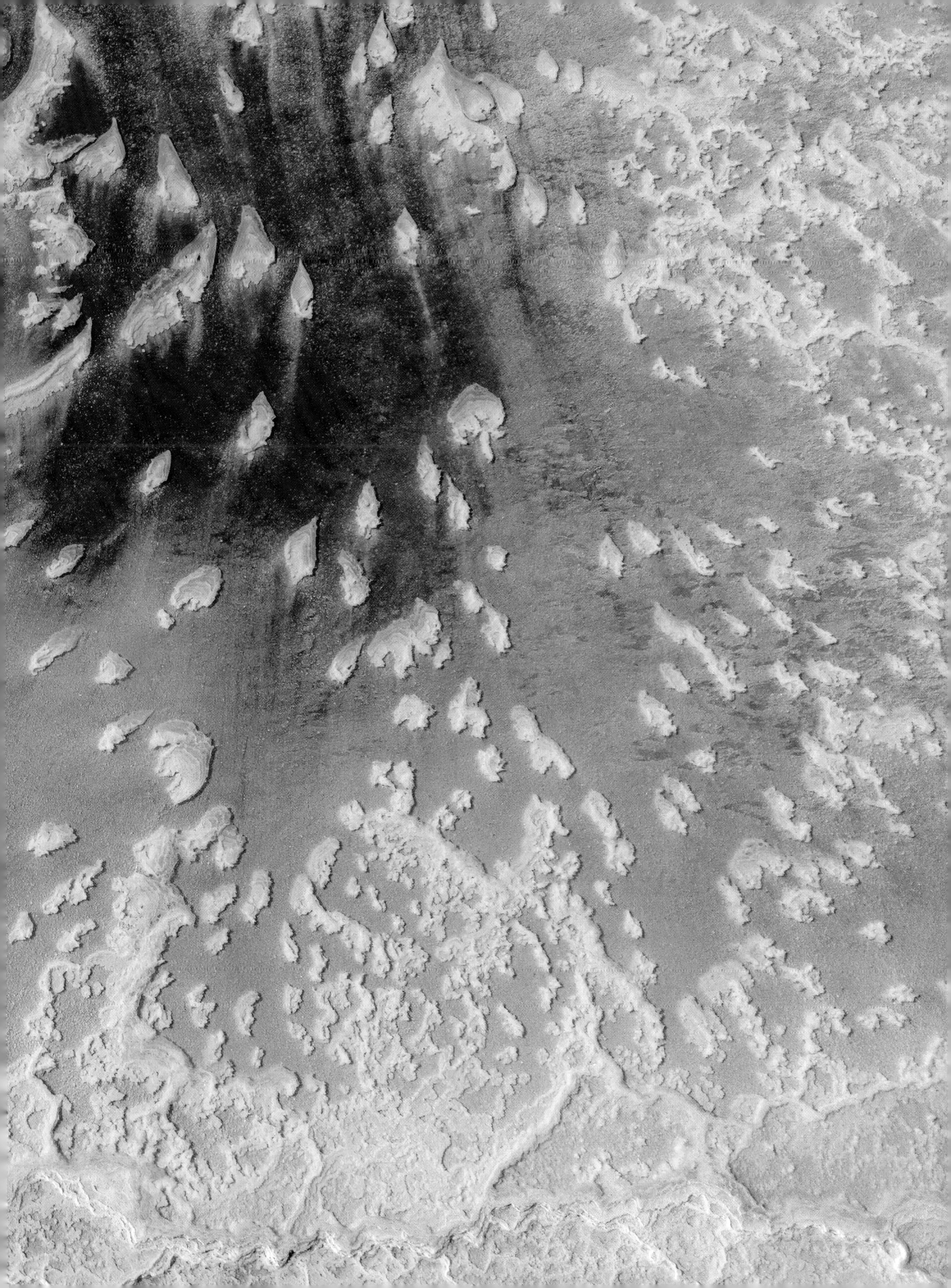

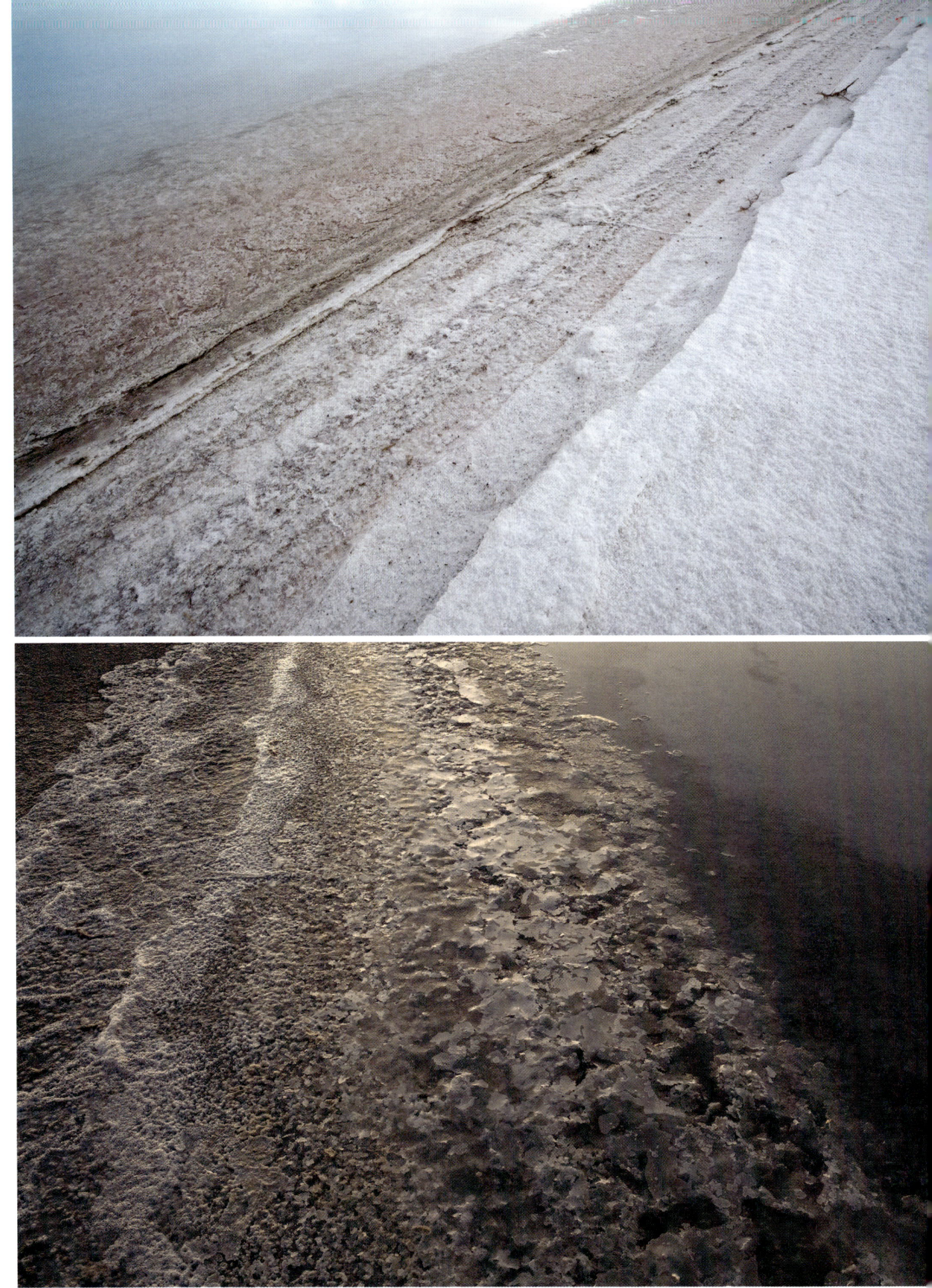

Salty shore, Stansbury Bay | J5 | 09.30.2024

Flaking salt evaporation pond, Morton Salt | K5 | 04.20.2024

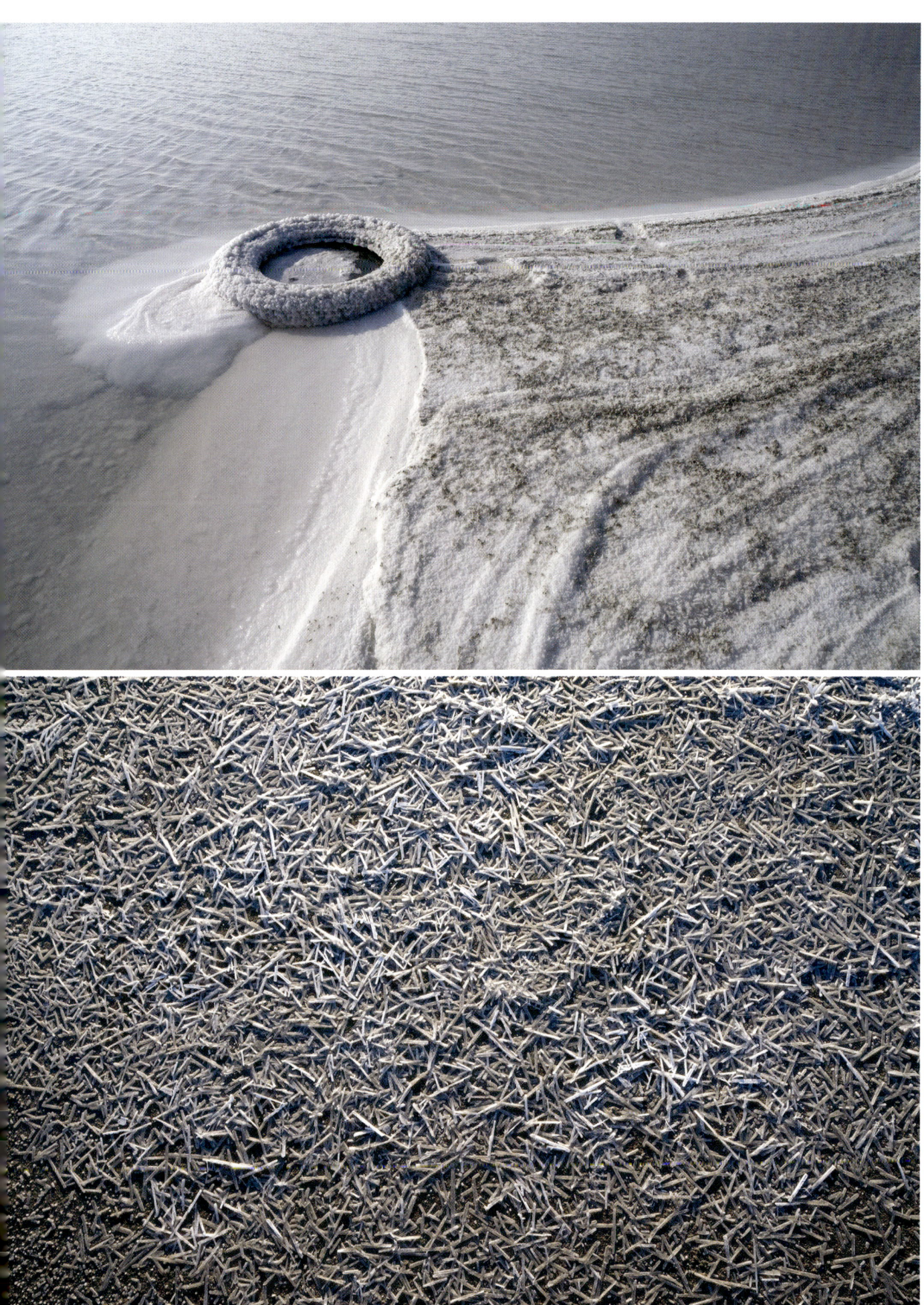

Salt-encrusted tire, Stansbury Bay | J5 | 05.25.2023

Mirabilite (hydrous sodium sulfate crystals), south shore | K8 | 11.20.2022

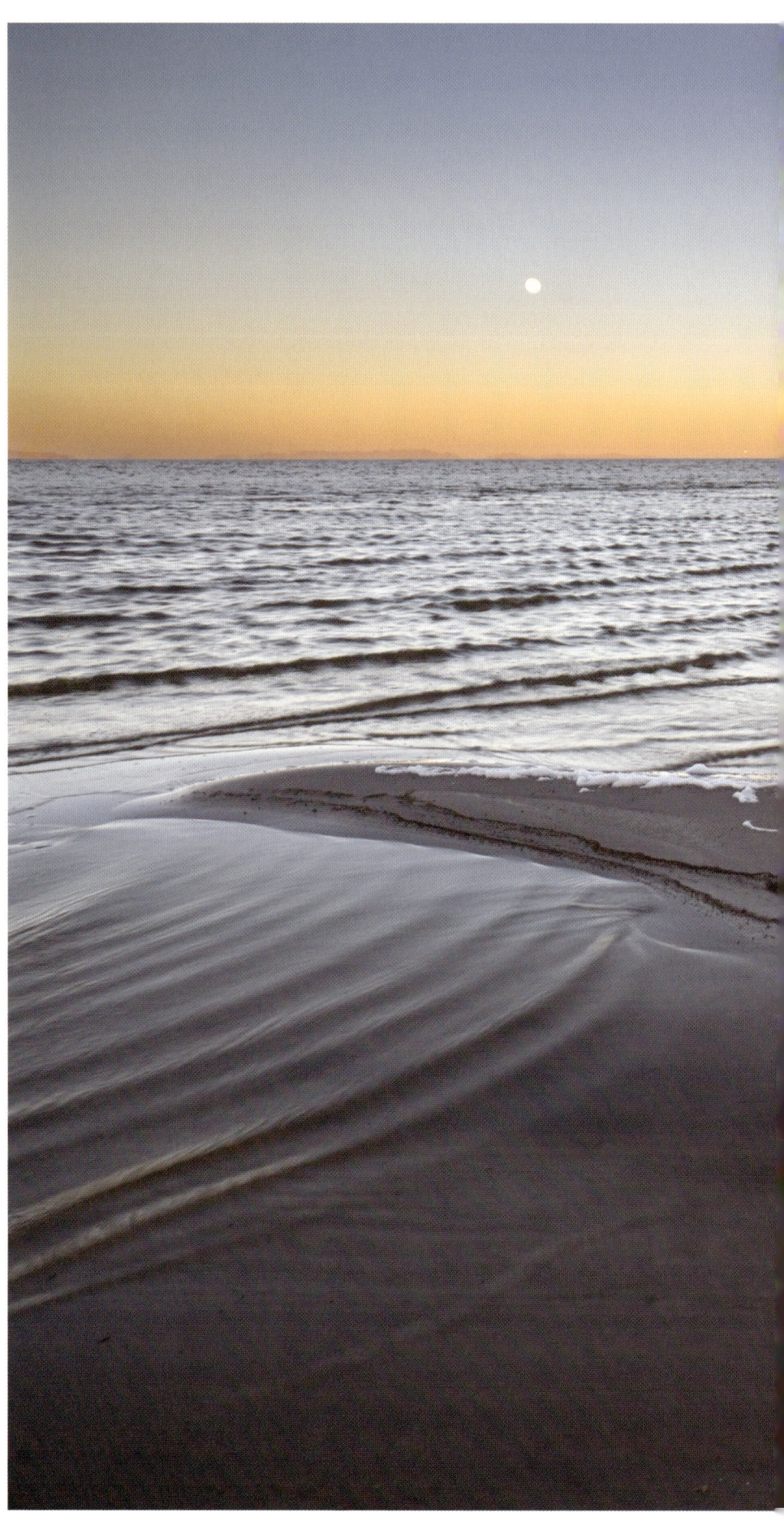

White Rock and moon | H8 | 10.29.2023

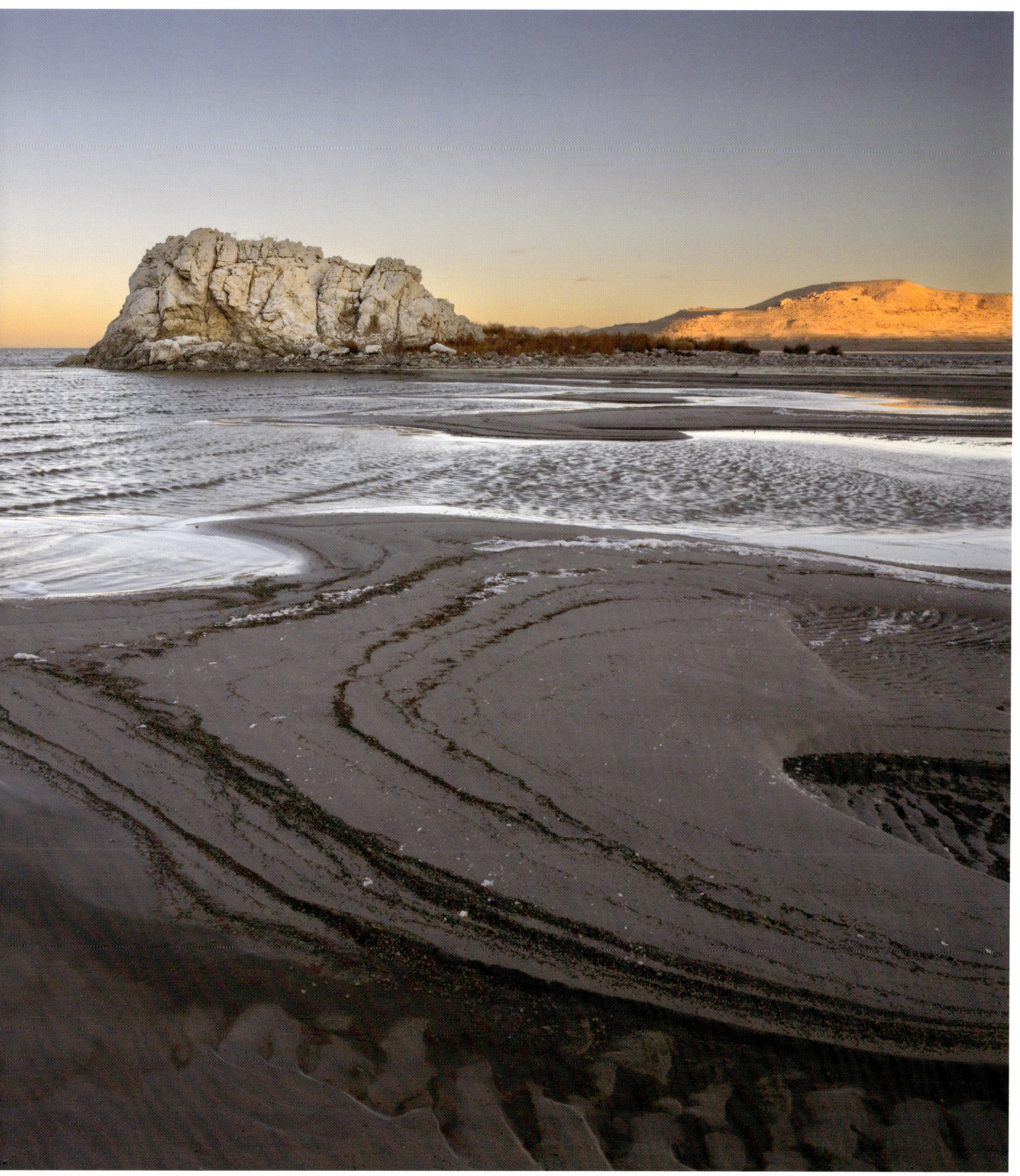

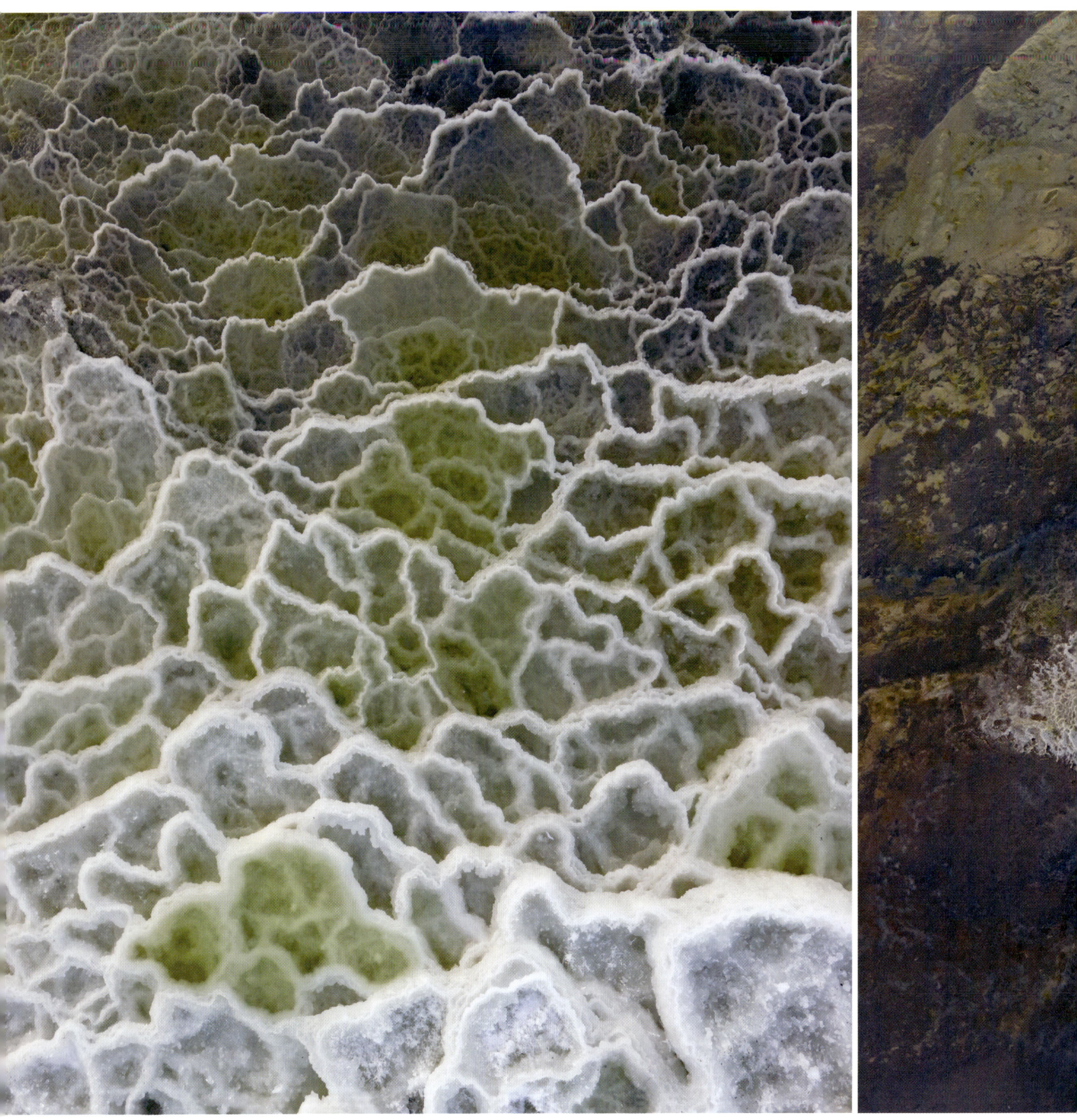

Mirabilite mound detail | K8 | 12.31.2023   Mirabilite mounds from 164 feet (50 m) | K8 | 12.31.2023

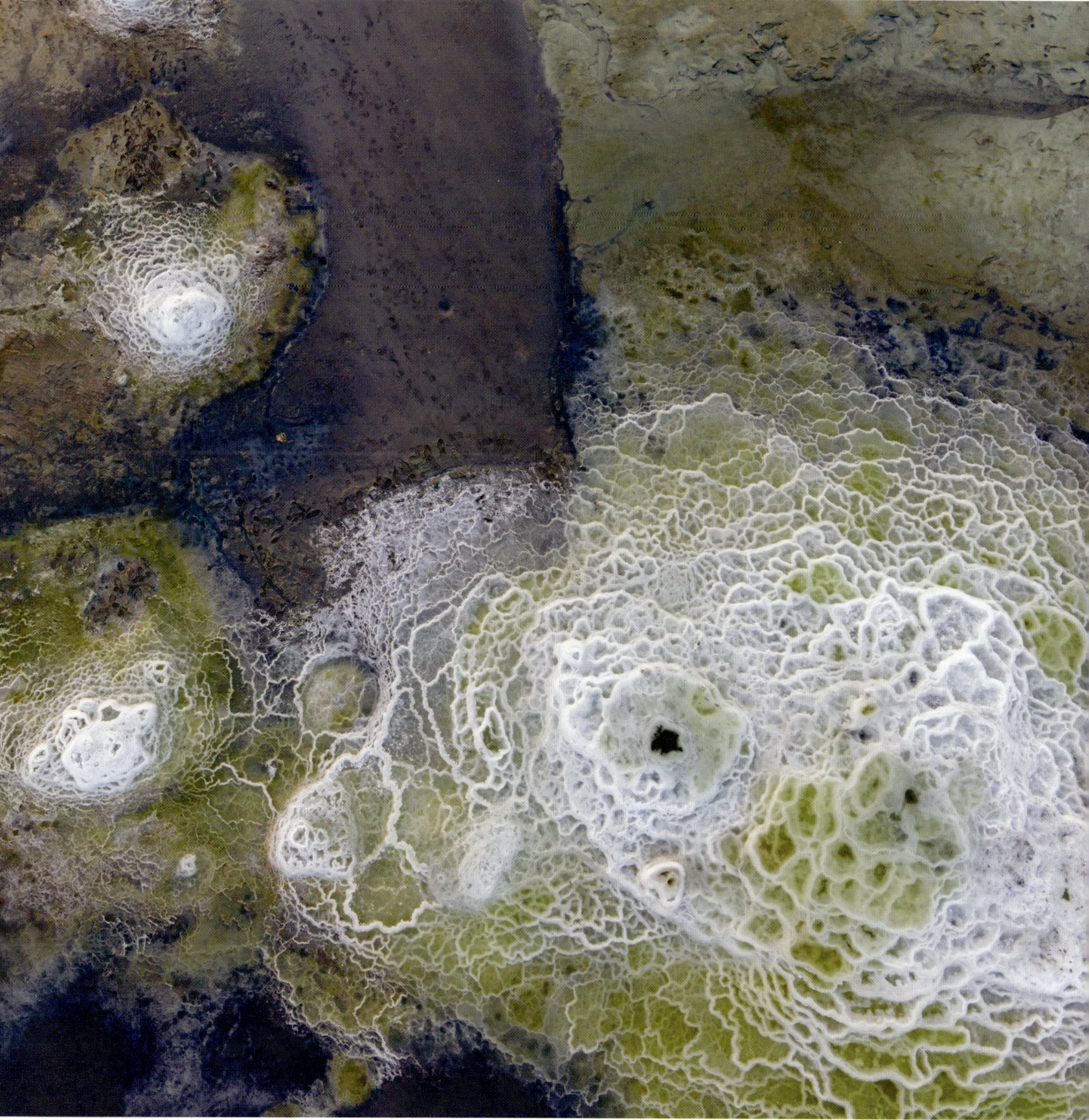

MIRABILITE MOUNDS

In the colder months, the lake's edges can develop mirabilite mounds. Mirabilite, a type of hydrated sodium sulfate, forms mounds and towers when the water evaporates and temperatures drop. These mounds are delicate and often dissolve quickly, leaving a fleeting yet fascinating mark on the landscape. The texture of mirabilite mounds is powdery and crystalline, contrasting with the harder salt flats and rocks around them. These formations are beautiful and serve as indicators of the changing environmental conditions around the lake. Mirabilite mounds are rare, found only in a few places on Earth, such as the Antarctic, and their appearance in Great Salt Lake is a unique occurrence tied to specific climatic and hydrological conditions. They provide insights into Earth's—and potentially Mars's—geological processes due to their formation in sulfate-rich environments.

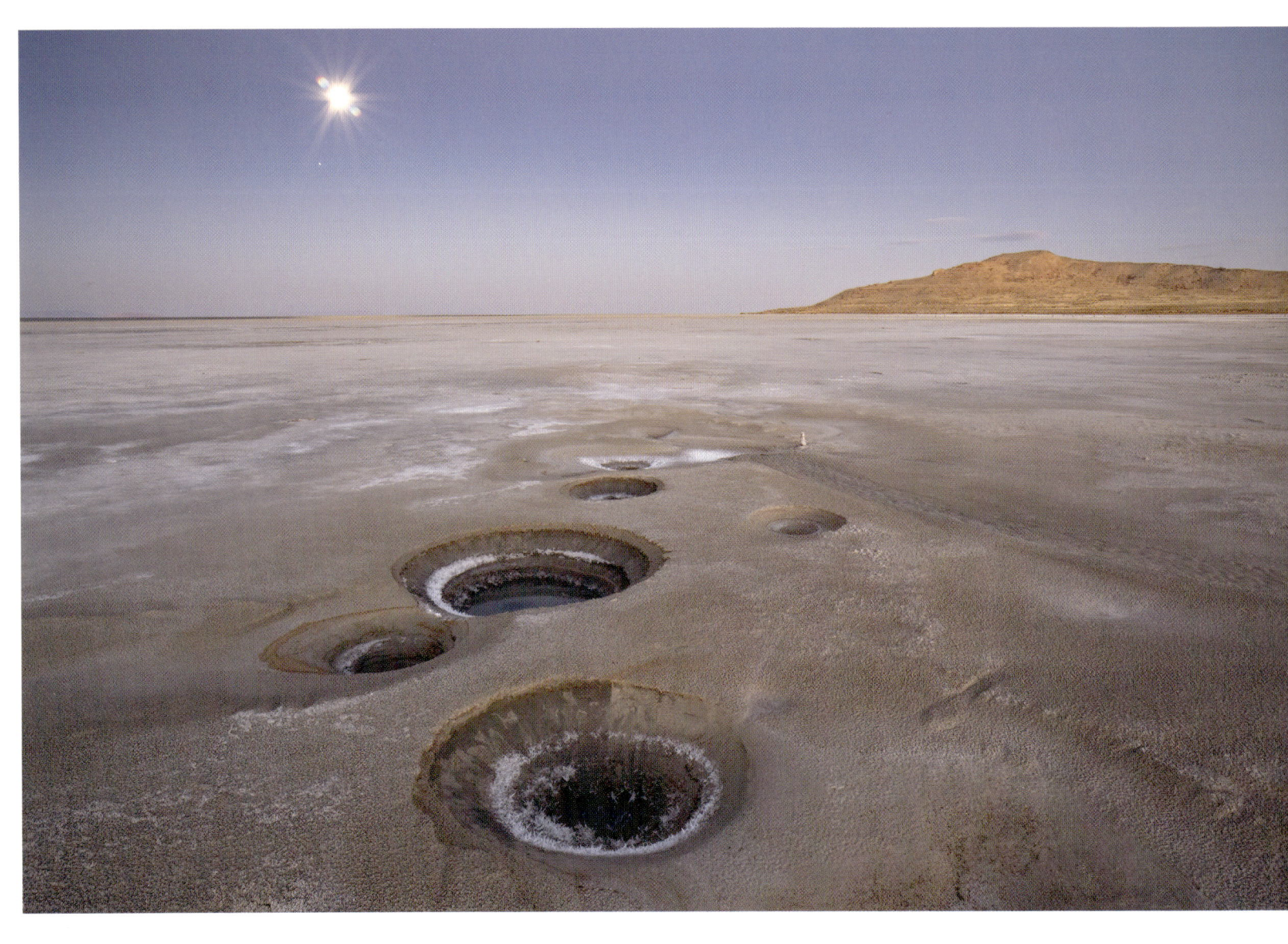

Salt pots and moon, White Rock Bay | H8 | 10.29.2023

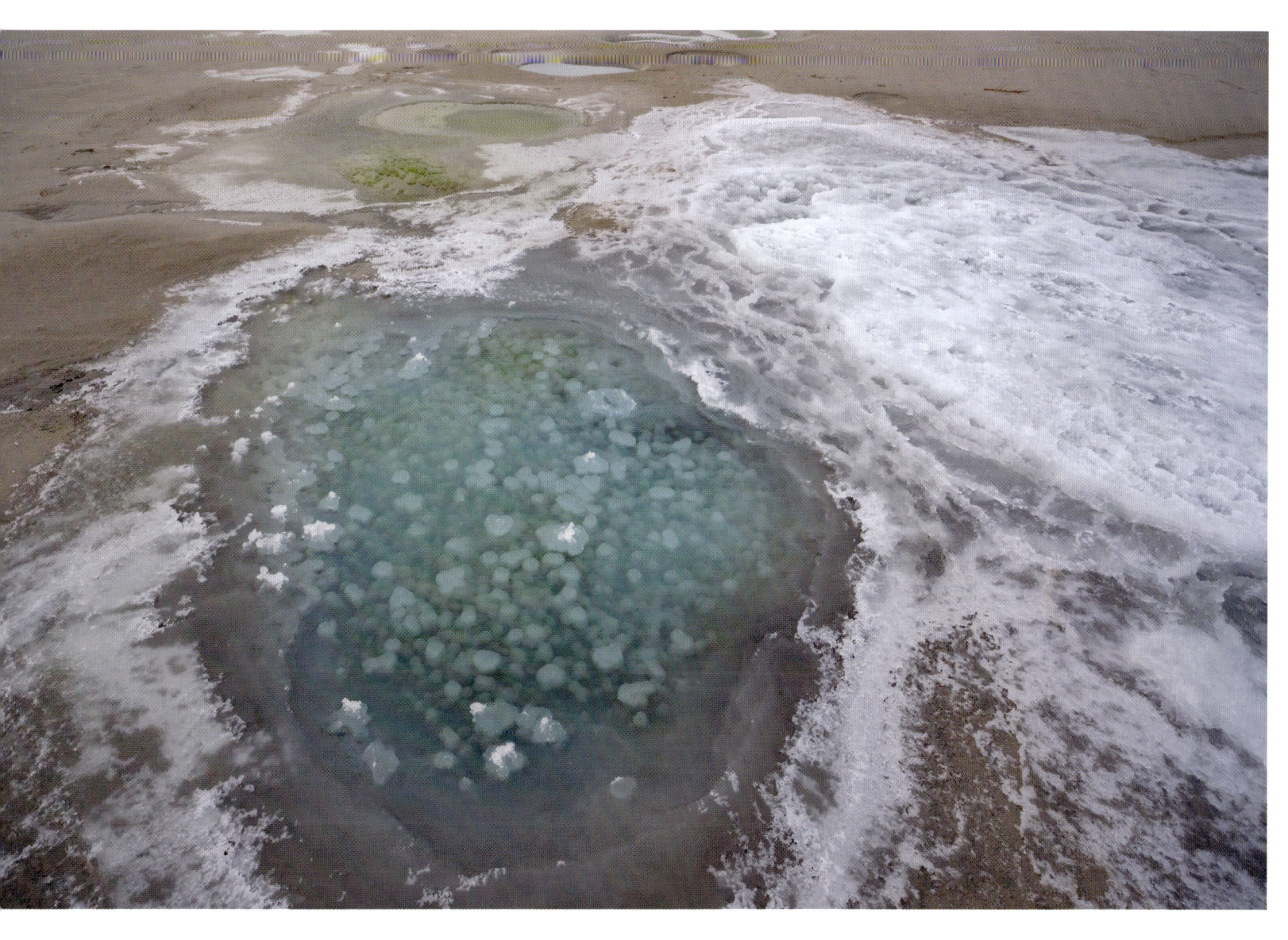

Salt spring, White Rock Bay | H8 | 12.27.2023

FOLLOWING PAGE: Brine pool and mud, Stansbury Island | J5 | 09.30.2023

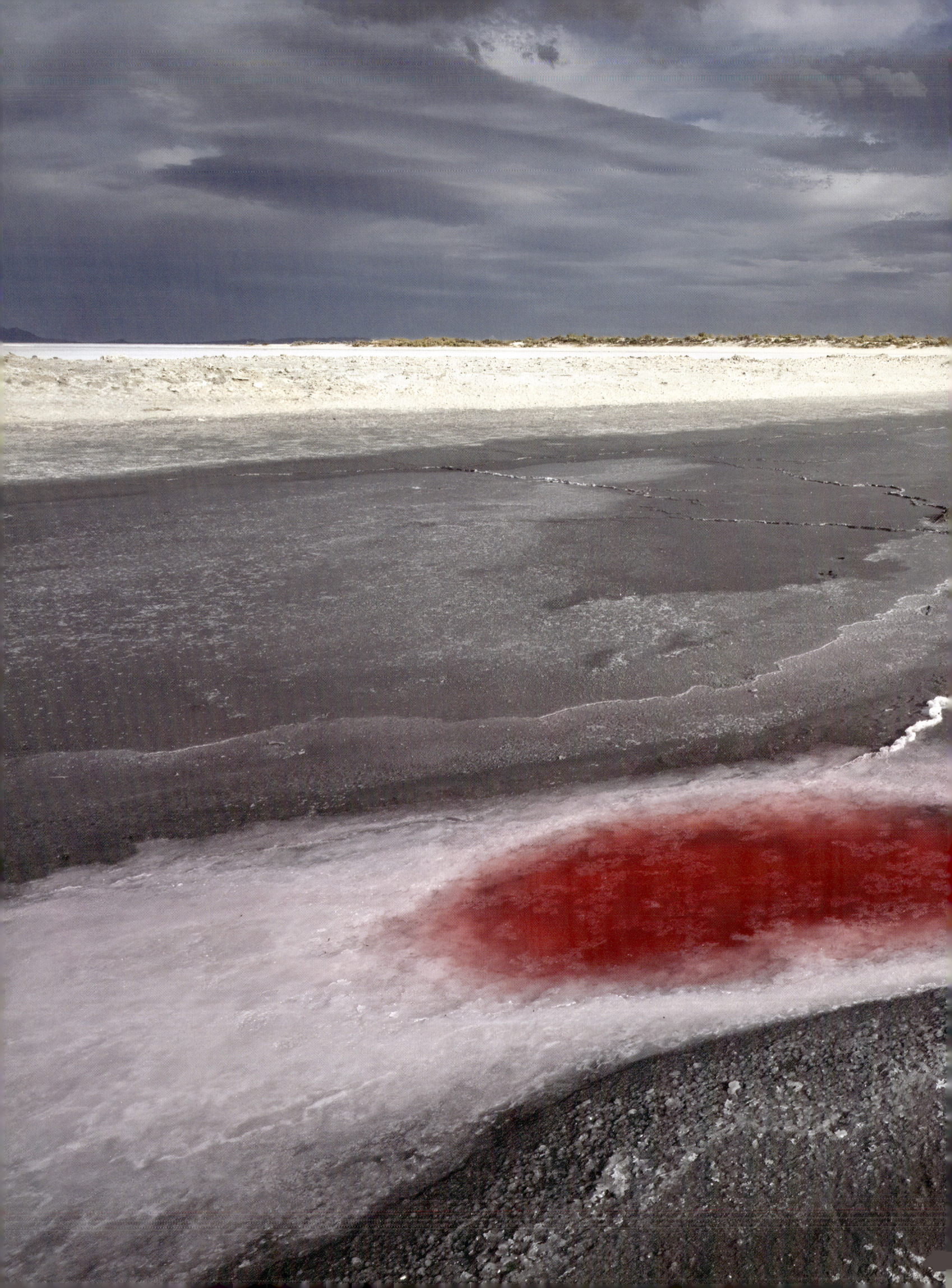

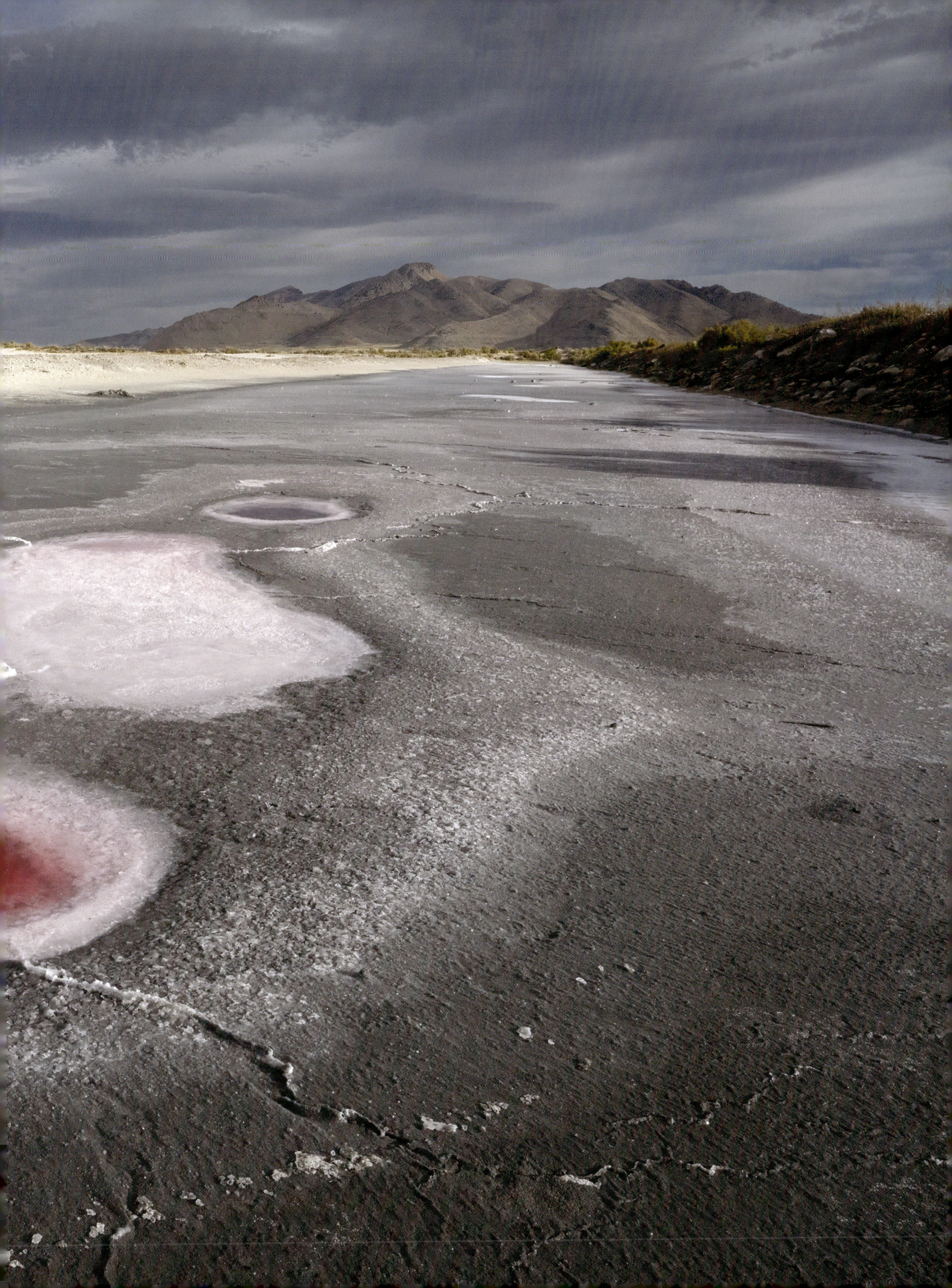

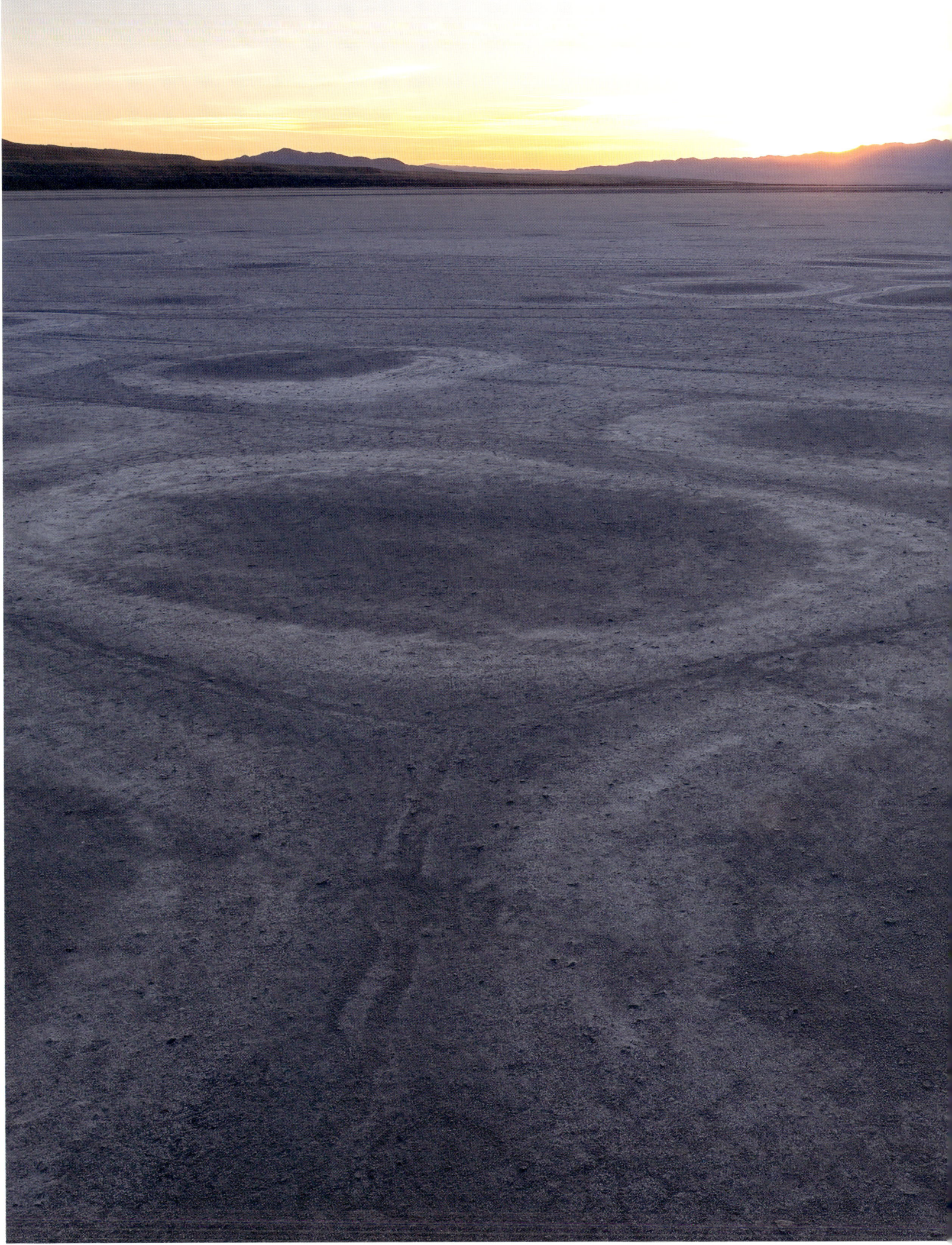

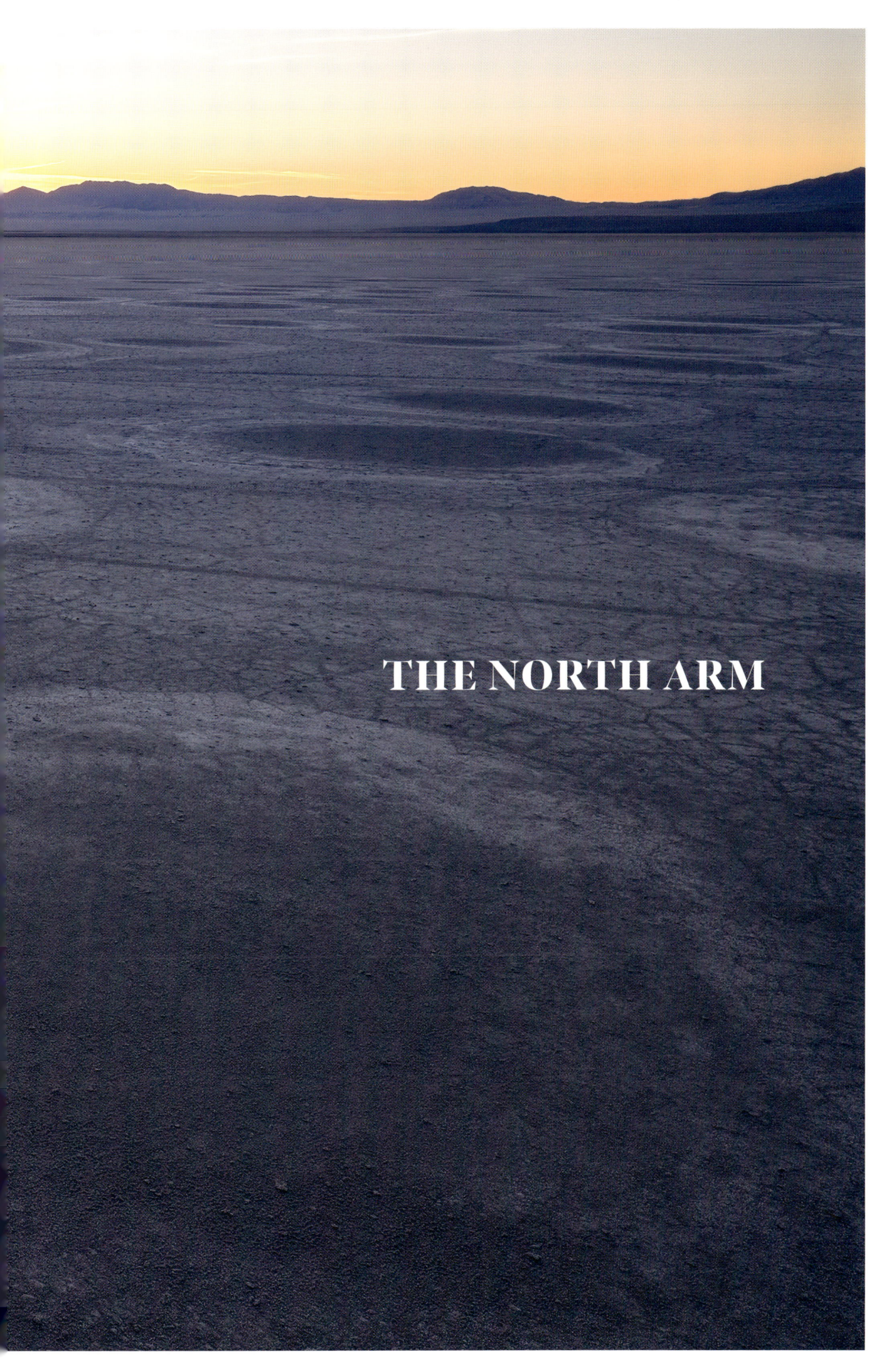

THE NORTH ARM

05.

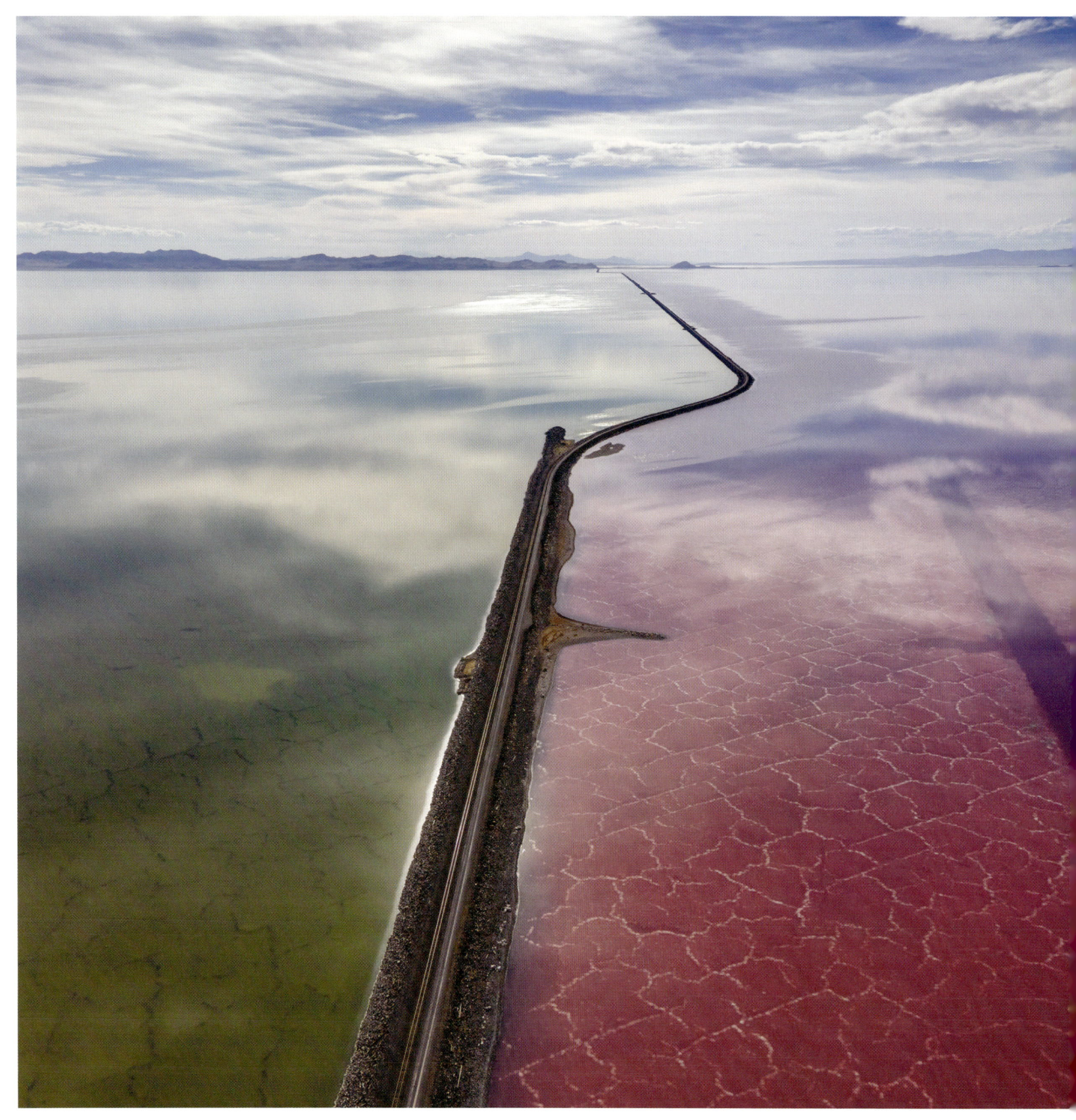

The Lucin Cutoff, Union Pacific Railroad causeway | F5 | 10.20.2021
PREVIOUS PAGE: Mineral circles on the playa, Spring Bay | B3 | 07.16.2023

A Vivid Paradox

THE NORTH ARM OF THE GREAT SALT LAKE is a realm of stark beauty and extremes. It is a place of vivid ironies—where a harsh environment meets striking pink waters. Known as Gunnison Bay, the North Arm is separated from its southern counterpart by the Union Pacific Railroad causeway, fostering a distinct and severe ecological divide. Water in the North Arm is often at a state where it cannot hold any more dissolved salt because it is at saturation with respect to halite, so solid salt forms on the lakebed.

Salinity levels in the North Arm exceed 30 percent, far higher than the south. These hypersaline conditions paint the waters in shades of vibrant pink and red, caused by halophilic bacteria and algae that thrive in such concentrated saline water. Covering around 850 square miles (2,201 sq km), the North Arm may be smaller than the South Arm but is no less significant—a stark environment showcasing the lake's brilliant diversity. The high salinity levels in Gunnison Bay cause extensive salt crusts and formations on the lakebed and along the shores. These formations, viewed from above, resemble a web of veins. The salt veins crisscross the landscape in an organic, almost vascular pattern, mimicking the complex pathways of blood vessels in the human body.

The ancient microbialites in the North Arm have a more difficult time here than in the South. Here, they provide insights relevant to astrobiology, simulating conditions that might exist on other planets. It is often said that the North Arm looks like another planet. Only the most resilient life forms can endure here. Otherwise hardy species like brine shrimp and brine flies now struggle as salinity pushes past survivable limits, nearly eradicating the once-thriving shrimp and fly populations, threatening the many bird species that depend on them.

In this extreme place, the iconic Spiral Jetty by Robert Smithson stands out—an earthwork sculpture extending 1,500 feet (457 m) into what used to be water in a coiling spiral form that shifts with the ebbs and flows of lake levels. It may be the most important piece of land art ever created, a poignant symbol of the intricate dance between human creativity and raw natural forces.

At the most northern part of Great Salt Lake lies Spring Bay, known for its bright red channels flowing into the lake and crystalline salt formations that glow ethereally at sunrise and sunset, creating landscapes that feel truly otherworldly.

The North Arm carries layers of human connection too. Indigenous tribes have long found spiritual and pragmatic value in its harsh beauty long before settlers and industries capitalized on its mineral-rich waters. Today, vivid evaporation ponds from salt extraction patchwork the landscapes on the east side of the Promontory Mountains.

The very existence of the North Arm is at stake because of intensifying challenges. Water diversions starve it of critical inflows, while climate change accelerates evaporation—a dual threat pushing salinity to inhospitable extremes.

The North Arm is a warning sign of what the South Arm could become. Within this struggle lies an urgent purpose: to balance human interference with ecological preservation. Researchers monitor salinity and water quality and track the health of unique species like the Wilson's Phalarope and Eared Grebe that still make the North Arm their home. The North Arm's greatness is reflected in its stark, rugged beauty and its role as an unforgiving yet nurturing habitat where life finds its way.

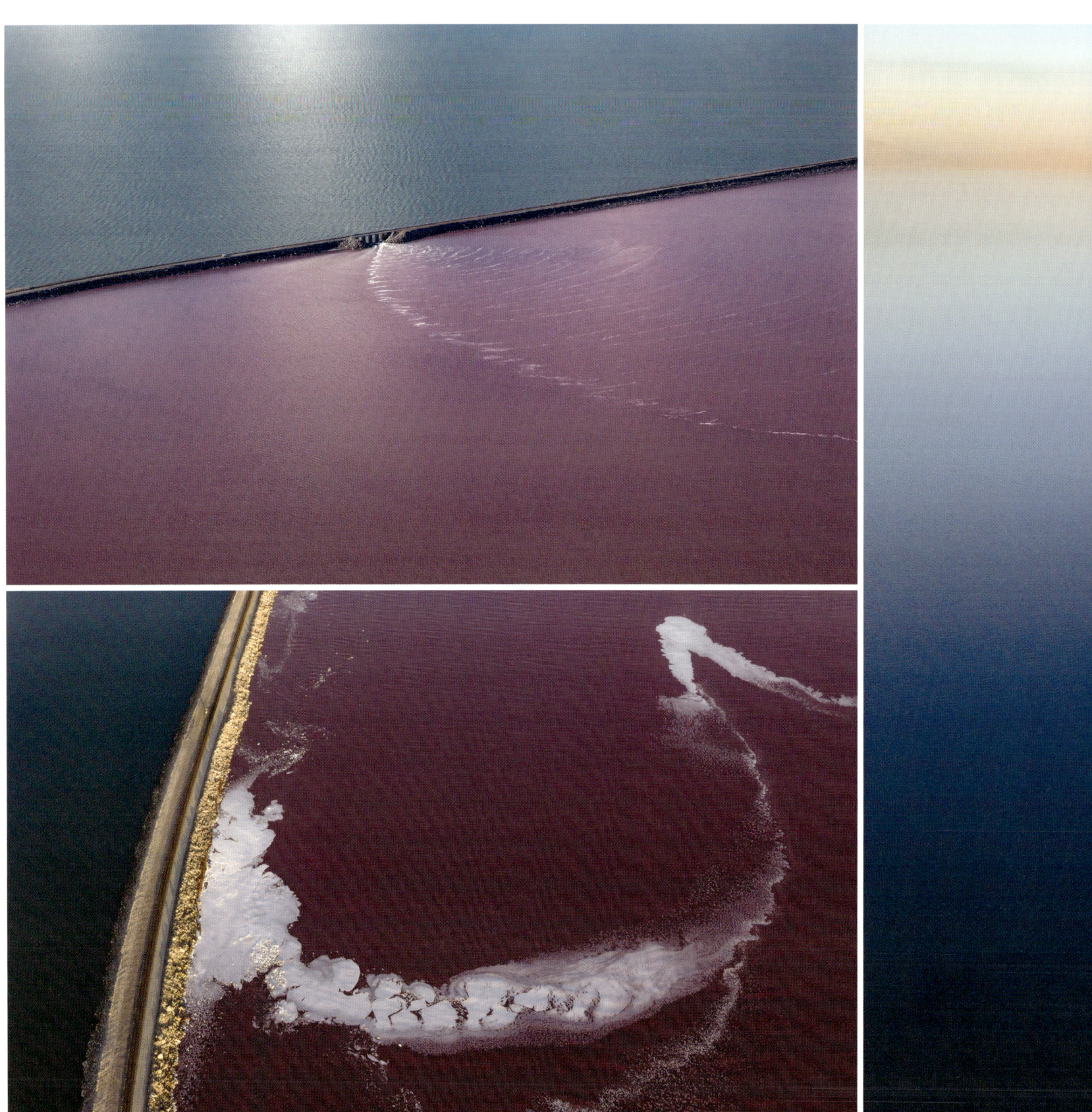

The Lucin Cutoff breach to allow water from the
South Arm to flow into the North Arm
F5 | 10.13.2023

The Lucin Cutoff, Union Pacific Railroad causeway
F5 | 10.07.2024

THE LUCIN CUTOFF

The Lucin Cutoff, constructed between 1902 and 1904, is a 102-mile (164-km) railroad line
that significantly altered Great Salt Lake's ecosystem. Originally built as a wooden trestle
and later replaced by an earthen causeway in the 1950s, the Cutoff divides the lake into two
distinct sections. The South Arm, receiving freshwater inflows from the Bear, Weber, and
Jordan rivers, has lower salinity and is characterized by blue-green algae, giving the water a
blue hue. Conversely, the North Arm, cut off from these freshwater sources, is a hypersaline
environment almost ten times saltier than the ocean. This extreme salinity supports unique
organisms like Dunaliella salina algae, which produce beta-carotene, giving the water its
distinctive red color.

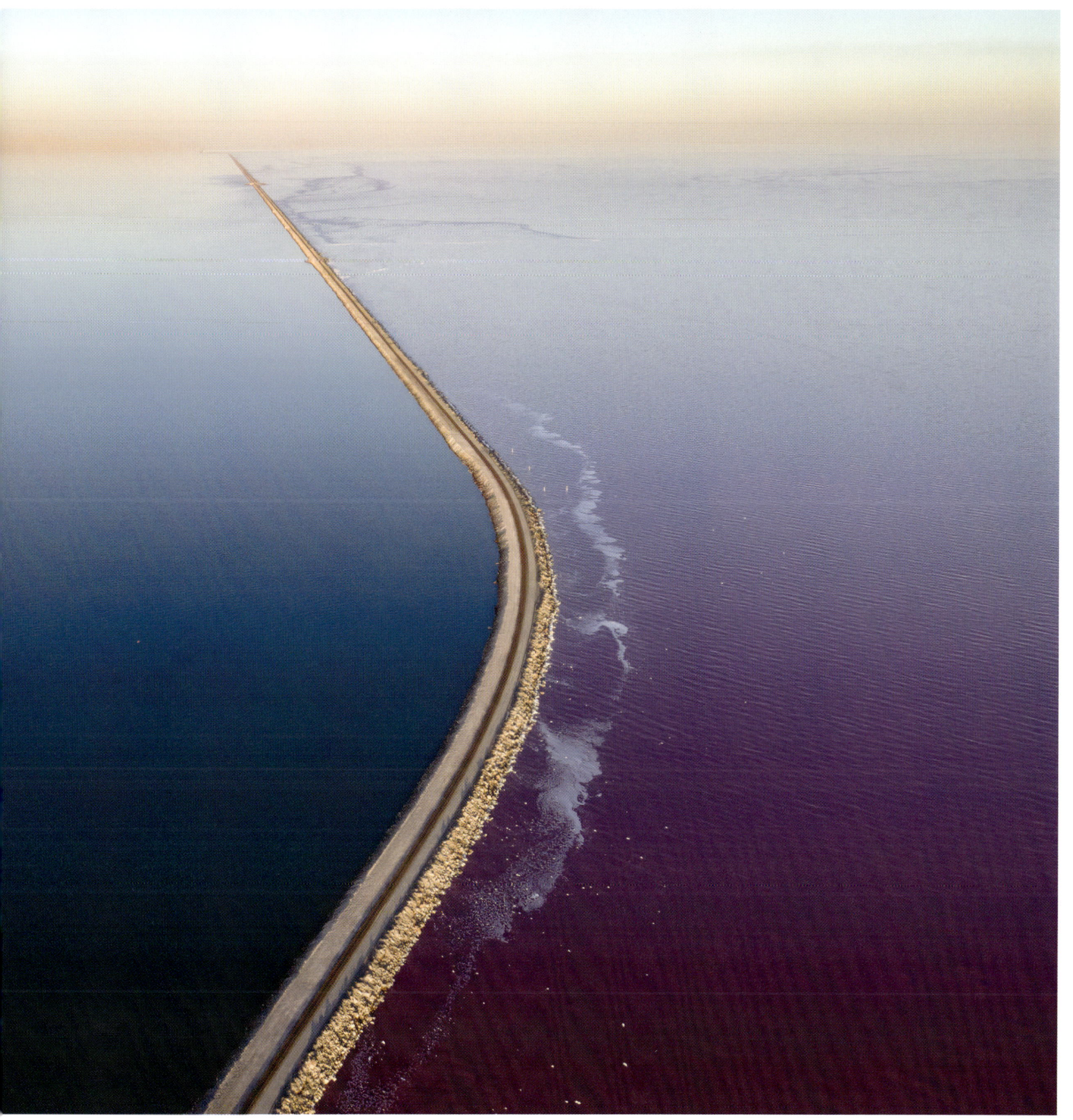

The construction of the Lucin Cutoff has had profound ecological impacts, altering natural water flow and creating two separate ecosystems within the lake. Efforts to mitigate these effects include creating breaches in the causeway to allow water exchange. In 2016, a new breach was made to help restore a more natural balance between the lake's arms. Despite its revolutionary impact on railway transport, the Lucin Cutoff continues to influence Great Salt Lake's physical characteristics and ecosystems, underscoring the complex interplay between infrastructure development and environmental conservation.

The Lucin Cutoff, Union Pacific Railroad causeway
F5 | 10.07.2024

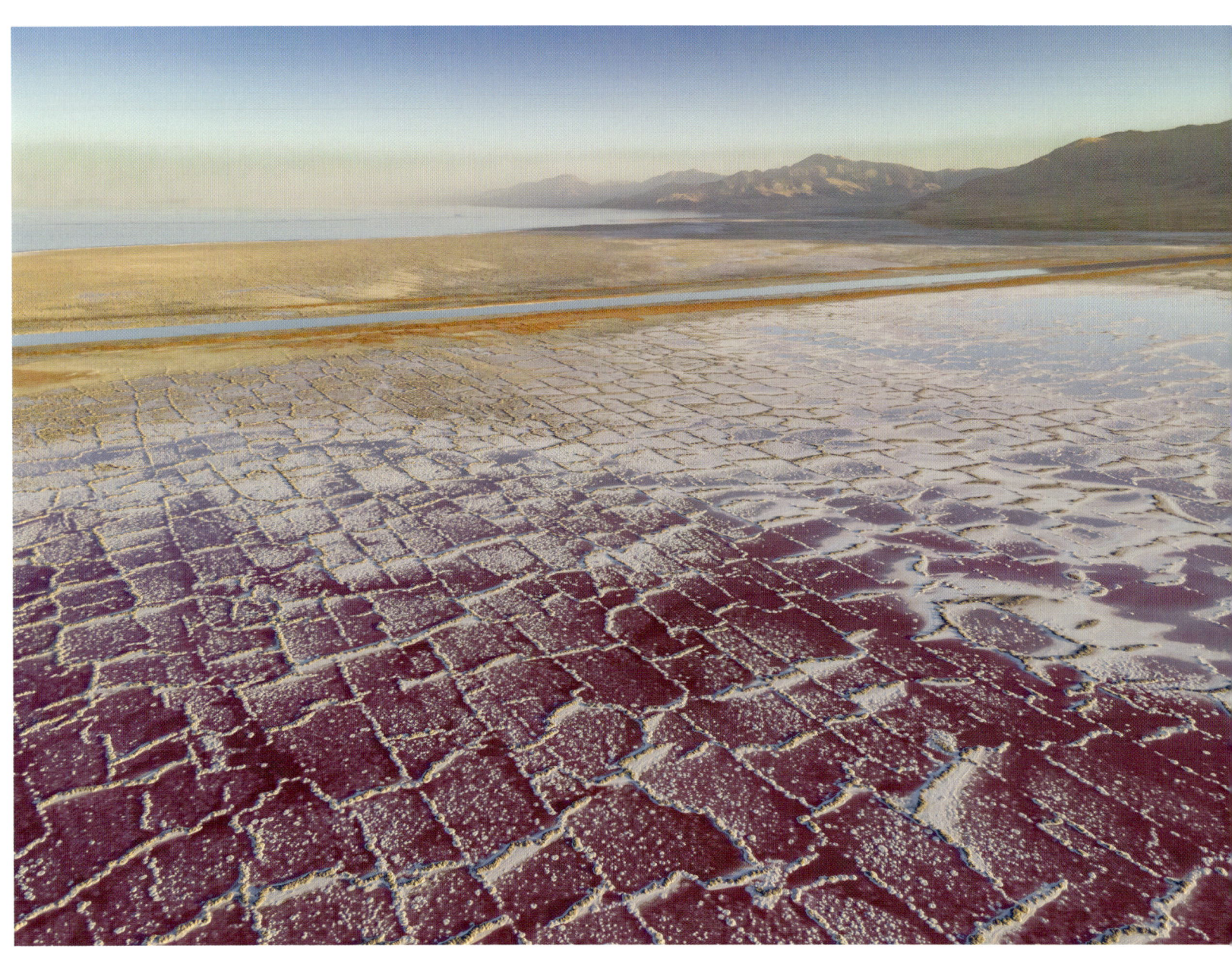

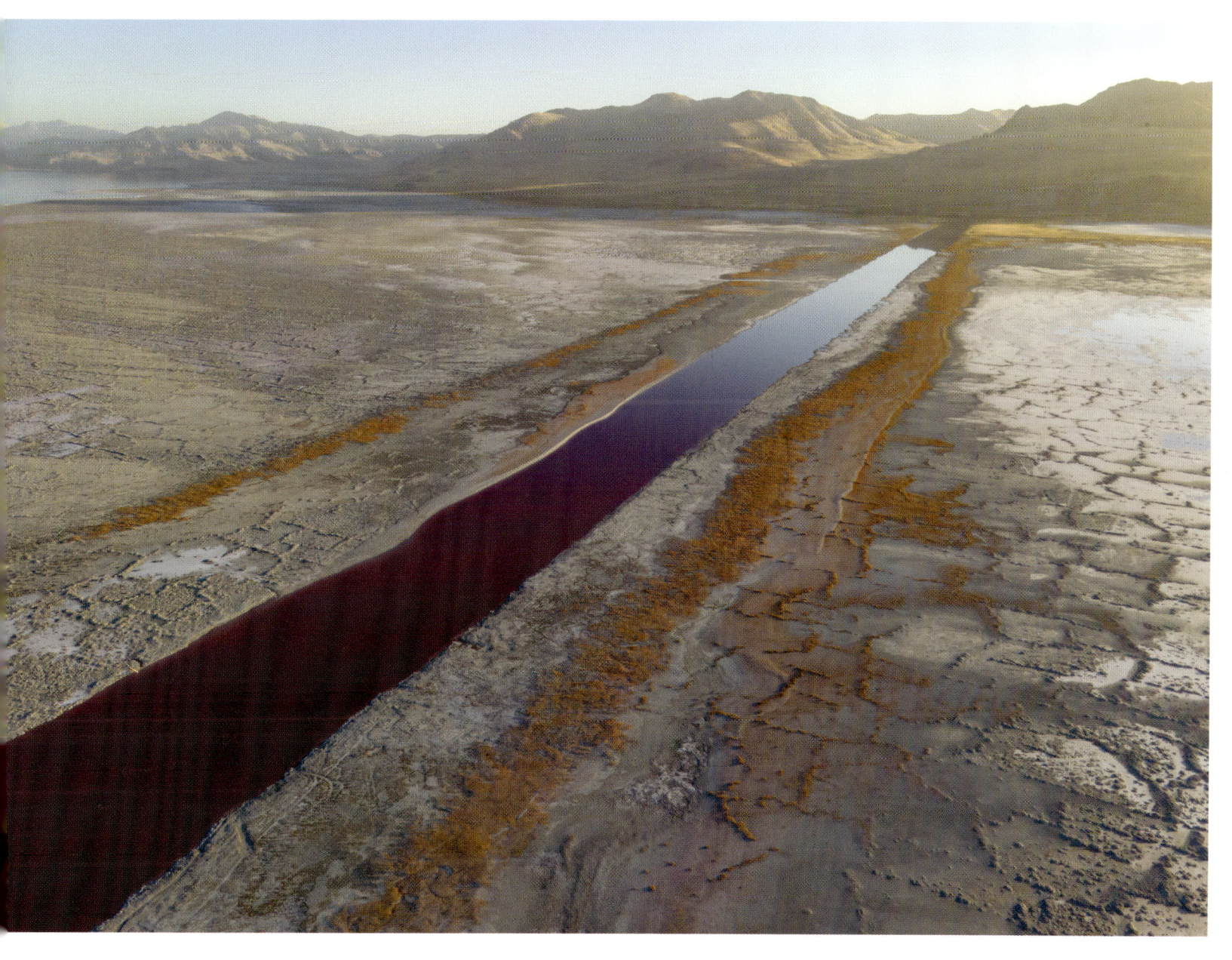

The west coast of Promontory Point, just north of the Lucin Cutoff | F6 | 10.07.2024

Shipping channel, west coast of Promontory Point | F6 | 10.07.2024

GUNNISON BAY

Gunnison Bay is isolated from freshwater inflows due to the construction of the Lucin Cutoff causeway, resulting in an extreme hypersaline environment. The salinity in this part of the lake is nearly ten times that of ocean water, which has led to the development of a unique ecosystem. This isolation has created a distinct habitat, making it one of the saltiest bodies of water in the world and a crucial area for studying extremophilic organisms.

The striking pink color of Gunnison Bay is primarily due to the presence of halophilic microorganisms, particularly the algae *Dunaliella salina* and *halophilic archaea*. These microorganisms thrive in hypersaline conditions and produce reddish pigments, such as beta-carotene, which give the water its distinctive pink hue. This phenomenon is similar to what is observed in other hypersaline environments around the world, where high salt concentrations lead to the growth of pigmented microorganisms. The unique coloration of Gunnison Bay makes it not only a visual marvel but also an important site for ecological and microbiological research.

Pink water, Gunnison Bay | D4 | 06.07.2023

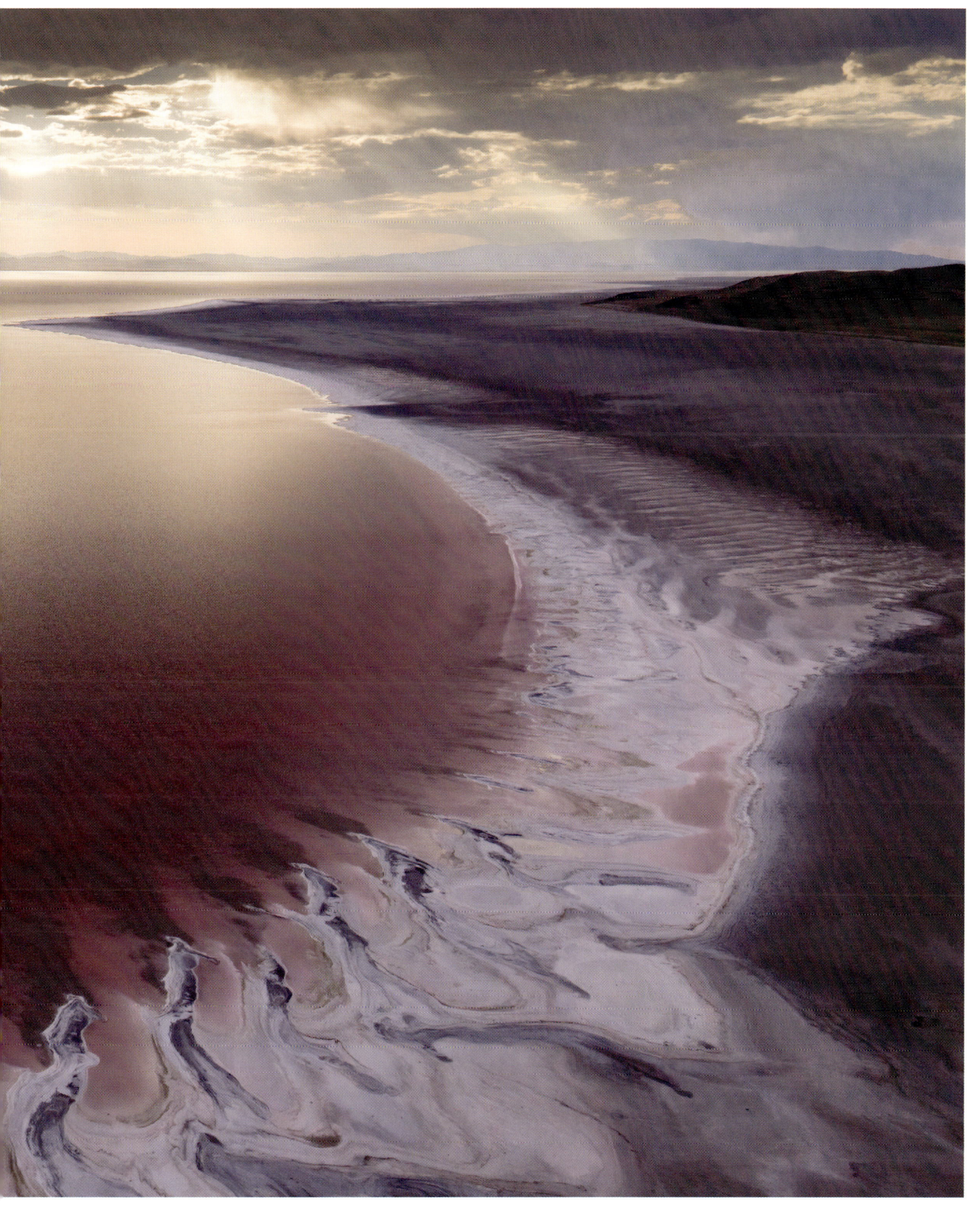

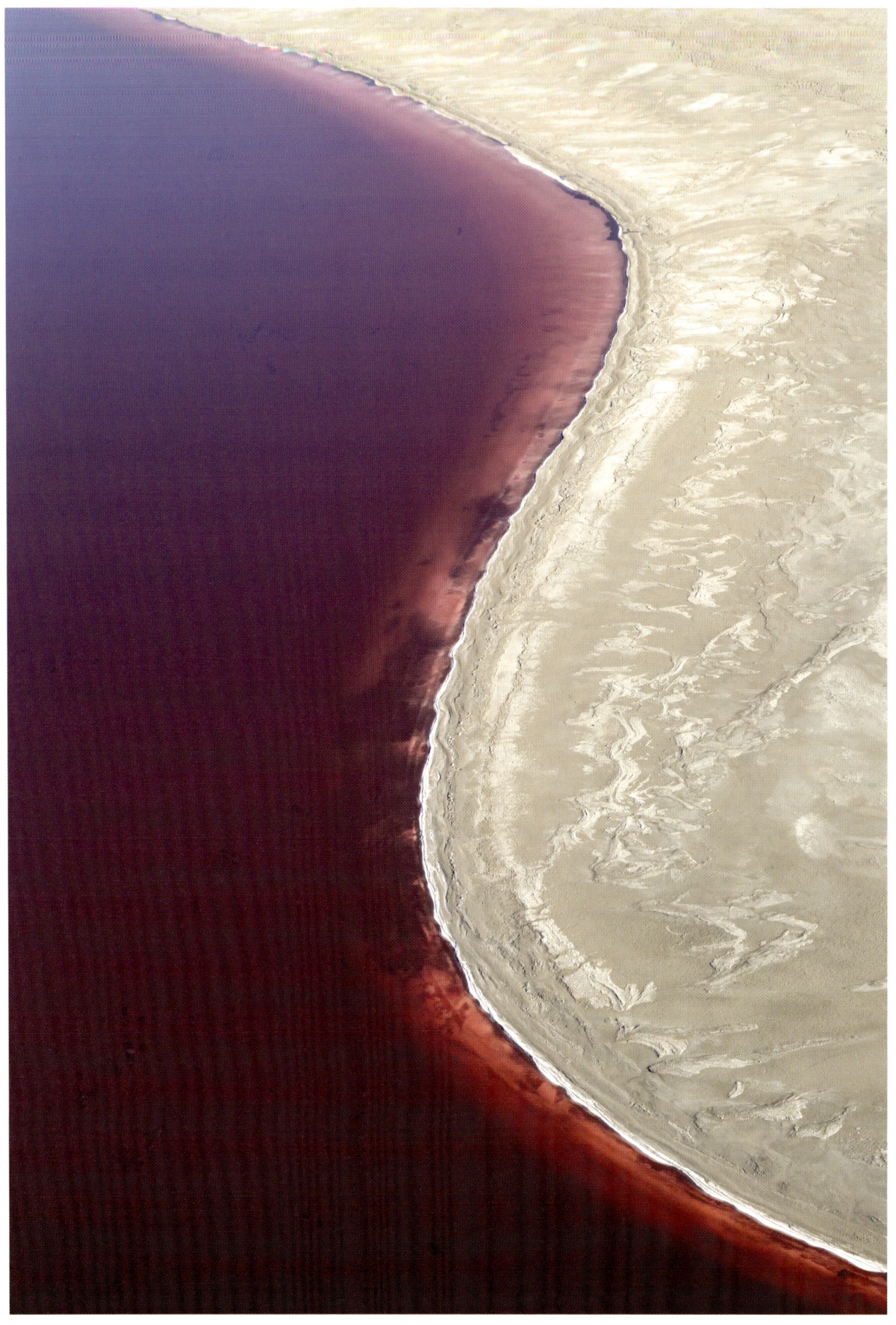

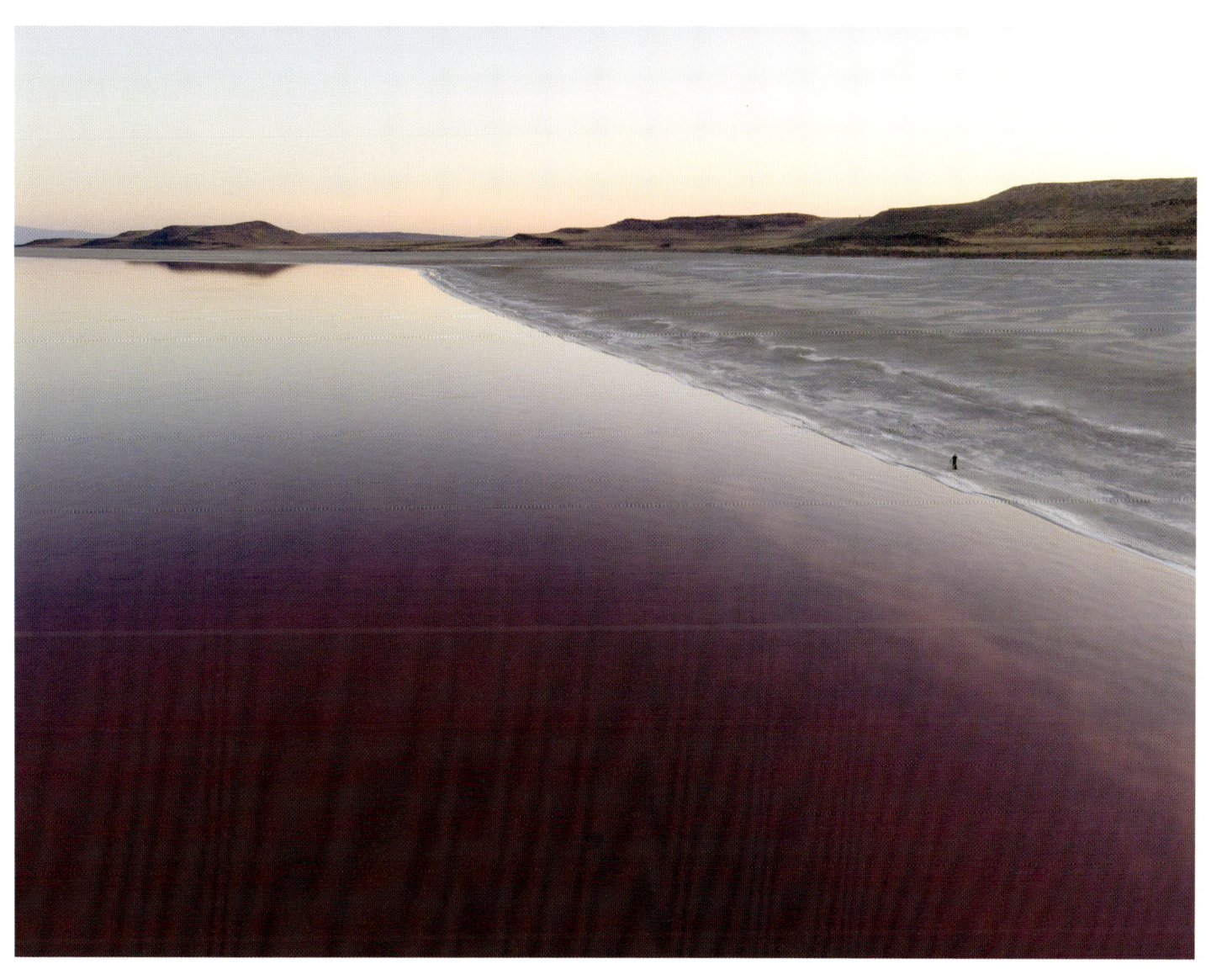

Pink shoreline curve from 7,000 feet (2,134 m) | E6 | 10.13.2023

Self-portrait at sunrise, Gunnison Bay | D4 | 06.24.2023

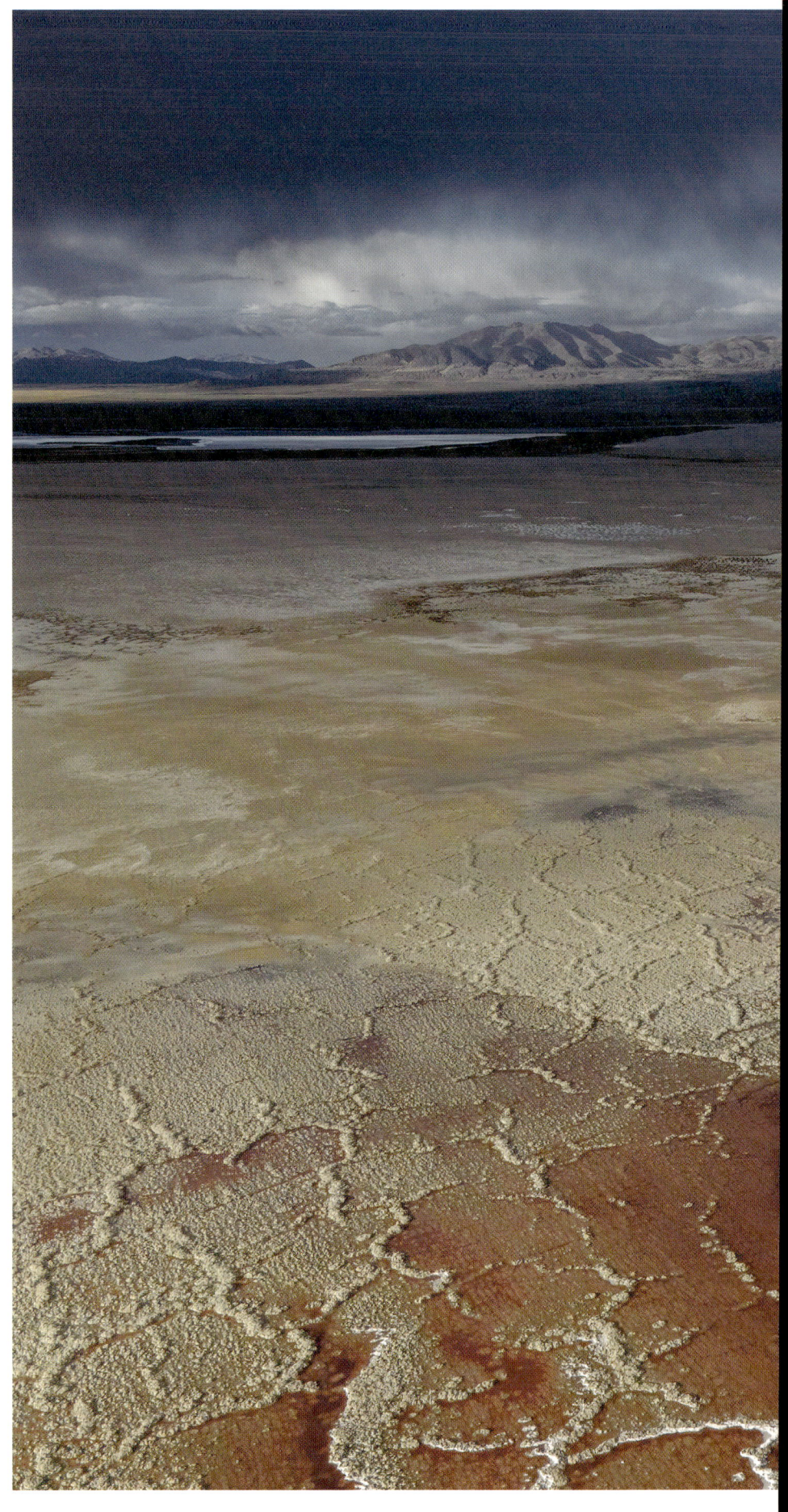

Pink water and salt coastline of Gunnison Bay | D4 | 04.07.2024

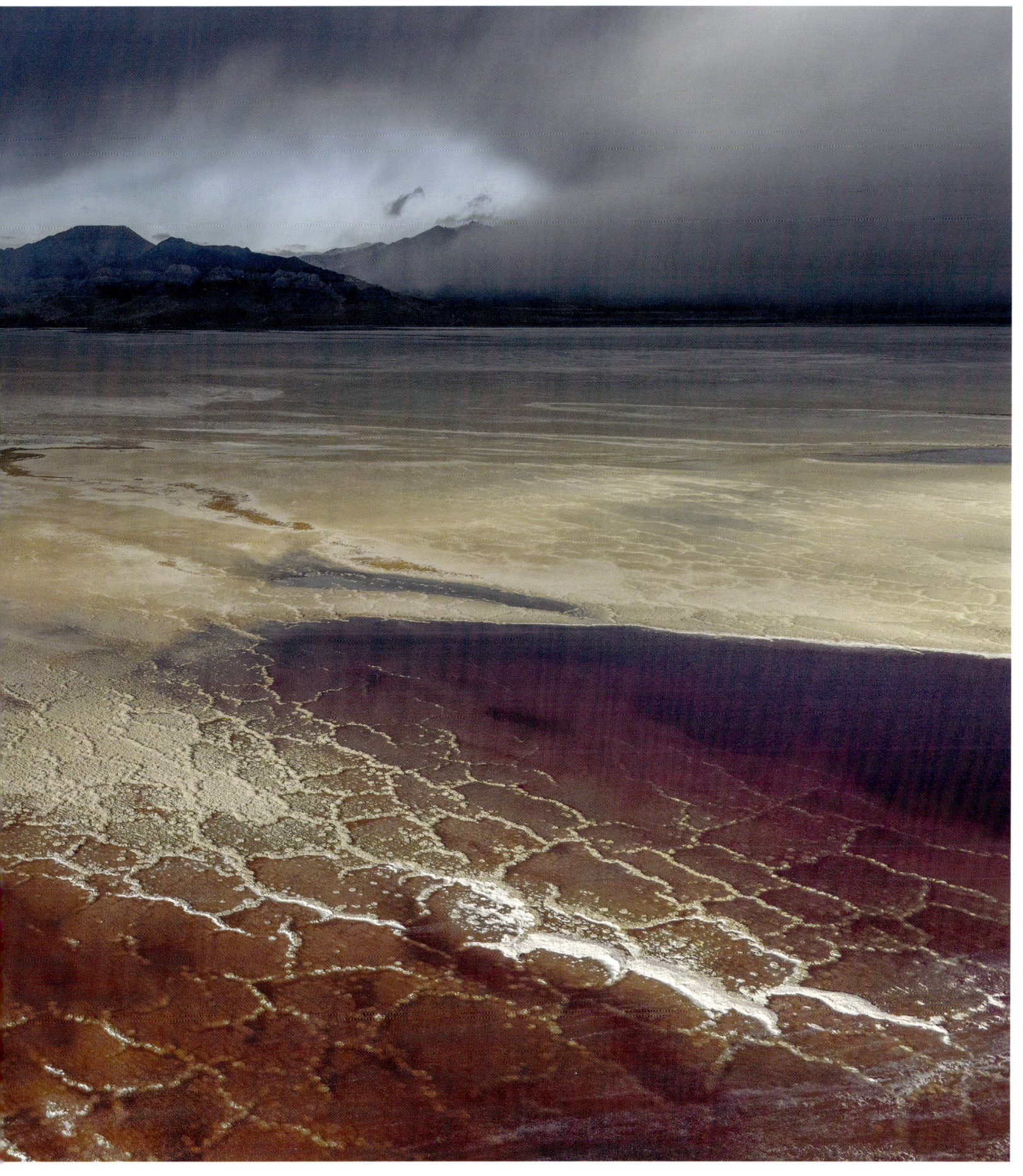

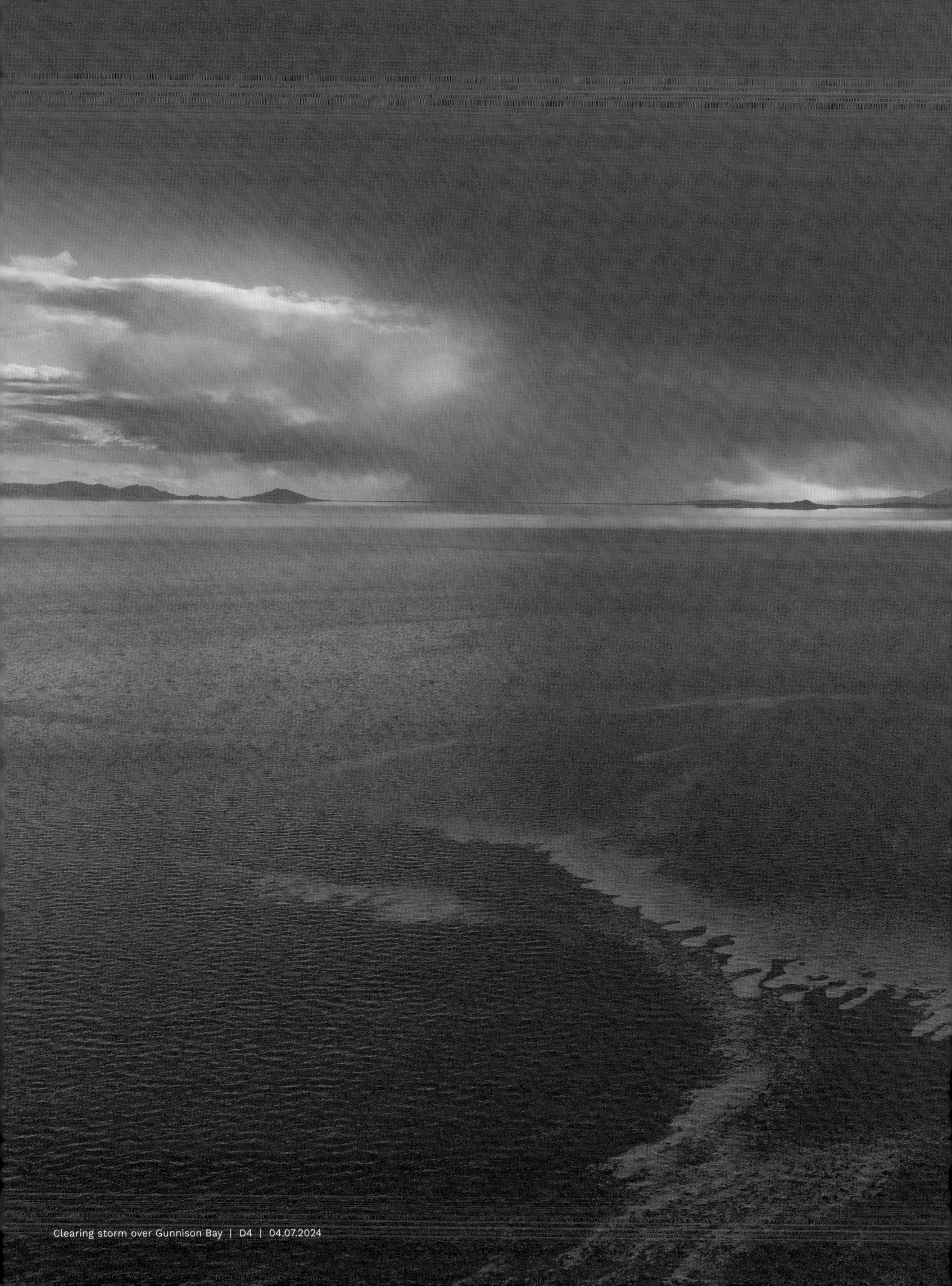

Clearing storm over Gunnison Bay | D4 | 04.07.2024

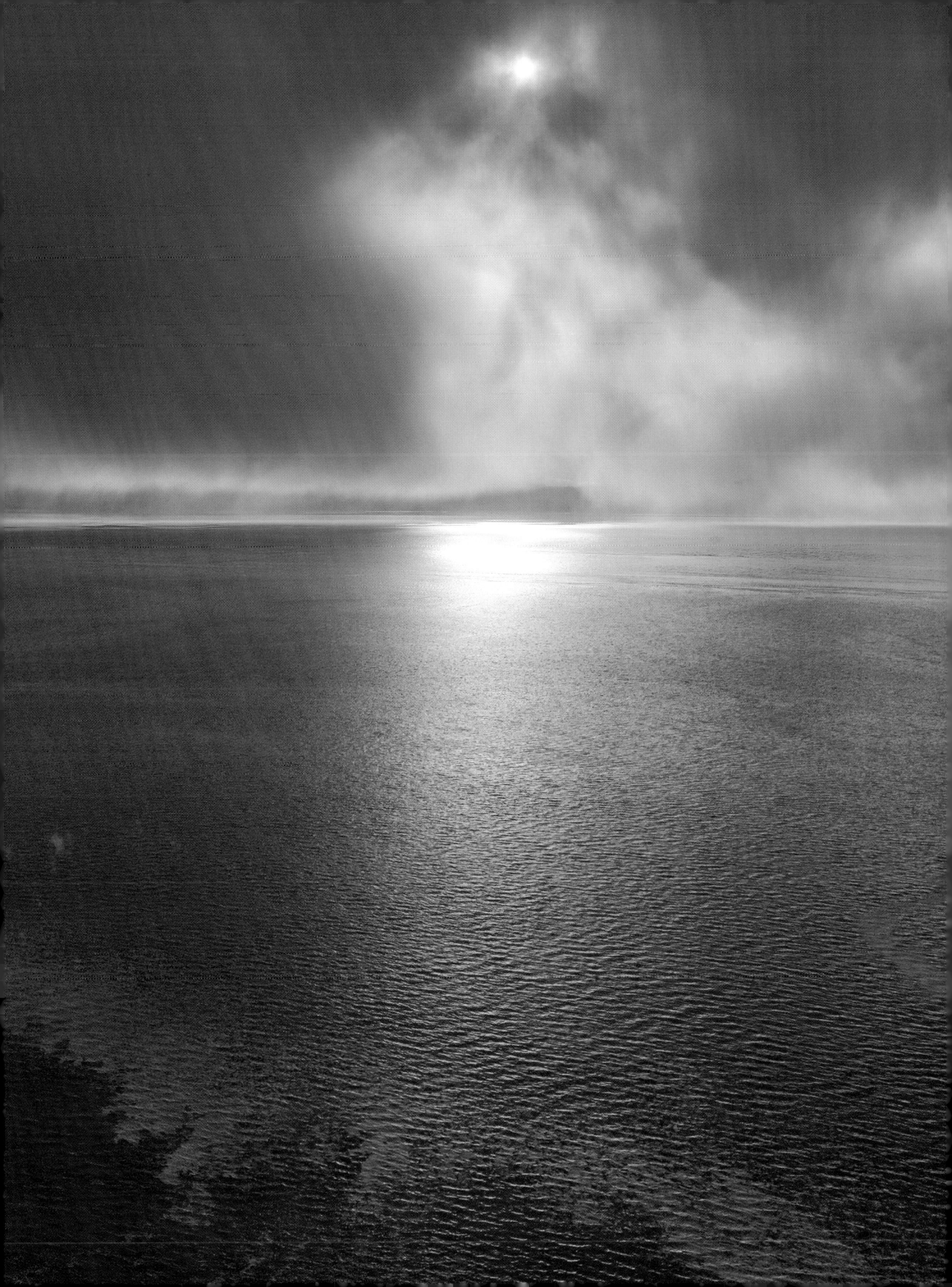

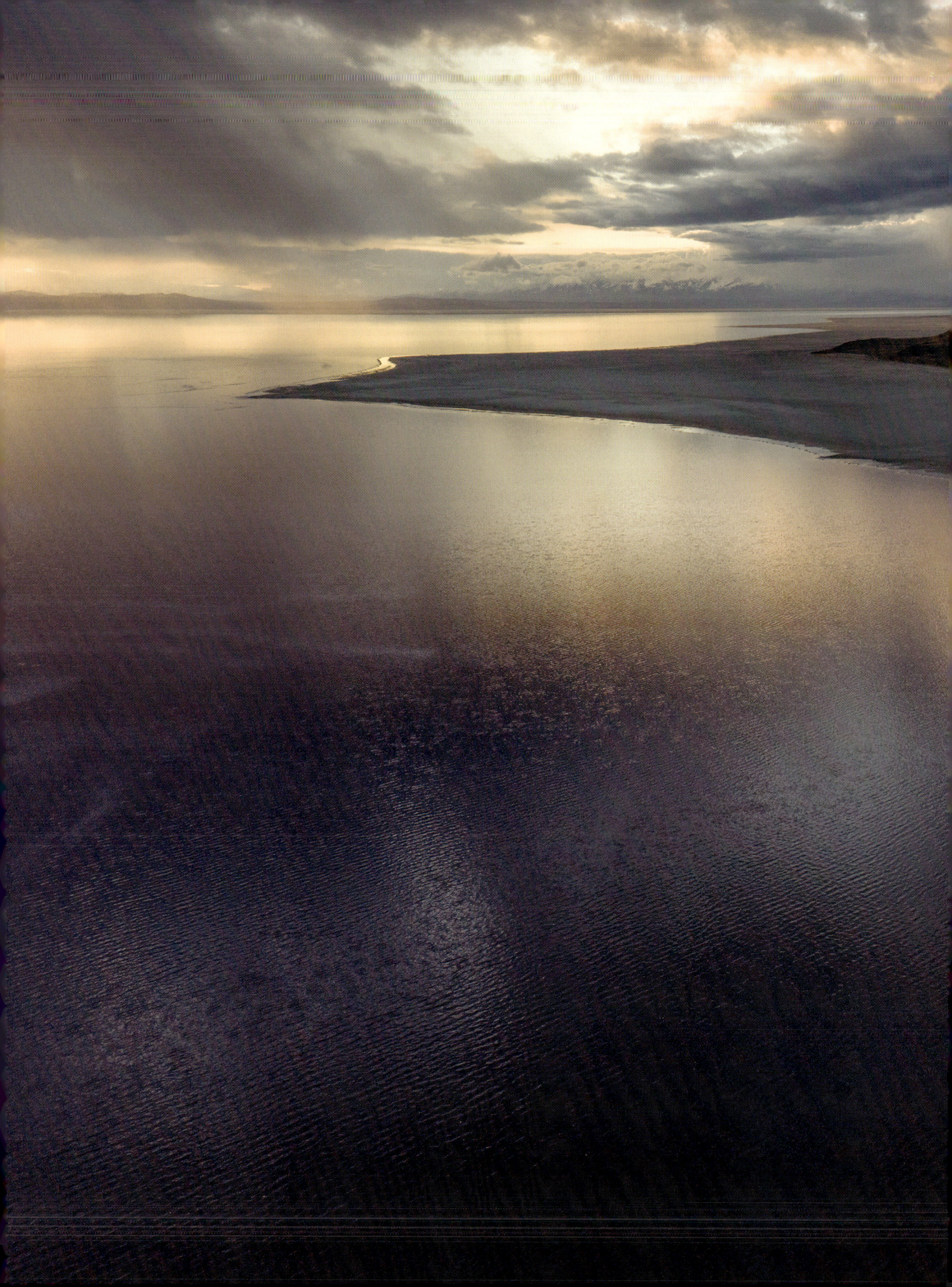

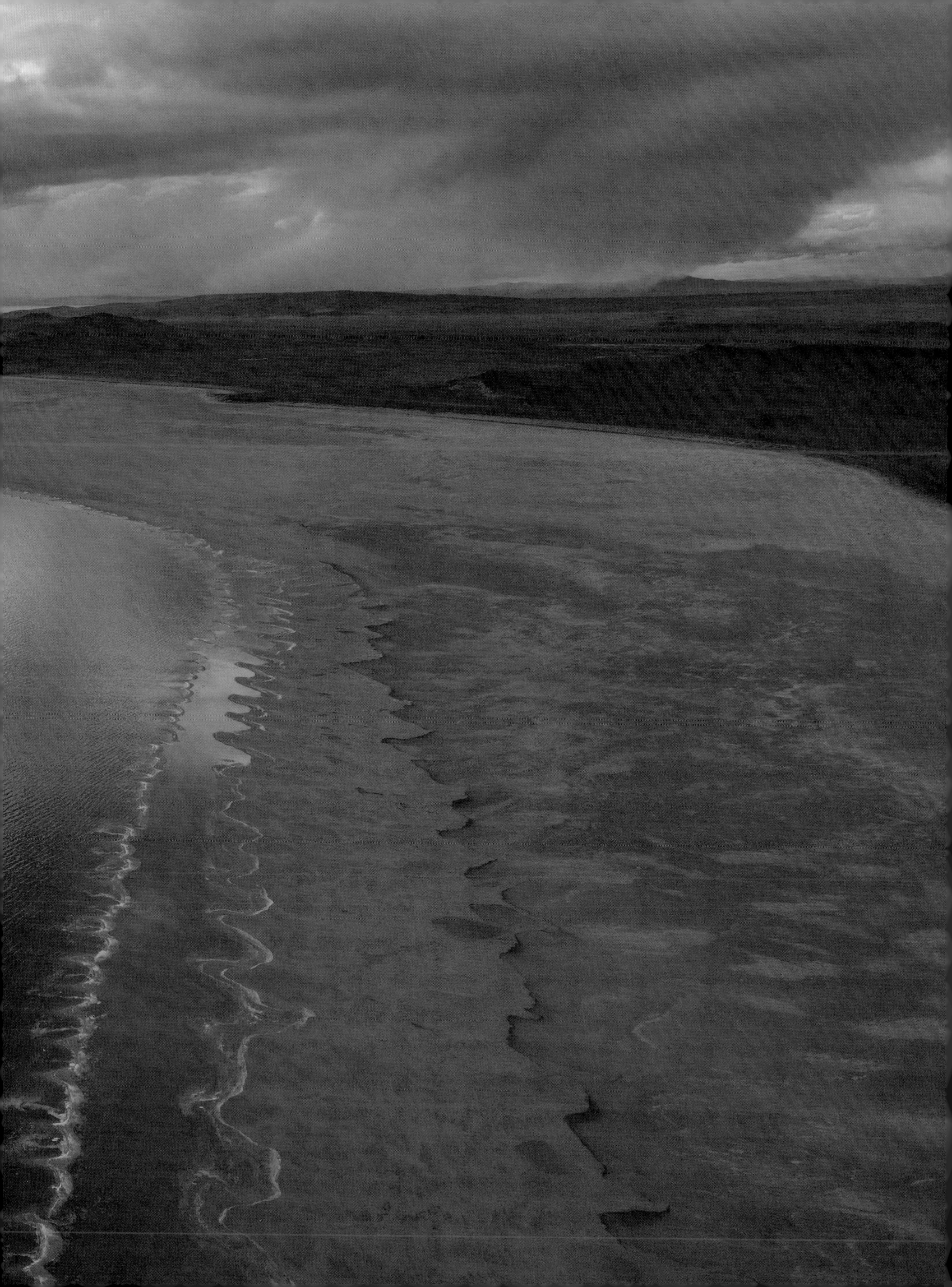

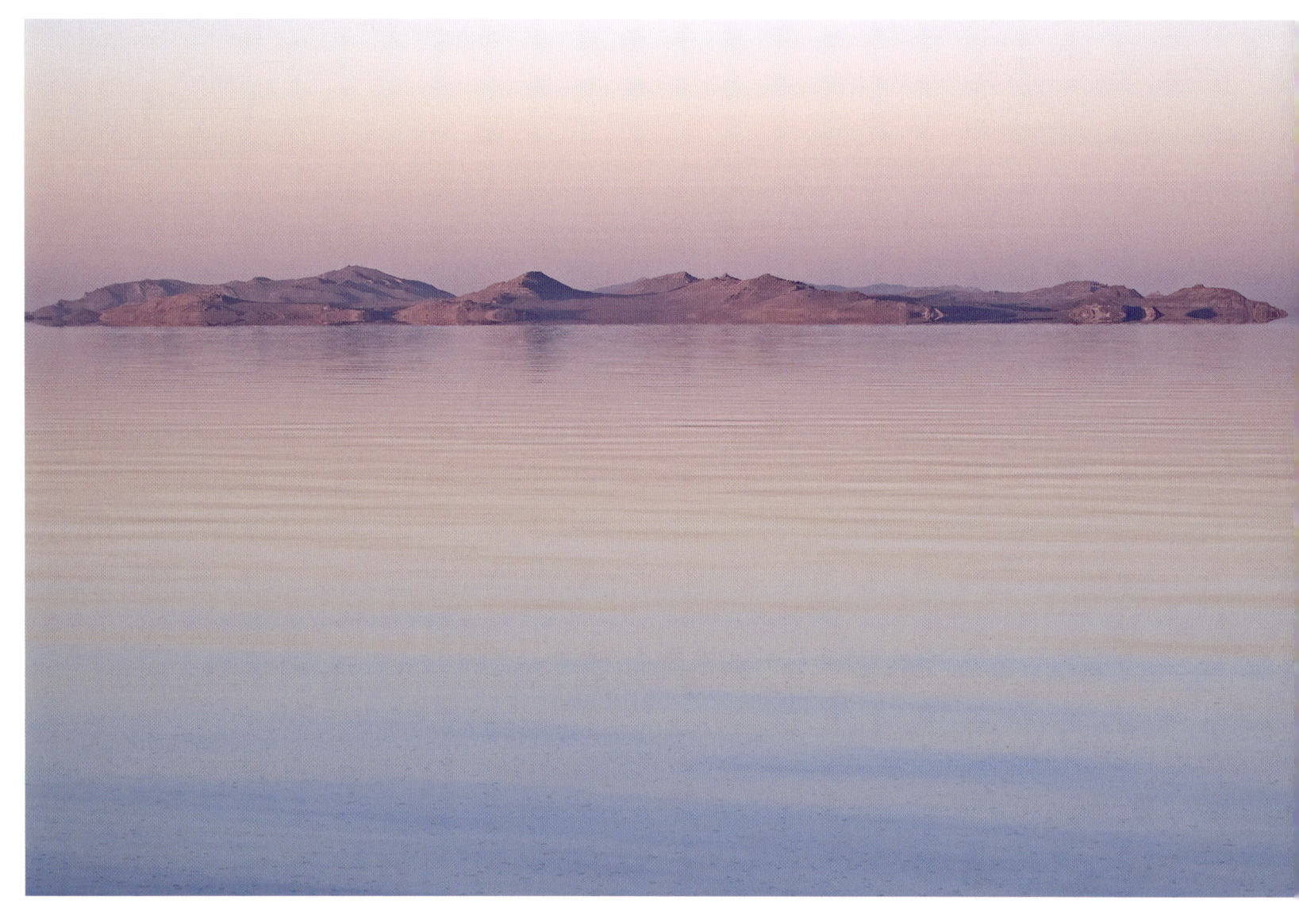

PREVIOUS PAGE: Gunnison Bay and breaking storms | D4 | 04.07.2024   Pink water at dawn, Gunnison Bay | D4 | 06.24.2023

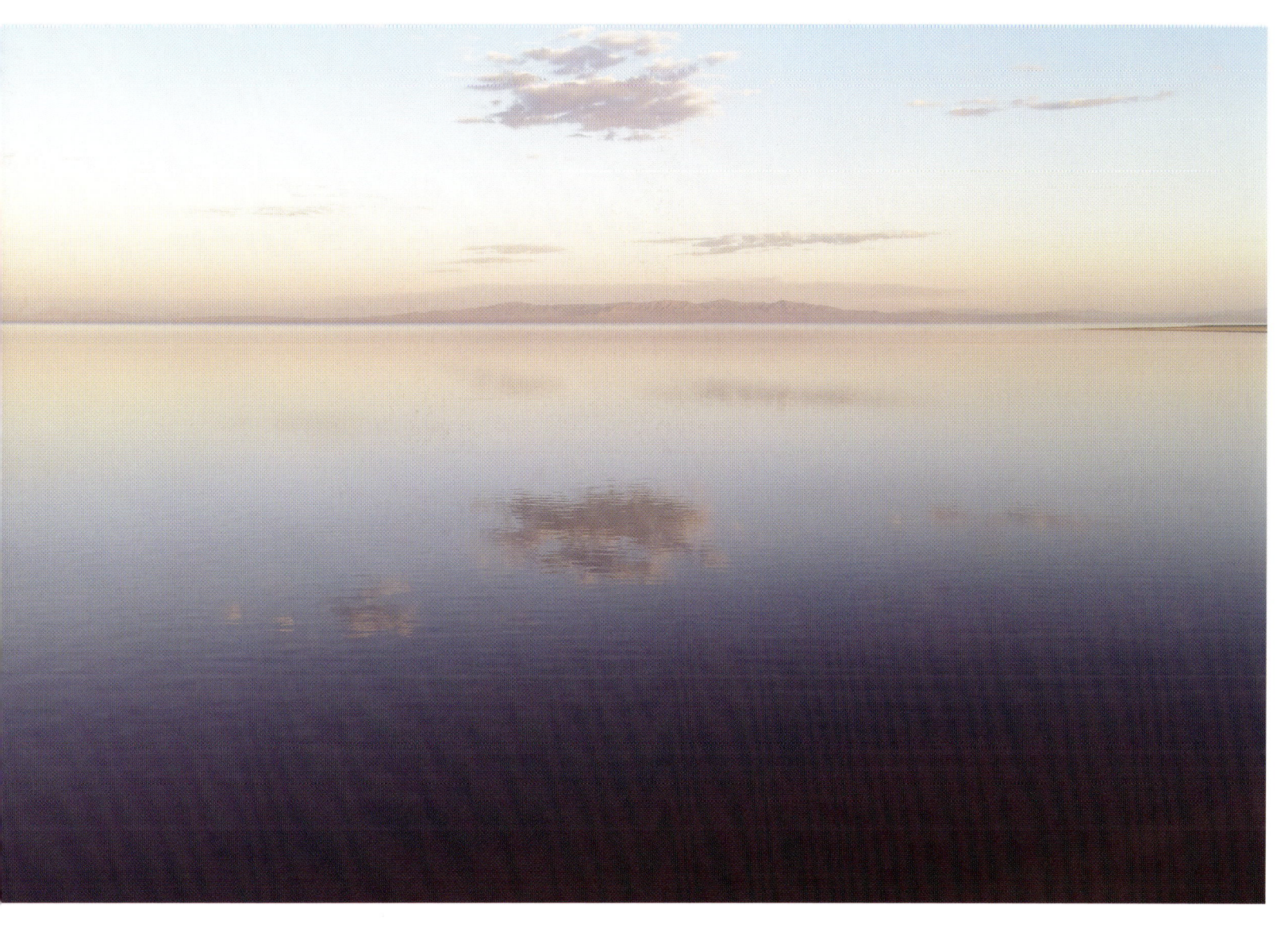

Purple water at dawn, Gunnison Bay | D4 | 06.24.2023

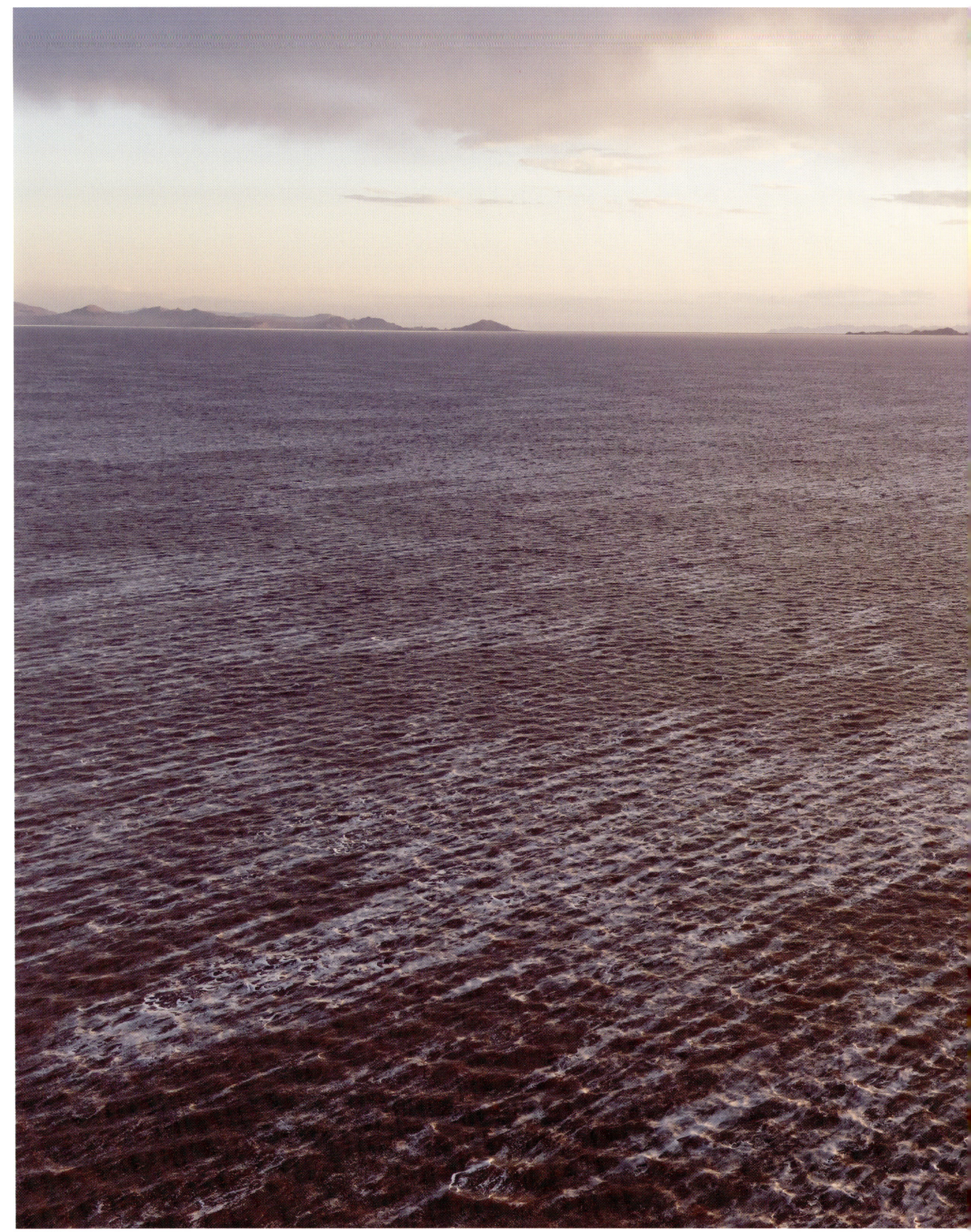

Windy water, Gunnison Bay | D3 | 06.26.2023

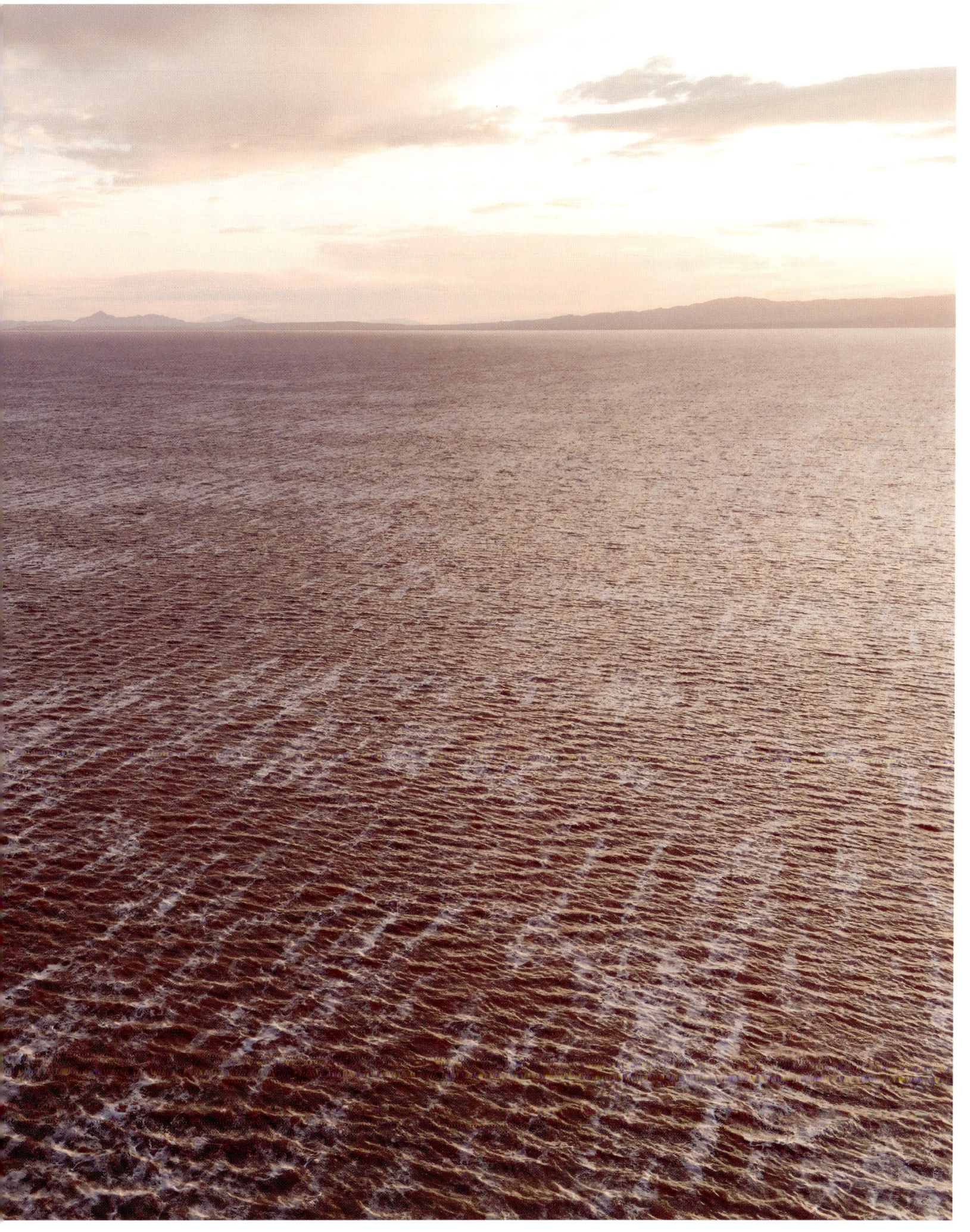

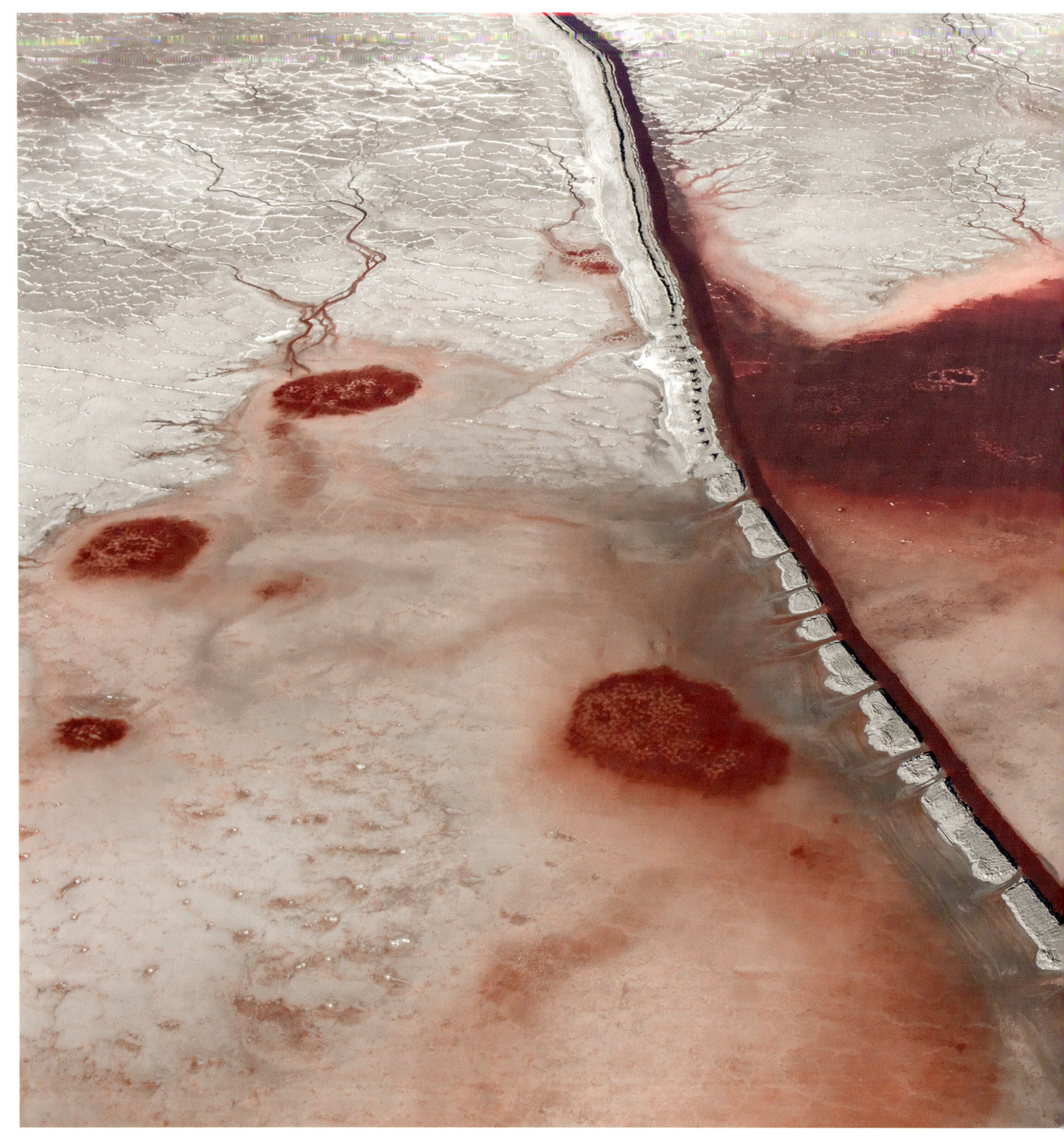

Hypersaline pools and salt mounds from 7,000 feet (2,134 m) | D2 | 10.13.2023

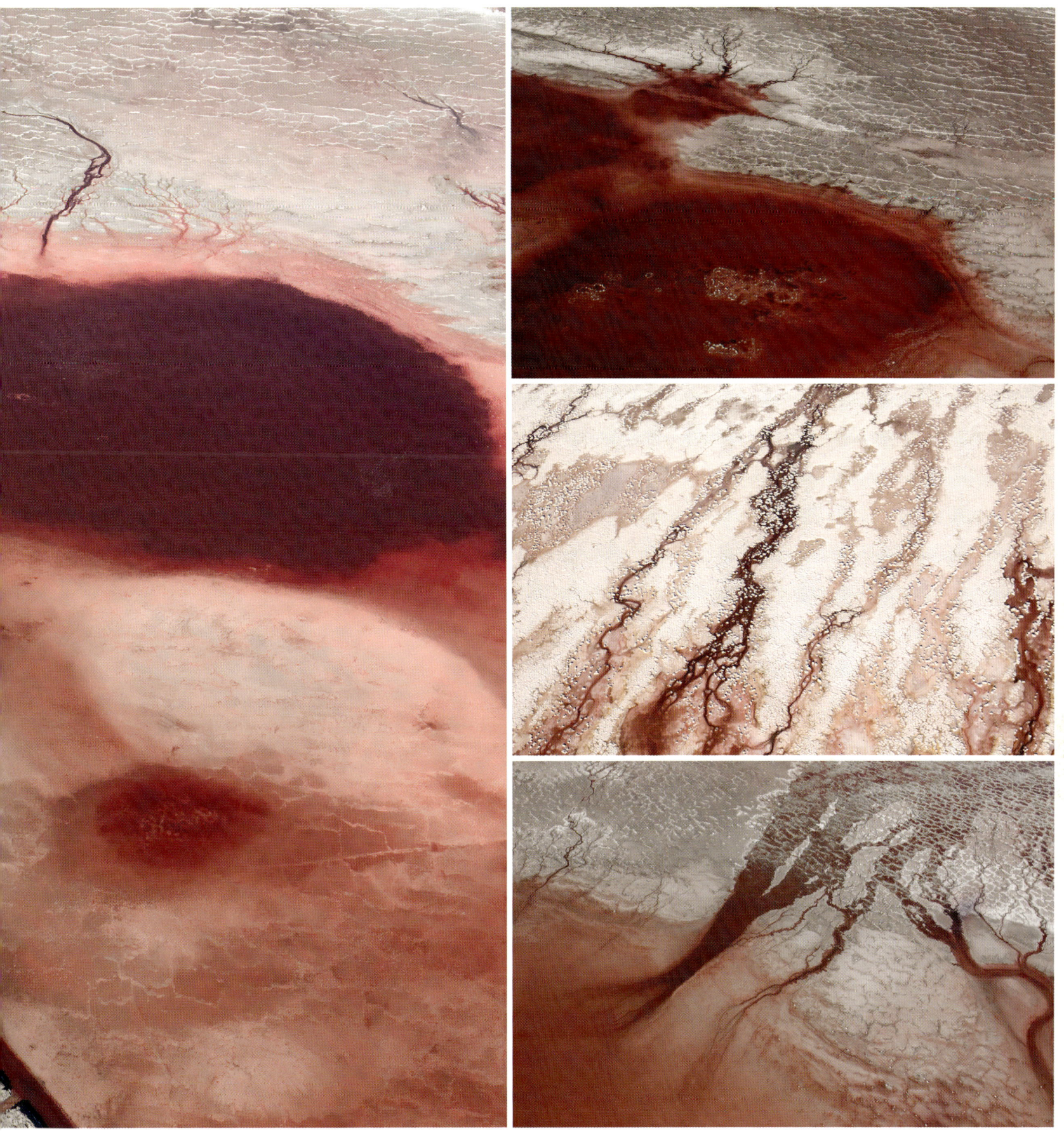

Hypersaline pools and salt mounds from 7,000 feet (2,134 m) | D2 | 10.13.2023
Hypersaline pools and salt crust from 7,000 feet (2,134 m) | D2 | 10.13.2023
Salt mounds and hypersaline channels from 7,000 feet (2,134 m) | D2 | 10.13.2023
FOLLOWING PAGE: Salt mounds from 7,000 feet (2,134 m) | D4 | 10.13.2023

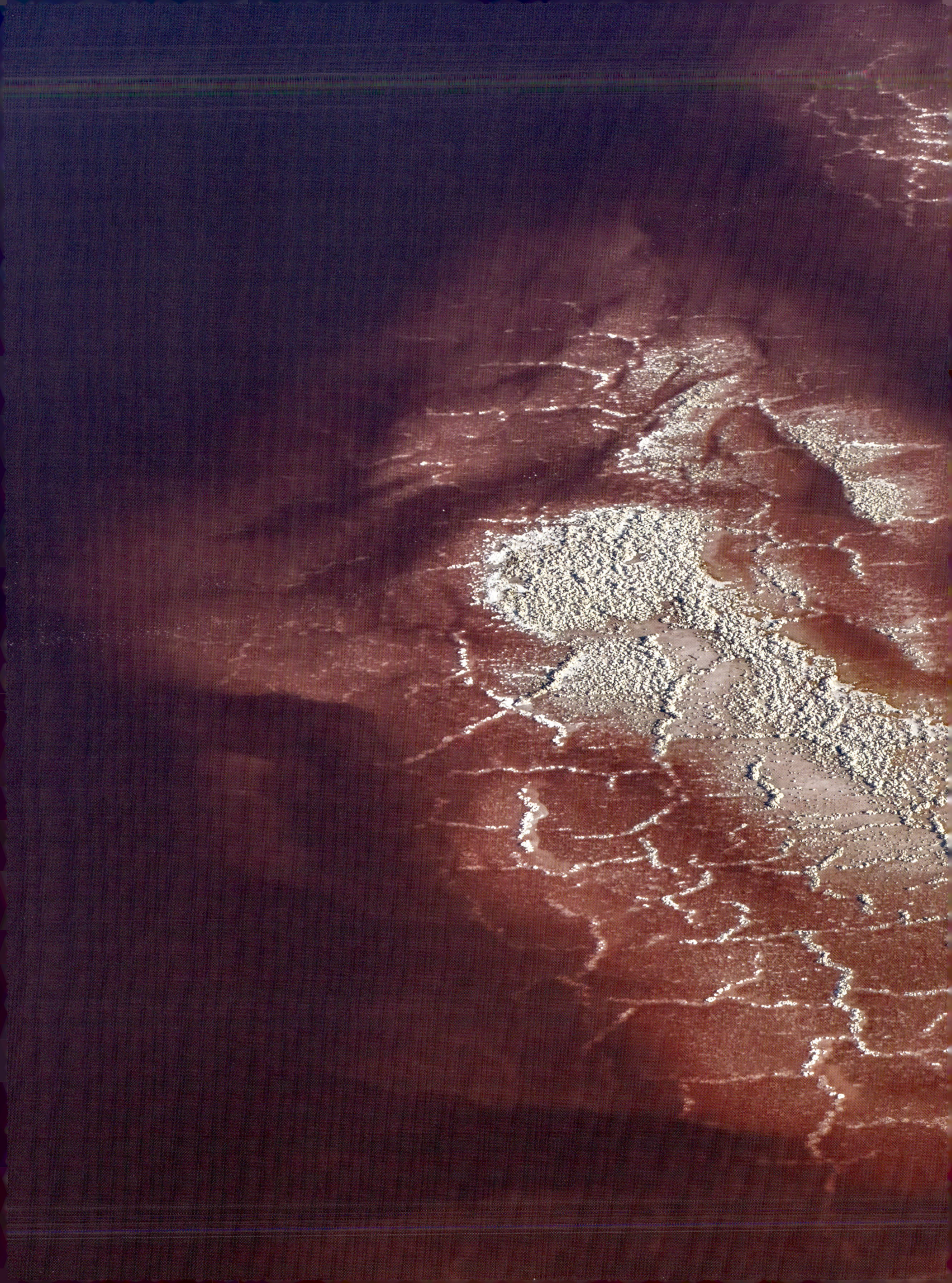

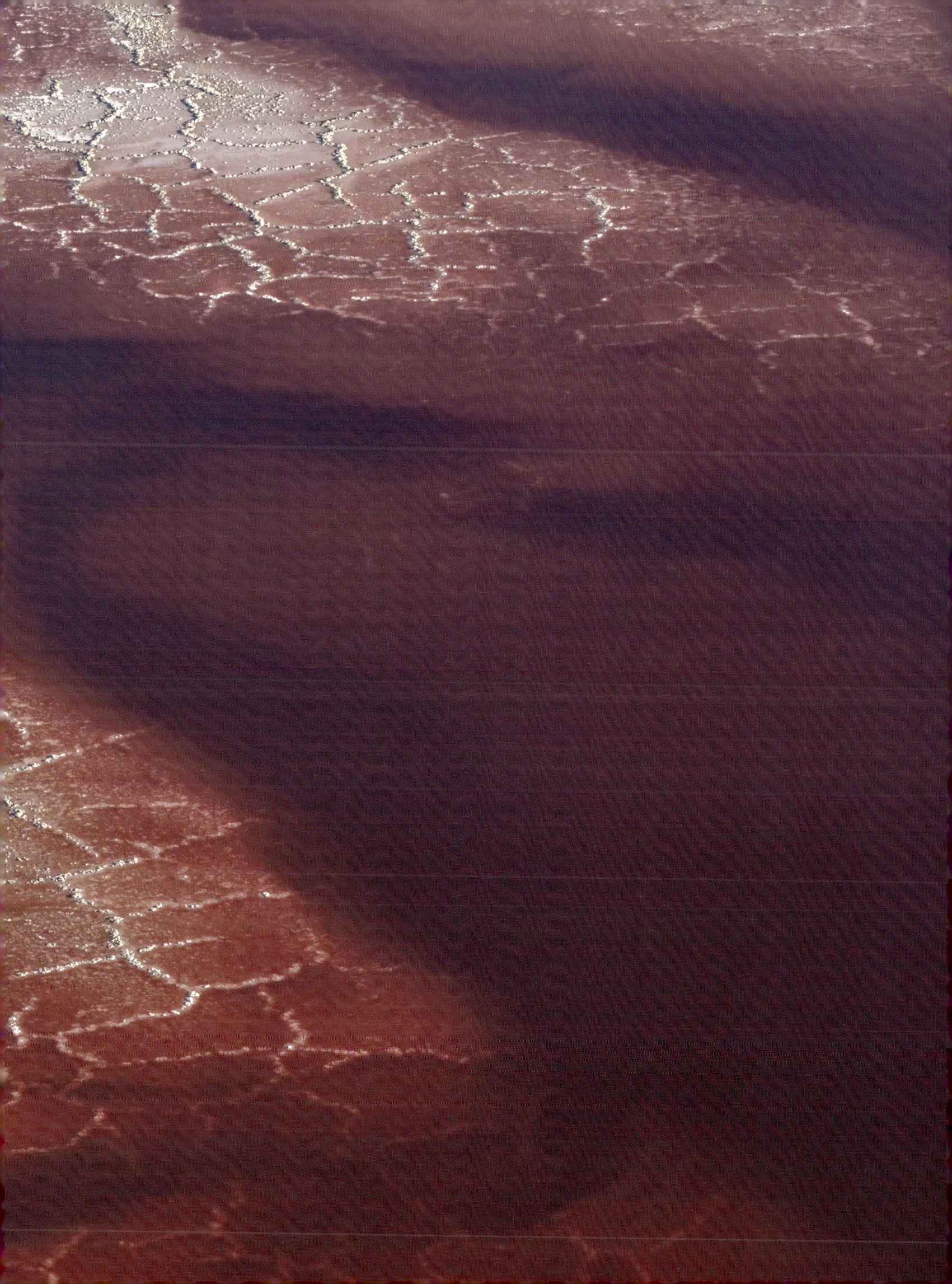

SPIRAL JETTY

Robert Smithson's Spiral Jetty is a monumental piece of land art, created in April 1970 on the shores of Gunnison Bay in the North Arm of the lake. This massive sculpture extends 1,500 feet (457 m) into the lake, forming a counterclockwise coil made from over 6,000 tons (5,443 tonnes) of black basalt rocks and earth. Smithson chose the site for its fluctuating water levels. The pinkish hue of the water perfectly captured his fascination with entropy and natural transformation.

The spiral shape of the Jetty represents infinity and continuous change, embodying Smithson's interest in the passage of time and natural decay. Since its creation, the Spiral Jetty has been submerged and re-emerged with changing water levels, highlighting its dynamic nature and Smithson's vision of an artwork constantly interacting with natural forces. However, in recent years, due to prolonged drought conditions and the receding waters of the lake, the Jetty has remained exposed, situated atop cracked, sun-scorched earth.

As a seminal piece in the land art movement, the Spiral Jetty challenges traditional notions of art by existing outside of galleries and in the natural environment. Over the decades, it has inspired countless artists and attracted visitors, scholars, and art enthusiasts, cementing its status as a significant work in contemporary art. The enduring presence of the Spiral Jetty stands as a testament to Smithson's innovative approach and as a profound commentary on humanity's relationship with nature.

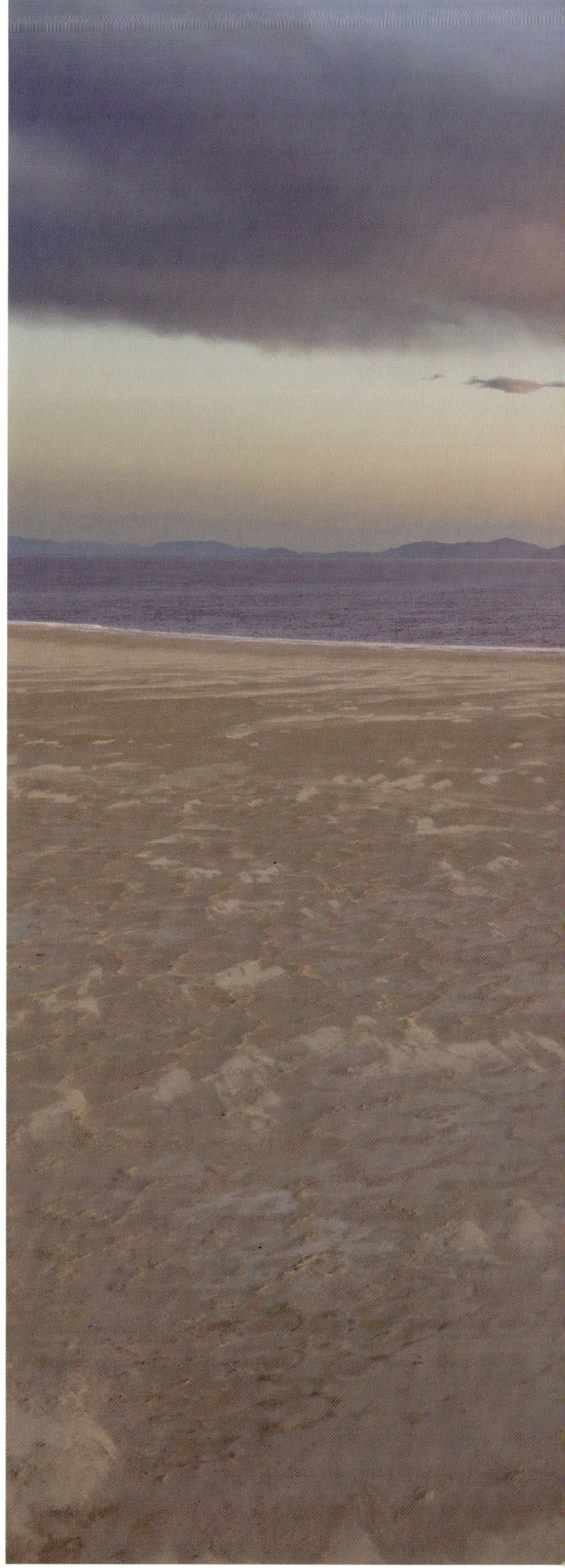

Sunset at Spiral Jetty | D4 | 06.23.2023
FOLLOWING PAGE: Self-portrait, Spiral Jetty | D4 | 04.07.2024

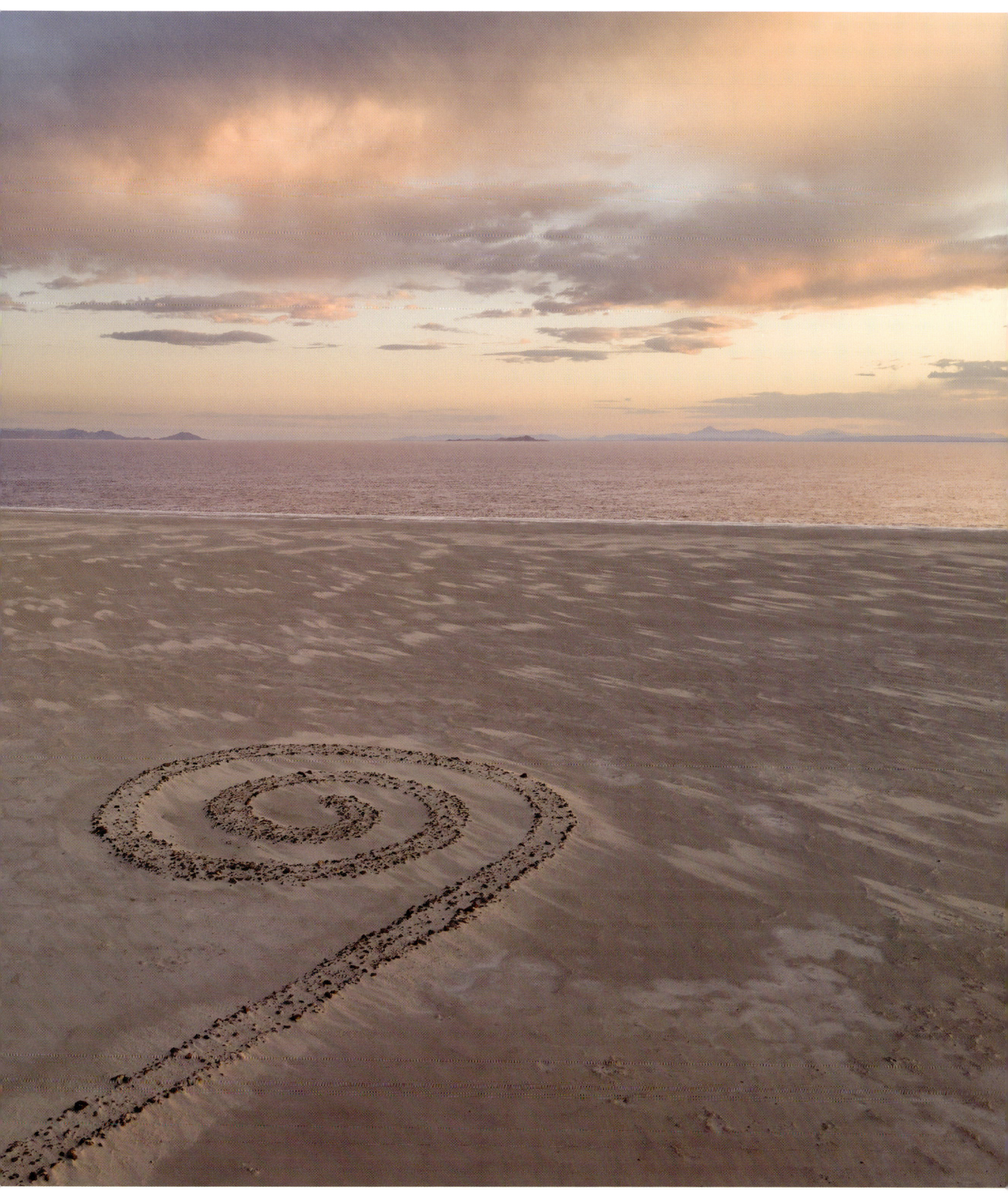

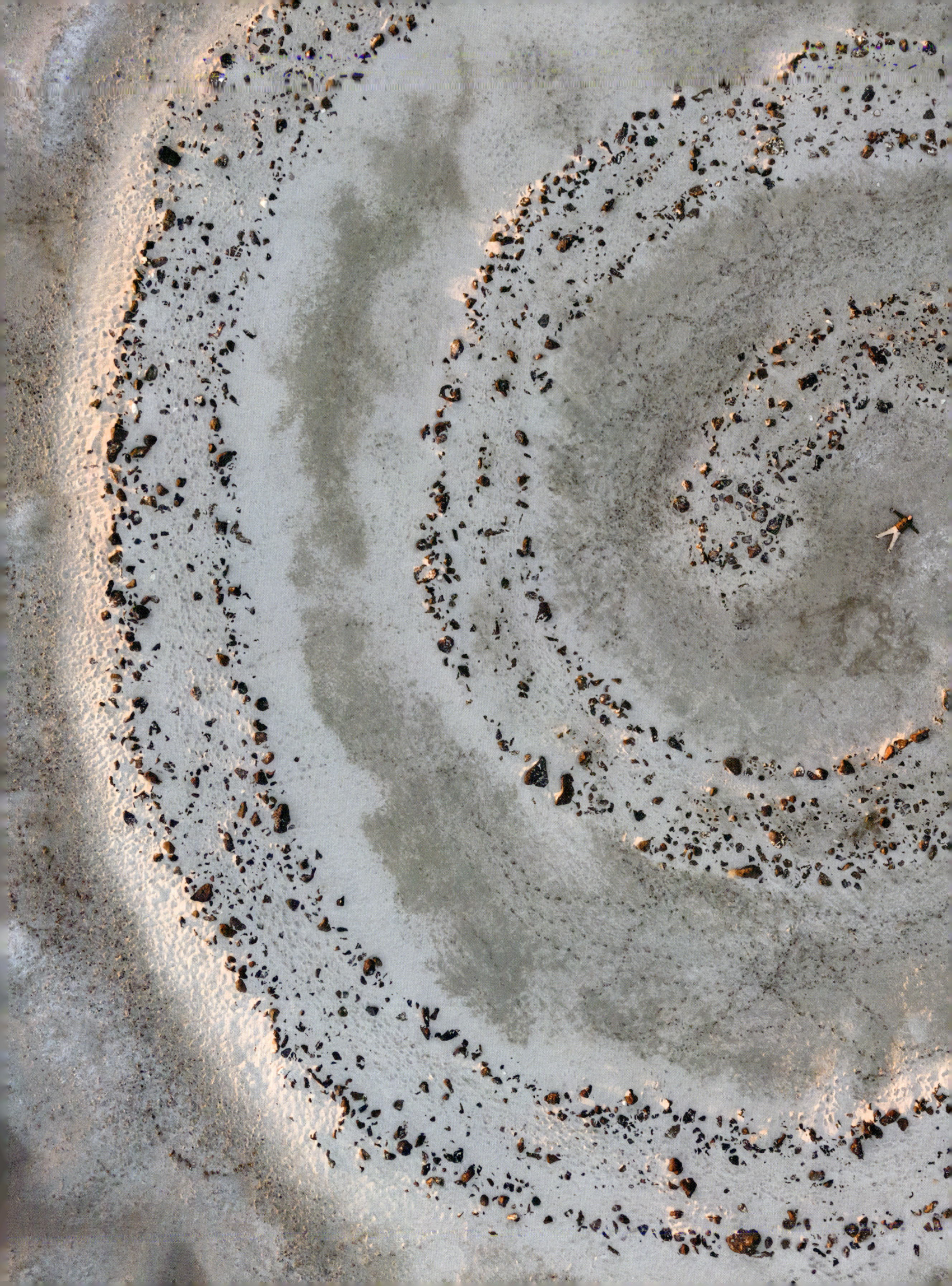

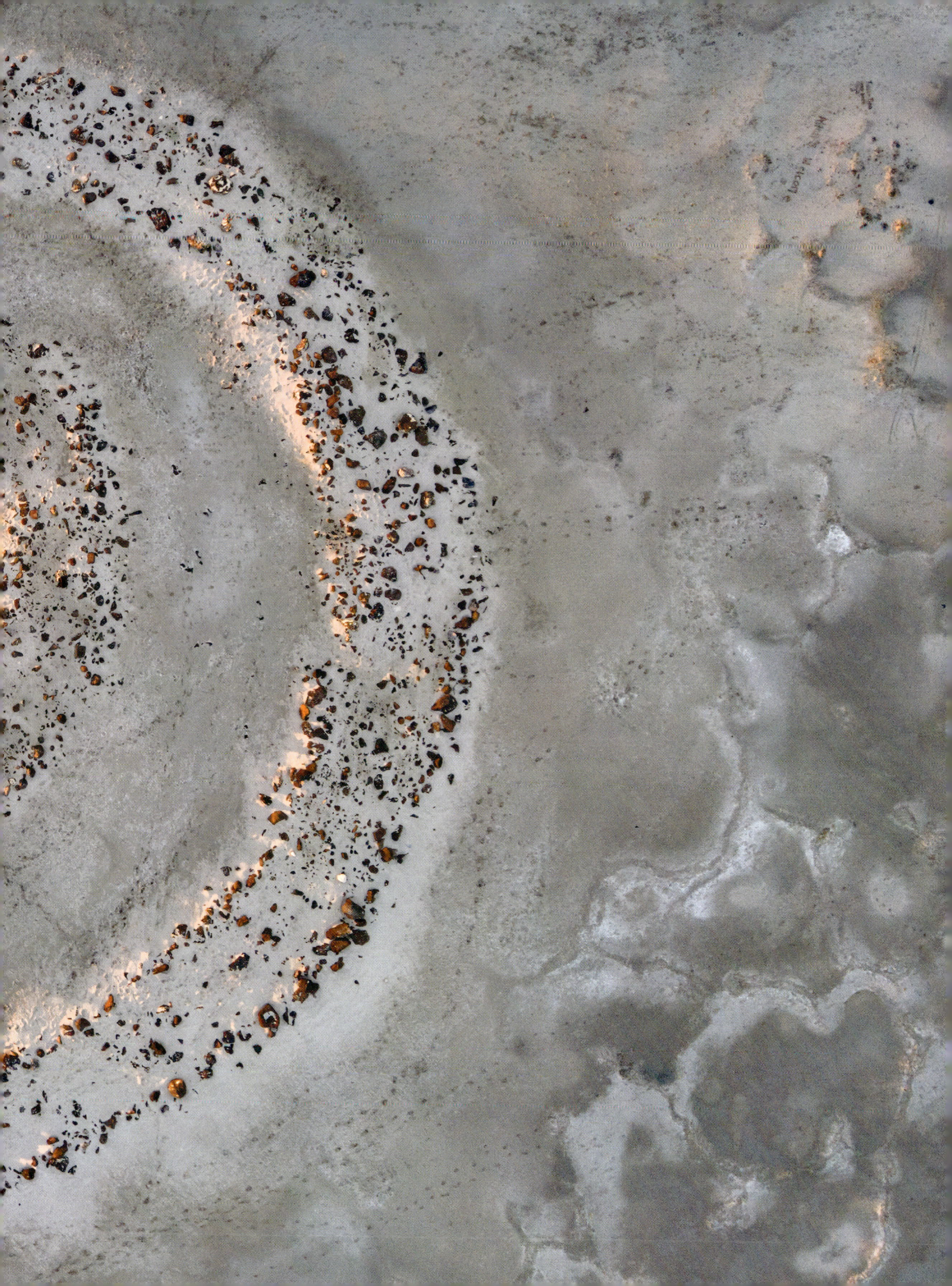

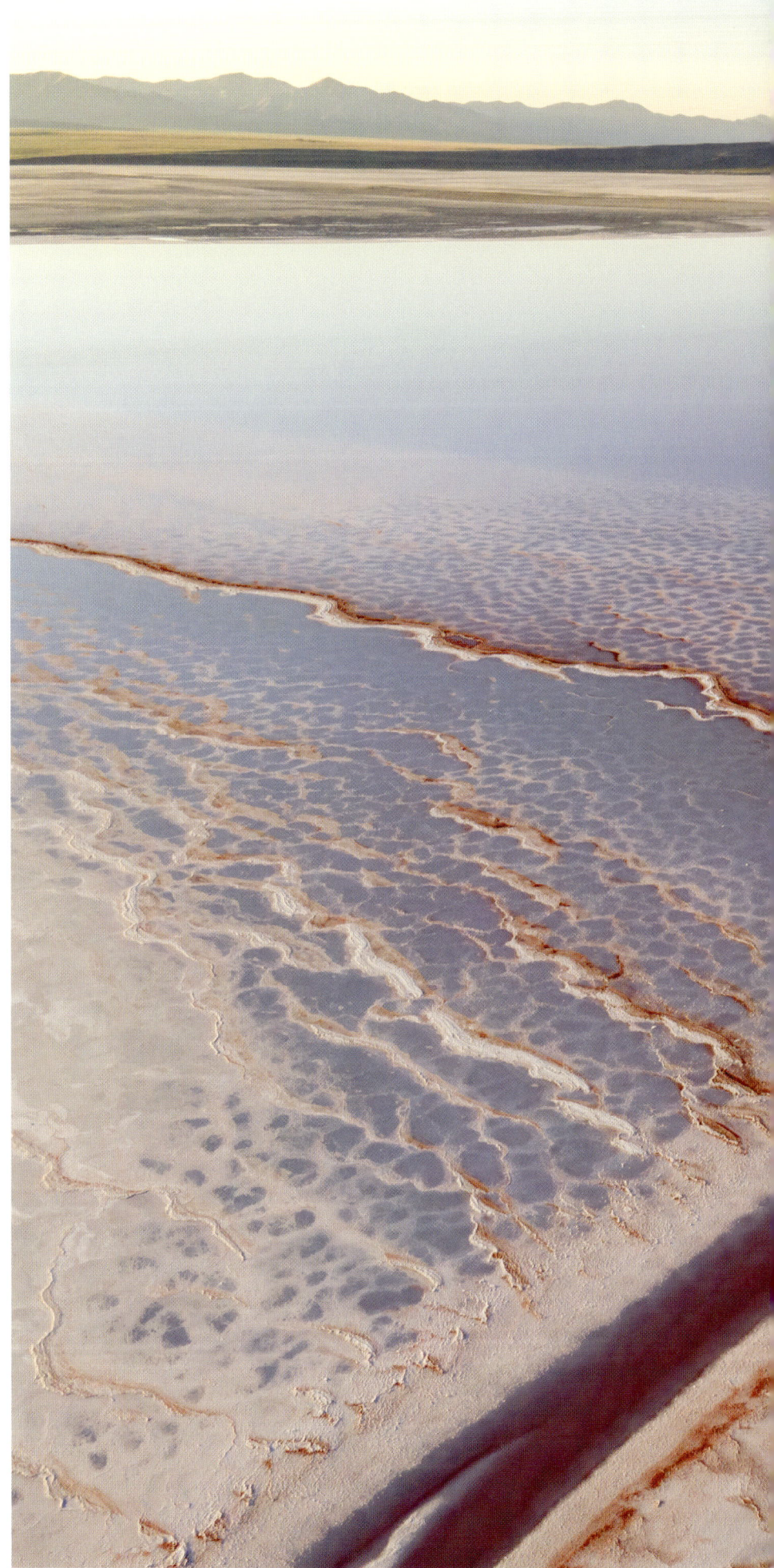

SPRING BAY

The reddish pigment in Spring Bay is hyper-salinity at its most extreme with halophilic microorganisms creating vibrant pink and bright red waters in greatest concentration. The interplay of water flow, sediment deposition, and microbial activity forms intricate, vein-like patterns in the salt flats, resembling the veins of the human body or the tail of a Chinese dragon. The bright, lighter areas are salt crusts formed as the water evaporates, leaving behind concentrated salts. Spring Bay's ephemeral beauty and unique geological features make it a captivating place unlike any on Earth.

Hypersaline channel from 656 feet (200 m) | B3 | 07.16.2023

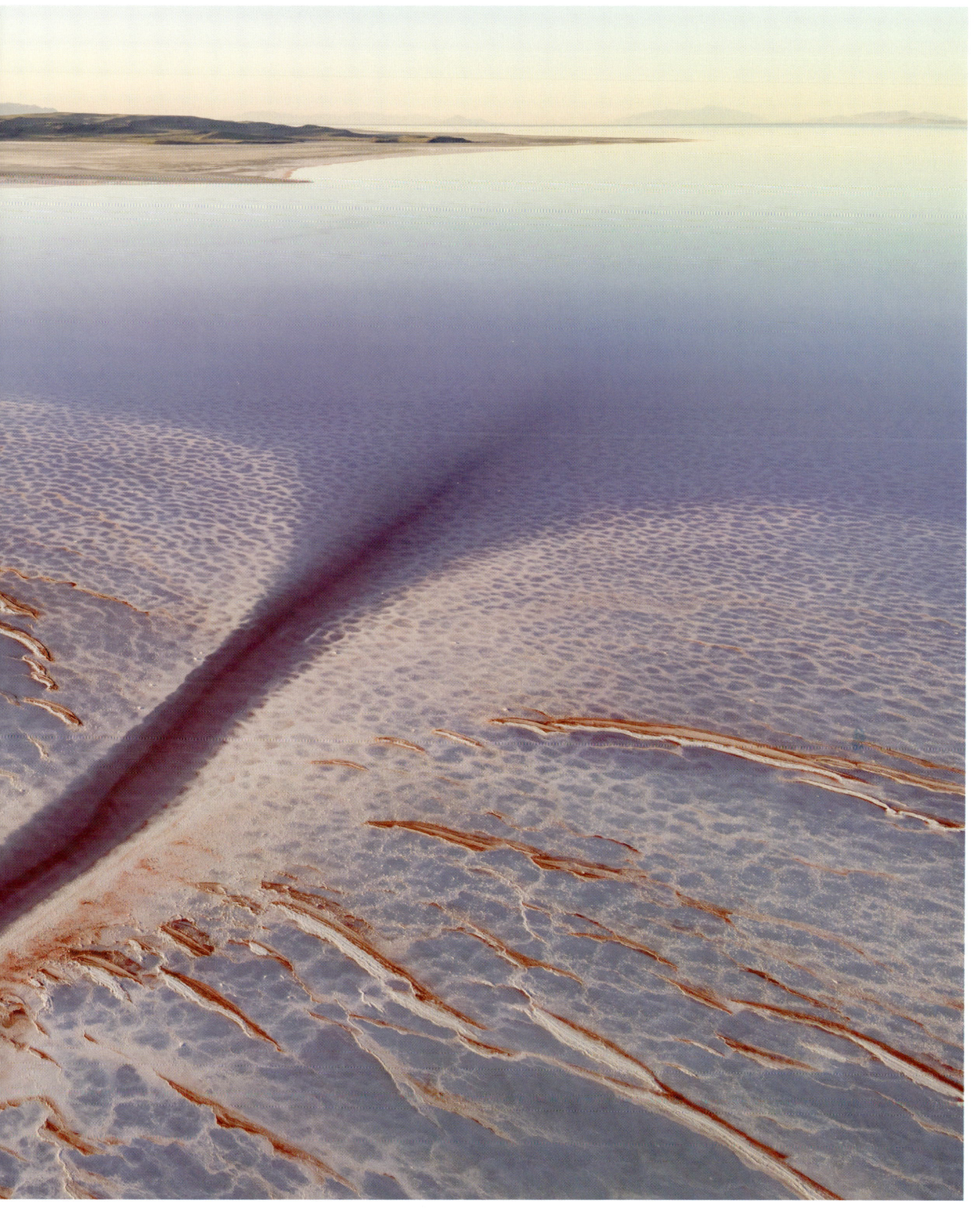

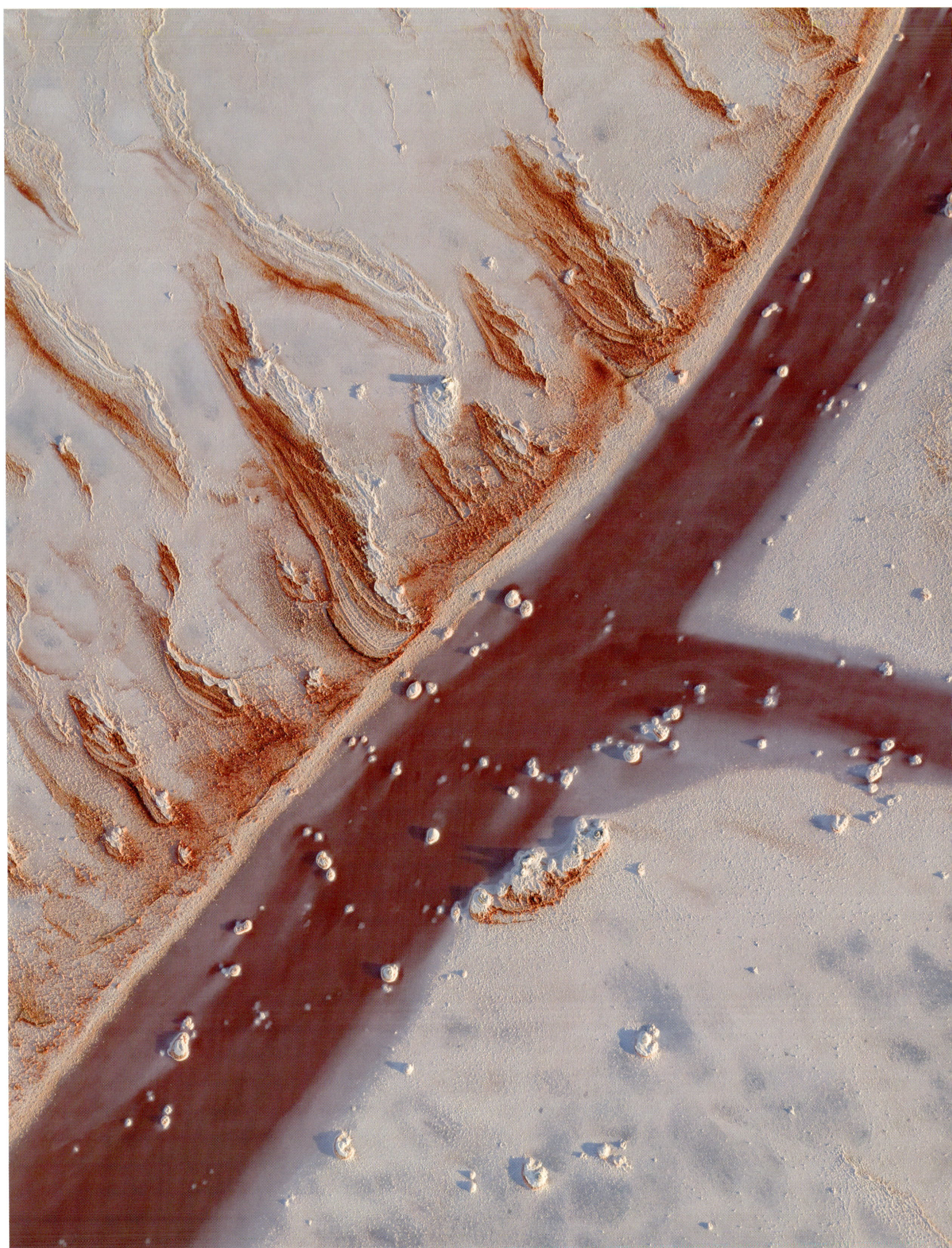

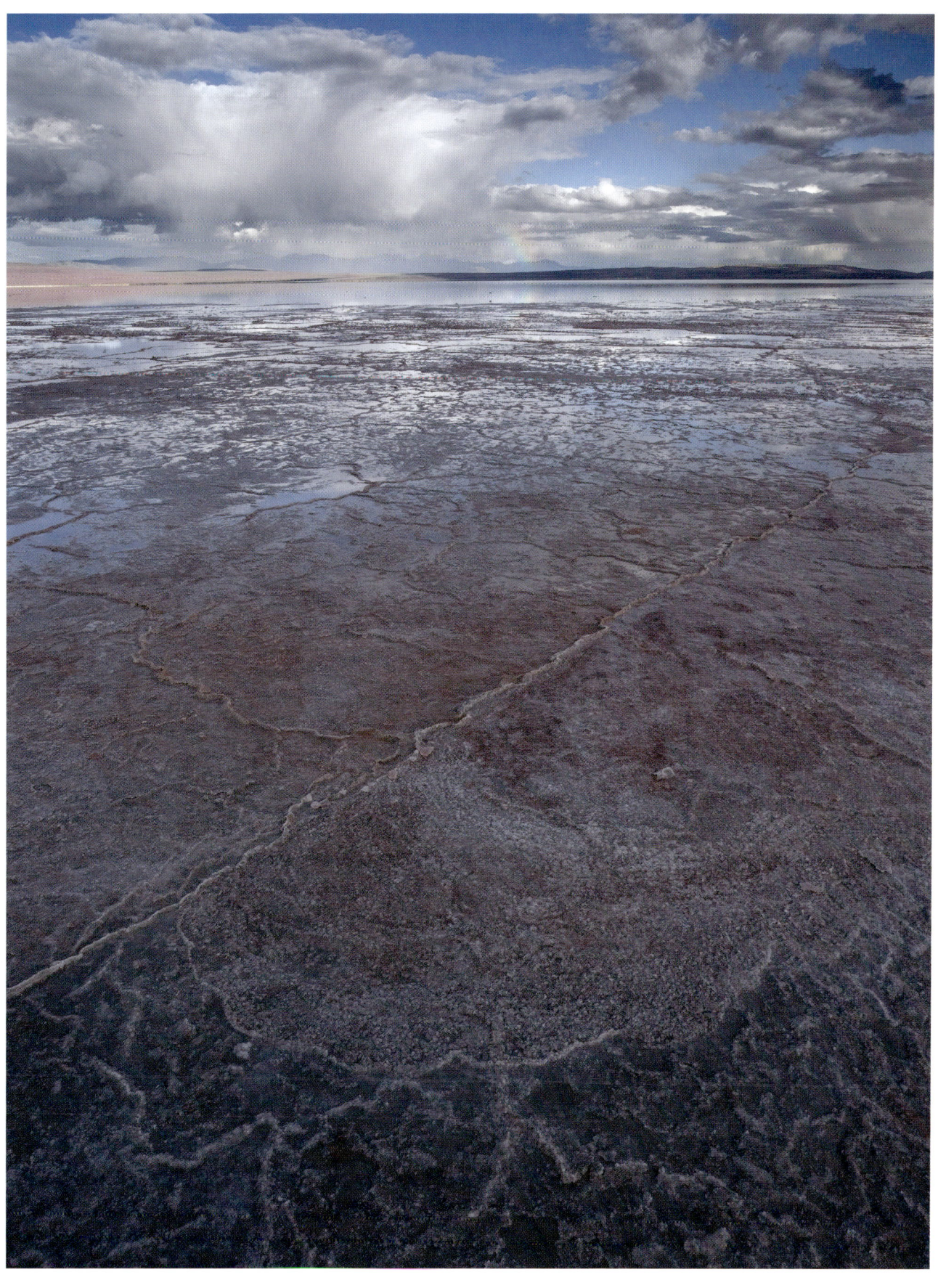

Hypersaline channel and salt mounds from 164 feet (50 m) | B3 | 07.16.2023

Salt crust, Spring Bay | B3 | 05.25.2024

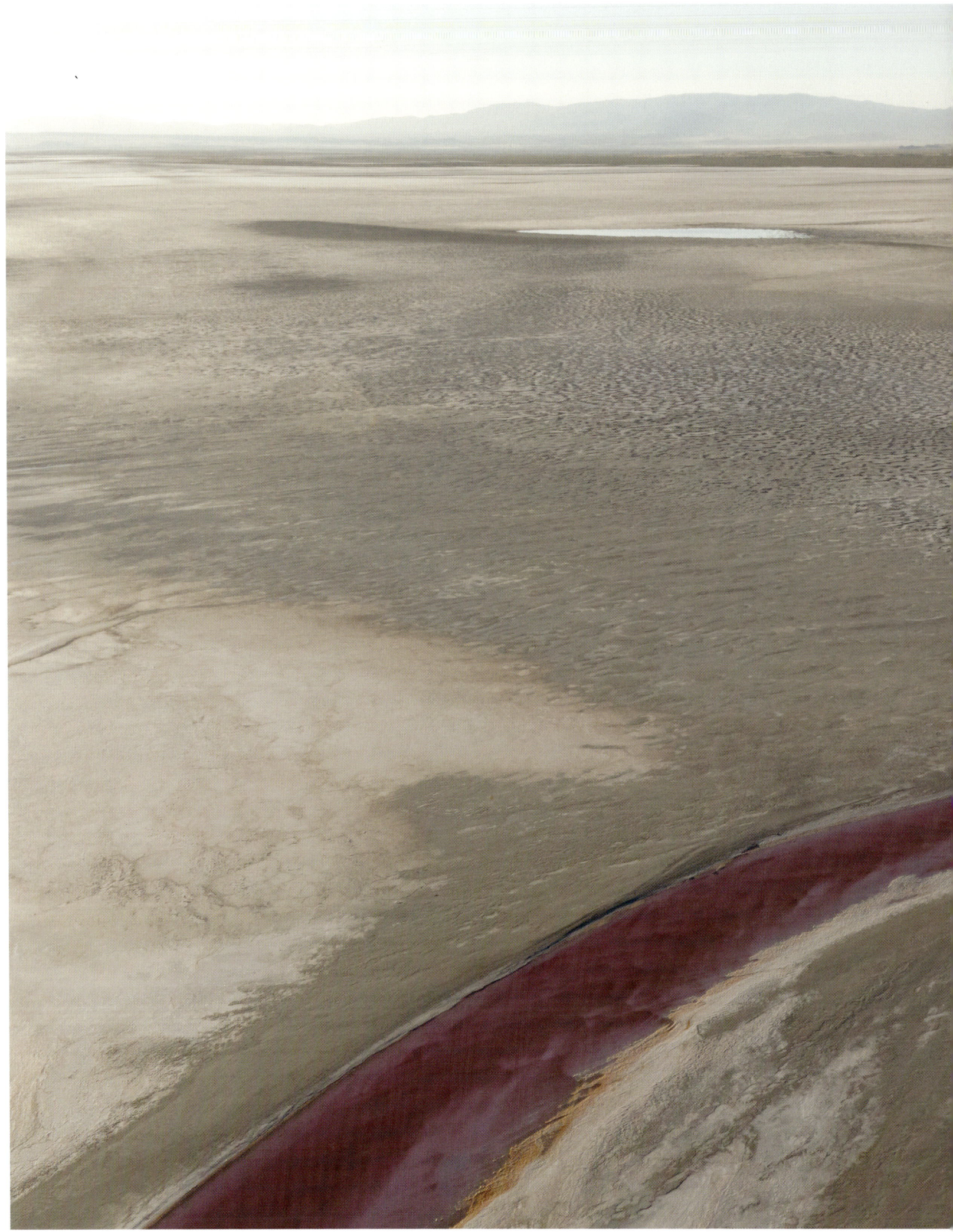

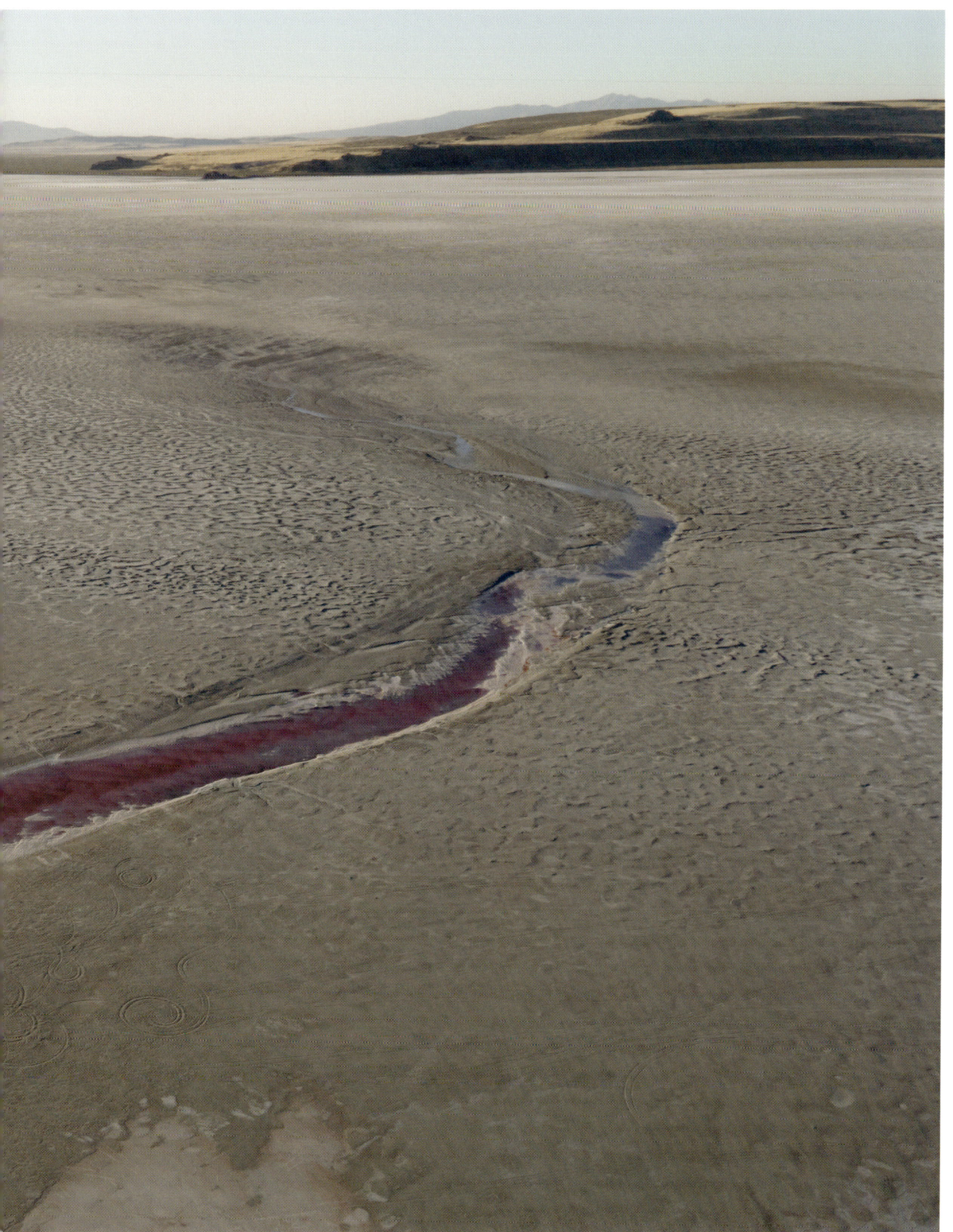

Pink slash of a hypersaline channel in the playa, Spring Bay | B3 | 05.25.2024

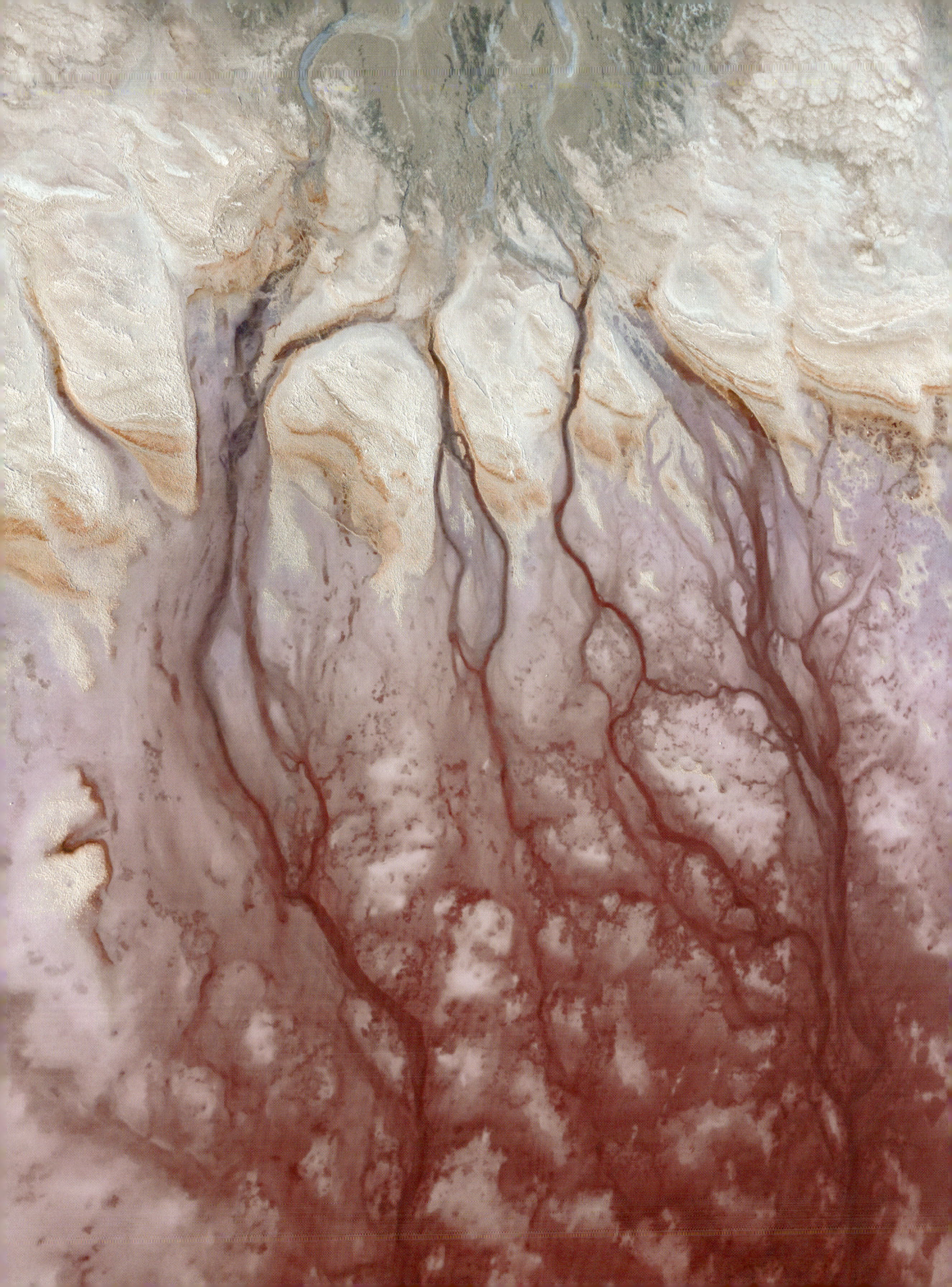

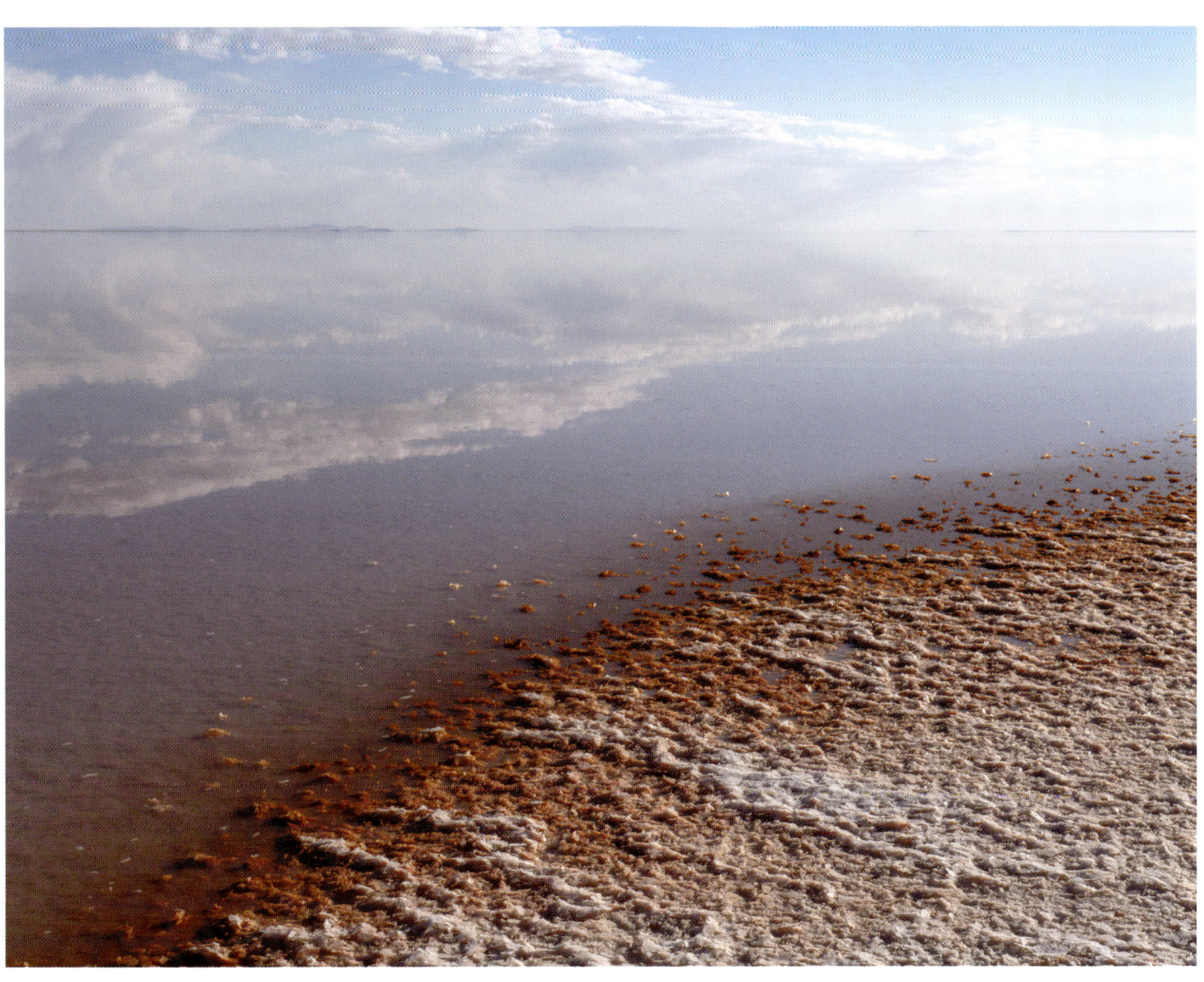

Hypersaline channels from 492 feet (150 m), Spring Bay | B3 | 10.05.2024

Red Salt Coast, Spring Bay | B3 | 10.05.2024

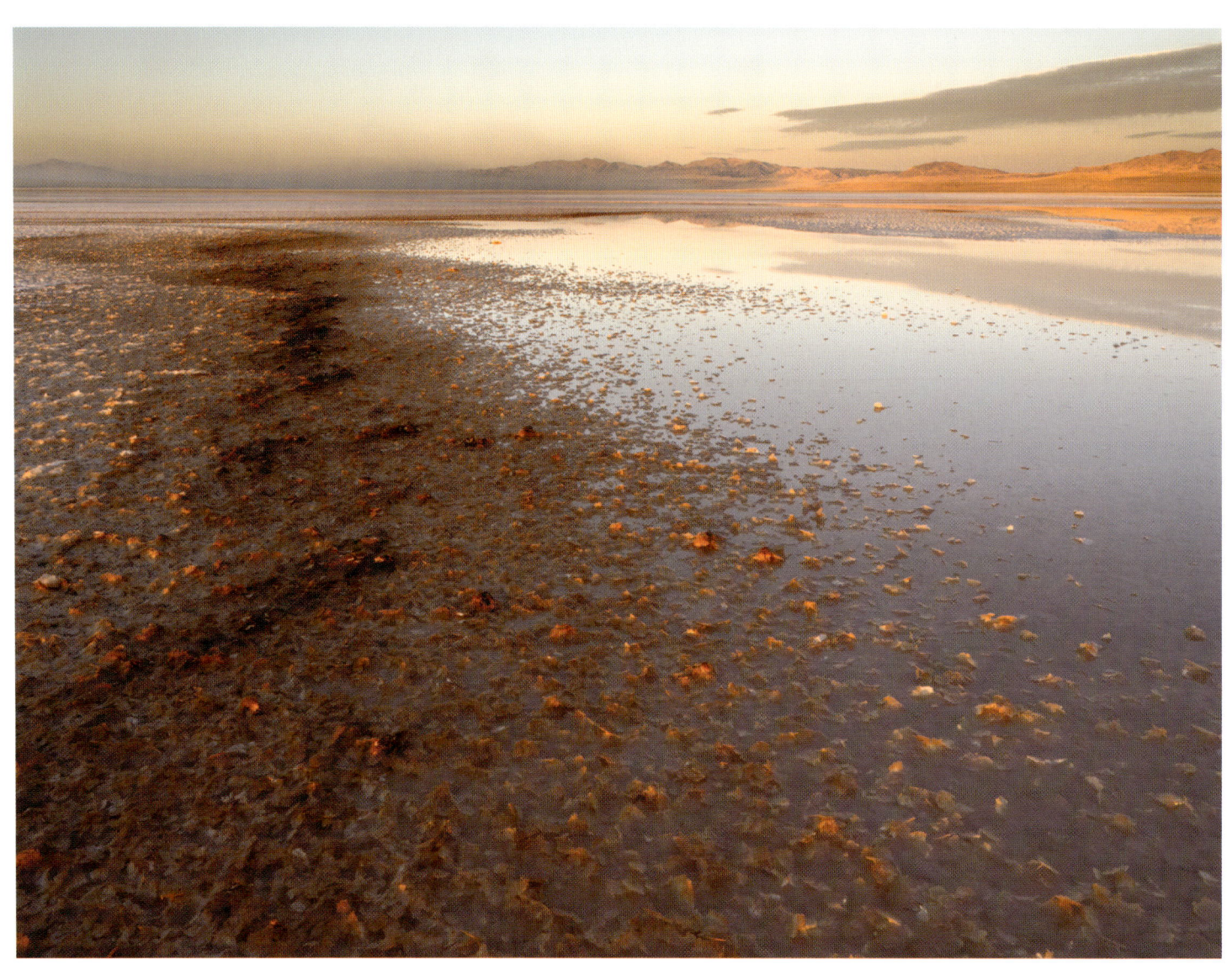

Salt shore at sunset, Spring Bay | B3 | 10.05.2024

Hypersaline channels from 492 feet (150 m), Spring Bay | B3 | 05.25.2024

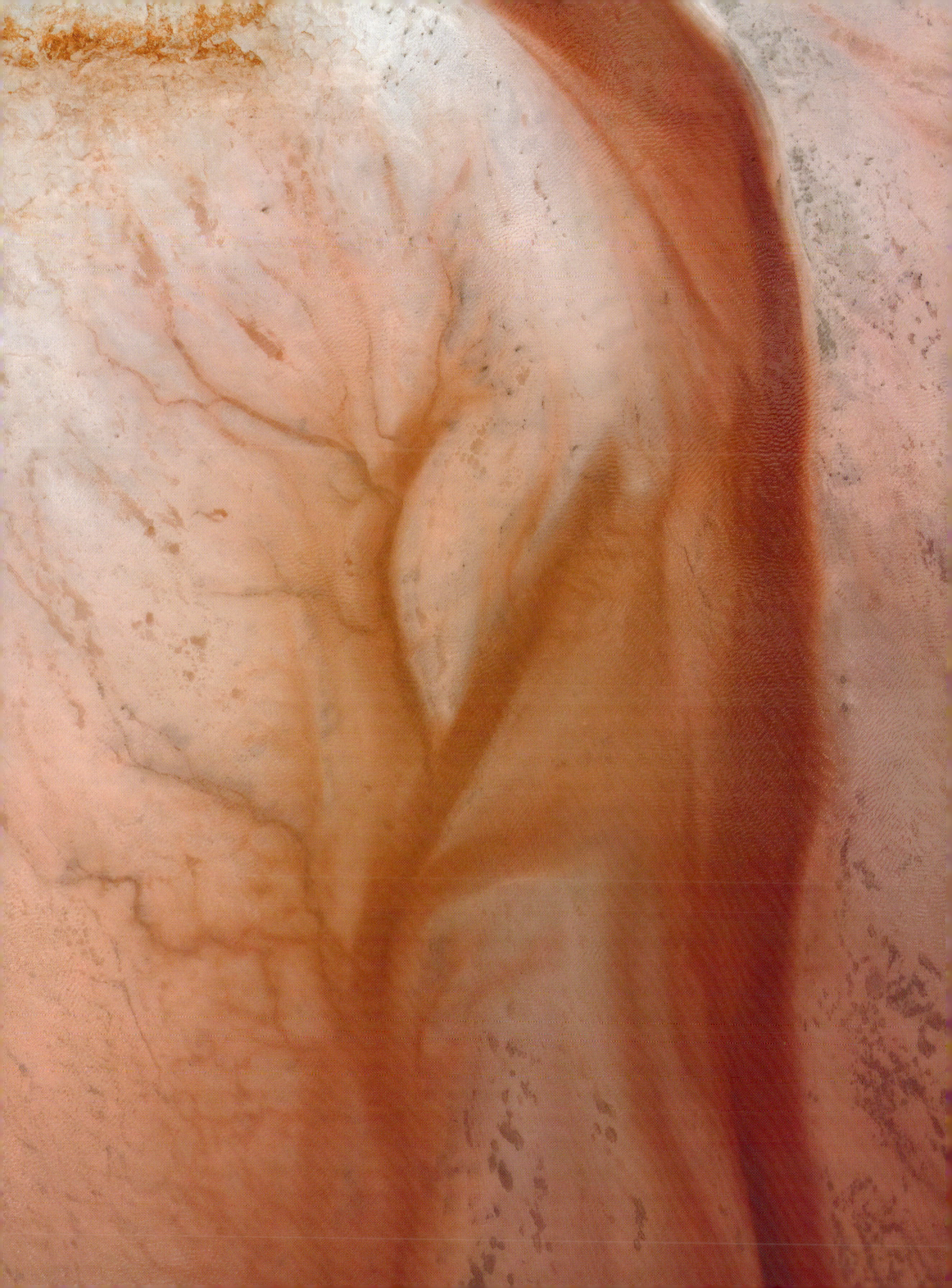

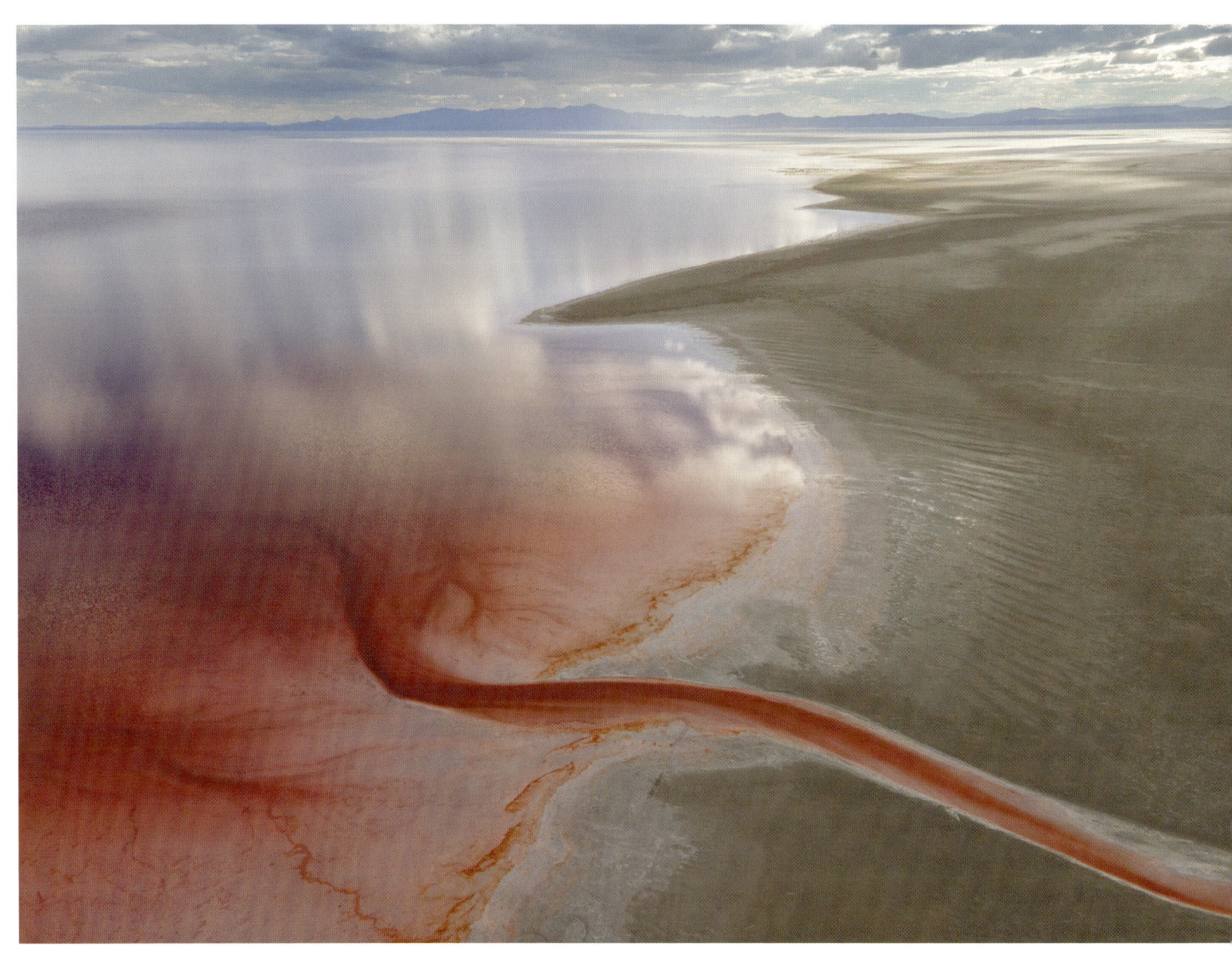

Hypersaline Spring Bay | B3 | 05.25.2024

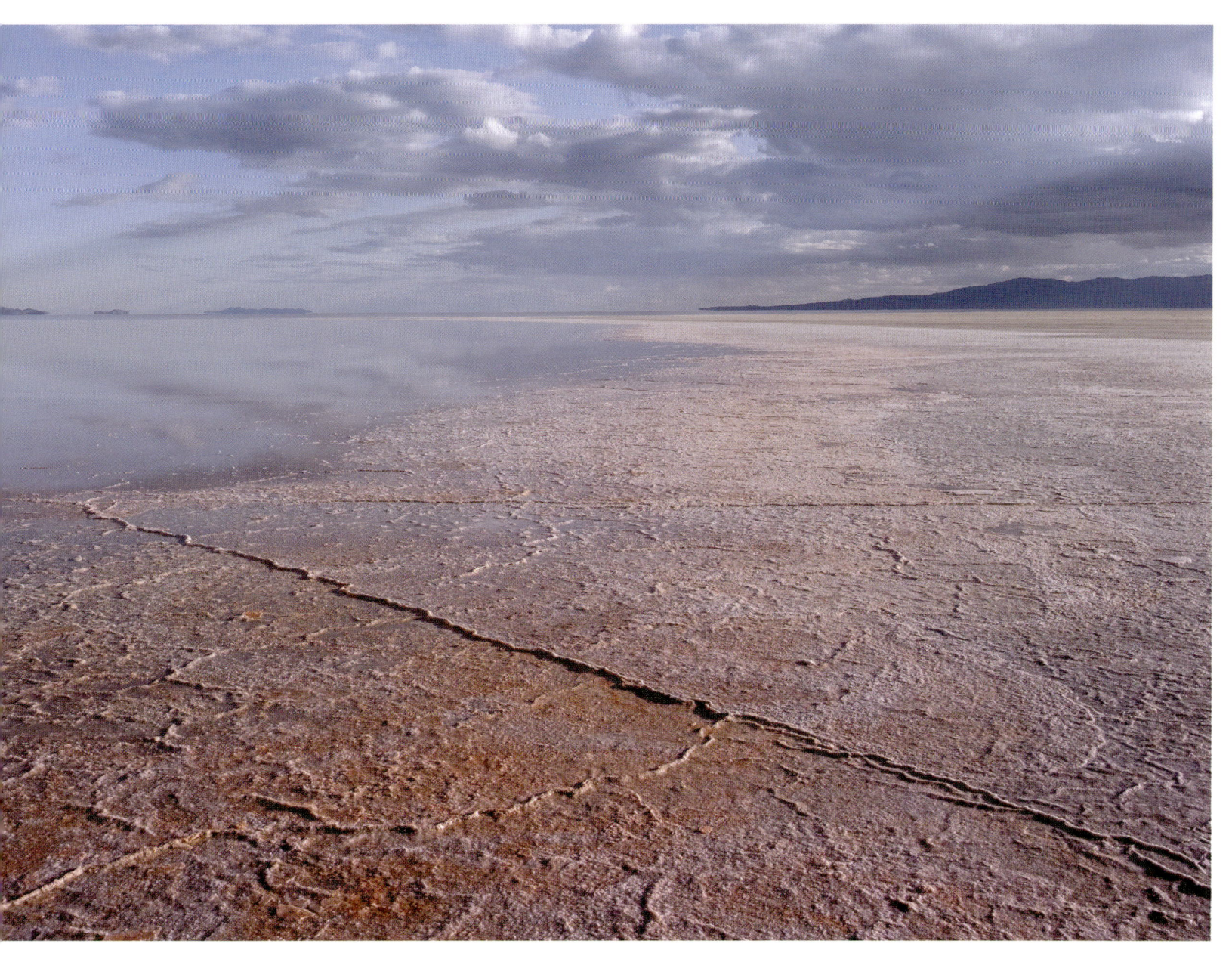

Pink salt crust, Spring Bay | B3 | 05.25.2024

FOLLOWING PAGE: Rainbow and pink salt, Spring Bay | B3 | 05.25.2024

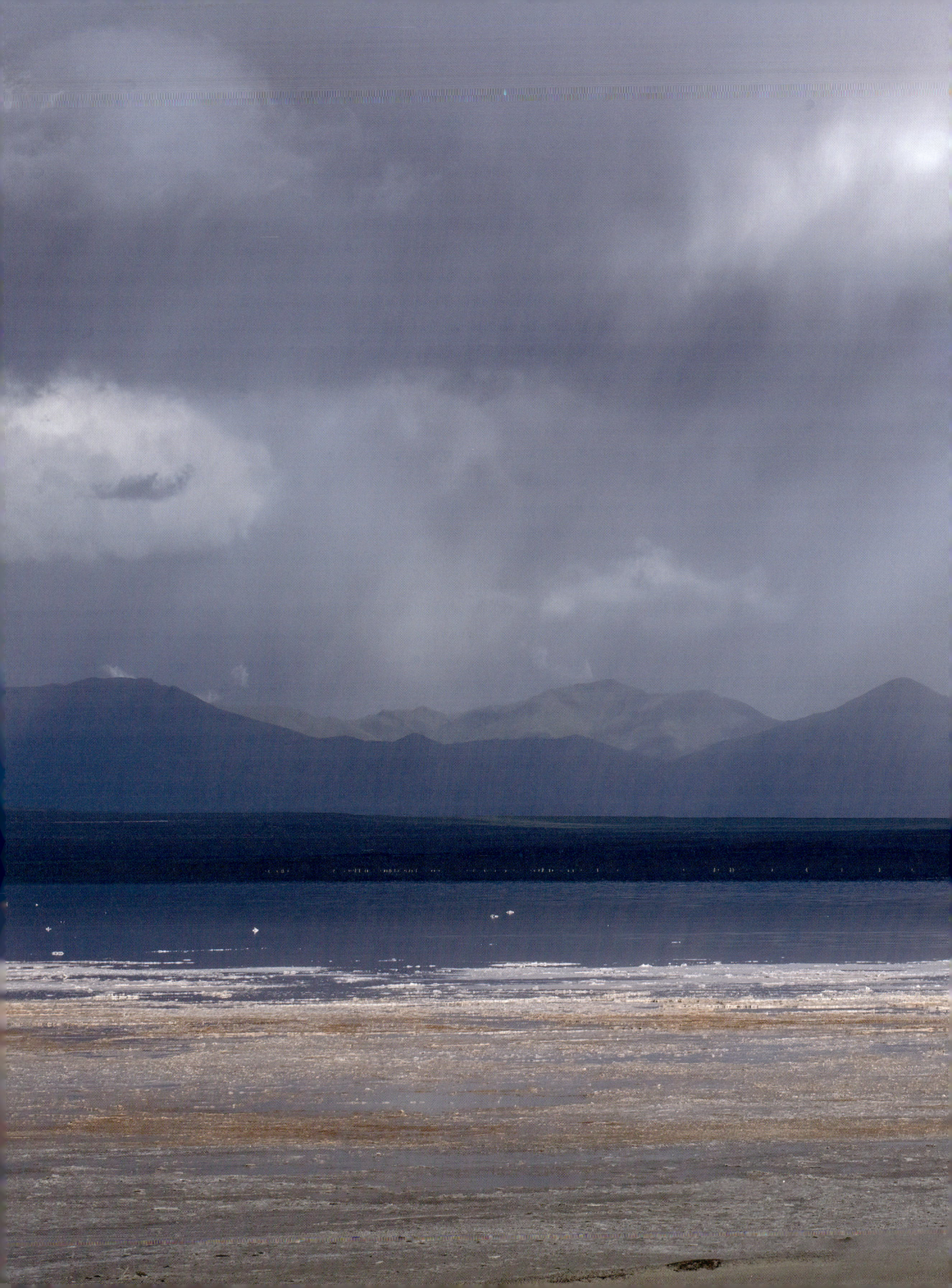

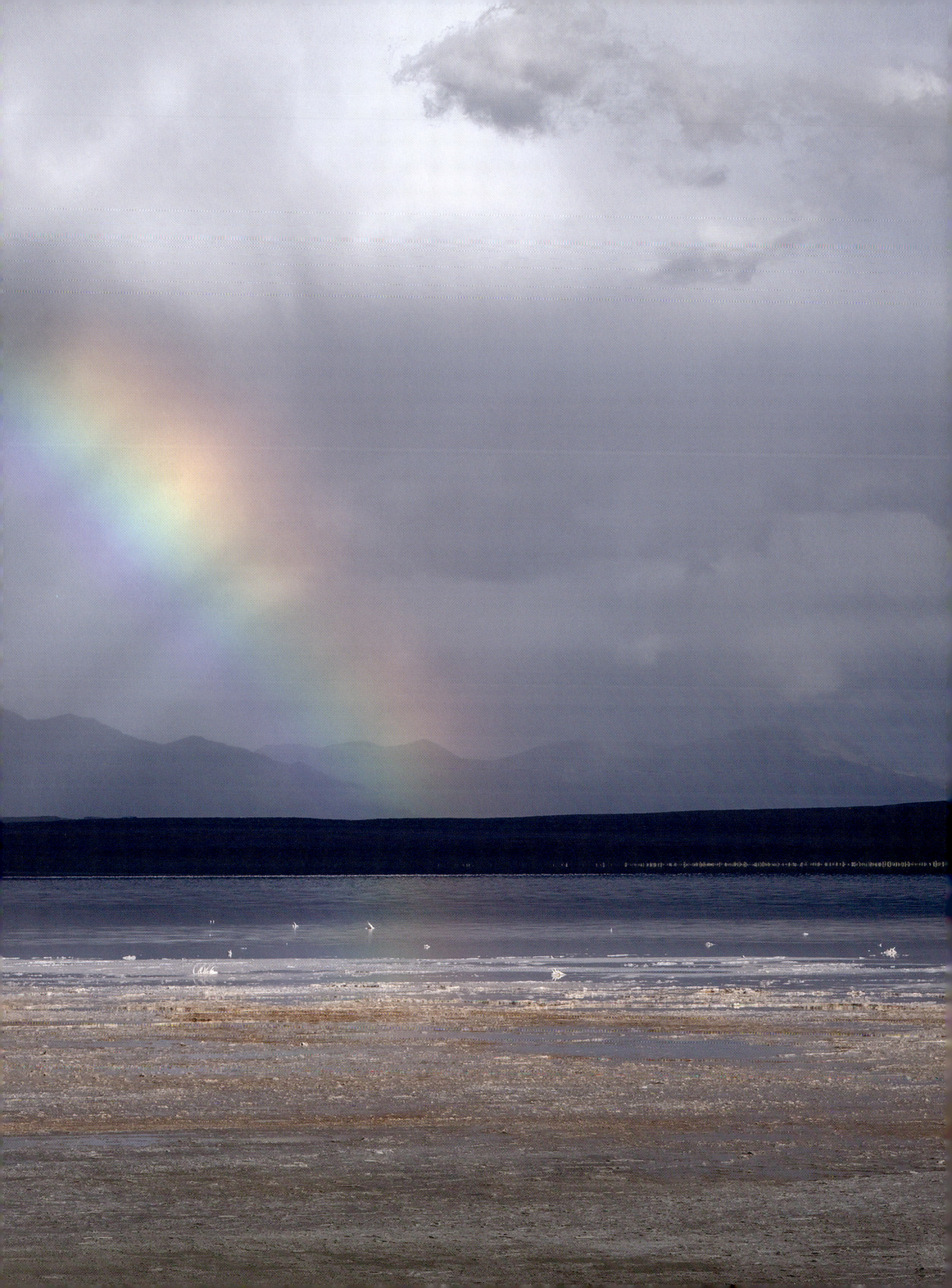

Acknowledgments

I want to begin by expressing my deepest gratitude to my parents. Thank you for standing by me when I chose to pursue a BFA in photography, even when it wasn't the most typical or expected path. Your belief in me has been a constant source of strength, and I am forever grateful for your unwavering support.

To my amazing wife and two boys: I cannot thank you enough. Your patience, love, and support have carried me through every step of this journey. You've been my rock, and I could never have reached this point without you by my side. You are the heart of everything I do.

A huge thank you to Jeremy Ames, who didn't just design this book—he became a true partner in every sense. Jeremy, your dedication and vision helped transform this project into something far beyond what I had ever imagined. You helped me capture the essence and beauty of Great Salt Lake in a way that will now live on, and I am endlessly grateful for that.

I also want to thank my sister, Samantha, for her incredible encouragement and for putting so much care and attention into editing the writing. Your feedback made all the difference, and your involvement has meant the world to me.

To Sheri Dew, Laurel Day, Chris Schoebinger, and the entire Shadow Mountain team— thank you for believing in this project and for taking a chance on me. Your trust and support turned this book into a reality.

I'm especially grateful to Abby Cox and Fraser Bullock for writing such a beautiful and thoughtful foreword that perfectly sets the tone for this book.

A special thanks to Bakcou Bicycles—your electric bike made it possible for me to reach remote, breathtaking parts of Great Salt Lake that would have otherwise been inaccessible.

To Brad Barrus, thank you for flying me over the lake! Without your support, some of the most unique shots in this book wouldn't have been possible.

Lastly, to my colleagues at Boncom—you inspire me every single day. Whether you were helping with photo editing, offering words of encouragement, or sharing your creative ideas, you pushed me to take risks and to believe in what this project could be. I'm especially grateful to Andrew Bagley and Steve Wright for their unwavering support from start to finish.

This book is the result of countless hands, hearts, and minds, and I couldn't be more grateful to each and every one of you. Thank you for taking this journey with me.

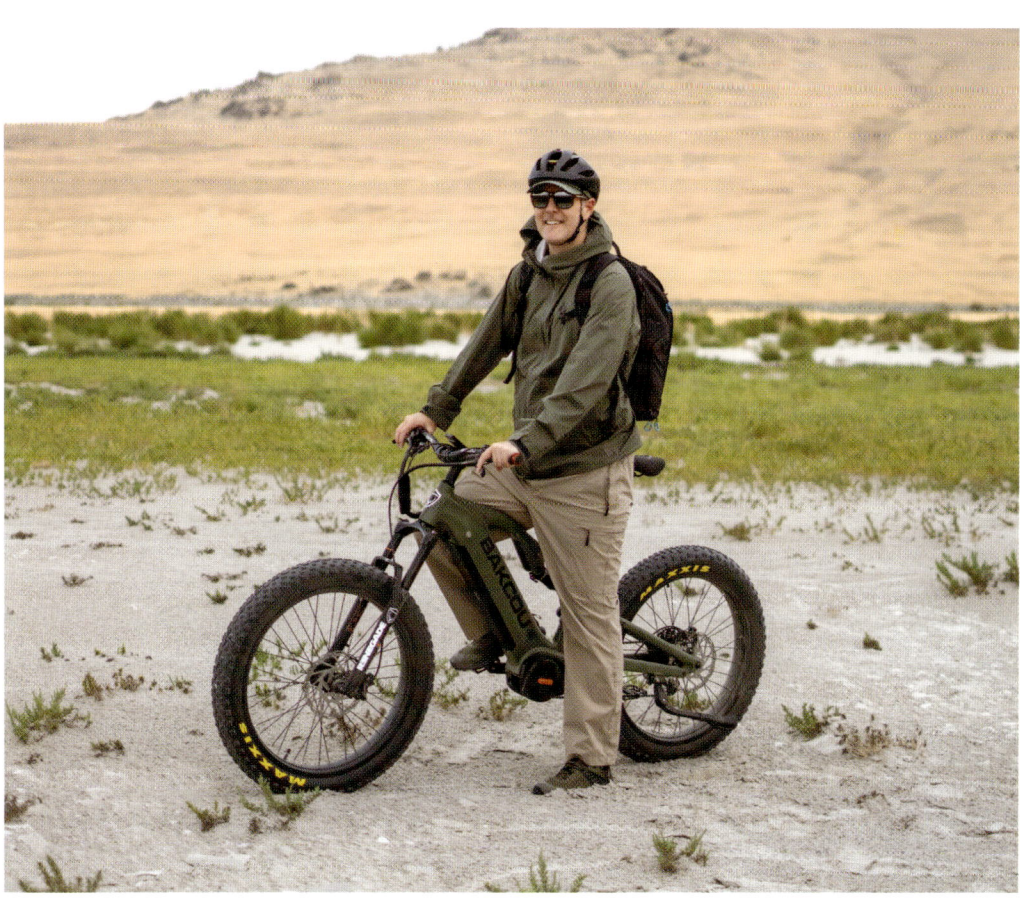

About the Artist

Chris Carlson is an artist with a BFA in photography from Brigham Young University. He is deeply connected to Great Salt Lake through his ancestry, which traces back to the earliest pioneer settlers on Antelope Island. Over the past three years, Chris has dedicated himself to capturing the lake's magnificence, using both traditional cameras and drones to craft expansive aerial views alongside detailed ground-level shots. His photographic approach skillfully reveals the lake's grandeur in vivid and unexpected detail.

Chris dedicates countless hours to perfecting his technique and finding new ways to capture Great Salt Lake's unique landscape, driven by his passion for environmental storytelling. His work aims to elevate public awareness and appreciation of Great Salt Lake's ecological significance. He believes in the power of photography to bring people together, building a community of conservationists who, despite their differing viewpoints, share a common goal: the preservation of Great Salt Lake for future generations.

Photo of Abby Cox on page ix courtesy of Utah Governor's Office.
Photo of Fraser Bullock on page ix courtesy of the Salt Lake Organizing Committee of the 2034 Winter Olympics.

Book design: © Shadow Mountain
Art direction: Garth Bruner
Design: Jeremy Ames

Text and images © 2025 Chris Carlson

Visit us at shadowmountain.com

Library of Congress Cataloging-in-Publication Data
Names: Carlson, Chris, 1972– author
Title: Preserving greatness : Great Salt Lake in photographs / Chris Carlson.
Description: Salt Lake City : Shadow Mountain, 2025. | Includes bibliographical references. | Summary: "*Preserving Greatness* captures the beauty and fragility of the Great Salt Lake as it recedes at an alarming rate. Photographer and author Chris Carlson spent three years documenting its stunning landscapes, diverse wildlife, and unique ecological features. Through breathtaking images and compelling insights, this collection inspires readers to appreciate and advocate for the preservation of this extraordinary natural wonder"—Provided by publisher.
Identifiers: LCCN 2025003196 (print) | LCCN 2025003197 (ebook) | ISBN 9781639934577 hardback | ISBN 9781649334763 ebook
Subjects: LCSH: Pictorial works | Natural history—Utah—Great Salt Lake—Pictorial works
Classification: LCC F832.G7 C37 2025 (print) | LCC F832.G7 (ebook) | DDC 917.92/25800222—dc23/eng/20250305
LC record available at https://lccn.loc.gov/2025003196
LC ebook record available at https://lccn.loc.gov/2025003197

Printed in China
RR Donnelley, Dongguan, China

10   9   8   7   6   5   4   3   2   1

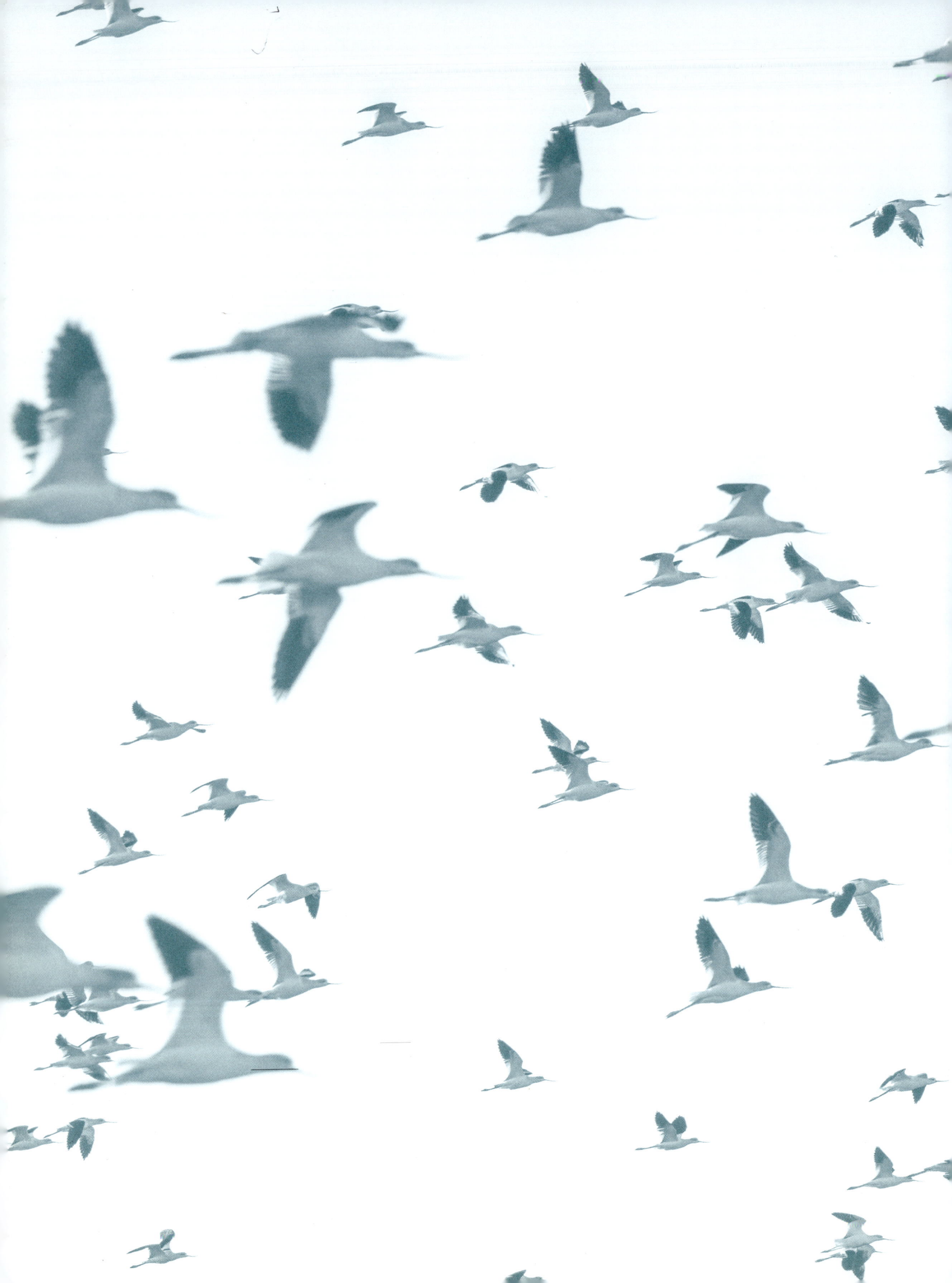